The UN World Food Programme (WFP), the world's largest humanitarian agency, with over 14,500 staff, 90 per cent of whom work in developing countries, provided food to over 101 million people in 75 countries in 2009, 80 per cent of which was purchased in the developing countries themselves. The organization has the largest network of partnership arrangements with working agreements with other major humanitarian agencies, other UN bodies, over 2,000 NGOs, and with major companies and foundations in the private sector.

This book gives the first comprehensive account of the transformation of the WFP, previously a major development organisation in the UN system, into the world's largest humanitarian agency, and of the conversion of food aid into food assistance interventions that end hunger and malnutrition in sustainable ways.

In doing so, it describes the strategic deployment of WFP staff throughout the developing world, how the agency has assumed responsibility for global logistics, telecommunications and food security operations on behalf of the entire international humanitarian system, and how it has established partnerships with other agencies in the non-governmental and private sectors to form the largest humanitarian network that now provides assistance annually to over 100 million people.

The World's Largest Humanitarian Agency will be required reading for students of development economics, sociology and human rights, as well as policy makers, NGOs and bilateral aid agencies.

D. JOHN SHAW was associated with the WFP for over thirty years, almost from the start of its operations in 1963, latterly as Economic Adviser and Chief, Policy Affairs Service. He was also consultant to the Commonwealth Secretariat, the Food and Agriculture Organization of the United Nations (FAO), and the World Bank. A postgraduate in Agricultural Economics at the University of Oxford, UK, he was Senior Lecturer in Rural Economy at the University of Khartoum, Sudan and Fellow in Agricultural Economics and founder member of the Institute of Development Studies at the University of Sussex, UK. He has written extensively on development, food security and food aid issues and now serves on the International Editorial Board of the Journal *Food Policy*. He can be contacted at djohnshawuk@aol.com

Also by *D. John Shaw*

GLOBAL FOOD AND AGRICULTURAL INSTITUTIONS

WORLD FOOD SECURITY
A History since 1945

SIR HANS SINGER
The Life and Work of a Development Economist

INTERNATIONAL DEVELOPMENT COOPERATION
Selected Essays by H. W. Singer on Aid and the United Nations System (*editor*)

THE UN WORLD FOOD PROGRAMME AND THE DEVELOPMENT OF FOOD AID

WORLD FOOD AID
Experiences of Recipients and Donors
(*edited with Edward Clay*)

THE QUEST FOR FOOD SECURITY IN THE TWENTY-FIRST CENTURY
(*edited with Helene Delisle*)

A FUTURE FOOD AID REGIME
Implications of the Final Act of the GATT Uruguay Round
(*with H. W. Singer*)

POVERTY, DEVELOPMENT AND FOOD
Essays in Honour of H. W. Singer on his 75th Birthday
(*edited with Edward Clay*)

THE WORLD FOOD PROGRAMME AND EMERGENCY RELIEF

FOOD POLICY, FOOD AID AND ECONOMIC ADJUSTMENT
(*edited with H. W. Singer*)

FOOD AID AND THE WELL-BEING OF CHILDREN IN THE DEVELOPING WORLD
(*edited with P. J. Greaves*)

The World's Largest Humanitarian Agency

The Transformation of the UN World Food Programme and of Food Aid

D. John Shaw

palgrave
macmillan

First published 2011 by
PALGRAVE MACMILLAN

Palgrave Macmillan in the UK is an imprint of Macmillan Publishers Limited, registered in England, company number 785998, of Houndmills, Basingstoke, Hampshire RG21 6XS.

Palgrave Macmillan in the US is a division of St Martin's Press LLC, 175 Fifth Avenue, New York, NY 10010.

Palgrave Macmillan is the global academic imprint of the above companies and has companies and representatives throughout the world.

ISBN: 978–0–230–58099–2

This book is printed on paper suitable for recycling and made from fully managed and sustained forest sources. Logging, pulping and manufacturing processes are expected to conform to the environmental regulations of the country of origin.

A catalogue record for this book is available from the British Library.

Library of Congress Cataloging-in-Publication Data

Shaw, D. John.
The world's largest humanitarian agency : the transformation of the UN World Food Programme and of food aid / by D. John Shaw.
p. cm.
Includes bibliographical references and index.
ISBN 978–0–230–58099–2 (alk. paper)
1. World Food Programme – History. 2. Food relief – International cooperation – History. I. Title.

JZ5009.5.W675S53 2011
363.8'83—dc22 2011012456

10 9 8 7 6 5 4 3 2 1
20 19 18 17 16 15 14 13 12 11

Printed and bound in Great Britain by
CPI Antony Rowe, Chippenham and Eastbourne

To the Staff of the UN World Food Programme
Past and Present
Women and Men
Locally and Internationally Recruited
In Developing Countries, Liaison Offices, and at Headquarters for
Their Dedication to Ending Hunger

By three methods we may learn wisdom:
first, by reflection, which is noblest;
second, by imitation, which is easiest;
and third by experience, which is the bitterest.

Confucius

Humanitarian assistance is the aid and action designed to save lives, alleviate suffering and maintain and protect human dignity during and in the aftermath of emergencies. To be classified as humanitarian, aid should be consistent with the humanitarian principles of humanity, impartiality, neutrality and independence.

Principles and Practice of
Good Humanitarian Donorship

There are no humanitarian solutions to humanitarian problems...

Humanitarian action may create space for political action but on its own can never substitute for it.

Sadako Ogata, UN High Commissioner
for Refugees (1990–2000)

Hunger is a complex, multidimensional challenge that requires bold and decisive action. The enormity of the problem, with its social, economic, human, [and political] consequences have been well-documented. If the first Millennium Development Goal of halving the proposition of hungry people by 2015 is to be achieved, then agencies such as WFP must seek out new partners and be open to new forms of partnership [and innovative interventions].

WFP's Private Sector Partnership and
Fundraising Strategy

Instead of managing poverty, we should help people out of poverty and avoid creating dependency.

US President Barack Obama, UN General
Assembly, 22 October 2010

Contents

Illustrations

Tables

Figures

Boxes

Acknowledgements

This book could not have been written without the help and cooperation of many people, particularly WFP staff. I begin my debts of gratitude with the four executive directors in charge of the WFP during the three decades from the beginning of the 1980s to the present. I acknowledge especially the role that James Ingram played in encouraging me to write this book, and the help he provided not only through his own book, *Bread and Stones* (Ingram, 2007), but also through the considerable personal correspondence he sent me in which he revealed his innermost thoughts concerning the WFP's transformation from a development to an emergency relief programme. His leadership role in strengthening the international response to emergencies was finally recognized when he was requested by the UN secretary-general to conduct humanitarian negotiations in the Horn of Africa on behalf of the United Nations. He commented in detail on the draft of Chapter 2.

I am indebted to Catherine Bertini for her detailed, personal account, *A Decade of Change: Renewal and Transformation of the World Food Programme, 1992–2002*, which was presented to the WFP's executive board in 2002 on the eve of her departure. The decentralization initiative she undertook with courage and conviction during her ten years in office eventually led to the creation of the world's largest humanitarian agency. She was appointed as the UN secretary-general's special envoy for drought in the Horn of Africa (2000–01). On leaving the WFP, she was under-secretary-general for management at the United Nations in New York (2003–05) and served for four years as chair of the UN Standing Committee on Nutrition (2002–06). She is now senior research fellow at the Bill and Melinda Gates Foundation and professor of public administration at Syracuse University in the United States.

James Morris took Catherine Bertini's work further during his period as executive director (2002–06) by encouraging the WFP to think 'strategically' in its work and in the role of food aid in achieving the Millennium Development Goals. He strengthened the WFP's capacity at headquarters to support the WFP's staff in its regional bureaux and country offices throughout the developing world, particularly in policy formulation, as can be seen from the bibliography listing documents presented to the WFP's executive board during his period of office. He created four deputy executive director positions at WFP headquarters – a senior position for the Operations Department, and three further positions for hunger solutions, external relations, and resources management – so that he could spend more time with WFP staff in developing countries in the front line of the WFP's work. In July 2002, he was appointed as the special envoy of the UN secretary-general for humanitarian needs in Southern Africa. He championed the fight against hunger and, with the WHO director-general, against HIV/AIDS. After leading a high-level mission to the Darfur region in the Sudan in April 2004, he is widely quoted to have drawn attention to the injustices in the humanitarian aid system in a statement to the UN Security Council when he said: 'Occasionally, I have thought the worst place for a hungry child to live in Africa today is in a country that is at peace with its neighbours and relatively stable. Funding levels rise with the incidence of violence and media interest'. He played a major personal role in forging partnerships with other bodies, particularly in the private sector, to increase the coverage, effectiveness and efficiency of the WFP's work.

Josette Sheeran's dynamic leadership is portrayed especially in the many speeches, addresses, and statements she has made in different forums since taking office in 2006. In her first address to the WFP's governing body on 4 June 2007, she stated: 'My long-term hope is that we can ultimately put WFP out of business, at least in chronic hunger. Let us make chronic hunger a part of history – to break the cycle of chronic food insecurity at its root' (Sheeran, 2007a). Later, she referred to WFP staff as the 'green berets of the humanitarian world' (Sheeran, 2007b) She laid the framework for the WFP's work over the seven years from 2008 in its *Strategic Plan (2008–2011)*, extended to 2013, which includes the transformation of food aid to food assistance programmes to support innovative interventions to end hunger. As she succinctly put it at International Food Aid Conference in Kansas City in the United States in April 2008, 'this is not your grandmother's food aid' (Sheeran, 2008).

The four executive directors would be the first to recognize that what they were able to achieve would not have been possible without the support and dedication of WFP staff, to whom this book is dedicated. I begin my appreciation of the help and cooperation afforded me by WFP staff with my thanks to David Stevenson, former director of the WFP's Policy, Planning and Strategy Division. He responded quickly and positively to my three requests made in 2008 for access to WFP papers and documentation, interviews with WFP staff, and the appointment of a contact officer to facilitate my work. He appointed Jacqueline Nivet. She efficiently arranged my appointments with a cross-section of WFP staff at WFP headquarters in September 2008, accompanied me throughout the interviews, and kept a record of the discussions that took place, and my requests for information and documentation. I am grateful to the following WFP staff I interviewed: Amir Abdulla, Lubna Alaman, Martin Bloem, Gianluca Bruni, François Buratto, Evelyn Chung, Jan Dalbaere, Amer Daoudi, Torben Due, Alzira Ferreira, Mario Fetz, Ugo Gentilini, Valerie Guarnieri, Menghestab Haile, Rebecca Hansen, Amy Horton, Jacob Kern, Monica Marshall, Mary Ellen McGroarty, Joop Menkveld, Tahir Nour, Steven Were Omamo, Robert Opp, Akldo Oiscina, Kofi Owusu, Gina Pattugalan, John Powell, Rebecca Richards, Issa Sanogo, Georgia Shaver, Sheila Sisulu, Terri Toyota, Sylvia Trulli, Paul Turnbull, Carlos Veloso, Claudia von Roehl and Edgardo Yu.

Earlier, in connection with my work on an earlier book on *Global Food and Agricultural Institutions* (Shaw, 2009), which includes the WFP, with the help of my contact points Paul Howe, Marco Cavalcante and Sylvia Trulli, I interviewed at WFP headquarters: John Aylieff, Tina van den Briel, Henk Jan Brinkman, Lisa Doughten, Francisco Espejo, Adama Faye, Jean-Jacques Graisse, Edith Heines, Deborah Hines, Robin Jackson, Sarah Laughton, Francis Mwanza, Haladou Salha, Joseph Scalise, Suresh Sharma, George Simon and Jamie Wickens.

The cooperation of Andreas Psoroulas, head of the WFP Library, was indispensible throughout the writing of this book. He replied to my many requests for information, papers, and documents quickly and efficiently. Steven Were Omamo commented on the entire draft manuscript. Many inputs and detailed comments on the drafts of Chapters 2 and 3, including the examples of WFP emergency operations, were provided by the former WFP staff members who had worked in a number of posts in developing countries and at WFP headquarters: Julian Lefevre, who was with the WFP for 35 years (1974–2009), including as chief evaluation officer in the WFP's Evaluation Service (2001–08); Trevor Page, who was with the WFP for 31 years (1966–96), including as director of the WFP's Emergency Service (1983–86); and Bronek Szynalski, who was with the WFP for over 30 years (1968–99), including as senior evaluation officer in the WFP's Evaluation Service (1984–86) – when he led a major evaluation of the WFP's response to the African food crisis – and chief, Disaster Relief Service, and director, Emergency Division (1986–94). Sarah Longford commented in detail on the draft of the section on the WFP's *Purchase for Progress* (P4P) programme in Chapter 6 and updated the data given. Carlo Scaramella provided additional information and documentation on the WFP's work on disaster risk reduction and climate change.

Allan Jury and Catherine Feeney at the WFP's Washington, DC office provided me with information on the US food aid programme and the US federal food stamp programme. A number of other former WFP staff members provided me with information, material and recollections, including: Bruce Crawshaw, Maurizio Gnocchi, Bern Kaess and Masood Hyder. Jens Schulthes gave me permission to refer to his article on monetization that appeared in an IDS *Bulletin* in 1992 and to his chapter 'Is There a Future for WFP as a Development Agency?' in the book edited by Edward Clay and Olav Stokke titled *Food Aid and Human Security* (Frank Cass, 2000: 256–73). Ron Ockwell informed me about the work he did as a WFP consultant on the pioneering training materials for WFP emergency operations and the part he played in early training programmes, and sent me his thematic evaluation on the recurring challenges of food assistance in complex emergencies (Ockwell, 1999).

Of the many others who helped me, I would particularly like to mention Dr Edward Clay, senior research associate at the Overseas Development (ODI) in London. He undertook a number of consultancies for the WFP, particularly at the time of the 'tipping points' at the start of the transformation of the WFP from a development to an emergency relief agency, and edited a book with me on *World Food Aid: Experiences of Recipients and Donors* (1993). He has subsequently written prolifically on food security and food aid issues, and on the WFP. He sent me a copy of his proposal for 'A Future Food Aid or Food Assistance Convention' (ODI,

2010). The staff at ALNAP and in the Humanitarian Policy Group at the Overseas Development Institute (ODI) in London, including John Mitchell, James Darcy, Joanna Macrae, Paul Harvey, Frances Stevensen and David White, responded to my many questions and made copies of their publications available to me. Jo Adcock, Jo Fottrell and Tom MacManus at ODI sent copies of my articles and book reviews published in the ODI journal *Development Policy Review.* I benefited considerably from the inspiring work of Roberta Cohen and Francis Deng, and Thomas Weiss on internally displaced persons and proposals to improve the UN humanitarian aid system.

Permission was obtained from Steven Were Omamo, Ugo Gentilini and Susanna Sandström to quote from the book they edited on *Revolution: From Food Aid to Food Assistance. Innovations in Overcoming Hunger* (WFP, 2010). Peter Walker, director of the Feinstein International Center at Tufts University in the United States, gave me permission to quote from the centre's publications, his article on 'Complexity and Context as the Determinants of the Future' (Opinion Paper, 7 July 2008), and the book he co-authored on *Shaping the Humanitarian World* (Walker and Maxwell, 2009). Rajul Pandya-Lorch, John Whitehead, Djhoanna Cruz and Michael Go at IFPRI gave me permission to use the institute's publication and sent me its documents. Cambridge University Press gave permission to refer to the book by Nicolas Stern on *The Economics of Climate Change* (2006). The Brookings Institution gave me permission to refer to the seminal book by Roberta Cohen and Francis M. Deng on *Masses in Flight. The Global Crisis of Internal Displacement* (1998) and the book they edited on *The Forsaken People: Case Studies of the Internally Displaced* (1998), and to quote from the foreword by the president of the Brookings Institution, Strobe Talbott, to the book edited by Lael Brainard and others on *Climate Change and Global Poverty. A Billion Lives in the Balance?* (2009). Wiley Publishing and the Production Manager gave permission to use my articles and book reviews that have appeared in the journals *Development Policy Review* and the *Canadian Journal of Development Studies.*

James Ingram gave permission to quote from his book *Bread and Stones* (2007). The Taylor & Francis Group gave permission for me to refer to my book on *Global Food and Agricultural Institutions* (2009). The Earth Policy Institute gave permission to refer to the books by Lester Brown on *Outgrowing the Earth* (2004) and *Plan B 3.0* (2008), and has sent me regularly the institute's releases on his *Plan B 4.0* (2010). Lawrence Haddad gave permission to quote from the Institute of Development Studies' publication on *Lifting the Curse. Overcoming Persistent Undernutrition in India* (2009). Thomas Weiss sent me a copy of his 'Humanitarian Shell Games. Whither UN Reform?' (*Security Dialogue*, 1998, 29(1)) and gave me permission to quote from his book on *What's Wrong with the United Nations and How to Fix it* (Weiss, 2009). Jennifer Clapp gave permission to quote from the books she co-edited on *Corporate Power in Global Agrifood Governance* (Clapp and Fuchs, 2009) and *The Global Food Crisis* (Clapp and Cohen, 2009). And Palgrave Macmillan gave permission for me to refer to my books on *The UN World Food Programme and the Development of Food Aid* (2001), *Sir Hans Singer. The Life and*

World of a Development Economist (2002), and to *World Food Security. A History since 1945* (2007).

John Mitchell gave permission to refer to and quote from ALNAP publications. The World Bank gave permission to refer to and quote from several World Bank publications. The chair of the Good Humanitarian Donorship gave permission to quote the definition of humanitarian aid given in the *Principles and Practice of Good Humanitarian Donorship.* Paul Harvey gave permission to quote from the publications he wrote or co-authored. David White gave permission to refer to the Humanitarian Policy Group's 'opinion' on Linda Polman's criticism of humanitarianism. And FAO gave permission to reproduce the statement made by George McGovern at the Intergovernmental Advisory Committee in Rome, Italy on 10 April 1961, included in its publication *Development through Food* (1961: 121–2), which led to the establishment of the WFP.

John Mitchell gave permission to refer to and quote from ALNAP publications. The World Bank gave permission to refer to and quote from several World Bank publications. The chair of the Good Humanitarian Donorship gave permission to quote the definition of humanitarian aid given in the *Principles and Practice of Good Humanitarian Donorship.* Paul Harvey gave permission to quote from the publications he wrote or co-authored. David White gave permission to refer to the Humanitarian Policy Group's 'opinion' on Linda Polman's criticism of humanitarianism. And the FAO gave permission to reproduce the statement made by George McGovern at the Intergovernmental Advisory Committee in Rome, Italy on 10 April 1961, included in its publication *Development through Food* (1961: 121–2), which led to the establishment of the WFP.

Christopher Delgado and Christopher Gerrard at the World Bank gave me publications by the Bank. Randolph Kent and Larry Minear referred me to their work on humanitarian aid. Panos Konandreas sent me the paper he prepared for the FAO Emergency Operations and Rehabilitation Division on 'Promoting agricultural inputs in the Food Aid Convention to increase food production in emergency-prone developing countries' (2010) Galina Konandreas kept me informed of the discussions in the WTO regarding the future of food aid. John Toye sent me a copy of the Joyce Pearce Memorial Lecture that James Ingram gave at the University of Oxford, UK in 1988, which was subsequently published in the *Journal of Refugee Studies* (1989) 2(3): 329–58.

I am grateful to Angela D'Ascenzi of the WFP's INTERFAIS unit who prepared Figure 3.2, to Elaine Johnson, who prepared Figure 7.1, and to my son Dr David Christian Shaw who prepared all the other figures and tables that appear in this book.

Last, and most important, I owe much to my wife, Ileana, and my son and daughter, David and Elizabeth, for their support and encouragement.

I would like to thank Taiba Batool, my commissioning editor at Palgrave Macmillan, for responding quickly and positively to my request to publish this book. This is the sixth book that Macmillan or Palgrave Macmillan have published that I have written, edited or co-edited. Ellie Shillito, editorial assistant, worked diligently in clearing the manuscript through to the production stage, and helped in the design of the book's cover. The text has benefited from the thorough copy-editing of Keith Povey and his assistant Marilyn Hamshere of Keith Povey Editorial Services Limited, the company that also copy-edited my history of WFP that was published by Palgrave Macmillan in 2001. The proof pages were prepared quickly and efficiently by Newgen Imaging Systems Pvt. Ltd. in India.

The draft manuscript of the book was sent to WFP staff for comment. The comments received were taken into consideration in finalizing the manuscript. However, I alone am responsible for the views expressed in this book and for any shortcomings or errors therein.

Notes on the Text

1. All monetary values are expressed in United States dollars ($), unless otherwise stated.
2. All quantities are given in metric tons, unless otherwise stated.
3. One billion equals 1,000 million.
4. All figures and tables have been produced from WFP documents, unless otherwise stated.
5. Low-income, food-deficit countries include all net cereal-importing countries with a per capita gross domestic product (GNP) not exceeding the level used by the World Bank to determine eligibility for lending from its International Development Association (IDA).
6. In its resolution 2768 (XXVI) of 18 November 1971, the United Nations General Assembly singled out the poorest countries for special attention. They were called 'least-developed countries' (LDCs) and were defined as: 'countries with severe long-term constraints on development assessed on three basic criteria: per capita gross domestic product (GDP) of $100 or less at 1970 prices; share of manufacturing of 10 per cent or less of GDP; and 20 per cent or less literate persons aged 15 years or more'. New criteria established in 1991 defined LDCs as 'those low-income countries that are suffering from long-term handicaps to growth, in particular low levels of human resource development and/or severe structural weaknesses'.
7. The current six WFP operational regions are: Asia; the Middle East, Central Asia and Eastern Europe; Latin America and the Caribbean; West Africa; Southern, Eastern and Central Africa; and Sudan.
8. Up until 1967, the WFP was written in the American spelling 'World Food Program'. Thereafter, it has been written in the English spelling 'World Food Programme'.
9. The WFP's governing body, originally called the Intergovernmental Committee (IGC), was reconstituted as the Committee on Food Aid Policies and Programmes (CFA) in 1976 following a resolution on 'An Improved Policy for Food Aid 'of the 1974 World Food Conference (UN, 1975), and changed to the Executive Committee in 1996 following UN General Assembly resolution 48/162, on 'Further Measures for the Restructuring of the United Nations in the Economic, Social and Related Fields' adopted on 20 December 1993.
10. Up to and including its twenty-second session in October 1986, the reports of CFA Sessions were referred to as the 'Report of the United Nations/FAO Committee on Food Aid Policies and Programmes'. Thereafter, they were called 'Report of the Committee on Food Aid Policies and Programmes'.

Abbreviations

ACABQ	United Nations Advisory Committee on Administrative and Budgetary Questions
ACC	Administrative Committee on Coordination (UN)
ACC/SCN	Administrative Committee on Coordination/Subcommittee on Nutrition, now called the UN Standing Committee on Nutrition
ACF	Action contre la faim
ALNAP	Active Learning Network for Accountability and Performance in Humanitarian Action (London: ODI)
CAP	Consolidated Appeals Process for emergencies (UN)
CARE	Cooperative for American Relief Everywhere (US)
CDS	Consultative Subcommittee on Surplus Disposal (FAO)
CFA	Committee on Food Aid Policies and Programmes
CFS	Committee on World Food Security (FAO)
CRS	Catholic Relief Services (US)
CSD	Consultative Subcommittee on Surplus Disposal
DAC/OECD	Development Assistance Committee of OECD
DHA	Department of Humanitarian Affairs (UN), now OCHA
EB	Executive Board (WFP)
EC	European Commission (Brussels, Belgium)
ECHA	Executive Committee on Humanitarian Affairs (UN)
ECHO	European Commission Humanitarian Office
ECOSOC	Economic and Social Council (UN)
EDP	Enabling development policy
EEC	European Economic Community (later, the European Union)
EMOP	Emergency operations (WFP)
ERC	Emergency Relief Coordinator (UN)
EU	European Union
FAC	Food Aid Convention
FAO	Food and Agriculture Organization of the United Nations
FEWS	Famine Early Warning System
FFHC	*Freedom from Hunger Campaign*
FFP	Food-for-Peace Program (US)
FFW	Food-for-work
FIVIMS	Food Insecurity Vulnerability Information and Mapping System (FAO)
FRESH	Focusing Resources on Effective School Health
GATT	General Agreement on Tariffs and Trade
GDP	Gross Domestic Product
GIEWS	Global Information and Early Warning System (FAO)
GNP	Gross National Product

HPG	Humanitarian Policy Group
IASC	Inter-Agency Standing Committee on emergencies (UN)
IBRD	International Bank for Reconstruction and Development (World Bank Group)
ICCH	International Commodity Clearing House
ICRC	International Committee of the Red Cross
IDA	International Development Association (World Bank Group)
IDP	Internally displaced person
IEFR	International Emergency Food Reserve
IFAD	International Fund for Agricultural Development
IFC	International Finance Corporation (World Bank Group)
IFPRI	International Food Policy Research Institute
IFRC	International Federation of the Red Cross and Red Crescent Societies
IGC	Intergovernmental Committee (WFP)
ILO	International Labour Organization
IMF	International Monetary Fund
INTERFAIS	International Food Aid Information System (WFP)
IOM	International Office for Migration
IPCC	Intergovernmental Panel on Climate Change
IRA	Immediate Response Account of the IEFR (WFP)
ITSH	Internal transport, storage and handling (of food aid in developing counties)
JIU	Joint Inspection Unit of the United Nations
LDC	Least-developed country
LIFDC	Low-income, food-deficit country
LWF	Lutheran World Federation
MDGs	Millennium Development Goals
MOU	Memorandum of Understanding
NGO	Non-governmental organization
OCHA	Office for the Coordination of Humanitarian Affairs (UN)
OHCHR	Office of the High Commissioner for Human Rights
OPEC	Organization of Petroleum Exporting Countries
PRO	Protracted relief operation
PRRO	Protracted relief and recovery operation
PSA	Programme Support and Administration budget/costs (WFP)
REACH	Renewed Efforts Against Child Hunger and Undernutrition
SADC	Southern Africa Development Community
SO	Strategic objective
UN	United Nations
UNBRO	United Nations Border Relief Operation (Thailand)
UNCTAD	United Nations Conference on Trade and Development
UNDP	United Nations Development Programme
UNEP	United Nations Environmental Programme
UNESCO	United Nations Educational, Scientific and Cultural Organization

UNFPA	United Nations Fund for Population Activities
UNGA	United Nations General Assembly
UNHCR	United Nations High Commissioner for Refugees
UNICEF	United Nations Children's Fund
UNRRA	United Nations Relief and Rehabilitation Administration
UNRWA	United Nations Relief and Works Administration for Palestine Refugees
UNTAB	United Nations Technical Assistance Board
USAID	United States Agency for International Development
USDA	United States Department of Agriculture
VAM	Vulnerability Analysis and Mapping (WFP)
WFC	World Food Council (1976–93) (UN)
WFP	United Nations World Food Programme
WHO	World Health Organization

Introduction

Fifty years have passed since the UN World Food Programme (WFP) was established in 1961. The past half century has witnessed the remarkable birth and transformation of this UN body. Few international organizations have been born in the personal and unusual way in which the WFP was created (Chapter 1). By the end of its first thirty years of operations at the beginning of the 1990s, the WFP was one of the largest UN development agencies. Only a decade later, at the start of the new millennium, it had been transformed into what was described, for the first time, as 'the world's largest humanitarian organization' in its *Annual Report 2001.*[1] In 2008, with the adoption of the WFP's *Strategic Plan (2008–2011),* later extended to 2013, another transformation of the WFP was begun: from a food aid to a food assistance programme.

This book is about these transformations and the work of the WFP. I have been stimulated to write it for three main reasons. First, to complete my history of the organization, *The UN World Food Programme and the Development of Food Aid,* that was published in 2001 (Shaw, 2001). This covered the period up to 1995 and focused mainly on its development work. Second, the desire to describe in some detail how these transformations took place to create an organization which is now indispensible in the international humanitarian system. And third, to contribute to the WFP's institutional memory while records and details are still fresh and available.

Some explanation is in order concerning the title of the book. With over 14,000 staff, 90 per cent of whom are located in developing countries, in 2009, the WFP provided food to more than 101 million hungry poor people in 75 countries, 80 per cent of which was purchased in the developing countries themselves. But the WFP does not work alone. The organization has established the largest network of partnership arrangements in the international humanitarian system, working closely with other major humanitarian agencies, other UN and international organizations, over 2,000 national and international non-governmental organizations, and major companies and foundations in the private sector. Co-operation has also been established with leading humanitarian research groups and institutions to draw on the latest state-of-the-art knowledge, policy formulation and operational procedures to provide assistance based on the humanitarian principles of humanity, impartiality, neutrality and independence.

My interest in the concept of food security – and the consequences of its antithesis, food insecurity, which dominates the lives and livelihoods of hungry poor people and households throughout the developing world – was kindled during field research when an undergraduate, and later a postgraduate at the University of Oxford, in such diverse places as western Ireland, what are now Bosnia and Croatia before the break-up of the Federal Republic of Yugoslavia, and Morocco. It continued during my time as senior lecturer in rural economy at the University of Khartoum in the Sudan, as fellow in agricultural economics and founder member of the Institute of Development Studies at the University of Sussex, UK (1959–68), when I was also a consultant to the Food and Agriculture Organization of the United Nations (FAO), the World Bank, and the WFP. This involved visits to many countries in North Africa, the Middle East and sub-Saharan Africa.

My interest and concerns were strengthened further when I was employed by the WFP at its headquarters in Rome, Italy, first as senior evaluation officer, then as senior economist and head of the Policy Unit in the Office of the Executive Director, then as economic adviser, and finally as chief of the WFP's Policy Affairs Service until my retirement in 1994. During this time, I visited many countries in Africa and Asia, and liaised with a number of UN and international organizations concerned with issues related to food security. Located at the WFP's headquarters in Rome, I was also able to consult the papers and documents of the early pioneering FAO work on food and nutrition security in its archives and library, and follow closely discussions in its principal committees. This eventually led to my *World Food Security. A History since 1945* (Palgrave Macmillan, 2007) and my *Global Food and Agricultural Institutions* (Routledge, 2009), which includes the FAO, the Agricultural and Rural Development Department of the World Bank, the WFP, the International Fund for Agricultural Development (IFAD), and the Consultative Group on International Agricultural Research (CGIAR).

For this book, Chapter 1 gives the historical background to the establishment of the WFP in order to understand the transformational processes that have later taken place in the organization. The pre-history of the WFP was dominated by the development of the United States food aid programme and the pioneering work of the FAO. The unusual way in which the WFP was born as a three-year experimental programme (1963–65) is outlined. This was largely due to the efforts of one man, George McGovern, who at the time was the first director of the US Food-for-Peace programme, supported by President John F. Kennedy. The results and lessons of the experimental period and the activities of the WFP over the next thirty years, following its continuation in 1965, are described.

Chapter 2 identifies the tipping points in the WFP's transformation from a development to an emergency organization, brought about by executive director James Ingram when it was still mainly a development agency, based on his book on *Bread and Stones. Leadership and the Struggle to Reform the United Nations World Food Programme* (Ingram, 2007)[2] and personal correspondence with him.

Chapter 3 describes the completion of the WFP's transformation into the world's largest humanitarian agency led by Ingram's successor, executive director Catherine Bertini. It also gives examples of WFP emergency operations following large-scale natural disasters including: the Indian Ocean tsunami of 2004; food insecurity and the impact of HIV/AIDS in Southern Africa in 2005–06; the massive Pakistan/Kashmir earthquake of 2005; the widespread damage of cyclone Sidr in Bangladesh in 2007; and relief and recovery operations in the Central American region in 2002. Examples of responses to complex conflict-induced disasters are also given, including: conflict and genocide in Rwanda in 1994–95;

armed conflict and civil unrest in coastal west Africa (1989–2004); relief and continuing recovery in Afghanistan; and the humanitarian crisis in Darfur, Sudan, one of the WFP's largest, most complex, and prolonged emergency operations from 1993 to the present. Finally, examples of fast-moving emergency operations are given, including: the war in Bosnia-Herzegovina (1992–95); the UN oil-for-food programme in Iraq; emergency operations in the Lebanon in 2006; assistance to cyclone victims in Myanmar (Burma) in 2008; and emergency aid to war victims in Georgia after the fall of the Soviet Union in 2008–09.

Chapter 4 describes in some detail the four main elements of what is called the 'anatomy' of WFP emergency operations in the shift from development to relief activities. First, was the strategic deployment of WFP staff and decision-making from WFP headquarters to regional bureaux and country offices in developing countries. Second, was the development and enlargement of the WFP's transport and logistics expertise. Third, were the benefits of the new communications and information technology. And, finally, was the development and strengthening of partnerships and co-operation with other major humanitarian agencies, other UN and international organizations, NGOs, and the private sector.

Chapter 5 describes the WFP's associate development programmes and projects in the fields of nutrition-improvement, school feeding, HIV/AIDS, and gender policy and mainstreaming, concluding with the initiative on *Ending Child Hunger and Undernutrition* (ECHUI), which has now been transformed into REACH, *Renewed Efforts Against Child Hunger and Undernutrition*.

Chapter 6 is concerned with transforming food aid into food assistance programmes, led by the WFP's current executive director, Josette Sheeran. Early experiences with the food aid modalities of monetization, triangular transactions, local food purchases, and commodity exchanges are given, followed by more recent activities in: local and regional food procurement; the WFP's *Purchase for Progress* (P4P) programme, which aims to increase the food production of small-scale farmers in developing countries and link them with local markets through its food purchases; and voucher and cash transfer schemes, leading to innovations in food assistance to end hunger. The chapter ends by identifying major changes in the food security architecture.

The final chapter concerns the way ahead for the WFP following the adoption of its *Strategic Plan (2008–2013)*, and the identification of future challenges and opportunities. These include: leadership and co-ordination in the international humanitarian system, of which the WFP is a part; the conflicting priorities of saving lives, maintaining human rights, and protection of the afflicted and vulnerable, and the need for close co-operation among the mandated bodies; and clear identification for responsibility for internally displaced persons (IDPs) in emergency operations. The WFP's resource-related problems and the important position of the United States as its major donor are described. The impact of climate change and the need for the WFP to adopt a strategy to address the predictable outcomes are outlined. A strategy of combining the WFP's comparative advantages with partnerships to end hunger is proposed. The need to complete a comprehensive policy statement of WFP emergency operations is suggested. The importance of implementing what is called the 'third transformation' of building the capacities in governments and people in developing countries to take over programmes currently supported by WFP, included as strategic objective five of WFP's *Strategic Plan (2008–2013)*, is emphasized. Measures are called for to ensure the professionalism and security of WFP staff, the main strength of the organization. The chapter ends with a proposal for an independent external evaluation of WFP activities, which should be called for and monitored by its executive board.

1
Historical Background

In order to understand the transformation process that has taken place in the WFP, and the transformation of food aid to food assistance that is in progress, it is necessary to take account of the historical background which led to the establishment of the WFP in 1961.[1]

The pre-history of the WFP

The pre-history of the WFP was dominated by the development of the United States food aid programme and closely tied up with the pioneering work of the Food and Agriculture Organization of the United Nations (FAO) in Rome, Italy and the United Nations (UN) in New York.

United States food aid programmes: growth and development

The early history of US food aid was to have a major effect on discussions that eventually led to the establishment of the WFP.[2] US food aid originated in relief assistance for the victims of natural disasters, famines and civil disturbances at the beginning of the nineteenth century. The first major food aid operation occurred during and after the First World War (1914–18) for relief and reconstruction programmes in the war-torn countries of Europe when over six million tons of food was provided. The importance of this US initiative lay not only in the amount of relief provided, but in establishing a precedent for operations of this type. It also involved prominent personalities, the most famous being President Herbert Hoover, and the general realization of the potential value of food aid as a politically stabilizing factor (Singer *et al.*, 1987).

When food aid operations ended after the First World War, the Unites States was still producing considerable surpluses of cereals that could not be sold commercially on the international market through a combination of government agricultural support measures and the introduction of new technology and modern farming methods. Ways were sought to dispose of these burdensome food stocks, which were costing the US taxpayer increasingly more for the federal government to store. During the economic depression of the 1930s, President

Franklin D. Roosevelt resolved to address the problem through price and production controls. But the end of the period between the two world wars was characterized by mounting agricultural surpluses and generally ineffective efforts to dispose of them, either through domestic programmes or increased agricultural trade and aid channels.

The Second World War (1939–45) gave a further boost to US food aid programmes. Some $6 million of agricultural products were provided to European allies and legislation was passed to allow the sale of US surplus agricultural commodities for local currencies. At the end of the war, the United States again came to the aid of European countries in a massive reconstruction effort that involved the largest aid programme in world history. Under this European Recovery Programme (popularly known as the Marshall Plan after its originator, George C. Marshall, President Truman's secretary of state), $13.5 billion of aid was provided between 1948 and 1952 – about 3 per cent of US annual GDP, almost one third of which consisted of food, feed and fertilizers. It demonstrated that, if well-administered and managed, and combined with financial assistance, food surpluses could contribute to reconstruction, stability and economic growth. The Marshall Plan was also a boon for US domestic agriculture, providing a guaranteed export market for US farm output at a time when high levels of peacetime production were resumed. But it took another major military conflict, the Korean War (1950–53), to provide temporary relief, when once again the growing surplus burden became a major asset.

The Marshall Plan and the Korean War were to prove to be a major watershed in US food aid policy. Explosion in the scale and pace of technological advance in US agriculture led to ever-increasing surpluses as supply outstripped domestic and international commercial demand (Benedict and Bauer, 1960: 60–1). Hoping that this problem would eventually go away, the US congress and the White House adopted *ad hoc* measures, which, in reality, supported high levels of production long after changes in the post-war demand for US farm products had indicated the need for a major adjustment in national agricultural policies. In the late 1940s, the United States faced new economic and political challenges as European countries began to emerge from the devastation of war and rebuild their economies, including their agricultural sectors.[3]

Despite persistent imbalance between agricultural production and demand, leading to huge surpluses, US farmers had benefited from a large and growing overseas market and a considerable and growing food aid programme. Now, new challenges were emerging. European agricultural production began to rebound, and demand for US farm commodities declined as competition increased and the need for large US food aid programmes in Europe receded. However, the US farm price support systems instituted in the 1930s remained largely in place, and the impact of new technologies helped to create enormous food stocks in government inventories, draining financial reserves, and leading to heated bipartisan debate about how to resolve the problem. This was not the first time that this situation had emerged, but the scale of the problem was unprecedented and demanded a long-term solution.

At the same time, the United States emerged as the world's pre-eminent economic power, a role that brought with it new global political leadership and responsibility. As a result, the United States began to assume a more vigorous leadership in world affairs, especially concerning halting the spread of communism, particularly in developing countries (Ruttan, 1996). This was also reflected in the pivotal roles the United States played in the creation of the UN, the Bretton Woods institutions of the IMF and World Bank, and the UN specialized agencies, including the FAO. One way of securing the alliance and co-operation of developing countries was to provide economic assistance, including, and especially, food aid. In theory at least, countries receiving US aid were more likely to be allies. If they received food aid, they could also eventually become commercial markets for US agricultural commodities as their economies developed. At the same time, it would relieve the economic pressures of mounting food stocks held by the federal government at taxpayers' expense, and avoid politically awkward domestic agricultural reform measures.

Public Law 480: the institutionalization of United States' food aid

It was at this point that a mixture of political, economic, commercial, social and humanitarian concerns and objectives were brought to bear in fashioning the US food aid programme, largely in the form that persisted almost to the present time. Out of these compounded interests came the historic Agricultural Trade Development and Assistance Act of 1954, which became widely known by its number, Public Law (PL) 480 (Baker, 1979; Epstein, 1987). The act was to institutionalize, and to provide the legal framework for, US food aid programmes. PL480 finally marked recognition that the paradox of US surplus food production alongside hunger and malnutrition in the world could no longer be considered to be isolated and temporary occurrences. It established an indelible relationship between US domestic agricultural, commercial, and foreign policy interests, and external economic and humanitarian assistance, which were often in conflict.

Under PL480, US food aid was originally classified into three categories or 'titles', reflecting the motives and objectives of different interest groups: sales for foreign currency, famine relief and other assistance, and general provisions.

Title I: Sales for foreign currency. The major part of US food aid was to be provided as bulk, programme aid, mainly for balance of payment or budgetary support, and sold in recipient countries on concessional credit terms. The sales proceeds were to be used for no fewer than eight purposes: the development of new markets for US agricultural commodities; purchase of strategic and critical materials; procurement of military equipment; financing the purchase of goods and services for other 'friendly countries'; promotion of balanced economic development and trade among nations; payment of US obligations abroad; loans to promote multilateral trade and economic development; and financing international educational exchange.

Title II: Famine relief and other assistance. Up to $300 million of food aid commodities provided under PL480 was earmarked for emergency assistance to meet famine or other urgent relief requirements through voluntary relief agencies (to the extent that was practicable) and international organizations, including the WFP after its establishment.

Title III: General provisions. Under this title, food commodities were made available to US private voluntary organizations for distribution in food assistance programmes in the United States and abroad. Barter of food aid commodities was also permitted for strategic materials and goods not produced in the United States.

The food aid debate

US food aid increased rapidly with the passage of PL480. By the time the WFP was established in 1961, it had reached over 18 million tons a year at a cost of $1.6 billion. At the same time, it became the subject of increasing debate and criticism by politicians and academics alike. Democratic politicians, led by Hubert Humphrey and George McGovern, called for major reform measures and the establishment of what was called a 'food for peace' programme (Humphrey, 1958). The debate swirled around the competing multiple interests and groups for which PL480 was said to be created.[4] Whatever other objectives were stated, US food aid was identified with two overriding objectives: the development of commercial markets for US food commodities; and the disposal of unwanted US food surpluses. PL480, therefore, became one of the most popular but, at the same time, most controversial of US assistance programmes. Feeding the hungry poor in distress appealed to the strong humanitarian instincts of the American people who were prepared to give generously of their bounty, but the question was repeatedly asked 'Who is helping whom?' The level of food aid tended to be conditioned more by stock and price levels than by the needs of developing countries. The paradox emerged of food aid being more available when least required, and less available when most needed.

Political support in the United States for financial and food assistance also differed (Ruttan, 1993: 1–36). The major constituency supporting financial aid was typically in the executive administration, foreign policy establishment, and economic development academic community. Food aid, on the other hand, traditionally enjoyed support from the American public, and especially the farm community; Congress; and special interest groups in agricultural commodities, shipping and handling. Simply put, food aid was the farmers' friend; financial aid was the taxpayers' enemy. Strikingly, while the US Congress always passed a food aid budget as requested by the president, other economic assistance budgets received a mauling.

From the enactment of PL480 in 1954, food aid was treated separately from other forms of US aid. It became an inextricable part of an omnibus farm bill, which was passed at periodic intervals of four to five years, financed out of US Department of Agriculture appropriations. This, in turn, led to marked differences in responsibility for policy, programming and operations between food aid and other forms of US assistance, and a lack of co-ordination among the different types of aid in country assistance programmes. Other differences emerged.

Different methods of appraisal, operational procedures and evaluation were used for food aid to those adopted for financial assistance. Food aid had to be 'disposed of' and was seen as a 'second class' resource to financial aid. More attention was given, for example, to accounting for the food commodities provided (for which elaborate and costly procedures were devised) than to evaluating the benefits (or otherwise) that food aid brought to its recipients.

The differences between US financial and food aid, and even within US food aid itself, led to sharp differences of view in the academic world (Ruttan, 1996: 1984–90). One school of thought represented a 'marriage of convenience' between the disposal of agricultural surpluses and development assistance. Surplus food was seen to form a 'policy bridge' through which the pressures of surpluses in the United States, and of population and income increases in developing countries, could be moderated (Cochrane, 1959, 1962). Adjustment time could be bought to solve the problems of developed and developing countries simultaneously. It was appreciated, however, that the use of farm surpluses alone, even on an increasing scale, would not solve the problems regarding the sustainable development of countries. Other considerations were necessary. It was suggested, for example, that competing nations burdened with agricultural surpluses might participate in a 'food for development' programme under some form of multilateral arrangement. In this way, a formal international food aid programme under the sponsorship of the UN might come into being, anticipating the birth of the WFP.

Another school of thought was sharply critical of the 'marriage of convenience' persuasion (Schultz, 1960). The potential benefits of a food for development programme in developing countries were considered to bear little resemblance to what actually happened on the ground. The cost of the PL480 programme to the United States was considered to be grossly exaggerated and the value of the food assistance provided to recipient countries overstated, except in times of emergencies and severe food shortages. The cost to the United States measured in terms of the marginal revenue forgone from export sales was probably close to zero, but only if it were assumed that the programmes that generated the surpluses must be taken as a 'fact of life', and no alternative resource uses could be considered. Except in emergencies, food aid could have a negative effect on domestic agricultural production and trade in recipient countries, and on decisions of recipient governments to invest in their own agriculture.

Yet another view was that of the food aid recipient countries themselves. As in the United States, so also in developing countries, the implications of food aid were not clear. When PL480 was first mooted, the public statements of some US spokesmen often differed from those of US officials at the conference table. The former tended to create the impression that, since agricultural surpluses were a burden for the United States, they could be given away as a free gift to needy countries and used for giving relief to the poor. US officials, on the other hand, tended to emphasize that these surpluses were a scarce resource for developing countries and that they would vie with one another to obtain them. Hence, they felt it their duty to impose conditions that would limit the amounts received to the minimum required, and to prevent misuse. They also felt that the surpluses could prove useful for inducing recipient countries to follow certain political, economic and social policies. Thus, the face that the United States presented to developing countries was a 'combination of a kind-hearted humanitarian, an anxious salesman, and a hard-headed negotiator' (Sen, 1960:1031).

Food aid given for emergency relief did not create the same controversy, and was always welcome. Furthermore, much debate disappeared when food aid was integrated with recipient countries' own programme of economic development. In the last analysis, it was realized that a soundly planned and executed food aid programme was mutually beneficial for the recipient country and for the United States. For the former, it could help to speed economic development. For the United States, it was necessary to avoid serious price and storage problems, which could jeopardize the stability of its economy, and politically awkward domestic agricultural reform measures. Recognition of this mutual self-interest was the basis for success.

Much of the academic debate and research on food aid over the decade following the enactment of PL480 centred on the arguments of these three schools of thought. An extensive specialized literature emerged.[5] But intellectual investment in the subject was much less than might have been expected, given the magnitude of food aid provided. With some notable exceptions, development economists tended to avoid the subject, or came to it with a preconceived dislike, largely because it was perceived as 'surplus disposal' as opposed to 'serious development assistance' (Witt, 1964). The issues were blurred by new participants in the food aid debate who produced populist literature on the world food problem that emphasized philosophical and moral arguments, and the responsibility of developed countries, particularly the United States, to 'feed the hungry' (Ruttan, 1996: 184–96).

It was not until the latter part of the 1970s that the contradictions in the economic literature on food aid were clearly revealed (Isenman and Singer, 1977: 223). Many economists viewed food aid from a different perspective than for other forms of development assistance. Most economists appeared to believe that financial aid should be used to increase investment, employment and output in accordance with well-conceived development plans and projects, or signals provided by market forces. They would be disturbed if it were used instead, like food aid, to increase consumption in the short-term, or for low priority development projects with uncertain impact. At the same time, it was inconsistent to insist that food aid should be used for short-term consumption increases or for *ad hoc* 'additional' projects not included as a top priority in development plans, and to criticize food aid because it benefited consumption, not investment. These contradictions were clearly evident in the 'conventional wisdom' on food aid by the time the WFP began its operations in 1963.[6]

By the beginning of the 1960s, before the WFP was created, the battleground between the food aid protagonists and their detractors was well-established in the burgeoning literature and international debate. The main advantages of food aid were seen to be its:

- particular relevance for addressing the problems of poor and hungry people;
- ability to support employment-creation programmes, through labour-intensive works projects, without creating inflation;

- the establishment of stable food prices for producers and consumers, if the timing of food aid supplies was right; and, significantly,
- its ready availability as an additional resource to financial assistance on account of strong support in donor countries by politicians and special interest groups, and the general public.

Set against these advantages, the main shortcomings of food aid were described as:

- the disincentives it created to increase domestic agricultural production in recipient countries through depressing food prices, disrupting trade and distorting government policies and priorities;
- the creation of a dependency syndrome through providing handouts;
- the political and commercial forces of donors that motivated food aid flows; and
- its inferiority to financial assistance as a doubly-tied aid resource, tied to the food commodities provided and to the places where they were delivered.

Pioneering work of the FAO

While these developments were taking place in the creation and enlargement of US food aid programmes, the WFP also had its antecedents in the various attempts to set up some form of multilateral world food security arrangement since the time of the League of Nations before the Second World War. These attempts tried to rationalize food production, supply and trade for the benefit of both producers and consumers, in developing and developed countries. Attention was focused on two basic concerns:

- to reconcile the interests of producers and consumers by protecting them from uncontrolled fluctuations in world agricultural production and prices; and
- to use agricultural output in excess of commercial market demand, the so-called 'agricultural surpluses', to assist economic and social development in the developing countries, without creating disincentive to their domestic agricultural production or disruption to local or international trade.

In this regard, the pre-history of the WFP is closely tied up with the work of the FAO in Rome, Italy, the UN in New York, and the interests of the IMF and World Bank in Washington, DC. The origins of multilateral food aid can be traced to two meetings that took place in 1943. In May of that year, US President Franklin D. Roosevelt convened the UN Conference on Food and Agriculture at Hot Springs, Virginia in the United States, which laid the foundation for the creation of the FAO. In November of the same year, an agreement was signed in Washington, DC that led to the establishment of the UN Relief and Rehabilitation Administration (UNRRA), the first significant 'experiment' of a multilateral agency dealing with food aid (Woodbridge, 1950). Two others, operating on a smaller scale, were the UN Relief and Works Agency for Palestinian Refugees (UNRWA) and the UN Korean Reconstruction Agency.

From its inception in 1945, the FAO persistently advocated the establishment of some form of multilateral world food security arrangement and the constructive use of surplus agricultural commodities for development and emergency relief in the developing countries. Equally important was the need to avoid potentially destructive effects through the dumping of unwanted surpluses in developing countries, thereby impeding agricultural development and trade. The FAO's first director-general, Sir John (later Lord) Boyd Orr, took a proactive stance on both issues. A first step was to form an 'International Emergency Food Council', a body with powers to cope with the immediate, short-term chaos caused by war devastation in Europe and Asia. But a more far-reaching proposal was his attempt to establish a 'World Food Board'. The board would have the functions of: stabilizing prices through buffer stock schemes; holding a world food reserve against famine; financing surplus disposal programmes to needy people; co-operating with a credit-issuing agency, which would assist developing countries to develop their agriculture and ancillary industries; and co-ordinating bodies dealing with individual food commodities (FAO, 1946). The proposal was considered at the first FAO Conference in Copenhagen, Denmark in September 1946 but was not approved.

The proposal was revived again in 1949 in the form of an 'International Commodity Clearing House' (ICCH) but was turned down just as decisively as the former proposal. The major industrialized countries, particularly the United Kingdom and United States, were adamantly opposed to any centralized and multilateral world food management and security arrangement. As Boyd Orr put it:

> Britain and America were not prepared to give either funds or authority to an organization over which they had not got full control. Britain might have lost her advantage of cheap food imports, while the US thought that she could do better for herself as a world power through bilateral aid to other countries. (Boyd Orr and Lubbock, 1953: 57)[7]

While these attempts did not succeed, the FAO secretariat continued to keep the issues alive throughout the 1950s in a series of seminal studies and reports.[8] Three issues were to have particular relevance for the WFP when it was eventually established in 1961. The first concerned the identification of principles and guidelines for the disposal of agricultural surpluses, first adopted in 1954 in the face of growing surpluses in the United States and the enactment of the PL480 food aid programme, which became known as the *FAO Principles of Surplus Disposal* (FAO, 1954). The *Principles*, which were not legally binding but which provided 'consultative obligations', were to form a cornerstone for all WFP activities. Three general principles were recommended. The solution to problems of agricultural surpluses should be sought, wherever possible, through efforts to increase consumption rather than through measures to restrict supplies. Disposal of excess stocks of agricultural products should be undertaken in an orderly manner to avoid sharp falls in prices on world markets. Also, there should be an undertaking on the part of both importing and exporting countries that disposal of surpluses would be made without harmful interference to normal patterns of agricultural production and international trade. A special Consultative Subcommittee on Surplus Disposal (CSD), a subcommittee of the FAO's Committee on Commodity Problems, was set up in Washington, DC to monitor adherence to these principles, which has remained in place until the present time.

The second issue concerned the use of agricultural surpluses to finance economic development in developing countries. A pilot investigation was carried out in India, which laid the foundation for the project approach to the use of food aid that was subsequently adopted by the WFP (FAO, 1955). It showed in detail how the large amounts of capital represented by food surpluses could be used to finance a general expansion of investment programmes in developing countries.

The third set of issues related to proposals to establish: a world food reserve; national food reserves in developing countries; and international commodity agreements. Few developing countries had established national food reserves, which strengthened the case for a world emergency food reserve to provide emergency relief quickly and effectively. Several alternative plans evolved. One proposal, called the 'Three Circles Plan', was designed to combine speed and flexibility of relief operations with the acceptance and use of different kinds of contributions. The 'three circles' of the plan consisted of an inner circle of financial contributions on an agreed scale, a second circle of contributions in kind, and an outer circle of *ad hoc* contributions. Although the plan, like other proposals, was found to be technically sound, it was not pursued. The main reason for lack of progress was the reluctance of governments, mainly in developed countries, to approve measures that might weaken their national initiatives and powers of control. The climate of opinion continued to be against multilateral action in operational fields, as distinct from advisory or informational roles.

An expanded programme of surplus food utilization: an expert study

The FAO's persistence eventually paid off. In the context of the *Freedom from Hunger Campaign* (FFHC), which the FAO director-general B. R. Sen had launched in 1960 (Sen, 1982: 137–72), a resolution was adopted by the UN General Assembly in October 1960 on the 'Provision of Food Surpluses to Food-Deficient People through the United Nations System' (resolution 1496 (XVI)). The resolution invited the FAO, in consultation with others, to establish 'without delay' procedures by which 'the largest practicable quantities of surplus food may be made available on mutually agreeable terms as a transitional measure against hunger' through the UN system.

The FAO director-general appointed a group of five 'high-level independent experts' to assist him in making his proposals.[9] The group met at the height of the Keynesian consensus with its emphasis on full employment, active government demand management, and the welfare state, and its members were fully of the Keynesian view. The whole emphasis of its report was to deal with the surplus problem not by curtailing production but, rather, by expanding demand. Food aid from the food surpluses that existed was seen to be an important part of the resources needed for economic development in developing countries. Far from being a waste, it could be a blessing, if matched by other resources and used as an essential part of a coherent aid programme (as it had been used in the Marshall Plan) and, to borrow from the Keynesian concept, would 'turn the stone of surpluses into the bread of development'.

A central part of the expert group's case was that surplus food products could form an important part of capital in its original sense of a 'subsistence fund'. They reasoned that if sufficient food could not be supplied in a country to meet the increased demand of additionally employed workers on construction or other investment projects, then either more resources would have to be spent for food imports, or the amount of additional investment would have to be reduced. Additionally employed workers would have to be fed during the construction period, before the fruits of their labour and of investment could supply their needs, or enable them to buy their subsistence. Without such a fund, additional investment would not be possible, and inflation would be rampant. Food surpluses used for economic development would enable hungry people to produce either their own food or other products to provide the funds to buy food. Freedom from hunger could ultimately be achieved only through freedom from poverty.

The group estimated that about $12.5 billion of agricultural commodities could become available as 'surpluses' over a five-year period for use outside normal commercial market channels, either bilaterally or through the UN system. It recommended that about two-thirds of these resources should be used in economic development programmes and one-third for social development. A small part should be used to establish food reserves in developing countries and an international emergency food reserve. While it recognized that the major part of food aid would continue to be provided bilaterally, the group recommended that it should be supplied within a consultative, multilateral framework. This would assure that bilateral and international aid activities would take place within coherent and consistent country programmes of assistance. The vital function of country programming for external assistance, including food aid, was highlighted, anticipating by more than three decades the country programme approach that was eventually adopted by the WFP (WFP, 1994a).

The report of the expert group was reproduced in full in the FAO direct-general's proposals to the UN Economic and Social Council (ECOSOC), which was fittingly published in the FFHC basic studies series with the apt title *Development through Food: A Strategy for Surplus Utilization* (FAO, 1961a). Although a number of the report's recommendations were well in advance of their time, their value was subsequently recognized. Crucially, they were well-received by officials in key positions in the United States.[10] In submitting his proposals, B. R. Sen set out four 'basic principles'. First, food surpluses in aid must be granted for the promotion of economic and social development. Second, the main decisions as to what course development should take should be decided by the food-aided countries themselves. Third, food aid would be more effective if it were integrated in national development programmes. Fourth, use of food surpluses should not endanger the balance of the national economy in such ways as to allow short-term advantages but result in long-term failure.

The birth of the WFP

In the meantime, significant events had occurred in the United States, which resulted in a sea change in attitude towards the UN and the multilateral approach to international co-operation, including food aid. During the US presidential election campaign of 1960, in which Senator John F. Kennedy faced the two-term vice-president Richard M. Nixon, both candidates had shown an interest in the establishment of some form of multilateral food aid facility. The first public document containing a US proposal for a multilateral food aid facility appears to have come from Nixon (Wallerstein, 1980: 167–9). His motives were mixed. The proposal would not be harmful to US friends and allies, since they were expected to participate in it. It would not be subjected to the same criticism that was directed against US bilateral food aid, as it would be administered through the UN. It would project a positive international image for the United States. And it would 'out innovate' his presidential opponent, who was also calling for a multilateral food aid mechanism. Ultimately, President Eisenhower announced to the UN General Assembly on 22 September 1960, when the presidential election campaign was in full swing, that the United States was 'ready to join with other Member States of the United Nations in devising a workable scheme to provide [food surpluses] to Member States through the United Nations system relying on the advice and assistance of the Food and Agriculture Organization' (UN, 1960).

Upon winning the election, President Kennedy lost no time in using US food surpluses to combat hunger at home and abroad, and as a tool for American foreign policy. In his inspiring inaugural address on 20 January 1961, Kennedy stated:

> The world is very different now. For man holds in his mortal hands the power to abolish all forms of human poverty and all forms of human life ... To those people in the huts and villages of half the globe struggling to break the bonds of mass misery, we pledge our best efforts to help them help themselves ... If a free society cannot help the many who are poor, it cannot save the few who are rich. (US, 1963: 1012–13)

His first executive order, issued on the day after his inauguration, provided for an expanded programme of food distribution to needy families in the United States. The second, issued three days later, outlined the responsibilities of the newly appointed director of the Food for Peace programme, George McGovern, who was located in the executive office of the president. In his 'State of the Union' address on 30 January 1961, ten days after his inauguration, he stated that his administration would expand the Food for Peace programme 'in every possible way' so that the 'product of our abundance must be used more effectively to relieve hunger and help economic growth in all corners of the globe'. And he stated that he had requested McGovern 'to recommend to him additional ways in which these surpluses could advance the interest of world peace – including the establishment of world food reserves' (US, 1961).[11]

In a 'Special Message to the Congress on Agriculture' on 16 March 1961, Kennedy outlined a policy framework that was designed to move the focus of the US food aid programme from the disposal of surpluses to the constructive use of abundance, both at home and abroad (US, 1962: 192–200). In a 'Special Message to Congress on Foreign Aid' on 22 March 1961, he called for a comprehensive overhaul of US foreign aid, noting that its aid programmes and concepts were 'largely unsatisfactory and unsuited for our needs and for the needs of the underdeveloped world as it enters the Sixties' (US, 1962: 203–12).

Kennedy capped these statements at his first address to the UN General Assembly on 25 September 1961 when he proposed that the decade of the 1960s should be designated as the 'United Nations Decade for Development' (US, 1963: 623). The UN General Assembly approved Kennedy's proposal. It ushered in a new era, and created an atmosphere for positive international action and burden-sharing. Hopes were raised, especially in the developing countries, that the United States and other developed countries would be prepared to make substantial increases in their aid programmes, including food aid, as part of the UN development decade. At the same time, the FAO's *Freedom from Hunger Campaign*, which was to last throughout the 1970s, heightened world attention to the problems and causes of hunger, and its powerful negative effects (Sen, 1982; Shaw, 2007: 77–84).

It was against this background that consideration was given to FAO director-general B. R. Sen's proposals for *Development through Food* (FAO, 1961a), and the personal and unusual way in which the WFP was born. Before submitting his report, Sen requested a meeting of an Intergovernmental Advisory Committee in Rome, Italy in April 1961 to obtain its views. President Kennedy asked George McGovern to represent the United States at the meeting, with the assistance of Raymond Ioanes of the US Department of Agriculture and Sidney Jacques from the US Department of State. As noted earlier, President Kennedy had asked McGovern to undertake an evaluation of the past operations of the US food aid programme and propose ways to improve it. The report, which Ioanes had helped to prepare, was submitted to the President on 28 March 1961, shortly before the meeting in Rome, Italy. In it, McGovern wrote, among other things:

> We should support an expanded role for FAO – a role where it will have responsibility for developing and executing a multi-lateral food distribution program. There should not be fear that a multi-lateral approach will conflict with the US Food for Peace Program. On the contrary, world food needs are so great that there is need for both approaches.[12]

At the meeting in Rome, recalling the evaluation he had recently submitted to President Kennedy, McGovern suggested to the other members of the US delegation that a concrete proposal be made in order to move the process forward. This came as a complete surprise. There had been no discussion, hence no agreement, on any proposal in Washington, DC prior to the departure of the US delegation for Rome. Moreover, the meeting had been called only to provide advice and comments, not to present government positions. McGovern's colleagues felt that there was insufficient time to get any proposal approved in Washington, DC. However, McGovern persisted. He requested the other members of the delegation to help draft a proposal while he undertook to get clearance from the White House.

This unconventional procedure was even more unusual in that permission to proceed was sought over a weekend. McGovern contacted his deputy in the Office of Food for Peace, James Symington, by telephone and requested him to speak about the draft proposal to Theodore Sorensen, special counsel to President Kennedy. Sorensen, a friend of McGovern who had the ear of the President, later spoke by telephone with McGovern, and 'within 24 hours' permission was obtained to go ahead. This showed the close relationship, and high regard, McGovern enjoyed with President Kennedy.

The multilateral food aid programme that McGovern proposed was circumscribed in a number of ways. (The full proposal is given as the Appendix at the end of this chapter because of its historical significance for the WFP.) It was to be a three-year experimental programme with a decision on its continuation dependent on an evaluation of experience. It was to be limited to $100 million in commodities and cash. The United States would be prepared to offer $40 million in commodities and possibly a supplementary cash contribution when, in 1961, the value of farm products shipped under the US food aid programme alone was $1.3 billion and US food surplus stocks had reached 112 million tons. The activities of the experimental programme were to be restricted to meeting emergencies and to the piloting of development interventions, such as school lunch programmes and labour-intensive projects, in order to test approaches and develop diversified experience. The US food aid programme was also engaged in pilot projects in these areas.

The multilateral food aid experiment was meant to be a supplement to, and not a competitor of, the bilateral food aid programmes. Large-scale programme food aid for balance of payment and budget support, and support for political and commercial objectives that the bilateral food aid programmes provided, was precluded. The proposal stressed its multilateral nature: the word 'multilateral' occurred four times. It was to be 'a truly multilateral program with the widest possible contributions by member countries'. This served notice that the United States was not prepare to address the food problems of developing countries alone. International burden-sharing was needed to tackle their dimensions, politically and financially. This would help both to meet the costs involved and to give an opportunity to all donors to contribute according to their comparative advantage in terms of food commodities and the kinds of food needed, money for transportation and administration, and services, such as shipping. The establishment of a small and circumscribed multilateral food aid experimental programme also provided a token to the UN system at a modest cost, and posed no threat to the large bilateral food aid programmes or to commercial trade.

McGovern's proposal, and the concise, yet detailed, way in which it was presented, caught the delegates from other countries by surprise. They called for an adjournment to consider how to respond. At the same time, officials in the US delegation to the UN were working on another, and much larger, multilateral food aid proposal to be administered through the UN Special Fund in New York. McGovern had been briefed on this proposal. He was not opposed to it but was sceptical that it would clear the various US departments in Washington, DC and the US Congress. That was why he went ahead with his proposal in Rome after obtaining approval from the White House. The two proposals had to be reconciled so that a common position could be presented by the US delegations at the FAO Conference and the UN General Assembly at the end of 1961.[13] McGovern initiated a meeting in New York with US representatives to the UN on 10 November 1961. A second meeting was held at the Department of State in Washington, DC four days later. The State Department generally favoured a limited experimental plan along the lines proposed by McGovern in Rome, and the larger food aid proposal was no longer pursued. It was recognized, however, that if the proposed three-year experimental multilateral food aid programme was successful, it could encourage, rather than foreclose, a larger food aid programme (McGovern, 1964: 109–110).

Both proposals were preferred to other proposed schemes. The Prime Minister of Canada, Lester Pearson, laid a proposal for a 'world food bank' before the UN General Assembly in 1959. A comprehensive commodity plan was also proposed (Haas, 1969: 155). These alternative proposals did not receive serious consideration – particularly after US opposition was known (Wallerstein, 1980: 170). Eventually, McGovern's proposal was accepted. In the new spirit of international solidarity and burden-sharing in development co-operation that the Kennedy administration had ushered in, the UN/FAO World Food Programme (WFP) was established in parallel resolutions passed by the FAO Conference and the UN General Assembly on 24 November and 19 December 1961, respectively (FAO, 1961b; UN, 1961a).[14]

As McGovern had proposed, the resolutions established an experimental three-year programme of approximately $100 million. It was to be undertaken jointly by the FAO and the UN. Critically, contributions were to be made on a voluntary basis, and not on an assessed basis and mandatory form as in the UN specialized agencies. Contributions could be made in the form of appropriate commodities, acceptable services, and cash aiming, in the aggregate, at a cash component of a least one third of total contributions. An Intergovernmental Committee (IGC) was established consisting of 20 members, (increased to 24 in 1963), half elected by the FAO Council and half by the ECOSOC, to provide guidance on policy, administration and operations, taking into account the need for balanced representation of economically developed countries and of less developed countries and other relevant factors, such as representation from both contributing and recipient countries, equitable geographical distribution and representation of countries with commercial interests in international trade in food stuffs, especially those highly dependent on such trade.

In the administration of the WFP, attention would be paid to establishing adequate and orderly procedures on a world basis for meeting emergency food needs and emergencies inherent in chronic malnutrition, which could include the establishment of food reserves. Also, assistance would be given with preschool and school feeding; and pilot projects would be implemented with the multilateral use of food as an aid to economic and social development, particularly when related to labour-intensive projects and rural welfare. Other forms of assistance and country plans for economic and social development should be taken into account in providing WFP food aid. Projects would be undertaken only in response to requests from the recipient country or countries concerned.

It was recognized that the administration of the WFP would require close co-operation, particularly on development projects, between the FAO and the UN, and other appropriate UN agencies and intergovernmental bodies. Food aid would be provided in accordance with the *FAO Principles of Surplus Disposal*. The work of the WFP was to be carried out by a joint FAO/UN administrative unit located at FAO headquarters in Rome, Italy, which would report both to the FAO director-general and the UN secretary-general. The costs of administration and operations would be met from contributions to the WFP. The UN resolution called for 'expert studies' to be undertaken, 'which would aid in the consideration of the future development of multilateral food programmes'.

The WFP constitution: a joint UN/FAO undertaking

As one writer has put it: 'In pursuing their desire to create a modest, experimental programme that would satisfy the myriad competing interests of the time, the founders of the WFP created a complex constitutional structure' (Charlton, 1992: 634). The unique and unprecedented nature of the WFP's original constitution was that the new experimental programme was to be undertaken *jointly* by the *parent* organizations of FAO in Rome, Italy and the UN in New York (WFP, 1963a). The rationale given for this unprecedented arrangement was that WFP activities were perceived to be included in the mandates of both organizations. The UN functioned 'in the general field of economic and social development', while the FAO had special responsibilities 'for securing improvements in nutrition and in the efficiency of food production and distribution'. In reality, there was a mixture of motives for establishing the 'joint undertaking'. One was to widen the appeal of the new organization among donors, particularly those in North America, who felt that they had greater influence on decision making at the UN in New York than at FAO in Rome, Italy. Another reason, voiced by the UN secretary-general, U Thant, was to portray the new body as a symbol of co-operation in the UN system and solidarity in the international community in the context of the UN Decade for Development, called for by President Kennedy and launched shortly before the WFP was established. He expressed the hope that 'the administration of the programme (WFP) will provide an outstanding example of concerted action within the United Nations family' (UN, 1961b).

The view was expressed at the FAO Conference in 1961 that FAO alone should administer the WFP and should co-operate with the UN 'as and when needed'. But FAO director-general B. R. Sen noted that while food surpluses could make a major contribution to rural development and welfare, plans for agricultural development must form part of the overall economic development of a country. This view was finally endorsed and the FAO Conference unanimously supported the joint operation of the WFP by the FAO and the UN. It was also expected that the WFP would provide substantial additional resources to support the work of both the FAO and UN. Therefore, neither would yield to the other and, as a compromise, the WFP was made a joint undertaking. The checks and balances written into the WFP's constitution were to ensure that neither organization would gain hegemony over the fledging programme.

A contrary view was that, given the negative experiences of the rapidly expanding US food aid programme, the political, commercial and economic dimensions of food aid required policy, economic and financial controls and guidance by the two organizations with the mandates, experience and responsibilities for the wider issues at stake. As a multilateral food aid entity, WFP operations could not be left only to an overseeing body in which donors would tend to have undue influence. Rather, it should be subject to intergovernmental authorities with larger and differently balanced memberships.

Other parts of the WFP's constitution sprang from this basic framework of a joint UN/FAO undertaking with the constant involvement not only of the executive heads of the parent organizations, but also of their principal governing bodies in a Byzantine vortex of controls and balances. The WFP's executive director was to be appointed by the UN secretary-general and FAO director-general, after consultation with the WFP's governing body. WFP senior officials were to be chosen by the executive director in agreement with the executive heads of the UN and FAO. The executive director was required to present a programme of work to the governing body once a year for consideration and approval, in consultation with, and with the approval of, the executive heads of the UN and FAO. In a joint *Note Verbale* of 11 June 1962, the UN and FAO executive heads delegated authority to the WFP executive director to conduct correspondence directly with governments on their behalf.

The executive heads of the UN and FAO were made jointly responsible for convening pledging conferences at UN headquarters in New York at which donors could announce their voluntary contributions to the WFP's resources. An elaborate process was established whereby the target levels of resources set for these conferences were approved by them, after being proposed by the WFP's executive director, then agreed by the WFP's governing body, approved by ECOSOC and the FAO Council, and endorsed by the UN General Assembly and the FAO Conference. The executive heads of the UN and FAO were also to ensure that any expert studies called for in the UN resolution establishing the WFP should, as much as possible, be made part of the regular activities of their organizations and of other interested and competent intergovernmental bodies.

WFP financial arrangements were entrusted to the FAO director-general rather than to the WFP's executive director. All contributions to the WFP's regular resources were credited to a special trust fund from which the cost of WFP operations and administration were to be met. The fund was to be administered by the FAO director-general in accordance with FAO financial regulations. WFP annual accounts were to be submitted to the FAO's external auditors but, to add to the complexity, WFP annual budgets and financial reports were to be reviewed not only by the FAO's Finance Committee, but also by its UN counterpart, the UN Advisory Committee on Administrative and Budgetary Questions (ACABQ) before they were passed to the WFP's governing body for approval.

In an arrangement that was to cause future friction, WFP emergency assistance was to be approved not by the WFP's executive director but by the FAO's director-general. Allocation of WFP resources for emergencies was to be reviewed by the WFP's governing body in consultation with the FAO's director-general. In cases of special need, the governing body could, at the request of the executive director, and in consultation with the FAO director-general, allocate further amounts for use by the director-general to meet emergency food needs. Once requests for emergency assistance were approved by the FAO director-general, the WFP's executive director concluded an agreement with the recipient government, and submitted progress and terminal reports to the WFP's governing body.

The founders of the WFP 'were as much influenced by what they did not want to create as to what they intended to do' (Charlton, 1992: 635). They did not want to set up a specialized, self-contained, agency and were concerned to create a structure that could be easily dismantled in the event that the WFP experiment did not succeed. The legal standing of the WFP's administrative unit or secretariat was questioned until, in a letter to UN secretary-general U Thant of 20 June 1962, FAO director-general B. R. Sen gave his view of what he regarded as its status:

> I am of the opinion that the administrative unit is neither exclusively an integral part of FAO nor of the United Nations... [It] is a joint one reporting both to the Secretary-General of the United Nations and the Director-General of FAO. It has its own supervisory and executive organ reporting to the FAO Council and to ECOSOC.[15]

The arrangements agreed upon were devised: to take account of the temporary and experimental nature of WFP activities, with an uncertain future; to avoid duplication of services already available in the UN system; to keep administrative costs as low as possible; and to stress the overriding operational nature of the WFP. Thus, 'in all stages of the development of its activities', the WFP was required to consult with, and seek advice and co-operation from, its parent bodies, the UN and FAO, and operate in close liaison with appropriate UN agencies and operating programmes, bilateral aid agencies and non-governmental organizations (NGOs).

A major anomaly was that while the WFP's executive director was made responsible for assuring that the development projects supported with WFP assistance were 'sound, carefully planned and directed toward valid objectives, for assuring the mobilization of the necessary technical and administrative skills, and for assessing the ability of recipient countries to carry out the project', and for 'correction of any inadequacies in project operations', the expertise required to undertake these tasks were not immediately available to the WFP but had to be contracted from other organizations. To assist the WFP in these and other matters, liaison officers were established at the UN, FAO, ILO, UNESCO and WHO, paid for by the WFP.

Every effort was made to keep WFP management and administrative costs to a minimum 'consistent with the maintenance of efficiency'. Instead of developing its own services, the general financial and administrative services of the FAO were called upon on a reimbursable basis. WFP staffing, and the level of their appointment, was kept low and closely monitored, with the governing body micro-managing and approving new staff at all levels, both professional and general service, and proposals for their upgrading and transfer at WFP headquarters.

Rather than appoint its own representatives in countries receiving WFP assistance, the country representatives of the UN Technical Assistance Board (UNTAB), later of the UNDP when it was established in 1965, were requested to perform that function, in addition to their other responsibilities. WFP field staff stationed in recipient countries formed part of their office, and national WFP staff were appointed and administered under UNDP rules and regulations, the cost of which was reimbursed by the WFP. One of the strangest paradoxes was that, for WFP staff members to become WFP representatives, they would have to resign their positions in the WFP and become staff members of the UNDP, although, in reality, few made that transition.

While the WFP's administrative costs were kept to the lowest level of any aid agency (between 6 and 7 per cent of operating costs), the tasks of the small WFP staff were increased manyfold. The two parent bodies had to be consulted and generally kept informed. Communications with other co-operating UN organizations had to be maintained. The twice-yearly meetings of the governing body had to be serviced and reports on those meetings submitted to both ECOSOC and the FAO Council. Requests for WFP assistance, and progress and evaluation reports had to be presented to the governing body for discussion, and approval was made on an individual project basis, not as country assistance programmes as in many UN bodies.

These complex and complicated institutional arrangements were to remain in force for thirty years until major changes in the WFP's constitution came into effect in 1992 (WFP, 1991b). For almost a decade from his appointment in 1982, WFP executive director James Ingram led a struggle for reform against the intransigence of FAO director-general Edouard Soauma. This confrontation is carefully and thoroughly documented in Ingram's book *Bread and Stones*, based on the diaries he kept throughout the period. As Ingram points out:

> In a sense this is a depressing tale that shows how dysfunctional the UN system of related agencies, created by governments and overseen by them,

can become. On the other hand it is a harbinger of hope. Reform is possible'. (Ingram, 2007: 1)

The legal opinion that Ingram requested from the UN to clarify the nature of the WFP's relationship with its parent bodies, and the powers and responsibilities of the WFP's executive director, noted that while the joint programme should be equally responsive to both parent organizations, it had the autonomous authority to decide on the disposition of resources approved by its governing body. It also noted that the provision of services to the WFP by the FAO had been introduced to assist the WFP to carry out its functions, and should not be interpreted as a mandate to control WFP activities, as Saouma had done.

Another cause of friction was the unequal partnership that was born and developed between the UN and FAO, and their executive heads, in executing their responsibilities regarding their joint undertaking. The UN secretaries-general had many other responsibilities. From them, the WFP was one of several UN bodies whose business was delegated to other UN senior staff. While constitutionally the executive heads of UN and FAO had equal responsibility for the appointment of WFP executive directors and senior staff, in consultation with the WFP's governing body, in reality it was the FAO director-general who took the initiative in identifying and appointing those he regarded as suitable.

Located in Rome, Italy, the work of the WFP could be closely followed and influenced by the FAO director-general. In addition, as most sessions of the WFP's governing body were held at FAO headquarters, policy papers presented to, and the draft reports of, the governing body could be vetted and controlled. FAO resident representatives from selected developing countries on the WFP's governing body were used as surrogates or channels to present the FAO director-general's views. These practices were well-known and allowed to continue throughout Saouma's long period of office, which was to last 18 years. They became so blatant that eventually the WFP's major donors insisted that basic changes would have to be made in the WFP's constitution if they were to continue their support of the Programme.

Ingram had an unexpected ally in his crusade to obtain the WFP's institutional freedom. In 1984, on his own initiative, Maurice Bertrand, an inspector of the UN Joint Inspection Unit, an independent unit in the UN system, prepared a report on personnel problems in the WFP. The report was highly critical of the WFP's personnel situation. The root of the problem was considered to be the WFP's outmoded constitutional structure, which was found to be 'neither rational nor workable'. The report concluded that the WFP's personnel problems were 'practically insoluble within the existing legal framework', and that:

> Since the development of a personnel policy is the first, absolutely essential step in enabling WFP to perform its mission properly, changes in the legal framework and the practices followed must be proposed and put into effect. (Bertrand, 1984: 3)

Far-reaching changes to the WFP's constitution were adopted by consensus by its governing body in 1991. They were written into the WFP's new general regulations, which came into force at the beginning of 1992. While the WFP was to remain a joint UN/FAO organ, its governing body was given full powers of oversight of the Programme and the WFP was given a 'legal capacity'. The number of members of the governing body was increased from 30 to 42, with 27 members from developing countries. The location of WFP headquarters was to remain in Rome, but no longer at FAO headquarters. And the executive director was given complete responsibility for the operation and administration of WFP resources, approval of emergency assistance up to a level delegated to him by the governing body, and staff appointments up to and including the D-2 level (UN, 1991a; FAO, 1991; WFP, 1991b: 12–30). The shackles that had impeded WFP growth and maturity had finally been lifted.

A special ceremony was held in honour of executive director Ingram at his final session of the WFP's governing body in December 1991 (WFP, 1991a). Tributes were paid by 26 delegates, some on behalf of country regional groups. While a few remarks were *pro forma*, most reflected a genuine feeling of respect and gratitude that he had brought the WFP through a very stormy sea to a safe haven. In so doing, he had helped to restore the self-confidence and self-respect both of the WFP's governing body and its secretariat to face the challenges and opportunities of the future.

The experimental years: 1963–65

As we have seen, the WFP did not begin its use of food aid with a clean slate. It acquired a number of legacies from its pre-history, some of which were positive, couched in the spirit of an idea whose time had come. Others were less favourable; some downright negative. Many of the basic ideas and concepts that the WFP acquired were developed in the FAO. The WFP owed its birth, in part, to the vision and tenacity of early FAO leadership, and support by senior management at the UN. The legacies from the United States were also profound. It was, after all, the initiative and leadership at the highest level in Washington, DC that was largely responsible for the birth of the WFP, and for its support. But there were less fortunate legacies that emerged from the policies and programmes of the US PL480 food aid programme that had begun operations almost a decade before WFP activities started. We shall see how these legacies affected the WFP in its experimental years (1963–65), before it was launched on a continuing basis in 1965.

By the end of the experimental period on 31 December 1965, 101 countries had participated in the experiment as donors or recipients, or both. Total resources contributed to the WFP reached $93.7 million, just short of the target of $100 million, which was later reduced to $84.5 million to take account of lapsing pledges and price changes. The main purpose of the three-year experiment was to explore *as widely as possible* (emphasis added) the ways in which a multilateral organization could use surplus food effectively as a resource to promote development, as well as to respond rapidly and effectively to emergency needs in the developing countries. This learning experience was to take place in the three specific areas mentioned in the FAO and UN resolutions establishing the WFP: meeting emergency food needs; assisting pre-school and school feeding; and implementing pilot economic and social development, labour-intensive and rural welfare projects.

Although 32 emergency operations were carried out in 25 countries during the experimental period, three problems faced the WFP in providing speedy and adequate relief assistance from the outset. First, an allocation was made (25 per cent) for emergencies from the limited resources available. Second, the WFP was unable to provide rapid emergency assistance. Food commodities pledged to the WFP were not held in storage by the Programme but kept in food stocks of donor countries around the world. The WFP did not have its own transport and logistics facilities but had to purchase them with its limited cash resources, which also restricted the purchase of food products close to where emergencies occurred. It took several months to deliver food from donor to recipient countries. More time was often required to synchronize the arrival of consignments of different food commodities that made up emergency rations from a number of donors. Third, there were basic operational problems, such as the sustained supply of staple and acceptable foodstuffs, the size and suitability of containers and packaging, and adequate transport, storage and handling facilities in developing countries. As a result, evaluating the experience at the end of the experimental period, the WFP's executive director, Addeke Boerma, wrote:

> The conclusion is reluctantly reached that it is important to make clear to countries suffering disasters the inevitable limitations to which the supply of World Food Program emergency food aid is subjected, in order to avoid the raising of hopes which cannot be fulfilled. (WFP, 1965c: 30)

The result was that, for the next thirty years, the WFP focused the major part of its assistance on development projects.

During the experimental period, 116 development projects were supported in a wide variety of economic and social development sectors. The largest number of approved projects was in Asia (41 per cent), followed by Africa (30 per cent), southern Europe (15 per cent), and Latin America and the Caribbean (14 per cent). Seventeen different types of development projects were approved. These could be grouped into four main categories as far as the use of food aid was concerned: food-for-work programmes, land settlement and reform, special feeding programmes, and animal production projects.

Food-for-work programmes

The largest category comprised labour-intensive works programmes. WFP food assistance was provided to workers and their families in the form of rations calculated to meet their nutritional requirements and as part of their money wages. Most of these projects were designed to promote agricultural development.

Others involved the construction and improvement of physical infrastructure. A small number were industrial and manufacturing projects. A common feature was the mobilization of unemployed and under-employed workers through the creation of useful employment, thereby improving their standard of living and speeding up economic and social development.

This early experience indicated that one of the greatest under-utilized resources of developing countries were the people themselves. The provision of food could help tap this resource. But assistance, both financial and technical, was also required to improve the quality, scope and speed of implementation of the works undertaken. For this reason, a number of the early pioneering projects were undertaken in co-operation with other UN agencies, bilateral aid programmes, and NGOs. They also showed that a great deal of organizing ability was required, which was often a scare factor, but that where work was carried out on a communal basis, much of the required organization could be provided by local leaders and the people themselves. As the WFP provided rations to a worker and his family, about one million people benefited directly from WFP assistance, and more indirectly from the work programmes carried out, giving an indication of the potential scope for future WFP activities, should they be continued after 1965.

Land settlement and reform

A second category of projects involved the settlement or resettlement of people in new agricultural schemes or after land reform measures had been implemented. Food was provided to settler families until they could produce their own food. Food aid could play a key role in easing the burden and hardship of settlers on new lands. However, it had to be carefully calibrated. It should not create a disincentive for settlers to attain their own food self-sufficiency as soon as possible. But neither should it be withdrawn too soon, thereby creating unnecessary hardship. These projects could only benefit from food aid if they were carefully planning and prepared, which was not always possible to ensure, given the often political environment within which they were implemented, and the short period of the WFP's experimental programme (see p. 23).

Special feeding programmes

The third category embraced pre-school, primary school, and various other types of educational and training programmes. Food aid was considered to act as a resource to improve nutrition and school performance, provide an incentive for children from poor households to attend school regularly, and help offset the cost of education and training programmes. While the original scope of WFP assistance in this field was limited to school feeding programmes, it was quickly realized that there was a much wider possibility for food aid to contribute to what came to be called the 'development of human resources'. This included: the improvement of nutrition of mothers and pre-school children; assistance to education and training programmes after the primary school stage, including literacy campaigns; and public health and hospital feeding programmes. But many of these programmes required a longer time span for their full benefits to be realized than the three-year experimental period allowed. Hence, the relatively small share of this category of projects in the totality of WFP activities during the experimental period.

Animal production projects

The fourth category involved projects for the promotion of livestock production in which feed, not food, aid was provided. Two main types of projects were involved: dairy production schemes designed to increase the production of milk and dairy products; and schemes to improve grazing conditions, particularly in semi-desert regions. Animal production was often encouraged as part of larger agricultural production projects as an incentive for mixed farming and improved land management, leading to increased farm incomes. Livestock projects of this kind presented opportunities for the conversion of low-value feed grains in surplus in donor countries into high-value protein foods in developing countries. Early experience made it clear, however, that other factors were essential for their success. These included a simultaneous effort to increase the domestic production of feed supplies in recipient developing countries, or to increase their ability to pay for imported feedstuffs on a commercial basis during the time that WFP aid was provided. At the same time, there should be a systematic plan to reduce livestock numbers on overgrazed land, and to improve the quality and productivity of breads. Also, technical advice and assistance should be closely integrated in planning and implementing projects in this field.

The lessons of the experimental period

That the experiment was regarded as successful, leading to the continuation of the WFP after 1965, was due to the dedication of a small band of ably-led pioneers in the WFP secretariat,[16] guided by an active and involved governing body; the support of many donors, from the developing and developed parts of the world; and the co-operation of officials in recipient countries, the two sponsoring organizations (the UN and FAO), other UN agencies, and NGOs. An important additional factor was the timing of the experiment. As we have seen, the WFP experiment was approved in the year that the Kennedy administration took office in the United States. Following President Kennedy's proposal, the 1960s had been designated as the 'United Nations Decade of Development', which ushered in the promise of increased aid for developing countries in a spirit of international burden-sharing, and in the context of a multilateral approach to international co-operation through the UN system, which enjoyed its halcyon years.

With hindsight, setting a time limit of three years was to prove to be a very short period in which to carry out the experiment, for which there were few established ground-rules to guide operations. Each task had to be performed in accordance with an inexorable timetable. In reality, the experiment was to take place over only two years. By the beginning of November 1964, almost all the high protein commodities and the cash resources provided to the WFP had been committed. There was little time left after that date to obtain more experience, even if more resources were made available, and to evaluate the results in order to make a decision on the future of the WFP after the end of 1965.

The experimental period did, however, establish basic WFP policies and administrative procedures that were to remain largely in place for the next three decades.

Policy considerations

Project aid

From inception, the WFP was restricted to providing assistance to specific, individual development projects or emergency operations executed by recipient developing country governments. This so-called 'project approach' was in marked contrast to the 'programme approach' adopted under the US and other bilateral food aid programmes, which provided food aid in bulk for balance of payments and budgetary support, and for supporting political and commercial objectives. A number of reasons were put forward for adopting this different approach. WFP food aid was to be supplementary to, and not in competition with, bilateral food aid, and should therefore be kept to a moderate size. It was much more difficult, and time-consuming, to disburse large amounts of aid – any aid – on a project-by-project basis than for macro-economic purposes using the bulk food aid programme approach.

Other reasons were given. The WFP experiment had been specifically proposed to test out the use of food aid in different types of development projects. The project approach facilitated evaluation of the effects of WFP food aid on economic and social development, and was made a mandatory requirement when the WFP was eventually continued beyond 1965. The project approach was also considered to be the best way of adhering to the *FAO Principles of Surplus Disposal*, and for avoiding any disincentive to agricultural production in the recipient countries and disruption to international trade that had been attributed to the US and other bilateral food aid programmes. In addition, it was hoped that the WFP would attract more donors and, hence, forestall the creation of other large-scale bilateral food aid programmes, which could compete with those already established. This particularly applied to Western Europe where, through the adoption of a Common Agricultural Policy (CAP) in the European Economic Community (EEC) (later the European Union – EU), large-scale food surpluses began to be created.

Nutritional considerations

Debate took place as to whether to take the nutritional or income-transfer value of the food commodities provided by the WFP into account in determining the rations to be supplied. The former approach was adopted in conformity with the *FAO Principles of Surplus Disposal*. The aim was to provide a food ration that, together with local foods, made up a complete and balanced diet. When beneficiaries were almost entirely dependent on the WFP for their subsistence, a full family balanced ration was provided. Where the quantity of local foods was more substantial, the WFP ration was reduced *pari passu* within the overall nutritional target. Where workers were separated from their families and WFP rations were distributed only to them, the calorie level was higher in order to take account of the level and conditions of the work undertaken. In feeding programmes, WFP rations were calculated to meet the particular nutritional needs of specific groups. This nutritional approach was to create operational problems in trying to synchronize the delivery of several food commodities from different donors in what was often disparagingly referred to as the 'supermarket approach', and to add significantly to supply costs.

Direct distribution in kind

Preference was given to the direct distribution of food commodities in kind, free of charge, to beneficiaries engaged in new activities. In this way, it was easier to verify that the commodities provided by the WFP did not displace existing supplies on the markets and that they resulted in a net increase in consumption.

Sales policy

It was recognized, however, that to meet some specific requirements of a project, it would be expedient to sell (monetize) some of the food commodities provided. These sales were restricted to limited amounts, for which a full explanation had to be provided. Three types of sales were envisaged. The first was sales on the open market in the recipient country. Sales inherent in the purpose of a WFP-supported project were permitted, such as dairy development schemes where tinned milk containing WFP-supplied dried skimmed milk was sold to augment local milk supplies, or price stabilization schemes where WFP-supplied grains were sold to stabilize prices and the proceeds used to replenish food reserves. The third category comprised sales to designated project beneficiaries outside normal markets at subsidized prices to augment wages, as at remote work-sites where food supplies were limited and at high prices.

Proceeds from the sale of WFP food commodities were to be spent in implementing the specific project that had been approved by the WFP's governing body, and should not go to meeting the costs of other projects, or to augment the budget of the recipient government. Sales proceeds could be used to buy locally produced tools, material or equipment required for the implementation of the approved WFP-assisted project. In these cases, it was reasoned that additional employment would be created and that the income generated would be spent mostly on locally produced food. Sales proceeds could also be used to help offset the internal costs of transporting, storing and handling the WFP food commodities provided in the recipient country.

Food as wages

From inception, the WFP adhered to the International Labour Organization (ILO) conventions governing work for which normal paid labour was employed in supplying food as wages (ILO, 1949).[17] Recipient governments were expected to pay at least 50 per cent of wages in cash to enable workers to meet their non-food needs.

This requirement also avoided placing workers in a position in which they would be obliged to sell some of the food aid commodities they received to buy non-food items. Family rations were provided to project workers based on the most adequate and well-balanced diet possible within the limits imposed by the level of wage rates in operation and the commodities available to the WFP. Wages-in-kind would then be appropriate both in composition to improve nutrition and energy, and as a proportion of the total wage to meet the needs of workers' families, without provoking sales.

Certain exceptions were recognized where WFP food commodities were provided in addition to the prevailing wage. This was done to attract workers to projects in remote areas or in difficult working conditions, where markets were weakly developed and local food prices high. WFP food commodities were provided through canteens or stores at the project work-sites at subsidized prices and within the principles established by the 1949 ILO convention. The goods and services bought with the sales proceeds were provided for the benefit of the workers and not for securing a profit. Exceptional cases were also recognized where governments were not able to pay 50 per cent of the wage in cash. In post-emergency, relief or public works programmes, for example, a rotation of labour was allowed so that the maximum number of people were employed. In these circumstances, it was judged that the gains from a wider spread of employment outweighed the disadvantages of lowering the level of remuneration or maintaining a smaller workforce.

WFP assistance was also provided to groups of voluntary workers engaged in community development projects to enable, or encourage, them to undertake work of benefit to their own community as a whole. The WFP abided by other ILO conventions which ensured that no coercion was applied in mobilizing and using community action (ILO, 1930, 1957). The attitude of workers to partial remuneration in food was taken into account. The WFP sought to ensure that the cash portion of the wage was fixed as an appropriate percentage of the wage for similar work in the locality of the WFP-supported project. The commodity component of the WFP ration was determined by those food items that workers' families wanted to eat. The scope for food aid therefore depended on the ability of the WFP to supply foods that the recipients wished to consume themselves. As a rule of thumb, voluntary workers were required to work a minimum of 24 hours a week for a basic WFP family ration. Participants working for lesser periods were entitled to supplementary rations in the form, for example, of selected protein-rich commodities to improve the dietary standard, although flexibility was allowed to take account of the precise conditions at each project site. The food ration was determined by nutritional need.

Administrative procedures

Procedures were laid down during the experimental period for requesting, approving and evaluating WFP aid that were to remain largely in place for almost thirty years. They were more elaborate and demanding than those of other UN bodies, not only because of the experimental nature of the WFP, and the need to observe closely the experience gained, but also because of the uncharted and uncertain nature of the effects of the type of aid provided, and the negative effects of the US and other bilateral food aid programmes.

Requests for WFP aid could originally only be made by governments in developing countries in accordance with a standard *pro forma* provided by the Programme. They were first scrutinized at WFP headquarters to ascertain that they complied with the Programme's rules and regulations. Satisfactory requests were then sent to the parent organizations, the UN and FAO, for scrutiny. They were also sent to the co-operating UN specialized agencies for appraisal of their technical and economic feasibility in accordance with their mandates: these were the ILO, where employment and training conditions and standards were involved; UNESCO, where education was concerned; and the World Health Organization (WHO) to check on health implications. At the same time, the Consultative Subcommittee on Surplus Disposal was consulted to ensure that requests for WFP aid complied with the *FAO Principles of Surplus Disposal.*

Requests that passed this scrutiny screening could be approved in one of three ways: by the governing body at one of its twice-yearly sessions; by governing body members through a correspondence procedure of up to 45 days when, for reasons of urgency, a request needed to be approved quickly between governing body sessions; and by the executive director through authority designated to him by the governing body if the food/feed value of the request, based on current international prices, did not exceed $500,000. A 'plan of operation' or a 'letter of understanding' was drawn up for each WFP-assisted development project or emergency operation, respectively, which laid down the terms and conditions on which WFP aid was provided. These legal instruments were signed by a representative of the recipient government and of the WFP. Even after signature, recipient governments were also required to submit to the WFP a 'letter of readiness' confirming that all preparatory measures had been taken to implement the approved project. This confirmation was examined at WFP headquarters. Upon finding it satisfactory, instructions were issued for the shipment of WFP commodities to commence.

Evaluation of development projects was mandatory. Standard clauses were therefore included in plans of operation making it obligatory on governments to allow the WFP to observe the implementation of food-assisted development projects. Recipient governments were also required to assist in project evaluation by providing information and data in accordance with specific guidelines give in an annex to plans of operation. Governments were also required to provide quarterly progress reports on the implementation of projects and annual audit accounts, together with a final certified audit account on the use of WFP aid at the end of project implementation. Progress, interim evaluation and terminal reports were presented to the governing body by the WFP secretariat. Any additional WFP assistance to ongoing projects was made conditional on their performance.

Priority was given to benefiting poor and food-insecure people in the rural areas of the neediest, food-deficit developing countries with the broad aims of promoting food and agricultural development and nutritional improvement, encouraged by one of its parent organizations, the FAO, in keeping with its mandate. Emphasis was placed on supporting development projects with specific objectives and identified groups of hungry poor people in keeping with the *FAO Principles of Surplus Disposal*. A multifaceted concept of additionality was made a keystone in the WFP's policies and programmes. WFP food aid was provided in order to increase the levels of consumption, education and training, employment, and income and investment beyond what would have been possible without such assistance.

The potential advantages of channelling food aid multilaterally through a UN organization were appreciated at the outset. Different food and other contributions could be made by many countries that could complement each other, leading to international burden-sharing, facilitating resource management, and making food deliveries more cost-effective and timely. A close rein was kept on administrative overheads, which were set at less than 6 per cent of total annual expenditure, one of the lowest of any development assistance agency. And food aid could be provided without any political or commercial strings attached, for which much of the food aid provided bilaterally by the major donor countries was criticized.

Even by the standards of the UN system at the time, and well in advance of today's emphasis on national execution and capacity-building in the developing countries, the WFP was expected to stand at the other end of the aid spectrum, away from neo-colonialism and paternalism, and to be non-interventionist (WFP, 1973). WFP food aid was provided to support governments in developing countries in the implementation of their own development plans and programmes. They were responsible for the utilization of WFP aid in accordance with agreed purposes. Ownership of the food commodities provided by the WFP passed to the recipient government at the port of arrival, or frontier station in the case of land-locked countries. The roles of WFP staff were restricted to providing assistance, advisory services and training.

But controversy in the food aid debate continued. For donors, the direct transfer of food aid to recipient countries was particularly attractive. It involved no balance of payment problems, was relatively inexpensive in terms of opportunity costs, and was overvalued in data on international aid. It was a politically convenient way of buying off farm pressure groups and shelving the problems of agricultural adjustment in food aid donor countries, while persuading consumers and taxpayers that they were helping to avoid some Malthusian catastrophe. At the same time, antagonists continued to regard food aid for anything other than responding to emergencies as the epitome of all that was worst in the aid business – highly tied, politically convenient to donors, and potentially harmful to recipients. Country case studies of the impact of the US food aid programme completed before the WFP began operations tended to confirm that view.

The critically short time of the experimental period, and the need to gain sufficient experience to qualify the WFP for continuation, led to adoption of procedures and practices that were to haunt a continuing WFP after the experimental period was over. The governing body meeting twice a year for little more than a week at a time could hardly be expected to give detailed attention to an array of policy and operational concerns. Delegates who had competence in the operational aspects of development projects and emergency operations did not necessarily have the same ability in policy matters. While the major donor-developed countries could fly in a number of officials from their capitals to form their delegations, developing countries were often represented by one official, usually the FAO country representative resident in Rome. Working under pressure, representatives of the major donor countries tended to dominate discussion. Two important precedents were set. No requests submitted to the governing body were rejected, although some were modified. And the governing body insisted that it was a technical rather than political body so that later, when the United States tried to turn down a project request from Vietnam, patently on political grounds, it was overruled.

The position of the United States was a cause of special concern. It had played a leading and prominent part in the proposal for the WFP experiment. It provided over half the resources made available for the experimental period. Such dependence on one donor could be destabilizing. The United States itself found this imbalance troubling. It hoped that the other donors would contribute more and that no other large-scale bilateral food aid programmes would be established in competition to PL480, particularly by the EEC.

The United States enjoyed other special advantages. It was the only major donor with detailed knowledge of WFP-assisted development projects and their performance, through the reports of USAID country missions. Under the terms of US participation in the WFP experiment, USAID country missions were required to clear a request for WFP assistance if US commodities were required, the only donor to impose bilateral restrictions on the multilateral programme. Requests might not be approved if either they contravened the technical provisions of the PL480 programme, or they conflicted with general US policies regarding which developing countries could be assisted. Other constraints were that US food aid commodities had to be transported in US ships, and three-quarters of US food aid commodities had to consist of bagged, fortified or processed products, to satisfy US food processing, shipping and handling interests. These requirements were resented by other members of the WFP's governing body, who feared that they could lead to the 'bilateralization' of the multilateral programme.

A major limitation was the size and level of appointment of staff in the WFP secretariat. From the outset, emphasis was placed on keeping programme and administrative costs to a minimum. The number and level of appointments in comparison to other UN bodies was such that the administrative overheads accounted for less than 6 per cent of total expenditure during the three-year experiment, the lowest of any UN body. This was diseconomically low in some critical areas of the WFP's work, and would need to be reviewed if WFP activities were to be significantly expanded. So, too, were the working relations between WFP headquarters and field staff. Under the pressures of the experimental period, there was little delegation of responsibility to WFP country offices.

Requests for WFP assistance were sent to the UN, co-operating specialized agencies for technical scrutiny with a tight deadline. The comments of officers in these agencies, made on top of their existing workload and for projects in which they had no stake or control, were often perfunctory and couched in general terms. This arrangement would also need to be reviewed if effective technical scrutiny were to be improved in the post-experimental period. The UN specialized agencies might also do more to draw the WFP's attention to development projects that they were supporting, thus ensuring a fusion of financial, technical and food aid. A particular problem was that each UN organization had its own planning, programming and budgetary cycle, which made it difficult to synchronize the assistance they provided.

The experimental period proved to be invaluable in revealing and addressing the practical operational problems that had to be overcome in using WFP assistance effectively and efficiently. Out of this experience, the WFP established a transportation and logistics service that gained a considerable reputation among donor and recipient governments for being able to move large amounts of food commodities, often in difficult circumstances, throughout the developing world. The cost of delivering WFP consignments, particularly those involving several food items in 'supermarket' rations in order to provide a full and balanced diet, was often more than the value of the foods provided. Small consignments were delivered on liner vessels at high unit costs.

With growing experience, transport and associated costs were reduced through improving shipping schedules and making combined shipments on charter vessels to a number of projects in the same recipient country at lower transport costs. Other practical problems concerned the size and durability of containers, packaging and the labelling of food commodities in different languages and in picture form so that it could be understood by illiterate people. Storage facilities in developing countries were a basic and serious concern. The WFP commissioned a survey of storage problems. One outcome was the decision that all WFP field officers should receive intensive training in storage practices in order to provide advice and training to staff in recipient countries. Faced with these difficulties, the achievements of the experimental period were even more remarkable. The survey also revealed the paradox that those countries most in need of food aid often had the least capacity to absorb it.

WFP study programme

As we saw above, the UN resolution establishing the WFP experimental programme called for 'expert studies which would aid in the consideration of the future development of multilateral food programs'. After taking into account the views of other bodies with special competence in the subject, the WFP's governing body recommended that studies be undertaken on five topics:

WFP Study No. 1: *The Demand for Food and Conditions Governing Food Aid during Development* (Dandekar, 1965);

WFP Study No. 2: *The Impact of Food Aid on Donor and Other Food Exporting Countries* (Allen, 1965);

WFP Study No. 3: *The Linking of Food Aid with Other Aid* (Chakravarty and Rosenstein-Rodan, 1965);
WFP Study No. 4: *Operational and Administrative Problems of Food Aid* (FitzGerald, 1965);
WFP Study No. 5: *The Role of Multilateral Food Aid Programs* (Dessau, 1965).

The studies were carried out by independent experts who were eminent authorities in their fields.[18] They were responsible for the views expressed. The studies covered three broad areas: the potentials and problems of food aid (Studies no. 1–3); operational and administrative problems (Study no. 4); and the scope for multilateral food aid (Study no. 5).

An important conclusion to emerge from the first three studies was that, while food surpluses were likely to accrue at an increasing rate in the future, the opportunities for using them effectively in developing countries might not expand commensurately. One inherent danger was that food aid programmes might retard the adaptation of agricultural production in developed countries to commercial demand and food production in recipient developing countries. Close international co-operation, especially between North America and Europe, would facilitate a readjustment in pledges to the WFP in order to respond better to the particular needs of developing countries. Ways and means had to be found of using food surpluses efficiently.

Divergent views were expressed on the use of food aid in labour-intensive projects. One view was that the scope for food aid was limited, as it was unlikely to cover a sufficient part of total project costs. Another, more optimistic, view was through what were called 'closed loop' projects, defined as those that could speed up the absorption of labour into productive work without draining away scarce resources from other sectors of the economy. Potential harmful effects could be avoided if food aid were granted as part of well-designed development plans in developing countries. The studies concluded that there was likely to be considerable cope for food aid in developing countries. Donor co-ordination might best be achieved by adopting a formula of 'bilateral aid within a multilateral framework', which could include international agreement of burden-sharing and international aid consortia. This had first been advocated in the FAO director-general's expert group report in 1961 (see p. 10).

The operational and administrative problems of food aid were considered by comparing project food aid provided by the United States and through the newly established WFP experiment. By mid-1964, US project food aid commitments were said to have a market value of about $125 million compared to about $53 million by the WFP. The United States already had a considerable development aid programme by the time the WFP experiment began. The operational and managerial facilities set up for the US bulk supply food aid programme could be used for its project food aid, thereby reducing costs. In addition, it was potentially easier to co-ordinate food aid with non-food assistance (financial, technical, material) for development projects from the aid resources provided by a single, large, donor country.

In comparison, administrative, managerial and operational procedures for the WFP experiment had to be developed from scratch under 'forced draft', owing to its limited duration. As the WFP was not a self-contained entity, there were additional and time-consuming procedures. The different views of donor and recipient countries had to be reconciled in the governing body. Food, cash and services had to be garnered and co-ordinated from many sources. And technical services and non-food inputs required for WFP-supported development projects had to be obtained from other UN organizations, bilateral aid agencies and NGOs.

But multilateral food aid had other potential advantages. It made possible the mobilization and co-ordination of food commodities from many countries, and permitted nutritionally adequate rations to be provided in keeping with food habits and customs in recipient countries. It supported the principle of burden-sharing, whereby each country could contribute according to its comparative advantage in food commodities, cash and services. It could draw on a wide range of professional and technical competence in the UN system in joint and co-funded programmes. And, most significantly, developing countries were given the choice of an alternative source of assistance, which took the politics out of food aid.

Special roles were identified for the WFP as a multilateral programme (Dessau, 1965: 37–8). It could create and centralize a knowledge base required to work out and disseminate the principles for using food aid as an effective resource for development, as well as for meeting emergencies. It could become a catalyst for, and promoter of, the harmonization of all food aid programmes. The likelihood of food surpluses occurring simultaneously in North America, Western Europe, some developing countries and in the centrally-planned economies could result in a 'surplus war' that could have disastrous repercussions both in international markets and on general economic development. Co-ordination of the use of food surpluses from a number of sources could best be undertaken by the WFP as a multilateral institution. The utilization of food surpluses in developing countries raised special problems, which a multilateral agency was best placed to resolve. The functions of food aid agencies needed to be defined and co-ordinated globally, so that they take the cohesive action most favourable for development. A multilateral agency could best help in these tasks.

Continuation of the WFP

The results of the experimental period, the conclusions of the study programme, and developments within and outside the UN system provided a strong case for the continuation of the WFP after 1965. But there was one factor above all others that justified the continuation and growth of the WFP to become a major and successful organization in the UN system – the development of expertise and experience in transportation and logistics.[19]

Transportation and logistics

Over the experimental years, the WFP gained a considerable international reputation for being able to move large amounts of food commodities, often in difficult circumstances, throughout the developing world. This particularly appealed to the major donors, who saw the food commodities that they had provided being moved quickly and efficiently to poor food-deficit countries and people, which led to their increased support. It also resulted in donors and NGOs requesting the WFP to help in the transportation and delivery of the food aid that they provided through their own programmes of assistance in addition to that provided through the WFP.

Complex food aid management

The nature and composition of WFP resources, and the chosen methods of their deployment, called for complex food aid management arrangements. Although the bulk of commodities made available by donors to the WFP consisted of different types of cereals, a wide variety of foods and feed for livestock were provided. A preference was given to providing food rations directly to beneficiaries, calculated on the basis of their nutritional requirements. The delivery of a number of food items from different countries had to be synchronized to arrive simultaneously in recipient countries. Each consignment had to be appropriately labelled and provided in containers the size and form of which facilitated distribution to beneficiaries.

A relatively small number of donors provided the majority of the WFP's resources but many nations, including developing countries, made small, but symbolically important, contributions. Over 100 countries made contributions to the WFP at one time or another. While this added to the strength and diversity of WFP resources, it called for management skills in co-ordinating these contributions to individual development projects and emergency operations in different parts of the developing world.

Although donors undertook to make their pledged commodities readily available to the WFP when required, it often took a minimum of three months for them to be acquisitioned by tender from their food stocks, packed, marked, labelled and assembled at the dockside ready for shipment. It then required time to transport them to recipient countries and distribute them accordingly. A further complication was that some donors placed restrictions on the countries to which they were prepared to allow their commodities to be provided, or only agreed to support selected emergency operations after they had occurred.

As the WFP developed, a series of resource 'windows' were opened up to address specific requirements or problems. By the beginning of the 1990s, no fewer than seven separate resource channels were established, each with its own individual terms and conditions. While they provided additional resources for WFP operations, their non-interchangeability added to the complexity of resource management. The main channel for the WFP's largest, 'regular' resources was through biennial pledging conferences that were held at the UN in New York, normally in the month of January before the next biennium began. Targets were set for each pledging conference by the WFP's governing body and approved by the UN General Assembly and FAO Conference.

Many donors were unable to announce their full contributions to the WFP at the time of the pledging conference. A number of donors made their pledges known in monetary terms, which were converted into commodities, services or cash as their pledges were drawn down. Only for three biennia (1969–70, 1973–74 and 1975–76) were the pledging targets surpassed. For all other biennia, the targets were not reached and, in some cases, significantly under-met. The United States, the WFP's largest donor, made pledges for the three biennia between 1966 and 1972 on the basis that they should not exceed 50 per cent of the total pledges of all donors, which was reduced to 40 per cent thereafter.

While donors were given an indication by the WFP secretariat of the kinds and amounts of commodities required for WFP operations, a high degree of mutual self-interest was shown in the commodities that each donor actually provided, including high-value products such as canned meat and fish. US food aid legislation also required that three-quarters of the commodities it provided should be in the form of bagged, fortified or processed products, thereby restricting the amount of whole cereals it could supply. In addition, under US cargo preference legislation, three-quarters of its food aid commodities had to be shipped in US vessels at shipping rates significantly above the international level.

Finally, added to the complexity and difficulties of WFP resource management was the Achilles' heel of shortage of cash resources. As the food aid organization of the UN system, the WFP was unique. The impressive growth in its resources was in large part due to the fact that food aid was, at least in part, additional to financial assistance. There was relatively little competition from other UN organizations for the kinds of resources that it was designed to deploy, and the WFP efficiently performed its functions at low financial cost, with overheads pegged at around 6 per cent of its expenditure. But the increasing demand for more voluntarily provided cash resources put the WFP in direct competition with other UN organizations that operated entirely with assessed and guaranteed financial resources.

It was originally estimated that the WFP's cash requirements would be met if at least one-third of total contributions were provided in cash and service. This estimate was made at a time when only a small proportion of WFP resources were devoted to emergency operations. At the same time, the one-third provision was applied not to individual donors but, rather, to all contributions 'in the aggregate', on the understanding that donors with food surpluses would contribute mainly food commodities while others with no food surpluses would provide cash and services, such as shipping. This did not happen, leaving the WFP increasingly with a cash resources problem when greater involvement in emergency operations led to higher cash requirements. Another factor was that, in 1972, the WFP's governing body agreed that the WFP should help meet the internal transport, storage and handling (ITSH) costs of the food aid it provided in the least-developed countries. Subsidizing these costs placed a heavy additional burden on the WFP's limited cash resources, particularly after the steep rise in world food and oil prices in the early 1970s. To take pressure off the WFP's limited cash resources, sale of cereals donated to the WFP was permitted in eligible countries to offset ITSH costs. This, too, created difficulties, as ITSH costs continued to rise and larger volumes of grain were needed for sale rather than to support development projects and emergency operations. WFP annual commitments to cover ITSH costs increased more than six times to reach $320 million by 1992.

The WFP also undercharged for the services provided to bilateral agencies and NGOs for the shipping, procurement and monitoring of their food aid supplies. An independent cost measurement study conducted in 1993 showed that, for all the services provided, the fees charged by the WFP were less than the actual costs incurred in providing them. The study concluded that 'with a stable financial base, WFP will be able to continue to provide quality food aid services, but that without the introduction of reliable, flexible revenue sources the quality of performance and the responsiveness of its operations will suffer' (WFP, 1994d: 14).

Ocean shipping

By the early years of the 1990s, thirty years after the start of operations, the WFP managed the annual transportation and delivery of over 4.7 million tons of food to over 90 developing countries at a total cost of $387 million. About one-third of this tonnage was handled on behalf of bilateral donors and NGOs. Some two-thirds of the tonnage involved ocean transport from donors to recipient countries. Another one-fifth was moved by inland transport arranged by the WFP within recipient countries. About 400,000 tons were delivered by surface transport to landlocked countries. And over 53,000 tons were transported by air in emergency operations.

Ocean shipping was the WFP's main transportation function in its first thirty years of operations, accounting for the largest proportion of its cash expenditure, when the WFP became a major user of the world's shipping lines. Standard and flexible procedures were developed over a number of years that could be quickly modified to respond to sudden emergencies. As a rule, small consignments of food commodities were shipped on liner vessels which ran on regular schedules and carried cargoes for a number of different shippers. By the early 1990s, the WFP had booked some 2,000 liners annually for a total freight expenditure of about $85 million. It was often possible to combine shipments from neighbouring donors, thereby strengthening the WFP's bargaining position with shipping lines for reduced freight rates and other concessions.

For larger consignments (usually above 3,000 tons), it was more cost-effective for the WFP to charter an entire ship. A number of small consignments were often consolidated into one shipment in order to benefit from the lower freight rate. Consolidated shipments could be arranged either by combining a number of single consignments from a single donor, or by combining cargoes from several donors, or by collaborating with bilateral donors and NGOs who therefore benefited from the WFP's information network and expertise. By the early 1990s, the WFP had arranged for about 200 charter vessels per year at an annual freight cost of about $108 million.

Not only was the WFP able to enjoy significant cost advantage in making use of chartered vessels, it was also strategically important. At any time, the WFP had a number of ships on charter with substantial food resources afloat that could be diverted at short notice to respond quickly to a sudden emergency. Food supplies from diverted chartered vessels were often the first deliveries of relief assistance to reach a stricken country. All concerned were kept informed by the WFP of the precise position of each ship from loading to discharge.

The WFP set up an international panel of chartering brokers in major maritime centres (such as London, New York and Tokyo) to cover the international ship chartering market. Through this network, the WFP was kept constantly informed of the most competitive charter rates. At the same time, the WFP's experienced chartering officers followed movements in the international freight markets through daily market reports. When a vessel was chartered, a contract was drawn up with the ship owner that gave details of the financial commitments, obligations and legal responsibilities.

The WFP also had its own customized contractual arrangements. In the mid-1980s, BIMCO (the world's largest association of ship-owners) and the WFP jointly drew up a contractual agreement for exclusive use by the WFP. Charter contracts are often subject to dispute, but the ratification by such a leading authority resulted in ship-owners unconditionally accepting the WFP's terms, thus reducing the likelihood of time-consuming and costly disputes and litigation. The WFP's special charter contract made provision for the WFP to be responsible for the loading and discharge of charter vessels. For those operations, the WFP entered into special stevedoring arrangements and employed a net work of charterers' protection agents to ensure that charter vessels were turned around in the ports of both loading and discharge with minimum delay and cost.

Insurance

All commodities shipped by the WFP are insured and carefully monitored to detect damage or loss during transportation. Each consignment is insured to the port of unloading, or the frontier station in the case of landlocked countries, where the title of the food commodities passes to the recipient government. Insurance is arranged on a global basis through one of the world's largest multinational brokers. The WFP appointed and supervised a network of superintendents and inspectors at about 150 locations as part of a comprehensive worldwide system. They assess the quantity and condition of all WFP consignments at the time they are delivered to recipient governments and report back to the WFP. Their reports are used as a basis for any claims against insurers and third parties, as well as for WFP accounting records. About ten 'general average' claims (contributions necessary to complete a voyage after an unexpected incident) per year were settled by insurers by the early 1990s. The superintendents also alert the WFP immediately the prospect of large losses or major problems arises so that remedial action can be taken. Losses were remarkably low over the years, amounting to less than 1 per cent of deliveries (in value terms) in the early 1990s. As well as cargo insurance, the WFP also arranged insurance to cover its liability as a charterer of ships. Claims were rare and no ship-owner succeeded in claiming against the WFP on the basis of charterer's liability. As a result, the premium was very low – less than $100,000 per year for over 200 vessels in the early 1990s.

Logistics

A logistics unit was established in the WFP secretariat in 1986 to handle the WFP's increasing involvement with surface transportation within and between developing countries. In addition, some 100 international staff and over 1,000 local staff were employed. In 1986, about 300,000 tons of food were transported within and between developing countries. By the early 1990s, that amount had increased to 1.6 million tons, mainly as a result of the WFP's increasing involvement in large-scale and complex human-made emergencies. With the WFP's increasing involvement in emergency and disaster relief operations (see Chapter 2), the unit took over responsibility for all kinds of new and unconventional transportation and logistics activities, including airlifts, parachute drops and water transport operations. In some developing countries, the WFP managed and operated fleets of trucks and trailers at the request of governments and the donor community to transport and distribute food aid provided from all sources.

Humanitarian diplomacy

From the beginning of the 1990s, the WFP became increasingly involved in negotiations with warring parties for the safe passage of relief supplies and personnel across disputed territory. For example, the WFP negotiated the re-opening of the port of Massawa, which allowed the delivery of relief food to Eritrea and northern Ethiopia during the war between the two countries. Cross-border transportation was organized from Kenya by a fleet of trucks and a large-scale airlift to deliver emergency relief assistance to southern Ethiopia. The WFP also played a role in the rehabilitation and upgrading of port facilities destroyed or damaged by war. The WFP commissioned a port management team to assess the war damage done to the Eritrean ports of Massawa and Assab. To repair the port of Massawa, the WFP purchased spare parts and basic equipment, and invested some $3 million in a tugboat, a pilot boat and generator sets. To increase Ethiopia's internal transport capacity, the WFP commissioned a feasibility study of the Djibouti–Ethiopia railway, which resulted in the supply of two locomotives, together with an assistance package of $4 million for the transportation of food aid.

Following the severe drought that affected countries in southern Africa at the beginning of the 1990s, the donor community asked the WFP to carry out a review of port and transport infrastructure to ensure that the large amount of food imports, including food aid, that was required could be quickly and efficiently delivered. And following a new working arrangement between the WFP and UNHCR in 1992, the WFP assume responsibility for providing basic commodities and for mobilizing funds required for their transport and delivery in all large-scale refugee operations.

The WFP's unique experience and expertise in transport and logistics was recognized by the international community. A study commissioned by the Nordic countries on the UN system in 1990 concluded that: 'Over the years the organization (WFP) has developed a supply system that is both professionally managed and appreciated by the recipients', and recommended that the WFP should 'be formally designated as the UN agency with primary responsibility for matters relating to logistics and transport for both food and non-food items, including assistance to countries in developing their own transport arrangements' (Nordic UN Project, 1990: 63 and 77).

An evaluation of food aid transport costs and options carried out by the EEC in 1992 stated that the WFP not only consistently achieved the most competitive freight rates but, overall, was the most effective agency (TechEcon, 1992). And in 2005, the Inter-Agency Standing Committee (IASC) designated the WFP as the lead agency for the global logistics cluster leader, in addition to being global cluster leader for food in situations of humanitarian emergency or where there was considered to be a need to strengthen leadership and partnership with other humanitarian actors (IASC, 2005). Obtaining the confidence of both donors and recipients has been particularly important in getting food to the hungry poor, particularly in emergency situations. With the knowledge that it had obtained that confidence, the WFP could charter the way ahead.

Future directions

The WFP's first executive director, Addeke Boerma, recommended what future WFP activities might be, assuming agreement was reached to extend the Programme beyond 1965 (WFP, 1965c: 69–93). He reiterated that while the WFP would continue to bear responsibility for providing food assistance in emergencies, experience had shown the difficulties of supplying food relief quickly. As a result, WFP assistance was likely to prove more effective in reconstruction and rehabilitation activities after emergencies, and in disaster prevention, preparedness and mitigation measures.

In his opinion, the main focus should, therefore, be support of economic and social development projects based on the free and direct distribution of food to beneficiaries, with limited sales in exceptional circumstances, in order to comply with the *FAO's Principles of Surplus Disposal*. But he considered that interpretation of the *FAO Principles* had been somewhat one-sided. More attention had been given to protecting the trading interests of exporting developed countries than to the possible disincentive effect to agricultural producers in food aid receiving countries. More balanced consideration should, therefore, be given in a future multilateral food aid programmes. Some relaxation of the WFP's sale policy might be in order. The disadvantage of possible temporary market displacement by sale of WFP commodities should be weighed against the countervailing advantages of increased efficiency and output of a WFP-assisted project and long-term market gain, as was later contemplated in a revision of the *FAO Principles* in 1992 (FAO, 1992: 23). He also suggested that consideration should also be given to experimenting with the country programme approach, which had been precluded from the experimental period, without prejudice to the continued development of the project approach, 'which should remain a primary and characteristic activity'.

In estimating the rate of growth of the WFP beyond 1965, the executive director projected that $833 million of aid in commodities and cash might be committed for the five years 1966–70. Of that total, 63 per cent should be for development projects, 30 per cent for support to the development plans of developing countries through a country programme approach, 4 per cent for emergencies, and 3 per cent for administration. About 70 per cent of total contributions were estimated to be in commodities and 30 per cent in cash. The original target of one-third of WFP donations in cash was predicated on operational needs related only to the project approach. Purchases of food to balance diets would not be necessary for aid to national development plans. And administrative costs were expected to fall as the scale of WFP operations increased.

The UN secretary-general and the FAO director-general presented their joint views on the WFP's continuation to the WFP's governing body.[20] They expressed 'broad agreement' with the recommendations of the WFP's executive director, and had 'no hesitation in stating our conclusion that the results of the ... experiment period ... have been sufficiently positive to warrant its (WFP) continuation and indeed expansion' (UN and FAO, 1965).

They noted that a considerable increase in food surpluses was expected in the future, with a wider spread in their geographical occurrence and commodity composition. The WFP had handled only about 2 per cent of total food aid during the experimental period. Even with the expansion proposed by the WFP executive director, it would still only handle about 10 per cent. Nevertheless, it would constitute an important addition and complement to assistance provided through the UN system.

The executive heads concluded that 'an expanded WFP must have as its primary objective to benefit the *people* [original emphasis] in developing countries, of whom most were farmers and their families. Benefits to the *rural* [original emphasis] population should be a special priority consideration for the WFP.' Assistance should not be limited to direct agricultural or rural development projects but should cover a range of projects for a maximum effort in economic and social development.

The WFP's governing body unanimously agreed to recommend the continuation of the Programme to the parent bodies, the UN and FAO, with food aid linked to specific development projects as its main activity. No agreement was reached on the WFP's involvement in the country programme approach, although the executive director was requested to carry out a detailed study on the subject (see p. 40). A target of $275 million was set for the three years 1966–68, of which at least 33 per cent should be in cash and services. It was considered that this would permit the purchase of commodities to balance diets and cope with emergency needs, which, 'as far as possible and economical, should be bought in exporting developing countries to help boost their exports'.

During the discussions on the future of the WFP, two specific proposals were made for its modification:[21] neither proposal influenced the decision on the WFP's continuation. The political climate was such that, within little more than six months of submitting the WFP governing body's recommendations to ECOSOC and the FAO Council, the UN General Assembly and the FAO Conference adopted parallel resolutions in December 1965. The resolutions approved the WFP's extension 'on a continuing basis for as long as multilateral food aid was found necessary' and 'on the understanding that the Program will be regularly reviewed ... and if circumstances so require, it may be enlarged, curtailed or terminated'. The 24-member governing body was retained, but a review of the WFP's general regulations was requested, which remained basically unchanged (UN, 1965; FAO, 1965).

Food for development

Although the WFP played important roles in emergencies, the main focus of attention for most of the next thirty years of its operations was on using food aid in support of economic and social development projects (Shaw, 2001: 67–144). Two distinct phases may be discerned during this period. The first was the decade to the major watershed of the 1974 World Food Conference, during which the WFP was faced with unstable and fluctuating resources, and the search for a distinct identity. Resources pledged to the WFP reached $187 million, failing to meet the target of $275 million set for the three-years 1966–68. The United States had issued a challenge and a warning at the 1966 pledging conference that, in order to emphasize the truly multilateral nature of the WFP, it was essential for it to keep its contribution in balance with those of other nations, and that it would reduce proportionately its contribution if there were a shortfall in the target level of $275 million. The second period after the 1974 World Food Conference lasted for much of the next twenty years, during which project food aid was fully developed and institutionalized.

An investigation into the use of programme food aid in support of a country's national development plan was carried out in Jamaica in 1965 (WFP, 1966a). The report of the Jamaica mission was sent to the FAO Committee on Commodity Problems and to the Consultative Subcommittee on Surplus Disposal. As expected, both warned of possible disruptions to commercial trade, reflecting the thinking of the main food exporting countries. The FAO director-general also expressed concern about the possible negative impact on domestic food production in food aid recipient countries. The comments of the major donors were particularly revealing. They showed that there was a general unwillingness for them to relinquish control over a substantial share of their own food aid resources. They argued that food and cash were too limited for the WFP to embark on programme assistance at a time when its resources represented less than 5 per cent of global food aid. 'Even more important', the US representative commented, 'the WFP staff was limited, and it had to concentrate on projects to obtain the best possible results. Good projects should not be sacrificed for a doubtful program approach' (WFP, 1966b).

The WFP's governing body did agreed that the executive director should prepare an outline for a further study on the feasibility of multilateral food aid in support of national development plans and programmes. But while the outline was being prepared, two significant developments took place. A Food Aid Convention (FAC) was established as part of a new International Grains Agreement in 1967, and a joint study of multilateral food aid was carried out by the UN and FAO. Both raised the prospect of substantial additional resources being made available to the

WFP, thereby removing one of the main objections raised to the WFP's involvement in country programme food aid, which did not materialize.

By the end of the first decade of WFP operations (1963–72), $1.2 billion of assistance had been committed to 540 development projects in 94 developing countries, and annual food aid disbursements had reached $170 million. An estimated 24 million people had benefited directly from WFP assistance, and many more had benefited indirectly (WFP, 1973). The next ten years were to witness a steady growth, refinement and institutionalization of WFP project food aid for development. By 1982, the WFP had committed about $5.3 billion of assistance to 1,100 development projects in 144 countries, directly benefiting 94 million people (WFP, 1983a). The WFP had become one of the major funding programmes of the UN system and a principal source of grant aid to poorest sections of the populations of developing countries.

By the end of the WFP's first thirty years of operations in 1992, it had invested over $13 billion (involving more than 40 million tons of food) in 1,600 development projects to combat hunger and to promote economic and social development throughout the developing world. In 1992 alone, WFP commitments to ongoing development projects totalled $3 billion and provided food to an estimated 52 million people. The WFP had become the largest source of grant development assistance to the poor in developing countries in the UN system. In the process, three notable WFP achievements stood out. The WFP was the largest source of assistance within the UN system to development projects involving and benefiting poor women in developing countries and was the largest provider of grant assistance for environmental protection and improvement activities in developing countries. Also, it was the largest purchaser of food and services in developing countries among UN agencies, and a major supporter of South–South trade (WFP, 1993a).

The WFP received high praise when its work was annually reviewed in the FAO Council and ECOSOC and periodically reviewed in the FAO Conference and the UN General Assembly. But outside the UN system, project food aid for development continued to be criticized (see, for example, Jackson, 1982). While food aid to meet emergencies was not questioned, calls were made to end food aid for development purposes to be replaced with 'aid for food' (Reutlinger, 1999). A comprehensive policy review of the future of food aid concluded that: 'The balance of evidence is that food aid is no longer an additional resource but must justify itself in competition with other uses of scarce aids funds' (Clay *et al.*, 1998: 63; ODI, 1998). The review found that food aid, as statistically recorded, had quickly become a marginal and uncertain component of aid globally, making it difficult for it to have a significant food security impact at the international level. It had become an increasingly marginal part of overseas development aid – 3–4 per cent, compared to 22 per cent in 1965 and 11 per cent in 1985.

A former WFP staff member addressed the question: 'Is there a future for WFP as a development agency? (Schulthes, 2000: 256–73).[22] His point of departure was that donors would only be prepared to support the WFP if they were persuaded that food aid still had a comparative advantage as a development resource, even after the disappearance of burdensome surpluses. Addressing the question in a series of 12 theses, he concluded that the most important and controversial thesis was that development food aid had a place only when it constituted an integral component of a firm, mainstream government policy of food security.

The WFP conducted a comprehensive review to strengthen steps throughout its project cycle from identification, preparation, appraisal and approval of WFP-assisted development projects to their implementation, monitoring and evaluation (WFP, 1984). Emphasis was given to placing poor and food-insecure people at the centre of all projects. A sequence of questions was raised at the beginning of the project cycle: Who are the poor and food insecure? What are the causes of their condition? What activities are best suited to improve their condition? Is food aid required? If so, in what ways and on what terms and conditions should food aid be provided? This anticipated by a decade the food security and vulnerability information and mapping systems adopted after the World Food Summit in 1994.

Over the first thirty years of WFP operations, changes in WFP development assistance manifested themselves in several ways. There was a gradual shift of focus to sub-Saharan Africa, which became the main recipient of the WFP's development assistance. There was a deliberate attempt to allocate development resources to the neediest people in the poorest countries. Priority was therefore given to countries classified as least-developed, low-income and food-deficient, to which an increasing proportion of WFP development aid was allocated.

A broad category of agricultural and rural development projects received about two-thirds of WFP development aid commitments, while projects for human resource development involving improvements in health, nutrition, education and training received one-third. Preference was given to the first group, as they promised to provide employment and income for the poor, yield quick returns, generate demand for food, and contribute toward self-reliance. Projects in the second group were less favoured because of their open-ended nature, and the difficulties of demonstrating their benefits. Three other types of development projects received WFP assistance – livestock production, industrial and mining development, and food reserves – but these involved only a small part of WFP development assistance.[23]

WFP experience in providing assistance to development projects showed that food aid could have a number of functions in achieving different objects. Each function raised different issues for project design, implementation and evaluation. At any point in time, a given unit of food aid could only achieve one function, but it was possible for food aid supplied to a development project to serve a number of functions. Nutritional improvement could be achieved when rations were supplied to people with deficient diets. Income transfer could take place, as when workers on labour-intensive works received part – or, in special cases, all – of their wages in food rations for themselves and their families. Incentives and enabling support could be offered to beneficiaries engaged in activities on their own land, or in community development schemes, or for children and students to attend school, other educational institutions and training centres. When farmers engaged in transforming their traditional farming systems, or when settlers worked on newly developed land until their crops came into production, they could be tided over. Budgetary support could be provided through the release of funds previously allocated for specific purposes by the provision of food aid, or by creating funds through the authorized sale of part of the WFP commodities provided for a project. Support could also be offered for policy change, as in food subsidy and safety-net programmes.

Development and/or emergency aid

Despite the WFP's impressive work through support to development projects, questions continued to be asked, with increasing regularity, as to what direction the Programme should take in the future. A policy debate thus began that was to take up much of the 1990s. There were two contradictory trends. Global food aid began to fall dramatically, to reach its lowest level for over twenty years in 1996. At the same time, the demand for food aid increased considerably with the escalation in the conflict-made emergencies early in the 1990s as states collapsed, civil war proliferated, and genocide and ethnic cleansing raged (Shawcross, 2000).

Not only were poor developing countries affected, particularly in sub-Saharan Africa, but new countries and regions were to suffer following the political collapse of the Soviet Union and the Federal Republic of Yugoslavia. More UN peace-keeping and peace-making operations were launched in the early years of the 1990s than in the previous twenty years (Annan, 1999a). Refugees and displaced persons reached unprecedented numbers, leading to an escalation in the need for emergency and relief food aid for more protracted periods (UNHCR, 1997). And more food aid was required when these afflicted people eventually returned home to begin the process of rehabilitation, reconstruction and renewed development.

At the same time, a process of reform of the UN system was initiated with the passage of a number of resolutions in the UN General Assembly that related to all UN bodies, including the WFP (Chapter 4). A series of UN-sponsored international conferences were held throughout the 1990s on subjects of global concern, leading up to the UN Millennium Summit in 2000 that set Millennium Development Goals (MDGs) as a framework for national and international action (Shaw, 2007: 271–368). To assist the process of arriving at a decision concerning the WFP's future directions, consultations were organized by the WFP secretariat, which brought together members of the WFP's governing body, other representatives of UN and FAO member states, staff from other UN agencies, NGOs and the WFP, and eminent academics. A joint study of food aid to sub-Saharan Africa was carried out by the World Bank and WFP (World Bank and WFP, 1991). And the WFP secretariat organized three regional seminars to mark the first thirty years of its operations and to learn from experience in shaping its future work.

Tripartite evaluation of the WFP

Divergent views were expressed among the major donors to the WFP as to whether it should retain its developmental focus or become an exclusively emergency agency. In an attempt to resolve the issue, three donor countries – Canada, the Netherlands and Norway – undertook a comprehensive evaluation of the WFP between 1991 and 1993, one of the most detailed assessments of any UN body up to that time (Chr. Michelsen Institute, 1994).[24] The evaluation did not produce recommendations but, rather, 'shared judgements' that might be taken into account in discussions concerning the WFP's future directions. And the findings were not formally discussed in the WFP's governing body. The evaluation concluded that the WFP's performance in relief and emergencies was 'impressive'. The 'judgement' put forward aimed at incremental improvements rather than radical change, and 'it would be in the interest of all countries, both donor and recipient, to maintain and strengthen WFP as the principal international organization for handling food relief'.

The analysis of the WFP's development activities noted some successes, but also identified a number of weaknesses. While the WFP performed well in the physical movement of food, it was considered to be less successful in the developmental aspects of the projects it supported. Three options were identified for improving the WFP's development performance: reducing the number of countries in which the WFP operated, concentrating on those with the lowest incomes, and especially in those countries that were disaster-prone; keeping the wide spread of countries receiving WFP assistance, but limiting activities to a much narrower band of types of projects in which food aid functioned well, such as natural resource management and human resource development; or phasing out all types of development projects, except for those that were relief-related, such as disaster preparedness, rehabilitation, and repatriation activities. The evaluation concluded:

> A development programme targeted at the poorest people in the poorest countries, organized by the UN system, based on bringing food to the hungry, and aimed at long-term impact as well as short-term benefits should surely be maintained by the donors as long as it can be run effectively and efficiently. The WFP membership should be thinking about improving their effectiveness and efficiency, not about winding up the Programme. (Chr. Michelsen Institute, 1994, abridged version: 29)
>
> Taking relief and development together, the evaluation concluded that: there is a clear value in retaining WFP as a hybrid organization. If relief is accepted as the main focus there is a strong case for combining – as a minimum development profile – an active programme oriented toward disaster preparedness, mitigation and rehabilitation. (Chr. Michelsen, 1994, abridged version: 32)

WFP mission statement

The conclusions of the tripartite evaluation were taken into account when a new mission statement for the WFP was unanimously approved by the WFP's governing body in 1994, the first since the WFP's original general regulations were formulated thirty years previously (WFP, 1994b). Charting the WFP's course into the twenty-first century, the statement recognized that WFP food aid could help to promote food security, which had become a *leitmotiv* in the food aid policies of the major food aid donors – Canada, the European Union and the United States – and should be oriented towards the objective of eradicating hunger and poverty. The WFP's core policies and strategies were defined as: saving lives in emergencies; improving the nutrition and quality of life of life of the most vulnerable people at critical times of their lives; and building assets and promoting the self-reliance of poor people, particularly through labour-intensive works programmes.

The WFP would concentrate its efforts and resources on the neediest people in the poorest countries. Targets were set that, by 1997, at least 90 per cent of the WFP's development assistance would be provided to low-income, food-deficient countries and 50 per cent to least-developed countries.[25] The WFP was described as being 'well placed' to play a major role in the continuum from emergency relief to development. WFP activities would be integrated at the country level so that they could respond to urgent needs while retaining core development objectives based on the national plans, policies and programmes of developing countries. The WFP would continue to provide its transport and logistics expertise and assistance to ensure rapid and efficient humanitarian aid. Bilateral services would be provided to donors, other UN agencies and NGOs on the basis of full cost recovery. Collaboration with other UN organizations, bilateral aid agencies and NGOs would be pursued. And the WFP would play its part in bringing the issue of hunger to the centre of the international agenda and in advocating policies, strategies and operations that directly benefited the poor and hungry.

Consultations on the future directions of the WFP were held right up to the end of the millennium. A joint WFP/UN University seminar on 'Ending the Inheritance of Hunger' was held at WFP headquarters in May 1997, which served to reinforce the conviction that tackling malnutrition in the early stages of life was a sound investment of scarce food aid resources (WFP and UNU, 1997). In May 1998, the WFP's executive board decided to undertake a policy review of WFP development assistance. A series of consultations were organized in an open review process under the theme: 'Time for Change: Food Aid for Development'. The executive director, Catherine Bertini, let it be known that she was 'not willing to concede that development food aid is over. It's got to be the basis of helping people help themselves out of poverty. If we don't do that, we are building a world of perpetual emergencies' (IFPRI, 1998: 4). In 1998, the WFP's executive board signalled the need for a policy review of the use of food aid as a development instrument, recognizing the need to further clarify the particular advantages of food assistance, and to define how and when the WFP should intervene with food aid.

Enabling development policy

At the end of the long-standing debate, which extended over most of the 1990s, the WFP secretariat produced a major policy paper, *Enabling Development* (WFP, 1999a). The paper was based on the perception that food aid had a crucial role to pay in enabling marginalized, food-insecure people to participate in the broad process of development. Food was a form of assistance which met one of the most basic needs of poor people, and was essential for health, growth and productivity. 'Nothing could replace it'. The prospect of achieving food security in a few years could not compensate for inadequate nutrition today. Targeted food aid was a fast track to reaching the poor. It reached them directly and immediately in ways many other types of assistance did not, providing help until the benefits of economic growth and increased productivity relieved food insecurity.

The enabling development policy (EDP) advocated focused on five basic objectives: enabling young children and expectant and nursing mothers to meet their special nutritional and nutrition-related health needs; enabling poor households to invest in human capital through education and training; making it possible for poor people to gain and preserve assets; mitigating the effects of natural disasters in areas vulnerable to recurring crises; and enabling households which depend on degraded natural resources for their food security to shift to more sustainable livelihoods.

The WFP would only provide food assistance when and where food consumption was inadequate for good health and productivity. Every WFP development intervention would be targeted on poor, food-insecure households. They would be designed to encourage investment and to leave behind physical assets or improved human capital to help households and communities after food aid came to an end. The targets would be urban and peri-urban areas with high concentrations of malnutrition, as well as food-insecure rural areas. The WFP would endeavour to intervene early, and would explicitly take seasonality into account in areas with wide fluctuations in food security. The poor themselves would be involved in order to gain a greater understanding of their problems and lasting solutions. And the WFP would be proactive in seeking partnerships with other aid organizations and in developing new approached in project design.

The rationale behind the EDP's formulation derived from the realization of the need to narrow and sharpen the WFP's role in development against the background of decreasing levels of overseas development aid and the continued questioning by some donors of the use of food aid for developmental purposes. The EDP recognized that WFP food aid should play a different but unique role in enabling poor and marginalized people to take part in the development process and to benefit from it. The main elements of the EDP were: five areas of focus (health and nutrition, education and training, asset creation, disaster mitigation, and sustainable livelihoods and natural resources), and identification of a set of measures to improve the quality of the WFP's development interventions (strengthened partnerships, enhanced community participation, better targeting, increased understanding of beneficiaries' circumstances, and greater attention to gender considerations).

The main changes that the EDP intended to introduce were essentially: a clearer and more focused definition of the potential beneficiaries of the WFP's development projects; streamlining and narrowing down the range of projects that could be supported by WFP food aid; emphasis on community management and ownership of the activities undertaken and of the assets created; focus on poor people's priorities and livelihoods; and re-orienting the role of food aid as a temporary support to poor people while their livelihoods improved, rather than as a form of payment in labour-intensive works programmes.

The WFP's executive board considered the secretariat's paper on the EDP at its annual session in May 1999. It expressed appreciation for the consultation process concerning food for development that the secretariat had organized, which had been 'open, thorough and participatory'. The recommendations contained in the secretariat's paper, including the focus on the five development objectives, were approved (WFP, 1999b). However, some representatives (unspecified) expressed reservations regarding food aid for development. They cautioned that the 'WFP's excellence in emergency operations should not be compromised by the requirements of implementing the new development policies'.

The executive director, Catherine Bertini, emphasized that emergency and recovery operations would not suffer from the organizational changes required by the new development policy. She emphasized that many of the changes in the new development portfolio would provide operational capacity in both emergency and protracted recovery operations. The executive board reiterated the importance of co-ordination and partnerships in carrying out the development policy recommendations. It stressed that a choice of the five priority areas, or their combination within a country programme of assistance, would depend on the specific needs of individual country. As food aid for development was a scarce resource, the best use should be made of it, and it should be targeted on the neediest countries and people (WFP, 1999c).

External evaluation of the enabling development policy

In 2003, four years after its approval by the WFP's governing body, representatives of seven WFP donor countries – Canada, Denmark, Finland, France, Germany, Italy and the United States – initiated an external evaluation of the progress achieved and difficulties encountered in implementing the EDF.[26] The evaluation was undertaken by an international consortium of consulting firms in the seven countries, and was managed by the evaluation offices of the international aid agencies of the seven countries in close co-operation with the WFP's Office of Evaluation and the support of two senior advisers. The evaluation, which took two years to complete, involved research at WFP headquarters, generating seven country studies conducted by teams consisting of two national and two international consultants in Ethiopia, Mali and Mozambique in sub-Saharan Africa, Bangladesh and Pakistan in Asia, and Bolivia and Honduras in Latin America. Considerable support was provided by WFP headquarters and field staff.

The main focus of the evaluation was not on food aid for development as such but, rather, on the effectiveness of the EDP as part of an ongoing process of change within the WFP, and on how the EDP contributed to meeting the MDGs. The results of the evaluation were expected to: provide the sponsoring donors with valuable insights and issues for consideration concerning their future support for WFP development activities; identify ways that could potentially enhance WFP effectiveness in the design and implementation of its development portfolio; and contribute, through empirical evidence, to a better understanding of the conditions for success or failure of food aid in development activities.

On the basis of interviews carried out with representatives of donor countries and a review of donors' policy documents during the course of the evaluation, four main reasons were identified as to why some donors were moving away from the use of food aid for development. Doubts were expressed as to whether food aid could be a valid instrument to foster development, which created a tendency to allocate resources away from food aid-based activities at a time when development resources were increasingly scarce. There was continuing concern about the potential negative impact of food aid on markets and production in recipient countries. There remained lack of strong evidence on the positive impact of the use of food aid for development. Also, for several donors, food aid was considered an expensive form of aid transfer, the additional costs of which had to be justified on the basis of clear comparative advantage.

The overall conclusions of the evaluation were, however, positive. The evaluation findings indicated that the WFP had put in place, 'albeit with limitations and delays', the policy directions envisaged in the EDP. The overarching goal of the EDP of enabling poor, marginalized people to take part in the development process and benefit from it, had been, or was being, achieved by the WFP, 'albeit with some limitations'. The EDP had been a crucial factor in this success. The EDP directions had contributed to the increased relevance of the WFP's interventions overall; to the achievement of results consistent with national poverty-reduction goals, which were broadly in line with the target group's priorities and expectations; and to increased sustainability of the results obtained.

The evaluation concluded that the EDP was a sound policy whose principles were worth further support and implementation by the WFP and donors, particularly in the light of their potential for improving the quality and relevance of WFP emergency operations. Implementation of the EDP had also helped to shed further light on the actual and potential roles of food aid in situations not strictly of an emergency or recovery nature. The evaluation confirmed one of the major assumptions of the EDP: that while food aid alone could not contribute to development in the same way as other measures, 'food assistance *can* [original emphasis] play a specific role within long-term poverty-reduction frameworks'.

The evaluation also identified EDP-related areas where improvements were necessary for enhancing the comparative advantage and overall relevance of WFP food aid for development activities. These improvements could provide the WFP with a clearer role as the leading UN agency that contributed food assistance and related know-how for the protection and nutrition-related needs of the most vulnerable groups. Three improvement measures were highlighted. There was need to improve the WFP's 'partnership strategies', from a concept that saw food aid as a resource around which to build interventions, towards a paradigm where food aid complemented other resources within national and local poverty reduction and recovery plans. WFP interventions required further refinement regarding the targeting that others are unable to undertake, as in labour-poor households, out-of-school children, and people living in remote areas. Consistent progress should be made on nutrition-related issues, which could be an important justification for the systematic use of food aid transfers in non-emergency situations and in the presence of functioning markets.

The evaluation report made seven main recommendations, each with a number of sub-recommendations that were addressed to WFP management, the executive board, WFP membership, and donors. The first three recommendations were considered to be 'strategic': further integration of WFP assistance within broader poverty-reduction frameworks, improving the targeting of the most vulnerable and excluded groups, mainstreaming the nutrition priorities within WFP development operations. The remainder related to 'implementation': close consideration of resourcing-related issues, including donors guaranteeing their resourcing at levels agreed by the executive board at project approval and through multi-year funding arrangements; strengthening results and efficiency analysis to facilitate informed decisions; reconsideration of the level of priority attributed to the five EDP strategic objectives in the light of current policy reduction frameworks and of WFP organizational changes; and the sustainability aspects of WFP development activities should receive more attention, including appropriate exit strategies and increased integration of WFP development operations into national poverty-reduction frameworks.

The EDP was reflected in the WFP's *Strategic Plan (2006–2009)*, which was approved by the WFP's executive board at its Annual Session in June 2005. The plan set the goals and objectives for all WFP activities over the four-year period (WFP, 2005a). The core programme goal was 'to contribute to meeting the MDGs through food-assisted interventions targeted on poor and hungry people'. In order to achieve that goal, WFP operations would be targeted on five strategic objectives (SOs): saving lives in crisis situations; protecting livelihoods in crisis situations and enhancing resilience to shocks; supporting the improved nutrition and health status of children, mothers and other vulnerable people; supporting access to education, and reducing gender disparities in access to education and skills training; and strengthening the capacities of countries and regions to establish and manage food assistance and hunger reduction programmes.

Transformation

The WFP secretariat welcomed the external evaluation as encouraging greater support for WFP development activities at a time when donor contributions for development were dwindling. It was felt that further investment in development would greatly improve vulnerable people's capacity to cope with shocks, thereby reducing the cost of emergency interventions. But the evaluation did not result in encouraging donors to give more resources to the WFP for development projects. The highest annual WFP commitment to development projects in current prices of $925 million occurred in 1984. From then, annual commitments for development projects were gradually reduced to $268 million in 2006. At the same time, WFP annual expenditure in emergency operations increased sharply from $234 million in 1984 to $1, 962 million in 2006. This transformation from one of the major development programmes of the UN system to the world's largest humanitarian agency is the subject of Chapter 2.

Appendix

Statement of the Honourable George S. McGovern, Delegate of the United States of America, Director of the Food for Peace Program, Executive Office of the President, (FAO Intergovernmental Advisory Committee, Rome, Italy: 10 April 1961) that led to the establishment of the WFP as a three-year experimental programme.

1. The United States favors a multilateral approach for the use of agricultural commodities as a supplement to bilateral arrangements.
2. We think FAO should have a major role in such a program, in co-operation with other UN organizations.
3. We believe this should be a truly multilateral program with the widest possible contributions by member countries.
4. We recognize that countries are here to advise the FAO Director-General on his report – not to take government positions on subjects covered in his report. Because of the need to move to the consideration of specific action proposals, however, we have been in touch with our Government over the weekend.
5. As a result, we are authorized to propose that an initial program on a multilateral basis might aim at a fund of $100 million in commodities and cash contributions. For its part, the United States would be prepared to offer $40 million in commodities, and the possibility of a supplementary cash contribution will be explored in Washington.
6. The $100 million total would be available for use over a fixed forward period. We are thinking of three years.
7. We recognize the desire of the (FAO) Director-General to make the widest possible use of commodities in alleviating malnutrition. However, we continue to believe that the primary aim of the program in its initial stage should be to meet emergency needs. At the same time, we would support use of the program

fund for pilot activities in other fields such as school lunch and labor-intensive projects, in order to develop some diversified experience.

8. Specifics including additional staffing would have to be worked out for consideration by governments. This could be the responsibility of the (FAO) Director-General in informal consultation with individual countries.
9. The purpose of our proposal is to help in launching a multilateral program utilizing food to test approaches. After such experience, we could then examine the question of future additional work.

Source: FAO (1961a) *Development Through Food: A Strategy for Surplus Utilization*. FFHC Basic Study No. 2 (Rome, Italy: FAO: 121–2).

2
From Development Projects to Emergency Operations: Tipping Points in the WFP's Transformation

In little more than a decade, the WFP was transformed from being a major UN development programme to the world's largest humanitarian agency. The transformation was not easy, partly because of the speed and scale by which events occurred that forced the change of direction (Margous, 2002). During its first decade of operations (1963–72), the WFP had invested less than 10 per cent of its resources in emergencies. In 1977, emergencies accounted for almost one-quarter of WFP commitments. That shift quickened and intensified until, by 2006, over 80 per cent of WFP food aid went to emergency relief (Figure 2.1). At the same time, there was a significant shift from assistance to emergencies caused by natural disasters and crop failures caused by drought, pests and diseases to relief for refugees and displaced persons, the victims of disasters caused by conflict, and to a focus on sub-Saharan Africa.

Increasing involvement in emergencies

We saw in Chapter 1 that, while the original intention was that the WFP should focus first on providing emergency assistance, the limitations to which the WFP was subjected in the supply of resources from donors led to the shift of focus to supporting development projects. In addition, and as a result, only a modest proportion of WFP resources were allocated for providing emergency relief. The net result was that emergency assistance was provided on a small scale. But there were exceptions, and some significant events may be singled out in the inexorable increase of the WFP's involvement in emergency operations. They are related here in chronological order, although there is some overlap between them.

Up to the beginning of the 1990s, the greater part of WFP resources were allocated to development projects. But the development and refinement of a transportation and logistics system to deliver food aid efficiently to WFP-supported development projects could also be drawn upon to serve WFP emergency operations. This was a major factor in gaining increasing recognition in the international

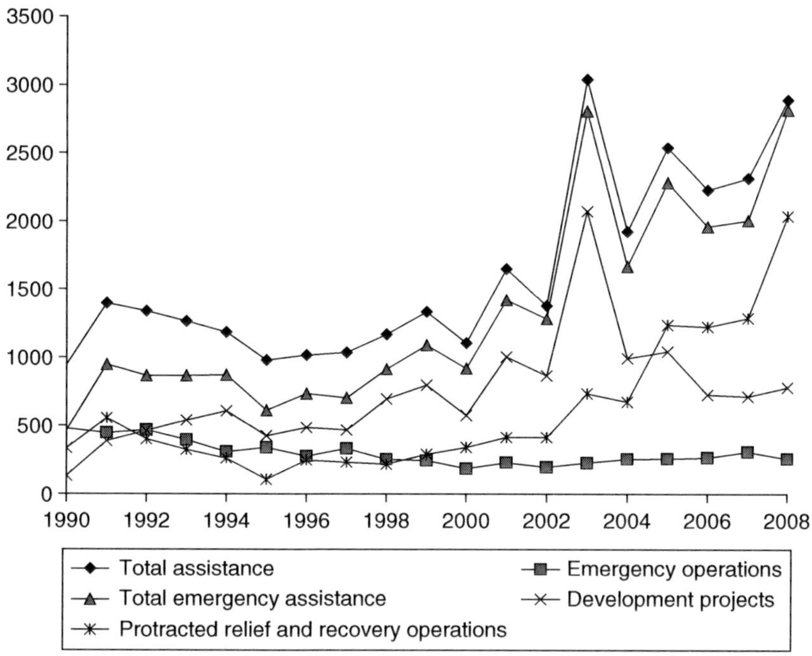

Figure 2.1 WFP development and emergency assistance 1998–2008 ($ millions)
Source: WFP Annual Reports.

community of the WFP's ability to address large-scale and complex humanitarian crises. Furthermore, as WFP development assistance expanded, this also assisted its work in emergencies, as stocks of WFP food commodities in recipient countries to support development projects could be drawn from on a replenishment basis to respond to emergencies quickly.

Civil war in Nigeria

The WFP had early experience in handling humanitarian operations in conflict-induced emergencies in the civil war in Nigeria and in subsequent recovery programmes, which were to become prominent some years later. In 1967, the secessionist state of Biafra in the south-eastern part of the country tried to become an independent state. A three-year civil war ensued during which up to two million people died from armed conflict, disease, and starvation, and many people were displaced from their homes. During the humanitarian crisis, the Nigerian government requested the WFP's help to solve the problems of port congestion, caused by international food aid arrived in an uncoordinated way, and internal transport and logistics difficulties, which impeded the rapid movement of food into areas of acute need. After the war, the WFP assisted nine projects at a total cost of $16 million for a major reconstruction and rehabilitation programme during which about 76,000 dwellings and 1,800 school buildings and teacher's quarters were built or repaired, and 105,000 workers and the families were fed. Well over half a million people were estimated to have benefited directly from the relief and reconstruction programme.

The African droughts of the 1970s

Before the early 1970s, there was virtually no international emergency food aid to Africa. Although food shortages occurred, they were mostly localized. But such incidences became increasingly more widespread, exacerbated by the growth of the population, and the failure to promote agricultural growth and development. Six successive years of drought in the Sahelian countries of West Africa called for a major international relief effort in the three years 1973–75. Seven countries (Chad, Gambia, Mali, Mauritania, Niger, Senegal, and Upper Volta), with a total population of 25 million people, were most seriously affected. When the drought started, no one could predict how long it would last. As the situation worsened into widespread starvation, the immediate priority was to provide relief food quickly and on a massive scale. During the three-year international emergency relief operation, over 2.5 million tons of cereals were delivered to the region. Notwithstanding the unprecedented relief effort, it was estimated that over 100,000 people died and one million head of cattle perished.

The UN secretary-general appointed the FAO as the lead agency for the large-scale international emergency relief operation. The FAO set up an Office of Sahelian Relief Operations (OSRO) to lead this task, to which WFP officers were seconded. By this time, a decade after it had commenced operations, the WFP had already built up an international reputation for its transportation and logistics expertise in delivering food aid throughout the developing world. This expertise proved to be invaluable in responding to the widespread emergency situation in some of Africa's most difficult terrain. WFP staff, along with many others, became inextricably involved in the wider aspects of emergency operations – information collection and dissemination, assessment of food requirements, monitoring the delivery of food commitments – that were to add up to the WFP being increasingly called upon by donors and recipients alike to play a co-ordinating role in large-scale international emergency food aid operations in the future.

Transportation by road, rail, river, and air was the biggest bottleneck. Monitoring relief supplies was a key operation. Continuous co-operative efforts were necessary to keep, at the peak period, as many as 1,000 trucks operating every day, delivering food, feed for livestock, and other basic relief supplies. WFP field staff worked with local officials and donor representatives in maintaining the flow of food supplies over long distances to, and within, landlocked countries.

Airlift and airdrop operations were necessary in remote areas. A number of donor countries made the necessary aircraft available, with WFP staff providing on-the-ground co-ordination and supervision. In 1973, 30 cargo aircraft from nine national air forces took part in the airlift operations. Some 25,000 tons of cereals and other foods were airlifted over a period of four months in round-the-clock operations. In 1974, most airlift and airdrop operations were discontinued as it was possible by that time to pre-position food and feed stocks in remote areas before the onset of the rainy season. Camel caravans were used to transport food and feed to the remote parts of Chad and Niger.

WFP staff also assisted in the design and implementation of a delivery system for the orderly shipment of food to nine West African ports and for co-ordinated inland distribution throughout the region. Some ports were not organized or equipped to handle the large volume of food required. Port handling and logistics specialists were assigned by donor countries to work with WFP staff at key locations throughout the food delivery chain. Task forces were set up to solve problems as they arose. Expansion of storage facilities became a matter of high priority as food stocks built up with the arrival of shipments at the ports. Emergency measures, such as the provision of portable silos, helped to alleviate the problem. Average clearance of food at ports and inland transport more than doubled. NGOs from many donor countries played an important role, especially in reaching the afflicted population in remote areas.

As in the Sahel region of West Africa, the drought in Ethiopia in 1973 was the culmination of several years of sub-normal rainfall. In April 1973, the Ethiopian government started a large-scale relief programme, established a National Drought Relief Committee, banned all grain exports, and requested international aid. During 1973, the WFP provided 20,000 tons of grain and $200,000 for its internal transportation, handling and distribution. WFP staff monitored bilateral food aid shipments, and assisted in tackling considerable logistical and communications difficulties. Some of the worst affected areas were almost completely inaccessible by surface transport and air drops were organized.

Lack of information and communications clouded the real magnitude of the disaster. Only when large numbers of starving people migrated from the interior to the main highways was the full scale of the catastrophe revealed. Aid measures had then to be improvised, concentrating on the provision of food and shelter along the roads. Once the real dimensions of the drought were known, action by the Ethiopian government and the international community gained momentum. By May 1974, international donations of food, medical supplies, transport equipment, technical assistance and cash grants amounted to over $80 million. The government's emphasis shifted to a long-term rehabilitation programme, and an increasing proportion of relief food supplies were used in food-for-work programmes, particularly for soil conservation, irrigation, and reforestation.

A number of lessons were learned from the African food crises of the 1970s. This was the first time that the international community confronted a disaster that affected so many countries simultaneously and covered such a large geographical area. A combined and co-ordinated effort was required by governments in the afflicted countries, the major donor countries, the concerned UN agencies, and the large number of international and national NGOs involved. Many weaknesses had to be overcome, including the reluctance of the governments of the afflicted countries to appeal for external humanitarian assistance until many people and livestock started to die, hence the late recognition of the full magnitude of the disaster. This resulted in delays in the response of donor countries, aid agencies and NGOs, and the resultant late delivery of urgently needed relief food. It also led to the ultimate recognition that the international community was simply unprepared to mount a sufficiently rapid relief operation on the scale required.

Important lessons were learned about the practical implementation of large-scale relief operations, and what was required to establish and maintain co-ordinated international action. One lasting benefit that was to emerge from the catastrophe was the creation and development of the FAO's Global Information and Early Warning System for Food and Agriculture in 1973. Since the establishment in 1968 of an early warning system for food shortages, FAO and WFP field staff had sent in monthly data to FAO headquarters for over 70 countries. The experience of the Sahelian countries and Ethiopia in the 1970s underlined the need to improve the system, which was endorsed by a resolution of the 1974 World Food Conference (UN, 1975). This system now provides vital early warning of impending emergencies caused by drought and crop failure. It has improved over time, especially after the introduction of satellite imagery, although it is recognized that more requires to be done to establish and improve response systems to react promptly and effectively to the early warning signals, and to develop and implement an early warning system for emergencies caused by armed conflict and civil unrest.

Special measures for least-developed countries: meeting internal costs

Another factor facilitating the WFP's increased involvement in emergency operations was the approval by its governing body of special measures to meet certain internal costs of the food aid it provided to least-developed countries (LDCs). In 1972, the UN General Assembly acknowledged the limited capacity of LDCs to absorb external aid. At the time, 25 countries had been designated as 'least-developed'. By 2008, that number had increased to 50, with 31 in sub-Saharan Africa, eight in Asia, and 11 island countries (UN, 2008a). The Canadian delegation to the WFP's governing body proposed that the WFP should help meet the internal transport, storage and handling (ITSH) costs in LDCs relating to the food aid provided by the WFP: this was approved. Subsidizing ITSH costs placed a heavy additional burden on the WFP's limited cash resources, particularly after the steep increase in world food and oil prices of the 1970s. To take the pressure off the WFP's limited cash resources, sale of cereals donated to the WFP was permitted in the eligible countries in order to offset ITSH costs. This, too, created difficulties, as ITSH costs rose and larger volumes of grains were needed for sale.

World Food Conference 1974: increased responsibilities for the WFP

The world food crisis of the early 1970s, the worst in modern history, led to the holding of a World Food Conference in Rome, Italy in November 1974.[1] The conference had two major implications for the WFP (UN, 1975). Resolution XVII, An Improved Policy for Food Aid, recommended that donor countries adopt the concept of forward planning of food aid, providing at least 10 million tons of grains for food aid per year, starting in 1975, and also 'adequate quantities' of other food commodities. The resolution also recommended that the WFP's governing body, the Intergovernmental Committee (IGC), be reconstituted as the Committee on Food Aid Policies and Programmes (CFA), and 'entrusted with the task of formulating proposals for the more effective co-ordination of multilateral, bilateral and non-governmental food aid programmes and of co-ordinating emergency food aid'. The CFA was established in 1976, increasing the WFP secretariat's responsibility to service it on matters relating to all food aid, including the international community's food aid response to emergencies and the co-ordination of emergency operations.

The conference also adopted a resolution on an International Undertaking on World Food Security (Resolution XVII), which urged all countries to build up and maintain world food-grain reserves large enough to cover foreseeable major food production shortfalls, and to be strategically located both nationally and regionally. It was proposed that the wheat and rice components of the reserves should be 30 million tons. In responding to the resolution, the UN General Assembly adopted its own resolution (3362 (S-VII)). The resolution established an International Emergency Food Reserve (IEFR) with a target of not less than 500,000 tons, to be placed at the disposal of the WFP to strengthen its capacity to respond to crisis situations in developing countries (UN, 1976).

The IEFR offered the prospect of additional resources for WFP emergency operations. Modalities for its operation were approved by the CFA in 1976, and revised and enlarged in 1978 after protracted deliberations in the WFP's governing body (WFP, 1978a). The reserve was seen as a continuing mechanism with yearly replenishments determined by the CFA. It was originally regarded as a multilateral standby arrangement to provide the WFP with an initial, quick-response capability to respond to emergencies whenever and wherever they occurred. It did not involve the WFP holding food stocks in strategic locations. Instead, contributors to the IEFR were required to announce their pledges to the reserve from their own food stocks one year in advance, which were to be provided in the most expeditious manner.

Contributors were also expected to meet transport and other related costs for the food aid provided under the reserve. Developing countries not in a position to make contributions to the reserve could make interest-free loans of commodities that the WFP could use in the initial stage of an emergency to speed up food deliveries. Part of the contributions to the reserve was to be made in food commodities, such as rice and white sorghum, to take account of the food habits of afflicted people. But the reserve was not a completely multilateral mechanism. Where contributions to the reserve were not placed at the disposal of the WFP, the participating country was required to keep the WFP informed about their uses in order to achieve co-ordination of the food assistance provided under the IEFR. Fatally, as we shall see later, the procedures already adopted for the approval of WFP emergency food assistance were applied to operations under the reserve. The CFA could consider changes in the existing procedures at a later stage in the light of experience. WFP executive director James Ingram tried to change the criteria for granting emergency aid but this was not accepted by the WFP's governing body (Ingram, 2007: 129–34).

While the IEFR did improve the WFP's ability to respond to emergencies, it did not live up fully to its original expectations. The reserve is not like a bank account readily available for the WFP's instant use; neither is it a stock of food kept by the WFP on standby to be instantly drawn from when emergencies strike. It is a voluntary arrangement to provide emergency food relief from food stocks and funds kept in contributing countries. Contributors have not fully respected the IEFR modalities that they approved after considerable deliberation in the WFP's governing body. Contributions have not been fully announced in advance. A high proportion of contributions have been tied and designated by donors to specific emergencies after they have occurred, which has eroded the multilateral nature of the reserve and made it difficult to respond rapidly and flexibly to emergencies no matter where or when they occurred.

Contributions to the reserve have fluctuated considerably and cash contributions have fallen short of requirements. Consequently, a timely and adequate response to all emergencies proved to be difficult, especially those less publicized. The end result is that the world still does not have an adequate and well-functioning multilateral emergency food reserve. A truly multilateral and fully subscribed emergency reserve would help to take the politics out of emergency aid, avoid the hardship and suffering that the afflicted populations might needlessly endure, and limit the costs and diversions of funds for development that result from a late and inadequate response to emergencies. These deficiencies were serious impediments to the effective and timely response to emergencies. To overcome some of the problems, the WFP's governing body agreed in 1991 to executive director Ingram's proposal to set up, as an integral part of the IEFR, an Immediate Response Account (IRA) with an annual target of $30 million in cash to enable rapid purchases of food and its transport close to where emergencies occurred.

Kampuchean emergency operation

WFP education in responding to the human and physical devastation caused by civil war was taken to a new height in the emergency relief and recovery operations that took place in Kampuchea (Cambodia) between 1979 and 1990, one of the most protracted and complex operations ever undertaken.[2] Between 1975 and 1979, paralyzed to act, the international community watched the internal destruction of an entire nation – immortalized in the film *The Killing Fields* – during which an estimated 1.5 million people were killed by war, massacre, starvation, lack of medical care, and forced labour. The entire economy of the country was in ruins as the urban population was forced to work in the countryside in the most primitive conditions. Malnutrition was severe, particularly among children and the elderly. Acute food shortages were reported in many parts of the country following the collapse of agricultural production. There was little transport, no public services or trade, and the government administration had been completely dismantled. In short, the country was on the brink of a total catastrophe (Shawcross, 1984).

Reports in early 1979 indicated that mass starvation would result if immediate action were not taken. The political complexity of an international relief effort was added to by the urgent needs of different people, in different locations, that had to be addressed simultaneously. Practically the entire population of five million people required emergency humanitarian assistance. In addition, a large migration of people had taken place to the Kampuchean/Thai border, causing dislocation and hardship to the Thai villagers in the area. The Kampuchean emergency operation began in response to UN Resolution 34/22. An international appeal was made for funds: $102 million were raised for the food component of an international relief programme. In 1982, a UN Border Relief Operation (UNBRO) was established to provide co-ordinated humanitarian assistance to refugees and displaced persons along the Kampuchean/Thai border under the overall authority of a special representative of the UN secretary-general. Initially, it was difficult to estimate the number of displaced persons along the border as there was much cross movement. One estimate put the number at around one million people but, by the time the WFP assumed management of UNBRO, the numbers had stabilized to around 250,000 to 300,000. A further complication was that Thai villagers, who in the north-east were of the same ethnic origin, tried to enter the border camps to be counted in order to benefit from a ration card. A special programme was established to mitigate any hardships experienced by the Thai border villagers.

The two parts of the relief operation were differently managed with little integration between them. The internal operation in Kampuchea, managed from Phnom Pehn, was managed along what at the time were fairly traditional lines. The WFP had a modest presence in the country for most of the early years, with support from the Swedish Disaster team. The WFP worked through the government, with some NGO partnerships. This contrasted with the management of the UNBRO operation. UNBRO had a total of about 40 international staff based in Bangkok and in offices along the Thai/Kampuchean border, with only a small number of WFP international professional staff. The UNBRO operation involved a number of innovations, including setting up a border medical co-ordination group to ensure uniform health treatment and common protocol in the camps set up for the large number of Kampucheans who had crossed over into Thailand, which went beyond the traditional WFP focus on the provision of food. The WHO sent missions to look at the health care provided and was complimentary of the work undertaken. The range of assistance co-ordinated by the WFP along the border included not only the provision of food and supplementary feeding programmes, but also primary health care, curative health care, the provision of safe water and sanitation facilities, shelter, primary education, social welfare, security and protection and pioneering technical support (such as radio systems for communications and security purposes).

The WFP assumed managerial oversight of UNBRO and became the lead agency for the delivery and monitoring of a complete package of relief aid provided by UNBRO, playing a number of roles in providing humanitarian assistance.

Well-rounded food rations were distributed consisting of cereals (mainly rice), vegetable oil, canned fish, pulses, and blended foods. Dried skimmed milk was also provided, but only a small quantity was used in pre-mixed and pre-cooked foods in supplementary feeding programmes in view of the danger that it might be used to bottle-feed infants, and most was exchanged in Bangkok and Singapore for fortified foods. Food purchases were made in Thailand, a major rice exporter. A food-processing programme was carried out to produce bread, biscuits, and noodles. Initially, food shipments to Kampuchea were hampered by limited port capacity, the breakdown of harbour facilities, and lack of storage and transport. The WFP organized work to overcome these obstacles with the help of financial, technical and material assistance. A central warehouse was established in Aranyaprathet, Thailand, and two sub-stores were set up near railway sidings and major roads to the border area. Trucking fleets were assembled in Kampuchea and Thailand to maintain the flow of supplies and the distribution of food and other relief assistance. In 1987, the WFP ceased its administration of one of the largest and longest relief operations, during which more than $180 million of assistance in cash and kind were provided.

Many problems were faced in carrying out this large and complex emergency operation. A WFP mission to evaluate UNBRO operations was instigated by executive director Ingram, which included a member of the Refugees Studies Programme of Oxford University, UK. It revealed a 'shocking abuse of human rights'. Operations were to be conducted in accordance with the Thai government policy of not encouraging permanent settlement at the border or of aid acting as a magnet to attract migration into that area. Kampucheans on the Thai border were denied refugee status by the Thai authorities, and were treated as 'political pawns' to western and Thai-Asian political priorities, without which they could have returned to Kampuchea long before (Reynell, 1989). At the same time, aid was to be provided in ways that retained the dignity, pride, national identity, and spirit of the recipients. Conflicting factions attempted to control the distribution of food to needy people for political ends. Food was diverted to the military. Quicker provision of development aid by donors, and in larger amounts, could have reduced the time over which emergency aid was needed. Transport and logistics difficulties were acute. Despite these problems, the operation succeeded in its basic aim of providing humanitarian assistance to people in extreme distress, thereby saving many lives.

UNBRO provided a number of important early lessons for the WFP in conducting emergency relief operations. It revealed the paradox of a UN humanitarian agency trying to save lives and mitigate human misery in the absence of a satisfactory political solution, which made resolution of the problem less urgent for the political negotiators and public opinion. It showed that WFP senior management needed to be seen to be politically even-handed and transparent in such politically sensitive operations, in line with the humanitarian principles of the UN, and to give clear guidance to WFP field staff. In such highly visible and sensitive relief operations, adequate numbers of competent, experienced and proven WFP staff should have been assigned from inception. Despite the obvious political problems, UNBRO was unique in that the WFP provided services that went far beyond the provision of food, thanks to the initiatives of its field staff. These, combined, added to the health, general well-being and security of the displaced Kampucheans, an important lesson for future emergency operations.

With the signing of the Paris Peace Agreement between the warring factions in 1990, the WFP was able gradually to transform its relief assistance into aid for development. Total bilateral contributions channelled through the WFP by 16 donors and the UN Transitional Authority in Cambodia amounting to over $70 million enabled the provision of 167,000 tons of food to be made for five purposes: repatriation of refugees; assistance to internally displaced persons; feeding of vulnerable groups of mothers, children, the sick and the elderly; assistance to demobilized soldiers to enable them to return to civilian life; and de-mining operations and food-for-work programmes for the reconstruction and rehabilitation of the country, especially the agricultural sector. This gave the farming community both physical strength and confidence to open the way to agricultural recovery, a vital step before food aid could be phased out. The WFP also assisted that process by helping to transport seed, fertilizer, and agricultural equipment along with food aid, and begin a food-for-seeds programme to collect rice seed.

Several factors contributed to the successful transition from relief to development: flexibility to respond to the changing needs of the people resulted from extensive delegation of authority to the WFP country office in Cambodia; funds were readily available to meet the costs of non-food inputs and administration; a high proportion of the staff was locally recruited; and extensive consultation was held with the local population in the selection and implementation of the development activities undertaken.

Afghan refugees in Pakistan

Another significant experience was the provision of humanitarian assistance to a large Afghan refugee population in Pakistan. This, among other things, involved the close co-operation of the WFP and the UNHCR that later was to become institutionalized. Internal political unrest in, and the invasion of Soviet Union forces into, Afghanistan resulted in a large influx of refugees into Pakistan and Iran at the beginning of the 1980s, one of the largest refugee populations ever recorded (Shaw and Clay, 1993: 83–4). At its height, there were over 3.5 million Afghans in Pakistan and 700,000 in Iran. In Pakistan, the registered refugee population lived on over 300 camps in various parts of the country. In addition, there was a large unregistered refugee population scattered throughout the country. Half of the registered refugees were children and one-quarter comprised women. This did not take account of the babies born in refugee camps during the 1980s, estimated by the UN to number around 700,000, and for whom no special emergency programme was initiated.

The Pakistan government appealed to the international community for humanitarian assistance in the form of food, shelter, and other basic needs. A number of donor countries and international aid agencies responded in a common large-scale humanitarian operation. Initially, the refugees were supplied with emergency relief items of food, water and health facilities, and blankets, quilts, clothes, and shelter materials to take care of extreme climatic and weather conditions. The infrastructure of the camps was gradually improved and services extended. About two-thirds of the food donations were channelled through the WFP, 15 per cent through the UNHCR and the remainder provided bilaterally. The WFP assumed full operational responsibility for the supply of all food commodities, including local purchases, transport, logistics, handling and monitoring. The UNHCR handled the larger part of external non-food assistance. The Pakistan government provided a small cash maintenance grant to each registered refugee. This contributed to the purchase in local markets of basic necessities, including food items not provided in the package of external assistance.

The original food basket for the Afghan refugees consisted of wheat, edible oil, dried skimmed milk, sugar, tea, dates, and high-nutrient biscuits. This was reduced to only two item, wheat and edible oil, when the other items were no longer forthcoming from donor countries. Wheat was drawn from Pakistan's national stocks on a replenishment basis. Delays and shortfalls in replacing the wheat occurred at a time when Pakistan had two bad wheat harvests due to drought. Imports of up to two million tons had to be bought commercially, at considerably higher foreign exchange costs, from an already ailing Pakistan economy. In addition, the food items no longer supplied in the international food aid programme were provided by Pakistan from its food imports, adding even further to the host country's costs of supporting the refugee population.

Any relief operation of such magnitude is likely to encounter formidable difficulties. This one went through a catalogue of problems. But it is testimony to the value of the overall approach adopted that the relief operation managed to withstand many technical and operational problems and to succeed in its basic objective of delivering humanitarian food and other basic needs to the large refugee population. Several factors contributed to the overall success: the level of its commitment and material support demonstrated the determination of the government to assume responsibility for the welfare of the refugees; from the outset, priority was assigned to the operation in terms of resources and manpower; strong administrative and institutional arrangements were set up for the refugee community; the government delegated technical and operational responsibilities to the aid agencies, while using existing administrative and political structures to retain overall control; and lastly, and particularly significantly, open consultation and co-ordination fostered by the government, and supported by all concerned, was invaluable not only in resolving problems, but also for applying constructive trial-and-error approaches.

Unfortunately, the ordeal of the Afghan refugees was far from over. Subsequently, the WFP supported a regional project for Afghanistan involving the return of 3.7 million refugees and displaced persons to their homes from Pakistan, Iran and within the country. But internal unrest and insecurity continues (see Chapter 3).

Tipping points

While these and other examples of WFP emergency operations were impressive, they did not result in tipping the balance of WFP resource allocation from development projects to disaster relief operations. That was to be initiated by the arrival of a new executive director, James Ingram, in 1982, and the implementation of his long-term vision for the future of the WFP.[3] Ingram was a former Australian diplomat and ambassador, and served for seven years as director-general of the Australian Development Assistance Bureau, during which he was Australia's representative at meetings of a number of UN and international bodies. He detected that the best route for getting the WFP's indispensible value into the minds of governments was through humanitarian assistance. As he put it, setting aside natural disasters, politics is at the root of humanitarian crises and governments are interested in politics. He detected that there was not the same interest in development aid. He felt that support for development food aid could easily evaporate but the WFP's role in relief would endure. He related that he attended many meetings with agencies, experts and governments when he was forced to defend WFP food aid for development projects to sceptical, even hostile, audiences. This experience reinforced his feeling that support in governments for food aid was fragile and that humanitarian aid should increasingly be the WFP's focus. At his final session of the WFP's governing body in December 1991, shortly before his retirement, he said:

> I find a tremendous ambivalence among governments about food aid itself, and where WFP should stand in relation to the three levels of food security, viz. household, national and global. So long as that ambivalence continues, the international community will be less successful than it could be in the hunger fight. (WFP, 1991a: 39)

Ingram gave a clear indication of his intentions in his statement to the first session of the WFP's governing body he attended in April 1982 at a time when the WFP's development assistance was growing rapidly and was to reach its zenith in 1984. He said: 'while WFP's main emphasis was on development, its work on emergencies was of great importance'. He laid stress on the humanitarian as well as the developmental aspects of the WFP's assistance, and underlined that the Programme must, therefore, 'apply the same high professional and administrative standards in its emergency operations as in its development projects' (WFP, 1982a: 13). In particular, he wished to see the high reputation that the WFP had acquired in its transportation and logistics activities emulated in other aspects of its emergency operations. At the same time, he went out of his way to establish close personal relationships with the executive heads of the UNHCR, ICRC, and the LRCS, and of international NGOs such as Oxfam and Save the Children.

But Ingram faced a constitutional problem and a mindset that the FAO director-general, Edouard Saouma, had formed. Saouma saw 'WFP exclusively as a logistics agency to deliver food to FAO-designed development projects and FAO-approved emergency operations' (Ingram, 2007: 309). Developing country governments requiring WFP emergency food assistance had to submit their request not to the WFP executive director but, rather, to the FAO's director-general, in accordance with the WFP's *General Regulations* approved by its governing body in 1962. The FAO director-general was to ask the WFP's executive director to examine the request and to decide upon it 'taking into account the recommendation of the executive director'. As Ingram explained, as the FAO regarded itself as primarily responsible for needs assessment, he could not appraise the validity of the request, for example, by sending an independent mission. Therefore, in practice, he could not do much more than consider whether there were resources available to meet the request. This system satisfied FAO director-general Saouma well, as he got the political credit from governments for the assistance provided while the WFP got the blame for allocating less than requested (Ingram, 2007: 294). Also, FAO country representatives informed governments of the approval of their requests for WFP emergency assistance by the FAO director-general before they were officially informed by the WFP.[4]

The FAO director-general sought to secure his advantages from this arrangement by proposing to convert the IEFR into a 'legally binding convention' and to increase its target to two million tons. These proposals were opposed by donor representatives on the WFP's governing body. They were reluctant to give the FAO director-general unrestricted authority over potentially much larger emergency resources. Their contributions to the IEFR were therefore much lower than anticipated. They also tied their contributions to emergency operations that they, not the FAO director-general, chose to support, weakening the original concept of the reserve as a multilateral facility to provide quick food relief to emergency operations whenever and wherever they occurred.

Establishment of a WFP emergency service

Ingram began the implementation of his vision by establishing an Emergency Service at WFP headquarters. He appointed Trevor Page as its director with effect from the beginning of 1983, with a view to ending the 'unprofessionalism' in its emergency operations.[5] Page had had substantial operational experience in emergencies, including secondment to the UNHCR during the East Pakistan (now Bangladesh) refugee crisis (1971–72), in Africa during the food crisis of the 1970s, and through secondment to the FAO's OSRO as chief logistics officer (1973–74). In taking this step, Ingram sought to rectify the imbalance in the WFP's workforce between work on development projects and work on emergency operations, to improve the assessment of emergency food needs and criteria for the provision of emergency food aid, and to build up an expertise in emergency operations to match that of the WFP's transport and logistics services. In short, as he put it, 'to stimulate WFP to a new level of creativity' (Ingram, 2007: 194). This came at an opportune time.

The African food crises of the 1980s: evaluation of the WFP response

Africa was to experience a series of food crises throughout the 1980s, even greater, and more complex, than those of the 1970s. Some 25 countries were affected. A core of some 15 countries remained 'at risk' throughout 1983–85. Out of a total population of about 150 million people, some 30 million were judged to need food assistance, of whom almost 10 million had abandoned their homes and land in search of food, water, and pasture for their livestock.[6] The FAO estimated cereal food aid requirements for 1983/84 at 2.9 million tons and for 1984/85, seven million tons. The WFP provided 774,000 tons of cereals through 87 emergency operations in 25 African countries for 19 million people during 1983–85. In addition, the WFP handled food aid on behalf of bilateral donors and 548,000 tons were provided for development projects, much of which went to the most affected countries. Overall, the WFP helped provide 14 per cent of the total food aid pledged for 1983–85.

Once the full magnitude of the disaster was recognized, the response of the international community to appeals for emergency aid was prompt and generous. Rarely before had so much food been mobilized so quickly and distributed to so many countries in such a short time.[7] At the height of the crisis in 1984–85, almost five million tons of cereal food aid was delivered to countries in sub-Saharan Africa, 40 per cent of global food aid deliveries, half of which was in the form of emergency food aid (World Bank and WFP, 1991).

As in the African food crises of the 1970s, the WFP played a number of vital roles in addition to being the largest single supplier of emergency food aid. It transported, purchased and monitored food aid for bilateral donors. It was the largest buyer of food produced in the region for use as food aid. Purchases averaged over 200,000 tons a year, including those made on behalf of donor countries. With the co-operation of donors and other aid agencies, the WFP strengthened logistics and management capacity in several African countries. In recognition of the WFP's ability and competence, the World Bank provided the WFP with a special grant of $5 million to help improve transport and logistics operations and to monitor food distribution. Food management units were established as an integral part of government administrations with WFP assistance, for which extensive training of national staff was provided with help from the UNDP. Shipping and logistics officers seconded from donor countries were deployed at strategic locations to facilitate co-ordination of all food aid deliveries and to accelerate port clearance and in-country transportation. They helped to introduce bulk handling arrangements at ports, organized transport to landlocked countries, and were largely responsible for speeding up emergency food aid distribution.

Large-scale trucking operations were set up, funded by donors and the massive public fund-raising programmes 'Band Aid' and 'Live Aid'. In Ethiopia, the WFP ran a fleet of over 220 trucks that delivered 10,000 tons of food per month from the ports to the drought-stricken areas inland.[8] In Sudan, the WFP assumed responsibility for the co-ordination of all food aid to the country and managed a fleet of 150 vehicles for the in-country transportation of relief food. In Chad, the WFP ran a fleet of 91 trucks from four regional logistics bases to transport food and other relief needs from the west coast of Africa to the landlocked interior. They provided a lifeline of support for large numbers of destitute and starving people.

Unlike as in the 1970s African food crises, however, Ingram established an Operational Task Force on Africa at WFP headquarters in November 1983 to assist in the co-ordination of emergency food supplies to Africa. The task force was supervised by a senior management committee, which met weekly under the chairmanship of Ingram or the deputy executive director, Salahuddin Ahmed. A mechanism was set up for the collection and dissemination of information to all concerned on requirements, pledges and deliveries of food supplies, and also on the capacities of port and inland transport and the supply system. In addition to monthly reports, weekly telex statements were issued on the rapidly changing food aid situation and related logistics in the most critically affected countries. This pioneering information service was later developed into the WFP's international food aid information service (INTERFAIS), which now provides a database for food aid operations worldwide.

Executive director Ingram also decided that an evaluation of WFP emergency operations in response to the African food crisis should be conducted during 1985, the first of its kind. A summary of the lessons learned was presented to the WFP's governing body in the form of a special report (WFP, 1986a).[9] The evaluation revealed a catalogue of shortcomings. It provided the WFP governing body members with the first frank account of the realities of emergency operations on the ground and found that:

> in the face of the sheer magnitude of the problem and the rapidity of the changing situation, neither recipient governments, nor the international donor community, nor international organizations, including WFP were prepared for, and reacted adequately to, the very specific needs of displaced people, i.e., both those seeking shelter across frontiers and local populations looking for help outside their own drought-ravaged regions. (WFP, 1986a)

The evaluation described in vivid detail the appalling conditions of people in desperate conditions in the most affected countries that had appeared on television throughout the western world. Drought had quickened the deterioration in Africa's food and agriculture that had been taking place over the past two decades owing to the neglect of the sector, which was central to the region's economic and social well-being. More than any other in the past, the crisis had provoked famine conditions leading to many of the displaced people arriving at relief shelters in a condition of severe distress, with acute malnutrition and severe illnesses, requiring immediate feeding and intensive health care. Throughout most of 1984/85, the most seriously affected countries were Ethiopia, Sudan and Chad. Not only was it difficult to assess the constantly fluctuating numbers of people in need, but also the effect of a massive influx of refugees into areas inhabited by almost destitute local populations was often disastrous, with increased pressure on already scarce resources.

A major finding of the evaluation was the need for a significant improvement in the assessment of emergency food aid needs as a basic requirement for improving emergency operations. Ample evidence of the impending crisis had been given to donor countries through the FAO's early warning system and the WFP's Operational Task Force on Africa, but they were slow to react as a result of scepticism concerning its validity, political considerations, and donor administrative and budgetary constraints. The system did not, however, provide enough operational data regarding detailed estimates of emergency food aid needs resulting directly from the drought. The evaluation showed the importance of a continuous assessment of emergency food aid needs at the country level and that short-term missions of brief duration were not an effective substitution.

Delays in requests for emergency assistance by governments in African countries also had a negative effect on the response to the food crisis. WFP field staff played an active role in only 28 per cent of the preparation of requests for WFP emergency assistance. They were uncertain as to how far they should go in assisting governments, as their mandate was to provide assistance 'as and when required'. Owing to staff constraints, the WFP's Emergency Service only occasionally participated in multi-donor missions. The evaluation concluded that more visits to African countries at the preparatory stage of government requests would have been 'extremely useful'. For the 25 countries evaluated, more than one-third of food provided arrived when the peak period of urgency was over.

The evaluation also showed that, in a situation of 'massive need', the limitations of the IEFR became 'very apparent'. The IEFR as an international standby arrangement to allow the WFP to respond quickly and effectively to emergencies, wherever they occurred, was not achieved. In particular, the inadequacy of the pledging procedure for the IEFR was revealed, which did not give the WFP sufficient timely information about the likely size of IEFR resources during the following year. Changes were introduced when the modalities of the IEFR were approved by the WFP's governing body in 1976, and revised and enlarged in 1978. Participating countries were required to indicate their contributions to the reserve, over and above their regular pledges to the WFP, from their primarily grains stocks 'at the beginning of each calendar year or other appropriate 12-month period' (WFP, 1978a). But shortcomings in the operation of the IEFR remained.

Major problems were encountered in the procurement and delivery of emergency food aid commodities. Transportation from the port of loading in a donor country to the delivery point in a recipient country was the only phase in the delivery process completely under WFP control. In spite of the high number of landlocked countries involved, 41 per cent of the main cereal commodity arrived within one month of being loaded, and a further 37 per cent in two months, testimony to the efficiency and expertise of the WFP's Transport Division. However, delays in donor countries resulted in less than 30 per cent of commodities arriving with three months of shipping instructions being issued, and 50 per cent between three and seven months.

Emergency operations were started with food commodities borrowed from government security stocks, WFP development projects, food aid stocks from other sources, and marketing boards in 17 of the 25 countries studied. But there were limitations. Borrowing food commodities other than cereals proved to be an 'almost impossible task'. And borrowing from neighbouring countries, as opposed to direct delivery from donor countries, proved to be only marginally quicker owing to political and legal implications. Where needs were most urgent and borrowing arrangements not possible, the WFP resorted to the diversion of shipments destined for other countries to expedite deliveries. The purchase of food produced locally was also limited; primarily because of limited availability, but also because of difficulties over prices, quality, and procurement rules. Transfer of funds for urgent logistics operations, including the purchase of spare parts or equipment, took a minimum of seven to 10 days.

The WFP was aware of the difficulties of food aid deliveries and had taken steps to overcome them. Two pre-positioning facilities had been set up at Rotterdam and Singapore, each with a capacity of 2,000 tons, primarily to store wheat flour and rice; these were called upon to meet emergency requests in West Africa and Asia and East Africa, respectively. Greater recourse to chartering vessels also gave additional flexibility by allowing diversion of vessels to Sudan, Ethiopia and the West African port of Douala for Chad. Bulk handling was introduced in several African ports, as well as block-train transport on the Chad transit route. There was a substantial increase in the international community's response to coping with major logistics and related problems early in 1985. Funds were provided, and equipment and logistics personnel loaned for specific tasks. Of particular value was the grant of $5 million from the World Bank to the WFP in 1984–85 for emergency operations. The grant was especially valuable in that it was untied, which indicated the importance of the WFP having access to untied cash resources to meet urgent logistics problems in major emergency operations as soon as they arose.

Recipient governments had major responsibility for arranging for the receipt of food aid commodities and their distribution to beneficiaries, and for monitoring and reporting on the implementation of emergency operations. The evaluation revealed that only in eight of the 25 country studies were the arrangements made satisfactory. Central management and administrative units were usually beset by budget problems and the lack of well-defined lines of responsibility, which caused bottlenecks in arranging for in-country food aid delivery and distribution. It also showed the greater need for continuous assessment and operational flexibility by donors and recipient governments to ensure constant adaptation of the relief programme to the changing requirements of the situation. Improvements in internal distribution, particularly in some of the most seriously affected countries, did not match the improvements made in external delivery arrangements. Lack of internal logistics capacity appeared to be the most important handicap. Not only did food sometimes fail to reach the beneficiaries, but also internal logistics problems caused donors either to delay shipments as consignments pilled up at ports or to delays in deliveries on pledges already made. This underlined the importance of adequate financial support by donors to meet ITSH costs.

WFP emergency assistance, as with that from other sources, was not specifically targeted for camps where destitute people had gathered but, rather, was intended for reportedly affected people in designated locations. Recipient governments did not always assign first priority to camp populations, with consequent interruptions in food supplies. As camps were seen as temporary shelters, relatively little was done to ensure an assured and stable supply of food and other basic needs. As they were expected to be only temporary structures, insufficient attention was given to their protracted requirements when they remained occupied for a long period. In addition, the WFP's food basket was very limited and did not normally cater for supplementary or special feeding. Other basic and complementary needs, such as an adequate and safe water supply and preventive or curative medicines to avoid the outbreak of large-scale epidemics, often received insufficient support. Lack of trained personnel and material resources, together with ineffective co-ordination among the many aid agencies present, also hampered emergency operations, and making recovery and rehabilitation programmes difficult.

The evaluation also revealed serious shortcomings in the WFP secretariat. An institutional structure and environment had been built up focused more on supporting development projects than responding rapidly and effectively to emergencies, with strong central control and little delegation of responsibilities to staff located in recipient countries. The administration of emergency food aid resources by WFP headquarters and country officers was found to be generally satisfactory. But the dispersal of responsibilities among the various administrative units at headquarters dealing with emergencies had led to some confusion, resulting in the establishment of the WFP Task Force for Africa in 1985. The staffing levels of WFP country offices were determined by the volume of development project assistance provided and not by emergency operational requirements, which were not envisaged as a permanent feature in the work programme. In only four of the 25 countries studied were additional staff assigned to take care of emergency operations. In the absence of delegation, WFP country officers felt that they had little authority to act independently in responding to emergency situations. These shortcomings pointed to the need to revise the WFP's management and administration structure, and to train WFP officers in emergency as well as development operations to ensure maximum flexibility between them and to enable them to cope with situations that may suddenly arise.

Much of the emergency food aid provided had a negative effect on efforts for post-emergency rehabilitation and reconstruction by virtue of its quantity, regularity and the lack of discrimination between those most seriously affected and those less in need. Free distribution of emergency food handouts organized on a regular basis over a number of years in the same area led to the creation of dependence, and raised the expectation that the international community would always provide assistance in times of 'crisis'. Guidelines were required to ensure that distribution of free food should not be made indiscriminately to everyone in a disaster situation but only to those in real need. It was unnecessary, even harmful, to prolong free food distribution after a disaster except to vulnerable groups of mothers and children and those unable to work. Distinction should also be made between structural food deficits and food shortages caused by disasters. Emergency food aid should be used, to the extent possible, in support of reconstruction and rehabilitation activities designed to prevent, prepare for, or mitigate, future emergencies. WFP-assisted development projects should be designed in such a way that they could be expanded rapidly to include the victims of disasters, which would reduce the need for free distribution of emergency food aid.

In the final analysis, the food crisis of the 1980s demonstrated that the multiple and longer-term developmental problems of Africa should be addressed. The crisis could not be attributed solely to drought. Africa had the potential to feed itself. Its vast land and water assets could be harnessed to expand food and agricultural production. But governments and donor countries and international aid agencies, including the World Bank, did not invest enough in African agricultural development, increasing the need for food aid to expand food supplies to poor, hungry and malnourished people, whose numbers were expected to increase (Shaw, 2009: 115–19). Projections indicated that, even with increased agricultural production, food imports would increase significantly. With few exceptions, African countries would not have the necessary foreign exchange for commercial imports. Food aid could help fill the import gap and help build African capacities by investing in people and strengthening infrastructure and the institutional framework required to provide an enabling framework for sustained development (Shaw, 2000).

The findings of a USAID evaluation of the US response to the African food crisis were similar to those of the WFP evaluation (Wood *et al.*, 1986). According to that evaluation, several key lessons had been learned. The widespread droughts and emergency food crises that affected large parts of Africa in the 1970s and 1980s were not extraordinary episodes separate from the development process that had been taking place in the region. The problems and setbacks caused by drought among the rural population should be seen as a syndrome of inadequate policies aimed at solving Africa's long-term food and agricultural problems and inadequate income growth, and not just as drought-induced manifestations of hunger, malnutrition and ill-health, which was the common perception. Development programmes and projects must consider the problems of drought-prone areas and pre-plan for food emergencies, particularly those that may affect isolated, difficult-to-reach rural areas. And African nations can, with early information, anticipate the need for emergency food assistance programmes and pre-plan accordingly, taking into account the development context in which such programmes occur.

The evaluation listed four key objectives for the future: help ensure that food emergency setbacks are anticipated and responded to effectively before they assumed crisis proportions; achieve equitable sharing of responsibility for dealing with food emergencies between host governments and the international community; realize the desired impact of emergency food assistance efforts – saving lives, reducing suffering and fostering additional longer-term development; attain cost-effective results from emergency food assistance efforts; and assess, document and report the results of emergency food assistance programmes.

Despite the shortcomings described in the two evaluations, the WFP and its partners in recipient and donor countries made a significant contribution towards the survival of millions of people who were at risk of starvation, although many had died and many more had suffered severely. The WFP evaluation made 41 proposals for addressing the deficiencies identified in the response to the African food crisis. When presenting the results of the evaluation to the WFP's governing body in October 1986, at the session when his period of office was extended for a further five years, executive director Ingram noted that the lessons of the past gave the WFP an opportunity to take steps to improve its management of emergency operations. He considered that a major review of the WFP's organization and management was needed, aimed at ensuring a better interface between its development and emergency work. He expected that a new structure would lead to a more timely response to emergencies and would facilitate the transition from emergency to development, which was essential for the prevention of many future emergency situations.

Comprehensive review of the WFP management: shifting the centre of gravity to the field

In 1986, executive director Ingram commissioned a comprehensive external review of the management of the WFP by the international consultants McKinsey & Co. He recalled that, at the time, WFP was the only organization in the UN system to take what was seen as a 'bold, even revolutionary, step of inviting in external reviewers and, moreover, to share their full report with the governing body' (Ingram, 2007: 194). The crux of the report was to 'shift the centre of gravity of WFP to the field' and to give greater emphasis to providing direction and support for field operations (WFP, 1986b).

The WFP's governing body commended the WFP secretariat for undertaking the extensive evaluation and particularly for the critical nature of the report, which highlighted the operational weaknesses of the WFP, donors, and recipients. There was broad agreement on the conclusions and recommendations contained in the evaluation report; whereupon, the executive director appointed Bronek Szynalski – the leader of the evaluation team who had written most of the evaluation report – as the next director of the WFP's Emergency Service, with the mandate to 'implement them' for the WFP's future emergency operations.[10]

Emergencies caused by conflict: WFP/UNHCR co-operation

Perhaps more than any other single factor, the escalation of disasters caused by conflict in the 1980s, and the concomitant new working arrangements between the WFP and the UNHCR greatly increased the WFP's involvement in emergency operations. The scale, complexity and duration of these disasters increased considerably. In 1970, there were 2.5 million refugees throughout the world. In 1980, that number had increased to 11 million. And there were countless more people displaced from their homes in their own countries. In 1985, almost three-quarters of the WFP's emergency assistance went to refugees.

Ingram sought to strengthen WFP emergency operations involving refugees and displaced persons by marrying the WFP's comparative advantage in handling emergency food aid with that of UNHCR, which had been set up in 1951 with the specific mandate to protect, and promote durable solutions for, refugees. No single UN or international body has been given the mandate to look after the interests of persons displaced within their own country (see pp. 723–7). The close collaboration between the two organizations was further strengthened in early 1985, when an agreement was reached on joint assessment of refugee food aid needs and the advance mobilization and programming of the required food. It was agreed that, around the middle of each calendar year, the WFP and UNHCR would jointly assess food required for all refugee operations so as to allow an adequate lead time to ensure a systematic flow of food aid for the coming year. These assessments would be followed by semi-annual joint reviews of any changes in the refugee situation due to fresh influxes or departures, as well as pledges and deliveries against requirements. For large-scale refugee emergency operations, joint headquarters missions would be fielded. These joint missions broadened the understanding of the problems related to refugees, and were expected to result in improved planning and implementation of refugee operations.

Protracted relief operations

Not only had the proportion of WFP assistance going to conflict-induced emergencies increased dramatically, but their protracted nature (defined as those lasting more than one year) had also increased. As a result, an ever-increasing share of WFP emergency aid was being allocated to these protracted emergencies, leaving less for meeting other types of emergencies. To address the problem, executive director Ingram organized a review of WFP-assisted protracted refugee and displaced person operations (PROs) in 1989 (WFP, 1989). It was found that PROs had special characteristics, which set them apart from other emergencies. Solutions to three particular problems had to be found: how to provide an assured and continuous supply of food that was not only adequate for good health, but was also sufficiently varied to avoid monotony and flexible enough to meet changing needs; how to co-ordinate food supplies with the provision of other essential non-food basic needs; and how to cater for the developmental as well as the survival needs of the victims caught up in protracted emergency situation in terms of the nutrition, health, education and training, and, where possible, how to provide employment and income-earning opportunities.

To meet these problems, the WFP's governing body agreed with Ingram's astute proposal that PROs should no longer be funded from the WFP's emergency assistance but, rather, from a special sub-set of its development resources. Donors were invited to make special contributions over and above their normal pledges to the WFP, supplemented by up to $30 million a year from the WFP's regular resources by amounts to be determined by the governing body. Previously, the FAO director-general's approval had to be obtained for each tranche of assistance (usually six months) to protracted relief operations. Now, except for operations costing less that $1.5 million, authority for which was delegated to the WFP executive director, it was the WFP's governing body which made decisions on PRO operations. It was hoped that this would encourage donors to put more resources through the WFP. The provision of an extra cash supplement enabled nutritionally better and more appropriate food rations, and smoother delivery to beneficiaries in PROs.

These measures undoubtedly strengthened the WFP's ability to cope with PROs. But they carried far-reaching implications for the WFP, which was now committed to respond to refugees' needs and PROs on a priority basis. If the WFP's development resources did not expand proportionately, an increasing share of those resources would go to PROs. Paradoxically, the WFP's assistance to other types of emergencies might also suffer from a declining development project portfolio. Not only would this limit the amount of borrowing of food commodities supplied to WFP-assisted development projects, but there could also be a reduction in WFP support for disaster prevention, preparedness, and mitigation activities.

Horn of Africa: personal recognition

In major complex emergencies, many UN agencies and NGOs are involved, resulting in the difficult issue of co-ordination. In the 1970s and 1980s, special arrangements were often necessary for each large-scale emergency, which usually took the form of the UN secretary-general inviting the executive head of the appropriate UN agency to act as his personal representative. In 1984, Ingram joined forces with the UNICEF executive director, James Grant, to persuade the UN secretary-general to bypass the usual bureaucratic processes and establish a special office in Ethiopia for emergency operations that would oversee and co-ordinate the work of many organizations concerned with famine relief in that country (Jansson *et al.*, 1987). The success of that operation led to the establishment in New York of the Office for Emergency Operations in Africa (OEOA) to co-ordinate the UN system response to the whole of the Africa emergency. OEOA was headed by Bradford Morse, the UNDP administrator.

Executive director Ingram gave his unreserved support to OEOA, seconded a WFP officer experienced in emergencies, and personally promoted OEOA's leadership effort (Ingram, 2007: 196).

Almost continuously for over a decade beginning in the late 1970s, the WFP was involved in humanitarian relief operations in countries in the Horn of Africa (Djibouti, Eritrea, Ethiopia, Kenya, Somalia and Sudan), where widespread famine and starvation were caused by a lethal combination of drought, civil war, and the breakdown of orderly government. Executive director Ingram's personal determination to strengthen and improve the WFP's emergency operations were at last recognized by the UN secretary-general, who requested him to conduct humanitarian negotiations in the region on behalf of the UN (Ingram, 2007: 298–301). He successfully conducted negotiations with the Ethiopian government and the Eritrean People's Liberation Front (EPLF), then engaged in civil war, to re-open the EPLF-controlled port of Massawa to enable the WFP to deliver food to Asmara, which was besieged by EPLF forces.

Following the collapse of the Marxist government in Ethiopia, the UN secretary-general requested Ingram to lead a mission comprising representatives from the UN operational agencies (UNICEF, UNHCR, UNDP and WFP) to assess the UN system's development/humanitarian response to the new political situation not only in Ethiopia, but also in Djibouti, Kenya and Sudan. The principal concern was to assess the impact of refugee flows. The WFP had been involved in two imaginative and spectacular operations – Operation Rainbow in 1986, and Operation Lifeline Sudan in 1989, providing humanitarian assistance to the large numbers of people in the southern Sudan caught up in the civil war between the Sudanese government and the Sudan People's Liberation Army. Executive director Ingram addressed a UN High-Level Meeting on Emergency Relief Operations in Khartoum in March 1989, which created Operation Lifeline Sudan, and made several visits to Sudan to help resolve the many problems that arose in WFP operations.[11] This involvement vindicated his conviction that 'these co-called humanitarian interventions in conflict situations were only feasible when political conditions are ripe' (Ingram, 2007: 301).

Ingram's legacy

At the end of his ten-year period as WFP executive director, Ingram was fully aware that the transformation he sought for the organization into a major humanitarian agency was not complete. A measure of his legacy might be seen in comparing the WFP's annual commitments to development projects and emergency and protracted relief operations in 1981, the year before he assumed office, and in 1991, his last year before leaving (see Table 2.1).

During his ten-year period of office, in the face of consistent opposition from the FAO's director-general, professional staff increased by only 50 per cent, while assistance provided by the WFP increased many fold. When he took over the leadership of the WFP in 1982, 'WFP was in a rut. What it did, it did well enough but it had ceased to innovate and, constrained as it was by FAO's oversight, lacked the will to do so' (Ingram, 2007: 309). By his example, this environment was to change. A large part of his success was due to the unification of WFP field and headquarters staff, which he initiated and his successor, Catherine Bertini, completed (see pp. 164–74).

Through his initiatives, each a tipping point in a ten-year deliberate strategy, Ingram laid the foundation for his successors to complete the transformation process. His period of office saw: the establishment of an emergency service; the evaluation of the WFP's response to the African food crisis of the 1980 and the implementation of its numerous recommendations; the comprehensive external review of the WFP's management, which led to a shift of gravity to the field and greater emphasis on providing direction and support for field operations; the close alliance with the UNHCR in strengthening emergency operations for

Table 2.1 WFP commitments by type of activity: 1981 and 1991 ($ millions)[1]

Activity	1981	1991
Development projects	543	448
Emergency operations	178	391
PROs[2]	–	558
Total	721	1,397

Notes: [1]Figures rounded; [2]WFP commitments to this category of operation began in 1989.

Source: WFP.

the benefit of refugees and displaced persons; reform of the IEFR; the creation of a new category of assistance for protracted emergencies from the WFP's development, not emergency, resources; and the wider recognition of the WFP's role as a co-ordinator of international emergency operations through his role as the personal representative of the UN secretary-general.

Significantly, the new *General Regulations* for the WFP that came into operation at the beginning of 1992 (see Chapter 1) took emergency food aid out of the shadow cast by the FAO director-general and gave responsibility to the WFP executive director up to a level of authority delegated to him by the WFP governing body. In cases exceeding that level, approval is accorded jointly by the FAO director-general and the WFP executive director. Governments requiring emergency food aid now submit requests to the WFP executive director. Upon approval of a request from emergency or protracted relief food aid, an agreement is concluded between the WFP executive director and the government of the recipient country.

The new General Regulations also contained a provision of historic importance:

> WFP may also provide emergency food aid and associated non-food items and logistics support assistance at the request of the [UN] Secretary-General. WFP assistance in such exceptional cases shall be fully coordinated with the United Nations system and efforts of governments, intergovernmental and non-governmental organizations in the areas concerned. (WFP, 1991b)[12]

Ingram regarded this addition as a 'most important innovation' (Ingram, 2007: 295). Previously, the WFP was only able to respond to requests for assistance submitted by governments. That requirement made it often difficult to intervene at the most appropriate time in support of all the victims of man-made emergencies. The basic idea behind this additional provision was to find a way around this restriction, which became increasingly inappropriate after the end of the Cold War when national sovereignty was no longer seen as sufficient reason to deny humanitarian assistance to the victims of internal conflict.

Ingram hoped that the new provision would provide the basis for a new dialogue between the WFP and the UN secretary-general that would help to bring about 'more consistent and disciplined humanitarian interventions' (Ingram, 2007: 295). In his opinion, many WFP humanitarian interventions served the political interests of particular states, rather than the community of UN member states. In such cases, he reasoned that interventions, including the imposition of sanctions, should be undertaken by UN agencies only with the direct sanction of the UN Security Council (Ingram, 1994).

He also observed that, for WFP interventions that furthered the political and strategic interests of the Western powers, it was relatively easy to raise resources from donors, compared to those that had no significant political interest for them. As he saw it, there was a fundamental dysfunction in the UN between its role as a political organization and the attempts of its humanitarian agencies, such as the WFP, UNICEF and UNHCR, to act as if they were politically neutral organizations in the same way as the ICRC (Ingram, 1993).

Nevertheless, he noted that WFP interventions saved many lives and relieved much human suffering. That was why he had no hesitation in doing all he could to improve the quality of the WFP's emergency operations, and to strengthen the WFP's relations with the UNHCR, UNICEF, ICRC and others. He also contrasted WFP interventions following man-made emergencies with those following natural disasters, where its role was unambiguous and indispensable. The new provision also reflected another strong conviction that Ingram formed from his involvement in complex emergencies and the need for coordinated action among the many agencies involved. By involving the UN secretary-general from the beginning, a more coherent international response could be set in place.

A special ceremony was held in Ingram's honour at the end of his final governing body session in December 1991 (WFP, 1991). Tributes were paid by 26 delegates, some on behalf of country regional groups. While a few remarks were *pro forma*, most reflected a genuine feeling of respect and gratitude that the executive director had brought the WFP through very stormy seas to a safe haven. On so doing, he had helped to restore the confidence and self-respect of both the governing body and its secretariat to face future challenges.

In his foreword to Ingram's book *Bread and Stones*, Gareth Evans, the former Australian foreign minister, president and chief executive officer of the International Crisis Group, and author of *The Responsibility to Protect. Ending Mass Atrocity Crimes Once and For All* (2008), wrote:

> The World Food Programme (WFP) is now not only the world's biggest humanitarian agency, but one of its most respected and effective. That it became so is very much the legacy of Jim Ingram ... It is also testament to another factor all too rare in public life. Ingram's willingness to take his personal interests out of the equation, and announce that he would seek no further public office when his reform task was done. Would that many more followed that lead ... Jim Ingram's book is both a handbook and an inspiration.

Motivation

Ingram gave an insight into what motivated him when he was invited to give the Joyce Pearce Memorial Lecture at the University of Oxford, UK in 1988 in recognition of his efforts to place WFP emergency food aid, particularly to refugees and displaced persons, on a more professional basis (Ingram, 1989).[13] Ingram began his lecture by paying tribute to Joyce Pearce's qualities and to the Refugee Studies Programme (RSP) for the research work it had carried out that had brought new and refreshing insights into how to respond to refugees' problems and needs. He considered that more should be known about the social, economic, and political and power structures of refugee populations, and felt that the research carried out by social scientists was of considerable value to all, including the WFP.

He observed that:

> without empathy, without a full recognition that refugees have the same concerns and aspirations as other human beings, without an understanding

> of their needs as they see them, the results of our interventions are likely to continue to be disappointing. (Ingram, 1989: 329)

The WFP was feeding some 8.5 million refugees and displaced persons in 1988, an increase of 2.3 million as compared to two years previously. The WFP's support for these groups of people had increased many fold over the decade from 1977 from 42,000 tons, valued at $16 million, to 577,000 tons, valued at $186 million in 1987, and the upsurge in numbers showed no sign of abating. The WFP's responsibility was to mobilize most of the food required by these vulnerable groups and to ensure that it was delivered to them on time. The WFP's partnership with the UNHCR had grown apace in recent years. The UNHCR saw the value in using the WFP as the primary vehicle for the provision of food aid. Since the WFP was an agency specialized in food logistics, this division of labour made the most cost-effective use of the limited management resources and money available to both organizations.

Ingram regarded better feeding programmes for these groups as an issue of 'enormous importance'. He had repeatedly urged governments to making the feeding of long-term refugees and displaced persons 'a first charge on their humanitarian food aid programmes'. In his view, there were no people of the Third World more deserving of help. They were 'not social misfits but truly victims of man's inhumanity'. The time had come for governments to consider an improved approach that would avoid the constraints he described. These included: the considerable difficulties of getting food regularly to refugees and displaced persons in remote and dangerous situations, 'at some risk to life and limb'; the constraints on the effective operation of the IEFR; the problem of providing appropriate food rations; severe restrictions on the sale of food aid commodities; the difficulty of assessing the numbers in need; the provision of food aid as an entitlement both for refugees and displaced persons, and the host populations who were often not better off; and the role of political factors in camp populations.

Ingram ended on a highly contentious point, which remains with the WFP to this day. In his view, the WFP was a humanitarian organization not a human rights organization, whose mandate was, *inter alia*, to provide, at the request of member states of the UN, succour to refugees and other disaster victims. He realized that such assistance could sometimes have political effects. But the WFP's 'only viable touchstone' was:

> will our interventions help suffering people?' If the answer was affirmative, WFP should proceed irrespective of the rights and wrongs of the situations that created suffering in the first place and irrespective of whether WFP interventions may make it easier for a state to pursue more vigorously the situation which had given rise to enforced migration.

Responding to questions at the end of his lecture, Ingram reiterated his view that the WFP was 'a humanitarian organization giving primacy to the right to life'.

On his way home to Australia at the end of his ten years as the WFP's executive director, Ingram stopped briefly at the Watson Institute of International Affairs at Brown University in the United States as a 'Distinguished Visitor', where he wrote his views on an improved arrangement for international humanitarian assistance. He suggested that 'human suffering arising from internal conflicts is in most situations likely to be dealt with best by an internationalized ICRC [International Committee of the Red Cross]' (Ingram, 1993: 190). One critic found the suggestion to be unworkable for three main reasons: the implausibility of altering the ICRC's Swiss character; the unwillingness of the ICRC to budge from its principle of consent, which would be a handicap in enforcement operations; and its ferocious need to maintain autonomy would not be conducive to being the servant of governments (Weiss, 1998: n. 32). Ingram also realized that his suggestion could not work, but offered it in order to define what he considered would be an ideal arrangement in comparison with the existing dysfunctional situation.[14]

He gave further views on a future architecture for international humanitarian assistance at a conference organized by the UN Institute for Training and Research (UNITAR) and others in Singapore in February 1997 (Ingram, 1997). He explained that during his period as the WFP executive director four elements critical to his thinking had emerged, which he considered were of continuing validity. The first element was that minimizing loss of life and life-threatening suffering, the accepted goal of humanitarian intervention, required that humanitarian agencies act even-handedly on gaining access to all affected civilians. The second element was that, while he was able to satisfy his conscience that one-sided humanitarian interventions were 'much better' than doing nothing at all, he remained concerned that in most instances they also 'overwhelmingly' served the political interests of donors, which in practice meant the United States and its allies. The third element was that, as a manager concerned with maximizing the humanitarian benefit of the financial and human resources available to UN agencies in complex emergencies, he was convinced that the UN was unable to overcome the 'incoherence and inefficiency' which beset the work of the many autonomous and semi-autonomous agencies claiming a role in such emergencies. To solve the problem, he considered that the 'most essential step' was to create a single humanitarian relief agency to take over the operational relief activities of the whole UN system. The final element was that the biggest impediment to institutional reform, both within the UN system and in the total international humanitarian response, was that governmental thinking was constrained by the existing institutional structure.

To Ingram the goal was clear: to maximize the impact of humanitarian assistance by accessing on an equal basis and to the greatest extent feasible all civilian victims of internal armed conflict. To achieve that goal, he considered that two things were required: the strengthening of the capability of the humanitarian arm of the UN to act as independently as possible of its political wing, with the realization that the UN is, first and foremost, a political agency; and the improvement of the effectiveness and efficiency of the UN's humanitarian operations and its capacity to provide leadership to the other operational actors. For this, the operational humanitarian activities of all existing agencies should be brought together and incorporated within the UN Department of Humanitarian Affairs (DHA), with its head made a deputy secretary-general and the appointment be confirmed by the UN General Assembly. The UN's capability to use diplomacy to prevent or mitigate the effects of conflict should also be strengthened, and humanitarian relief should not be used as a tool of peace-making unless sanctioned by the UN Security Council.

At the end of his ten-year term of office, Ingram received the Alan Shawn Feinstein World Hunger Award for his leadership of the WFP in 1991 and was the first recipient, with George McGovern, of the WFP's Food for Life Award in 2000. Governments pressed UN secretary-general, Boutros Boutros-Gali, to appoint Ingram to the position of UN undersecretary-general for humanitarian affairs. There was also strong pressure from within the UN secretariat, so much so that Ingram wrote to the UN secretary-general to advise him that he did not wish to be considered for the post.[15] With so many players involved both inside and outside the UN system, Ingram expressed scepticism that the new co-ordination arrangements would work.

When the incumbent, Jan Eliasson, left the post as head of the DHA, the Australian government was again approached to nominate Ingram to take up the role of UN humanitarian affairs co-ordinator, which it was willing to do, but Ingram again declined. On retirement, Ingram was pressed to join the Refugee Studies Programme at the University of Oxford, UK and a similar organization at the University of Toronto in Canada. But after the long time spent abroad, he preferred to return to his native Australia. Since returning home, he has been, *inter alia,* director of the Australian Institute for International Affairs; has continued to write on improved arrangements for the provision of international humanitarian assistance (Ingram, 1993a, 1993b, 1994, 1997); and, most recently, was chairman of the Crawford Fund Task Force report *A Food Secure World: How Australia Can Help* (2008), which includes chapters on reform of the international food aid response and improvement of the international post-emergency response.

Chapter 3 will show the full effects of Ingram's legacy and how, through the determination and leadership of his successor, Catherine Bertini, the WFP finally emerged as the world's largest humanitarian agency.

3
Emergency Assistance: Transformation Accomplished

The WFP's transformation to become the world's largest humanitarian agency was not completed with the departure of executive director James Ingram. This was brought about by his successor, Catherine Bertini, a US citizen and the first women to head the WFP. She had been assistant secretary of Agriculture of Food and Consumer Services in the United States Department of Agriculture, which involved the management of all US federal domestic food assistance programmes, and had displayed a special interest in child nutrition and the advancement of women. During her ten years in office (1992–2002), she led a re-examination of almost every aspect of the WFP's work and brought about major changes in WFP management and organization, which hastened its transformation (see Chapter 4) (WFP, 2002a).

At her final session of the WFP's executive board on 14 February 2002, the board paid tribute to her and expressed its 'profound admiration for her leadership, vision and remarkable dedication as Executive Director of the organization whose progress and evolution she had spearheaded over the last decade'. The board also noted her 'dedication to improve the situation of women and children around the world and the human touch she brought to her dealings with beneficiaries, in particular the way she met individuals and made them feel special. Her outstanding commitment to those in need had shaped WFP into the organization it is today' (WFP, 2002i).

Escalation in emergencies

Early in the 1990s, the number, scale, duration and complexity of conflict-made emergencies increased as states collapsed, civil war proliferated, and genocide and ethnic cleansing raged (Shawcross, 2000). Each emergency was a saga of man's inhumanity to man; the fortitude of the civilian population, particularly of women, in the face of appalling suffering; and the dedication and suffering of relief workers, national and international, a number of whom lost their lives or were seriously injured. Not only were poor developing countries affected, particularly in sub-Saharan Africa, but new countries and regions were to suffer following the political collapse of the Soviet Union and the Federal

Republic of Yugoslavia. More UN peacekeeping operations were launched in the early years of the 1990s than in the previous forty years (Annan, 1999a). Refugees and displaced persons reached unprecedented numbers, leading to an escalation in the need for emergency and protracted relief food aid (UNHCR, 1997). And more food aid was required when these afflicted people eventually returned home to begin the process of rehabilitation, reconstruction, and renewed development.

A new, large and additional dimension was added to WFP emergency operations in 1992 following the break-up of the Soviet Union and the Federal Republic of Yugoslavia, and the formation of new states. Civil war in the former Yugoslavia and the process of 'ethnic cleansing' in the newly formed republic of Bosnia-Herzegovina, and later Kosovo, were vividly shown on television across the world. Given its experience and expertise in handling emergencies throughout the developing world, the WFP was called upon to assist with the food aid aspects of large and complex international relief operations. The WFP accepted that role on the understanding that it would be financed entirely from contributions additional to its multilateral resources, so that its assistance to developing countries would not be impaired. Much less in the news, but just as devastating, was the human tragedy that unfolded in the newly created Commonwealth of Independent States (CIS) in the Caucasus and Central Asia region of the former Soviet Union, where the WFP helped in what amounted to the reconstruction of the entire food supply system. The WFP was also requested to assist and monitor food supplies in Iraq in the aftermath of the Gulf War, the imposition of economic sanctions, and the implementation of a UN Security Council resolution, which later allowed the sale of Iraqi oil to pay for food and other essential imports.

While no two conflict-made disasters were the same, the large and complex emergency operations required to address them shared common features. Their costs, particularly of transport and logistics, were often very high and were difficult to resource fully and constantly. The warring parties created serious obstacles to food delivery that threatened large-scale malnutrition, starvation, and death. They often took on a regional dimension as they straddled the frontiers of several countries, further complicating relief operations. Ingenuity and versatility often had to be deployed in finding solutions to transport and logistics problems in very difficult physical and political circumstances, in order to get food through to the civilian population in dire need caught up the fighting. Relief workers, national and international, were exposed to considerable risks and, tragically, to loss of life. Overall administration was difficult to control as often there was little government or other capacity to plan and implement these large-scale and complex programmes of assistance. Co-ordination among the many government and aid agencies involved was necessary but difficult to maintain not only to provide the food required, but also other essential basic needs including water, fuel, shelter, medicines, security and human rights. And the close interplay between peace-making, peacekeeping and humanitarian relief operations caused confusion, and sometimes resulted in food aid becoming part of the problem rather than the solution.

The powerful role of the media, especially television, in exposing national authorities and drawing the attention of the international community to the horrors of conflict-made disasters, leading to action and the positive response to public appeals for assistance, became increasingly evident. But there was a downside. The provision of emergency relief, particularly during and after man-made disasters, remains a highly emotive subject. In the glare of the world's media, the basic instinct was to dispatch food with the greatest possible speed to people in distress without a clear and precise understanding of what caused the problem, and whether food aid was the best response. In attempting to solve an immediate problem, other difficulties could be created later for the process of rehabilitation, reconstruction, and subsequent development. Early WFP experience showed the need for a clear policy framework based on an understanding of the causes of different types of emergencies, how they affected different people, and the best ways to provide external assistance. And the process of constructing such a policy framework could be assisted if more attention were given to evaluating the results of emergency operations and understanding the lessons learned.

Issues and concerns

Many issues and concerns emerged in the response to emergencies, as the examples at the end of this chapter show. Experience showed the need for strong leadership and co-ordinated action among the many organizations involved in providing emergency aid, both within and outside the UN system, and for establishing consolidated appeals for assistance both globally and regionally. Experience also showed that the effects of emergencies should be disaggregated both to better understand their full effects and to design and implement intervention programmes that addressed their causes and impact, especially on poor people. It was understood that the poor do not comprise a homogeneous group. There are significant differences between them and between the solutions to their problems. Distinction should also be made between the poor and very poor – those who have the least assets are more prone to mortality, illness, and low physical performance, often associated with chronic malnutrition and related diseases – who may not be able to respond quickly to assistance and to improved conditions (Wilmshurst *et al.*, 1992).

This highlighted the importance of emergency needs assessment and targeting as key concerns in the design and implementation of emergency feeding operations and strategic factors in facilitating access and outreach to the afflicted population. Four factors have had an especially important bearing on the effectiveness or otherwise of targeting: the criteria set; administrative feasibility and costs; participation by the afflicted people themselves; and the type, form, level and method of the resource transfer. In the absence of an improved assessment of need, donors mistrusted the number of people requiring assistance and the amount of assistance required. As a result, too much or too little aid was provided, leading to waste of scarce resources and corruption, or to unnecessary hardship and suffering, especially among the less-influential and most vulnerable, particularly women and children, who most needed help. Steps were taken to improve needs assessment and targeting through WFP/UNHCR co-operation, which included setting up a common method for establishing the numbers eligible to receive food assistance as part of their new working relationship.

Considerable controversy surrounded what should be an appropriate daily ration during emergencies. Evidence showed that, while generous, the international response to emergencies was inconsistent, sometimes based more on political considerations than on real need. The avoidance of high malnutrition rates and mortality in certain man-made emergencies, for example, contrasted starkly with the lack of success in others (Seaman and Rivers, 1988; Toole, 1993, Jaspars and Young, 1996). However, there were real practical constraints. The logistics involved in providing an adequate food ration consistently to the victims of disasters in remote areas in Africa and elsewhere were formidable and costly. But innovative and pioneering efforts were made – such as the use of triangular transactions, local purchase and food exchange arrangements, between and within countries – to expedite the provision of adequate and appropriate food rations.

The special problems of providing adequate rations to refugees and displaced persons, including micronutrients and variety in the food basket, were recognized. A special statement was issued by the UN Administrative Co-ordination Committee (ACC) (the highest administrative body in the UN system consisting of heads of the UN bodies under the chairmanship of the UN secretary-general), on the advice of the ACC Sub-committee on Nutrition (now called the UN Standing Committee on Nutrition), which recommended that 'the protection and promotion of the nutritional well-being of affected populations be fundamental goals of [UN] agency policy and programmes concerning refugees and displaced persons' (ACC/SCN, 1993). The WFP and UNHCR agreed that, when refugees had no other resources, food rations should meet all their nutritional requirements.[1] While access to adequate food is vital in emergencies, other basic needs are also essential, including safe drinking water, basic medicines, shelter, fuel, and human security, both for disaster victims and relief workers. Without these basic human needs, morbidity and mortality occur despite the availability of adequate food. A major problem was that different lead times are provided by many different aid agencies and NGOs. Co-ordinating and synchronizing their provision was often deficient, and ways were needed of ensuring their combined and simultaneous provision.

Emerging new concepts had also been taken into consideration. In the major famines of the past, starvation and death occurred not only (or so much) because food was not available but, rather, because poor people lost access ('entitlement') to it through loss of purchasing power (Sen, 1981). There was also distinction between chronic and transitory food insecurity, for which different policies and programmes were required (World Bank, 1986). A concept of 'human security' was developed which combined two major components: freedom from fear, and freedom from want (UNDP, 1994). Food security is regarded as a prerequisite to human security along with economic, health, environmental, personal, community, and political security.

The rise of the human rights movement in the 1980s led to a proposal to shift the focus from 'political will' – which had been the commitment at international conferences throughout the 1990s to solve many of the world's problems, including food insecurity – towards 'obligations' in addressing world hunger and poverty (Eide and Kracht, 2005, 2007). This would be in keeping with the right to adequate food as a basic human right of all people everywhere and the role of the UN, as stipulated in its *Charter*, 'to reaffirm faith in fundamental human rights, in the dignity and worth of the human person, in the equal rights of men and women and of nations large and small'. It is argued that people have a right to adequate food, and to be free from hunger, as a matter of international law. This right is articulated in the *Universal Declaration on Human Rights*, adopted by the UN General Assembly over 60 years ago (UN, 1948), the *International Convention on Economic, Social and Cultural Rights* (UN, 1966), and other international instruments. States that are parties to these agreements have made a commitment to ensure the realization of these rights. More recently, a case has been made to ensure responsibility to protect the victims of man-made emergencies (Evans, 2008).

What distinguishes a human rights approach to the elimination of hunger and poverty, and the realization of other basic socio-economic goals, is the focus on the dignity of human beings, as recognized in the UN *Charter*, their role as subjects and agents of change, and as rights-holders. The argument in favour of the human rights approach is that policy objectives come and go with changing governments, and the numerous declarations of intent to end world hunger and poverty are not legally binding. The imperative of human rights based on human dignity with consequent legal obligations would remain of constant value beyond the volatility of politics. Getting all countries to adopt this approach – particularly powerful nations such as the United States that have shown aversion in the past – and translating the content of legal commitments into operational strategies and action would still present formidable challenges. Several UN bodies have adopted a statement of common understanding regarding a rights-based approach to their co-operation and assistance programmes (UN, 2003). The FAO Council has adopted a set of voluntary guidelines to support the progressive realization of the right to adequate food in the context of national food security (FAO, 2005). It remains to be seen whether the human rights approach will prove to be more successful than the other commitments made over the past 60 years based on political will.

It also became painfully clear that there are significant differences between responding to emergencies caused by war and civil conflict, and those arising from natural disasters (Macrea and Zwi, 1994). Western reaction to the atrocities and tragedies of the 1990s unleashed a humanitarian impulse in what became known as 'humanitarian emergencies' in which ensuring better access to, and treatment of, victims came to preoccupy policy-makers, parliamentarians, and the general public (Vayrynen, 1996).[2] The role of UN agencies such as the WFP in emergency operations following natural disasters such as earthquakes, floods, hurricanes and drought are clear and generally appreciated. Conversely, the linkages between providing humanitarian aid and peace-making and peacekeeping operations remains dangerously confused. The role of the UN system in providing relief to those civilians caught up in the fighting in war zones may be accepted, but how far should the UN go to prevent, contain, or mitigate the fighting. Taking the example of Somalia, should the UN cross the 'Mogadishu line' between peacekeeping and peace-making, transcend national sovereignty, cut out the political process, and 'leave it to the military', even though there may be serious political differences among UN member countries, and a selective application of UN mandates and resolutions (WFP, 2000d)?

Humanitarian assistance has become closely linked with the dynamic of violence (Charlton, 1997). This is difficult territory for the UN system, which has conventionally respected the principle of state sovereignty in conformity with the *Charter of the United Nations* (UN, 1945). But the Charter also states that this principle 'shall not prejudice the application of enforcement measures under Charter VI concerning Action with Respect to Threats to the Peace, Breaches of the Peace and Actions of Aggression (UN, 1945, ch. 1, art. 2.7). And, more recently, two concepts of sovereignty were redefined by UN secretary-general, Kofi Annan (Annan, 1999b). First, states are now widely understood to be instruments at the service of their people, and not vice versa. Second, individual sovereignty has been enhanced by a renewed and spreading consciousness of individual rights. The aim of the UN *Charter* is therefore seen as to protect individual human beings, and not to protect those who abuse them. This has cast in stark relief the dilemma of so-called 'humanitarian interventions', and forced a re-examination of how the UN systems and others should respond to humanitarian crises. It was Ingram's conviction that humanitarian interventions in conflict situations were only feasible when political conditions were ripe (Ingram, 2007: 301).

There are, as yet, no clearly established rules, guidelines and modalities; neither are there any easy solutions. Much will depend on the nature of the conflict in each emergency operation. Humanitarian interventions following man-made disasters remain marked by *ad hoc* reactions and crisis management. Full identification of responsibilities and areas of collaboration on the ground have yet to be achieved. This may be understandable, given the nature and increasing number and complexities of man-mad emergencies in recent years. But progress should be quickened in implementing the many proposals that have been made. The general public remains moved by the compassionate case for saving civilians from horrific violence. But, as one writer has put it, 'tough questions must be asked':

> Even if war proceeds from humanitarian motives, does it actually have humanitarian consequences? It is not so simple. The guarantee of international protection may cause civilians at risk to let down their guard, and when tragedy ensues turns out to be an empty one (Srebrenica, Rwanda)...killers are much quicker than interveners. (Easterly, 2008: 54)

At the same time, an unprecedented increase in the number and scale of both natural and conflict-made disasters occurred. From the 1990s, natural disasters killed 58,000 people on average each year and affected another 225 million people. In 2005 alone, 92,000 people died in 150 natural disasters. These disasters struck rich and poor countries alike, but had a greater negative impact on developing countries because of their lack of financial and material resources to protect people and livelihoods. Half of the world's least developed countries faced high levels of disaster risk. Of these, six were hit by between two and eight large disasters every year (UNDP, 2001).

Africa and Asia bear a disproportionate burden of losses due to the impact of natural disasters. About 88 per cent of all people reported killed and 96 per cent of people reported as being affected by natural disasters live in these two regions (CRED, 2004). From the 1950s, the economic costs associated with natural disasters increased from $3.9 billion per year to $63 billion per year in the 1990s. In 2005 alone, losses were at about $220 billion. The World Bank estimated that losses caused by natural disasters in developing countries, as a percentage of their gross natural product, were 20 times higher than those in developed countries (World Bank, website).

The 1990s were therefore described as a 'decade of undeclared war on women, adolescents and children as poverty, conflict, chronic social instability and preventable diseases such as HIV/AIDS threatened their human rights and sabotaged their development' (UNICEF, 1999: 19). Among the many lessons of development during the second half of the twentieth century were that political integrity, leadership and economic stability are essential; economic growth does not usually trickle down; no single policy will trigger development everywhere; people and their institutions really matter; and 'what matters most is putting people ... at the heart of the development agenda for the 21st century' (World Bank, 2000: 1).

As a result, humanitarian assistance increased considerably. Between 1990 and 2006, humanitarian assistance provided by DAC/OECD countries, the major donors, more than doubled in constant terms. This took place in two escalating 'waves' – 1990–1994 and 2000–2005 – in response to the occurrence of large-scale and complex emergencies (Development Initiatives, 2009) (see Figure 3.1). Total DAC/OECD country humanitarian assistance averaged over $5 billion a year from the beginning of the 1990s, more than double the $2 billion average in the 1980s. This assistance has grown more rapidly as bilateral aid provided directly to governments in afflicted countries than as multilateral aid provided through UN agencies.

In addition, NGOs in DAC/OECD countries provided an estimated $4.2 billion in humanitarian assistance funded by voluntary contributions from the general public and from official donors (Development Initiatives, 2009). Africa and Asia have received the major share of DAC/OECD country humanitarian assistance. In 2006, they received 46 per cent and 34 per cent respectively, with the Middle East receiving 15 per cent. This assistance has been focused on a small number of countries in recent years. Sudan has received the most (18 per cent) followed by the Palestine Occupied Territories (10 per cent), with the Democratic Republic of the Congo, Pakistan, Indonesia, Lebanon and Ethiopia receiving 5 per cent each.

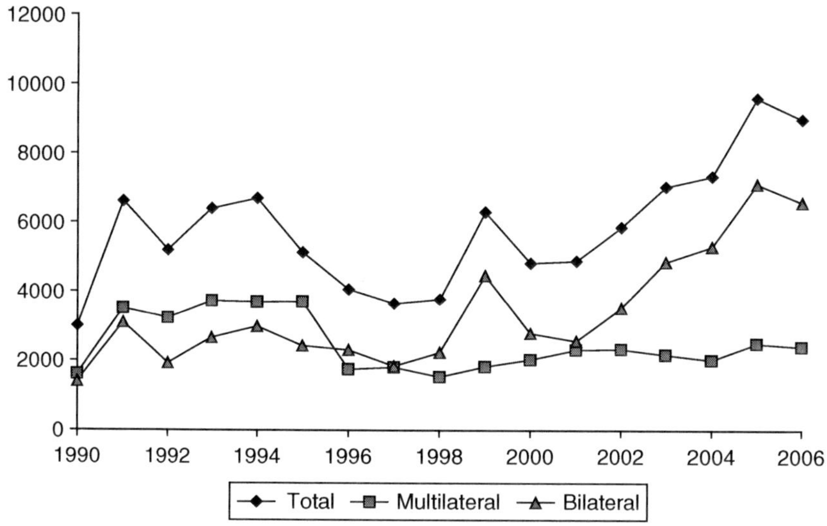

Figure 3.1 Official humanitarian assistance provided by DAC/OECD countries 1990–2006 ($ millions, constant 2005)

Source: Global Humanitarian Assistance (2007–08).

But these figures should be put into perspective. DAC/OECD country humanitarian assistance has remained a small part of their overall ODA, ranging between 6 and 10 per cent for each of the 16 years between 1990 and 2006. Although it reached almost $9 billion (in 2005 constant prices) in 2006, it still only accounted for 9 per cent of their ODA. Moreover, more than one-quarter of the highest priority humanitarian needs were unmet in 2006. Furthermore, this does not include the humanitarian assistance provided by non-DAC/OECD countries, and other NGOs, the private sector, and local responses, and remittances that are very significant for saving lives, but not yet fully reported.[3]

Transformation completed

Against this background, within the decade of executive director Catherine Bertini's leadership (1992–2002), the WFP's transformation from a development programme into a mainly emergency relief agency was completed (see Figure 2.1). What motivated her to build so strongly and quickly on the platform that James Ingram had left? (WFP, 2002a:11). At the time of Ingram's departure in 1992, some 60 per cent of WFP resources were being devoted to emergencies. Following his lead, donors were increasingly interested in supporting the WFP's emergency interventions, particularly in the form of protracted emergency operations (PROs). At the same time, humanitarian interventions were becoming increasingly more necessary, and larger in scale and complexity, as civil war, massive displacement of people, and cross-border operations

Table 3.1 Contributions to WFP resources by category, 1996–2008 ($ millions)

Year	Total	DP	IEFR	IRA	PRRO	SO	Others
1996	1,445	399	628	19	342	32	18
1997	1,311	347	547	17	319	16	64
1998	1,727	346	991	15	322	21	32
1999	1,555	275	792	24	382	49	35
2000	1,751	226	1,030	18	381	26	70
2001	1,904	270	1,036	12	510	55	20
2002	1,807	215	1,048	12	470	37	25
2003	2,600	240	1,389	19	824	46	50
2004	2,206	276	1,109	25	616	94	84
2005	2,766	269	756	19	1,381	262	79
2006	2,705	248	1,044	32	1,095	203	84
2007	2,705	277	878	27	1,324	162	87
2008	5,042	408	1,347	59	2,312	172	745

Key:

DP	Development Projects
IEFR	International Emergency Food Reserve
IRA	Immediate Response Account
PRRO	Protracted Relief and Recovery Operations
SO	Special Operations
Others	Contributions to Trust Funds, Special Accounts and the General Funds

Source: WFP Annual Reports.

required more food aid and more sophisticated co-ordination mechanisms. In addition, civil conflict and economic disruption arising from the post-Cold War break-up of states in the former Soviet Union and the Balkans increased demand for humanitarian food aid in a part of the world that had not previously received it (Table 3.1).

To make matters more difficult, the impact of the Uruguay Round of multilateral trade negotiations on agricultural commodity surpluses was uncertain (Shaw and Singer, 1995). It could no longer be assumed that the large food surpluses of the past would continue indefinitely. Global food aid flows had begun a long-term downward trend, creating insecurity regarding the amount of food aid that might be available to the WFP (see Figure 3.2). During this period, ODA and development resources were also declining worldwide, and some donors and critics started to question the validity of food aid as a development resource. All these factors put severe pressure on the food aid available for development projects that had been the core of WFP activities until the late 1980s. These changes also seemed to be threatening the traditional basis for WFP resourcing.

The response was to create a new type of programme for WFP assistance in 1998, called Protracted Relief and Recovery Operations (PRROs), in place of the PROs that executive director Ingram had created. It will be recalled that in the WFP's mission statement approved by its governing body in 1984, the WFP was described as being 'well placed' to play a major role in the continuum from emergency relief

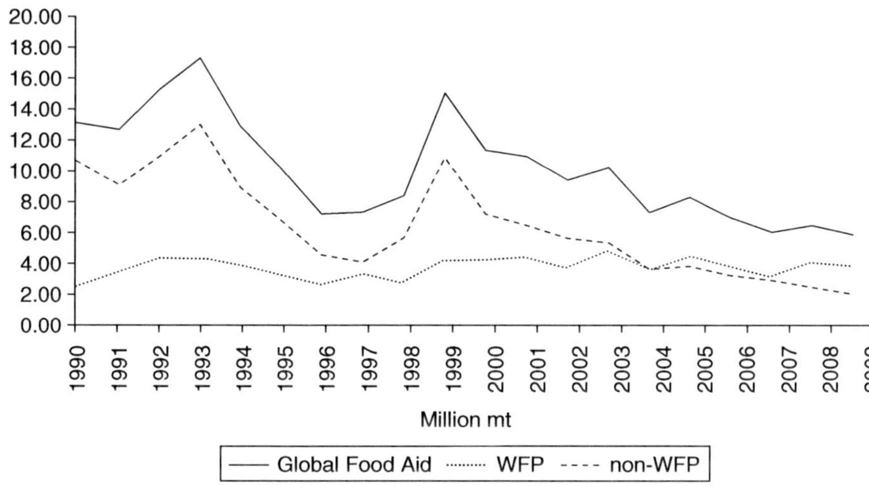

Figure 3.2 Food aid flows 1990–2009
Source: WFP, The Food Aid Flow 2009, Rome, Italy, 2010.

to development (WFP, 1994b). In 1998, executive director Bertini championed the WFP's dual role and strongly supported the developmental uses of WFP food aid to help people help themselves out of poverty (IFPRI, 1998) (see Chapter 1).

In 1998, a policy paper was presented to the WFP's executive board entitled 'From Crisis to Recovery', which gave the rationale for establishing PRROs. It was predicted that recovery from natural and conflict crises would continue to represent one of the major challenges confronting humanitarian and development agencies in the coming decade (WFP, 1998a). Since 1980, over 50 countries had faced protracted conflicts, many of which were still ongoing. About 35 million people were displaced from their homes in 30 low- and middle-income countries. Accompanying populations displaced and exposure to violence was the erosion of social structures and human capital, public and private infrastructure, and reduced productive capacity. The magnitude of the crises was apparent in the profile of WFP beneficiaries. In 1996, the WFP assisted 16 million displaced persons, 4.5 million refugees, and 4.1 million victims of natural disasters, about 4 million more than the 20.7 million reached through WFP-supported development projects.

The international community had responded to the proliferation of crises with a range of relief, peace-keeping, rehabilitation, disaster mitigation, and development measures, in addition to exploring new mechanisms for co-ordination among the many aid agencies involved. The result had been a shift away from development aid towards the provision of immediate and short-term relief assistance for those most in need. For the WFP, this shift had been significant. At the end of the 1980s, most of its resources went to development projects. By 1996, 70 per cent of WFP assistance was targeted to relief needs.

The WFP's experience in protracted or complex emergency operations had demonstrated that treating a crisis as an abnormal, short-term event distinct from development was often inadequate in addressing the real needs of people trying to stabilize and secure their livelihoods in and out of a conflict situation. Development activities in support of humanitarian efforts could help prevent further deterioration in social and economic structures, establish foundations for recovery and reconciliation, and help avert future conflict-related emergencies. Hence the need for integrating relief and development activities, and the development of strategies that better integrated relief and development programmes. The WFP's dual mandate of providing relief and development assistance placed it in a key position, in co-operation with partners, to assist the transition from crisis to recovery.

In preparing for this policy paper, the WFP conducted a major literature review and study of humanitarian relief operations. Lessons were drawn from operations conducted by the EC Commission, DAC/OECD, FAO, IFAD, DHA/OCHA, UNDP, UNHCR, UNICEF, and the World Bank, complemented by field assessments of recovery issues in Angola, Cambodia, Mozambique and Sudan, and case studies in transition in Ethiopia, Guatemala, Kenya, Mali and Pakistan. Six important lessons were drawn from this extensive review: recovery from crises was often haphazard, uneven, and complex; there was need for a strategy to integrate development, relief, and recovery operations; prior planning was important for logistics operations; situation-specific responses worked best; standards needed to be adopted for recovery; and funding arrangements needed to be assured for emergency operations, but also to facilitate recovery.

The policy paper made a number of proposals, which were approved by the WFP's executive board. PROs would henceforth be called PRROs, and emergency operations (EMPOs) would respond to acute emergency needs. Only in exceptional circumstances would PRROs exceed a period of two years. The WFP's support for PRROs would be guided by a recovery strategy that would propose activities and funding; the WFP would work in consultation with partners and through inter-agency mechanisms; and detailed operational guidelines for PRROs would be drawn up for WFP field staff.[4]

The guidelines were issued in January 1999 (WFP, 1999d). They stated that PRROs would contain three clearly identified components: protracted relief, refugee feeding, and recovery. They would provide the most flexibility for donors to contribute to PRROs from available sources of funding. Donors would be asked to support PRROs as a whole but, should they chose to direct contributions to certain components only, the WFP would retain the flexibility to redirect resources between the components of a PRRO, with donor consent. When a PRRO contained two or all three components, they would be linked in a strategic manner to ensure that the planned activities were mutually reinforcing and complementary.

Regarding the recovery component, the guidelines noted that different agencies and organizations used different terms when referring to the post-emergency phase, such as 'reconstruction' or 'rehabilitation'. The guidelines emphasized that development activities should be introduced as early on in a crisis as possible, even if a strategic planning process were not yet in place. This would provide a better response to the needs of the beneficiaries. They had the potential to improve the cost-effectiveness of operations, reduce dependency on food aid, encourage local production, and regenerate food market activities.

To assist PRROs, a category of 'Special Operations' was introduced for donor funding (WFP, 2004a). These were defined in the amended *General Rules* governing WFP operations as 'rehabilitating and enhancing transport and logistics infrastructure, and carrying out or providing technical assistance, to permit timely and efficient delivery of food assistance, especially to meet emergency and protracted relief needs'. They were also meant to 'enhance co-ordination within the UN system and with other partners through the provision of designated common services', which led to the WFP's designation as the lead UN agency for transport and logistics operations (see Chapter 4).

The introduction of the PRRO concept was clearly intended to maintain the WFP's dual mandate of providing development and relief assistance, and to attract donor contributions to its flagging resources, especially those related to development. It was also a genuine attempt to prevent the re-emergence of emergencies, and to provide an effective exit strategy for the WFP. In reality, it was to have unforeseen contorting effects. As the PROs before them, PRROs are funded by contributions to the WFP's general resources and not from contributions for its emergency operations. Since this category of assistance was introduced in 1998, it has attracted increasing amounts of resources to emerge as the largest component of WFP aid, and accounting for more beneficiaries than development projects or emergency operations combined (Figure 3.3). It has also resulted in an increasing

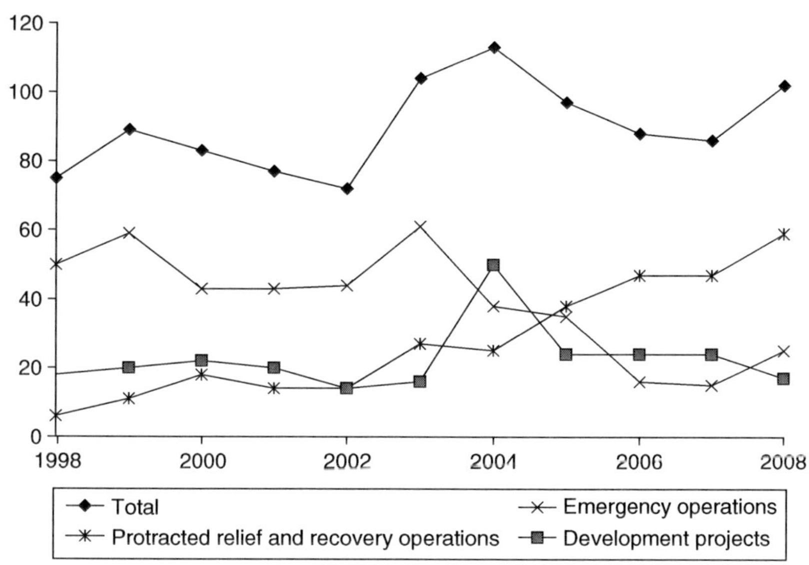

Figure 3.3 Beneficiaries of WFP assistance, 1998–2008 (million)
Source: WFP Annual Reports.

concentration of assistance in sub-Saharan Africa and, to a lesser extent, Asia, where most of the PRROs have been located.

There have been other complications. As PRROs have increased in size and duration, increasing amounts of WFP food aid have been locked up in these operations in a smaller portfolio of overall assistance. Allowing donors to contribute to certain components of PRROs encouraged them to provide the oxymoron of what became known as 'directed multilateral' resources. And the recovery component of PRROs involves activities well beyond the WFP's mandate of providing food aid, calling for integrated action by a number of partners whose co-operation had to be sought.

As Figure 3.2 shows, the WFP emergency assistance reached new heights after 2002 with the occurrence of major natural and conflict-induced disasters – such as the earthquake that hit Pakistan/Kashmir; the Indian Ocean tsunami; the large-scale humanitarian disaster in Darfur, Sudan; and the special operation in Iraq, where the WFP was called upon to assist in feeding the entire population after the Gulf War through resources made available from the oil-for-food programme that had been approved by the UN Security Council.

Profile of WFP operations (2010–11)

The legacies of past policies and operations, as well as the outbreak of recent emergency situations, have helped to fashion the current profile of WFP operations. A snapshot of WFP assistance for the succeeding two years was given at the end of 2009 (WFP, 2009a). It should be emphasized that the profile has been subject to change as new emergencies have occurred since 2009. In addition, the WFP operational regions in southern, eastern and central Africa were merged into

Table 3.2 Profile of WFP assistance by operational region, 2010–11

	ODB	ODC	ODP	ODD	ODJ	ODS	Total SSA	Total
Countries (no.)	14	11	10	19	18	1	37	72
Operations (no.)	41	21	20	43	39	7	89	171
Food volume (million tons)	1.8	0.9	0.3	1.0	3.3	1.3	5.6	8.4
Operational budget ($ million)	1,421	780	350	1,153	3,086	1,578	5,617	8,168
Beneficiaries (millions)	27	7	6	11	26	6	43	83

Key:
ODB Asia
ODC Middle East, Central Asia and Eastern Europe
ODP Latin America and Caribbean
ODD West Africa
ODJ Southern, Eastern and Central Africa
ODS Sudan
SSA Sub-Saharan Africa

Source: WFP Biennial Management Plan (2008–09).

Table 3.3 Profile of WFP assistance in operational regions by type of operation, 2010–11 ($ millions)

Type of operation	ODB	ODC	ODP	ODD	ODJ	ODS	Total SSA	Total
EMOP	43	110	4	356	668	1,387	2,412	2,569
PRRO	1,117	620	297	553	1,983	–	2,537	4,571
DP	203	50	48	196	365	12	572	873
SO	58	–	1	47	70	178	296	354
Total	1,421	780	350	1,153	3,086	1,578	5,817	8,368
%	17	9	4	14	37	19	70	100

Note: Figures rounded to the nearest $ million.

Key:

EMOP	Emergency Operations
PRRO	Protracted Relief and Recovery Operations
DP	Development Projects
SO	Special Operations
ODB	Asia
ODC	Middle East, Central Asia and Eastern Europe
ODP	Latin America and Caribbean
ODD	West Africa
ODJ	Southern, Eastern and Central Africa
ODS	Sudan
SSA	Sub-Saharan Africa

Source: WFP Biennial Management Plan (2008–09).

one operational region with the regional bureau in Johannesburg, South Africa (see Chapter 4).

Commitments to approved programmes and their logical extensions, if fully funded, are shown in Table 3.2. They reveal how, over the years, the WFP has become the world's largest humanitarian agency working on the frontlines of hunger through 171 operations in 72 countries to reach 83 million people with 8.4 million tons of food at an operating cost of $8.0 billion for the two years 2010–11.

WFP assistance is now concentrated in sub-Saharan Africa where 70 per cent of commitments for the two years 2010–11 are allocated. By marked contrast, the Asia operational region is expected to receive 17 per cent, and the Middle East, central Asia and eastern European and the Latin America and Caribbean operational regions are expected to receive 9 per cent and 4 per cent, respectively.

Table 3.3 shows the dominance of emergency operations in the WFP's overall assistance programmes, with commitments to PRROs likely to be almost double that for EMOPs, and development projects accounting for just over 10 per cent of total commitments.

Sub-Saharan Africa

The situation in sub-Saharan Africa is particularly disquieting. The 19 countries that make up the WFP's west Africa operating region have mutually reinforcing problems of conflict, recurring natural disasters, chronic poverty, and food insecurity that potentially can quickly become large-scale emergencies. The WFP considers all countries of this operating region as high priority. They are low-income, food-deficit countries of which 16 are classified as least-developed countries, indicating that they have the highest priority for WFP assistance. The region has the highest under-five mortality rate in the world. The UNDP human development index lists 15 of the countries in the bottom 20 per cent in the world. Although long-lasting conflicts in the region have been settled, many countries continue to suffer from political instability.

The region continues to be severely affected by high food and fuel prices, the global financial crisis, and weakening of government structures. Attempts are being made to enhance local food procurement and strengthen market access for poor farmers through the WFP's *Purchase for Progress* (P4P) programmes. Another tool contributing to safety nets are the school meal programmes implemented in all countries in the region, targeting 3.9 million school children, and representing almost one-quarter of the region's overall assistance portfolio.

The situation in the WFP's southern, eastern and central Africa operating region is characterized as one of the most vulnerable in the world. Drought, floods, cyclones and civil war have affected the region. As a result, it has received WFP emergency assistance continuously for many years. A multitude of factors – HIV/AIDS, weather-related shocks, environmental degradation, political instability, deep poverty accentuated further by recent high food, fuel and input prices and the global financial crisis – have combined to create more complex hunger and nutrition challenges. A large number of people are vulnerable even to small crises that can have immediate and serious consequences, leading to population movements within countries and across borders. It is planned to implement 21 PRROs in this region, accounting for two-thirds of its operational requirements, with the largest in Ethiopia, the Democratic Republic of the Congo, and Zimbabwe. An emergency operation in Somalia will account for 22 per cent of the region's operational requirements.

An additional factor in southern Africa is the occurrence of HIV/AIDS. Nine of the countries with the highest prevalence rates in the world are found in this operational region, which is where 41 per cent of the world's AIDS orphans are found. The WFP will focus on working with partners, emergency preparedness and response, and disaster risk reduction. Priority will be given to support for food-insecure households affected by shocks, universal access to HIV/AIDS care and treatment, nutritional support and protection for agricultural-based livelihoods. These interventions, and WFP collaboration with the FAO in the Horn of Africa Food Security Strategy, where more than 18 million people require relief assistance, are expected to reduce vulnerability and decrease the need for emergency interventions. During 2010–11, it is planned to purchase about 34 per cent of the region's food aid requirements at competitive prices on local and regional markets in Africa to assist 26 million beneficiaries.

Sudan receives more WFP emergency assistance than any other country in the world. The WFP operates throughout much of the country with four large sub-offices: Darfur in western Sudan; southern Sudan; in the three areas of Abyei, Blue Nile and South Kordofan; and in eastern Sudan. There are currently seven emergency operations, planned to reach 6 million beneficiaries in 2010–11 with 1.3 million tons of food at an operating cost of $1.6 billion. This represents 19 per cent of total WFP operational requirements for 2010–11. The continued presence of large numbers of internally displaced people and conflict-affected households in Darfur, and insecurity and political instability in other parts of the country, has led to substantial population displacement.

Most of the aid provided is therefore for internally displaced persons, refugees, and returnees. Life-saving assistance for the population of Darfur, caught up currently in the world's largest and longest humanitarian crisis, accounts for 70 per cent of WFP assistance provided for Sudan. Large areas of the country lack infrastructure. Logistics challenges include the high cost of road transport and expensive air transport of food to locations inaccessible during the rainy season. Efforts are being made to reduce costs by pre-positioning food before the rainy season and limiting airlifts only to cases where sudden emergency arises.

The cost of providing direct programme support, management, and administration in insecure areas also significantly affects WFP costs. As a result, 70 per cent of the WFP's budget for Sudan is non-food costs. Another special feature of WFP assistance to the Sudan is that the WFP manages three special operations on behalf of all aid agencies: the UN Humanitarian Air Service; the UN Joint Logistics Centre; and a road rehabilitation project in the south of the country. The WFP plans to continue its emergency assistance as the insecurity situation and instability continues to result in food dependence and food insecurity. School feeding is expected to reach 1 million children. Partnership with UNICEF and FAO will continue to expand to provide meals for school children and their families, but much will depend on attempts to reduce political tensions. These political tensions have recently been heightened by the International Criminal Court issuing a warrant for the arrest of Sudan's president on a charge of war crimes; crimes against humanity; and, most recently, genocide in Darfur. A further consideration is the 2011 national referendum on the future of the southern Sudan, which resulted in an overwhelming vote to separate from the northern part of the country (see pp. 132–3).

Asia

The WFP's programme of assistance to the 14 countries in its Asia operating region shows a better balance between emergency and development operations. The 17 PRROs planned for 2010–11 account for 69 per cent of the food requirements for the region to assist 21 million people. Increasing operational costs are mainly due to the increasing number of internally displaced persons in Pakistan and Sri Lanka (most of whom will continue to require assistance as they return to their home areas), and to food-insecure people greatly affected by high food prices in Afghanistan, Bangladesh, Cambodia and Nepal. At the same time, nine planned development projects account for the remaining 31 per cent of food requirements for the region to assist 6 million beneficiaries. WFP operations range from post-conflict disaster recovery and assistance to refugees to mother and child nutrition programmes, school feeding, and communal asset creation, and help for governments in planning and managing national food-security policies and programmes. The WFP also aims to enhance emergency preparedness and response mechanisms and to set up early-warning and food-security monitoring systems following the large-scale natural disasters that have occurred in the region in recent years. Emergency preparedness and response will, therefore, be a priority, including the building up of capabilities at the regional level and the establishment of an Asian regional emergency preparedness and response training facility. A 'green initiative' will also be implemented to develop models for more environmentally sustainable operations.

Middle East, central Asia and eastern Europe

The situation in this WFP operational region presents a variegated picture, but also shows a gradual withdrawal of WFP assistance in certain countries. The region is affect by natural disasters and protracted conflict. Post conflict and refugee needs result from vulnerability to hunger and insecurity. In some countries, however, there has been economic growth and increased government capacity to provide social safety nets. In these cases, the WFP intends to hand over PRROs to government and local counterparts. This applies to Armenia, Azerbaijan, Georgia and Tajikistan. As the situation improves in Chechnya and Ingushetia, the WFP expects to phase out the PRRO in the Russian Federation in 2008 and hand over activities to local counterparts. WFP-assisted development projects in Algeria, Egypt, Iran, Iraq, the Occupied Palestinian Territory, Syria, and Yemen focus on education and health, and are planned to reach 716,000 beneficiaries. A development project in Syria focuses on capacity-building for the government to manage a food-for-education programme. A large government contribution will increase progressively as part of a strategy for the eventual handing over of operations to the government. The WFP also intends to hand over to the government the WFP-assisted development project in Jordan.

The WFP plans to use new initiatives to address the needs of beneficiaries in this region. For example, the emergency operation in the Occupied Palestinian Territory includes a cash voucher component to address high food prices and to inject new investment into the Palestinian economy (see Chapter 6). The use of food vouchers will also be considered in the design of a new PRRO for Yemen to assist malnourished children aged under five years, pregnant and lactating women, and infants. The WFP will also continue to work with partner organizations to provide food assistance in this operational region. In Egypt, for example, the WFP is working with the Global Alliance for Improved Nutrition (GAIN) on the vitamin A fortification of vegetable oil.

Latin America and the Caribbean

The WFP operates in ten countries in its Latin America and the Caribbean operation region, which has the most unequal distribution of income in the world. Progress in hunger reduction has been uneven, and gains have not been proportionally reflected among countries or the population as a whole. Chronic undernutrition affects 9 million children (16 per cent) aged under five years, increasing to 70 per cent among the indigenous populations. Micronutrient deficiency results in public nutrition and health problems in most countries. The vulnerability of at-risk populations has been exacerbated by recurrent natural disasters, including the massive earthquake that hit the capital city of Haiti. Six planned PRROs account for three-quarters of food requirements for the region to assist 4 million people.

There are 11 planned development projects to account for the remaining one-quarter of food requirements to assist 2 million people. Development activities focus on the eradication of inter-generational chronic undernutrition through integrated programmes, school feeding and the protection of livelihoods from unexpected shocks. The WFP will assist governments in implementing food-based programmes such as school feeding and mother and child nutrition improvement programmes. There will also be a continued focus on supporting governments in emergency preparedness and response, with increased emphasis on enhancing capacities at the community and household levels. PRROs will include assistance for displaced persons in Colombia, vulnerable groups in Haiti, and indigenous populations in Central America and the Andean region to build resilience to natural disasters and other shocks.

The global financial crisis has already led to a significant reduction in employment and remittances from people working abroad. Rural households are suffering from high prices for food, agricultural inputs, and raw materials. The WFP is piloting its P4P initiative in the countries of Central America to provide a platform for sustainable development by increasing agricultural production, while improving the livelihoods of smallholder farmers with an emphasis on linking farmers to government food-based programmes and private industry. The WFP is also working closely with governments to complement and strengthen food-based social safety net programmes that ensure access to food for the most vulnerable and marginalized groups, including indigenous people, afro-descendents, and people with HIV. Work on the development and improvement of fortified foods and micronutrient supplements designed to improve the nutrition of young children and pregnant women will also continue in countries in Central America and the Andean region of South America.

Some examples of WFP emergency operations

The number, scale, duration and complexity of WFP emergency operations have all increased in recent years. The case studies chosen to describe the WFP's emergency operations in greater detail may be classified into three types: large-scale natural disasters, complex conflict-made disasters, and special or 'new wave' emergency operations.

While the WFP has often been the *de facto* lead agency in tackling large-scale natural disasters, particularly because of its logistics and transportation expertise and experience, conflict-induced disasters have an additional element of complexity, which significantly affects the WFP's ability to deliver assistance quickly and effectively. They involve the political concerns of the warring parties and issues of human rights and protection that are beyond the WFP's mandate, requiring co-ordination and co-operation with other agencies and organizations.

The special or 'new wave' emergencies in which the WFP has engaged in 'quick in, quick out' operations have been more controversial. While some have recognized that the WFP should use its particular comparative advantages in responding to these emergencies, which could gain it additional resources, others are concerned that they could deflect the WFP from its essential role in responding to emergencies in developing countries, and could tarnish its multilateral image.

Unless otherwise stated, the descriptions that follow are drawn mainly from evaluation reports submitted to the WFP's executive board.[5] They show the shortcomings as well as the strengths of WFP operations, adding lessons to the WFP's institutional memory. In selecting the case studies, consideration has been given to describing examples in different geographical regions and to show a range of WFP activities in response to different kinds of emergency situations. Their number is restricted by the space available.

Large-scale natural disasters

Indian Ocean Tsunami 2004

On 26 December 2004, a massive earthquake under the Indian Ocean off the west coast of north-eastern Sumatra, Indonesia generated a series of tidal waves (tsunami) that killed people and caused massive damage in the coastal areas in 14 countries around the Indian Ocean in one of the largest natural disasters in living memory. Indonesia, Sri Lanka, the Maldives, India and Thailand were the hardest hit. Over 227,000 people lost their lives and some 1.7 million people were displaced from their homes. The total economic cost of the damage and consequent losses across the affected region was estimated at $9.9 billion.

The tasks, complexity, and scale of the disaster facing the citizens and governments of the affected countries and the international community were enormous. In the most rapidly and generously funded disaster response in history, $13.5 billion were pledged or donated by the international community, including more than $5.5 billion from the general public, and private donations broke many records. Over 40 aid agencies from the UN system, donor governments, and NGOs, took part in one of the largest humanitarian operations ever undertaken (Telford and Cosgrave, 2006).

The WFP's contribution should be seen in the context of this massive, overall, international emergency operation. A real-time evaluation of the WFP's response to the Indian Ocean tsunami was carried out in 2005 (WFP, 2005b). The WFP focused particularly on providing logistics support to the entire humanitarian community. The two objectives of the WFP's operation were: to save lives by preventing deterioration of the nutritional status of vulnerable mothers and children; and to promote rehabilitation of housing, community infrastructure, and livelihoods. In addition, the WFP's emergency operation was supported by three special operations: provision of logistics support to get food to those in acute need (at a cost of $24.37 million); provision of air services to move food supplies quickly (at a cost of $42.42 million); and at the WFP's initiative, to establish a UN Joint Logistics Centre (UNJLC) to co-ordinate inter-agency logistics support and activities (at a cost of $3.92 million). Total WFP support for the relief operations over a period of six months amounted to $256 million.

Within hours of the tsunami hitting the coasts of the affected countries, key WFP staff gathered at the WFP's Asian regional headquarters in Bangkok, Thailand and WFP offices in the affected countries. WFP-hired ships at sea carrying rice were diverted to the disaster areas. An airlift was launched to provide emergency supplies of food, trucks, generators, and other essential equipment from the WFP-managed UN Humanitarian Response Depot in Brindisi, Italy and from the WFP's Asia Emergency Response Facility just outside Phnom Penh, Cambodia. Communications and computer equipment were delivered from the WFP's support facility in Dubai. Vitamin- and mineral-enriched biscuits were sent from storage in India and Bangladesh to needy people in Sri Lanka and the Maldives. Transportable warehouses were delivered from Oslo, Norway, while more vehicles were supplied from Alicante, Spain and Perth, Australia.

The logistics challenges of providing some 2 million people with urgently needed food supplies in a region that stretched from south-east Asia through south Asia to the east coast of Africa were immense. Overcoming these logistical obstacles demanded drawing on the WFP's considerable expertise and experience. New supply routes were opened using helicopters, landing craft, and floating warehouses. New WFP field offices were opened in the worst hit areas. More than 280 WFP officers were flown in from duty stations around the world, and 250 national staff were locally recruited. A new strategic humanitarian air hub was put into operation at the Subang military airbase in Malaysia, which proved to be crucially important in moving large amounts of food to the stricken areas. A shortage of transport vehicles was overcome with the help of WFP private sector partners, including TNT (the global mail and express delivery company), the Dutch multinational company Unilever, and Citigroup (the corporate investment bank).

By the end of January, one month after the tsunami occurred, the WFP had delivered by air, land, and sea, a total of 18,350 tons of food to 1.27 million disaster victims in six most affected countries spread across two continents. In June 2005, the WFP operation entered a new phase, with the focus moving from emergency relief to longer-term recovery. A real-time evaluation of the WFP's response to the disaster took place over four weeks in May/June 2005, some four months after the tsunami occurred (WFP, 2005b).[6] The evaluation focused on emergency operations in Indonesia and Sri Lanka, the worst-hit countries. It showed in sharp relief the strengths, versatility, and weaknesses of WFP operations in responding to this massive and complex natural disaster, and provided valuable lessons for further emergency operations. The overall conclusion was that the WFP acted promptly and effectively to this disaster. The WFP staff involved were commended for their commitment in difficult circumstances. A regional, rather than individual country, approach adopted for this emergency operation was considered to be appropriate in giving flexibility to WFP activities and the deployment of resources. WFP assistance was found to make a major contribution to achieving the first objective of the operation, preventing deterioration of the nutritional status of mothers and children. Few deaths were reported from malnutrition or disease. The second objective, rehabilitation and recovery, was more difficult to achieve in the optimistic timetable foreseen. While slower than expected, food aid provided a safety net for people in need and an income transfer for the displaced population.

The findings and recommendations of the detailed evaluation reports of the Tsunami Evaluation Coalition (TEC) – a multi-agency learning and accountability initiative in the humanitarian sector set up in February 2005 in the wake of the disaster – were also instructive.[7] In a foreword to the TEC reports, the UN Secretary-General's Special Envoy for Tsunami Recovery, former US president William J. Clinton, pointed to three overriding messages to emerge from the international response to the disaster: to do better at utilizing and working alongside the local communities and structure; to invest much more in risk reduction and preparedness measures; and to translate good intentions into meaningful reform of the international humanitarian system. The TEC report identified critical systemic challenges for the humanitarian community, many of which had been analyzed at length in the aftermath of the Rwanda crisis (see pp. 112–16), and had already been included in a range of standards and codes of conduct (Telford and Cosgrave, 2006: 3–4).

Four major recommendations were made. First, the international humanitarian community needed a fundamental reorientation from supplying aid to supporting and facilitating affected communities' own relief and recovery priorities. Second, all actors should strive to increase their disaster response capabilities, and to improve the linkages and coherence between them and other actors in the international disaster response system, including those from the affected countries themselves. Third, the international relief system should establish an accreditation and certification system to distinguish agencies that work to a professional standard in a particular sector. And, finally, all actors need to make the current funding system impartial and more efficient, flexible, transparent, and better aligned with principles of good donorship.

Three key issues stood out regarding the co-ordination of international humanitarian assistance (Bennett *et al.*, 2006). The number and diversity of organizations involved made co-ordination simultaneously more expensive and less effective. The large amounts of funding, especially from the private sector, reduced organizations' incentive to co-ordinate. In some cases, the competitiveness associated with funding, reduced organizations' interest in co-ordination. Some aid agencies were said to go about their work in a spirit of competition, leading to them adopting what was called a 'me-first' mind-set (Mitchell, 1997: 14).

Despite the best efforts of OCHA to harness and broadcast information and technical know-how within the humanitarian community, it had neither the authority nor, in some cases, the influence to direct events. The TEC evaluation on co-ordination concluded that, while the sheer scale of the tsunami disaster magnified inherent flaws in the humanitarian system, it also highlighted opportunities for fundamental change. International co-ordination standards and principles could be strengthened, perhaps through a major international consultation that drew on the lessons from the tsunami and other recent emergencies, and outlined a programme for the further rationalization and professional performance of the humanitarian sector as a whole.

The whole humanitarian community benefited from the logistics and telecommunications support that the WFP and its partners provided. It remains to be seen whether the humanitarian community will take account of the profound experience of responding to this massive disaster when the next major natural disaster strikes.

Southern Africa: food insecurity and the impact of HIV/AIDS, 2005–07

The WFP has responded to the food crises of countries in southern Africa for more than thirty years. As a result of drought in the early 1990s, one of the worst in recent history, an estimated 18 million people in ten countries in the region faced the spectre of famine and starvation. A major catastrophe was avoided by relief operations carried out with almost textbook precision (WFP, 1994c). The drought was identified in its early stages. Co-ordination was established with all affected countries through the Southern Africa Development Community (SADC) secretariat and South African Railways. An overall food aid delivery plan was drawn up and information was disseminated through a SADC/WFP Logistics Advisory Centre in Harare, Zimbabwe to governments throughout the region. Over $5.5 million was spent from a donor logistics fund to reduce bottlenecks and improve co-ordination. A joint USAID/WFP telecommunications project linked the major agencies involved in delivering and monitoring emergency aid; and much of the food aid required was purchased from Zimbabwe, then a grain exporting country and the grain basket of the region, through a system of triangular transactions and World Bank loans.

Ten years later, in 2002, another major food security crisis occurred in the region. Nearly 13 million people in six countries were considered at risk of extreme food shortages and starvation before the next harvest was due in 2003. There were significant differences between the food crisis of the early years of the new millennium and that of ten years previously. By 2002, a 'triple threat' had emerged to threaten the food security of the region once again. In addition to severe and chronic poverty, the onset of an HIV/AIDS epidemic, together with weakened governance capacity and inappropriate policies, had contributed to a serious decline in economic and social development. Zimbabwe, once a major food exporting country, had become a food aid recipient following years of internal political and civil unrest.

The WFP's executive board approved a regional PRRO for southern Africa in October 2004 for people vulnerable to food insecurity and to the impact of HIV/AIDS (WFP, 2004b). The PRRO provided for 5.5 million people, over half of whom were women, for a period of three years (2005–07) at a total cost to the WFP of $404.5 million. Approximately one-third of WFP assistance was assigned to relief assistance and two-third to recovery activities. The PRRO, which started in January 2005, had multiple objectives. There needed to be improvement in food security, livelihoods, and productive capacity among the vulnerable poor, including people infected and affected by HIV/AIDS. It was also desired to increase households' access to food and ability to manage shocks, and to reduce the impact of HIV/AIDS on food security among vulnerable people in high-priority districts. The nutritional needs of vulnerable people needed to be met, and sustainable increases needed to be made in school enrolment, attendance and ability to learn and concentration, while reducing gender disparities.

It was also planned that gender equity would be promoted through access to WFP resources, managing community food aid systems, and providing an integrated inter-agency response; and a shift would be made from large-scale general food distribution to a more targeted approach. This approach would take place in four main areas: food security; HIV/AIDS care and support for affected households, including orphans and other vulnerable children; heath and nutrition; and education.

A mid-term evaluation recognized the challenges faced by the WFP's regional bureau and country offices in implementing simultaneously the multiple activities contained in the PRRO (WFP, 2007b).[8] Several positive achievements were recorded. The WFP's support increased access to food for 9 million beneficiaries during the 2005–06 lean season. WFP assistance reached large numbers of people with HIV and AIDS, possibly because the epidemic touched almost every community. At the end of 2005, the high rates of HIV transmission affected a large proportion of PRRO beneficiaries. WFP food assistance was crucial in encouraging beneficiary participation, and ensuring treatment and care in school feeding programmes for orphans and other vulnerable children, and to home-based care providers. Beneficiaries stated that food aid was critical to household food security, especially during illness or drought, or following the death of an income earner.

The WFP addressed the nutritional needs of vulnerable groups by fortifying milled cereals and providing vegetable oil fortified with vitamins A and D, and corn-soya blend. Because of resistance by certain governments in the region about the acceptance of genetically modified foods, the WFP switched primarily to local maize purchases, installed a milling programme, and expanded local and regional purchases of maize meal and fortified blended food. Almost 487,000 tons of maize was purchased in the two years to the end of 2006, a small fraction of grain production of the countries of the region, which had little effect on food prices.

But beneficiaries did not always receive a complete food ration, or the full amount of each commodity, mainly because of breaks in food supplies. In some cases, aid organizations (co-operating as partners with the WFP) enrolled more beneficiaries than planned and were obliged to divide food supplies among more people, thereby reducing the nutritional benefit. In most countries, school enrolment and attendance rates reached or exceeded the planned number as a result of the school feeding programme but, in some schools, children did not receive a complete food ration, which also reduced the nutritional benefit. The quality of education might have also suffered because of inadequate investment in infrastructure and teaching capacity and quality to meet increased demand. But parents and teaching staff praised school feeding despite its shortcomings, particularly in community schools in areas with little government support.

The evaluation also recorded some fundamental strengths and weaknesses of WFP operations. Regional co-ordination among governments, UN agencies, and NGOs was strong. The fact that eight UN agencies were located in Johannesburg, South Africa enabled them to work jointly both before and during the PRRO. A Regional Inter-Agency Co-ordination and Supply Office, set up during the emergency period and chaired by the WFP, was active throughout the PRRO. Inter-agency vulnerability assessment committees operated in all PRRO countries, supported by the SADC, led to improved food security data collection, analysis, dissemination and decision-making.

While the regional approach adopted by the PRRO benefited certain activities, such as food aid management, it was not suitable for others, such as the care and support of HIV/AIDS-affected households and communities, which required national and targeted attention. Cohesion and integration among the various PRRO activities was also weakened. They were often implemented in a parallel, rather than convergent, manner as different co-operating partners did not always target the same districts, communities, or populations. The WFP's shift from relief to recovery and development programming was considered to be appropriate, but weaknesses in their funding and programmatic cycles indicated that both the WFP and its donors were not prepared for this shift.

Technical expertise in food security analysis and livelihood programmes was often limited in the WFP's regional bureau and country offices and sub-offices. The WFP's definition of food security needed to be broadened. Until recently, the concept of food security and related measures was largely limited to acute food insecurity rather than sustainable food and livelihood security. The evaluation team considered that the WFP and its partners should continue to improve their techniques for identifying chronic, as opposed to transitory, food insecurity groups before an emergency occurred.

A basic problem concerned the sustained financing of PRRO activities. Late donor funding, and only partially successful borrowing of funds, resulted in a slow start to local and regional procurement of food at higher costs. Some in-kind donations arrived late, leading to increased costs. Late deliveries led to competition for transport during the period of peak demand when transport rates were at their highest. Also, difficulties were encountered as some deliveries had to take place during the rainy season.

An important objective of the PRRO was the mainstreaming of gender concerns. In all PRRO countries, girls outnumbered boys in school feeding programmes.

But involving a majority of women in food-for-work activities presented a challenge, and insufficient attention was paid to women's needs and their access to, and use of, the assets created. Work norms were modified to ensure that women could participate without being overburdened, and ration cards were issued in the name of each participant. Women were generally well-represented in food distribution committees, despite cultural barriers. But lack of WFP staff dedicated to gender mainstreaming hampered gender-related activities. Gender focal points normally had other responsibilities, reducing the time they had for gender issues. Senior country office staff rarely held gender focal point positions, creating decision-making difficulties. In the evaluation team's view, senior management commitment was essential to successful gender mainstreaming.

The experience in responding to this emergency has helped the WFP in addressing the recurrence of food insecurity in the region. The establishment of a telecommunications network, the first of its kind to be used in major emergency situations, was a significant factor in averting death and starvation. It provided a basis for future WFP work in this field, which eventually resulted in the WFP being designated as co-lead agency in the global telecommunication cluster for emergencies established by the IASC (see Chapter 4).

Pakistan/Kashmir earthquake, 2005

A huge earthquake measuring 7.6 on the Richter scale struck the mountainous region of Pakistan-administered Kashmir (PK) and the North West Frontier Province (NWFP) of Pakistan on 8 October 2005, devastating the lives of 3.5 million people (WFP, 2006c). An estimated 73,000 people were killed and 79,000 injured and disabled. Some 2.8 million people lost their homes, assets and livelihoods. About 84 per cent of the homes, hospitals, schools, and other public infrastructure in NWFP, and 36 per cent in PK, were damaged or destroyed. More than 2,700 villages were affected, some of them completely destroyed. Aftershocks and landslides severed rural roads, trapping 745,000 people in mountain valleys and forcing 250,000 people into tented camps.

The impact on health and education was profound. Over 18,000 school children and over 850 teachers lost their lives. Over 570 health facilities and 4,800 schools were destroyed. Some 955,000 school age children had their education disrupted. There was significant destabilization of land and serious environmental damage. Irrigation and community water systems were damaged or buried. Natural springs dried up as a result of seismic shifts. And terraces and retaining walls required widespread repair.

The WFP response to this massive natural disaster was swift and measured. It called upon all of the emergency instruments and procedures that the WFP had at its disposal, in association with the government of Pakistan and its aid partners. From the outset, an overall plan was implemented that moved incrementally from the provision of immediate relief to sustainable recovery. An immediate emergency operation was approved by the WFP country director two days after the earthquake struck to provide high-energy biscuits to 400,000 beneficiaries in the worst-affected areas for a period of 30 days. One day later, the WFP's executive director and the FAO's director-general jointly approved a larger emergency operation to provide nutritionally fortified, ready-to-eat, food commodities for six months to 1 million earthquake victims, at a total WFP cost of $55.8 million, priority being given to those located in the more remote areas lacking cooking facilities. On 22 February 2006, the WFP's executive board approved a PRRO to benefit just under 1 million people for two years at a total cost to the WFP of $67.9 million. The total overall cost to the WFP of these three step-by-step operations was over $124 million.

The interventions included in the WFP's PRRO were identified by an inter-agency appraisal mission with representatives from the FAO, IFAD, UNDP, and WFP in December 2005 as part of a joint area development programme. A corps of social mobilizers was established to undertake agricultural extension work and to provide technical advice and inputs, such as seeds and saplings. Some 2,000 community organizations and 11 cluster bodies were created to implement relief and recovery activities.

The PRRO included general food distribution to 1 million earthquake survivors, including 250,000 people in tented camps, 5,000 hospital patients, and 745,000 people trapped in remote mountainous locations accessible only by helicopter, off-road vehicles, and pack mules. The WFP also provided supplementary feeding for 150,000 children in tented schools. The government requested that communities be given access to food-for training and food-for-work activities to ensure that funds were used for reconstruction. A high proportion of WFP costs was attributed to logistical difficulties in getting food quickly to people in desperate need in areas difficult to reach.

Within the first week after the earthquake, some 76,000 people in 35 villages were reached using trucks, two helicopters, pack horses and mules, and soldiers of the Pakistan army, who carried supplies on foot to inaccessible villages. Food was procured locally, subject to its availability and cash resources. When imported, it was transported by WFP-appointed transporters to WFP warehouses close to affected areas. Temporary storage was also set up close to final distribution points. Off-road vehicles and pack animals were used in the mountainous areas.

A special feature of the emergency operation was a combined WFP/Pakistan/donor helicopter operation, which was vital in the immediate aftermath of the earthquake and before the winter set in. The WFP requested donors to provide $100 million to keep the helicopter operation going for six moths as part of the UN Humanitarian Air Service (UNHAS). By the end of 2005, only about half the amount requested had been achieved. Despite this problem, the WFP succeeded in mounting the biggest helicopter airlift in its history. A fleet of 18 helicopters was deployed, each capable of carrying a payload of 20 tons. The Pakistan army also provided some 45 helicopters for the relief effort, as well as the UK and US air forces. In all, by mid-January 2006, UNHAS had airlifted 7,750 tons of food, 2,000 tons of non-food items, including tents and tools, and nearly 16,000 passengers. Most of the passengers were from remote mountain villages and were injured or destitute people seeking medical attention or accommodation in camps set up in the lower valleys.

Another special feature of the WFP's PRRO was the fortification of wheat flour with micronutrients to improve the nutrition and health status of children, mothers, and other vulnerable people. This programme was based on several years of experience in fortifying wheat flour in Pakistan for WFP operations in Afghanistan. The WFP and its aid partners collaborated in installing micro-feeders in the eight largest roller mills in the earthquake-affected areas to provide a pre-mix and training for one year until fortification was fully adopted and commercial mills imported and pre-mixed nutrients economically, in adherence with government standards.

The WFP should distil the profound experience of responding to this major earthquake and provide a guide for operational decision-makers and relief programme managers, drawing on the briefing paper produced by ALNAP in 2008 on the accumulated experience of responding to earthquakes (ALNAP, 2008).

Bangladesh: Cyclone Sidr, 2007

Bangladesh is one of the countries most exposed to natural disasters, as well as being one of the most densely populated in the world. It regularly suffers from major floods, devastating cyclones, and tidal waves from the Bay of Bengal. As a least-developed, food-deficit country, with an estimated 40 per cent of its population living below the poverty line, and widespread undernutrition among children, Bangladesh is a WFP priority country and has been one of the largest recipients of its assistance. That assistance has played a major role in relief operations. It has also been used in development projects to build and improve cyclone and flood protection infrastructure, including dykes, embankments, and cyclone protection shelters, and to renovate and improve irrigation systems. The WFP's long association with the country has also resulted in increasing national capacity to cope with recurring disasters through emergency preparedness and mitigation measures.

These measures were brought into action when Cyclone Sidr, a major category 4 tropical storm over the Bay of Bengal, hit the coast of Bangladesh on the evening of 15 November 2007. Winds of up to 240 km an hour lashed the shore, creating widespread destruction to homes, businesses, roads and bridges, and agricultural livestock and fisheries production, and markets. Some 3,800 people were killed, along with thousands of livestock. Over 4.7 million people lost their homes and livelihoods: 2.2 million were in need of immediate food assistance. The government estimated the total cost of the damage at more than $2.2 billion.

The Bangladesh cyclone preparedness programme and the government's early warning system (built up in past years with the WFP and other assistance and support) allowed 3.2 million people to be evacuated before the cyclone made landfall. More than 2,000 shelters previously constructed with WFP development assistance were activated, and 42,000 volunteers recruited to help in relief and recovery activities. These measures, combined with the construction of dykes and embankments against floods, and a radio alerts system set up with WFP assistance over past years since the devastating cyclone of 1970, considerably reduced the number of casualties.

Following the 1970 cyclone, which killed half a million people, the government and the Red Crescent Society began working together to improve coastal warnings and evacuation plans as part of a national cyclone preparedness programme. The backbone of the programme is a cadre of village volunteers, organized into local teams. They are equipped with radios to monitor weather bulletins, megaphones and hand-operated sirens, first aid kits, rescue equipment, and protective clothing. They receive travel costs and daily allowances to attend training sessions. The programme is costly and requires ongoing funding from the government and aid agencies. Extending its coverage and improving its operational effectiveness are continuing challenges.

On 26 November, 11 days after the cyclone struck, the WFP's executive director and the FAO's director-general jointly approved an emergency operation for 2.2 million people, at a total cost to the WFP of $51.8 million. The emergency operation was to: meet the immediate food needs of the affected population; prevent deterioration of the nutritional status of women and children, and reduce child mortality; restore livelihoods and rural community infrastructure in the affected areas; and encourage continued school attendance.

The operation was designed to take place in two phases. The first phase (November 2007–February 2008) focused on the provision of relief assistance and micro-nutrient supplements to prevent further deterioration in the nutritional status of the affected population. The second phase (February–May 2008) turned to the recovery and rebuilding of livelihoods through food-for-work and cash-for-work schemes to reconstruct shelter; to rebuild roads, embankments, small bridges and culverts; plant trees and repair schools; and an emergency school feeding programme to get children back to school as quickly as possible, during which the WFP assistance was closely co-ordinated with that provided by the government.

The lessons learned from emergency operations following previous cyclones were applied in this case. Surveys showed that, in the wake of a cyclone, there was likely to be a double peak of acute distress in the affected areas: the first peak was expected two or three months after the disaster occurred, largely due to diarrhoea and infectious diseases; the second peak would arise due to food insecurity in the months leading up to the next harvest. It was important that targeted feeding for children began as soon as feasible and continued until the harvest arrived in the non-affected areas of the country. The WFP, in collaboration with UNICEF and Helen Keller International, monitored the impact of the cyclone through a supplementary feeding programme implemented by WFP partners.

Studies had also shown that malnutrition in Bangladesh is highly correlated with the prices of rice and non-grain food expenditures. Commodity prices rose significantly prior to the cyclone, which had an even greater impact on child malnutrition. In the recovery phase of the emergency operation, food-for-work and cash-for-work schemes were implemented. Beneficiary families with no able-bodied members capable of participating in the work schemes received standard food rations through special targeted and distribution programmes. One of the underlying problems of access to food was insufficient household purchasing power. Cash-for-work schemes were therefore considered when local food supplies improved and food markets became more functional. Cash was delivered through bank transfers to WFP partner NGO accounts and cash payments to workers made in the presence of local authorities and the local community, monitored by WFP officers.

The WFP country office and WFP staff deployed from other countries on a temporary basis provided assistance in the implementation of emergency operation activities. NGO partners and local government officials selected the beneficiaries in the severely affected areas, with WFP staff closely monitoring the targeting process. Field monitors were located in each severely affected district to follow activities closely. NGOs carried out food distribution, and reported to an emergency co-ordinator. The nutritional status of the targeted beneficiaries was closely monitored through nutritional surveys in partnership with UNICEF and WHO.

It was originally planned to phase out the emergency operation by the next harvest season in May 2008, and to hand over the maintenance of the communal assets created to village communities and local government bodies. In the event, the recovery phase took longer than anticipated and the emergency operation was extended to the end of 2008, with a budget increase of $26.4 million, bringing the total WFP cost of the operation to $78.8 million. In this extended phase, 575,000 people were employed in food-for-work schemes in areas where limited food was available in local markets, and $2.5 million was provided for cash-for-work schemes. The WFP also provided tools and equipment, and training for NGOs and local government officers in the management and implementation of the work schemes.

Incremental improvements in the Bangladesh cyclone preparedness programme and the government's early warning system backed by consistent support from the WFP and other aid agencies saved the lives of many people in the cyclone-stricken areas. It showed the classical application of the weather tracking system that the WFP had developed with the Meteo Institute in Torino, Italy and the Bangladesh government, which enabled the path of the cyclone to be predicted accurately. This allowed organized local teams and WFP staff to be deployed in advance as the cyclone progressed. The emergency operation also showed the versatility of the WFP in deploying the range of emergency tools at its disposal, both in responding quickly and efficiently to relief needs, and in helping to set in motion activities to assist in speedy recovery from the disaster. The lessons learned will be particularly valuable in assisting the government to plan for, and respond to, future disasters of this nature, which are likely to occur even more frequently, and on an even greater scale, as climate change and global warming take effect.

Central America region: relief and recovery operations, 2002

Natural disasters – drought, earthquakes, floods and tropical storms – are endemic occurrences in Central America, regularly affecting the countries of the region. These events negatively affect the food, livelihoods, and human safety of the people of the region, particularly the indigenous population. One shock has followed another: the poorest and most food-insecure have increasingly exhausted their coping strategies, condemning them to inter-generational hunger and poverty.

In 1999, the presidents of four Central American countries – El Salvador, Guatemala, Honduras and Nicaragua – agreed to establish a five year programme (2000–04) to reduce the impact of natural disasters, supported by the international community. This provided a framework for concrete, cohesive, and consistent initiatives. A Central America Coordination Centre for the Prevention of Natural Disasters was established to address issues at the regional level. It played a key role as an integrating body for ensuring policy consistency throughout the region, exchanging information, and co-ordinating relief activities.

A Regional Disaster Reduction Plan provided a mechanism by which governments co-ordinated policies, priorities, and disaster-mitigation activities. Effective co-ordination among the government ministries, international agencies, donors, and local officials was recognized as essential for effective and efficient responses to the recurrent natural disasters. Strategic links had already been established between the WFP and the Pan-American Health Organization (PAHO), which served as a framework for supporting the regional initiatives.

Against this background, as part of a comprehensive regional programme, in October 2002 the WFP's executive board approved a three-year (2003–06) Central American PRRO to provide targeted food assistance for people affected by natural disasters, and for the recovery of their livelihoods. The PRRO was planned to benefit 690,000 people each year in the four countries of the region at a total cost to the WFP of $56.6 million. The total cost to the governments of the region was estimated at $10.2 million.

WFP assistance had three roles in a balanced programme of assistance between providing relief and supporting recovery. It would provide: nutritional support for families affected by natural disasters, particularly women and children; an enabling environment for asset-creation to mitigate the effects of shocks and improve household food supplies; and direct support to help stabilize enrolment rate and keep children in school. Communities would be targeted where food needs were greatest. Activities would be identified and planned at the local level using rapid and participatory approaches. The WFP and its aid partners would work through existing local committees and local authorities. Regular and joint consultation would be maintained with appropriate government authorities, UN partners (UNICEF, UN Office of Project Services, PAHO), NGOs, and community-based organizations.

An independent mid-term evaluation of the PRRO was carried out in April 2006 (WFP, 2006a).[9] The evaluation team found that the WFP delivered assistance to the most affected communities in spite of difficult access, and was often the only international agency present. Malnutrition rates among infants and children under five had fallen by 25 per cent, although this was not only attributable to WFP assistance. In spite of the results achieved, rates of malnutrition and stunting remained high and required continued attention in the ensuing years. School feeding had reduced drop-out rates. Available resources from donors for food-for-work activities, however, were insufficient to achieve sustainable outcomes.

At mid-term, as a result of a serious shortfall in donor funding, only 27 per cent of the food assistance had been distributed; only 31 per cent of the funding target had been met; and assistance was spread over a large-number of beneficiaries in many municipalities, which diluted impact and complicated monitoring. The low implementation rate was not only the result of low levels of contributions from donors, but also the slow implementation by WFP co-operating partners of food-for-work and food-for-training activities. The low level of funding also prevented the strengthening of capacities, and hampered monitoring by WFP country offices and its regional bureau.

Despite the regional design of the PRRO, different implementation in each of the four countries made it difficult to measure progress towards regional objectives. Faced with low funding and limited implementation capacity, the WFP offices in the four countries made considerable efforts to reach optimal levels of food distribution and to maintain the balance between relief and recovery objectives. WFP country offices also made significant efforts to find new partners to increase the capacity to deliver food. Working in consultation with municipalities and civil society organizations outweighed the effects of cuts in government ministries budgets and improved needs assessment. The decision to establish WFP sub-offices also improved monitoring and capacity-building by partners and communities. But the overall effectiveness of the PRRO was diminished by increasing the number of distribution sites and beneficiaries, reflecting a desire to respond to all needs in all places, and using beneficiary numbers as the main indicator, instead of maximizing its impact on smaller, more needy population groups.

Some important outcomes, previously unreported, were observed. The provision of corn-soya blend in the WFP's food basket played a fundamental role in providing a high concentration of nutrients and facilitated participatory education work. Beneficiaries learned many new recipes, which helped to diversify eating habits. Activities carried out under the PRRO were usually part of longer-term programmes, such as social investment funds, where objectives extended beyond those of the food aid component, and acting as leverage for greater impact. Food contributions produced a spirit of initiative in the communities and a positive impact on the work of other institutions. The PRRO had an under-reported multiplier effect on other sectors of rural development, particularly social capital and market access, which improved through renovation of small-scale infrastructure.

School feeding gave the PRRO a focus on vulnerable groups and contributed to human capital through increased school attendance and social capital through parents' associations. These associations sometimes emerged as the most representative and permanent in the community. In some cases, they were also involved in disaster preparation, which had an impact in the community beyond their initial purpose. In all four countries, women accounted for 50 per cent of leadership positions in management committees and food distribution.

The experience of this regional emergency showed that, while certain problems are best handled on a regional basis, others are more effectively dealt with on a national or local basis. It also showed the importance of donors abiding by their commitments on time to have effective impact.

Complex conflict-induced emergencies

Recurring challenges

A thematic evaluation of the recurring problems and dilemmas faced by the WFP and its partners in providing food assistance in complex conflict-induced emergencies was presented to the WFP's executive board in 1999 (Ockwell, 1999).[10] It showed: the need to combine operational capabilities with careful and continuous analysis and political sensitivity; how to adapt to rapidly-changing circumstances; and when to terminate assistance. While acknowledging the enormous efforts made and initiatives taken by the WFP and its partners in complex emergencies, it identified aspects of policy, procedures, and practices that required further consideration and action.

The WFP and other humanitarian agencies follow the humanitarian principles of humanity, neutrality, impartiality, and independence in providing assistance to victims in complex emergency situations caused by conflict and civilian unrest. But experience had shown that the assistance provided, especially food aid, had not been without consequences both for the course of events and the actions of the warring parties. Lives had been saved but many people were not reached, and there were unintended side effects. Delivery costs were high and food had been lost, stolen or misused. Increasing numbers of WFP and other humanitarian workers had been killed or injured.[11] In many conflict situations, food had been used as a weapon. In some cases, warring parties had profited from, or sought to impede, food assistance operations.

Access to affected civilian populations and delivery of supplies often had to be negotiated with the parties to the conflict. Even then, agreed arrangements were not always respected and serious issues of humanitarian principles had arisen. The motivations of the different parties to the conflict and their relationships to the civilian populations in the areas they controlled were among a number of critical factors that influenced relations between the WFP and their partners and the parties to the conflict. Such motivations also affected the possibility of devising meaningful agreements on access and safe passage. Assessing needs, including both the number of people requiring assistance and the level and type of assistance needed, and keeping pace with changing needs were difficult in most conflicts, as was monitoring the impact and distribution of the assistance provided. Targeting to the neediest was particularly difficult.

Security systems had been developed among UN agencies in the southern Sudan and Somalia. The WFP took broad-ranging measures in the Great Lakes region of

Africa and instituted a worldwide security awareness training programme, but a number of issues relating to staff security remained. Ground rules and codes of conduct were drawn up for emergency operations. But many operations did not benefit from a clearly-defined framework of operating principles, particularly between humanitarian aid workers and military personnel in peacemaking and peace-keeping operations. And WFP staff had not received adequate training or guidance concerning the dilemmas they often confronted and the difficult judgements they had to make in war zones.

Six principle recommendations were made. There should be clarification of the WFP's policy and basic principles for assistance in complex emergencies, including providing guidance to staff on human rights and protection issues, and the circumstances when suspension of assistance may be necessary. Continuation and enhancement of the WFP's engagement was required in ongoing interagency processes relating to the co-ordination of international assistance and the interaction between humanitarian, political, and human rights issues, emphasizing adherence to humanitarian principles. An in-depth review of experience and the development of operational guidelines with WFP partners and in consultation with donors should be undertaken. There should be consolidation and refinement of arrangements for resource mobilization on a regional basis, where necessary, to respond to changing needs between neighbouring countries. There should also be consolidation and refinement of staff security measures and training in collaboration with the UN security co-ordinator, other operational UN agencies, and NGO partners. Finally, provision should be made of detailed and country-specific briefing to staff assigned in conflict situations, with particular attention to inter-personal and negotiating skills in the selection and training of all staff in such situations. The WFP has taken steps to respond to these recommendations, as will be seen in later chapters of this book.

Conflict and genocide in Rwanda, 1994–95

There had been many warnings of the uneasy relationship between the majority Hutu tribe and the minority ruling Tutsis in Rwanda, as revealed in many accounts (see, for example, Dallaire, 2003; Melvern, 2000, 2004). Of the many

Table 3.4 Rwandan refugees in neighbouring countries, March 1995

Country of asylum	Number of refugees
Burundi	243,000
Tanzania	589,000
Uganda	4,000
Zaire	1,149,000
Total	1,985,000

Source: UNHCR. Special Unit for Rwanda and Burundi, March 1995; also quoted in Minear and Kent (1998): 62.

studies on the Rwanda crisis, the most comprehensive was the international evaluation of emergency assistance to Rwanda (*The International Response to Conflict and Genocide: Lessons from the Rwanda Experience*, 1996).[12]

Despite the many warning signs, the international community was taken by surprise when the genocide happened, triggered by the shooting down of the plane carrying the Tutsi president of Rwanda and the Hutu president of Burundi on 6 April 1994. Out of a total population of some 8 million at the beginning of the 1990s, an estimated up to 1 million people, mostly Tutsis, were slaughtered in little more than 100 days. Some 2 million people were displaced within Rwanda's borders during the last eight months of 1994, and close to another 2 million fled as refugees to neighbouring countries (Table 3.4).

First Tutsis, then Hutus fled *en masse* as the genocide continued. Many Tutsis returned when their army entered the country, which explains why Hutus could not seek refuge in the north.

At least seven UN agencies and the DHA were directly involved in the Rwandan emergency operations together with the IOM, about 250 NGOs, some eight military contingents, the ICRC and the IFRC. With so many organizations involved, there was a critical need for a strong capacity at the centre to provide leadership and overall co-ordination. Over 20 donor organizations provided resources for the emergency operations. Over the period April to December 1994, $1.4 billion were allocated by the international community for relief operations. About half of the total allocations was expended by, or channelled through, UN agencies, with the WFP and UNHCR accounting for over 85 per cent. A substantial proportion of the resources channelled through these two UN agencies were allocated to NGO implementing partners involved in the distribution of humanitarian assistance and who played a vital part in avoiding mass starvation.

Along with the many other humanitarian agencies, the WFP responded swiftly to the Rwandan catastrophe. Implementing, for the first time, the WFP's policy of deploying rapid response teams at the onset of major emergencies, senior and experienced officers were quickly at the scene.[13] Rapid and highly innovative solutions were provided by the WFP's transport and logistics service. The WFP began airlift operations within 48 hours of the refugees' main exodus from Rwanda into Zaire (now the Democratic Republic of the Congo). Food from the WFP's main procurement and logistics centre in Uganda was immediately redeployed for refugees and IDPs as soon as emergency operations were approved. The WFP's trucking fleet in Uganda was strengthened with long-haul vehicles from WFP operations in other countries in the region.

A WFP food aid co-ordination and information centre was set up in Nairobi, Kenya to monitor and co-ordinate the flow of relief supplies. The WFP also negotiated and maintained the transportation of food supplies through Tanzania, where 250,000 Rwandan refugees had fled over a 24-hour period in what the UNHCR described as the largest and fastest exodus in modern times, before the exodus to Goma occurred (see p. 114). In contrast to the situation in Zaire, which remained a 'no-man's land', the Tanzanian government allocated land for refugee camps, creating problems for the host populations. And close collaboration was established between the WFP and donor countries, which allowed flexible use of the resources provided.

The main focus of the initial relief operations was on getting food to the refugees living in camps outside Rwanda, particularly at Goma, just across the border in Zaire, where in only five days in July 1994, some 850,000 refugees had congregated. Enormous transport, logistical, and security problems were presented by the speed and magnitude of the exodus, the creation of some of the largest refugee camps ever known, and their location in some of the most inhospitable and unsuitable areas. Large amounts of food needed to be delivered quickly if starvation were to be avoided. An additional and serious problem was that of the protection and safety of the refugees. The perpetrators of the genocide had infiltrated the camps with their weapons. They interfered with humanitarian operations within the camp, and engaged in political and military manoeuvres to reassert their hold over Rwanda. In the circumstances, 'there [was] no delineation between feeding soldiers and non-soldiers and no opportunity to so do' (Bertini, 1994). The spectacle of aid agencies feeding the perpetrators of the Rwanda genocide in refugee camps alongside their victims presented harsh lessons about interventions based on the principle of 'doing no harm' and making no distinction between the receivers of humanitarian aid (Barnett and Weiss, 2008: 7).

The international evaluation of the humanitarian aid operations found that the response 'contained many highly commendable efforts'. The food aid supply system established by the WFP was vital for the survival of both refuges and internally displaced people, and 'performed well'. Given the magnitude and scale of the population movements and the distance from coastal ports, this was a 'substantial achievement'. But humanitarian operations within Rwanda were severely constrained not only by the high levels of violence, but also by the failure of the established international co-ordination mechanism in Kigali, Rwanda's capital city, to heed to the warning signals and sound the alarm. With the exception of Goma, the large-scale movement of Rwandans into camps in neighbouring countries enabled easier access but, at the same time, created substantial humanitarian needs and problems of co-existence with local communities.

A number of critical lessons were drawn from the Rwanda experience. Above all, it demonstrated the need for much closer association between humanitarian and political policies in the principal donor countries and the UN system, and in neighbouring countries and regional bodies, such as the OAU (now the AU). The Rwandan crisis was characterized by the lack of a co-ordinated political strategy within the international community. This was created by differences among key members of the UN Security Council and the governments of neighbouring countries regarding the different political factions in Rwanda, and their inability to confront and overcome these differences. This contrasted sharply with the readiness of the international community to fund humanitarian assistance generously as TV and newspaper images graphically displayed the magnitude of the suffering.

In addition to the heavy presence of military forces, the humanitarian response involved an unprecedented number of aid agencies and NGOs, increasing overall costs and the difficulties of ensuring a co-ordinated response. Co-ordination arrangements were unsatisfactory, leading to the international evaluation study to adopt the term 'hollow core' as a characterization of the centre of the humanitarian relief system. There was lack of clarity in the division of responsibilities among senior UN officials (who had various leadership and co-ordination functions) and their relationship with senior personnel of UN agencies. In addition, the roles of the special representative of the UN secretary-general, the UNAMIR force commander, and the UN humanitarian co-ordinator were limited to operations within Rwanda.

This hampered co-ordination between policies and operations inside Rwanda and those relating to refugees in neighbouring countries. On several occasions, the UN humanitarian agencies and NGOs were accused of undercutting the UN secretary-general's representative's initiatives by rushing ahead with aid deliveries without reference to the overall political and human rights objectives being pursued. Institutional and financial difficulties, lack of control over the funding of the UN agencies, and ambiguity over its representation in the field made the DHA unable to provide strong leadership and direct co-ordination.

The international response to the crisis in Rwanda involved an unprecedented number of NGOs, reflecting not only a genuine and widespread desire to provide assistance, but also the reality that participation in large-scale, high-profile relief operations had become an important factor in their formation and development. A substantial proportion of the resources channelled through the WFP and UNHCR were allocated onwards to NGO implementing partners for distribution to the victims of the genocide. The performance of many NGOs was 'highly impressive' and many co-operated closely with each other. There were numerous examples, however, where this was not the case. Some NGOs openly competed with each other to get to trouble-spots first. Others sent inadequately trained and equipped personnel; some undertook to cover only a particular sector of need and failed; and others were unwilling to be co-ordinated. The conclusion was drawn that the mechanism for ensuring that NGOs adhered to certain professional standards was inadequate.

Perhaps the most important finding of the international evaluation of the Rwandan emergency operation was that: 'Humanitarian action cannot substitute for political action'. In his report on the UN and the Rwanda crisis, the UN secretary-general wrote:

> We must all recognize that...we have failed in our response to the agony of Rwanda, and thus have acquiesced in the continued loss of human life. Our readiness and capacity for action has been demonstrated to be inadequate at best, and deplorable at worst, owing to the absence of a collective political will. (UN, 1994a)

One authority considered that the absence of meaningful military peacekeeping in Rwanda was 'the single worse decision the United Nations ever made' (Kennedy,

2006: 103) Another view was that the 'Rwanda genocide, probably more than any other event, shattered humanitarians' self-confidence in its own virtue and opened the floodgates to critical interpretation' (Barnett and Weiss, 2008: 6).

The international evaluation noted that one of the hallmarks of a complex emergency is that the political/diplomatic (including conflict resolution), human rights, humanitarian, military/peacekeeping and development aspects 'get inextricably intertwined' before, during, and after the peak of the crisis. It found that, in the case of Rwanda, the problem was that policy and strategy formulation by the international community 'seldom, if ever, took these elements into account in an integrated manner'. At the field level, there was tension among the agencies involved stemming from the lack of an overall agreed understanding of the complexity of the situation and an unclear division of labour.

The international evaluation found that insufficient reliance had been placed on the regional and sub-regional groups in Africa, particularly the OAU and the Economic Community of the Great Lakes countries. It identified three options for strengthening co-ordination among the large number of agencies involved in the international humanitarian assistance network: strengthening and extending existing inter-agency co-ordination arrangements and mechanisms; considerably strengthening the central co-ordinating role of the DHA; and creating a new, expertly-led and staffed UN operational mechanism that would consolidate the emergency response functions of the principal UN humanitarian agencies (DHA, UNHCR, UNICEF, WFP). This last option was favoured by the team devoted to the humanitarian aid and effects aspects of the international evaluation. Regarding equitable food distribution, it was recommended that operational guidelines should be developed for direct food distribution at the household level, and that the desirability and feasibility of direct provision to women should be explored, which the WFP implemented.

Two seasoned analysts considered that 'Rwanda ... offers lessons too important to leave unexamined' (Minear and Kent, 1998: 89).[14] The international evaluation of emergency assistance to Rwanda called for increased professionalism in the humanitarian sector. This led to the establishment of ALNAP (Active Learning Network for Accountability and Performance in Humanitarian Action) in 1997 as a mechanism for the many different organizations involved to keep each other and the wider humanitarian community informed of their performance-related activities. The humanitarian system, including the WFP, is now benefiting from the many services that ALNAP provides.[15]

Armed conflict and civil unrest in coastal west Africa, 1989–2004

The WFP's humanitarian operations were severely tested during armed conflict and civil unrest in four countries in the coastal region of west Africa – Côte d'Ivoire, Guinea, Liberia, and Sierra Leone – over a period of 15 years from 1989 (WFP, 2004c). Most of the political instability and civil unrest could be traced back to the civil war in Liberia that started in December 1989. Conflict there quickly took on a regional dimension as civilians sought sanctuary in neighbouring countries. Armed factions in Liberia linked up with a number of different groups, loosely associated with different ethnic affiliations across national frontiers, often with large numbers of young children, and adding to the overall chaos and hindering efforts to find peace.

WFP assistance to the war-torn region began in 1990 with a series of short-term, county-specific, emergency operations. Humanitarian aid was severely hampered by continuing insecurity both to the local population and aid staff. Humanitarian operations were made increasingly complex by unpredictable population movements, within and between countries, requiring constant adjustments to food delivery plans and distributions. Consequently, a regional approach was adopted to increase flexibility of programming, logistics, and resource allocations.

The rationale for a regional approach was to facilitate the planning and implementation of assistance. A single overall budget was expected to increase flexibility and allow rapid regional and local decision-making in resource allocation and reallocation according to internal and cross-border population movements involving internally displaced persons, refugees, returnees, and war-affected host populations. A Regional Humanitarian Co-ordination and Support Office was established in Abidjan, Côte d'Ivoire. At the country level, WFP country directors were responsible for co-ordinating and implementing in-country relief and recovery activities. As years of civil conflict had seriously weakened the capacity of government institutions in all countries in the region, the WFP contracted partnerships with international and national NGOs to deliver food aid to the beneficiaries. The WFP contributed to meeting their costs for food distribution to displaced persons at an agreed rate per ton. UNHCR contributed to their costs for food distribution to refugees.

Until the mid-1990s, the main focus of WFP assistance was on free general food distribution, as the prevailing security situation severely restricted opportunities to support meaningful recovery activities. In 1996, the WFP evaluated its experience with the relief operations in Liberia. The evaluation recommended phasing down general food distribution and strengthening targeted recovery activities. The upsurge in violence in 2000 and 2001, which continued into the summer of 2003, curtailed the expansion of recovery activities. As a result, general relief food distribution still accounted for 60 per cent of WFP assistance in 2003 and 2004.

In 2003, three phases of a PRRO were approved with food distribution in Guinea, Liberia, Sierra Leone, and Côte d'Ivoire. This represented the largest and most prolonged operation in west Africa for 750,000 beneficiaries, with a total cost to the WFP of $75 million, to deliver 124,000 tons of food. All phases of the PRRO had the same objectives: to provide relief assistance to the most vulnerable victims of civil strife, refugees, and displaced people; to facilitate their return once the situation stabilized; and to rehabilitate social and productive infrastructure, and improve household food security.

In 2004, an evaluation of the PRRO was conducted.[16] General food distribution for relief interventions involved a number of feeding programmes, including: therapeutic feeding, provided in government hospitals outside camps, for severely malnourished children; supplementary feeding in camps for moderately malnourished children; and mother and child feeding programmes for pregnant and lactating women. The evaluation mission found that outbreaks of severe violence in Liberia in 2002/03, combined with increased civil unrest in Côte d'Ivoire, resulted in overall relief requirements being 50 per cent higher than originally planned as the countries of the region struggled to cope with new waves of IDPs and refugees, although numbers may have been significantly exaggerated (see p. 119).

Curative feeding interventions seemed to become increasingly more effective in 2003, particularly in Guinea. Targeted feeding programmes in camps were also available to mothers and children from surrounding villages, where malnutrition rates were often higher than in the camps. In 2003, most of the beneficiaries in these programmes were IDPs from the host populations. The evaluation mission found WFP relief interventions to be effective. There were 'no reports of death through starvation' and the mortality rate for children aged under five years was 'generally low and stable'. Most quantitative data on the effectiveness of WFP relief interventions was collected from refugee camps in Guinea and Sierra Leone. These data showed that WFP relief activities had 'successfully met their objectives'. Under-five mortality rates were low and stable in all refugee camps, where wasting was also lower or similar to that of the surrounding host population.

There was therefore strong evidence that WFP general food distribution, combined with selective curative feeding programmes, significantly contributed to saving lives; restoring, maintaining, and improving food security; and maintaining the nutritional status of the beneficiaries. But food availability was only one of a number of factors influencing nutrition status. Clean water, appropriate sanitation arrangements, and good health care were also vital. In addition, the effectiveness of the WFP's curative feeding interventions depended on NGOs providing medical care and medicines paid for by the UNHCR.

On the other hand, designing and implementing meaningful and effective recovery activities using WFP food aid was 'the greatest challenge'. The major weakness was considered to be 'lack of clarity as to the specific objectives of the recovery interventions', which had implications for the phasing out of WFP aid. The recovery activities included: emergency school feeding; food for training; food for work; food for agricultural development through seed protection; and support to returnees, including disarmament programmes. The evaluation mission found that the range of recovery activities supported in each country exceeded the capacities of WFP country offices. Sound project design and implementation, as well as monitoring and assessment, were difficult to ensure, given the limited number of programme staff and the limited technical support available from the WFP's regional office. The capacity of government departments to implement recovery activities and provide non-food inputs was also limited.

The nature of the crisis over the ten years was a cyclical pattern of extreme violence – when only general food relief assistance was possible, followed by periods of calm – when recovery or targeted interventions were introduced. There was lack of clarity and uncertainty as to when to shift from relief to recovery interventions. The UNHCR pressured the WFP to introduce targeted interventions in combination with general relief food distribution in refugee camps as soon as possible. The WFP resisted this until general food distribution rations were reduced, thus making targeting food distribution more attractive to camp inhabitants. It was foreseen that school feeding in refugee camps would be introduced when the general food ration was reduced to a certain level.

For non-camp beneficiaries, there was little evidence that recovery activities were introduced following specific assessments of changes in the situation or their condition. The growth in emergency school feeding in 2003 in Guinea and Liberia was particularly noteworthy as a means of supporting the communities hosting the largest numbers of displaced people and a means of rectifying the imbalance between supporting them and the refugees. The expansion of emergency school feeding overshadowed the generally 'rather dismal' performance of other recovery activities. It was particularly difficult to establish effective food-for-work programmes, partly because of the social attitude towards working for food and also because of the serious lack of implementing partners with appropriate technical expertise and capacity to execute food-for-work activities. Food-for-training interventions were also much more difficult to implement; again, lack of appropriate implementing partners being one reason. Limited information was available on the benefits of recovery activities, such as on expanding livelihood capacity or creating sustainable assets.

The evaluation revealed the difficulty of meeting PRRO costs as it moved from the relief to the recovery phase. Typically, relief interventions had lower management and programming costs than recovery activities and involved distributing more food against which, according to the WFP financial arrangement, charges could be made. Mobilization of resources for the regional PRRO was good, with 17 countries donating contributions, while donors were hesitant to provide assistance for development to a region in crisis. The United States and the European Union provided about four-fifths of total resources that donors gave generously. Thus, governments and other agencies looked to the WFP to support activities for which food aid had a lower comparative advantage, creating additional burdens on the limited and already stretched capacities of WFP country office staff.

Targeting of general food distribution in refugee camps in Guinea and the camps for the IDPs in Liberia was particularly difficult. For refugee numbers, the WFP basically relied on the UNHCR: identifying and registering IDPs outside camps was far more difficult, especially in Liberia where people were forced to flee several times. Their number was significantly exaggerated, resulting in the sale by beneficiaries of maize meal provided as food aid by the WFP. Sale of a 50 kg bag of maize meal was only sufficient to buy 5 or 6 cups of rice, about 1.5 kg. Yet, there were no signs that the nutrition of the beneficiaries had been adversely affected, suggesting that many of the beneficiaries were not reliant on WFP relief food rations to meet all, or even most, of their nutritional needs.

The evaluation mission found that there were two consequences of targeted general food distribution in Liberia. First, many of the inhabitants of the camps established for IDPs became long-term residents, having received free food from the WFP over a number of years. For them, the WFP food ration had become an 'entitlement'. Second, many people, including the IDPs, lived in other types of accommodation, called 'spontaneous settlements'. They often lived precariously, without humanitarian assistance, and their living conditions were usually more insecure than the inhabitants of camps.

The overall efficiency of WFP operations was hampered by the high level of turnover of international staff. UN security regulations for UN agency field staff in crisis situations were strengthened in 2004 with the aim of improving their safety. This had significant implications for the work and workload of WFP country office programme staff. In Liberia, basic field monitoring trips now required considerable bureaucratic and administrative procedures to obtain all the necessary clearances, both within the country and from the UN in New York. Single staff and vehicle travel was not permitted in large parts of the country. One consequence was that routine travel to monitor operational performance was passed to implementing NGO partners, who were less constrained to travel but had limited experience with food aid programmes. Reporting demands on WFP country office programme staff was also heavy, seriously diverting them from managing and monitoring food aid operations. Large amounts of quantitative data were collected in the field and presented in reports to WFP headquarters, where much of the demand for data originated, reducing the amount of time devoted to in-country programming issues.

As insecurity was all-pervasive, a review of protection measures was undertaken, within the framework of the overall evaluation described above, and included as an annex in the evaluation mission's report (WFP, 2004d).[17] The review identified protection as an issue cutting across all WFP interventions. Protection was the responsibility of states, but when they were unable or unwilling to do so, responsibility passed to the international community. Some UN agencies and the ICRC were specifically tasked with protecting certain rights or certain categories of the population. The WFP was mandated to save lives through providing food aid, thus safeguarding the most fundamental right of all, the right to life.

In addition, there were UN agencies whose mandates were the protection of the vulnerable and promotion of human rights. The WFP therefore had a responsibility to work in accordance with UN human rights principles and instruments. The UN secretary-general had also encouraged all UN agencies to expand and strengthen the protection of civilians in complex emergencies in conformity with international humanitarian law. The WFP also operated on the basis of a set of humanitarian principles by which it was committed to 'provide assistance in ways that respect life, health and dignity' and to 'uphold recognized human rights' (WFP, 2004c).

The review mission therefore reasoned that the issue of protection should not involve a reconsideration of the WFP's mandate. It should examine its operations through a 'protection lens'. This involved identifying and understanding the context in which the WFP carried out its operations. In west Africa, the food insecurity that had prompted WFP action had been caused by violence and violation of human rights. This required an understanding of what constituted violence under international law. Food aid could have an effect on these violations, positively or negatively. It also involved understanding the role of other actors, referring those violations that could not be solved by the WFP alone to them; and what role the WFP could play in advocacy.

Most WFP staff expressed a strong interest in protection issues to the review mission, but their awareness and understanding of the WFP's role with regard to protection, human rights, and humanitarian law varied across the region. This had an impact on the design and implementation of WFP-assisted programmes and ability to monitor protection issues. Many WFP officers requested guidance on protection measures. The review mission concluded that: 'There was a need for a common understanding on protection concerns, why WFP should be concerned, and guidance on when to intervene'.

The regional approach adopted in implementing the PRRO had several positive aspects. It increased flexibility in pipeline management, enabling adjustments in food deliveries in light of changing needs both within and between countries, thereby increasing flexibility in budget allocations. It facilitated the introduction of regional standards, most notably in the allocation of food rations. Decentralization of decision-making to the WFP regional office in Dakar, Senegal was also beneficial, in that it increased the level and frequency of technical support provided by the WFP regional technical advisers and facilitated direct contact with locally-based donors.

The WFP subsequently took action in responding to the review mission recommendations, as related in the following chapters of this book.

Relief and recovery in Afghanistan

WFP assistance to Afghanistan has shown the considerable difficulties of trying to respond to the special problems of a country emerging from many years of bitter internal conflict and foreign invasion, which led to widespread destruction and loss of life, and large numbers of refugees and IDPs.

For many years up to the beginning of the new millennium, the WFP provided assistance to Afghanistan through a series of emergency operations for the victims of long drawn-out conflict, civil unrest, and drought, both to the large numbers of people displaced within the country and to the many refugees in neighbouring countries. The downfall of the Taliban regime in November 2001, and the establishment of a new interim government during the second half of 2002, provided a new opportunity to change the focus of assistance from relief to recovery and sustainable development. A more open approach could now be adopted in the selection of beneficiaries of WFP assistance, especially women and girls who were previously difficult to access.

A national development framework (NDF) was formulated that called for systematic provision of basic social services. It also involved, as part of an environmentally sustainable development process, the creation of new, and the recovery of former, livelihoods destroyed through many years of conflict Food aid, and relief food in particular, came under criticism from both the new government and from within the donor community following the high levels of relief food distributed during the protracted emergencies of the past, greater availability of food in local markets, and the government's preference for cash-based interventions. The government also expressed its desire to minimize food aid in order to reduce dependency, enhance local food production, and distribute food aid to food-deficit areas only when it had a comparative advantage over other aid instruments.

Against this background, the WFP changed its support from providing assistance through short-term emergency interventions to a PRRO designed to support the nation-building objectives of the NDF in consultation with the government, donors, other UN agencies, and NGOs. The PRRO had two components. One aimed at providing relief and the other at livelihood recovery, which, in reality, often merged during implementation. About 28 per cent of the PRRO's resources were allocated for relief and 72 per cent for recovery interventions.

The relief component included: feeding of IDPs in camps; food packages for returnees; support for vulnerable people in rural and urban areas; institutional feeding; support for tuberculosis patients; and supplementary feeding. The recovery component involved: food-for-work activities; food-for-education and school feeding; food for supplementing teachers' salaries; food for teacher training; food for non-formal education; and support for the re-integration of demobilized soldiers.

A mid-term evaluation of the implementation of the PRRO was carried out in 2004.[18] The evaluation mission found that the WFP staff in Afghanistan was doing a 'commendable job' in implementing the WFP's mandate in the country despite the security situation, which had worsened since the PRRO was designed at the end of 2002 (WFP, 2004f). The operation had a number of strengths, such as strong synergy between its design and government priorities, effective logistics and pipeline management in providing the food aid commodities, and creative and innovative project design, especially in activities related to improving nutrition.

However, it was difficult to obtain reliable data on beneficiary numbers and on project results due to a monitoring system that was weakened by the deteriorating security situation. Support for IDPs in camps was found to be 'very effective' but, otherwise, the relief objectives were not fully met. Recovery objectives were partially met through a combination of food-for-work, food-for-training, and FFE. The effectiveness of school feeding was reduced, however, by the unreliable supply of biscuits. Performance in asset creation was highly satisfactory in one province (Badakhshan), where the WFP had supported food-for-work activities for over a decade.

The evaluation found that food-for-work only partially met the immediate food needs of the most vulnerable. Food-for-work was restricted to areas where between 60 and 80 per cent of the population were acutely or highly food-insecure. But only 27 per cent of the food aid commodities were programmed for such areas and was therefore thinly spread. Weak targeting resulted in the inclusion of non-food-insecure households and the exclusion of many food-insecure families. Food-for-work was also weakly self-targeting on the poor, even though food rations were below market wages, because village leaders selected the beneficiaries, and rations were redistributed within the community. It was uncertain whether food-for-work helped poor households cope with crises, retain assets, or reduce expenditure on food in total household expenditure, because systematic collection of data was lacking. There was evidence, however, that work opportunities through food-for-work helped to reduce out-migration.

Recorded physical outputs from one year of food-for-work activities were found to be 'impressive'. Rehabilitation of community assets, roads, and drinking water benefited women and poor households equally, but repair of irrigation systems benefited landlords more. Tree nurseries and reforestation mainly benefited public institutions. Construction of new roads enabled the inhabitants of isolated villages previously without access to roads to bring in consumer goods, send produce to market, and reach health services.

But food-for-work did not achieve an optimum relationship between the costs involved, the quality of work undertaken, and the time taken to complete work. For food-insecure people, transaction costs were high, food assistance of short duration, and results were modest in terms of asset creation. In food-secure areas, cash-for-work often had a comparative advantage over food-for-work and was preferred by better-off households in food surplus areas near markets. Afghans tended to prefer food aid in winter and spring, and cash assistance in summer and autumn. Poor households and women in food-deficit areas with poor market access preferred food aid all year round, but better-off households in food surplus areas near markets preferred cash assistance.

Vulnerable people in four major cities were supported through 86 bakeries that employed 900 poor women and 60 poor men, and which supplied subsidized bread daily to over 167,000 beneficiaries. The bakeries received free wheat flour and iodized salt from the WFP and sold bread at a subsidy ranging from 67 to 83 per cent. The bakeries may have been effective at their conception during the time of the Taliban regime, but the changed political environment, together with greater cash-based employment opportunities in the towns, made the bakeries less effective in addressing the needs of the vulnerable urban population.

WFP support was highly relevant to national priorities because the voluntary return and reintegration of Afghan refugees and displaced persons into their original communities was a main pillar of the NDF. Three types of assistance were provided: food transfers to returnees on their way home; food assistance in the places of return; and feeding of displaced persons in camps. Returnee re-integration was lower than expected. Free relief food provided to IDPs in camps was effective, reaching over 123,000 beneficiaries. The UNHCR expressed satisfaction with the WFP's performance, reporting that its partnership with WFP had worked well. The WFP's assistance had been timely and had contributed to meeting legitimate food needs. Severe wasting among children aged under five was prevented. IDPs returning home were slower in southern Afghanistan than elsewhere because of insecurity, unresolved land rights issues, and continuing drought.

The considerable increase in school enrolment following the overthrow of the Taliban regime in 2001 was mainly the result of the changed political environment, a successful UNICEF-supported back-to-school campaign, and the influx of returning Afghans. Take-home wheat rations were distributed in place of biscuits in remote mountain areas, which contributed to increased enrolment. A take-home cooking oil ration was also an incentive for girls to enrol and helped to reduce the gender gap. Food aid may have contributed to women's enrolment in literacy classes, although centres were well-attended that did not offer food rations.

The WFP identified chronic, as opposed to acute, malnutrition as more serious in Afghanistan and shifted resources from the original focus on hospital-based treatment to food fortification, nutrition/health/hygiene awareness raising, water supply, sanitation improvement and de-worming. The food incentive for tuberculosis treatment was effective in reducing the drop-out rate as it attracted poor rural people, enabling them to stay long enough to complete the treatment, and ensuring their return for follow-up visits. Raising nutrition and health awareness also took place under food-for-training and food-for-education.

The WFP country office was commended for its efforts to build capacity in two government ministries: the Ministry of Rural Reconstruction and Development, and the Ministry of Education. Impressive progress was made in risk and vulnerability assessment in the evolution from the WFP's VAM system to national risk and vulnerability assessment. But the duration and timing of assistance were often inadequate to address the food gap, partly because of remoteness, insecurity, shortage of implementing partners to distribute food aid, and inadequate co-ordination with cash-based programmes.

The geographical targeting of assistance was deficient. Food-for-work was to be restricted to areas of acute and very high food-insecurity, but only a small part of food-for-work assistance was programmed to these areas. Food-for-work interventions tended to be concentrated in irrigated valleys to the neglect of rain-fed areas, and to concentrate around provincial and district capitals. Monitoring focused on food deliveries and only partially covered progress toward achieving planned targets. Three well-prepared studies found no overall effect of the provision of food aid on the prices of locally produced food. There could have been short-term effects, however, because markets were separated by poor roads, transport costs were high, and storage was limited. There was no evidence to support the possibility that food aid might have increased farmers' incentive to grow opium poppy.

The experience of implementing the PRRO in Afghanistan echoed some of the findings of conducting PRROs in other countries. One common problem was the difficulty of addressing relief and recovery in a single operation, and getting the balance right. Another was to decrease the level of general relief food distributions in favour of more targeted interventions to promote self-reliance and asset creation. There was a widespread misconception in Afghanistan that the PRRO was a time-bound exit strategy for phasing out WFP relief assistance and for converting to recovery activities. In the face of criticism of food aid in the government and among the donor community, the evaluation mission considered that the WFP had made commendable efforts to reduce free relief food distributions, to target its assistance more effectively to food deficit areas, and to expand recovery activities. There was so much concern about avoiding criticism of free relief food that some of the legitimate relief needs of the rural vulnerable population may have been neglected. Some of those needs were to be met through cash-based programmes, which started late and faced a number of the same targeting problems that the WFP had with its food aid.

In the face of formidable difficulties, the main achievements of WFP interventions were: the return of refugees, and their reintegration in Afghanistan; the creation of physical assets; and the improvement of nutrition, particularly of school children. Afghanistan remains a WFP priority country and one of the main recipients of its assistance. WFP humanitarian assistance is continuing through protracted relief and recovery operations.

Darfur, Sudan: one of the WFP's largest, most complex, and prolonged emergency operations

As was seen earlier in this chapter (pp. 94–5), Sudan has received more WFP assistance than any other country, starting with the first WFP-assisted development project in 1963. Since that time, the WFP has providing development and relief assistance over many years to the Sudanese population, including those affected by war and civil unrest in the southern, eastern, and central parts of the country. Another large-scale humanitarian crisis began in the Darfur region in its far west of the country in 2003. This new crisis, now in its eighth year, has developed into the WFP's largest, most complex, and prolonged emergency operation. The intervention has an intricate web of local, national, and international interests and groups, played out in a vast and remote region with poor communications and restricted access.

The causes of the conflict have been widely discussed and documented.[19] The emergency was seen as, first and foremost, a human rights crisis created by the Sudanese government, but opinions differed as to whether this amounted to the specific charge of genocide.[20] It was also seen as a crisis in protection – particularly of women and children, who were rampantly attacked and violated. In late April 2004, a high-level UN mission, led by WFP executive director James Morris, visited the Darfur region and raised serious concern about the protection of the crisis-affected population. But while the UNHCR had the responsibility to protect refugees, no UN agency had a clear mandate to protect the much larger numbers of IDPs, despite the 1998 UN Guiding Principles on Internal Displacement, which clarified their legal position. With some 2 million IDPs, of whom 1.4 million were in camps and the remainder living among host populations, and 200,000 refugees in Chad, in early 2005 the Darfur crisis was clearly primarily one of people displaced within their own country.

The WFP had begun operations to deliver food to drought-affected people in the Darfur region in April 2002. These operations were scaled up to provide food assistance to the war-torn people of Darfur soon after the inception of the crisis in 2003. And the WFP was at the forefront of efforts to bring relief to the traumatized community in 2004. The main objectives were, and have remained, saving lives and reducing or stabilizing malnutrition among the conflict-affected and displaced population that have experienced loss of access to the sources of their livelihoods. Since then, the WFP's assistance programme has grown and evolved.[21]

The WFP's country office in Khartoum manages WFP food operations throughout the Sudan, including Darfur, working with co-operating partners, the government's Humanitarian Aid Commission, and national NGOs, which it has advocated and encouraged to operate in the Darfur region. The WFP is also represented on the UN humanitarian co-ordinator's task force on Darfur, which regularly reviews the security situation, protection of the civilian population, and co-ordination of response among all the humanitarian agencies involved. The WFP's country office hosts monthly NGO co-ordination meetings on key operational issues.

Up until May 2004, humanitarian assistance was severely restricted as WFP staff and those of other humanitarian organizations were not allowed access to many areas of Darfur. During 2003 and 2004, the WFP rapidly expanded its assistance programme by addressing the major logistical constraints in getting food to one of the most remote regions in the interior of Africa. WFP staffing levels were increased during 2004 to the point when 65 international and 300 national officers were employed in Darfur itself, and more than 100 international officers worked in support of the Darfur operation in Sudan. Three WFP area offices and 11 field offices were located strategically throughout the region. The field offices and forward warehousing, located close to IDP camps in relatively remote locations, were particularly important in facilitating assessments needs and monitoring operations, and in supporting co-operating partners. Significantly, the WFP established food relief committees (FRCs) to empower local communities to participate actively in food distributions and to ensure their continuity in the event that security situations deteriorated to the point that even the staff of WFP's co-operating partners could not reach distribution points.

A series of special operations were approved from 2005 to support the WFP's emergency operations in Darfur, ranging from augmenting logistical capacity to deliver food assistance to running the UN Humanitarian Air Service (UNHAS) to transport humanitarian personnel (government, donors, UN representatives, and NGOs) over the vast areas of the country, quickly and at short notice. In a public statement, 14 international aid agencies wrote: 'Much of our work of meeting the enormous humanitarian and development needs across Sudan would not be possible without these flights...for months at a time, vast areas are flooded and completely impassable. Without UNHAS to fly in, there is no way the needs of the areas could be met' (WFP, 2009l: 35).

Three main target groups were identified to receive WFP food assistance in Darfur: IDPs in camps, IDPs outside camps and their host populations, and rural non-displaced people. The primary sources of information for planning and targeting relief food distribution included annual food security and nutrition assessments, and more localized needs assessments conducted in response to changes in local situations brought about by new attacks by armed groups. Distribution lists were set up by a registration process conducted in 2005. Ration cards were issued to heads of households, which recorded their dependents. Most of the annual forward planning of targeted resource needs was based on what happened in the previous year or by localized needs assessments that were conducted as allowed by local events and circumstances. The WFP entered into contracts with co-operating partners to distribute the food it provided to those in need, in line with its policy commitment of beneficiary involvement in the distribution of its food assistance (WFP, 2004g).[22]

An evaluation of the WFP emergency assistance programme in Darfur was carried out in 2007.[23] It concluded that WFP staff in the Sudan had worked hard to fill the food gap in Darfur in very difficult circumstances. Over 560,000 tons of food had been distributed between April 2004 and December 2005, which was described as a 'triumph'. In 2005, the Darfur operation, one of the largest that the WFP had ever undertaken, accounted for over 20 per cent of total WFP expenditure. In the view of the evaluation team, without this massive food assistance there would have been significant nutritional distress, increased illness, and death. To avert such a disaster was an achievement that 'justifies the existence of WFP'.

The WFP showed that it was highly capable of meeting formidable logistical difficulties. Road, rail and, when necessary, air transport was used in getting food to Darfur. The region was isolated from the main food markets in Sudan, and the amount of food needed was larger than the normal market mechanism could provide quickly. The long distances from the landing ports in Sudan, Libya, and Cameroon made it difficult to reach the remote areas of Darfur timely and consistently. Darfur is 2,000 km from Port Sudan. The route from the port of Douala in Cameroun through Chad is extremely hazardous in the rainy season. An alternative route, unaffected by seasonal rains, was opened with the agreement of the Libyan government through the Saharan desert, but trucks take at least three weeks to cover the 2,800 km to Darfur.

Road transport is hampered by poor infrastructure and the lack of paved roads. Large areas are inaccessible during the rainy season between July and October. The rail link to Darfur is slow and unreliable. Further constraints on logistics capacity are experienced through competition for transport from the agricultural sector and the expanding oil industry, and lack of fuel and spare parts for local transport contractors. Reliable transport is required to transport food over long and difficult routes. The WFP purchased 120 all-terrain 6x6 trucks from the Netherlands and planned the purchase of a further 150 heavy-duty trucks. A dedicated fleet of leased trucks was nearly 350-strong by the end of 2004, in addition to others hired on a piece-work basis.

Insecurity is another major constraining factor for both humanitarian staff and operations. Many of the most important roads of the Darfur region were closed to UN personnel for lengthy periods, often the result of random acts of banditry, which became increasingly more frequent during 2004. In some cases, insecurity forced the WFP to evacuate its staff from locations particularly at risk. In August 2004, three WFP staff and three employees of the Sudan Red Crescent were abducted in north Darfur and released four days later. In October 2004, a British and a Sudanese aid work were killed when their vehicle hit a landmine. In 2005, direct assaults on the humanitarian community began with attacks on clearly marked convoys; and UN and NGO staff were robbed, intimidated, and harassed. In October 2005, three Nigerian peacekeepers of the joint UN/AU forced were killed. Attacks on aid workers in Darfur accelerated in the latter half of 2005 when 12 Sudanese relief workers were killed. More than 400 UN and NGO staff were evacuated during 31 separate incidents in the last six months of 2006. In December 2006, armed insurgents broke into the world's largest IDP camp in Darfur and attacked aid workers. As a result, one of the WFP's co-operating partners was forced to withdraw, leaving 130,000 people without food until the ICRC could take over.

Trucks carrying WFP food were targeted by armed looters, and the railway line into Darfur was attacked on several occasions. In the first nine months of 2007, 98 vehicles were high-jacked, 61 convoys ambushed, 100 staff kidnapped, 66 assaulted, and five killed (WFP, 2007c). In 2008, 110 trucks delivering WFP food were hijacked before reaching the IDP camps. These factors significantly increased the cost of the WFP's food assistance programme. Innovative measures were taken by the WFP country office to improve efficiency and effectiveness including: borrowing from other emergency operations in Sudan; assisting local contractors to get trucks; providing a security team to clear areas; and establishing a distribution storage network with pre-positioned stocks to enable food distribution to continue during the rainy season.

Despite the considerable difficulties, the WFP remained committed to the principle of broad-based participation of beneficiaries, national and local government, civil-society organizations, and other parties in its food assistance programmes, to 'contribute their knowledge, skills and resources to processes that influence their lives' (WFP, 2004g). The WFP involved women and men beneficiaries in all activities wherever possible, and worked closely with governments at the national and local levels to plan and implement its food assistance.

A series of studies was commissioned by the WFP into targeting its assistance in complex emergencies with the support of the European Commission's Humanitarian Aid Office (ECHO), the Canadian International Development Agency (CIDA), and the United Kingdom Department for International Development (DFID). One study conducted in Darfur in October 2008 provided one of the most compelling insights into the interplay of forces at work within complex, protracted emergency situations (Young and Maxwell, 2009).[24] Although a literature review suggested that community-based targeting worked best in slow-onset emergencies with no conflict or population displacement, participatory approaches to targeting assistance had been attempted in complex emergencies, either directly by elected relief committees, or indirectly through unelected but representative leaders. The study examined community participation throughout the food aid programme cycle, from initial assessment to final evaluation, to understand the role of recipient committees in the targeting of food assistance under the conflict conditions pertaining in Darfur.

The study found that understanding local governance, including humanitarian governance, was crucial to identifying options for enhancing local participation in targeting food distributions. This included an analysis of the role of the FRCs set up by the WFP, which represented a new governance institution with its own system and rules. The study also investigated the role food assistance played in humanitarian protection. Fifteen different stakeholder groups were found to be involved in the WFP's food assistance programme cycle. This showing the complexities in which targeting of food assistance was directly and indirectly influenced and affected by a wide range of interest groups. The degree of influence of the stakeholders varied depending on location and circumstances. Some of their roles were formal and some more informal.[25]

The views and positions of these interest groups became more entrenched as the Darfur crisis became prolonged. This particularly applied to the IDPs, especially those in camps. They depended entirely on food assistance and had no access to alternative livelihoods. As the study revealed, they came to claim a 'right to food', which was closely interwoven with the 'right to protection' more broadly. This, in turn, was closely intertwined with other politicized claims that lay at the heart of what was called 'the IDP identity'. While the categorization of beneficiaries as IDPs was a pragmatic and practical response to the problem of targeting, the risk was that it reinforced a political claim to food assistance. The study therefore concluded that, as long as food entitlements were closely linked with wider and more highly politicized claims, 'there remains very limited potential for community-based targeting in this complex setting' (Young and Maxwell, 2009: 9).

The WFP was responsible for many elements of the food assistance process, including overall policy and targeting. Although many other parties were involved, it had primary responsibility for the registration of beneficiaries. Holding a WFP ration card was the primary form of IDP identification. Field-level agreements with co-operating partners set distribution programmes for periods of six months. The WFP conducted the major needs assessments that determined the level of needs for donor response, as well as conducting occasional market assessments. Crucially, the WFP was also responsible for the logistics of the food assistance operation and for food pipeline management that ensured that food assistance was supplied consistently.

The WFP's co-operating partners were responsible for more local-level assessments of food needs. They played a significant role in the registration of beneficiaries and were responsible for food distribution, training, and oversight of the FRCs, and for conducting post-distribution monitoring. The IOM was responsible for verifying food recipient lists and for maintaining a database on population displacements that was also designed to track the movement of IDPs from one camp or location to another. The OCHA had responsibility for the overall co-ordination of the humanitarian response. The Humanitarian Aid

Committee was the main government office involved in the policy and administration of humanitarian assistance, and was widely believed to have a security function.

The initial registration of those in need was particularly difficult not only because of the large number of people involved, spread out over a vast area, but also because they were constantly moving, displaced by new insurgencies, which also restricted access to them due to high levels of insecurity. Inevitably, there were errors of inclusion (which led to multiple food card holders) and exclusion (especially of people located outside camps). Registration and ration cards were controlled by local leaders in the larger, more politicized IDP camps. Resistance to improved registration by local leaders who had acquired multiple ration cards became a significant security issue. Rumour was also rife that the Humanitarian Aid Commission set up by the Sudanese government was intent on getting the IDPs out of camps and sent back to their villages, many of which had been totally destroyed during the insurgency.

These factors made the re-registration process that was carried out by the WFP, IOM and OCHA in 2005 much more difficult and dangerous. In many places, the re-registration process was undermined. The resulting lists were not an accurate reflection of the actual numbers of IDPs. It was largely successful, however, in rationalizing the number of people living in camps at the time. But a comprehensive means of tracking the movement of IDPs was not established, and remains an unresolved issue.[26] In 2005, the inclusion error for IDP households in camps (those judged by their assets and income to be able to afford an adequate diet from their own means) was calculated at 12.9 per cent. The exclusion error (those eligible but who did not receive food assistance) was estimated at 4.9 per cent. By 2007, the exclusion error was recalculated at 28 per cent and the inclusion error at 22 per cent. A common exclusion error was said to be that households now had more members than were recorded on their ration cards.

An important feature of the WFP's food assistance programme was the establishment of the FRCs. Originally, it was envisaged that at least 50 per cent of FRC members would be women. The FRCs created a new institution within the humanitarian governance system that linked tribal leaders to government. It brought with it its own system and rules in the form of humanitarian principles, overarching policies, and operational guidelines, thereby creating additional tiers of local government administration, and adding to the complexity of food assistance operations.

The FACs fell short of their original objectives in a number of ways. The participation of women was generally weak, and certainly not equal, reflecting women's position in traditional Sudanese society. The FACs were generally controlled by local tribal leaders. Members were usually chosen by local tribal leaders, rather than elected as representatives of their communities. Their main function tended to be limited to helping in the distribution of food assistance, particularly in IDP camps. They ensured continuity of food distribution when the security situation deteriorated to the point that staff of the WFP's co-operating partners could not reach distribution points. FACs proved to be particularly valuable when international and national NGOs were expelled from Darfur in March 2009.

The complexity of the Darfur crisis was carried to the international level by the dysfunction between those concerned with saving lives and those intent on addressing human rights issues and bringing to justice the perpetrators of the human catastrophe. The UN Security Council referred the Darfur crisis to the International Criminal Court (ICC). On 4 March 2009, the ICC issued warrants for the arrest of senior Sudanese government officials, and later the president of Sudan himself, for war crimes and crimes against humanity. The charge of genocide was dropped, but could be reinstated with more evidence. The governments that ratified the Rome treaty creating the ICC are obliged to bring the accused to justice. The Sudanese government's reaction was as swift as it was predictable. Thirteen international NGOs were expelled from Darfur and three national NGOs had their licenses revoked (ALNAP/HPG, 2009).[27] A total of over 600 aid workers were involved, about half of whom were international staff and half national. About 40 per cent of the aid workers present in Darfur at the time were expelled. They had delivered over half of the total amount of aid provided to over 2.7 million IDPs and an unknown number of victims of the crisis outside camps.

After the expulsions, the WFP continued to operate its logistics system of getting food to distribution points through private contractors. The WFP was also able to organize an emergency distribution through the FRCs and, with the help of 200 national staff, borrowed from some of the expelled NGOs on a temporary basis. The role and importance of the FRCs was therefore significantly increased, although without supervision. It was appreciated that any reductions in food assistance, or unequal distribution between different areas and camps, could increase the risk of violence, especially in the camps themselves. Also, ensuring the protection of civilians would become more difficult. The mandated protection agencies – the ICRC, UNHCR, and UNCEF – were not expelled, but their work was significantly increased by the expulsions. A sudden decrease in aid could further destabilize the security situation in Darfur, especially in the already overcrowded camps, and could result in significant population movements.

In June 2006, the WFP and the Feinstein International Center at Tufts University in the United States organized a three-day forum in Khartoum, Sudan on the future of WFP programming in Sudan.[28] The most consistently raised question at the forum was 'What is the WFP'? Was it a food delivery agency, an emergency food security agency, or an emergency intervention agency? The question was asked because the potential for the WFP to evolve was seen in its track record, its unparalleled presence in Sudan, and its innovations in responding to large-scale and complex emergency situations. The WFP's partners seemed unsure about whether this added up to a changing WFP, or just to adaptations to the moment. An answer to the question was necessary if the WFP were to build the partnerships based on trust that would be necessary for the future (Gelsdorf *et al.*, 2007: S7).

In August 2008, the WFP embarked upon an ambitious new programme in north Darfur. This was designed to help bridge the lean season between harvests when malnutrition particularly affected children between the ages of six months and five years. Initially, it targeted 180,000 children with supplementary feeding in addition to the WFP's general food distribution programme. Training is also provided to mothers and community leaders to raise awareness about malnutrition and its relation to food, health, and care-giving practices. They also learn about the composition of the WFP blended food ration, consisting of a mixture of dried skimmed milk, sugar, and corn-soya blend enriched with essential vitamins, minerals, and other micronutrients.

At the time of writing (March 2011), there is still no sign that this protracted humanitarian catastrophe can be brought to an end. At the same time, the Sudanese government appears to be encouraged by US President Obama's talk of engaging with nations, rather than isolating them. UN officials said that there was little evidence that the government was sponsoring ethnic violence, as it was accused of doing in the past. The cataclysmic predictions of the past few years had not come true. The big Sudanese government offensive that many feared would take place in 2006 and 2007, the attacks by large numbers of marauding bandits against refugee camps, and widespread disease and death as a result of the expulsion of foreign aid organization did not occur. The hybrid African Union-UN peacekeeping mission, the most expensive in the world at $1.6 billion per year, was in place.

This has raised the question of what the future holds. The Comprehensive Peace Agreement for Darfur is still in place. But many of the displaced appear not to be ready to venture home. If they did, they fear there would be tribal war resulting from one of the biggest problems in Darfur, fighting between different ethnic groups over shrinking grazing land, and the reinstating of livelihoods (Young, 2007). Some camp dwellers have begun to take up jobs in nearby towns (Young, 2009). Also, markets are beginning to function more fully. The focus in Sudan seems to be steadily shifting south, where rebels have fought a separatist war for decades. The region voted on its independence in January 2011 and overwhelmingly decided to separate from the northern part of the country, which is scheduled to take place in July 2011. According to UN officials, more than 2,000 people were killed in 2009, many more than in Darfur.

The root cause of conflict in the southern Sudan and Darfur remains the same: their marginalization. One glimmer of hope is that, for the first time, camp elders, religious figures, and women leaders are being given prominent roles in the peace talks. In the meantime, in April 2010 the Sudanese president won the first national election in 25 years held by a wide margin. The global arrest warrant for the president issued by the ICC citing charges of war crimes and crimes against humanity, to which was later added genocide for his role in the humanitarian crisis in Darfur, has restricted his movements abroad, especially to any of the 111 countries that have joined the ICC, 30 of which are in Africa. While governments have seemingly stopped trying to undermine this rare warrant for a sitting head of state, there was also broad recognition that the president could play a critical role in carrying out a peaceful referendum in 2011, which he did. The referendum resulted in overwhelming support for the independence of southern Sudan. Meanwhile, the Sudanese president has visited Chad and Kenya, both signatories to the ICC, without being arrested. He has also announced that he will not seek another term as president.

Special, 'new wave', emergency operations

War in Bosnia-Herzegovina 1992–95: UNHCR/WFP joint operations

With the collapse of the Federal Republic of Yugoslavia in 1991, war broke out between the newly formed republics that resulted in some of the worst atrocities seen in Europe since the Second World War (1939–45). Conflict was particularly severe in Bosnia and Herzegovina (BiH) between the Muslim Bosnian, Croatian, and Serbian populations, with all sides being accused of ethnic cleansing and genocide.[29] Continuation of these acts by the Bosnian Serbs eventually resulted in a massive NATO bombing campaign targeting Serbian artillery positions throughout Bosnia that led to a peace agreement on 21 December 1995. Bosnia was divided into two main parts, known as the Muslim-Croat Federation and the Bosnian Serb Republic. By this time, an estimated over 200,000 Muslims had been systematically murdered, over 20,000 people were missing, and over 2 million had become refugees or displaced persons.

Against this background, humanitarian assistance operations were launched which, at the time, were among the largest ever undertaken by the international community. Between 1992 and 1996, an average of 2.6 million people were given humanitarian assistance, the majority of them in BiH. At the height of the conflict in BiH, there were some 1.2 million displaced persons and another 1.4 million people with no means of support. It was estimated that 80 per cent of the population of BiH received food assistance provided by the UNHCR and WFP at one time or another. Beneficiaries in all the former Yugoslav republics increased from 500,000 in December 1991 to over 3 million in December 1992.

The scale and complexity of the situation called for close co-operation between the UNHCR and WFP in difficult and dangerous joint wartime operations. A joint UNHCR/WFP evaluation of humanitarian operations in BiH in 1998 established that co-operative arrangements between the two organizations were divided into three phases (WFP, 1998e). Between 1991 and late 1992, the UNHCR became the lead agency for humanitarian relief supply and distribution. The second phase of co-operation was between late 1992 and 1995. During the first half of 1992, the seriousness of the crisis and scale of humanitarian operations required became increasingly evident. The UN system, and the UNHCR in particular, requested the WFP to assume the role of co-ordinating and managing resource mobilization and delivery of food to extended delivery points, based on working arrangements already agreed upon between the UNHCR and WFP, in recognition of the WFP's capacity as a manager of large-scale international relief operations. In assuming this operational role, it was understood that the WFP's resource mobilization efforts should only involve and generate *additional* (original emphasis) multilateral and bilateral commodity pledges without in any way detracting from or diverting necessary food resources from other WFP activities. The third phase of co-operation was between 1995 and 1997, when the peace agreement was negotiated and hostilities ended, and the management of the food chain within BiH was handed over to the WFP.

The humanitarian operations provided an extreme example of the difficulties confronting humanitarian agencies in complex, war-induced, emergency situations. The joint UNHCR/WFP evaluation mission found that it was to the credit of both organizations that, even under the extremely difficult and politically complex conditions of war, food assistance reached the neediest, and widespread hunger and malnutrition were averted. For isolated populations in besieged cities and towns, however, insecurity and inaccessibility made food distribution particularly difficult. When access by land was denied, distribution was made by air transport, as in the difficult and relatively successful air-drop operations on Srebrenica, Gorazde, and Zepa.

The protracted airlift operations into Sarajevo added considerably to the total cost of humanitarian operations. The evaluation mission suggested that more attention should have been paid to maximizing the amount of food delivered by providing a food basket constituted of food items with high nutritional value in relation to their volume. Irregular and unpredictable food supplies were experienced, which resulted in urgent and frequent calls to donors. Targeting became increasingly possible, so that localized levels of under- and over-supply were gradually corrected. Overall, co-operation and communications between the two organizations were described as 'remarkably good', although there were some difficulties during the transfer of responsibility from UNHCR to WFP.

The evaluation mission was asked to address the controversial question of the time as to whether provision of humanitarian assistance had prolonged the conflict. It could be argued that, by giving generous support to food assistance, donors were able to defend themselves against the charge of inaction in Bosnia. By so doing, the military intervention needed to end the conflict was postponed. The evaluation mission found that this was a criticism of the priorities and political will of the international community, rather than of food aid itself. It found no evidence that providing humanitarian assistance deflected public opinion from supporting military action. On the contrary, it noted that the provision of such assistance brought with it additional international media coverage, which it found to be 'a precursor to eventual decisive intervention'.

But did humanitarian assistance prolong the war by giving material assistance to the combatants? In the view of the evaluation mission, the conflict might have been shorter but the suffering greater, and the outcome could have been the division of BiH among its neighbours. It found no convincing case that the risk of increased suffering that would have occurred in the absence of humanitarian supports could have been justified by an increase in the prospect of a swifter and more satisfying outcome of the conflict.

There were some unavoidable negative political effects of the humanitarian operation. Distribution of assistance was under the control of the authorities *in situ*. Bargaining with them and agreeing to use the channels they controlled inevitably reinforced their authority to some extent. In some cases, taxes were levied by the military authorities to allow food convoys to pass. These were systematically resisted by UNHCR field staff, who were given specific and repeated instructions not to do so. Occasionally, field staff underwent pressure to relinquish aid and, on some occasions, food was seized, sometimes at gun point, illustrating the tense context to which humanitarian aid workers are subjected and the difficult duties they have to perform.

In 1997, the WFP's executive director and the FAO's director-general jointly approved an extension of emergency food assistance for 1.7 million returnees, refugees, IDPs, and other war affected people in the republics of the former Yugoslavia. Although the local availability of fresh food had improved significantly, the limited purchasing power of large parts of the population restricted access to it. The resettlement of IDPs and the return of refugees were described as being 'exasperatingly slow', and large-scale return was not expected to begin in earnest until after the winter months. In BiH, the economic and social infrastructure was shattered and employment prospects were, for the most part, 'bleak'.

In the still fragile peace environment, the UN foresaw the need for continued humanitarian assistance over a two-year stabilization period. Emergency food assistance was gradually phased down and redirected. In BiH, the number of beneficiaries was reduced from 2 million in December 1996 to 1 million in December 1997, and assistance focused on the neediest. General food distribution was scaled down and gradually shifted from its initial role of providing nutritional support to that of income support for vulnerable groups. This was achieved primarily through directing food distribution on a more selective basis to the most vulnerable through support of employment creation and other income-generating activities. Small-scale rehabilitation activities were community-based, gender focused, and time-limited. A project to rehabilitate kindergartens, managed by the international NGO Action Contre la Faim, received WFP food assistance to provide school meals for 1,500 children. Other schemes were explored, such as support for women's groups, and public works programmes with the World Bank. The WFP assisted municipalities in selecting beneficiaries and food distribution as part of its capacity-building strategy.

Iraq: UN oil-for-food programme

In 2003, at the request of the UN Security Council, the WFP was mandated to ensure that the national food distribution system in Iraq was kept working. Through the UN oil-for-food programme, proceeds from the sale of Iraqi oil were used to import food and other basic needs.[30] During more than a decade of war and economic sanctions, the entire population of Iraq of 27 million had become increasingly reliant on the public food-distribution system. The nutritional status of the vulnerable groups, particularly children, had deteriorated as a result of government policies and a failing social infrastructure, including the national health system. The challenges of setting up and maintaining a national food distribution system in a country and region affected by war and insecurity were considerable.

Food distribution was continued despite bombing in Baghdad by the warring factions, which led to serious destruction to the UN headquarters and the killing of the UN humanitarian co-ordinator, Sergio de Mello, and other UN staff.

To fulfil its mandate, the WFP transferred 375 international staff to Iraq and to neighbouring countries to work with 1,100 Iraqi staff. Another 118 personnel were obtained through standby arrangements with donor relief agencies. The WFP carried out its largest ever logistical operation (WFP, 2004h). Between April and November 2003, a joint WFP/Iraq Ministry of Trade team negotiated 409 international oil-for-food contracts involving 2.76 million tons of food, valued at $1.41 billion. The WFP delivered over 2 million tons of food into Iraq from the UN oil-for-food programme and 750,000 tons of contributions from donors. This was enough to cover a seven-monthly distribution cycle to the national population, including Iraqis returning from neighbouring countries and people internally displaced throughout Iraq. A supplementary feeding programme for school children, pregnant and lactating women, and other vulnerable groups was also expanded. With training and support, Iraqi national staff and officials were increasing able to take over the management of the national food distribution system as WFP staff phased out.

Given the unprecedented size of the Iraq operation, the WFP considered that having all aspects of the operation, from planning through procurement to shipping and final delivery, under one chain of command within the WFP Iraq country office was 'extremely beneficial', and a key element in the success of the operation (WFP, 2004h).

In 2004, the WFP continued to support the Ministry of Trade in Iraq to ensure a regular food ration to the Iraqi people, despite the volatile situation in the country. The WFP procured and secured the transport of 1.6 million tons of food on behalf of the ministry to establish a three-month buffer stock. This was the largest single amount ever procured by the WFP. In addition, the WFP also provided food through the public distribution system to the large number of Iraqis returning home from neighbouring countries and to internally displaced people. Although WFP international staff had been relocated outside Iraq, these operations were successfully carried out through an effective network established between out-posted WFP international staff, and Iraqi national staff and government officials.

In 2004, a baseline food security survey was carried out in Iraq. The survey, the first of its kind to be conducted in the country, found that some 6.5 million people (25 per cent of the entire population) were highly dependent on food rations through the public distribution system. Some 2.6 million were so poor that they had to sell part of their food rations to buy other basic necessities, such as medicines and clothes. A further 3.6 million (14 per cent of the country's population) would become food-insecure if the rationing system were discontinued. In June 2004, the WFP and the World Bank jointly published a study analyzing the functioning of Iraq's food grain market, and the relative roles of the public and private sectors. In August 2004, the two organizations signed a 'letter of intent' outlining their collaboration in analyzing the likely impact of various reform proposals for the public distribution system. This collaboration was carried further in 2005, with a view to providing the Iraqi government with policy advice on food security and safety net options.

Emergency operation in the Lebanon

On 13 July 2006, in response to a series of rocket attacks on northern Israel by the Hezbollah militia organization based in southern Lebanon, and the kidnapping of two Israeli solders the previous day, Israel launched a series of air strikes not only on Hezbollah positions, but also on key transport infrastructure – roads, bridges and ports – throughout the country, and on Beirut International Airport. More than half a million people were forced to flee their homes. Many sought refuge in northern Lebanon. Some 95,000 displaced people packed into schools, public buildings, and parks in Beirut, joined by many from the Hezbollah-occupied parts of Beirut's southern suburbs. A further 140,000 people fled across the border into Syria. In southern Lebanon, which bore the brunt of the bombing and shelling, those who could not leave – the oldest, weakest and poorest – faced immediate hardship. Goods and services disappeared as shops and markets closed, and electricity and water supplies were cut off. A major humanitarian crisis loomed.

The government, civil society, and NGOs in Lebanon acted swiftly with the resources they had on hand to help the war-affected displaced population. However, the suddenness and magnitude of the destruction was such that the government requested humanitarian assistance from the international community. The WFP geared up fast to respond to the crisis (WFP, 2006d: 13–18). Within a week, an assessment team was on the ground to work out the requirements for food, logistics and security support. An emergency plan to provide food to those in greatest need was finalized as part of a $130 million UN Flash Appeal. Initially, the WFP planned to supply some 300,000 people with food, valued at $8.9 million. As many beneficiaries did not have access to cooking facilities, ready-to-eat foods were provided, including high-energy biscuits and canned products. Flour was also provided to support bread production through NGOs and commercial bakeries.

All WFP activities were carried out in close co-ordination with the Lebanese government, particularly its High Relief Committee and the Ministry of Social Affairs. As the lead UN logistics agency, the WFP also assumed responsibility for transporting all UN aid supplies within the Lebanon, as well as on behalf of a number of NGOs. In total, the WFP transported 25,500 tons of food and non-food relief items for 38 organizations by land, sea, and air. Among the non-food relief items were fuel, shelter materials, water, and medical equipment. The WFP also helped the government import 12,300 tons of wheat during the period of the Israeli blockade. There were formidable logistical and security challenges. The air strikes had paralyzed the country. WFP food convoys had to take circuitous mountain routes over narrow dirt roads and across temporary river bridges jammed with fleeing civilians to bypass the broken road system, adding considerably to the time taken to reach people in desperate need. Constant bombing meant that new routes had to be regularly explored. There was also the constant danger of a large number of unexploded bombs and ordnance. As the conflict wore on, it became harder to find haulage companies and drivers prepared to join the aid convoys. Movement of humanitarian supplies was also hampered by a shortage of trucks suitable for crossing difficult and rugged terrain.

The supply by the Swedish Rescue Service Agency of a fleet of heavy trucks and support vehicles, with drivers and mechanics, made a crucial difference to the WFP's ability to deliver aid on behalf of the entire humanitarian community. Security of aid deliveries was another major problem. The WFP developed a system of 'concurrence on safety', whereby all sides in the conflict were provided with details of each convoy the day before its planned departure, including the number of trucks and escort vehicles, the exact route, and the planned times of departure and arrival. No WFP convoy would proceed without receiving concurrence from all sides. As a result, no WFP convoy came under attack at any time.[31]

The cessation of hostilities brought a new phase to the WFP emergency operations. The lifting of the Israeli blockade gave far greater access with the reopening of Beirut International Airport and renewed access to the sea ports of Beirut, Tripoli, and Tyre to international shipping. During the hostilities, WFP efforts had been concentrated on providing relief assistance to the displaced population throughout the country. Now, relief efforts were directed to all affected by the war. These included those who had been unable to leave their homes and the large number of people returning to their former locations, many to find that their houses had been destroyed.

During the time taken for normal activities and regular commerce to be re-established, the humanitarian assistance provided by the WFP was vital to fill the gap in basic needs. In late August and early September 2006, WFP staff carried out a two-week assessment to establish whether there was a need for continuing humanitarian assistance. It was found that, while some people were still suffering the effects of the war, especially those whose homes had been destroyed, food was again available at affordable prices throughout the country, including the southern parts where markets were showing encouraging signs of recovery.

The assessment recommended that the WFP continue food assistance to those in need until the end of October 2006. Over the previous three months, the WFP had built up an operation – run, at its peak, by 150 international and national staff – to provide 13,000 tons of food to some 824,000 people, and to deliver more than 2,000 tons of non-food items, carried out in the midst of conflict and its aftermath. At the end of October 2006, WFP staff left as quickly as they arrived as humanitarian operations were brought to a successful end.[32]

Myanmar: swift assistance to cyclone victims

On 2 May 2008, cyclone Nargis swept across southern Myanmar leaving a trail of death and destruction. Whole villages were obliterated and more than 140,000 people died in the first 24 hours. Over 2.4 million people were left without homes, food, or livelihoods as the cyclone shattered infrastructure and destroyed food stores, seeds, and livestock. The Ayeyarwady delta, the country's rice bowl and a rich fishing ground, bore the brunt of the storm. Large-scale crop losses, combined with the destruction of farm tools and equipment, and fishing boats and gear, crippled almost all income-generating opportunities in the region. The condition of the poor, dependent on waged labour for survival, was particularly serious.

Within four days of the cyclone striking Myanmar, a quick-response emergency operation was approved under the delegated authority of the WFP country director for 40,000 people to provide food for one month as a tidying-over measure until further assistance could be approved. Six days later, the WFP's executive director and the FAO's director-general jointly approved an emergency operation to provide 924,000 beneficiaries with food for one year at a total cost to the WFP of $69.5 million. In addition, a special operation was approved to expedite the movement and delivery of food at a cost of $39 million.

WFP intervention was decisive in two respects (WFP, 2009n). First, teaming up with other international and UN agencies, the WFP led the way in securing the military government's permission to gain international access to the country and to co-ordinate the much-needed relief efforts that helped prevent further loss of life from disease and exposure in the aftermath of the storm. Second, under the WFP's special operation, an uninterrupted supply chain of relief supplies to affected areas was established by setting up common logistics and telecommunications services. Activities included: establishing an air hub in Bangkok; providing an air bridge between Bangkok and Yangon in Myanmar; marshalling air, land, and water transport within the delta region; managing logistics hubs with storage facilities; and providing inter-agency telecommunications infrastructure and services.

More than 230 air cargo flights carried 5,000 tons of relief materials into Yangon from Bangkok. Some 10,400 tons of supplies were delivered deep into the delta by road and waterways, and about 30,000 square metres of storage space was created. In the early stages of the relief operation, the WFP deployed ten helicopters to ferry goods, including water purification units, and humanitarian aid workers to areas severely affected by the cyclone. As land and water transport gradually improved, the helicopter fleet was concomitantly reduced. This service had proved invaluable, flying almost 1,900 hours while carrying 22,000 aid workers and more than 1,000 tons of light cargo for 41 UN and government agencies, as well as local and international NGOs.

That the WFP was able to mount such a quick emergency response was largely due to the presence and initiatives of the WFP's national staff in Myanmar. This was particularly needed in the immediate aftermath of the cyclone when the military government imposed travel restrictions and delayed granting visas to foreign aid workers. In the first thirty days, the WFP's local staff delivered almost 500 tons of emergency rations to more than 24,000 displaced people in temporary shelters, including monasteries and public buildings. Rations were shared among those in the shelters as the numbers seeking refuge grew daily.

For those without cooking facilities and utensils, the WFP provided 17 tons of high-energy biscuits. More than 49,000 beneficiaries also received cash assistance for several weeks in Yangon, where markets were still functioning, until the government suspended this element of the emergency operation in June 2008. Some 76,000 people were also supported though food-for-work activities including the reconstruction of dykes, footpaths, and fish ponds. At the height of this large-scale emergency operation, the WFP had used a combination of helicopter, tracks, and barges to deliver relief food assistance to more than 1 million people.

Georgia: the aftermath of the fall of the Soviet Union

The sudden collapse of the Soviet Union and the emergence of new independent states on the southern border of the Russian Federation led to conflict and humanitarian crises throughout the north Caucasus region (Hansen, 1998). Different ethnic groups, backed by militias, paramilitary forces, and self-styled partisans, sought to gain authority. The conflict assumed an international dimension by creating political tension between Russia and the United States and the European Union.

One example of the resulting conflict, political tensions, and humanitarian action was that of Georgia, which declared its independence in 1991(Hansen, 2009). The borders of the new state encompassed two enclaves on its northern frontier with the Russian Federation, Abkhazia and South Ossetia, which for ethnic and historical reasons sought secession from Georgia, a claim supported by Russia. The conflict was taken to a new height when Georgian forces attacked South Ossetia in August 2008. They were repulsed by the Russian army, which invaded, Georgia cutting off strategic transport routes. The UNHCR estimated that some 163,000 people were forced to flee their homes as a result of the new conflict. The displaced persons were added to those who had been displaced by previous conflicts. Any prospect of their returning home was now made even more remote. There were over 1,000 collective centres in Georgia for displaced people from previous conflicts, many in a terrible condition.

The conflict showed a number of cross-cutting issues and concerns that appeared in similar conflict situations elsewhere, including: donor and military dominance; the need for coherence between political, military, and humanitarian agencies, and between military and humanitarian workers; the problem of maintaining neutral, impartial, and independent assistance in the spirit of Good Humanitarian Donorship; and widespread insecurity among aid beneficiaries and humanitarian workers.

The WFP was able to respond quickly to the humanitarian crisis caused by the August 2008 war by using food stocks from its existing emergency operations in the region to feed 212,000 vulnerable people in Georgia, many of whom were newly displaced by the fighting (WFP, 2009n).[33] Initially, WFP assistance was restricted to the capital, Tbilisi, where, only two days after the crisis erupted, the WFP was able to provide a ten-day ration of wheat flour, vegetable oil, beans, sugar, and salt to displaced people in shelters. The WFP emergency operation was soon expanded to other parts of the country. By the end of August 2008, more than 138,000 people had been reached, including those displaced and the local population affected by the conflict.

In the early days of the conflict, fighting cut off access to the combat zones. On 27 August, the WFP opened a sub-office in Gori, and established warehouses to supply the town and surrounding villages in the 'buffer zone'. Flour was delivered to three bakeries in Gori to supply bread to some 9,000 people. Tensions eased on 8 September 2008, when Russia agreed to withdraw its forces from all Georgian territory outside South Ossetia and Abkhazia, and to dismantle its checkpoints in other parts of Georgia. The first distribution in the buffer zone took place on 11 September after the WFP negotiated access with the general commanding Russian forces.

Since many of the shelters accommodating displaced people were without cooking facilities, the WFP endeavoured to provide prepared foods, such as bread and high-energy biscuits, wherever possible. It also provided food to soup kitchens set up by the Georgian government and charities to supply hot meals. By the end of 2008, the WFP had reached 244,000 beneficiaries with 8,500 tons of food. In October, the UN launched a revised flash appeal, putting the food security sector needs at $32 million, with $20 million for the WFP. In addition, the WFP appealed for $2.5 million to provide logistics co-ordination and inter-agency storage capacity and transport.

The overall response to the August 2008 conflict in Georgia was ultimately far more political than humanitarian (Hansen, 2009: 31). The humanitarian response highlighted that the humanitarian system is largely ineffective when confronted by the blatant and dangerous politicization of humanitarian responses by donors who disregard the Good Humanitarian Donorship guidelines, to which they have given an undertaken, on the use of the military.[34] The future of the many displaced by the recent and previous conflicts was placed in jeopardy by heightened political instability and the failure of the combatants to reach a political settlement. Unable to return home, they were left in desperate situations, dependent on continued humanitarian assistance.

The new humanitarian crisis was superimposed on top of earlier crises, with the underlying issues ineffectively addressed. The scaling down of donor support for a number of years in the 1990s and early 2000s, only to be reactivated in August 2008, confirmed the need for a continuous and consistent long-term multilateral humanitarian effort that takes the needs of all those adversely affected into equal account, including support of the action plan for the Georgian government's strategy for the displaced population adopted in May 2009. Russia and Georgia agreed to reopen their major border crossing on 24 December 2009, signalling the first thawing of relations between the two countries since they went to war in August 2008. The two countries have not had diplomatic relations since then. Russia insists that it will have no direct contact with the Georgian president, but has expressed more willingness to lessen its pressure on Georgia. Much will also depend on the future stance of the United States and the EU over the conflict in Georgia. In the meantime, the appalling conditions endured by the displaced population on both sides of the conflict line continue to contribute to the political instability of the country.

Chapter 4 will look more closely at the main elements of what is called the 'anatomy' of WFP emergency operations.

4
Anatomy of WFP Emergency Operations

This chapter dissects the complex structure of WFP emergency operations to examine the four main elements that were involved in the WFP's shift of focus from development to relief assistance:

- the strategic redeployment of WFP staff and of decision-making from headquarters to the WFP regional bureaux and country offices in developing countries;
- the WFP's transport and logistics expertise and experience;
- the benefits of new communications and information technology; and
- the development and strengthening of partnerships and co-operation with other major humanitarian agencies, other UN and international organizations, NGOs, and the private sector.

In reality, these four elements were implemented at the same time. They are discussed separately here to obtain a clear understanding of their importance. But for all this to happen in a consistent and cohesive way, a new policy and operational framework was required that pulled the strands together, and provided guidelines and training for WFP field staff and partners to implement them.

Towards a comprehensive policy and operational framework for WFP emergency operations

As the focus shifted from providing development assistance to emergency relief operations, the policy and operational framework to guide the WFP's work had also to change. A series of policy and operational proposals that reflected this shift in emphasis were presented by the WFP secretariat to the executive board for approval. These proposals took into account the established policy contained in the WFP's *General Regulations* (2008), the WFP *Mission Statement* (1994) concerning the purposes and functions of the WFP and, later, the objectives laid out in the WFP *Strategic Plan (2008–11)*, which was extended to 2013.

The WFP secretariat also took into account the UN General Assembly resolutions that led to reform in the UN system. The governing bodies of the WFP and of the other UN funds and programmes (UNDP, UNFPA and UNICEF) were transformed into executive boards in order to ensure effective interaction between the UN General Assembly, ECOSOC, and the individual executive boards. Also, there was co-ordination of UN humanitarian assistance; and Millennium Development Goals were established, which the UN agencies, including the WFP, are committed to achieve. The policy and operational proposals were also influenced by the international principles governing the effectiveness of aid as set out in the *Paris Declaration on Aid Effectiveness* (2005) and by the *ACCRA High-level Forum on Aid Effectiveness* (2008). Also, some policy formulations endeavoured to extend the frontiers of traditional food aid into food assistance programmes to fight hunger in more finely-tuned or nuanced ways.

Definition of emergencies

Providing emergency relief is a complex operation, both conceptually and operationally. The approved definition of what constitutes an emergency sets the appropriate general framework for what events qualify for WFP relief assistance. At the beginning of WFP operations, emergency situations qualifying for WFP assistance were defined as arising out of 'critical food shortages or famines resulting from sudden or unexpected occurrences' (WFP, 1964). In the light of experience, that definition was considered to be too general and was amended in 1970 to:

> urgent situations in which there is clear evidence that an event has occurred which causes human suffering or loss of livestock and which the government concerned has not the means to remedy; and it is a demonstrably abnormal event which produces dislocation in the life of a community on an exceptional scale. (WFP, 1970)

Even this expanded definition was to cause problems, and three types of emergencies were identified: sudden, natural calamities, such as earthquakes, floods and hurricanes; slower-maturing emergencies arising from food shortages caused by drought, crop failures, and pests and diseases; and conflict-induced emergencies resulting in refugees and persons displaced within their own country.

In 1986, the WFP's governing body endorsed this definition and approved broad criteria for the release of WFP emergency resources. The basic principles for a WFP response were established as: famine was unacceptable, the poorest countries should receive priority attention, the gross national product (GNP) alone should not be the measure of a country's capacity to respond, interventions should be rapid and not subjected to excessive bureaucratic formalities and prescriptive criteria, and assistance should be temporary (WFP, 1986c).

The definition of emergencies was changed again in 2005 to reflect the major changes that had taken place in the world in which the WFP operated since the last definition was approved in 1970 (2005d). As we saw in Chapter 3, there was a dramatic shift in the focus of WFP assistance from development to emergencies and protracted crises during the 1990s. At the same time, WFP emergency responses shifted increasingly to conflict and post-conflict situations, and to the effects of the slow onslaught or sudden occurrence of economic crises. The WFP and other humanitarian agencies broadened their understanding of the importance of livelihoods in emergencies beyond the loss of livestock alone, and of other factors, such as HIV/AIDS and economic collapse. The new definition read:

> For purposes of WFP emergency operations (EMOPs), emergencies are defined as urgent situations in which there is clear evidence that an event or series of events has occurred which causes human suffering or imminently threatened human lives or livelihoods and which the government concerned has not the means to remedy; and it is a demonstrably abnormal event or series of events which produces dislocation in the life of a community on an exceptional scale. The event or series of events may comprise one or a combination of the following:
>
> (a) sudden calamities such as earthquakes, floods, locust infestations and similar unforeseen disasters;
> (b) human-made emergencies resulting in an influx of refugees or the internal displacement of populations, or in the suffering of otherwise affected populations;
> (c) food scarcity conditions owing to slow-onset events such as drought, crop failures, pests and diseases that result in an erosion of the capacity of communities and vulnerable populations to meet their food needs;
> (d) severe food access or availability conditions resulting from sudden economic shocks, market failure or economic collapse that result in an erosion of the capacity of communities and vulnerable populations to meet their food needs; and
> (e) a complex emergency for which the government of the affected country or the secretary-general of the United Nations has requested the support to urgent human food needs in diverse and unpredictable situations. (WFP, 2005e)

WFP emergency operations would continue to be based on assessed needs, taking into account any other considerations that may be decided upon by the WFP's executive board consistent with the WFP's *General Regulations, Rules and Mandate*.

The new definition followed a comprehensive review of the definitions adopted by other UN, NGO, and donor agencies. Primacy was given to 'flexibility' to respond to urgent human food needs in diverse and unpredictable situations. The modifications incorporated in the new definition reflected more recent thinking on the types of emergencies and their causes. The new definition also explicitly recognized loss of livelihoods generally as an integral part of emergencies, and not only loss of livestock mentioned in the previous definition, but also the acceptance of 'complex emergencies' as a category on its own,[1] and the role of a rapid and professional assessment of need for emergency food assistance based on a variety of situation-specific factors and the use of a number of assessment tools. These included emergency needs assessment to analyze the nutritional situation, and the extent to which food scarcity for vulnerable people was the result of lack of food availability and/or a lack of access to food.

As in the past, member states of the UN, or members of any UN specialized agency or of the IAEA, were eligible to submit requests for WFP emergency assistance. The WFP could also provide emergency food aid and associated non-food items and logistics support at the request the UN secretary-general, when WFP assistance was to be fully co-ordinated with the UN system and efforts of governments and intergovernmental and non-governmental organizations in the areas concerned in accordance with the WFP's *General Regulations* (WFP, 2008g).

While the WFP's new definition was widely accepted in UN humanitarian circles, it was criticized in that it tended to imply that an emergency was a stand-alone 'event', whereas, in reality, many emergencies may be the acute manifestation of an underlying process, such as protracted conflict, or political and economic turmoil, climate change, long-term environmental degradation, and chronic vulnerability or poverty (Maxwell *et al.*, 2008: 9). In addition, the new definition did not explicitly differentiate between transitory and chronic food insecurity and hunger, which required different policy and programme solutions (World Bank, 1986).

Exiting emergencies

The WFP also appreciated that knowing how to end a response to an emergency was as effective as knowing when to begin one. Its strong capacity for emergency intervention needed to be accompanied by an appropriate exit strategy. When and how to move out of an emergency response depended on a range of factors, and exits could take a number of forms. For the WFP, an exit meant 'either a phase-out, a withdrawal of WFP assistance from an emergency operation or from a country, or a shift to longer-term programmes to protect and improve livelihoods and resilience' (WFP, 2005f). Knowing the appropriate time to exit involved identifying context-specific criteria, or indicators that would trigger a decision to exit.

The WFP recognized that a realistic and deliberate exit strategy, planned with government and other partners and clearly stated at the beginning of an emergency operation, could help to facilitate more effective country responses after the initial stage of an emergency had passed. The overall objective for most emergency interventions was 'to restore to pre-emergency levels the capacity of communities and vulnerable populations to access food'. WFP emergency aid would be part of broader national and international efforts to achieve that outcome, and would be joined with other forms of assistance, including appropriate non-food assistance. Exit strategies from emergencies would aim to withdraw WFP support without compromising communities' regained ability to meet their own food needs. Emergency responses, particularly in relation to recurrent shocks, were more effective when they were carried out in the context of a longer-term strategy for capacity-building and resilience.

Humanitarian principles

As the work of the WFP and other humanitarian agencies rapidly expanded during the 1990s, the need was felt to put in place more professional and global standards for their work. By the beginning of the new millennium, the need for new humanitarian principles to guide their activities was acutely felt. As human suffering in the world accelerated, the spirit of humanitarianism – compassion towards fellow human beings in need, combined with responsibility to help people when they had nowhere else to turn – intensified. This spirit was reflected in the *United Nations Millennium Declaration* at the end of the UN Millennium Summit in 2000, in which world leaders stated:

> We have a collective responsibility to uphold the principles of human dignity, equality and equity at the global level. As leaders, we have a duty therefore to all the world's people, especially the most vulnerable and, in particular, the children of the world, to whom the future belongs. (UN, 2000)

In June 2003, representatives of 16 donor governments, the European Union (EU), OECD, UN agencies (including the WFP), the ICRC and other agencies met in Stockholm, Sweden to endorse the *Principles and Good Practices of Humanitarian Donorship*, a set of 23 principles and best practices for donors. They reaffirmed that humanitarian action should be defined and guided by the four overarching humanitarian principles of humanity, impartiality, neutrality and independence. Assistance should be provided to save lives and alleviate suffering according to need, funding should be adequate, predictable and flexible, and donors should be accountable and seek to learn from experience.[2]

At its third session in December 2003, the WFP's executive board requested the WFP secretariat to clarify the humanitarian principles that specifically guided WFP assistance. The proposed statement of humanitarian principles prepared by the secretariat was constructed within international humanitarian law and other institutional efforts to standardize humanitarian principles (WFP, 2004e).[3] It reflected the belief that the global community must act when families and local and national institutions are unable to meet the needs of vulnerable people. It also recognized the importance of ensuring that aid should build on the capacities available in communities and nations, and that assistance is appropriate and well-co-ordinated.

Ten humanitarian principles were approved by the executive board for WFP assistance in 2004, prefaced by the following statement:

> WFP is driven by the need to respond to human suffering and assist fellow human beings when they have nowhere else to turn. WFP will use food and related assistance to meet the immediate needs and improve food security. It is committed to the purposes and principles of the United Nations Charter and to the values and principles expressed in the Millennium Declaration. WFP will not use food at any time or under any circumstances as a means of applying political or economic pressure. WFP will adhere to the principles set out

below when providing food aid, non-food assistance and technical support in response to humanitarian needs. (WFP, 2004p)

The ten humanitarian principles comprise core humanitarian principles, principles that form the foundations of effective humanitarian action, and standards of accountability and professionalism.

Core humanitarian principles

1. *Humanity.* The WFP will seek to prevent and alleviate human suffering wherever it is found and respond with food aid when appropriate. It will provide assistance in ways that respect life, health, and dignity.
2. *Impartiality.* The WFP's assistance will be guided solely by need and will not discriminate in terms of ethnic origin, nationality, political opinion, gender, race or religion. Assistance will be targeted to those most at risk from the consequences of food shortages, following a sound assessment that takes into account different needs and vulnerabilities of women, men, and children.
3. *Neutrality.* The WFP will not take sides in a conflict and will not engage in controversies of a political, racial, religious, or ideological nature. Aid will not be provided to active combatants.

Foundations of effective humanitarian action

4. *Respect.* The WFP will respect the sovereignty, territorial integrity and unity of the state in which it is working. The WFP will respect the local customs and traditions, upholding internationally recognized human rights. The WFP will act in accordance with the United Nations Charter and consistent with international humanitarian law and refugee law. The WFP will also take into account the Guiding Principles of Internal Displacement, when applicable.
5. *Self-reliance.* The WFP will provide humanitarian assistance with the primary objective of saving lives, in ways that support livelihoods, reduce vulnerability to future food scarcities, and support durable solutions. The WFP will work to ensure that food aid does not undermine local agricultural production, marketing or coping strategies, or disturb normal migratory patterns, or foster dependency. WFP programmes will be planned and implemented in ways that facilitate the link from relief to development.
6. *Participation.* The WFP will involve women and men beneficiaries wherever possible in all activities and will work closely with governments at the national and local levels to plan and implement assistance.
7. *Capacity-building.* Within its own capacity and resources, the WFP will strengthen the capacity of affected countries and local communities to prevent, prepare for, and respond to humanitarian crises. The WFP will ensure participation by women's organizations and will integrate a gender perspective in capacity-building activities.
8. *Co-ordination.* The WFP will provide assistance with the consent of the affected country and, in principle, on the basis of an appeal by the affected country. All

states members of the United Nations or members or associate members of any specialized agency or of the IAEA are eligible to submit requests for consideration by the WFP. The WFP may also provide emergency food aid and associated non-food items and logistics support at the request of the secretary-general of the United Nations. The WFP will work within the established United Nations co-ordination structures at the global and field levels. This will include working with other humanitarian actors such as NGOs and the International Red Cross and Red Crescent Movements.

Standards of accountability and professionalism

9. *Accountability.* The WFP will keep donors, host country governments, beneficiaries, and other relevant stakeholders informed of its activities and their impact through regular reporting.
10. *Professionalism.* The WFP will maintain the highest standards of professionalism and integrity among its international and national staff to ensure that its programmes are carried out efficiently, effectively, ethically, and safely. All staff will adhere to the Standard Code of Conduct for the International Civil Service and the UN secretary- general's Bulletin on Sexual Abuse and Exploitation in Humanitarian Crisis and Other Operations.

Targeting in emergencies

It is axiomatic that any aid, especially emergency food assistance, designed to help and support the poor and hungry in distress must reach them effectively and efficiently to have any benefit. Targeting is therefore a central element in WFP emergency operations. And as emergencies develop and population needs change, the target group and targeting methods must also evolve. Successful targeting requires regular and systematic analysis of a multiplicity of factors. Setting clear objectives from the start of an emergency operation may allow flexibility in targeting without compromising goals.

WFP experience has shown that four considerations have an especially important bearing on the effectiveness or otherwise of the targeting approaches adopted:

Balance. A balance may need to be struck between criteria that focus on the poorest people and less exacting criteria that address affliction on a community or area basis, without dissipating scarce resources and impact on hunger and poverty, or biasing in favour of any one particular group. Risk assessment and vulnerability mapping could provide useful operational tools for focusing on people and areas most in need. In the absence of reliable data, appropriate rapid appraisal and beneficiary participation techniques could be used to establish the parameters for targeting, which could be refined as emergency operations are implemented.

Administrative feasibility and costs. Targeted interventions may fail because they may be either unfeasible, or too costly to administer on a sustainable basis. The result may, at best, be only intermittent outreach to those most in need, or access only to those who are not so seriously affected, leading to errors of exclusion and inclusion. These problems may be overcome or minimized if a third consideration is taken into account.

Implementation, monitoring, and evaluation. Involvement of the target group itself in the implementation, monitoring, and evaluation of the emergency operation designed to help them through a participatory approach. But there is no universal model, or single way, of implementing that approach. To be undertaken thoroughly and well, the approach requires commitment and professional understanding. And it should not be seen as a soft option for solving the problems of governments or aid agencies (Herbinger *et al.*, 1999).

Aid transfer. The final consideration relates to the type, form, level, and method of the aid transfer. Decisions on these factors should relate to the specific emergency situation, and its causes, in which poor and food-secure people find themselves. Whatever the type and form of the aid transfer, premiums should be placed on its prompt and adequate provision, as these considerations generally increase both the effectiveness and efficiency of the intervention.

To help develop a policy on the subject of targeting, the WFP's Office of Evaluation commissioned a thematic review of targeting in relief operations (WFP, 2006j).[4] The review noted that WFP policy statements and guidelines on targeting were dispersed across a number of WFP documents (Hoskins, 2004). But the WFP's extensive experience in targeting had been neither systematically analyzed nor incorporated into policy and operational documents. There was evidently need to consolidate experience and to identify lessons learned. The WFP used a variety of mechanisms to target its food aid (including vulnerability analysis and mapping, and community-based targeting and distribution that utilized the knowledge and resources of whole communities) so as to identify those most in need of food aid and to manage its distribution.

The review identified three main reasons for the importance of targeting in relief operations against which performance should be measured: to reach those most in need; to maximize the use and impact of limited resources; and to prevent over-supply of food aid.

Three types of targeting approaches were used to evaluate results:

Administrative targeting implemented outside the beneficiary group by geographical area. Institutions were involved in drawing up lists of those eligible for registration and the issue of rations cards. These institutions included schools and mother and child care centres, and communities in which there were village heads, clan leaders, and administrative officials. The review found that, while this approach offered the opportunity to identify the largest number of needy people, it should always be based on credible and transparent analysis employing a variety of data related to food security.

Community-based targeting and distribution. With this approach, beneficiaries were selected by democratic and transparent methods to receive food aid, and community structures used to distribute it. The review concluded that this approach could lead to improved accuracy, transparency, fairness, and accountability, and could reduce costs, even though costs to the community were increased. However, it was felt more evidence was needed to develop guidelines to help decide whether to adopt this approach in a particular context.

Self-selection. Individuals and households were given the choice to become beneficiaries in food-aided schemes, such as food-for-work, or the distribution of low-value/low-status but nutritious food commodities. Here, the review concluded that the modalities should be selected primarily on the basis of priority objectives, and that they reached the target group and had maximum impact.

The overall finding was that targeting was difficult, as it often took place in complex political, social, and logistical environments. The case studies examined showed the diversity of security, political, gender, cultural, and institutional factors that could influence the targeting process and its outcomes. WFP staff and partners had shown strong commitment to identifying and addressing the problems of targeting, and to learning from experience, but this was not adequately or systematically applied in targeting decisions. A well-designed monitoring and evaluation system was required to determine whether the target approach adopted was successful, whether the people in greatest need were reached, and whether the programme objectives were achieved. More WFP staff training was needed, for which appropriate guidance and training materials should be developed.

The WFP secretariat produced a proposed policy document on targeting in emergencies which took into account the findings of the thematic review (WFP, 2006k). After much discussion at its first regular session in 2006, the executive board endorsed the following policy, which was incorporated into the *Consolidated Framework on WFP Policies* (WFP, 2009h):

> It is WFP policy that targeting is a central element of an integrated and comprehensive emergency needs assessment and response strategy. WFP should continue to respond immediately and in a cost-effective manner to emergencies and, in so doing, aim to meet conditions for effective targeting such as:
>
> (i) food assistance is required to save or protect lives and livelihoods;
> (ii) the most vulnerable target groups are identified;
> (iii) type and form of food assistance best suited to the needs of the target groups are identified; and
> (iv) ongoing adjustments are made to the above on the basis of appropriate assessments and modifications of activities according to changing needs.

Targeting should be a conscious and integral management activity at all stages of the programme cycle. As an emergency develops and populations needs change, target groups, targeting methods, and WFP practices must also evolve. Successful targeting requires regular, systematic analysis of a multiplicity of factors, including the gender dimensions of emergencies. Setting clear project objectives from the start that take these factors into account will later allow for targeting flexibility without compromising the goals of a project. The selection of programme and delivery mechanisms that ensure that food reaches those who need it is an equally important aspect of targeting.

The main targeting objective of the WFP in emergencies is to achieve a balance between targeting exclusion errors, which can be life-threatening, and potentially disruptive or wasteful inclusion errors. In acute emergencies, due to the urgency of the situation, it may well be necessary to accept inclusion errors in order to save lives or protect livelihoods. Other targeting objectives include providing a safe environment for food deliveries and maintaining flexibility to adapt to rapidly changing situations.

Targeting costs increase in proportion to the level and detail of targeting. The WFP should analysis benefits and budget for costs associated with different targeting approaches, keeping in mind that cost-efficiency for the WFP may imply increased transaction or opportunity costs for recipients.

From crisis to recovery: special needs

In 1998, the WFP correctly predicted that 'recovery from natural and manmade crises will continue to represent one of the major challenges confronting humanitarian and development agencies in the coming decades' (WFP, 1998a: 3). The WFP's extensive experience showed that traditional relief responses that treated an emergency as essentially an abnormal short-term event, calling for a short-term response, were often inadequate in addressing real needs of people trying to stabilize and secure their livelihoods in conflict situations. Developmental assistance in support of a humanitarian effort could help prevent further deterioration in social and economic conditions, establish foundations for recovery and reconciliation, and avert conflict-related disasters.

The UN Administrative Committee on Coordination (ACC), composed of the heads of UN bodies and chaired by the UN secretary-general, supported the necessity for complementing relief and development activities, and the development of strategies that better integrated relief and development programmes in a continuum of action. The WFP's *Mission Statement* of 1994 recognized that: 'WFP is well placed to play a major role in the continuum from emergency relief to development' (WFP, 1994b: 3). In 1998, the WFP's executive board endorsed the recommendation that the WFP's protracted relief operations (PROs) be renamed protracted relief and recovery operations (PRROs) to respond to protracted relief and recovery needs (WFP, 1998d: 4).

In protracted crisis and recovery situations, WFP assistance often went to refugees, displaced persons, and surrounding communities – and, at times, to demobilized soldiers and their families – helping these groups to build food security during times of displacement, encampment, resettlement, or return. Efforts to deliver food or restore food security during or after conflicts may be hindered by landmines. These issues were addressed by the WFP's executive board when discussing the policy paper *From Crisis to Recovery* (WFP, 1998a). In this context, the board agreed to the following actions.

> WFP will periodically review the effectiveness of the food assistance in each country where there is a refugee situation, in collaboration with governments, donors, NGOs and the Office of the United Nations High Commissioner

for Refugees (UNHCR). In providing assistance to refugees and displaced persons, WFP will take into consideration the needs of the populations of host areas in the vicinity of concentrations of refugees, returnees or other displaced persons. When mine clearing is needed to facilitate humanitarian food responses, WFP may provide food aid to support demining only in such situations where food aid complements and strengthens the work of other agencies. WFP may support demobilization processes in countries emerging from conflict when food aid support is implemented as part of a United Nations strategy and when it is provided after armed personnel are demobilized. This could include weapon-exchange programmes in selected cases where food is a suitable element within the context of an integrated programme.

Emergencies in urban areas

The WFP predicted that poverty, food insecurity and malnutrition in the urban areas of developing countries were likely to worsen as cities and towns continued to grow, and could be acutely exacerbated when natural or conflict-induced disasters occurred (WFP, 2002e).[5] To respond, the WFP and its partners would need to consider many factors that affected the food and livelihood security of the urban poor. These included: greater dependence on cash income and less reliance on agriculture and natural resources than their rural counterparts; low wages from work in insecure jobs, often in the informal sector outside the main economy; a large number of women working outside the home; legal obstacles, including insecure land and housing tenure; inadequate access to safe water, sanitation, and health services; and frequently weak social networks.

It was recognized that the urban poor would not be able to lift themselves out of poverty unless they had access to employment. Targeted food programmes would continue to be necessary as safety-net interventions, especially in situations of dramatic economic downturns and emergencies. The lessons drawn from ongoing and previous programmes would be critical for future responses, including: the need for a good diagnosis to understand vulnerability in urban areas, the challenges of targeting in heterogeneous settings, the importance of complementary programming to address the poor service delivery in slum areas, the nature of partnering in highly politicized environments, and the need for well-thought-out exit strategies so that prolonged food assistance does not have a negative effect on the economy.

To respond to these challenges and to lessons learned from experience, the WFP's executive board approved the following policy:

> WFP food assistance in emergency and development settings should address urban food insecurity when appropriate. WFP will expand its analysis of food needs in urban settings, and its efforts in urban programming, as the number of people experiencing poverty, food insecurity and malnutrition in urban areas increases. Urban programming will be consistent with existing WFP policies. WFP will develop a set of guidelines to assist [WFP] country offices in

programming more effectively in urban settings, drawing on its own experience and that of other aid agencies. While urban food insecurity is a growing problem requiring greater attention, the majority of WFP interventions will continue to be in rural areas. (WFP, 2009h)

Livelihoods in emergencies

The WFP, together with other humanitarian agencies, recognized the importance of livelihoods in crisis situations both in terms of the impact of their collapse in emergencies, and their support and revival during and after disasters. Yet, humanitarian assistance had traditionally focused only on saving lives and reducing suffering in the short term. Experience had shown that the impact of emergencies continued over time. Most people who survived a disaster had depleted assets and a diminished capacity to cope. Many owed their survival not to relief assistance alone, but also by using their own resources, networks, and coping strategies. Understanding and supporting those strategies should, therefore, form an important component of an emergency response. These experiences prompted academics and practitioners to take a closer look at livelihoods and how they were affected by, and mitigated, the impact of crises.[6]

The WFP launched a policy process to explore ways of using food aid to preserve assets and to support livelihoods in emergencies (WFP, 2003d). Many WFP emergency operations had objectives and related activities that were aimed at supporting livelihoods and preserving assets. These provided a repository of operational information, but had not been systematically analyzed. Field reviews were conducted in Angola, Guinea, and the Democratic Republic of the Congo to capture the challenges and successes from its experience. It was found that, by helping households preserve their assets and pursue their own livelihood strategies, the WFP could expand its life-saving support beyond those individuals who directly received food aid to include their extended family relations and those community members who relied on them, thereby quickening recovery. By using food aid to support and enhance local capacities to cope with crises, the WFP could help build vulnerable people's resilience and ability to cope with future hazards. This could be done by taking a number of steps. More could be invested in early warning systems and baselines, and vulnerability information and analysis through VAM. Livelihood assessments could be further and more systematically integrated into emergency needs assessment. The timing of emergency food aid interventions could be improved to reduce the need for negative coping strategies, such as selling or mortgaging essential household assets or incurring prohibitive debt. The WFP could advocate for the needs of those at risk of losing their livelihoods in addition to those whose lives were at risk. There could be promotion of partnerships with organizations that understood the needs of communities and the importance of livelihoods. The capacities of the staff of the WFP and its partners to appreciate and analyze the importance of livelihoods could be built up; and livelihoods could be more thoroughly and systematically included in the monitoring and evaluation of WFP emergency operations.

Following its review of the WFP's policy document at its annual session in 2003, the executive board approved the following policy statement:

> WFP will systematically assess and analyse livelihood-related issues in emergencies and determine where food aid can play a role in supporting livelihoods. WFP will strengthen staff capacity to design, implement and monitor programmes that save and protect livelihoods. WFP will also promote greater coherence between its emergency and longer-term interventions and will strengthen partnerships with national governments, local authorities, donors, United Nations agencies, international financial institutions, NGOs and community-based organizations, in particular for common analysis and design of appropriate livelihood interventions. (WFP, 2009l)

Food-based safety nets for emergencies

The WFP has sought more flexible and innovative tools to address emergency situations. There are good reasons for this. The WFP operates in places of extreme poverty, where lives and livelihoods are at risk. By the time an emergency response is mounted, livelihoods may be severely damaged, and may take many years to rebuild. In other cases, the cumulative effects of crises over time undermine the livelihoods of specific groups who suffer an ongoing 'silent emergency' of malnutrition and ill-health, and inter-generational poverty. Well-defined safety nets can ensure that livelihoods are not lost. The WFP presented a policy paper on the subject for the consideration of its executive board in 2004 (WFP, 2004q).

The paper revealed that, in the past, WFP country offices had been engaged in safety-net programmes along a spectrum based on a range of national factors and circumstances. At one end of the spectrum were countries with no formal safety-net or social protection systems. At the other end were countries with well-established and fully-functioning food-based safety nets as part of an integrated social protection programme. The WFP focused its conditional food transfers on beneficiaries undertaking certain desirable activities, such as asset creation in food-for-work programmes, vocational training in food-for-training schemes, and education and health and nutrition improvement programmes. Unconditional food transfers were targeted to vulnerable groups, such as the sick, HIV/AIDS affected, seriously malnourished, disabled, and the elderly.

In this way, the WFP engaged in a number of different types of safety-net programmes, but these were neither systematically nor comprehensively analyzed. From WFP inception, preference was given by its governing body to the direct distribution of food aid commodities from donors to beneficiaries. In addition, safety nets were often viewed as being simple relief transfers with limited long-term benefit and involved the danger of creating dependency. But experience had shown that properly designed safety nets could provide a predictable set of institutionalized mechanisms to help poor and food-insecure households and communities in distress cope with shocks and meet minimum consumption requirements. If correctly implemented by governments and supported by external assistance, they had the potential not only to protect, but also significantly to promote the livelihoods of poor people.[7]

There are many types of safety nets that can be provided in cash or in kind. Food-based safety nets provided food to beneficiaries either directly in kind or indirectly through food stamps, vouchers, and coupons (WFP, 2004q). Both cash and food-based programmes provided a transfer of income to increase recipients' purchasing power. But food-based programmes have other objectives, such as increasing household food consumption and addressing hunger and malnutrition, and micronutrient deficiencies.

In designing safety-net interventions, the comparative advantages of cash and food should be carefully analyzed on the basis of local conditions, taking into consideration a set of factors, including: the level of market integration and food supply, financial infrastructure and administrative capacity, inflation effects, food consumption levels, and micronutrient deficiencies. Often, it will not be a question of either cash/vouchers or food but, rather, how best to combine the two to achieve optimum results.

Designing good safety-net programming required five basic principles: integration into the broader national contexts, policies, and programmes; targeting those most in need of a transfer; availability in periods of need; taking a long-term perspective; and being as predictable and productive; as possible. It was concluded that safety-nets represented a potentially important tool for poverty eradication when used as part of national social protection strategies to complement broader development and food-security programmes. The WFP's extensive experience with food aid had shown the basic features of safety-net programmes. It could play a number of roles at different stages in their development including: in the transition towards a national safety-net programme; establishing national safety-net programmes; and improving an already established one. A major concern was to ensure that there was a clear-cut exit strategy.

The executive board reviewed the policy paper at its third regular session in 2004 and approved the following policy concerning the WFP's use of food-based safety nets:

> In order to participate with governments and other partners at each of the stages of implementation of national safety-net programmes, WFP will:
>
> - Enhance its capacity to advise and advocate for food-based safety nets, where appropriate, during the formulation of national poverty reduction strategies.
> - Measures relating to training and staffing should ensure that country offices, with the support of regional bureaux and headquarters, have sufficient in-house expertise.
> - Develop guidelines on the design and implementation of safety nets. Particular attention should be paid to:
>
>   (i) the most effective safety-net modalities for local circumstances,
>   (ii) the optimal combination of food and cash transfers,

(iii) the potential for safety nets to act as a bridge between emergencies, recovery and development, and
(iv) the design of safety-net activities.

- Strengthen its ability to improve existing national safety-net programmes.
- Best practices in WFP's experiences with safety-nets should be shared across regional bureaux and country offices as part of a larger system for knowledge and information sharing within the organization.
- WFP should also collaborate with partners including national governments, the World Bank, NGOs and other United Nations organizations to identify cross-agency best practices for safety nets;
- Explore appropriate funding mechanisms for its involvement in safety nets. These efforts may include expanding its donor base and addressing issues specific to safety nets, such as multi-year finding. (WFP, 2009h)

Vouchers and cash transfers as food assistance instruments: opportunities and challenges

The WFP secretariat presented a policy document to the executive board in 2008 containing proposals for the use of vouchers and cash transfers. The intention was that these could be used as complements or alternatives to existing food assistance modalities as part of the move towards more flexible tools for addressing hunger issues (WFP, 2008h). This was the first WFP policy document to relate explicitly to the use of vouchers and cash transfers. However, a number of other WFP policies had, over the years, gradually laid the foundation for a corporate policy on such transfers, including those described in Chapter 6. The WFP's proposed policy would be 'context-specific and evidence-based'. It would recognize that: beneficiaries are often in the best position to know their urgent and most important needs; food-insecure people would be able to obtain commodities where they were readily available; adequate and accessible financial partner institutions and appropriate monitoring, reporting, and control systems were essential for their efficient use, and that such conditions were not always present in the most food-insecure, unstable, and marginalized environments; vouchers and cash transfers were generally more cost-efficient than food transfers when markets operated well and capacities to implement them were adequately developed; it would fit well into the WFP's participatory approach, and would ensure the empowerment and involvement of communities, and give them greater choice; it would facilitate gender mainstreaming; and it would be fully in line with the objectives contained within the WFP's *Strategic Plan (2008–13)*.

Food assistance was defined as a set of instruments for addressing the food needs of vulnerable people, and could take the form of in-kind food transfers and voucher and cash schemes (Gentilini, 2007; Harvey, 2007). While programme objectives, design, and operational arrangements differed, they shared a similar market-based approach of transferring income or purchasing power to the beneficiaries to access food. While in-kind food transfers delivered food commodities to the beneficiaries, cash transfers provided money to purchase food.

Voucher transfer programmes involved the provision of coupons or stamps for use in selected stores or outlets to purchase a fixed quantity of food (commodity-based vouchers), or food for a fixed monetary value (value-based vouchers).

The policy document noted that interest in the use of vouchers or cash transfers had grown significantly for a number of reasons. The functioning of markets in many developing countries had improved: food systems had become more integrated; the pace of urbanization had accelerated; basic financial services had grown and spread into rural areas; and the international prices of food and fuel had risen sharply, which had a particularly negative effect on in-kind food transfers. The use of vouchers or cash transfers was expected to have outcomes and impacts for beneficiaries, developing countries, and the WFP as an organization.

Beneficiaries could benefit from receiving food assistance in ways and forms linked to meeting their specific needs. It could also help increase their capacity to manage risks, enhance their livelihoods, and improve their nutritional status by allowing them to make choices and prioritize needs. At the country level, benefits could include enhancing coherence and alignment of WFP interventions into national strategic priorities, policies and programmes for food security and nutrition, education, social protection, and poverty reduction. It could also create new opportunities to hand over activities to partners and governments as beneficiaries improved their livelihoods and capacities. For the WFP, the use of diversified food assistance instruments could: enhance the organization's ability to tailor its food assistance to specific country or local situations, meet identified needs in a more timely and flexible fashion, and support its strategic aim of transforming food aid into food assistance programmes.

The appropriateness of each of the transfer mechanisms depended on a number of factors, including, and especially, the robustness of markets, and capacities to implement them. They were not necessarily mutually exclusive: The variety of market conditions and capacities, even within the same country, suggested possible complementarities among them. Food transfers might be used when markets functioned poorly and cash transfers when they functioned well, with adjustments made to changing conditions. Differences in food availabilities and prices at different times of the year suggested that the various forms of transfer could be combined seasonally. Other combinations could occur: in the transition from emergency to post-emergency situations, in the promotion of livelihoods, and in the pathways out of poverty; or in improving the cost-efficiency in situations of high food prices and high transport costs, faster response time, improved social protection, and programming in urban areas.

But limitations were also identified in making greater use of vouchers and cash transfers. These included: short-term and small-scale experience in their use by the WFP, especially in emergency situations; limited capacity among the WFP's partners; risks for beneficiaries in rapidly changing conditions of food availability and price; and problems of fraud and corruption. However, the WFP was seen to have a number of comparative advantages in using these instruments, including: unparalleled field presence, outreach, and capacity to implement large-scale programmes, particularly in remote and risky environments; extensive experience in working with partners, including governments, other UN agencies, and a large number of NGOs, the majority of which were national and community-based organizations; analytical capacity in vulnerability, needs, and market assessments at the national, regional, community, and household levels; capacity to identify the appropriateness and feasibility of voucher and cash transfer programmes; significant synergies with the WFP's programme platform for the design, implementation, and evaluation of vouchers and cash transfers; multi-year and ongoing practical implementation experience; and the potential for the consistent provision of vouchers, cash, and food transfers according to local circumstances, and the flexibility to switch their use as circumstances changed over time.

A number of key issues would have to be addressed, however, to enable the WFP *gradually* (original emphasis) to engage more widely in voucher and cash transfer programmes.

Operational guidelines would have to be developed. Needs assessments, in transitional and development contexts, and market analysis capacities would require strengthening. Guidelines on financial management should be produced. The capabilities of partner institutions should be assessed. And WFP staff would require strengthening to undertake voucher and cash transfer programmes through the recruitment of officers with the appropriate technical background, secondment of staff from other agencies, and training.

Partnerships would be a key ingredient for effective and efficient vouchers and cash transfers.

Governments were crucial partners and should be involved in linking such transfer programmes with national priorities, strategies, and policies. Donors had a vital role to play in funding vouchers and cash transfers, in contributing to capacity-building, and in documenting best practices and lessons learned. Partnerships with other UN agencies would include new collaborations with their ongoing and planned programmes. The range of opportunities to work with the World Bank would be broadened. The main NGO partners would be those with the capacity to implement vouchers and cash transfers. And new forms of partnerships with financial institutions and retailers in the private sector would be required.

In reviewing the policy document at its second regular session in 2008, executive board members agreed that the use of vouchers and cash transfer systems could serve to maximize the effects of food interventions, and to help markets and farmers in recipient countries. They also noted that they reflected the general move towards context-based operations. They cautioned, however, that the WFP should proceed with care, given the risks involved and the need to ensure that such systems complemented national programmes. They emphasized that they were likely to be most effective in transition and development situations, and where markets were functioning, but could be used in emergencies should there be appropriate implementing conditions (WFP, 2008e).

As a result, the following statement was included in the *Consolidated Framework of WFP's Policies* (WFP, 2009h).

> The voucher and cash transfer policy enhances WFP's capacity to tailor assistance to more context-specific needs. Cash transfers and vouchers can be implemented as complements or alternatives to food transfer programmes: cash transfer programmes provide people with money; voucher schemes include coupons for a fixed quantity of food or its value in identified stores. WFP will only use cash and vouchers in the context of food assistance for vulnerable people.
>
> When appropriate market and implementation capacities are in place, WFP cash transfers and vouchers can foster economic multipliers, empower beneficiaries and improve the cost-efficiency of interventions. WFP recognizes that partnerships are crucial for effective implementation. The instruments give opportunities for new partnerships, for example, with private-sector entities and financial service providers. Cash transfers and vouchers should be implemented in line with country-led initiatives, such as social protection and safety net systems, whenever possible.

Disaster risk reduction

WFP *General Regulations* (Article 11b) state that one of the organization's principle purposes is: 'to assist in the continuum from emergency relief to development by giving priority to supporting disaster prevention, preparedness and mitigation and post-disaster rehabilitation activities' (1992b). A strategic approach to disaster mitigation was presented to the WFP's governing body in 2000 (WFP, 2000c) following which guidelines for WFP assistance for disaster mitigation were drawn up (WFP, 2000d).

Based on the experience gathered, the WFP's secretariat presented a proposed policy document on disaster risk reduction to the WFP's executive board in 2009 with the aim of enhancing the capacities of national governments and communities in developing countries to develop and implement disaster risk reduction systems (WFP, 2009j). The WFP's focus would be threefold: to reduce the risks of hunger, using vulnerability assessments and early-warning systems, to help governments institute what was called a 'culture of resilience'; to support the adaptation of livelihoods and physical preparations to meet disasters; and to develop detailed disaster management plans in line with national frameworks.

The policy document outlined the WFP's proposed overarching approach to the prevention and mitigation of disasters within a disaster risk reduction framework.[8] In 2005, over 180 countries adopted the *Hyogo Framework for Action 2005–15*, followed in 2007 by the *Bali Action Plan* to combat climate change. The second strategic objective of the WFP's *Strategic Plan (2008–13)* recognized the need for the WFP: to further engage in disaster risk address, and respond to acute hunger arising from disasters; and to support and strengthen resilience of communities to shocks through safety-nets or asset creation, including adaptation to climate change. It called on the WFP to 'invest in disaster preparedness and mitigation measures' as part of its efforts to prevent acute hunger. These events and strategic objectives inspired the WFP to take more concerted and coherent action to support government and communities' disaster risk reduction and climate change adaptation efforts. Hence the need for a clear policy in this area of WFP work.

The WFP responded to disasters and helped in rebuilding livelihoods, thereby reducing disaster risk.[9] Nonetheless, it was felt that the WFP needed to define its guiding principles for coherent and focused programmes addressing disaster risk reduction in varying country contexts, which would also help bridge the gap between relief and development.

It was recognized that the extra resources spent on prevention and preparedness in the developing world today, saved lives, livelihoods, and additional resources tomorrow. The increasing frequency and severity of disasters, due in part to climate change, had resulted in increasing humanitarian needs. In addition, soaring food and fuel prices, together with the threat of pandemics, created new types of vulnerability. Demographic pressure and marginalization in many developing countries resulted in the growing overall impact of disasters, with a corresponding increase in human, social, and economic costs.

The policy document stressed that governments had the primary responsibility for sustainable development and consistent disaster risk reduction policy. But given increasing global interdependence for disaster reduction, the WFP could be relied on even more for its ability to act rapidly and would engage with national policies and other UN agencies to strengthen the coherence and co-ordination of action to reduce the risk of disaster. Climate change threatened already fragile food systems throughout the developing world. As climate change was expected to cause more frequent disasters, prevention and preparation for such occurrences could help countries adapt to climate change. Collective action and substantial investment in the mitigation of, and adaptation to, the negative effects of climate change was required, particularly in the poorest and most vulnerable countries. Drought-affected areas were likely to increase, and increasingly frequent heavy rainfall would increase the risk of flooding.

It would be WFP policy to continue to support governments to reduce the risk of disasters and to adapt to climate change through a number of measures, including vulnerability analysis and mapping (VAM), emergency needs and response assessments, and multi-hazard early warning systems. These measures, combined with the transfer of knowledge, could help strengthen governments' capacity in disaster preparedness and response.[10] Food-for-training activities could help train community leaders and women representatives on committees to build a culture of safety and resilience. Vouchers and cash transfer schemes may also be used in disaster preparedness programmes. Timely support to protect livelihoods would limit the economic damage of disasters (Hess and Im, 2007). The WFP's contingency planning was a critical tool at the country level to assist government disaster preparedness measures, and could be extended to the global level in the event of pandemics.[11]

It was noted that the WFP with the FAO were leaders among UN agencies in the fields of early warning, early impact analysis, and crisis management for both natural and human-induced disasters. This leadership was further enhanced by the WFP's strong involvement with communities through safety-net and food-for-asset creation programmes. The WFP's comparative advantage for disaster prevention and preparedness activities derived from its operational nature, extensive field presence, and competence in disaster management. These factors provided local knowledge and gave the WFP credibility with governments in developing countries.

The WFP's proposed policy framework and overarching approach to disaster risk reduction was based on the strategic goals contained in its *Strategic Plan (2008–13)* and three interrelated tasks: to identify and ensure understanding of risk; to prevent disasters by lowering risks; and to prepare for disasters.[12] In the long term, all prevention and preparedness efforts aimed to substantially reduce loss of life and damage to the assets of communities and countries (*Hyogo Framework for Action 2005–15*: 5). In the meantime, the WFP's proposed policy aimed at the following outcomes for disaster risk reduction programmes: identification and understanding of hazard risks at all levels of government and within communities; preparing governments and communities to respond to disasters; and preparing governments and communities to be resilient to disasters. The WFP would focus on reducing those disaster risks that were likely to result in acute hunger.

The WFP's proposed disaster risk reduction policy stressed that government ownership was paramount to successful disaster prevention and preparedness. The WFP's role was to support governments in identifying and filling gaps to make their activities more effective. That role would also be guided by the UN Development Group and the Inter-Agency Standing Committee (IASC), and at the country level by the UN Development Assistance Framework, together with recovery and humanitarian assistance frameworks. Given that disasters did not respect national boundaries, there was a need for strong regional information-sharing and co-ordinated action. In addition, the WFP's effectiveness in contributing to disaster risk reduction came through working in partnership with governments, regional entities, other UN agencies, NGOs, and the private sector.[13]

A background document on disaster risk reduction strategies was presented to the January 2008 joint meeting of the executive boards of the UNUP/UNFPA, UNICEF and WFP. It called on the WFP to mainstream disaster risk reduction into its programming and to comply with the *Hyogo Framework for Action*. The WFP participated in drafting the IASC *Operational Guidelines on Human Rights and Natural Disasters* in 2006. An IASC working group producing guidelines on good disaster risk reduction principles in emergencies suggested that WFP prevention interventions be targeted on households whose coping capacity was insufficient to meet their food needs in the face of a disaster, which would erode vital livelihood assets. It was also recognized that gender relations played an important role in disaster mitigation strategies, and that local monitoring and evaluation systems should be set up from the outset of all interventions.

The policy document recognized that support of a country disaster risk reduction framework, as opposed to reaction to a disaster to save lives, required a shift in thinking within the humanitarian community. Pre-disaster work needed performance indicators that went beyond food delivery targets. The WFP could build on substantial experience and competence in disaster risk reduction to improve its programmes. This would require an enhanced role in the poverty reduction strategy process. Mainstreaming disaster prevention and preparedness entailed new ways of defining and rewarding programme success, and new expected outcomes required new targets and monitoring frameworks.

WFP programme guidelines should be reviewed in order to consider how to integrate pre-disaster work into its operations and intervene earlier to prevent acute hunger. Also, appropriate funding mechanisms would be needed to fund disaster risk reduction activities. Programme officers with skills in disaster prevention and mitigation would be posted in selected WFP country offices supported by disaster risk reduction knowledge and experience at WFP headquarters and regional bureaux.

When reviewing the proposed WFP policy for disaster risk reduction, the executive board recommended that it be discussed further with partners and experts from all regions in order to develop a more systematic and integrated approach (WFP, 2009m). The importance of partnerships was emphasized, particularly because of the requirement for expertise in various fields outside the WFP's core operations. The WFP was urged to define its role in the overall scheme of disaster risk reduction to maximize complementarities with other actors. Each country would have its own needs, and access to appropriate technologies would have to be arranged. The WFP's policy should also be expressed in internationally recognized terminology to avoid misunderstanding and confusion, and to ensure that governments clearly understood what was being proposed.

The following statement was incorporated into the *Consolidated Framework of WFP Policies* (WFP, 2009h):

> In line with the Hyogo Framework for Action, the Bali Action Plan and Strategic Objective 2 in the *Strategic Plan (2008–2011)*,* WFP is investing further in disaster risk reduction (DRR). DRR activities frequently form part of WFP's work programme: food-for-work activities for example often aim to improve livelihood opportunities and make communities more resilient, while vulnerability assessments provide a good basis for DRR work. For WFP, DRR also means complementing emergency response and preparedness with targeted prevention and preparedness activities before disaster strikes. Guided by governments and working with partners, WFP can contribute to national DRR and climate change adaptation frameworks thanks to its disaster management competency, experience, services and deep field presence. WFP has a record of rebuilding livelihoods and reducing disaster risk at all levels, often turning the aftermath of disasters into windows of opportunity for DRR. With this policy, WFP puts its comparative advantage to work in support of governments and partners.
>
> *Note*: * Extended to 2013.

The board reaffirmed its commitment to preventing hunger through disaster preparedness and other risk reduction measures by: strengthening capacities of governments to prepare for, assess and respond to hunger arising from disasters; assisting communities to build resilience to shocks within the WFP's specific mandate; and requesting the Secretariat to undertake further consultations on the policy with experts and partners from all regions (WFP, 2009k).

Strategic deployment of the WFP staff throughout the developing world

The first and most important factor in the transformation of the WFP into the world's largest humanitarian agency was the widespread deployment of its staff throughout the developing world, and the devolvement of decision-making to them from WFP headquarters, in a major restructuring of the organization that was to take most of the decade of the 1990s to accomplish. No one could have envisaged at the beginning of the decade the extent to which external and concomitant internal pressures would lead to a re-examination of almost every aspect of WFP activities.[14]

What stood out was the courage and steadfastness of WFP executive director Catherine Bertini in pursuing her decentralization initiative. But, as she knew, she could not have succeeded without the full support of her deputy, Namanga Ngongi, and senior management, and the thoughtful and considerate way in which WFP staff were involved and won over.[15] The final result was the most fundamental and far-reaching transformation of any UN organization. A detailed account of the transformation is provided here so that a full account of the many steps that were taken, and their effects, can be given.

The decentralization process[16]

In her first meeting with staff on taking up her appointment in April 1992, executive director Bertini emphasized three points that were to frame her consistent and sustained drive towards reorganization. First, decisions should be made at the lowest possible levels within the organization. Second, the gender imbalance in WFP staff should be rectified by the appointment of more women, particularly at the senior levels. And third, she quoted from Edmund Burke: 'The only thing necessary for the triumph of evil is for good men to do nothing'.

In what was called a 'new era of governance', member states through the governing body, senior management, and staff were engaged in a dialogue on options for strengthening and transforming the WFP. Discussions were carried out within the constraints inherent in an organization that was multilateral in nature, with a complex governance structure linked to higher UN bodies, and an amalgam of administrative frameworks.[17] At the same time, a process of reform of the UN system was initiated with the passage of a number of resolutions in the UN General Assembly on development and emergency assistance that related to all UN bodies, including the WFP and its governing body. Simultaneously, the outbreak of large and complex emergencies had to be addressed.

Against this background, the early years of the 1990s were a period of intense discussion and debate. At the outset of the new decade, the WFP's governing body began to consider what directions the WFP might take in that decade. For this purpose, the WFP secretariat produced a paper which noted that, while the need for food aid was expected to grow, studies by the FAO and others had indicated that food aid could become a more scarce resource for development (WFP, 1991d). Three WFP strengths were listed that were considered to be particularly important for the future: its multilateral character; its institutional infrastructure with professional officers experienced in targeting and delivering food aid and field offices serving over 90 developing countries; and its focus on providing assistance to poor and hungry people.

But important constraints were also identified that could restrict WFP operations. Increasing demand for emergency and refugee operations, together with growing requests for bilateral services to assist donor agencies and NGOs to deliver their food aid, were putting pressure on the WFP's limited resources, leaving disproportionately less for development projects. This left two options. One was for donors to provide the WFP with more resources, thus enabling it to restore and continue its historical emphasis on development. The other was to concentrate WFP activities in certain key areas, which would increase the national impact of its assistance, through co-operation with other aid agencies working for similar goals, including NGOs.

No single prescription was offered for the WFP's future, but two conclusions were reached. For the WFP to continue to meet emergencies and provide services to bilateral food aid programmes, it would have to retain adequate staff, both in the field and at headquarters, and receive full compensation for the actual expenses incurred. As the development work of the WFP sustained its capacity to respond to emergencies, a revised financial formula was needed to support the WFP that took account of the interdependence of its activities. Otherwise, emergencies and bilateral services might increase constraints on the WFP's development work to the point that they undercut its strengths.

It was suggested that the 1990s could be used as a time to shift direction. One possibility might be to help national food systems through more focused projects. Moving in that direction would concentrate the WFP's development efforts on food-insecure countries and on activities that had substantial benefit for food supplies to poor and hungry people. As a multilateral agency, the WFP was in a strong position to help co-ordinate food aid from all sources in that direction.

The governing body's reaction to the secretariat's paper was to request, for its consideration, identification of the 'most significant issues' in food aid policies and programmes, and of the WFP's role in the 1990s (WFP, 1991a). Thus began a policy debate that was to take up much of the decade. To assist the debate, the World Bank and the WFP carried out a joint study of food aid to sub-Saharan Africa, which produced an agenda for food aid to the region in the 1990s (World Bank and WFP, 1991). A special programme of food assistance to sub-Saharan Africa was approved by the governing body in 1992 which focused on disaster prevention and mitigation (WFP, 1992a). Three regional seminars were organized in Asia, Africa, and Latin America by the WFP's secretariat to mark the first thirty years of WFP operations and to learn from its experience in shaping its future (WFP, 1994f, 1995b, 1995c).

In 1994, the conclusions of a tripartite evaluation of the WFP carried out by three donors countries (Canada, the Netherlands and Norway) between 1991 and 1993 were published (Chr. Michelsen Institute, 1994). This was one of the most detailed external assessments of any UN body at the time.[18] Taking the relief and development activities of the WFP together, the evaluation concluded:

> There is clear value in retaining WFP as a hybrid organization. If relief is accepted as the main focus there is still a strong case for combining – as a minimum development profile – an active programme oriented toward disaster preparedness, mitigation and rehabilitation. (Chr. Michelsen Institute, 1994, abridged version: 32)

In October 1993, the governing body decided to conduct a major review of WFP policies, objectives, and strategies. The secretariat was requested to prepare a paper to assist it in its discussions at its session in May 1994, which stated:

> Food aid cannot do everything. WFP should not attempt to do everything. WFP should concentrate on what it is best suited to do, with the resources available to it. This basic premise is an essential starting point on the road to WFP's transformation. (WFP, 1994g)

Informal consultations were held with governing body members and drafts of the policy review paper were circulated to them for comment. A policy seminar was held in February 1994 with the theme 'Hunger and Social Action', which brought together eminent persons, academics, and practitioners from UN organizations, NGOs, and other agencies with governing body members and observers.[19] The policy review also drew on extensive consultations among WFP staff, including a global meeting of WFP country directors, as well as senior staff of other UN agencies, and the findings of the WFP/World Bank joint study, the WFP regional seminars, and the tripartite evaluation.

Following this process of widespread involvement and discussion, a draft of a WFP mission statement was prepared by the WFP secretariat, which was reviewed and finalized by a working group consisting of 14 members of the governing body.[20] The *Mission Statement* was approved unanimously by the governing body in December 1994, the first since the WFP's original *General Regulations* were formulated thirty years previously. This represented a landmark in the WFP's history, and charted its course into the twenty-first century (WFP, 1994b).

The *Mission Statement* declared, amongst other things:

> The policies governing the use of World Food Programme food aid must be oriented towards the objective of eradicating hunger and poverty.

> Targeted interventions are needed to help improve the lives of the poorest people – people who, either permanently or during crisis periods, are unable to produce enough food or do not have the resources to otherwise obtain the food that they and their households require for active and healthy lives.

The core policies and strategies governing WFP activities were identified as providing food aid to: save lives in refugee and other emergency situations; improve the nutrition and quality of life of the most vulnerable people at critical times in their lives; and help build assets and promote the self-reliance of poor people and communities, particularly through labour-intensive works programmes. Having decided what the WFP should do, the next question was how to do it most effectively and efficiently. The momentous and inevitable answer was that the WFP should become a field-based organization. From that crucial decision, a number of other interrelated questions arose, including: what should be the strategic deployment of WFP's field staff throughout the developing world; what should be their main duties; what guidance and training materials should be developed and training programmes put in place; and, critically, what changes should take place at WFP headquarters to provide essential support services for its field staff?

Executive director Bertini recalled that 'a phased but critical shift of power to the field was required' (WFP, 2002: 22). A measured and deliberate process was set in motion. She issued two key documents, which laid out her vision for the WFP's future: 'Preparing WFP for the Future: An Organization to Meet our Mandate' (July 1996), and 'Implementing Organizational Change' (February 1997). The timing was linked to the broad UN reform process that was launched by the UN secretary-general in 1997. The short-term priority was to strengthen WFP country offices. The longer-term objective was to establish the WFP on the basis of field-driven strategies, thinking, and analysis, with flexible staff able to move quickly and work where needed. A cornerstone of the decentralization initiative was that more senior staff and decision-making should be in the field, close to the beneficiaries of WFP assistance. Authority would gradually shift from headquarters, which would focus on providing support to WFP field staff. Decentralization would also facilitate the corporate objectives for resource mobilization and advocacy.

One of the main dilemmas in 1996 concerned the tension between the need to put structural changes in place, and the importance of developing necessary systems and guidelines to support those changes. It was decided to do both at the same time to maintain the momentum for change. WFP staff were advised that the change process would go ahead in early 1997. The far-reaching implications were twofold: within the framework of policies and strategies, and the allocation of resources determined by senior management at WFP headquarters, WFP field managers would have full responsibility for managing food aid operations and the resources entrusted to them; and many of the services and advisory functions provided from WFP headquarters would, in future, be provided from the country offices or regional bureaux.

A period of uncertainty and frustration was inevitable during the early stages of the transformation process. The participation of WFP staff at every level was a key aspect of managing the change process. Their involvement was critical in their assuming ownership of the change process and for ensuring the success of the organizational changes brought about. Five task teams were set up that brought field and headquarters staff together.[21] The teams developed the practical side of the new vision of a restructured organization in such areas as decentralization, the streamlining of procedures, field-headquarters relations, advocacy, resource mobilization, staffing and training. Considerable efforts were made to communicate and interact with all WFP staff.

An organizational change team was established to facilitate, catalyze and integrate the work of the various task teams. This team produced newsletters, held several briefing sessions with managers and staff, and consolidated the suggestions and conclusions of the task teams. A change implementation strategy was announced in February 1997 (WFP, 1997g). A change manager was brought in to monitor the implementation of the decisions made and to advise WFP managers. Later, a management oversight committee was established. Progress in the change process was discussed at WFP executive staff meetings. The governing body was kept informed: it requested the WFP secretariat to prepare a paper for presentation to ECOSOC and the FAO Council on the many and wide-ranging reform efforts undertaken (WFP, 1996a).

In 1997, the WFP was able to report on the main elements of the organizational changes that had taken place in 1996 (WFP, 1997g: 3–4): more senior and specialized staff would work in the field; more authority would be delegated to the field, facilitating timely decision-making guided by practical knowledge of the situation on the ground; regional offices were being established in strategic locations throughout the developing world to plan and manage regional operations; regional managers would provide technical support and managerial guidance to WFP country directors; the country directors would broaden their understanding of the food security and food aid situation in their country of assignment; the WFP would be more active in advocating for the hungry poor, both at headquarters and in the field; most WFP staff would be capable of managing both emergency and development situations, for which expanded training programmes would be provided; and communications within the organization and with its stakeholders would be improved, and procedures and processes streamlined.

Through a process of trial and error that would take five years to complete, a new organizational structure for the field was introduced. The first approach was based on a cluster of countries under the responsibility of experienced regional managers located in what were called cluster (regional) offices strategically located throughout the developing world. This arrangement enabled the WFP to place senior managers closer to field operations and the supervision of WFP country offices, and represented the first stage in the decentralization process. Starting in 1997, 13 cluster offices were created:[22] these offices were to provide technical, programme, and managerial guidance to the WFP country offices in their cluster. To facilitate this arrangement, specialist functions were devolved to the field in such areas as programming, logistics, food procurement, public information, finance and management, and human resources management. The cluster offices also directly managed operations involving regional and cross-border relief assistance. The cluster offices were designed so that they could be re-aligned or dismantled flexibly, which gave the WFP the option for swift selection of the most appropriate organizational structure to meet rapidly changing needs.

The establishment of cluster offices was intended to support the WFP's country office, which remained the key organizational unit in the field. The process of building their capacities continued. Many WFP field offices tended to be small, headed by what were called directors of operation, who could be quite junior in grade. They reported to the WFP country representative, who was still, at the time, the UNDP resident representative (see p. 18). Most of the country offices were development-oriented and staffed by development advisers who helped the government design development projects, and monitored the implementation of the food programme. In countries with sizeable emergency operations, the WFP's Division of Transport and Logistics tended to take the lead and established its own units in countries where it operated. Development and emergency programmes were sometimes run independently, with different reporting lines to WFP headquarters.

In the process of institutional reform and restructuring, several changes were introduced to strengthen WFP country offices. It was decided that all staff in WFP country offices should report to the head of each office, which gave them responsibility for both development and emergency programmes. When the heads of the WFP country offices became WFP country representatives (see pp. 180–1), the management and administrative functions previous handled by the UNDP were transferred to them. Increased delegated authority was given to approve expenditures on emergency operations, hire staff and consultants, and sign food procurement contracts. Delegation of authority was also increased in the areas of programme approval, logistics, finance, and resource mobilization. The decisions to rotate WFP staff between its headquarters and the field, and to increase the numbers of women and nationals of developing countries in the WFP workforce, also helped to strengthen WFP country offices, although rotation also created tensions among staff and led to some resignations.

However, one outstanding question in the process of devolution remained. When WFP cluster offices were created, there was strong concern that this would add an additional bureaucratic layer between WFP headquarters and its field operation. There were already regional bureaux at WFP headquarters controlling and guiding field operations on a regional basis. It was argued that they were needed particularly in times of large and complex emergencies, and would certainly be required while reform and change initiatives were being implemented. But the commitment to decentralization had been firmly established. It was therefore decided that, on an experimental basis, two of the regional bureaux should be out-posted to the field. The Middle East and North Africa regional bureau was moved to Cairo, Egypt and the Latin American and Caribbean regional bureau was located in Managua, Nicaragua. The experiment proved to be successful and led to all regional bureaux being out-posted to the field.[23]

It was eventually decided that seven WFP regional bureaux would be established. But where were they to be located? The main criteria used for the selection of host countries were: staff security; logistics; financial aspects; and living conditions. For staff security, the UN security ratings and security incident reports were consulted. A wide range of matters had to be taken into account: logistics, which included international and regional air travel networks, telecommunications infrastructure, the regional presence of other UN and international bodies, and facilities such as conference space and hotel accommodation; financial considerations, which included the cost of office space (possibly provided free or partially by the host government), cost of international and local staff, banking facilities, audit and inspection track record, taxation regimes, and diplomatic privileges; living conditions, which included the cost of living, medical and recreational facilities, international schooling, spouse employment opportunities, availability of consumer items, functionality of utilities, climate, and geography.

Each regional bureau would cover an average of 12 WFP country offices. The complexity of the WFP's assistance portfolio would balance out differences in the average volumes of resources to oversee. It was agreed that each regional bureau would have a target of 16 core-funded international staff, which would include: the regional director and the deputy regional director; programme advisers and support officers specializing in logistics; food commodity pipeline management; human resources; finance and administration; food procurement; information and communications technology; and public information and media affairs.

In December 2000, the deputy director of the Operations Department at WFP headquarters, Jamie Wickens, was designated as decentralization project manager (DPM), under the guidance of the WFP Director of Operations and assisted by WFP staff and consultants, to work on specific key issues including: formalizing the WFP's relations with host governments in agreements on regional bureaux; mastering the wide complexities and implications relating to staffing; and setting up the infrastructure for the new regional bureaux. Host governments were requested to accredit WFP country directors as WFP representatives and recognize WFP regional directors as representatives of the region in which they were located, thus according them the usual immunities and privileges. The DPM hired a consultant to work full-time for about four months on the complex and delicate human resources issues including: liaising with managers and staff of existing regional offices in the field and in Rome; listening to their concerns; facilitating the transition by helping them to identify opportunities in the new structure and related matters such as personnel redeployment; local and national staff separations; pensions; general service staff mobility; and liaison with other UN agencies and staff associations.

A major mid-2001 staff reassignment process involved more than 300 staff considered for transfer with no overall increase in WFP staff members. A total of 31 international professional staff posts previously at WFP headquarters were relocated to the field in the final phase of decentralization. Most of the general service staff posts were relocated to different headquarters divisions and liaison offices. Once the decision concerning where to locate all the regional bureaux was finalized around April 2001, the WFP moved rapidly to ensure that they would be operational by no later than 1 September 2001, which coincided with the WFP's major mid-year staff reassignment cycle. The executive director approved a budget of about $4 million to meet the costs of the establishment and functioning of the new regional bureaux and their telecommunication and security facilities. By September 2001, the decentralization process was complete (Table 4.1).

The decentralization, devolution and delegation measures that were initiated in 1996 had a major effect on the role and organization of WFP headquarters, particularly the Operations Department. In early October 1999, a consultant was hired to identify the major impediments to the effective implementation of the WFP's decentralization strategy, focusing particularly on the Operations Department. In mid-2000, a report was produced, 'Making Decentralization Work', which identified a series of issues including that: real decentralization must be accompanied by more decision-making power and delegation of authority to field-based managers; normative technical services were required to maintain a corporate profile; the regional bureaux should not become separate mini-WFPs; WFP corporate information systems must be fully implemented, especially in the field; clear definitions of the linkages, roles, and responsibilities of WFP headquarters and the field should be made in new and high-profile emergencies; face-to-face contact should be maintained among senior managers dispersed throughout the world; an effective corporate memory should be built up for an organization that continued to learn; and it be recognized that the management of change will never finish and will be a continuous process.

Table 4.1 WFP regional bureaux and country offices after full decentralization, September 2001

WFP operational region	Location of WFP regional bureau	Number of WFP country offices
West Africa	Dakar, Senegal	12
Eastern and Southern Africa	Kampala, Uganda	15[1]
Central Africa	Yaounde, Cameroon	9
Latin America and Caribbean	Managua, Nicaragua	10[2]
Asia	Bangkok, Thailand	12
ODC	Cairo, Egypt	13[3]
Eastern Europe	Rome, Italy	6

Notes: [1] Including the Maputo, Mozambique cluster with five country offices. [2] A resources office was located at Lima, Peru. [3] Including the Islamabad, Pakistan cluster of four country offices.

Key: ODC Mediterranean, Middle East and Central Asia region

Source: WFP *Status report on WFP's decentralization initiative* (WFP/EB.3/2001/11-B, annex).

The Operations Department was reorganized by September 2001, with two wings. The first wing comprised: a Transport Division with a Logistics Service; an Ocean Transport Service; an Insurance and Legal Branch; and a Freight Analysis and Support Branch. The second wing comprised a series of support services, under the Department's deputy director, including: an Office for Development Activities; an Office for Humanitarian Affairs; a Bureaux of Liaison Offices, reporting directly to regional bureaux in the field; a senior adviser for Africa; a Programming Service, and a Vulnerability Assessment and Mapping (VAM) unit.

Restructuring at headquarters took place with the aim of providing normative guidance, advice, and support to WFP regional bureaux and country offices. This was facilitated by the move of WFP headquarters to new and greatly improved accommodation in the late 1990s. Procedures, tools, and guidelines were developed to assist managers in WFP field offices in assuming their responsibilities and reducing the need to control individual decisions and transactions. Also, standards were established and systems put in place to ensure that the procedures, tools, and guidelines were respected, achieved through audit and evaluation reports, the monitoring of programme quality, and organizational learning.

Especially important was the need to carry out training and recruitment programmes to meet the skills demanded by the new organizational structure focused on the field and to fill the gaps created by departing staff unable to come to terms with changing demands and expectations. In 1996, a staff training change team was set up to manage a comprehensive training strategy and training programmes in most aspects of WFP work. Particular attention was given to staff security and safety because of the nature and location of their work, including staff counselling programmes to provide psychological support. In 2000, a peer support volunteer programme was established with confidential counselling and referral services for all WFP employees and their families, and a WFP ombudsman was appointed to hear staff problems. In 2006, a WFP ombudsman was appointed, reporting directly to the executive director, to provide staff and management with the services of an impartial and independent person and office where employment-related complaints and grievances could be informally addressed in a totally confidential setting.

The work undertaken on recruitment, skills profiling, and staff development played an important part in responding to the decision to have a mobile and versatile workforce that could be moved smoothly between positions at headquarters and the field, and to different locations in the field, as well as deployed to different and often difficult field situations at short notice. Another step was to provide managers with broad exposure to different work settings, field posts, and programmes. Through the recruitment, promotions, and transfer process, priority was given to bringing senior managers to headquarters and transferring them from headquarters to the field. Prior relevant field experience was a prerequisite for promotion to senior levels. In 1996, there were few senior-level managers in the field. By the beginning of the new millennium, half of the total number of WFP senior-level managers headed the regional bureaux and country offices. Also, as part of a rapid response team, by the end of 2001 the WFP had 100 staff members trained and on standby for deployment within 48 hours to an emergency anywhere in the world.

These changes encouraged staff to understand the importance of mobility in determining their careers and in transforming the headquarters–field divide. Deliberate progress was also made in meeting the targets set for the proportions of women and nationals of developing countries in the workforce. The proportion of women among the WFP's international professional staff increased from 17 per cent in January 1992 to 39 per cent in June 2001, with significant increases in the number of women in senior management positions. Other undertakings were made to women following the statement made by executive director Bertini on the WFP's behalf at the *Fourth United Nations Conference on Women* in Beijing, China in 1995, which improved WFP activities, particularly in emergency operations (see Gender policy, Chapter 5).

A target was also set for 40 per cent of WFP international professional staff to be from developing countries, which was exceeded by the turn of the new millennium. Stress was placed on the recruitment of national staff in WFP country offices, rather than on significantly increasing the number of internationally recruited officers. This policy produced a number of benefits. It helped to build national capacity, reduce operating costs, and provided more opportunities to hire qualified women, as well as contributing to programme continuity and institutional memory.

The focus on improving managers was helped by two other critical decisions. The first was to remove the historical legacy of under-grading WFP posts. Approval was obtained from the WFP's executive board to upgrade many existing posts in relation to their responsibilities and to the relative grades of counterparts in other UN agencies. The second was critically to shift managers' focus from the management of food to the management of people and the impact of WFP assistance on the hungry poor. During the last half of the 1990s, more than 300 managers were trained, starting at senior level then proceeding to middle-management and, finally, to the training of more junior professional officers in basic supervisory skills. The training programme increased WFP management capacity and created opportunities to increase communication throughout the organization. A key part of the efforts to enhance the WFP's management culture was the emphasis on building management teams at various levels to think strategically together, to formulate decisions, and to ensure a collegial and disciplined approach to the implementation of those decisions.

New institutional arrangements were established at WFP headquarters in 2001. A small executive group composed of the executive director, deputy executive director, the two assistant executive directors, and the director of the Office of the Executive Director was established to act as the senior management team for key management and operational decisions. This group was complemented by an executive staff unit to deal with the broad strategic, policy and managerial issues facing the WFP. The executive staff unit was composed of 20 members, including the executive group and 15 senior managers: 11 from developing countries and nine from developed countries, 13 of whom were male and seven female.

The executive staff unit met four times a year at one annual retreat and three working sessions immediately after meetings of the WFP's executive board, plus occasional teleconferences. Management teams were also created within each department and division at WFP headquarters, and in WFP regional bureaux and country offices. The nurturing of the WFP's organizational culture was a constant preoccupation of senior management from the beginning of the 1990s, reflecting the belief that true transformation would occur only when new principles and behaviour were embedded in the organizational culture.

Assessments of the decentralization initiative

Between 2002 and 2007, assessments of the decentralization initiative were conducted. In 2002, as part of his audited biennial accounts for 2000–01, the WFP's external auditor carried out a review of the decentralization process (WFP, 2002h).[24] The review was critical of the way in which host countries were chosen to locate the new regional bureaux. No formal evaluation was conducted, as previously recommended by the external auditor. The work done by a consultant was said to focus on procedures and responsibilities, and did not analyze the impact in terms of staff and other costs. It was recommended that, for the establishment of any further regional bureaux in the future, a comparative study be conducted and kept on record. Agreements signed with host countries should, notably, detail the form of the government's contribution and also indicate precisely who should pay for utilities, maintenance, and repairs.

As part of the review, a questionnaire was distributed to WFP country directors who had been out-posted from headquarters to the WFP's Latin America and Caribbean, and the Mediterranean, Middle East and Central Asian regions. The questionnaire contained five sections: electronic connections between WFP headquarters and the field; the restructuring of the Operational Department to serve WFP regional bureaux and country offices; the empowerment of WFP country offices; the performance of the regional bureaux and headquarters in supporting WFP country office staff; and the accomplishments of the decentralization process so far, and the challenges for the future. There was a high rate of replies (89 per cent). Analysis of the replies showed a wide range of views, confusion over the aims of decentralization, and concern over the image that the process might create in developing countries, especially with governments.[25]

In October 2001, the executive board requested a review of decentralization, including aspects of cost efficiency and the effects on programming. This review was carried out in May and June 2003 by a team of independent consultants.[26] The review showed that staff and non-staff costs over the period of decentralization (1996–2003) increased by $20.3 million (49 per cent). The steep decline in headquarters' costs to $23.1 million (55 per cent) was offset by the higher costs of setting up and operating the regional structures. Over the same period, international professional staff at headquarters decreased from 100 to 48, and general service staff from 102 to 69 – an overall decrease of 42 per cent. Field staff increased from 100 professional and 102 general service staff to 137 professional and 183 general service staff – an overall increase of 58 per cent. At the same time, the workload expressed by turnover (total expenditure) increased substantially from $2.7 million and 4.9 million tons of food to $4.4 million and 8.7 million tons of food.

One of the major objectives of decentralization was to upgrade the competence and professional standing of staff in a field structure with expanded authority and out-posted senior decision-makers. The number of senior professional officers (grades D1 and D2) increased from 13 to 41, while middle-level management professional staff (grades P3–P5) increased from 300 to 342, and junior professional staff (grades P1 and P2) increased from 56 to 130.

The review found that significant progress had been made towards meeting the original objectives of decentralization. Authority had been delegated to the field for project design and approval, financial management, human resources, food procurement, inventory control, transport, acceptance of contributions and budget revisions. Regional directors chaired programme review committees. Country directors found it particularly helpful to be granted the WFP representative status, formerly held by UNDP resident representatives, which enhanced the WFP's profile and standing in their host countries and with other agencies. But the review noted that new authority and representation placed considerable, and sometimes excessive, strain on field staff and capacities, especially for small offices, and affected programme quality. The WFP had not yet identified consistent measures of programme quality, but the establishment of the Office of Performance Measurement and Reporting at WFP headquarters was regarded as a major step in this regard.

The regional bureaux had been established to support WFP country offices but, the review observed, the responsibilities and authority of the bureaux needed to be clarified. They had to balance involvement in corporate and strategic thinking with hands-on support for the country offices under their supervision. The roles, responsibilities and workings of the regional bureaux should therefore be reviewed. It was questioned whether they had enough staff with the right skills to support country offices consistently.

Progress had been made in transforming WFP headquarters' controlling role to that of supporting WFP field offices, with a focus on providing normative guidance, standards and corporate strategies, and priorities. By the end of January 2003, there were 66 professional staff in the Operational Department at headquarters, including transport and logistics personnel, compared to 110 in 1997. Significant progress had been made in improving normative guidance, especially in enhancing access to guidance manuals, directives, circulars and other information that was placed on the WFP internal Intranet, making it instantly available to all WFP staff in the field and at headquarters. Especially helpful were a revised *Programme Design Manual*, an *Emergency Response Manual*, and a manual on the *Administration of Local Staff*, previously handled by the UNDP. The Operations Department also produced the primary document providing guidance on decentralization entitled *Guidelines for Model Structures, Unit Definitions, Distribution and Allocation of Functions, Functional Statements, Work Flow and Delegation of Authority for the Bureaux* (OD/2000/004, 10 November

2000), which, it was acknowledged, required to be updated in the light of experience with out-posting.

WFP field staff reported that there may be too much guidance material rather than too little, and requested more co-ordinated guidance from the various headquarters offices. Much of the guidance material, which had been written by consultants, needed to be reformulated in accordance with a corporate policy on format and style. Also, more consultation should take place with WFP field offices, and for them to adjust, before guidance was approved.

Progress was also made in involving WFP country directors and regional managers in mobilizing resources locally and in increasing advocacy for improvements in national food security policies. In January 2003, public information officers were placed in four regional bureaux and seven large country offices, resulting in a significant increase in the WFP's visibility. Some high-profile successes were recorded.[27]

An objective of decentralization was to increase knowledge-sharing among the WFP field offices in each region by capturing lessons learned and innovative practices. This was being done more in some regions than in others. The example was given of the annual regional logistics meetings for corporate knowledge-sharing with outcomes and recommendations that were reviewed at WFP headquarters and incorporated into the WFP's *Transport Manual*.

The review noted that the emerging decentralization structure magnified staffing and capacity issues. The uneven capacities observed among WFP country directors called for clearer career paths, and better and earlier training of new applicants, consistent with a system of monitoring by experienced country directors. Concern was expressed that fewer headquarters staff accepted reassignment to the field. A staffing analysis was required to assess the impact of decentralization. An objective was to enable all staff to handle new responsibilities and to work in both emergency and development operations. Field managers suggested that training should be more demand-driven and respond to needs identified by them.

The review concluded that, despite progress and the benefits of decentralization, several challenges and potential obstacles remained. Out-posting regional bureaux had resulted in some confusion and overlapping of roles and responsibilities among country offices and regional bureaux, and, to a greater extent, between headquarters and regional bureaux. The costs of decentralization were neutral (and close to staff neutral) in the context of workload changes. Significant progress had been made towards the main objectives of decentralization. Maintaining the effectiveness and cost-efficiency of out-posted regional bureaux would require regular review and a willingness to make periodic adjustments. The structure, staffing and, perhaps, location of regional bureaux would have to remain adaptable to changes in the WFP's workload and priorities, and the support needs of WFP country offices. Staff would have to accept the ongoing changes that flexibility brought. Two consecutive executive directors had endorsed what was now a managerial philosophy that should be applied, maintained, and constantly improved.

In 2007, the WFP's external auditor was requested to examine whether decentralization had met the WFP's operational needs at a time when a significant reduction in the WFP's programme and support administrative budget resulted in substantial reductions in its staff, particularly at headquarters (WFP, 2007k).[28] The main objective of the review was to examine the impact of decentralization on the use of resources. Three questions were asked. Had decentralization: led to appropriate, properly controlled and timely allocation of country and regional resources; focused resources effectively to best support operational needs; and given rise to cost-effective and efficient use of resources overall? Progress made in decentralization was also looked at against the five strategic objectives of the WFP's approved *Strategic Plan* for 2006–09, especially strategic objective 5: to strengthen the capacities of countries and regions to establish and manage food-assistance and hunger reduction programmes (WFP, 2005a).

The external auditor's report considered the impact of decentralization on the WFP's regional structure and headquarters. It concluded that management decision-making was now closer to operations, and country offices in general were better supported and managed through the regional structure. However, the need for WFP assistance was constantly changing among and within developing countries and regions. As a time-lag may occur before any modification in the decentralization structure could take effect, the WFP could therefore benefit from a more flexible structure to respond to changing needs. Comparisons with the decentralization structures of similar UN agencies might be useful. Options might include co-locating WFP offices with other bodies in the UN system, or maintaining one central office for each continent.

The report noted that there had been considerable changes in the workloads of the WFP's regional bureaux for two main reasons: the changing nature of emergency needs; and decisions to move responsibility for country offices between regional bureaux. There was a limit to the number of country offices that could be cost-effectively supported by a regional bureau, depending on the staff resources allocated to a regional bureau, logistical constraints, and the overall operational needs of a region. Despite improvements in controls, there remained lack of clarity about who should exercise oversight and a clearer definition was required of responsibilities between country offices, regional bureaux and headquarters.

International professional staff increased from 312 in 2002 to 503 in 2007, an increase of over 60 per cent. General service staff increased from 75 to 310 over the same period, an increase of 24 per cent. Total WFP staff numbers increased from 622 in 2002 to 888 in 2007. Decentralization did not seem to have resulted in reduced staffing levels at headquarters in the way that might have been expected from the decentralization process, and there was greater reliance on the flexibility of consultant contracts, which increased significantly. Many consultants originally recruited to assist the WFP in responding to emergencies or to provide specialist expertise were retained for relatively long, continuous periods. The report concluded that increases in the number of field offices and staff, combined with proportionately greater increases in headquarters staff and the continuous use of consultants, were not factors which, taken together, indicated increasing efficiency or, perhaps, effectiveness in the use of WFP resources. It recommended that a rationalization of the regional infrastructure be undertaken in line with need and that more economic alternatives be explored.

Despite many problems and difficulties, the decentralization of staff and decision-making had been achieved, a major accomplishment that took place during a period when the WFP was asked to respond to an increasing number of large and complex emergency operations. Also, decentralization was indispensable for creating the world's largest humanitarian agency.

Resource problems: WFP *Biennial Management Plan (2008–09)*

The WFP's decentralization process faced resourcing problems in 2007, which seriously affected its *Biennial Management Plan (2008–09)* (WFP, 2007a). The management plan rested on the assumption that the United Nations and its member states required the global humanitarian operations and programme activities of the WFP, and were ready to fund it on a voluntary basis. The funding model for the WFP differs significantly from other UN bodies in that it has no predictable income for its programme support and administrative (PSA) expenditures. The PSA budget covers all staff and non-staff costs at WFP headquarters and liaison offices, the majority of costs in its regional bureaux, and some of the management costs of its country offices. These costs are funded solely by income derived from a certain percentage, set at 7 per cent, of the voluntary contribution received from donors.[29]

Given the uncertainties inherent in this funding model, a main challenge facing the WFP leadership and member states is to maintain a managerial and operational support capacity that has certain basic features. It has to be both robust and flexible, and be able to meet the commitments made to its beneficiaries in operations and programmes approved by its executive board. At the same time, it has to maintain a rapid response and preparedness capacity in terms of staff, equipment, and systems, ready to be mobilized immediately at the onset of unforeseen emergencies.

This funding model served well in years when the volume of WFP work and resources increased considerably with the onset and increased frequency of major natural and human-made disasters. When fewer or no major emergencies occurred, the 7 per cent formula was unable to meet the management costs that had been built up in the crisis year. An additional factor is that the funding model has lacked a mechanism to compensate for significant increases in the price of food and fuel, and US dollar/European euro exchange rate variations (see Chapter 7). The US dollar exchange rate against the European euro has fallen sharply in recent years. Most of the WFP's PSA expenditures are incurred in European euros at WFP headquarters in Rome, Italy.

As a result, the PSA budget for the 2009–09 biennium was reduced by 21 per cent in real terms and WFP staff reduced by around 290 posts. With retirements and voluntary early separations, around 50 staff did not have their contracts extended. The aim was to manage these reductions in ways that did not harm the hungry and most vulnerable beneficiaries. Consequently, headquarters, liaison offices and regional bureaux had greater PSA reductions than country offices. The regional bureaux for southern, eastern and central Africa were merged under one regional director based in Johannesburg, South Africa, with key regional functions in Kampala, Uganda under a deputy regional director. However, it could not be excluded that activities in critical areas would be reduced to a level at which efficiency gains could not be compensated for the loss of capacities and competencies.

The impact of UN system reform

At the same time as the WFP's transformation process was under way, a series of major reforms of the UN system was taking place. These reforms had a direct effect on the WFP and its operations. In 1991, a UN General Assembly resolution was passed calling for the strengthening of the co-ordination of humanitarian emergency assistance provided through the UN system (UN, 1991b). The resolution led to: the creation of the post of UN emergency relief co-ordinator; the establishment of a UN Department of Humanitarian Affairs (DHA) to strengthen UN co-ordination, co-operation, and leadership in emergency operations; the setting up of a UN Inter-Agency Standing Committee(IASC) for emergencies, of which the WFP became a member; and the development of the concept of a 'continuum' of action and support from relief to rehabilitation and development, which became the framework for UN emergency operations. The WFP's *Mission Statement* recognized that 'WFP is well placed to play a major role in the continuum from emergency relief to development' and would 'give priority to supporting disaster prevention, preparedness and mitigation and post-disaster rehabilitation activities as part of development programmes'. The *Mission Statement* also recognized that:

> No single agency has either the resources or the capacity to deal with the problems of hunger and underdevelopment. Hence the importance WFP attaches to collaboration with other agencies, particularly with its parent bodies, the United Nations and FAO. WFP will continue to work closely with the United Nations Department of Humanitarian Affairs, UNHCR, other relevant agencies and non-governmental organizations (NGOs) in response to emergencies and humanitarian crises. (WFP, 1994b)

In 1992, the WFP responded to UN General Assembly resolution 44/211, which recommended that: 'Non-emergency food aid channelled through the organizations of the UN system should be programmed coherently so as to ensure its full integration with the development programmes of governments'. The UN director-general for development and international economic co-operation recommended that, within the context of the UN General Assembly resolution, the WFP 'be invited to recommend steps to bring about the greater integration of food aid with other assistance provided by the United Nations system' (ECOSOC, 1990: para. 201).

The WFP report presented, in a frank and systematic way, the factors that had been known for some time to inhibit both the integration of WFP food aid into recipient government development programmes, and its co-ordination with other forms of assistance provided by other UN organizations.[30] National development programmes were not always coherently articulated and co-ordinating the work of government ministries was often weak. The governments that WFP support faced severe budgetary constraints, and often civil strife, which distorted their development priorities or brought meaningful development initiatives to a halt.

Systematic and sustained collaboration between the WFP and other UN organizations was constrained by a number of factors, including lack of appreciation of the comparative advantage of WFP food aid. The system of WFP representation at the country level prohibited WFP aid from being brought into the mainstream of development assistance planning. Proposals were made to counter misconceptions and ignorance about WFP assistance, and to present concrete ideas for its use in World Bank and UNDP-sponsored consultative group meetings, which covered all aid to developing countries. Other specific proposals were made, including the adoption of a country programming approach to the planning and implementation of WFP assistance, which was recommended in the study leading to the establishment of WFP in 1961 (see Chapter 1: FAO 1961b) and started in 1994 as the 'cornerstone' of WFP strategy for providing assistance to developing countries (WFP, 1994a).

A further proposal arose out of the findings of the WFP report which, although not completely surprising, had been downplayed or largely ignored. From its inception, the WFP did not appoint its own independent representatives in recipient developing countries. Instead, the resident representatives of the UN Technical Assistance Board, which in 1965, together with the UN Special Fund, became the UNDP, were appointed as representatives of the WFP in addition to their other responsibilities. This arrangement was agreed to for three main reasons. First, the WFP was originally set up as an experimental programme for a short period of three years with an uncertain future, for which it was considered unwise to establish an elaborate self-contained administrative structure. Second, administrative and management costs should be kept to a minimum, consistent with operational efficiency. And third, the WFP experiment was approved at a time when a high premium was placed on the strengthening of co-ordination among the bodies of the UN system in the context of the first UN Decade for Development of the 1960s, which could be facilitated by having the UNDP resident representative as also the representative of the WFP.

By 1994, over thirty years after the WFP began operations, it was generally recognized that the arrangement by which the WFP was represented in developing countries was inconsistent with the importance WFP assistance had assumed in the totality of UN system development aid. It was therefore decided, in 1995, to designate WFP representatives from among its own staff in countries receiving its assistance. This ensured their dialogue with key government officials and freed UNDP resident representatives for the more active pursuit of their growing responsibilities as UN resident co-ordinators (WFP, 1995a: 11).

Yet another UN General Assembly resolution was passed in 1992, this time focused on the co-ordination of development assistance provided through the UN system (UN, 1992a). As with the resolution passed in 1991 on the co-ordination of UN-system emergency assistance, this one was born out of a sense of frustration that the UN system was not working cohesively to ensure that maximum benefit would be obtained from all the development assistance provided. A major implication was that notice was served on the UN system to 'get its act together', and that failure to respond could have serious consequences for the future level, flow, and direction of multilateral development assistance.

The centrepiece of the resolution was the call for country strategies for UN-system development assistance for individual developing countries. For this purpose, a 'country strategy note' (CSN) should be formulated by recipient governments with the assistance of the UN system under the leadership of the UN resident co-ordinator. The CSN would provide the framework for a country programme approach for all UN-system development assistance, including food aid, in which the various components of aid would be interrelated and linked. Critically, the resolution urged the governing bodies of the UN agencies to ensure the delegation of authority to field offices, and stressed the importance of supporting national priorities and national execution and the building up of national capacity in developing countries. This fitted well with the country programme approach that the WFP had adopted and the general tenor of its assistance strategy.

In 1993, the UN General Assembly passed another resolution, which transformed the WFP's governing body (UN, 1993). It will be recalled that the WFP's governing body had been enlarged and its duties changed with effect from the beginning of 1992. The resolution transformed the governing bodies of the UN funds and programmes (UNDP, UNFPA, UNICEF, and WFP) into executive boards of identical size and composition, and with similar functions and responsibilities. Each board would consist of 36 members composed of eight members from African states, seven from Asian states, four from Eastern European states, five from Latin American and Caribbean states, and 12 from Western European and other states. Common functions and working methods were established for the executive boards, under the authority of ECOSOC, although the joint undertaking of the WFP as a UN/FAO organ was retained.

The functions of the executive boards were to: implement the policies formulated by the UN General Assembly and the co-ordination and guidance received from ECOSOC; receive information from, and give guidance to, the executive head of each organization; ensure that the activities and operational strategies pursued were consistent with the overall policy guidance given by the UN General Assembly and ECOSOC; monitor the performance of each organization; approve programmes of assistance; decide on administrative and financial plans and budgets; recommend new initiatives to ECOSOC and the UN General Assembly; and submit annual reports to ECOSOC, with a common structure, in order to ensure effective interaction between the UN General Assembly, ECOSOC, and the individual executive boards. It was evident that the main purpose behind the resolution was to achieve greater discipline and co-ordination among these UN bodies in line with UN General Assembly and ECOSOC directives and guidance.[31]

A comprehensive reform of the UN system was carried out by the newly-appointed UN secretary-general, Kofi Annan, in 1997, which he described as 'the most extensive and far-reaching reforms in the 52-year history of our Organization', in order 'To bring greater unity of purpose, greater coherence of effort, and greater agility in responding to the increasingly dynamic and complex world'. The reform measures were intended to 'enhance our ability to promote development and address the root causes of poverty and conflict' (Annan, 1997). They focused on the UN secretariat in New York and the UN funds and programmes, and did not include the World Bank, or the IMF, or the other UN specialized agencies, thereby weakening its impact.

Five areas were identified that comprised what were referred to as the 'core missions' of the UN: peace and security, economic and social affairs, development co-operation, humanitarian affairs, and human rights. Executive committees were established to co-ordinate work in the first four areas, while human rights was designated as a 'cross-cutting' concern and therefore included in the work of all four committees. The WFP was designated to take part in the UN development executive committee, which led the reform process in the area of UN development activities. The WFP also became a member of the UN executive committee on humanitarian affairs in addition to taking part in the UN inter-agency standing committee for the co-ordination of humanitarian emergency relief, and participating in the joint meetings of the UN executive committees on peace and security, and economic and social development with the UN development and humanitarian affairs executive committees.

Through participation in these various executive committees, the WFP now had the opportunity to co-ordinate its food aid with financial and technical assistance provided by other UN agencies for both development and emergency operations. The reform measures also included the establishment of one 'UN house' in each developing country to accommodate and provide common services, security, and safety arrangements for all UN organizations with aid programmes under a UN resident co-ordinator. Later, through the implementation of the 'cluster system', the WFP was designated as the lead agency in the UN system for providing logistics support, with UNICEF for providing common telecommunications support, and with the FAO for food security (see pp. 187–9).

Transport and logistics expertise

We saw in Chapter 2 that the WFP's expertise and experience in transport and logistics played a prominent part in the advancement of the organization in its first thirty years. Subsequently, the WFP has built on this strong foundation by establishing rapid response to emergencies in a number of ways, so that executive director Sheeran was able to state in 2008 that: 'Today, we manage a global lifeline that can reach any corner of the world in 48 hours' (Sheeran, 2008). On any given day, the WFP operates an average of 60 aircraft, 40 ships, and 5,000 trucks. In 2009, the WFP reached 101.8 million beneficiaries in 75 countries with food assistance. To achieve this goal, the WFP drew from its impressive logistics capacity using surface transport, shipping, and aviation. About half the food distributed by the WFP is sourced directly within the country or region where it is needed. The other half is shipped by sea and unloaded in some 78 cargo ports around the world.

Augmented Logistics Intervention Teams for Emergencies (ALITE)

Starting with the response to the humanitarian crisis in Rwanda in 1994, the WFP established a mechanism for rapidly despatching teams of experienced WFP staff to the scene of large-scale and complex emergencies to provide immediate and effective emergency services to support WFP field operations. ALITE has provide to be particularly effective when it is important to co-ordinate the use of military and civil defence assets in humanitarian operations and in assisting WFP country offices overcome logistics bottlenecks. The most recent example has been the WFP's response to the massive earthquake in Haiti in 2010, when an ALITE force of 150 WFP staff was deployed from 24 WFP duty stations (Sheeran, 2010a).

Virtual food stocks

In times of crisis, the WFP has a number of ways of responding quickly to emergency food needs when disasters occur. Food stocks set up to assist WFP-supported development projects in developing countries can be drawn upon, although the ability to do this has been reduced as WFP assistance for development projects has declined. The WFP is also in command of a large floating stock of food. On any given day, the WFP has 40 ships at sea moving cargoes from 60 loading ports to some 75 discharge ports as it carries food commodities for distribution in more than 70 countries worldwide. This allows the WFP to re-route cargoes to unexpected emergencies when required. And food can be borrowed from the stocks of developing countries on a replenishment basis through bilateral arrangements with recipient countries to meet emergency needs.

Special operations

The WFP's Transport and Logistics Division launches special operations pragmatically in support of WFP emergency operations to overcome bottlenecks that hinder the smooth and effective flow of crucially needed relief food to afflicted people. In 1996, special operations became a WFP official funding programme category. Previously, the cost of such operations were met, in part, through a subsidy to meet the internal transport, storage, and handling (ITSH) costs that the WFP's governing body had approved in 1972, which led to a marked increase in the need for additional cash resources (see Chapter 2). But donors preferred to contribute to additional logistics costs through specifically identified and assessed special operations.

Funding of special operations increased dramatically, as Table 3.1 (pp. 183–5) shows, but shortfalls led to an evaluation of their performance and results. The WFP's Transport and Logistics Division requested WFP's Office of Evaluation to conduct an evaluation of special operations in 2002 (WFP, 2002g).[32] The evaluation found that a large part of the special operations were infrastructure works directly related to the WFP's first priority, to deliver relief food on time to beneficiaries in dire need. It noted that the WFP had had expensive experience in dealing with logistics bottlenecks that hindered meeting that priority. The ability of WFP field staff to deal with them, with the backing of the WFP's Transport and Logistics Division at headquarters, was seen as a major factor in the WFP becoming the lead UN agency in transport and logistics matters. WFP successes had triggered the development of WFP logistics services not only for the transport of urgently needed relief food supplies, but also for all aspects of humanitarian operations for the benefit of the entire humanitarian community. Thus, whereas special operations were, in essence, originally meant to be short-term, complementing exceptional operations, some became longer-term, stand-alone operations, or were for the benefit of other humanitarian operators as well as the WFP.

The evaluation mission felt that a number of special operations were logistics components of WFP emergency operations and should remain so, rather than become stand-alone operations. Many of the logistics bottlenecks could have been foreseen at the start of an emergency operation. On other occasions, contingency planning should have been included in logistics plans. Advanced planning, and accurate and detailed assessments of logistics requirements and constraints could probably have avoided the need for some special operations. And regular, technically qualified assessments would have been of help, as assessments were not always correct.

A recurrent phenomenon was an overestimation of special operations budgets and inadequate budget control, resulting in funds being unspent, wrongly earmarked, or overspent. Delays had been experienced in the donor funding of special operations. Considering the urgent need for most special operations, on which the success of a whole emergency operation often depended, the evaluation mission recommended the establishment of a fast-track administrative mechanism, and guaranteed swift access to funds, through a reserve fund pending the arrival of donor contributions, and operational procedures and guidelines drawn up in place of *ad hoc* arrangements.

The evaluation mission recommended that only two kinds of special operations should remain: infrastructure operations for unforeseeable logistics obstacles and for large-scale infrastructure works that could benefit a whole region and a number of emergency operations, which could be considered a project in itself; and inter-agency co-ordination operations, as in air services, telecommunications, joint logistics management, or co-ordination services.

Whatever weaknesses were found, the evaluation mission considered that the larger part of the special operations activities undertaken were 'justified, well implemented and effective', and that a 'dedicated and competent field staff was one of the major factors ensuring operation success'. The ability of WFP field staff to identify logistics bottlenecks and deal with them was considered to be a major factor in the WFP's success as the UN food aid agency. Over the years, the WFP had become increasingly the lead UN organization in logistics, as other agencies turned increasingly to the WFP to take on the co-ordination of logistics in emergency operations. In 2004, the WFP *General Regulations* were amended to include special operations as a programme category and defined in ways recommended by the evaluation mission (see Chapter 2).

Lead agency in logistics

At the onset of an emergency, it is crucial that emergency relief supplies required in an immediate response be deployed to the location of need in the fastest and most efficient way, and co-ordinated with the humanitarian agencies involved. During the humanitarian crisis in Eastern Zaire (now the Democratic Republic of the Congo) in 1996, the UNHCR, UNICEF and WFP combined their resources to airlift relief assistance into, and refugees out of, the war zone. This, and similar initiatives, resulted in the UN Interagency Standing Committee (IASC) Working Group on emergencies requesting the WFP to take the lead in developing the concept of a UN Joint Logistics Centre (UNJLC) to complement and co-ordinate the logistics capabilities of co-operating humanitarian agencies in large-scale emergencies. In 2002, the core unit of this mechanism was established at WFP headquarters in Rome, Italy. The core unit launches and manages field operations at the request of a UN country team or UN humanitarian co-ordinator. It prepares terms of reference for the IASC Working Group, whose approval can be obtained in 48 hours; at the same time, a special operation (see pp. 183–4) is prepared to support the field operations.

The WFP established its first humanitarian response depot in Brindisi, Italy in June 2000. In 2006, based on the WFP's own needs and at its own cost, the WFP replicated the Brindisi model by establishing two other regional humanitarian response depots to respond quickly to emergency situations in Africa, Asia, and Latin America. The operational success of these facilities resulted in the IASC establishing a UN Humanitarian Relief Depot (UNHRD) network administered by the WFP in strategic locations throughout the world, with depots located in Brindisi, Italy; Accra, Ghana; Panama City, Panama; Phom Penh, Cambodia; and Dubai, United Arab Emirates.[33] The purpose is to provide services that enable international humanitarian organizations to better co-ordinate a cohesive response and to minimize the time required to respond to emergencies. This is done through the pre-positioning of supplies at these strategic locations. At the same time, procurement and transport costs are minimized through economies of scale. The goal is that the network will host 50 users, provide 70 per cent of supplies in the first wave of a response to emergencies, will be completely self-sustaining, and will be adaptable to different locations and situations.

The UNHRD network provides the humanitarian community with standard services (free of charge) of storage, inspection, stock management, customs procedures, and visibility through a web-site and publications. The UNHRD also provides services on a competitive full-cost recovery basis including: procurement of non-food items and services, handling, kitting, repackaging, refurbishing, transport, stock insurance, rapid response teams, and other *ad hoc* services. The UNHRD focuses on establishing and strengthening partnerships with donors and users through presentations, interagency meetings, donor relations and communications, including a website. The aim is to increase the number of users by offering a diversity of services and reducing running costs through enhanced common planning and response to emergencies, including strengthening ties with the UN Logistics Cluster (see p. 188) and other UN clusters (such as in shelter, and water and sanitation), which will enhance co-ordination, common planning, and collective response to emergencies. Training is being provided to authorized users within the UNHRD in technical field operations, and logistics response and workshops, including a logistics cluster workshop. The depot in Brindisi, Italy will be developed into a centre of excellence for humanitarian logistics training.

The UNHRD network is funded by 14 donors: Australia, Canada, the European Commission's Humanitarian Aid Department (ECHO), France, Greece, Ghana, Ireland, Norway, Italy, Malaysia, the Netherlands, Panama, United Arab Emirates, and the United States. The capacity of the UNHRD network is designed to respond to four corporate emergencies at any one time and to enable the humanitarian community to respond to emergencies in a faster, more efficient, and cost-effective way. In 2009, 36 organizations including UN agencies, governmental bodies and NGOs joined the network as authorized users, the network performing over 450 shipments on behalf of 25 organizations, delivering over 2 million tons of humanitarian supplies at a total cost of over $36.5 million.

UN Humanitarian Air Service

A new and important dimension has been added to the WFP's arsenal to respond to emergency situations. The WFP helped to co-ordinate the airlifting and airdropping of relief supplies during the Africa food crisis of the 1980s (see Chapter 3). Since then, WFP Aviation's role has gradually shifted to take on the responsibility of co-ordinating passenger flights in order to facilitate the movement of the WFP and staff from other humanitarian agencies involved in relief operations, especially for the assessment of needs and the distribution of food. WFP Aviation is manned by qualified aviation professionals and provides technical support, financial resources for special operations, and aviation training to build up the capacities of national civil aviation authorities and other partners. In 2001, an air safety unit was established in WFP Aviation to provide close oversight of operators' compliance with air safety regulations and to ensure that operations are conducted in the safest manner. WFP Aviation also administers air operations on behalf of UNHCR and facilitates *ad hoc* cargo and passenger services for various clients at their expense.

The WFP's expertise and experience in this area was recognized by the UN High Level Committee on Management when it requested the WFP to administer a UN Humanitarian Air Service (UNHAS) on behalf of the entire humanitarian community in June 2003. UNHAS is funded by donors, private companies, and sources such as the UN's Central Emergency Response Fund (CERF). In 2009, UNHAS served 700 agencies and over 323,000 passengers, and carried a cargo of over 12,000 tons of relief supplies at a total cost of $144 million, using an average of 53 aircraft a month. Medical evacuations were carried out on 135 occasions and 782 security evacuations were conducted. Without this service, humanitarian workers and food, medicinal care, water, and sanitation and other crucial relief supplies would not have reached people in desperate need in many emergency situations due to insecurity risks and impassable land access, a fact recognized by aid agencies in the special UNHAS operations carried out in Afghanistan, the Central African Republic, Congo Brazzaville, Chad, the Democratic Republic of Congo, Ethiopia, Kenya, Nepal, Niger, Sudan, Tanzania, and the West Africa coastal area. The use of helicopters was particularly effective in emergency operations following the hurricanes and floods in the Philippines, Myanmar, and Haiti. WFP Aviation also performed 38 strategic airlifts to transport 1,790 tons of cargo at a cost of $7.5 million.

WFP's Aviation Safety Unit (LINHAS) is an independent unit that ensures an adequate level of safety in all UNHAS operation by continuously monitoring safety assessments, occurrence reporting, and safety communications systems. Over 100 operation risk evaluations were carried out in 2009 through the three regional safety offices in Johannesburg, Nairobi, and Sharjah, and at WFP headquarters. The unit organized the first Global Aviation Safety Conference for Humanitarian Air Operations in Abu Dhabi in 2009. AFP Aviation, in collaboration with TNT, provided training for almost 300 persons in 2009, bringing the total of personnel trained between 2006 and 2009 to 1,000.

UN cluster lead in logistics

In November 2006, the IASC designated the WFP as the UN global cluster lead for logistics, which recognized the roles the WFP played in the UNJLC, UNHRD, and UNHAS (IASC, 2006). In December 2005, the agencies represented on the IASC had generally welcomed the concept of a 'cluster approach' as a mechanism that could help address identified gaps in the international response to emergencies and enhance the quality of humanitarian action. This was seen as part of a wider reform process aimed at improving the effectiveness of humanitarian response by ensuring greater predictability and accountability, and strengthening partnerships between NGOs, international organizations, the International Red Cross and Red Crescent Movement, and the UN agencies.[34]

The IASC noted that, in the past, in international responses to humanitarian crises, some sectors or areas had benefited from having clearly mandated lead agencies, while other had not. This had led to *ad hoc* humanitarian responses, 'with inevitable capacity and response gaps in some areas'. To address this shortcoming, the IASC agreed to designate global cluster lead agencies specifically for humanitarian emergencies in nine sectors or areas of activity and also, with some flexibility, at the country level. The nine sectors or areas were divided into three types (Box 4.1).

Box 4.1 Global cluster lead agencies

Technical areas

1. Nutrition (UNICEF)
2. Health (WHO)
3. Water and sanitation (UNICEF)
4. Emergency shelter – for IDPs in conflict situations (UNHCR) – in disaster situations (IFRC – convenor)*

Cross-cutting areas

5. Camp coordinators/managers – for IDPs in conflict situations (UNHCR) – in disaster situations (IOM)
6. Protection – for IDPs in conflict situations (UNHCR) – for civilians other than IDPs (UNHCR, OCHR, UNICEF)**
7. Early recovery (UNDP)

Common services

8. Logistics (WFP)
9. Emergency telecommunications (OCHA, UNICEF, WFP)

Notes: *The IFRC was designated 'convenor' rather the 'cluster lead'. In a MOU with the OCHA, the IFRC neither committed to being a provider of last resort nor to be accountable to any part of the UN system; **UNHCR was designated as lead for the global protection cluster. At the country level or in complex emergencies involving displacement, the three 'core protection- mandated agencies' (the UNHCR, UNICEF and OHCHR) would consult closely and under the overall leadership of the UN humanitarian coordinator or resident coordinator agree which of the three agencies would assume the role of lead for protection.

Source: IASC, 2006.

Cluster leadership at the global level among the nine clusters did not include areas where leadership and accountability among international humanitarian actors was already clear, as for agriculture (FAO), for food (WFP), for refugees (UNHCR), and for education (UNICEF). A global cluster appeal for $39 million was launched in March 2006 to help build capacity at the global level in these nine areas. A second appeal was launched in 2007. Thereafter, costs associated with cluster leadership were incorporated into agencies' normal fund raising mechanisms. The IFRC appealed separately for emergency shelter in emergencies resulting from natural disasters. Cluster leaders are responsible for standards and policy setting, building response capacity, and providing operational support in their cluster areas.

At the country level, the aim is to strengthen humanitarian response by: demanding high standards of predictability, accountability, and partnership in all sectors or areas of activity; achieving more strategic responses; better prioritization of available resources by clarifying the division of labour among organizations; better definition of the roles and responsibilities of the humanitarian organizations within each sector; and providing the UN humanitarian co-ordinator with both a first point of call and a provider of last resort in all the key sectors or areas of activity.

The success of the cluster approach would be judged in terms of 'the impact it has on improving the humanitarian response to those affected by crises'. The aim is, eventually, to apply the cluster approach to all countries with UN humanitarian co-ordinators. These countries would, by definition, be those with humanitarian crises beyond the scope of any one agency's mandate, and where needs are of sufficient scale and complexity to justify a multi- sectoral response through the engagement of a wide range of humanitarian actors in both conflict-related emergencies and disasters caused by nature. It was expected that the cluster approach would 'significantly improve the quality of international response to major new emergencies through a substantial strengthening of the collaborative response'.

At the country level, the intention is to strengthen (rather than replace) sectoral co-ordination under the overall leadership of the UN humanitarian co-ordinator, who, in consultation with humanitarian country teams, is responsible for securing agreement on the establishment of appropriate sector groups and sector leads. Responsibilities of cluster leads at the country level include ensuring tasks are carried out, and that appropriate links are established with government and local authorities, state institutions, local civil society, and other stakeholders, for which they are accountable to the UN humanitarian co-ordinator. The designation of 'provider of last resort' implied a commitment of cluster leaders to ensure an adequate and appropriate response to meeting agreed priority needs and for organizing frequent meetings, supported by the UN humanitarian co-ordinator and the emergency relief co-ordinator. The UN humanitarian co-ordinator, with the support of OCHA, is responsible for ensuring an adequate, coherent, and effective response through the overall humanitarian operations, and is accountable to the emergency relief co-ordinator. OCHA will provide support to the UN humanitarian co-ordinator in four main areas: coordination, information management, advocacy and resource mobilization, and policy development.

When clusters are needed, the UN humanitarian co-ordinator informs the UN emergency relief co-ordinator who, in turn, informs the global cluster lead agency. At the country level, clusters are activated according to the scale and nature of emergency needs. In 2009, the WFP-led logistics cluster responded to emergencies in Benin, Indonesia, Laos, the Occupied Palestinian Territory, Pakistan, the Philippines, Samoa, and Zimbabwe. By mid-2010, the WFP was leading logistics clusters to enable humanitarian relief supplies to get to the afflicted population in the Democratic Republic of Congo, Gaza, Philippines, Somalia, Sri Lanka, and Sudan.

Information and communications technology

The rapid development of information and communications technology brought significant benefits for humanitarian operations and the ways in which humanitarian work is done (*The Economist*, 2007). Now, when an emergency occurs, often the first humanitarian workers on the ground are technicians setting up information and communications networks to keep all involved simultaneously informed – government, donors, aid agencies, and the victims themselves – of the many steps involved in responding to disasters, including tracking the supplies of humanitarian relief items by air, sea, and land. Better communications can help facilitate information-sharing, co-ordination, surveillance, assessment, and evaluation among humanitarian aid agencies. Also, critically, they can help in communicating with the afflicted population, often in remote and inaccessible locations, to find out their urgent needs and learn from them how best to respond in providing immediate, life-saving assistance and rapid emergency support.

Technology, including the use of websites and mobile phones, can now be used to help the victims of disasters contact, and be reunited with, relatives, who might help with a range of goods and services from food to mobile phone credits and remittances. The benefits of the new technology are tempered by problems, such as the expense of equipment and co-ordination difficulties caused by different technical standards and systems. But, on balance, the benefits can outweigh the problems, though the gains are often still uneven. And aid agencies are reorganizing themselves around the latest technology.

WFP Information Network and Global System (WINGS)

Early on, the WFP recognized the potential benefits of information and communications technology. One of the first actions of executive director Catherine Bertini, on taking office in 1992, was to 'modernize' the organization by distributing computers widely among WFP staff – not only at headquarters, but also in its field offices – and to set up an e-mail communication system. This was backed up with a determined and prolonged effort to establish a comprehensive communications system that could be accessed by all WFP staff simultaneously, whether at headquarters or in the most remote WFP field office.

WINGS was the main product of a financial management improvement programme (FMIP) that was established in 1995 to address shortcomings in the WFP's ability to control its resources and to report on their uses (WFP, 2010b). The ambitious but essential aim was to have one fully integrated system that would enable the management of staff, food, and finance while facilitating accountability, cost-effectiveness, control, transparency, and real-time reporting. With modifications, WINGS became operational in January 2001 and was gradually made available to all WFP country offices. It was an historical achievement that had taken 15 years to finalize, and it was the first enterprise resource planning information model in the UN system.

Without WINGS, the WFP would not have been able to carry out the fundamental transformation of the organization through the delegation of authority and accountability for operations to its country offices and the decentralization of its structure that was completed in 2001. WINGS allowed automation and control of all financial activities at the point of transaction. It provided WFP staff with access to the basic information needed to better manage their financial transactions. WINGS is linked to the WFP's commodity movement processing and analysis system (COMPAS), its resource mobilization system, and other internal systems. In 2009, WINGS was transformed into WINGS II, which re-engineered processes to fit more standard software.

With WINGS II, the WFP has, for the first time, a consistent, global view of the WFP's inventory, easily accessible to managers in the field and at headquarters. It provides the tools for effective management of the global supply chain, including better use of inventory within and between geographical regions. It has improved the quality of stock information, including warehouse data, allowing senior management better control over a critical risk area and monitoring how operations are performing against approved budgets. Managers in the field can now regularly generate country-specific income and balance sheet statements, and better manage operations and offices under their control. Also, financial statements can be produced that are compliant with the WFP's recently-adopted international public sector accounting standards.

The technological aspects of WINGS II are now the responsibility of the WFP's Information Technology and Management Division. A budget allocation of $56.5 million was made for the development and finalization of WINGS II, with contributions from the Australian government ($0.4 million), the Capital Asset Fund (2006–07) ($15.0 million), and the General Fund ($41.1 million), of which $54.8 million had been spent by the end of December 2009. The estimated value of the WINGS II intangible assets in 2009 was $45.4 million.

Fast information technology and telecommunications emergency and support team (FITTEST)

FITTEST acts as the WFP's first response to emergencies. Its responsibility is the rapid establishment of communications networks to facilitate the transportation of food and other vital relief items to the hardest hit areas in emergencies. The team is on call 24 hours a day, seven days a week, to response to any emergency. Its objective is to have equipment and staff *en route* within 48 hours following notification of a new emergency, if funds are available. FITTEST was relocated to the WFP humanitarian response depot in Dubai in early 2002 following the merger of two teams previously based in Kampala, Uganda and in Islamabad, Pakistan. Dubai was chosen because it provides ready access to a worldwide transportation hub at Dubai International Airport close to WFP major programmes and an accessible supplier base covering western Europe, northern and central Asia, the Middle East, and western Asia.

The team consists of dedicated technicians who respond rapidly to requests for its assistance from WFP country offices channelled through WFP regional bureaux. The team handles requests for assistance in establishing information technology networks and telecommunications and electricity systems (ICT), both for the WFP and for UN inter-agency projects. This is undertaken as part of an existing project or as a complete stand-alone solution, involving the total co-ordination of the project, technical support, assistance with all required documentation, and budgeting. Initially, FITTEST develops mission-specific terms of reference and a cost estimate. Once the project proposal has been approved by the country or target cluster involved, security clearance and travel authorization are requested. Upon receipt of all clearances, the chief of FITTEST or head of operations is given the final clearance for the mission, and deploys the required staff and resources to the country concerned.

FITTEST employs specialists in the fields of information technology and telecommunications and electricity systems. In addition to emergency preparedness and response, the team is mandated to implement the UN system-wide Minimum Operating Security Standards (MOSS) for the WFP and other UN operations worldwide. Thus, FITTEST technicians support ICT operations in the most demanding environments, with the primary goal of improving staff security in the field. FITTEST has a wide variety of kits and stock available, essential for the delivery of comprehensive ICT services, including radio, telephone, and satellite equipment; wiring; power rectification materials; generators; and computer hardware and software. The current stock, worth $3.1 million, is sufficient to address three complex emergencies simultaneously. FITTEST is mandated to provide its services on a full-cost recovery basis.

Recognizing the value of information and communications to the WFP in its emergency operations, both operationally and economically, the WFP's external auditor proposed a review of FITTEST in the programme of work for the 2004–05 biennium (WFP, 2004r). The review was carried out in 2004 and the findings presented to the WFP's executive board in 2005 (WFP, 2005g).[35] It noted that FITTEST operations had grown rapidly in the period 2002–05 in response to demand. During 2004–05, FITTEST supported WFP programmes in Afghanistan, Chad, Iraq, Lebanon, Sudan, and the countries affected by the Indian Ocean tsunami.

The review concluded that there were clear operational benefits in flexibly and rapidly deploying a separate FITTEST team against the alternative arrangement of expanding technical expertise at a regional, large country office, or headquarters level. It was recognized that FITTEST teams operated under conditions where it was difficult to assess in advance whether rapid procurement was more cost-effective than procuring routinely, and incurring handling, storage, maintenance, and (possibly) obsolescence costs. The number of technical staff changed with demand or through transfers to and from projects in WFP country offices. Contracts were managed for technical expertise and equipment was obtained when needed, outside WFP administrative control, to avoid any risk of emergencies not providing work and funding, and incurring overhead costs. The review recommended that FITTEST develop standard operating procedures to maximize its effectiveness, including close co-operation with local and/or regional ICT structures, which were subsequently established.

Emergency preparedness and response

To heighten its awareness of potential and impending emergencies, and to conduct a rapid response, the WFP established an Emergency Preparedness and Response Branch in its Operations Department at WFP headquarters as its corporate focal point in 2003. Based on the lesson of its long experience in meeting emergencies that prevention is better than cure and that, if disasters occur, rapid response mitigates their effects, a situation room was set up as the information management and operational support centre during breaking crises and as the interface with similar nodal points in other UN agencies and NGOs.

Strengthening its early warning capacity has been one of the WFP's strategic priorities. Since the establishment in 1968 of an early warning system for food shortages, FAO and WFP field staff have sent in monthly data for over 70 countries. The experience of the Sahelian countries of West Africa – where six years of successive drought resulted in a major international relief effort during the three years 1973–75, and in which the WFP played a prominent role (see Chapter 3) – underlined the need to improve this service. In 1973, the FAO Conference decided to institute a Global Information and Early Warning System, which was endorsed in one of the resolutions of the World Food Conference in 1974 (UN, 1975). Subsequently, joint FAO/WFP missions have been sent to disaster areas to estimate the extent of destruction and the effect on the food supply situation so that arrangements can be made for the speedy provision of food aid.

This work was taken a stage further when it was agreed at the World Food Summit in 1996 to establish a Food Insecurity and Vulnerability Information and Mapping System (FIVIMS) to identify population groups and households particularly vulnerable to food insecurity, together with the reasons for their precarious state (FAO, 1996). The FAO was requested to provide the technical secretariat for an inter-agency working group of over 25 members from bilateral and multilateral organizations, international NGOs, and regional bodies (FAO, 2000). The WFP is a close collaborator in FIVIMS and created its own Vulnerability Analysis and Mapping (VAM) system in 1994 (WFP, 2004s). While FIVIMS provides guidance on the norms and standards for use by national information and mapping systems, VAM supports the application of these common approaches at the country level.

VAM has proved to be a particularly effective system for identifying those who are food- insecure or vulnerable to food insecurity, why this is so, and where they are located, and is now widely used in emergency situations. VAM is a network of more than 120 experienced specialists in food security, nutrition, economics, and data collection, deployed in more than 50 developing countries. In Africa, VAM has staff in more than 20 countries where the WFP is operating, as well as in WFP regional offices. Comprehensive food security and vulnerability analysis has been carried out in 27 priority countries, providing a baseline for structural food insecurity and vulnerability issues at the household, community, and national levels in the countries concerned.

The situation room at WFP headquarters keeps constant track of emerging disasters throughout the world and of the responses to them. Instant and continuous communications are maintained with WFP field staff and all those involved in responding to disasters through information and communication networks. An impressive array of early warning tools has been developed for planning purposes and to support management in the decision-making process. An early warning team monitors over 160 specialized sources on a daily basis, and highlights the latest events and forecasts of concern that may trigger or accelerate the development of a humanitarian crisis. An early warning executive brief that gives a global overview of countries of concern is produced monthly, which provides global early warning updates of monthly trends and situations relating to both potential socio-political and natural disasters that may require food assistance. Countries of concern are divided into three categories: those with the potential to develop a new crisis; those with a current emergency that show signs of deteriorating conditions; and those with the potential for stability and peace, and hence repatriation and humanitarian access possibilities.

Maps highlighting countries of concern are produced on a monthly basis, coloured to show high, medium and low risk, in deteriorating, unchanged, or improving situations. An annual global hazard calendar provides a picture of possible hazards occurring, including floods, locust infestation, storm seasons, drought watch, and planting and harvesting seasons, by country. An alert and breaking news service provides rapid information of major events that may lead to a need for rapid WFP assistance, including the sudden onset of emergencies caused by nature (such as earthquakes, flash floods, and volcanic eruptions), and political and civil unrest.

A critical date watch calendar is regularly produced that presents an overview of key events (such as elections, transition dates, and disarmament deadlines) that could potentially affect the situation in a given country or region, and hence have implications for WFP operations. An early warning slide show and screen-saver is available daily within the WFP to highlight current natural hazards and socio-political situations with a potential to deteriorate into a disaster. An inter-agency website (HEWweb) has been developed by the WFP, which provides the first global 'one-stop-shop' for early warning information. An early warning-early action report is produced quarterly to foster inter-agency early warning and preparedness to meet the demands of a new humanitarian crisis, or dramatic changes in existing situations that are likely to occur during the next six months.

Co-operation with other agencies

Writing in December 2005, WFP executive director Morris stated:

> No organization can hope to conquer hunger and malnutrition alone. Every action we take in the fight against hunger is made better and more effective when it is taken together in genuine partnership with and for the people we serve. (Morris, 2005)

Now, the WFP has the largest network of partnership arrangements in the world with working agreements signed with the major international humanitarian agencies, other UN bodies, approaching 3,000 NGOs (national and international), and firms, companies and foundations in the private sector.

Major international humanitarian agencies: working arrangements

UNHCR. Even before the conclusion of a Memorandum of Understanding (MOU) in 1985, the UNHCR and WFP had established a close partnership of action in the service of refugees. This was significantly strengthened by a new working arrangement introduced progressively from the start of 1992. A revised MOU, reflecting experience with these new working arrangements, became effective at the start of 1994. In 1997, a new MOU was entered into reflecting working experience since 1994 (WFP, 1997g). The MOU set out its objectives and scope, established the division of responsibility between the two organizations, and gives details of arrangements for needs assessment, food mobilization, logistics, aid appeals, monitoring, nutrition surveillance, reporting, and co-ordination.

The 1951 *Statute* of UNHCR mandates it, within the UN system, to assume the function of providing international protection to refugees and of seeking permanent solutions to their problems, including voluntary repatriation, local integration, and settlement in a third country. Subsequently, UN General Assembly resolutions have given UNHCR certain responsibilities in respect of stateless persons and returnees. In specific situations, and further to a request from the UN secretary-general or a competent principal organ of the UN, the UNHCR may act on behalf of persons displaced internally for refugee-like reasons and threatened with displacement.

Within the scope of the MOU, the WFP has lead responsibility for mobilizing basic food commodities and the resources to deliver them. Through the timely provision of the right quantity of the right foods and related non-food items, the UNHCR and WFP seek to ensure the restoration and/or maintenance of a sound nutritional status through a food basket that meets the assessed requirements, is nutritionally balanced, and is culturally acceptable. The two organizations also seek to promote as much self-reliance as possible through the implementation of appropriate programmes to develop food production or generate self-employment, which would be facilitated by a progressive shift from general relief food distribution towards sustainable development-oriented activities.

Both organizations are committed to ensure that the food provided is targeted at the household level, reaches the most vulnerable, respects the guiding principles of humanitarian action, and involves the beneficiary community (especially women) in all aspects of the management of food aid. The MOU provides a management tool to achieve these objectives. It sets out clearly the respective responsibilities and arrangements for co-operation between them, which seeks to maximize their strengths and comparative advantages. It covers co-operation in the provision of food aid to refugees, returnees in specific situations, as defined, provided the beneficiary number is at least 5,000.

The 1997 MOU was superseded by a new MOU in July 2002, which recognized the importance of examining both food and non-food aspects relevant to food security, and of capitalizing on opportunities to increase self-reliance. This was followed up by a joint UNHCR/WFP document of 216 pages giving detailed guidelines, together with tools and resource materials. This document was the result of a joint effort to distil experience, institutionalize what had worked well, and agree on practical approaches to deal with problem issues (UNHCR/WFP, 2004). The document drew on previous joint studies and statements, including: *Guidelines for Selecting Feeding Programmes in Emergency Situations* (1997); *Guidelines for the Location and Management of EDP (extended delivery points)* (1997); *Model Tripartite Agreement among UNHCR, WFP and the Implementing Partner* (1998); *Food Security Assessment, Self-Reliance, Targeting and Phasing Out of Ongoing Emergency Situation*, Summary report of an inter-agency workshop held in WFP, Rome, November 1999 (2000); and *Food and Nutrition Needs in Emergencies* (UNHCR, UNICEF, WFP and WHO) (2002).

ICRC. The basic principles and terms of co-operation between the ICRC and WFP in emergency situations were set out in an exchange of letters between the heads of the two organizations in September 1996 They provided for the conclusion of *ad hoc* field agreements regarding the exchange of food commodities between the two organizations, either on a loan/reimbursement basis or as a donation. The exchange of letters was supplemented by an *aide-memoire* in December 1999 to facilitate the drafting of field agreements between the ICRC and WFP when an understanding had been reached that the two organizations would co-operate in the area of food aid (WFP, 1999i). The field agreements covered logistics plans, financial arrangements, reporting, validation of agreements, and arbitration procedures.

The *aide-memoire* noted that the WFP could donate food to the ICRC, particularly at the onset of an emergency due to conflict, whereas the ICRC could donate food stocks to the WFP, particularly in transition or post-conflict situations, and when either organization faced temporary food supply problems. Any disputes arising therefrom would be settled by mutual agreement or by arbitration in accordance with the UNCITRAL Arbitration Rules currently in force.

The general framework of the relationship between the ICRC and the WFP was laid out in a document in 2004 (WFP, 2004v). It noted that the primary aim of relief operations in conflict situations was 'to protect the lives, the livelihoods and the moral and physical integrity of victims', and 'to ensure that displacement and internment and the consequences of disease, injury or hunger do not jeopardise their future'. It emphasized that when the ICRC and the WFP provided humanitarian aid, 'it is not a partisan or political act', and 'efforts should undertaken to ensure that this action is not viewed as such'.

The provision of food aid would be based on a thorough assessment of the needs of the victims of conflict and the local capacities already in place to meet those needs. The amount of assistance provided would be consistent with the needs identified. Food aid would be provided to achieve short- and long-term solutions, both for basic survival and to restore self-reliance, and thus reduce future vulnerability to disasters. Efforts would be made, whenever possible, to involve the full participation of the afflicted community; to ensure that their culture, structures, and food habits are respected; and to address the specific needs of girls and women.

Where feasible and appropriate, the WFP and the ICRC would consult each other before and after carrying out assessments of food and economic security and logistics at the local, national, and regional levels in areas of joint operations. Joint assessments were expected to provide added value, depending on agreement between the ICRC head of delegation and the WFP country director. Regarding emergency preparedness, both organizations would inform each other of important technical issues, and would share information and the results of evaluations and reviews, where appropriate. The WFP and ICRC nutrition staff would maintain regular contact on issues of common interest. They would consult on thematic, technical guidelines and on new internal policies on nutrition. On women and gender issues, the focal points in both organizations would regularly exchange information on research, guidance, training, and programmes related to women. Co-operation would also take place in staff training programmes, security issues, logistics, and the use of air services.

UNICEF. Close and fruitful collaboration has existed between UNICEF and the WFP almost from the start of WFP operations in 1963, both in short-term emergency relief and rehabilitation, and in longer-term development programmes. A MOU between the two organizations signed in 1976 covered the aspects of consultation and exchange of information, joint action in assistance programmes, collaboration in development and nutrition policies, and policies and programmes for emergency preparedness. In November 1985, a joint workshop on *Food Aid and the Well-Being of Children in the Developing World* was held in New York in order to obtain a clearer and more comprehensive understanding of the various ways in which food aid, along with other forms of international co-operation, could help alleviate the problems of children in the developing world, especially in times of economic recession. The critical roles of women were also analyzed, as well as the improved design, operation, monitoring, and evaluation of projects and programmes for children and women (Greaves and Shaw, 1985).

Joint consultations in 1985 resulted in the identification of additional ways in which the two organizations could co-operate in the planning and implementation of emergency responses. Given the increase in the number and complexity of emergencies to which the UN system had be called upon to respond, they agreed to clarify their roles and responsibilities, to strengthen collaboration arrangements, and to further improve their responses in emergencies. This led to a far-reaching agreement on collaboration in a MOU in 1998, which built on previous agreements and experience, and provided an operational framework for programmes in which they worked together (WFP, 1998h).

The MOU noted that UNICEF was mandated by the United Nations to advocate for the protection of children's rights, and the fulfilment of their needs and opportunities. UNICEF responded in emergencies to protect the rights of children and to relieve their suffering and that of their families. Both organizations were committed to the principles articulated in the *Declaration and Plan of Action of the International Conference on Nutrition* of 1992, the *Convention on the Rights of the Child* of 1989, and the *Convention to End All Forms of Discrimination against Women* (UN General Assembly resolution 34/80). In emergencies, both organizations were committed to strengthening and sustaining the capacities of households to meet their basic needs for food, care of children and women, health services, and water and sanitation.

The MOU aimed 'to encourage and facilitate systematic, predictable and co-operative action between the two organizations' to achieve those objectives. It was regarded as a 'management tool' that sought 'to build on the recognized comparative advantages of each organization and to establish operational modalities to maximize the benefits of collaboration'. They shared a common commitment to actions in emergencies that helped ensure relief, recovery, and rehabilitation. The WFP would ensure that families had adequate access to food through the provision of external assistance, as required. UNICEF's priority activities in emergencies were to ensure care and protection of children and those who cared for them, and social and family reintegration of children and women who were the victims of violence. UNICEF also supported the delivery of services in the areas of child and maternal health, primary education, and water and environmental sanitation.

UNICEF and the WFP would collaborate in assessing the needs of the affected population as early as possible in the development of a crisis, and in addressing the food and non-food needs of the population. They shared a commitment to prevent and mitigate emergencies and their worst human consequences, to eliminate famine-related deaths, to end nutritional deficiency diseases in communities affected by emergencies, and to promote early recovery and rehabilitation of the affected population. They recognized that adequate nutrition was an outcome of the intake of food that was adequate in quantity and quality as well as access to health services, potable water and sanitation facilities, and adequate capacity to provide special necessary care for young children and women. These needs, especially child care, food preparation, and feeding, were best met by families. Both organizations were therefore committed to strengthening the capacity of the family as a unit to meet the basic needs of all family members for food, health, water and sanitation, and special care. Where this was not possible, supplementary feeding programmes were needed until adequate basic rations could be provided, as well as therapeutic feeding programmes for the rehabilitation of the severely malnourished with special foods and intensive medical care by well-trained staff.

Each organization would take care of the logistics arrangements for the international and in-country transport, storage, and handling of food and non-food items for which it was responsible. They would collaborate in the use of their respective emergency stockpile facilities, including UNICEF's warehouse in Copenhagen, Denmark and the WFP's stock of high-nutrition food in Brindisi, Italy, and non-food items in Nairobi, Kenya. They would collaborate in establishing operational arrangements to expedite deliveries in the most cost-effective ways. At UNICEF's request and its expense, the WFP would arrange international and in-country transport and storage of supplies provided by UNICEF up to agreed delivery points. Each would help the other improve its emergency response through a regular exchange of information and experience, and by developing innovative ways of responding to emergencies. In complex emergencies, they agreed to co-operate fully within the broader framework of inter-agency agreements and decisions relevant to in-country co-ordination, advocacy, and resource mobilization. They also agreed to collaborate in making appeals to donors and in sharing training facilities. Meetings would be arranged no less than once annually to review the MOU, to assess its application and impact on collaboration, and to revise it as appropriate.

Collaboration among the UN Rome-based agencies

Given the close complementarities of their missions and mandates, calls have been made over a number of years for the three UN agencies based in Rome, Italy (the FAO, IFAD, and WFP) to work together more closely (Shaw, 2009: 214).[36] They all work for or with food. They all seek to end hunger and alleviate poverty. They all subscribe to achieving the Millennium Development Goals. And, to a large extent, they share common members. The High-Level Panel on UN System-Wide Coherence has recommended that 'to build long-term food security and break the cycle of recurring famines, especially in sub-Saharan Africa, WFP, FAO and IFAD should review their respective approaches and enhance interagency coordination' (UN, 2006). The three agencies are now taking deliberate steps to co-operate more closely, although the memory of the head of one of the organizations (FAO) endeavouring to dominate another (WFP) has left an unfortunate legacy that has militated against closer working relations. That experience showed the importance of leadership, and the qualities needed for effective leadership, of UN bodies. It also showed the important roles that governments should play in the governing bodies of the UN agencies, and that reform is possible through working together (Ingram, 2007).

At the request of its governing body, the WFP presented an initial attempt to map all forms of collaboration that existed among the three UN bodies in 2007 (WFP, 2007j). They had agreed to organize information on their collaboration at the global, regional, and country levels around four 'pillars': agricultural investment – increased investment in agricultural and rural development; policy formulation, capacity-building, knowledge management, and advocacy; emergencies and rehabilitation, including risk management; and administration and procurement. The mapping exercises took 1 January 2006 as the starting point. At the global level, collaboration had taken place in 64 per cent of the activities undertaken on administrative issues, including procurement, human resources, finance, information technology, conferences, protocol, and knowledge-sharing services; 24 per cent in advocacy; and 12 per cent in emergencies and recovery.

In policy and advocacy, the three agencies have focused particularly on creating awareness and better understanding of the causes and costs of poverty and hunger. A joint paper was presented to the *International Conference on Financing for Development* at Monterrey, Mexico in 2002 on 'Reducing Poverty and Hunger: The Critical Role of Financing for Food, Agricultural and Rural Development' (FAO/IFAD/WFP, 2002). The paper argued that hunger, malnutrition, and poverty were intricately interlinked. Poverty was generally regarded as the root cause of hunger and malnutrition. What was not always understood, however, was that hunger and malnutrition can, in turn, be major causes of poverty. They could affect the capabilities and capacities of individuals attempting to escape from poverty in several ways, including: reducing the capacity for physical activity and, hence, the productive potential of the labour (usually their only asset) of those who suffer from hunger; impairing people' ability to develop physically and mentally, retarding child growth, reducing cognitive ability, and seriously inhibiting school attendance and performance, thus compromising the effectiveness of investment in education; causing serious long-term damage to health, linked to higher rates of disease and premature death; causing inter-generational disadvantages – for example, hungry mothers give birth to underweight children who start life with a severe handicap; and contributing to social and political instability that further undermine government capacity to reduce poverty.

Childhood poverty and malnutrition have been found to portend high costs in adult life. Children who grow up poor and malnourished can cost the country in which they live because as adults they are less productive, earn less, have more health-related expenses, and may resort to crime as members of a marginalized underclass. This indicates that investing resources in the reduction of poverty and hunger is more cost-effective than generally thought. One measure used to quantify the impact of malnutrition on both poor health and increased mortality is called 'disability-adjusted life years' (DALYs), the sum of years lost as a result of premature death and disabilities, adjusted for severity. A study sponsored by the WHO and the World Bank on *A Global Burden of Disease* ranked being underweight as the single-most significant risk factor for DALYs worldwide, and for both death and DALYs in the group of high-mortality developing countries (WHO and World Bank, 2006). This group includes almost 70 countries with a combined population of more than 2.3 billion people. Overall, childhood and maternal undernutrition are estimated to cost more than 220 million DALYs in developing countries. When other nutrition-related risk factors are taken into account, the toll rises to 340 million DALYs, representing a loss of productivity to having a disaster kill or disable the entire population of a country larger than the United States.

While the human cost of hunger is morally unacceptable, the economic costs of hunger are unaffordable, not only for the individuals concerned, but also for the economic development and prosperity of the nations in which they live (Shaw, 2007: 396–7). The costs of hunger come in several different forms. The direct medical expenditure of treatment throughout the developing world is estimated at around $30 billion a year. These direct costs are dwarfed by the indirect costs of low productivity and income caused by premature death, disability, absenteeism, and lower educational and occupational opportunities.

Coming at the costs of hunger from another direction, the FAO conducted a macro-economic study to estimate the benefits of reducing undernourishment by an amount sufficient to meet 1996 World Food Summit and 2000 MDG targets of reducing the number and proportion of hungry people by half by 2015 (FAO, 2004). The study estimated the value of increased production that would be unleashed if the targets were met. Based only on increased life expectancy, the total discounted value of the years up to 2015 was estimated at about $3 trillion, which translates into an annuity benefit of $120 billion a year as a result of longer and healthier lives.

The three agencies have worked together at, and for statements to, UN intergovernmental meetings (including the UN General Assembly and ECOSOC, and the 2006 International Forum on the Eradication of Poverty) to raise awareness and political support for reducing hunger and rural poverty. Their joint advocacy messages are based on the twin-track strategy of direct action to alleviate hunger immediately for the most vulnerable and the longer-term agricultural, food security, nutrition, and rural development programmes to eliminate the causes of hunger.

The three agencies were co-founders of the *International Alliance Against Hunger* in October 2005 (FAO, 2002). As a result, national alliances have been established, or are being developed, in developing countries, providing a forum for mobilizing a range of government, UN, and civil society actions advocating action to fight hunger at the national level. They have also established common positions in the UN Standing Committee on Nutrition (CSN) and in the OECD Development Assistance Committee's Network on Gender. The WFP and FAO were active in the Food Force created video game *Feeding Minds. Fighting Hunger.* The three agencies are members of the Inter-Agency Network on Women and Gender Equity, and have contributed to the Gender and Rural Livelihoods Sourcebook.

The WFP and FAO collaborated in Strengthening Emergency Needs Assessment Capacity (SENAC), funded by the European Union, to improve emergency needs assessment and post-crisis information. They also collaborated in developing the UN Consolidated Appeals Process (CAP) needs analysis framework and guidelines for crop and food supply assessment missions. They have co-chaired the UN Geographic Information Working Group, which is responsible for co-ordinating and facilitating the use of geographical information among UN agencies, and the development and maintenance of GeoNetwork, a software that allows improved sharing of geographically refined information between different organizations through the Internet.

To stimulate agricultural development by expanding local markets through the purchase of home-grown commodities, the WFP and FAO have worked together in launching a Home-Grown School Feeding programme, which links school feeding to increased food production. The WFP has also worked with the FAO in improving the FAO's supply and logistics chain. The WFP has trained officers in the FAO's Emergency Operations and Rehabilitation Unit and the FAO has become a member of the UN Human Response Depots (UNHRD) network, which is managed by the WFP.

At the regional level, 56 per cent of the three agencies collaborative activities have been in emergencies and recovery, 22 per cent in investment in agricultural development, and 22 per cent in advocacy and capacity-building. Several initiatives have been undertaken to improve food security by working with the regional bodies for the Sahelian countries of West Africa, the Horn of Africa, with the Southern African Development Community in Southern Africa, and with regional organizations in Latin America and the Caribbean.

At the country level, 63 per cent of the collaborative activities of the three agencies have been in emergencies and recovery, 26 per cent in investment in agricultural development, 10 per cent in advocacy, and 1 per cent in administration. The WFP and FAO have collaborated in 55 countries working on 84 projects and activities. The WFP and IFAD have collaborated in 10 projects in 8 countries.

Co-operation with UN agencies beyond Rome and with international organizations

Of the 208 WFP-supported operations worldwide in 2009, 173 (83 per cent) were conducted in partnership with UN agencies and international organizations (IOs) in 45 countries, a significant increase in collaborative ventures over the past three years (WFP, 2010a). The number and proportion of collaborative operations increased from 55 (22 per cent) in 2007 to 74 (36 per cent) in 2008, which is attributable to the WFP's participation in joint programming with UN country teams. UNICEF remained the WFP's main partner in 2009 with collaboration in 138 operations. Other partners in the UN system include the UNDP, WHO, UNHCR, UNFPA, UNAIDS, World Bank, IOM, and ILO. In June 2009, the WFP signed a MOU with the WMO. The number of partnerships with IOs remained the same in 2009, with collaboration in 11 countries on 12 operations with the ICRC and in 8 countries on 8 operations with the IFRC.

Partnerships with non-governmental organizations

One of the most remarkable features in the WFP's transformation to become the world's largest humanitarian agency, and which helped to make that possible, was the explosion in the establishment of partnerships with NGOs around the world. This, together with the deployment of WFP staff to the developing countries and the devolution of decision-making from headquarters to the field, resulted in the largest humanitarian network throughout the developing world.

Executive director Morris wrote in 2005:

> The World Food Programme is proud to work with nearly 2,000 non-governmental organizations around the globe – from small grass roots groups deep in the field to large international aid agencies. Without their collaboration, our efforts to bring much- needed food to more than 100 million people in 80 countries would be jeopardized. Without their vocal moral support, our efforts to put hunger at the top of the international agenda would be far less successful.
>
> We value our non-governmental partners tremendously. WFP is committed to being the best partner we can possibly be.... By understanding each other's policies and practices better, our working relationships can only improve. And

that has to be good news for the hungry children, women and men who need our help so much. (Morris, 2005)

The motivation to seek partnerships with NGOs came from the realization that, to reach those in need, especially in emergency situations, and to provide other vital inputs as well as food to address their hunger, the WFP depended on the collaboration of other agencies, particularly at the grass-roots level. In addition, the WFP's commitment to involve the beneficiaries of its assistance in a participatory approach to saving lives and ending hunger could be strongly supported. This realization took a long time to mature. It resulted in a flurry of activity, with surveys and papers to the WFP's governing body between 1998 and 2002, resulting in a global framework for WFP/NGO partnership, and a handbook for NGOs in December 2005 entitled *How to Work with WFP* (WFP, 2005h).[37]

In a paper to the governing body in 1999 on 'Partnerships with NGOs', it was emphasized that, as a UN agency, the WFP had a mandate to work with national governments as their primary partners (WFP, 1999e). But experience had shown that many poor and WFP-priority countries had limited capacity to provide the matching resources and skills required to absorb external assistance, and to make effective use of food aid. As a special measure, the WFP's governing body had agreed to the WFP helping to meet the internal transport, storage and transport costs relating to its food aid in the least-developed countries in 1972, but this did not address other shortcomings that limited their capacities. The executive board therefore recommended that the WFP should invest in building up the capacity of developing countries, particularly through NGOs and community groups, and work closely with NGOs to strengthen programming (WFP, 1997c).

The NGO community was a 'world of complexity and nuance, ranging from worldwide organizations to small community organizations working at the village level'. The traditional distinction between North and South, and international and national NGOs, was becoming more complex. Most international NGOs were increasingly linked to local partners, and had expanded and decentralized their processes that brought them into closer contact with conditions at the grass-roots level. Large faith-based networks had developed extended parochial or community structures that had both northern and southern members.

There had been a phenomenal increase in the number of NGOs, especially in developing countries. The OECD estimated the number of national NGOs in the South increased from 12,000 in 1988 to 50,000 in 1994, compared to 5,000 in the North. Besides the many small grass-roots organizations, there were also large national NGOs with highly-developed expertise and capacities. Results of a survey conducted in 1998 showed a rapid growth in WFP co-operation with NGOs. In that year, collaboration had been established with an estimated 1,120 NGOs worldwide, 250 international and 870 national or local, compared to a total of only 300 on 1989. In the thirty years since the WFP began operations in 1963, NGOs had acquired a critical role in the international community, and become a major channel for development and humanitarian assistance. They handled 29 per cent of all food aid deliveries in 1997, compared to 13 per cent in 1963.

It was considered that there were many opportunities to strengthen the national capacity of recipient governments and to enhance the effectiveness of WFP activities by increasing the participation of NGOs along the whole programme cycle, from planning and programming to implementation, monitoring, and evaluation. The WFP would strive to strengthen even further its partnership with NGOs, nationally and internationally.

Thematic evaluation of WFP/NGO partnerships

To pursue the subject further, a thematic evaluation of WFP–NGO partnerships was conducted in 1999 (WFP, 2000e).[38] The evaluation report noted that food aid was only one of several inputs needed to tackle food security problems, and that, in realizing its mandate and priorities, the WFP depended on collaboration with partners to complement food aid with organizational and technical capacities, and essential non-food inputs for the effective planning and implementation of emergency operations and development projects. National governments were not always able or prepared to fulfil those functions.

Based on the findings of studies in eight countries, the following factors were found to limit the capacities of national governments in developing countries: conflict, civil strife and their consequences, and post-conflict situations; major sudden natural disasters; prolonged adverse climatic conditions; combined with limited economic and/or political-economic transformation and ongoing structural adjustment programmes. NGOs often operated in certain sectors or localities not, or only partly, covered by government services. In such circumstances, the WFP pursued partnerships with them 'as there is virtually no other alternative'. Partnerships may then shift back to national government authorities as their capacities and resources improve. WFP–NGO partnerships were found to yield synergetic effects in terms of increased effectiveness and efficiency by making good use of their complementary capacities, resources, and comparative advantages. In so doing, they did not bypass national government authorities.

It was noted that, in 1999, NGOs delivered more ODA than the entire UN system, excluding the IMF and the World Bank, and channelled about one-third of global food aid. In 1998, the UN Secretary-General, Kofi Annan, described NGOs as 'indispensible partners' of the UN in preventing displacement, humanitarian work, development, and the promotion of human rights (Annan, 1997). NGOs differed in size, capacities, and focus so that forms of co-operation with the WFP varied considerably. Partnerships also took place at different levels. At the global level, they occurred through annual consultations and MOUs with the major international NGOs at headquarters level. This began in 1995 to enhance policy dialogue between the WFP and the major NGO partners, and to set up a general framework for collaboration. At the country level, partnerships occurred through major or country-wide programmes of assistance, often formalized by MOUs or agreements, particularly if some kind of resource transfers was involved. And at the field level, co-operation took place through specific projects, operations or activities. Some tripartite agreements were signed between national government authorities, the WFP, and NGOs.

Partnerships took place in many fields of activities, or as part of informal relations and *ad hoc* forms of co-operation.

In emergency relief operations, when large amounts of food and other relief items were involved, the WFP's main tasks were the rapid mobilization of the relief food required and arranging for transport and logistics in areas of need, while NGOs took care of final delivery and distribution to disaster victims. Both parties usually collaborated in assessing food requirements, setting targeting criteria, determining the composition of food relief rations, and designing distribution modalities, based on the WFP's global experience and NGOs' knowledge of local communities and conditions. While NGOs relied on the WFP as the provider of relief food, they mobilized other necessary relief needs, including drinking water supplies, sanitation facilities, shelter, tents, blankets, medical supplies, tools and equipment, from other sources, and monitored operations.

The evaluation confirmed that the comparative advantages of the WFP and NGOs, and the complementarities of their resources and capabilities, permitted expansion of the scope and scale of operations, and the more effective achievement of common humanitarian and development objectives. WFP–NGO partnerships in development projects were found to be more complex and diversified than in emergency operations, and the spectrum and intensity of collaboration varied considerably from country to country.

An impressive list of benefits accruing to the WFP from working with NGOs was drawn up, including: familiarity with local socio-cultural and environmental conditions in remote areas with difficult access; participatory approaches through the involvement of the beneficiary community, thereby facilitating innovatory and flexibly operations; provision of complementary inputs and technical and managerial capacities to distribute and manage food distribution; low-cost operations through the use of simple, appropriate technologies; employment of local staff and volunteers; streamlined services; and moderate overhead costs, although larger differences were experienced between international and national/local NGOs; advocacy concerning nutrition, food security, gender, and humanitarian issues; and research and training. The benefits to NGOs of working with the WFP were identified as: provision of food aid for relief, rehabilitation, and development; drawing on WFP food aid procurement and logistics capacity, and experience in food aid assessment and management; using the WFP's VAM to better target food aid to those in most need; co-operation in building the capacities of NGOs, government authorities, and local communities; and gaining recognition and credibility, and mediating and improving relations between government authorities and NGOs.

The evaluation also revealed a number of constraints that inhibited WFP–NGO partnerships. These included mistrust and little co-operation between government national and local authorities and NGOs in many developing countries. In addition, NGOs, particularly national and local ones, often perceived their relationship with international NGOs as contractor–client rather than as equal partners. NGOs were often less involved in the planning and programming stages of operations and projects in which their co-operation was later sought. WFP processes and procedures were perceived by NGOs to be overly bureaucratic and centralized. Also, WFP reporting formats and requirements were considered by them to be too complicated, difficult, and time-consuming.

The NGOs themselves had large differences in their capacities, competences, reliability, and credibility, partly the result of unreliable or irregular donor funding. Similarly, the WFP relied on voluntary contributions, which sometimes led to delays in food deliveries and distribution. Frequent changes in staff at the international professional level on both sides could disrupt continuity in collaboration. Cost-sharing and cost recovery arrangements were not satisfactorily regulated and frequently led to disputes. Some NGOs were not prepared or able to adapt their approaches to changing conditions, particularly in the transition from relief to development. And local-level agreements were often not sufficiently comprehensive to cover the concerns of both parties.

Despite these constraints, the evaluation 'confirmed the vital importance of WFP–NGO partnerships at the field level' but that this 'does not and should not mean by-passing government authorities'. It found that the complementarities of the WFP and NGO capacities and resources 'yield the additional advantages of increasing the efficiency of resource use and effectiveness and scope of interventions'. Overall, while satisfactory, there was scope for strengthening collaboration, building on the respective comparative advantages, and alleviating identified constraints. Among the evaluation's recommendations were: improvement of data and information exchange; clarification of NGOs' policy, advocacy, and capacity-building roles; establishment of clearer criteria for the selection of NGOs to engage in partnership with the WFP; and adoption of flexible financial and management tools to facilitate NGO partnerships.

Global framework for WFP–non-governmental organization partnerships

The thematic evaluation led to the executive board's request for greater clarity on how the WFP should pursue partnerships with NGOs in the future, and to the realization on the part of the WFP secretariat that a global framework for partnership was required (WFP, 2001b). At the beginning of the new millennium, the WFP was working with over 1,100 NGOs, some 80 per cent of which were national or local organizations and 20 per cent international. About 90 per cent of WFP country offices collaborated to some extent with NGOs, particularly in relief operations, where, in 80 per cent of the cases, NGOs were the implementing partners.

'Partnership' was defined as 'a mutually beneficial alliance between organizations where roles, responsibilities and accountabilities are clearly defined' and 'based on a shared vision regarding objectives and purposes of work ... involving joint resource contributions, shared risks and joint control of information'. The WFP had a range of collaborative arrangements with NGOs. One was partnerships, as defined here. Another was through contracts involving the provision of services, with little joint planning and decision-making. Yet another was through consortiums or networks, often involving numerous organizations aligned around a common purpose or for information exchange. A fourth involved joint ventures by two or more organizations that engaged in common design, implementation or management of an operation or project with a finite duration.

The WFP secretariat wished to enter into long-term partnerships with NGOs, as was evident in the MOUs outlining strategic ways of working with them, already numbering 16. The partnerships with major international NGOs were evolving into such long-term relationships that they went beyond operation or project boundaries. A similar relationship was sought with national and local NGOs, but was found not to be a realistic objective in many situations. WFP commitment had been reflected in a number of its policy papers and evaluation reports, but clear guidance was now required as to how this was to be achieved. This involved a number of structural issues, such as staff capacity, administrative procedures, and donor accountability that had, at times, made it difficult for the WFP to establish viable partnerships that translated into concrete operational activities, and inhibited effective partnerships.

To pursue the concept of establishing a global framework for partnership, further detailed studies were conducted in five countries to identify the current status of, and constraints on, partnerships with NGOs. In all five countries, the WFP was collaborating with both international and national NGOs. They represented a cross-section of partnerships that took place under different relief/development conditions, and in different operational environments.[39] The case studies documented lessons learned and contained specific recommendations for improving field-level partnerships. They provided the basis for the framework for partnerships globally, which was extensively discussed with NGO partners. An informal e-mail working group of NGO and WFP field and headquarters staff also contributed to the formulation of the framework.

The lessons learned highlighted the benefits of working with NGOs, diversity within the NGO community, an understanding of how partnerships evolved, the different points of view of governments and NGOs, and the organizational requirements and the resource implication of partnerships. Capacity-building had emerged as a central concern for all UN operational activities. According to an ACC guidance note, capacity-building and sustainability should be explicitly articulated as an operational goal at the country level.[40] In explaining the need for a framework for WFP–NGO partnerships, it was noted that such partnerships did not 'just happen'. Building on the strengths of NGOs and the potential of complementarities, a number of UN organizations had developed NGO partnership strategies in recent years.[41]

It was considered that to move WFP's relationships with NGOs towards full partnerships, a global framework for collaboration was needed that covered two types of association: contractual, and partnerships founded on a shared vision, mutual accountability, and the contribution of resources. The global framework would be based on: shared goals, mutual respect and trust; joint decision-making, design and activities; commitment to building and nurturing partnerships; willingness to give up a certain amount of independence to pursue joint projects; and commitment to accountability and transparency. The need for a country-level NGO partnership plan was also recognized. Given the diversity of NGO and WFP country programmes, specific operational elements should be developed at the country level. A global WFP–NGO partnership framework would help facilitate country-specific planning for NGO partnerships and help the WFP better select its partners and the partnership process.

The key components of the framework should be: a set of partnership principles; a statement of purpose or strategic direction; a shared vision, values and interests; recognition of the importance of building trust and working in a transparent manner; respect of differences and emphasis on compatibilities; recognition that partnerships changed and evolved, and were a learning process; mutual accountability, risk-sharing and joint decision-making; and flexibility. Each relationship would be influenced by context, and would be unique. Regarding strategic purpose and direction, each WFP country office had to be clear about the objectives it sought to accomplish. The objectives of a country-specific framework would indicate clearly the 'value added' of the partnership.

Partnership selection criteria for selecting appropriate partners would be a mutual process. It was recognized that it would not being easy. Stakeholder analysis would be conducted to assess institutional capacity, for which a number of analytical tools had been developed. Capacity-building would be an ongoing process in which individuals and organizations expanded their abilities to achieve their purposes. Advocacy would be strengthened with NGO partners. Good relations would be fostered and the resource implications of partnerships assessed, and each country would plan NGO partnerships at the country level.

The executive board approved the recommendations on how WFP–NGO partnerships should be pursued at it annual session in 2001 (WFP, 2001c). Those recommendations were that: the WFP would work in partnership with NGOs, in particular local NGOs, to reach its target populations more effectively when appropriate; the WFP would facilitate government, NGO and WFP tripartite arrangements to the extent feasible as a normal course of action and leading, where possible, to formal agreements; the WFP would adopt an NGO partnership framework that defines the key elements for strengthening partnerships with both international and local NGOs; country offices would plan at the country level for partnerships, developing country-specific partnership arrangements based on the WFP – NGO partnership framework; key planning elements would be summarized and included in the country strategy outline, country programme, and recovery strategy; country-level partnership planning with NGOs would be consistent with existing WFP policies and approaches to financial accountability and management.

The WFP would support capacity-building with its NGO partners and WFP staff, within available resources; capacity-building would focus on food logistics and management (in emergency settings), programme planning and design (including exit strategies), gender assessments, monitoring of results, budgeting, reporting and accountability procedures, as these activities are associated with existing WFP programmes; as appropriate, the WFP would engage in joint partnership advocacy initiatives on behalf of the hungry poor; the WFP would also facilitate better working relationships among NGOs, governments, and donors to secure additional non-food resources in support of WFP programmes; the WFP would also commit itself to the timely delivery of agreed-upon food commodities and associated non-food items; formal agreements would define roles and responsibilities, but be flexible enough to allow for amendments as circumstances change; the WFP would include programmatic roles and responsibilities in NGO partnership agreements, in addition to the agreed-upon financial and administrative conditions – these arrangements would be reflected in country-level agreements, or letters of understanding, operational contracts, plans of operations, and NGO partnership agreements; the WFP welcomes partnerships where both partners contribute resources of their own, based on individual capabilities; however, given the WFP's strong desire to work with local NGOs and civil-based organizations, the WFP would give priority to international and national NGOs that facilitated local NGO involvement; the WFP would expand the range of partnerships and capacity-building measures with local NGOs in consultation with governments in beneficiary countries and in conformity with WFP cost structures; the WFP encouraged donors to support its efforts in meeting capacity-building objectives.

Global Humanitarian Platform (GHP)

The GHP, created in July 2006, brought together UN and non-UN humanitarian organizations on an equal footing and with mutual respect between members of the partnership, irrespective of size and power. It also established respect of each other's mandates, objectives, and independence, and recognized each other's constraints and commitments. Constructive discussion would take place through dialogue on an equal footing, which should result in action that was reality-based and results-oriented, built on effective capabilities and concrete operational experience.

The platform recognized that humanitarian organizations had an ethical obligation to each other to accompany their technical responsibilities with integrity and in a relevant, complementary and appropriate way. It also recognized that diversity of the humanitarian community was an asset if it were built on comparative advantages and complemented each other's contribution. Local capacity on which to build was one of the main assets that should be enhanced.

Handbook for WFP–non-governmental organization partnerships

Following the decision of the executive board, operational guidelines for the planning and implementation of NGO partnership activities would be prepared. But the WFP secretariat went one better and published a handbook for NGOs on *How to work with WFP* (WFP, 2005h).[42] The handbook was divided into three sections. The first section explained what the WFP was, its work and objectives. For potential NGO partners, the WFP described itself as the 'United Nation's food aid agency and the world's front-line agency in the fight against hunger', working through 80 operational country offices and six regional bureaux. It was pointed out that any UN member state and state members of any of the UN specialized agencies could request WFP assistance, but that priority was given to requests from low-income, food-deficit countries and from the UN secretary-general when there was no recognized government or when an existing government's capacity was undermined by a crisis.

The structure of a WFP country office was described in detail to help in the understanding of how partnerships with NGOs were created and maintained. The WFP country director was responsible for overseeing that a WFP operation was managed effectively, alongside national authorities and NGO partners, who would promote and co-ordinate joint programming with other UN agencies, donors, and NGOs 'whenever possible'. At WFP country offices, NGO staff would mainly be in contact with the programme staff for issues related to programme implementation, logistics staff concerning the receipt of commodities, and financial staff on payments. Steps in the WFP's programme cycle and food supply chains were also described for the benefit of potential NGO partners.

The handbook also described who the WFP's partners were, pointing out that, while the WFP's main partner was the government in developing countries, partnerships had also been established with other UN agencies, international organizations, and NGOs. It was pointed out that, in 2004, the WFP worked with a total of 1,943 NGOs, 224 international NGOs, and 1,719 national or local NGOs. It was stated that NGOs played a 'fundamental role' in the distribution and monitoring of WFP food to beneficiaries. Around 85 per cent of NGOs working with the WFP were involved in those activities. They were also involved with the WFP in other activities, including early warning activities, food security assessments, advocacy for food/nutrition-related issues, and the co-ordination of food-security activities in an area or region.

The detailed criteria for an NGO to work with the WFP were identified. First and foremost, an NGO had to agree with WFP aims and principles. It also had to have a certain specified institutional profile including: acceptance by the recipient government of WFP assistance; extensive experience in humanitarian and relief operations; sound programmes of food distribution and/or on issues related to food assistance, food security, advocacy, and development, which corresponded to the WFP's general priorities and target groups; adequate personnel and in-country organizational structures; reliable, qualified, and suitably experienced staff, with reasonable continuity in assignments; a transparent institutional framework, active grass-roots participation, information systems and documentation, technical knowledge, and geographical presence; and willingness and ability to work with communities and community-based organizations.

While the WFP may reimburse operational costs relating to food aid distribution, an NGO should be able to cover part or all complementary inputs, including non-food items, staffing, and equipment. An NGO would need to provide detailed plans for distributing food to intended beneficiaries and have staff with basic skills in project and financial management, analysis, and capacity in areas of commodity tracking, food distribution, and beneficiary participation, and be able to comply with the WFP's monitoring and reporting requirements, with sound, reliable financial and accounting systems. Finally, a NGO would need to show a willingness to work with responsible governments authorities at all levels, and co-ordinate with other agencies and organizations; ideally, the NGO should be an active participant in any established co-ordination mechanism for an operation and any separate NGO co-ordinating body.

What could NGOs therefore expect from the WFP, particularly from co-operating partnerships? The WFP would cover the costs related to the physical distribution and storage of WFP food. The WFP would provide the quality and quantity of food, and at the time, agreed on. Information would be provided on the time of arrival of food and on any anticipated breaks in the delivery pipeline. Training would be provided to NGO staff, as required. NGOs would work with qualified WFP personnel and have access to WFP communications equipment. The WFP would liaise with local authorities on behalf of NGOs, and share information on the food-security situation and operational security in the country, region or area. And NGOs would benefit from the WFP's commitment to the promotion of gender equality and women's empowerment in all aspects of its work.

What could the WFP expect to gain from its partnerships with NGOs? NGOs would be responsible for the reception, storage, and handling of food at agreed delivery points and distribution to beneficiaries. They would ensure that food reached the intended people, and keep records and accounts of all WFP commodities received. NGOs would provide suitably qualified personnel and adequate means necessary for the successful implementation and supervision of activities, and monitor and report to the WFP. They would encourage the formation and involvement of community organizations, and share information with them. They would retain empty packaging and display the WFP's logo alongside their own. And they would adhere to WFP gender commitments and comply with the code of conduct of the International Red Cross and Red Crescent Movement and NGOs in disaster relief.

The second section of the handbook contained the general principles in creating a WFP–NGO partnership. Working together was said to ensure that: efforts were not duplicated and resources not wasted; competition for resources and for visibility were reduced; organizations could increase their resources and better advocate for their beneficiaries; and resources could be used in a complementary way to meet common objectives which could not be meet individually. At the highest level, through full partnership, working together allowed organizations to create new resources and ideas that they could not have been able to create alone. Making partnerships work required clear goals, roles, and procedures.

It was pointed out that the WFP worked with five categories of NGOs: large international NGOs; smaller international NGOs; large national NGOs working in their own country of origin; local NGOs; and community-based organizations such as local associations and local church groups. The WFP had a variety of relationships with these different types of NGOs, which were identified as: co-operating, complementary and co-ordinating partnerships. Details of the financial agreement established with each NGO were given, as well as of the different types of written agreements signed between the WFP and NGOs, including: field level agreements; global MOUs on collaborative working arrangements; MOUs on standby arrangements; and tripartite agreements between the WFP, UNHCR and NGOs. The standard agreement between the WFP and NGO partners is the Field Level Agreement (FLA). An FLA is drawn up at the country level for each operation or project that the WFP and its HGO partner collaborate on that involves distributing food to beneficiaries. It outlines the objectives of the partnership; the WFP's and NGO's specific roles and responsibilities; details of the food quantities, rations, and distribution mechanisms; reporting and financial management requirements; and payment procedures.

The final section of the handbook covered the principles of NGO involvement in a whole range of WFP activities, including: emergency preparedness; food security assessment; identifying response options; targeting; project design; food storage and handling; distribution; and monitoring and evaluation.

Increased WFP–non-governmental organization operational relationships

The handbook was highly successful, judged by the considerable increase that took place in WFP–NGO partnerships after its publication in 2005. By the end of 2008, the WFP had 2,837 NGO partners, of which 2,607 were national or local NGOs and 230 were international NGOs (WFP, 2009l). WFP international NGO partners came from 34 countries, over half in Europe (mainly from France, Italy, and the UK). The United States had the highest number of NGOs collaborating with the WFP (64), a 25 per cent increase since 2007. Some of the WFP's main international NGO partners are organized as federations with international structures, with headquarters and funding offices in developed countries, and operating offices in developing countries.

The full extent of collaboration could be seen when it was noted that 60 of the 80 WFP country offices had collaboration of one kind or another with NGOs: 174 of the 244 operations carried out by the WFP were undertaken in co-operation with NGOs. The main NGO partners were World Vision International (in 28 countries), CARE International (25 countries), and CRS (14 countries). Over 40 per cent of WFP country offices had 20 or more NGO partners. The main countries with the most NGO partnerships were Colombia, Sudan, and Somalia. Some 48 per cent of WFP food distribution in 2008 took place through NGOs. The main activity of WFP–NGO co-operation was food distribution; the main programme category of collaboration was PRROs and the main sectors of collaborations were primary schools, food for training programmes, and free relief food assessment. Close to 94 per cent of the WFP's NGO partners carried out food distribution activities in 2008, 45 per cent were involved in monitoring, and 29 per cent engaged in storage.

The WFP *Strategic Plan (2008–13)* states that: 'Partnerships are essential for WFP to accomplish its mission and achieve its objectives'. NGOs were described as 'instruments in increasing WFP's deep field presence', and were 'essential in both short-term and long-term responses to hunger' (WFP, 2008k). Success in saving the lives of the most vulnerable would depend not only on the WFP's own capacity, but also on the extent to which the WFP managed to be a partner for others, especially NGOs. Although the WFP mainly partnered with NGOs on operational lines, consultations were often held with its main operational NGO partners to discuss issues of common interest, and share views of common interest and on the latest developments in the humanitarian world. Consultations were held with partners on the WFP *Strategic Plan (2008–13)* before it was finalized. In March 2008, high-level consultations were held with the IFRC and ICRC to discuss issues brought about by rising food prices. In June 2008, a technical meeting was held with NGOs to discuss the WFP's response to the global food crisis, the use of cash and vouchers, programming in urban areas, social problems, and enhanced collaboration.

In the shift from a food aid agency to a food assistance agency, the WFP recognized that partnership with NGOs is 'essential' to reach those in need through innovative ways, such as cash and voucher schemes, and the *Purchase for Progress* (P4P) programme. Areas where collaboration with NGOs in the agricultural sector may be increased include: strengthening the capacity of, and enhancing the participation of women farmers' organizations; strengthening food quality control and assessment; developing strategies and post-harvest handling to reduce food losses; and facilitating access to credit, and agricultural inputs and services.

Co-operation with private donors

Background

Early in the new millennium, another dimension was added to the WFP's activities in the form of WFP–private donor partnerships. This new initiative was due to the leadership provided by former UN secretary-general, Kofi Annan, which was followed up by the personal initiatives of executive director James Morris. It brought with it three substantial benefits. First, it widened the appeal and advocacy for the fight against world hunger, and introduced the work of the WFP to the general public as never before. Second, the WFP itself came into contact with corporations and people beyond governments and the public sector, enriched by their knowledge and experience. And third, it led to additional resources for activities, such as school feeding programmes, nutrition improvement, and anti-HIV/AIDS activities, for which dwindling contributions were forthcoming from public donors. But it also brought the realization that adequate staff and administrative resources were needed to maintain and expand private donor support.

The many years of scepticism, even hostility, within the UN to co-operation and involvement with the private sector, fuelled largely by the fear of conflict of interest, was ended in preparations leading up to the UN Millennium Summit in 2000. In an address to chief executives in 1999, the UN secretary-general, Kofi Annan, proposed that businesses and the UN jointly initiate a global compact of shared valued and principles, to give a human face to the global market. The following year, the United Nations Global Compact (UNGC) was established. The compact is a call on companies everywhere voluntarily to align their operations and strategies with ten universally accepted core principles in the areas of human rights, labour standards, the environment and anti-corruption, and to take action in support of UN goals, including the MDGs (Box 4.2).[43]

Only 47 companies were present when the compact was launched in July 2000. A decade later, it had become the largest corporate responsibility initiative

Box 4.2 The United Nations Global Compact: ten core principles

Human rights

1. Businesses should support and respect the protection of internationally proclaimed human rights, and
2. make sure that they are not compliant in human rights abuses.

Labour

3. Businesses should uphold the freedom of association and the effective recognition of the right of collective bargaining,
4. elimination of all forms of forced and compulsory labour,
5. effective abolition of child labour, and
6. elimination of discrimination in respect of employment and occupation.

Environment

7. businesses should support a precautionary approach to environmental changes,
8. undertake initiatives to promote greater environmental responsibility, and
9. encourage the development and diffusion of environmentally friendly technologies.

Anti-corruption

10. Businesses should work against corruption in all its forms, including extortion and bribery.

Source: The UN Global Compact, 2000.

in the world with over 8,000 signatories, 6,000 from businesses and 2,000 for civil society and other non-business groups, in more than 135 countries (Hall, 2010). In addition, global compact local networks had been established in over 90 countries. Financial support was also provided by business participants to the Foundation for the Global Compact, which in 2009 reached $1.7 million, and funded a number of important programmes and events.

In his report to the UN General Assembly in 2001, Cooperation between the United Nations and All Relevant Partners, in particular the Private Sector, Kofi Annan stated:

> Our experience has shown that a large part of the work for development is about preparing the ground for sufficient private sector activity to provide the jobs and incomes needed to build a more equitable and prosperous society. Yet the United Nations has only sporadically tapped the power that can be drawn from engaging the private sector in development. (Annan, 2001)

This led, in July 2003, to the establishment of a United Nations Commission on the Private Sector and Development, which helped to unleash and engage the private sector in the development process in developing countries (UNDP, 2004). The commission believed that the primary responsibility for achieving growth and equitable development rested with the developing countries themselves. But there was also the realization that the savings, investment, and innovations that led to development were undertaken largely by private individuals, corporations, and communities. The private sector could alleviate poverty by contributing to economic growth, job creation, and poor people's incomes. It could also empower poor people by providing a broad range of products and services at low cost. Small and medium-sized enterprises could be 'engines' for job creation and 'sea-beds' for innovation and entrepreneurship. But, in many poor countries, they were marginalized in the domestic ecosystem and encountered many obstacles. Many operated outside the formal legal system, in the informal sector with its low productivity, and lack of access to financing and long-term capital.

Motivated by the UN secretary-general's leadership, WFP executive director Morris played a key role in fostering WFP–private donor partnerships. He informed the WFP's executive board, at its third session in 2003, that he would endeavour to broaden the WFP donor base in order to meet the financial challenges that the WFP faced. He stated: 'WFP planned to engage emerging donors, strengthen private-sector partnerships, and encourage traditional donors to meet the current OECD average of $2 per capita '(Morris, 2003). In 2003, he set up a new Fund-Raising and Communications Department to expand the WFP donor base by working with emerging donors and the private sector, and appointed John Powell as deputy executive director of External Affairs and Resource Development.[44] The WFP had unprecedented demands on its resources in 2003. But, at a time of growing hunger and poverty, aid resources, including food aid, were declining. Even without the Iraq emergency, the WFP's largest-ever operation, the WFP increased its food assistance in 2003 by more than 40 per cent over 2002. But shortfalls had occurred between the demand contained in the WFP's approved emergency operations and development projects and the contributions made to them. Morris stated:

> The global humanitarian community is losing the battle against hunger. FAO figures show 18 million more undernourished people in the developing world since 1997. There is no excuse for hunger in a world of food surpluses. (Morris, 2003)

He called for more partnerships in the fight against hunger, including private-sector support. The executive board commended the WFP's efforts to reach the private sector but emphasized that:

> private-sector relations must be conducted within the purview of the board. There needed to be dialogue, consultation and reports back to the board on the initiatives with the private sector. In the same spirit, it was important that private sector partners fully understood the role and responsibilities of the board. (WFP, 2003e)

In 2002, executive director Morris took the personal initiative of meeting with Peter Bakker, the chief executive officer of the multinational company TNT. The Dutch global logistics firm, specializing in the mail and express delivery business, became the WFP's first private sector partner. An account of their meeting is instructive.[45] Bakker came to the meeting having already primed himself on the problems of world hunger. He felt that, hunger in emergency situations was, to a large extent, a logistics problem. He realized that TNT, with over 16,000 employees in 63 countries, was in a unique position to make a contribution to solving that problem. He had discussed his ideas with the company's senior managers and, with their support, began developing the notion of a support programme on a global scale. They had also considered which organization they might support, with the right organizational and emotional fit. At their first meeting, Bakker found 'an emotional fit'. He recalled that:

> Morris showed strong signs of commitment and motivation, pointing out the many areas in which WFP could benefit from TNT's expertise. Most important, we recognized in him the same driving values and vision that guided us in our partner search process. (Tomasini and Van Wassenhove, 2009: 152)

The WFP's logistics agenda was explained, revealing areas in which the WFP could benefit from TNT's co-operation. For TNT, this validated the fact that the WFP was ready to assume change and co-operate on an equal basis with a partner. The next step was to establish interactive channels to enable both partners to define tangible, realistic projects with clear goals, and to involve and to commit the staff of both organizations to the partnership. It was decided to carry out this step during a retreat in Tanzania by senior management teams from both sides. Refugee camps, school feeding programmes, and regional emergency relief projects were visited. The teams interacted with the victims of political unrest, people with HIV/AIDS, and a large number of orphans, during which they witnessed extreme poverty in areas that had limited access to vital resources, care, and education. The TNT team began to understand that the main elements of emergency logistics were high uncertainty, limited resources (both human and capital), and an extreme sense of urgency. It also became apparent how the core competencies of TNT could add value through partnership.

Following the retreat, a presentation was made to the TNT board explaining the need for the partnership and indicating the potential benefits of choosing to work with the WFP. The partnership would not so much involve donations in cash but, rather, an exchange of capabilities and expertise that would also benefit TNT's competitiveness in its business. While it was difficult to show a formula, or even an estimate, for the return on investment, the presentation assured the TNT board of the potential gains from the partnership. Members were asked personally to adopt the initiative and devote time to its development.

A partnership agreement was signed between the two parties in December 2002 that launched a ground-breaking, multi-million dollar partnership called 'Moving the World', to help fight global hunger. The key objectives were to improve the lives of the hungry poor, increase awareness of world hunger, and strengthen the global image of both partners. The focus was on four main areas of work: knowledge transfer, hands-on support, awareness and fundraising, and becoming more responsible. Once the partnership was established, keeping its momentum and growing its potential were critical to its success. Difficulties could be expected, but these could be overcome by both partners being open and honest, learning from experience, being willing to adapt and adjust, and by spreading ownership of the partnership among staff internally and communicating successes.

When Bakker was asked what he had learned after two years of partnership with the WFP, he replied that 'businesses are not humanitarian agencies', reinforcing the idea that saving lives is a humanitarian task and that the role of business is to provide support to humanitarian operations. Clearly defined roles and expectations helped to break the barriers of stereotypes, but nothing surpassed the benefits of networking and personal relationships. Not surprisingly, humanitarians under pressure were more likely to call on the people they knew well and have met personally. But to work well, partnerships required a substantial investment of time and commitment.

Following his experience with TNT, executive director Morris proposed that he and the chief executive officer of the Boston Consulting Group (BGC), Carl Stern, make a joint visit to Bangladesh in December 2003 to give BCG first-hand exposure to the WFP's work in that country. BCG is an international strategy and general management consulting firm whose mission is to help corporations create and sustain comparative advantage. The WFP partnership with BCG had started in April 2003 with an in-kind consultancy valued at $1.8 million. The visit resulted in BGC's commitment to a partnership with the WFP. In June 2004, a MOU was signed between the two partners that established the procedures of working together.

Expanding and diversifying the WFP's donor base

The executive board requested a paper outlining the WFP's strategy to engage additional governments and the private sector to broaden the WFP resource base. A draft paper was prepared by the WFP secretariat and two informal consultations were held with WFP members during 2004 before a revised paper that reflected their views was presented to the executive board at its third session in 2004 (WFP, 2004t).

As global food aid requirements continued to grow, more donors were required to share the burden of support. WFP strategy was designed to 'seek and accept only contributions that are required to meet beneficiary needs or to help WFP to meet them'. The WFP aspired to have all member states, inter-governmental organizations, and the private sector as donors. It was therefore proposed to change the definitions of 'traditional' and 'non-traditional' donors and to use the single term 'donor', but to distinguish between 'public' and 'private' donors. Public donors were defined as contributors to the WFP who were members of the UN, FAO, an intergovernmental organization, or other public organizations. Private donors were contributors to the WFP that were either a for-profit corporation or business association; a foundation; a social, educational, or service organization; an NGO; or an individual, who would be approved on a case-by-case basis.

All contributions to the WFP were made on a voluntary basis so that the application of full-cost recovery was essential. To support member states unable to do so, and to ensure the application of objective criteria to determine which states were eligible for special efforts, the WFP proposed using per capita gross national income (GNI) to allow twinning with another member state, a twinning fund, or twinning with a private donor. The WFP also had a small fund of $4 million per year to help donors meet full-cost recovery allowing up to $1 million per eligible donor per year.

With modest growth in 2003–04, the WFP aspired to raise 10 per cent of its resources from private donors by 2007. The WFP's primary aim in co-operation with private donors was 'to expand its fight against global hunger by sharing the burden of the costs, resources and efforts required to achieve the goal of feeding all identified beneficiaries through approved programmes'. The rules of engagement with private donors should be defined, taking inspiration from the UN Global Compact, the UN Commission on the Private Sector, and the leadership shown by the UN secretary-general. It had been recognized that the private sector had significant roles to play in developing countries. However, in order to protect the reputation of the UN and its agencies, to avoid conflicts of interest, and to ensure that value was created from working with the private sector, UN agencies should 'take proper measures and manage expectations to ensure that no private sector partner benefits commercially from its relationship with the United Nations and is not granted exclusivity with any single private sector partner' (Annan, 2001). In addition, private contributions should not serve as a substitute for member states' funding. Furthermore, private donors should not compromise the independence and neutrality of the UN and its agencies, and should not replace the role of member states.

There were many ways of working with private donors, ranging from a single contribution to a long-term relationship. The WFP would explore all opportunities. Given that the WFP operations were rarely fully-funded, it was unlikely that private donations for a particular operation would substitute for member states' contributions. When a private donor provided a gift-in-kind for programme support and administration, the WFP would treat the donation in the same manner as special funds provided for such purposes by a public donor and ensure that it was consistent with the management priorities agreed through WFP management plans.

The WFP would seek private contributions that were aligned with its priority needs and could best serve its beneficiaries, including: increasing the speed and efficiency of emergency operations; building better supply chains for emergency donors; enhancing the nutrition, health, and education of beneficiaries; building awareness and support in the fight against global hunger; increasing technological support; strengthening management and human resources; and improving WFP business processes.

Private donations would be subject to the same WFP policies established for public donors (contained in WFP General Regulation XIII.4) and could be accepted in cash and gifts-in-kind – commodities, services, expertise or products.

In return, important non-profit benefits would accrue to private donors – for example, through demonstrating their social responsibility, a private donor's image would be enhanced, which would: increase positive exposure; improve employee morale; and strengthen staff performance, recruitment, and retention. For the WFP, co-operation with private donors created opportunities to engage in the fight against hunger, intellectually and emotionally, with organizations and people outside government circles. More specifically, private donors could provide resources, expertise, and skills to help the WFP to: assist more people by expanding its resource base; build a stronger institution by decreasing response times, improving operational efficiency, strengthening capacity, and sharpening skills; and multiply awareness and visibility of the WFP's fight against hunger.

Regarding the criteria for the selection of private donors for co-operation with the WFP, the WFP would only accept contributions from those that: had a record of social responsibility and a positive public, and/or product or service image; respected human rights; and abided by the ten core principles of United Nations Global Compact. The WFP would ensure compliance with its donor criteria by: requiring private donors to adhere to the WFP Code of Conduct (see below); and providing for review and standard exit or termination clauses in all agreements with private donors that required their continuous observation of WFP policies. The WFP executive director could, at his/her discretion, decline contributions from potential private donors deemed to be not in the best interest of the WFP. And WFP governance and policy would remain the sole purview of WFP member states, exercised through its executive board.

In order to ensure the integrity of the WFP's commercial relationships and fairness to all bidders in its procurement processes, the WFP would maintain a 'firewall' between its private fundraising and procurement processes to ensure that commercial relationships with private donors would remain independent and be managed separately. The WFP would create a 'Business Advisory Council', a global network of chief executive officers and corporate leaders, to discuss management issues with the WFP's executive management on an advisory basis. The objective would be to learn from their experiences and insights for the benefit of WFP programmes. And the WFP's executive director would report annually to the executive board on the WFP's work with private donors.

A 'Code of Conduct' was proposed for private donors containing 'fundamental principles' that they would agree to follow, 'interpreting their rights and obligations and as a guide for their conduct in all forms of co-operation with WFP'. The proposed code contained the principle of conformity with the WFP's mandate and policies, 'stringent' criteria for the selection of private donors, and 'rigorous' screening before acceptance of contributions from them. Individual donors would be dealt with on case-by-case basis. The proposed code also stressed non-exclusivity, non-preferential treatment, and impartiality in WFP dealings with private donors. Information on WFP–private donor activities would be made publicly available to ensure transparency and accountability.

Private donors would agree to allocate sufficient time, resources and capabilities to carry out activities in co-operation with the WFP. Monitoring and evaluation would be built into the design of joint projects. The WFP's name and emblem could be used only in a manner agreed in writing between the partners. Agreement would be reached between the WFP and private donors regarding the ownership of copyright, patent, or other intellectual property rights generated through joint activities. Private donors would be acknowledged for their contributions, and agreement in writing would be made on any communications or publicity concerning joint activities. Also, the parties involved would enter into a written agreement that stipulated the terms and conditions under which all activities would be conducted.

The executive board endorsed the proposed strategy for broadening the WFP donor base and requested periodic updates regarding its implementation (WFP, 2004u). It accepted the revised definition of public and private donors, the criteria to be used in the selection of private donors to co-operate with the WFP, and the Code of Conduct to be used for all forms of co-operation with private donors.

WFP private sector partnership and fundraising strategy

Following adoption by the WFP's executive board of the proposals to extend and diversify the WFP donor base, outreach to private donors was extended and intensified. The WFP's approach was lauded because it engaged strategic support from major corporations willing to leverage their core competences to ensure that the WFP had access to the cutting-edge of private sector approaches, technology, and competence without creating a conflict of interest. It was also realized that the WFP's goal of ending hunger presented a complex, multi-dimensional challenge that required bold and decisive action. The enormity of the problem, with its social, economic, human, and political consequences, had been well-documented. And it was agreed that if the first MDG of halving the proportion of hungry people by 2015 were to be achieved, then agencies such as the WFP should seek out new partners and be open to new forms of partnerships.

Finding the most efficient and effective means of responding to the needs of hungry poor people was perceived as the WFP's primary challenge. An overarching strategy was required to help the WFP respond to that challenge. This included strong donor partnerships and more innovative fund-raising mechanisms to raise additional resources. Nutrition strategies needed to be developed to reach the key beneficiary groups with the right nutritious food at the right time. And improving management systems would provide more accurate feedback on outcomes and outputs, ultimately helping to reinforce programme design and organizational management systems.

Against this background, the WFP secretariat presented a paper on the WFP's private sector partnership and fundraising strategy to the executive board at its first session in 2008, the paper having previously been discussed in informal consultations (WFP, 2008i). The paper reviewed experience with private donor partnerships since 2003 and proposed a self-financing model for fund-raising with private donors, the target being to raise over $200 million in cash by 2017,

50–60 per cent from corporations and 40–50 per cent from individuals and foundations.

A number of lessons were learned from WFP partnerships with private donors between 2003 and 2008. It proved sound to concentrate initially on a limited number of major corporate partnerships from which the WFP benefited both from expertise and knowledge transfer to improve its work and direct cash to support its operations. However, corporate partnerships required a significant level of services in terms of engagement, communications, and reporting. There was substantial potential for private donor partnerships and fund raising in all regions of the world that had not yet been tapped. At the same time, administrative arrangements to put these potential opportunities into operation needed to be regularly reviewed and adjusted in the light of experience in order to maximize efficiency and minimize costs. Foundations were willing to partner with the WFP on ventures of mutual interest, such as VAM, SENAC and ICT technology. Strong research and due diligence were required to ensure that the WFP minimized potential risk to its reputation. Public information was crucial and a sustainable strategy for marketing, communications, and branding was essential. WFP field officers were willing to reach out to potential private sector donors, but they needed to be supported by corporate guidance, training, and access to specialist advice. Private donors accepted that there were costs involved in raising funds that were higher than seeking public funds. Discussion with them revealed that they were willing to see up to 25 per cent of their donations used to offset fund-raising costs, which would enable the WFP to finance the costs of increased private sector fund-raising. Far more funds could be obtained from individual donors by engaging them more proactively. In 2003, the WFP raised around $250,000 through the internet. In 2006, with a modest investment, it was raised to $1.3 million. The better the WFP was known, the greater the potential for private donor partnerships and fund-raising. And effective public policy and advocacy enhanced the understanding of hunger issues and laid the foundation for effective partnerships.

Investment was required to build WFP in-house capacity for both private donor partnerships and fund-raising. It was therefore proposed to increase the personnel budget for these purposes from $6.5 million in 2008 to $11.1 million in 2017. It was projected that this would increase private donor contributions from $81 million in 2008 (of which $43 million were gifts-in-kind and $38 million in cash) to $270 million in 2017 ($70 million in gifts-in-kind and $200 million in cash). The WFP would ensure that private donor contributions were demand-driven, particularly gifts-in-kind, which would match WFP needs with donors' capacity to give. The WFP would manage the costs involved to ensure that the investment-to-income ratio did not exceed the global standard of four dollars raised for every dollar invested. The WFP intended to work well within that norm by focusing on proven cost-effective approaches and avoiding costly mechanisms, such as direct mail and purchased advertising.

The WFP intended to recruit around 15 global humanitarian partners willing to engage in a multi-year, multi-faceted relationship, which would involve a substantial cash contribution. They would be identified on the basis of WFP analysis of the best match between its needs and corporations' potential to donate, regardless of where they were located. A robust research and screening process had been developed to identify companies that could enhance the WFP's operations and image, screen out those who could endanger the WFP's reputation, and produce comprehensive donor profiles to ensure they met criteria approved by the WFP's executive board.

The WFP's executive board endorsed the proposed strategy for expanding private donor partnerships and fund-raising (WFP, 2008j). It approved a financing arrangement to cover the costs involved and accepted the concept of a self-financing model. Requests would be included in the WFP's biennial management plans with annual reporting in the annual performance reports. The self-financing model would be reconsidered in the context of the *Strategic Plan (2008–13)* and the changing funding environment.

Private donations to the WFP

As a result of partnerships with private corporations and foundations, and contributions from the general public and individuals, total private donations to the WFP rose significantly from \$28.6 million in 2003 to \$143.8 million in 2008, not including extraordinary gifts-in-kind, and were \$117.2 for 2010 at the end of September of that year (see Table 4.2). Of the total donations, cash contributions, including gifts-in-kind that offset WFP budgets, increased from \$5.5 million in 2003 to \$104.5 million in 2009. The value of gifts-in-kind increased over the same period from \$23.1 million to \$40.7 million. In 2009, approximately 65 per cent of the cash contribution received from private donors was invested in EMOPs and PRROs, and 20 per cent in school feeding, HIV/AIDS, and nutrition improvement programmes.

Table 4.2 Private donations to WFP 2003–09 (\$ millions)

Year	Cash[1]	Gift-in-kind[2]	Total
2003	5.5	23.1	28.6
2004	21.3	43.6	64.9
2005	27.0	45.5	72.5
2006	38.0[3]	37.4	75.4
2007	50.0[3]	45.2	95.2
2008[4]	145.5	48.8	194.3
2009[5]	104.6	40.7	145.3

Notes: [1]Included gift-in-kind donations that offset WFP budgets; [2]Donations that did not offset WFP budgets, including advertising; [3]2005 and 2006 cash figures exclude American Red Cross contribution to the Indian Ocean tsunami affected region; [4]Excludes \$66 million donation from the Bill and Melinda Gates Foundation for Purchase for Progress; [5]Provisional figures.

Source: WFP.

At the special session of the UN General Assembly in September 2010 to review progress in meeting the MDGs, WFP executive director Josette Sheeran announced a 'bold partnership with the private sector to combat hunger', following a major gathering of private sector companies (WFP, 2010f). She said:

> It is crystal clear that we need the ingenuity, power and reach of the private sector and the civil society and with sustainable solutions can we halve the number of people who go hungry every day...This kind of innovation is opening a world of possibility in combating hunger. Our private sector companies have put us on the cutting edge of hunger solutions.

She added that the WFP's newest private sector partner, Zynga Games, would help roll out its most innovative and wide-reaching grass-roots social media campaign to fight hunger to the 215 million people who play Zynga's games each month. The WFP's campaign 'WeFeedback' would start in October 2010; it encourages people online to use the feedback calculator to turn their favourite food item into a donation to feed the hungry. Through this innovative programme, people can spread the word by activating their personal networks through popular social sites such as Facebook and Google.

Other innovations to reach the hungry include Yum! Brands, which is about to enter its fourth World Hunger Relief Campaign. To date, $60 million has been raised from its offering its employees and customers a chance to participate in online giving through a special widget developed by the WFP. The WFP has joined with the WHO, UNICEF, FAO, and international companies in a partnership called 'Project Laser Beam', aimed at reducing child malnutrition in Bangladesh and Indonesia, with Unilever and Kraft as lead partners.

The WFP's partnering with Vodafone to train and deploy technology experts for emergencies has enabled the WFP to send telecommunications experts to Haiti within 12 hours of the earthquake striking in January 2010. These specialists were instrumental in re-establishing communications for use by the entire humanitarian community. The WFP partnership with TNT continues with cargo planes, warehouses, and specialized logistics staff being provided in emergency operations, as well as contributions from TNT employees for school meals programmes. The WFP has established a partnership with DSM to make its food assistance products and those of other partner companies more nutritious, and to explore the development of new nutritious food products.[46] DSM received the 'World Business Development Award' for its work towards achieving the MDGs in the field of hidden hunger.

Examples of WFP corporate private sector partners

The WFP has entered into partnership arrangements with a range of major corporations in the private sector. Brief descriptions of some of these partnerships are given below to indicate the kinds of corporations involved and the ways in which the WFP's work is strengthened, particularly in logistics, emergency telecommunications technology, improved nutrition, school feeding, advocacy, and awareness-raising.

TNT. The Dutch multinational corporation TNT, the WFP's first private corporate partner, is a global leader in the mail and express delivery business, with over 160,000 employees in 63 countries, working in over 200 nations. TNT has not only placed it considerable logistics expertise and capacity at the WFP's disposal, but also has raised funds for, and awareness of, the WFP's work. As one of the world's largest companies specializing in logistics, TNT is helping to improve the speed and efficiency of WFP emergency operations in some of the most difficult and dangerous locations. Its state-of-the-art commodity tracking system and improved supply chain delivery methodologies have helped to increase the delivery of WFP assistance in the fastest and most efficient ways.

TNT has an emergency response team on standby to help the WFP in any emergency situation. When an emergency strikes, TNT can make its skilled staff, warehouses, aircraft, and vehicle fleets available to the WFP within 48 hours, and use its experience in clearing goods through ports and customs, for a quicker and more efficient delivery of emergency supplies where they are needed. Fleet Forum, the first independent knowledge centre on humanitarian transport (an interagency partnership managed by TNT, ICRC, World Vision International, and the WFP), focuses on the key issues of truck fleet safety and security, efficiency and effectiveness, and environmental impact.

Through its Joint Supply Chain initiative, TNT has brought expertise from the commercial sector and its joint operations with the WFP to the forum. North Star Foundation is a public–private partnership that has established a network of roadside health clinics at major truck stops and border crossings in Africa, India, and China. These wellness centres offer a practical, low-cost response to the transmission of HIV and other sexually transmitted infections in the transport industry. Among other things, TNT has helped the WFP through airlifts in emergencies in Iraq, Liberia, Sudan, and Haiti; air operations training and customs expertise; the redesign of the UN humanitarian response depots; and the implementation of WFP fleet management systems.

TNT has motivated its employees to carry out fund-raising and awareness activities for the WFP through consumer and stakeholder events. These include a high profile 'Walk the World' initiative, the world's largest annual global fund-raising event for the WFP. This was first launched by TNT in 2003, and is a 24-hour relay with participants in each of the world's time zones walking five kilometres to raise money for the WFP. On average, over 360,000 people have taken part in 210 locations around the world to raise money for WFP school meals programmes in the world's poorest countries.

Other TNT awareness raising initiatives on behalf of the WFP include: an annual presence by TNT and the WFP at the World Economic Form in Davos, Switzerland to raise awareness among the political and business communities of the hunger problem and the work of the WFP; cause-related marketing through TNT's customer networks to encourage donations and raise awareness for the WFP; the Global Experience Programme, a special partnership with the world's largest international student association, AIESEC, through which students are sent to complete a humanitarian development internship in a developing country; Colour the World, a children's colouring competition open to the children of TNT employees designed to promote awareness of world hunger among young people; and Kids Moving the World, an educational game for children in primary schools in the Netherlands that addresses hunger issues. TNT has supported the WFP in more than 30 emergency operations and raised funds for WFP school feeding programmes in many countries, including Cambodia, Gambia, Malawi, Nicaragua, and Tanzania.

Boston Consulting Group. BGC is an international strategy and general management consulting firm whose mission is to help corporations create and sustain competitive advantage. It supports the WFP's increasing effectiveness by drawing on its strategic, organizational, and other functional expertise, and by providing an external perspective. It has no *a priori* agenda, and seeks to help set direction and achieve change using a more analytical, fact-based, and forward-thinking approach. BGC was the WFP's second corporate partner, an arrangement which started in April 2003. Since then, partnerships have taken place annually on a range of subjects. In 2003, BGC assisted the WFP in developing its private sector fund-raising strategy. It conducted a business process review to obtain more efficient utilization of resources and on-time food availability. A new methodology was developed to forecast WFP donations.

A long-term strategic vision was presented at the global meeting of WFP staff in Dublin, Ireland in June 2004 to define the WFP's role in achieving the MDG of halving the proportion of hungry people in the world by 2015. A review was conducted of the WFP supply chain to upgrade operations to state-of-the-art private sector best-practice. In the context of the WFP's decentralization process, a review was conducted to shape the organizational and governance structure that ensured that WFP country offices were most effective. During the major Indian Ocean tsunami emergency, BCG deployed four staff to the WFP's regional office in Bangkok, Thailand to assist in preparing the WFP's website for the emergency. And BGC provided support to the WFP's country office in Sudan to manage the WFP's largest country-wide emergency operation. Every year since 2003, the WFP's Private Sector Fund-raising Department assists BCG in the organization and presentation of the annual BCG–WFP business course for 30 short-listed candidates to be hired by BCG. BCG staff actively participate in the Walk the World event.

Caterpillar. The American corporation Caterpillar is the world's largest producer of construction equipment, especially heavy equipment. It is using its knowledge and expertise on the ground to help the WFP respond to emergencies more effectively by helping the WFP co-ordinate access to equipment and dealers across the world in times of disasters. It has assisted in the setting up of logistics hubs and mobile storage units that have proved to be vital in transporting food and other relief supplies to afflicted areas (for example, in places such as Ethiopia). The corporation's employees have also raised funds for WFP emergency operations in the Democratic Republic of Congo, Haiti, Pakistan, Somalia, and Tanzania. The corporation has made a donation to the WFP's school feeding programme in Haiti, which helped to expand its coverage to provide school meals to 500,000 children and take-home rations to their families.

DSM. The Nutritional Products Division of DSM is one of the world's largest producers of biochemicals and fine chemicals for nutritional use. It is at the cutting edge of research and development on the fortification of food products to improve their nutritional content. The corporation has a strong history of social responsibility focused on fighting nutritional deficiencies. In April 2007, the WFP and DSM signed a three-year agreement whereby DSM donated the equivalent of more than $9 million in cash, micronutrients, and in-kind services. The overall objective of what was called the 'Improving Nutrition, Improving Lives' partnership is to ensure that the nutritional needs of all WFP beneficiaries are met through the creation of cost-effective micronutrient interventions to improve the WFP's general food basket.

The partnership is composed of two initiatives. The first, which is the cornerstone of the partnership, is nutrition enhancement. DSM food technology, packaging and other experts work with the WFP to research and develop new or enhanced fortified foods, and to measure their effects on the nutritional state of WFP beneficiaries. Pilot projects are being conducted in selected countries to test food fortification solutions in different contexts (climate, temperature, malaria-affected beneficiaries, and the like) to help the WFP find cost-effective and sustainable nutritious food solutions for the hungry poor. The second initiative is to engage DSM employees and raise their awareness of, and enthusiasm for, the partnership with the WFP in DSM's offices and production sites in 50 countries around the world. This includes advocacy and fund-raising events, and specialist and generalist volunteers dedicated to helping selected WFP regional bureaux and country offices with specific needs.

LG (Life's Good). The 'Partnership of Hope' between LG and the WFP provides food to improve the education and health of vulnerable children across the Horn of Africa, with a focus on Ethiopia and Kenya, and to support environmental management schemes through food-for-work projects in the region. LG, a Korean-based corporation, is a global leader in consumer electronics, mobile communications, and home appliances. Through partnership with the WFP, it seeks to improve the lives of disadvantaged and vulnerable children in the Horn of Africa. LG is helping the WFP to reach needy children through investing in sustainable programmes, including school meals, nutritional assistance, HIV/AIDS, orphanages, and environmental projects. LG is the first WFP public–private partnership where a major Asian company has made a significant donation to support development programmes in Africa reaching, for example, some 23,000 of the poorest and most vulnerable people in the Nairobi slums in Kenya and in the remote areas of Ethiopia.

NPL, the Dutch National Postcode Lottery. NPL was created in 1990 and is the largest charity lottery in the Netherlands. It has distributed over two billion euros to charities. Half of the revenue generated by the lottery has been donated to 53 humanitarian organizations in the areas of development corporations, nature and the environment, human rights, and social cohesion. Starting in January 2005, NPL donated one million euros each year for the next five years to support WFP school feeding activities in Niger. In addition, in 2006 NPL donated 240,000 euros to the WFP food-for-work programme in Mali and, in 2008, made a donation of one million euros to support WFP cereal banks in Niger.

The main objective of the NPL-supported school feeding programme is to improve access to primary education, particularly for girls, in the nomadic, food-insecure areas of Niger. The donation in 2008 to the cereal banks in Niger was used to purchase 1,800 tons of cereals, enough to ensure sufficient cereal rations for a whole school year for 17,600 school children. The school feeding activities in Niger have helped increase the enrolment of girls, particularly in rural areas. The proportion of girls enrolled rose from 36 per cent in 2000 to 43 per cent in 2006. The schools receiving WFP school meals have a five per cent higher proportion of girls than schools without WFP assistance. NPL's donation to the WFP's cereal banks project in Niger allowed the establishment of 170 women-managed cereal banks in preparation for the 2008 lean season. With recurrent food crises in the country, the donation benefited around 85,000 families at risk of food shortage. The contribution also covered the procurement of millet, pulses, and vegetable oil for food-for-training activities for the women managing the cereal banks, giving them crucial skills at managing a sustainable business.

Pepsico Foundation. PepsiCo is one of the world's largest food and beverage companies employing over 190,000 people and selling products in 200 countries. The company uses its supply chain expertise to enhance the WFP's ability to delivery relief food supplies to afflicted communities in emergencies. It provides enhanced tools, metrics, and training for WFP logistics operations helping to bring more relief to more people in less time.

Unilever. Unilever is one of the world's largest manufacturers of consumer goods producing some of the most recognizable brands in foods, and home and personal care, with a worldwide workforce of more than 220,000 employees. It uses it expertise in nutrition, health, and marketing alongside its enormous customer base to raise funds and awareness for the WFP. The 'Together for Child Vitality' partnership aims to improve life for children through school meals programmes. Unilever became a WFP donor in 2005, when money and gifts-in-kind were given for the WFP's Indian Ocean tsunami emergency operations. Its employees in the United Sates conducted fund-raising activities. It conducted a cause-related marketing campaign in Singapore, and it donated ten trucks and money to transport relief food in Sri Lanka. It employees participated in the 'Walk the World' event in Ghana to raise funds to support WFP operations in that country. It also sold fortified vegetable oil at cost to the WFP, which provided substantial savings for WFP emergency operations in Mali and Niger. The company is helping to feed school children and to educate them and their teachers in nutrition and hygiene campaigns in Colombia, Ghana, Kenya, Indonesia, Pakistan, the Philippines, and Sri Lanka.

Vodafone Foundation and United Nations Foundation. These two foundations, together with the WFP, launched the first-ever Global Partnership for Emergency Communications to help the WFP and the entire humanitarian community improve the response when disasters strike, thereby saving lives, by training a network of hand-picked specialists. Vodafone is the WFP's emergency technology partner. It has significantly increased the WFP's ability to respond to emergencies. When roads, telegraph, and electricity lines are destroyed, it is crucial that relief workers are able to communicate. Telecommunications and information technology expertise are now often the first on the scene in emergencies to set up communication networks. ICT rapid response expert teams are dispersed in the immediate aftermath of humanitarian crises thanks to the availability of advanced funds, training, and the provision of new technologies such as wireless LAN and new radios. Attacks on UN offices in places such as Baghdad, Algiers, Pakistan, Beirut, and Sudan are changing the rules of engagement, with aid workers being directly attacked. Two-week security training courses are partly funded through this partnership as part of a three-year programme organized by the WFP.

YUM! Brands Inc. This is the world's largest restaurant company with some 36,000 restaurants in 110 countries, serving some 125 million customers worldwide. It is a crucial partner in raising awareness about issues of world hunger through its consumer outreach campaign 'World Hunger Relief'. By raising funds through its award winning campaign, it is helping WFP operations in some 26 countries. Over $60 million has been raised to date.

Zynga. This is the world's largest social games company, connecting people to the issues of world hunger through its games programme 'Fighting Hunger Online'. Players can buy special WFP-themed items, including the iconic red plastic cup that executive director Sheeran uses to advertise the WFP's school feeding programmes and the practicality of providing improved nutrition to children at low cost.

At least another 20 corporate supporters are assisting the WFP in its emergency operations and in nutrition improvement and school meals programmes for vulnerable children in some of the poorest countries, particularly in Africa.

Co-operation with foundations

The WFP also partners with leading philanthropic organizations to feed the hungry, enhance organizational capacity, and develop and implement strategic initiatives. Strong support has been given for emergency operations, particularly in Haiti.

Clinton Foundation. The foundation set up by former US President William J. Clinton has provided support for the provision of dietary and nutritional supplements to enhance the effectiveness of care and treatment for HIV positive children in Lesotho. In Haiti, it has helped in the distribution of high-energy biscuits and in the airlift of food from WFP emergency hubs to survivors of the massive earthquake in January 2010.

Community Chest of Korea (CCK). CCK has also provided generous support to provide food assistance to earthquake survivors in Haiti and to the WFP mother and child health and nutrition improvement programmes to address malnutrition among the most vulnerable. It has partnered the WFP in the food-for-education programme in Myanmar and school feeding programmes in Laos.

EIF (Entertainment Industry Foundation). The EIF has also provided generous support of WFP emergency assistance in Haiti through the Hope for Haiti Now Fund.

Bill and Melinda Gates Foundation. This major philanthropic organization is helping to tackle urgent issues that impede food security throughout the developing world. It is assisting the WFP to implement its *Purchase for Progress* (P4P) programme through which small-scale farmers in developing countries are given access to markets, thereby increasing their incomes. The Foundation is also assisting in a comprehensive food security and vulnerability study in 16 countries in sub-Saharan Africa, and supporting the WFP in fighting hunger in Burkina Faso, Côte d'Ivoire, and Niger, caused as a result of rising global food prices.

GAIN (Global Alliance for Improved Nutrition). In partnership with the WFP, the development of dietary foods products and the scaling up of access to them by malnourished people is taking place, including new fortified products for complementary feeding of infants and young children, and people living with HIV/AIDS and other infectious diseases. Assistance is also given with the delivery of food in emergency and non-emergency situations. The WFP is the executing agency for GAIN's large-scale *baladi* (local) bread fortification project in Egypt.

Howard G. Buffett Foundation. This foundation is another key supporter of the WFP's P4P programme. It also funds food assistance activities (including school feeding in Guatemala, Sierra Leone, Tajikistan, and Ethiopia), and contributes to improving logistics capacity in Central African Republic, Malawi, and Uganda.

Rockefeller Foundation. The WFP is being assisted by this foundation to restructure international natural disaster relief assistance from a largely *ad hoc* post-emergency system to an optimized global risk management system, with particular focus on coping with climate-related food crises in Africa. This is being undertaken in the context of two special initiatives. The first is through developing resilience to climate change by helping communities cope with the consequences of climate change. The second, launched with the Bill and Melinda Gates Foundation in 2006, is the Alliance for a Green Revolution in Africa (AGRA), which increases smallholder agricultural productivity through better seeds, soils, and markets.

While the greater part of WFP resources is now devoted to emergency operations, Chapter 5 will look at the development projects the WFP is undertaking.

5
Associated Development Programmes and Projects

While the greater part of WFP assistance has gone to emergency operations, support has still been provided for specific and associated development programmes and projects. These activities are linked to the WFP's work in emergencies and have helped towards meeting the Millennium Development Goals (MDGs) and the objectives of the WFP's *Strategic Plan (2008–13)*.

Nutrition policies and programmes

The WFP is well-known for its ability to deliver food quickly and efficiently throughout the developing world, even to the most difficult of locations. Relatively little is known, however, about its efforts to ensure that the food it delivers not only provides enough calories for survival, but also the vitamins and minerals needed for healthy growth and development. Given the importance of nutrition in combating malnutrition and poverty, and in meeting the MDGs, the WFP has taken steps to mainstream nutrition concerns into all its activities, including emergency operations. It has also joined with other concerned UN bodies in advocating and encouraging nutrition improvement throughout the developing world.

Nutritional considerations have been important to the WFP since its inception. At the outset, it was decided to provide its food assistance on the basis of nutritional objectives as additional food consumption. This was done to avoid any counter-productive effects on agricultural production in recipient countries and on international trade, in conformity with the *FAO's Principles of Surplus Disposal* (FAO, 1954).[1] WFP rations were calculated to meet the particular nutritional needs of specific groups. The aim was to provide a food ration which, together with local foods, made up a complete and balanced diet. When beneficiaries were almost entirely dependent on the WFP for their sustenance, a full family ration was provided. Where the quantity of local foods available was more substantial, the WFP ration was reduced *pari passu* within the overall nutritional target. Where workers were separated from their families and WFP food rations were only distributed to them, the calorie level aimed at was higher to take account of the level and conditions of work.

The special problems of providing adequate rations constantly and consistently to refugees and displaced persons in emergency situations was recognized at the conference on 'Nutrition in Times of Disaster', organized by the UN Standing Committee on Nutrition (SCN) and the International Nutrition Planners Forum, held in Geneva, Switzerland in September 1988. It was recommended that for emergency food rations, 'a practical working figure for the minimum energy requirement should be 1,900 kilocalories/person/day for a sedentary population'.[2] A special statement was issued in 1993 by the UN Administrative Committee on Coordination (ACC), the highest administrative body in the UN system, on the advice of the SCN, which recommended that 'the protection and promotion of the nutritional well-being of afflicted populations be fundamental goals of agency policy and programmes concerning refugees and displaced persons' (ACC/SCN, 1993).[3] Guidelines were subsequently agreed between the WFP and UNHCR on food rations for refugees. When refugees were dependent entirely on external food aid, the total food available to them from all sources should provide an intake of no less than 1, 900 kilocalories of energy per person per day, of which at least 8 per cent should be in the form of protein and 10 per cent in the form of fat. The calories of energy could be modified depending on the circumstances of the refugee population.

While generous, the international response to emergencies has been inconsistent, sometimes based more on political considerations than on real need. The avoidance of high malnutrition rates and mortality in certain emergencies, for example, contrasts starkly with the lack of success in others. The logistics involved in reaching afflicted people, and providing them with adequate food rations consistently, can be formidable and costly. But pioneering and innovative efforts have been made, such as using triangular transactions, food exchange arrangements, and especially local food purchases, to expedite and maintain the provision of adequate and appropriate food rations.

Recognizing the importance of nutrition for combating malnutrition, disease, and poverty, and for achieving the MDGs, the WFP has undertaken to mainstream nutrition concerns into all its operations (WFP, 2004k). The 1974 World Food Conference passed a resolution on 'Policies and programmes to improve nutrition', which called on the concerned bodies of the UN system, including the WFP, to prepare projects for assisting governments in developing countries to improve nutrition (UN, 1975).[4] From inception of operations in 1963, the WFP provided assistance to nutrition improvement programmes for mothers and pre-school children. By the end of 1995, the WFP had committed assistance to 196 projects in this field, valued at $1.5 billion.

The provision of supplementary food to mothers and children remains central to many WFP activities, but much has changed in recent decades in three important senses. First, food delivery is no longer the only objective, and programmes are better tailored to the problems they seek to overcome. Second, increased attention has been given to maximizing the nutritional value of the food rations provided. And third, the scope of nutrition programming has extended to other interventions. Good problem analysis clarifies the role of food. Complementary resources and skills are needed for nutrition interventions. Also, the focus has moved to preventing malnutrition, not merely treating it.

The WFP has placed emphasis on enhancing the quality of the food it provides not only through balanced food rations, but also by adding nutritional value through micronutrient fortification. The WFP has collaborated with the UNHCR and the University of London Institute for Child Health to develop a software tool to enable staff to better assess and compare alternative food ration compositions. A technical advisory group of experts under the auspices of the United Nations University has worked on the WFP's behalf to review potential new commodities in terms of quality, safety, nutritional value, and operational feasibility bearing in mind WFP shipment, storage, and handling requirements. The WFP is also expanding its role in food fortification measures. Other ways are being pursued to enhance the contribution of nutrition. In school feeding programmes, for example, nutrition education is being introduced to increase awareness of its importance, and micronutrient deficiencies are being reduced through school meals. De-worming is also being practised on a growing scale to ensure that the food consumed by the child provides maximum nutritional benefit. In income-generating activities, the WFP encourages the local production of fortified blended foods to help tackle micronutrient deficiencies.

Chronic malnutrition, the silent killer, often goes unnoticed, while good nutrition is largely invisible. A major problem is weak human and institutional capacity in developing countries, often where it is most needed. Interventions are hampered by the limited outreach of delivery infrastructure, a lack of skills in disciplines beyond medical training, and limited availability of non-food resources. A greater shift towards community programming is one way to overcome institutional weaknesses, but it is not an easy option, requiring investment in time and effort in community training. Among competing priorities, nutrition may still be sidelined by poor communities who often focus on pressing tangible needs, such as clean water, sanitation, or roads. The WFP seeks to overcome these problems through establishing partnerships with other UN bodies, institutions, and NGOs with similar interests and concerns, by helping to obtain non-food resources, and through the better documentation of nutritional impact.

The WFP has undertaken to pursue two other approaches to enhance the nutritional impact of its assistance. Nutrition problems in emergencies are now being systematically analyzed and the most appropriate responses defined, based on up-to-date knowledge and best practice (WFP, 2004l).[5] A joint statement has been issued by the WHO, WFP, and UNICEF on 'Preventing and controlling micronutrient deficiencies in populations affected by an emergency', involving the use of multiple vitamin and mineral supplements for pregnant and lactating women and for children aged six to 59 months. Special efforts are also being made to ensure that nutritionally adequate foods are provided in a timely manner. WFP staff are designing and implementing effective nutrition-related objectives and reporting on results. Collaboration with partners that offer complementary nutrition skill is being increased, including major private companies. Increased funding is being sought to enhance WFP cash resources to support nutrition objectives. And more attention is being paid to the underlying causes of malnutrition not only during emergencies, but also in longer-term development activities.

The WFP is increasing its efforts to meet micronutrient deficiencies among the beneficiaries of its assistance through the distribution of appropriately fortified foods (WFP, 2004m).[6] Support is also being given for national and international fortification initiatives, particularly for people in emergencies, and those living with HIV/AIDS. This is being done while respecting WFP procurement specifications and quality control procedures. The effectiveness and impact of food fortification is now being documented. The WFP is expanding its local initiatives to produce fortified blended foods and biscuits, and in the local milling and fortification of the cereals it provides. Much of the food the WFP delivers is now fortified with iron, vitamin A and other micronutrients before it is shipped. The WFP has pioneered the use of iodized salt and vitamin A. But there are good reasons to mill and fortify food as close to the beneficiaries as possible, including: helping to overcome the problems of a short shelf-life of whole fortified maize meal; enhancing the nutritional value of locally procured cereals; and fostering demand for fortified foods among local consumers, thereby nurturing an industry with potentially significant benefits for the health of the entire community.

Fortifying food in Afghanistan, Angola, and Zambia has showed the potential benefits and problems involved (Van den Briel *et al.*, 2006). All efforts were successful, but they showed that a considerable amount of staff time and supervision was involved, as well as external technical expertise. Involving the private milling sector, as well as governments, was also crucial, but difficult. In very isolated locations, strong, specialized partners were required, but these were often few in number. In such locations, other approaches to improve the diet may be more appropriate, such as the use of multi-micronutrient formulations, packed for individual or household use.

A joint statement was issued by the WHO, WFP, the SCN, and UNICEF in 2007 on 'Community-based management of severe acute malnutrition'. Severe, acute malnutrition remains a major killer of children under five years of age. Until recently, treatment had been restricted to facility-based and institutional approaches, generally limiting its coverage and impact. New evidence suggests that large numbers of children can be treated in their communities. The community-based approach involves timely detection of severe acute malnutrition in the community, and provision of treatment for those children without medical complications with ready-to-use therapeutic foods or other nutrient-dense foods at home. If properly combined with a facility-based approach, and implemented on a large scale, community-based management of severe acute malnutrition could save the lives of hundreds of thousands of children. It would also fit into the WFP's strategy of community involvement in participatory action.

School feeding programmes

The WFP, the world's largest humanitarian agency, is also the world's largest implementer of school feeding programmes. How did this come about, and why?

In his proposal for an experimental, multilateral food aid programme, made on 10 April 1961 (see Appendix in Chapter 1), which was to become the WFP, George McGovern identified school feeding as one of its proposed pilot activities. This was no surprise. At the end of his period of office as the first director of the US Food for Peace programme, McGovern had resigned in order to seek election to the US Senate. In his letter of resignation to President Kennedy on 18 July 1962, in which he summed up the multiple achievements of his 18 months as director, he had singled out one 'priority recommendation'. He strongly urged that 'the United States take an even more active lead in providing a daily school lunch for every child in the world'. He considered that 'no form of overseas assistance could return greater dividends for so little cost'. He advocated undertaking this task with renewed energy 'because it is right'.[7] School feeding as one of the WFP's objectives was incorporated into the FAO and UN parallel resolutions that established the WFP as a three-year experimental programme in November and December 1961, and in its *General Regulations* when it began operations in 1963. It was reiterated when the WFP was established on a continuing basis in 1965.

School feeding was, therefore, identified as one of the WFP's main activities from its inception. Three interrelated objectives were established: improving child nutrition and health; increasing the range of school enrolment to include the children of poor households, including girls; and encouraging greater regularity of school attendance, and reducing drop-out rates; thereby, improving school performance. Nutrition and health conditions were found to have important effects on educational performance and to be a major cause of 'educational wastage' throughout the developing world, representing one of the most significant educational problems, and involving high human and capital costs (Pollitt, 1984, 1990; WFP, 2006f). There were other reasons for the popularity of school feeding programmes. They had been found to be effective in a number of developed countries over many years. They were perceived to be basically important for the development of human resources, which was essential for economic and social development (Singer, 1972). They were strongly supported by the general public and by politicians alike in developed and developing countries. And they were considered to be relatively easy to implement and to create no displacement effects, as they involved additional consumption.

By the end of 1995, 33 years after the WFP began operations, over $2 billion (10.3 per cent) of WFP resources had been committed to 200 primary school feeding programmes throughout the developing world. While the number of primary school children reached was small compared to their total number, to say nothing of the number who did not attend school, the number of beneficiaries was more noticeable in some countries and regions. In Africa, for example, most of the primary school children in Botswana, Lesotho, Mauritius, and Swaziland were reached. In other countries, such as Algeria, Brazil, Colombia, and Sudan, considerable numbers of school children benefited.

At an early stage in its operations, however, the WFP recognized that to launch large-scale, nationwide, school feeding programmes, as many governments wished to do, would be less than responsible until the financial, technical, logistical, and administrative resources required for their sustained implementation were firmly secured from internal resources and external aid (WFP, 1969). Many donors were reluctant to provide support out of concern that they would be trapped into committing a large, and increasing, part of their aid resources to school feeding programmes as governments in developing countries failed to meet their own commitments, creating political as well as developmental tensions and problems.

In addition, the extensive evaluation literature on school feeding programmes that emerged showed that the nutritional, health, and educational benefits they promised were difficult to achieve in the reality of many developing countries (WFP, 1968, 1978c; Burgess, 1982; Levinger, 1983, 1984; Clay and Singer, 1985; Figa-Talamanca, 1985). The general obstacles to educational progress in developing countries, particularly in Africa, reduced the gains that food aid could potentially assist in achieving. Investment in teacher training and school infrastructure was often inadequate. The effectiveness of school feeding depended crucially on the degree to which governments in developing countries were taking steps, within their capabilities, to improve the basic education system.

School feeding programmes addressed an age group that has passed the greatest risk of acute malnutrition. It was difficult to repair the effects of inadequate food intake in the pre-school years in catch-up programmes. Dependence on imported food could create inappropriate food habits, which could be counter-productive to attempts to reach self-sufficiency. In the absence of adequate personnel, teachers were diverted from their educational roles to engage in food preparation and distribution. The neediest children – those who did not go to school, or attended infrequently – were not reached, particularly those in rural areas that had the poorest educational facilities. Evaluators therefore concluded that school meals programmes had a built-in bias against the rural poor, and for urban areas (Maxwell, 1978); Stevens, 1979).

An additional factor, which was often overlooked, was that the opportunity cost to poor households of sending children to school presented a barrier to school attendance (Schuh, 1983). Children of poor families make significant contributions to total household subsistence and income. Rather than providing only a meal at school, it might be necessary to give additional assistance to the family as a whole as an inducement to send children to school. This would augment the stock of human capital by improving nutrition and health, and increasing schooling. It would also provide an income transfer to poor and disadvantaged families to enable them, perhaps for the first time, to make longer-term investments in education that would raise their productivity and increase their income-generating potential. Seen in this way, food aid would be demand-enhancing rather than merely supply-augmenting.

Despite these criticisms, the basic validity of school feeding programmes remained. The WFP and other food aid agencies took steps to address the problems that were within their domain. It was recognized that continuity and regularity of school feeding programmes were essential if parents were to be motivated to send their children to school, and keep them there. Adequate administration and efficient logistics were necessary to keep a steady supply of food. The WFP and UNESCO, in co-operation with the FAO, UNICEF and WHO, carried out joint workshops and published guidelines to improve these aspects of the management of school feeding programmes (WFP, 1965; UNESCO, 1980, 1983; Guruge, 1983; FAO, 1993). Areas and schools with the highest prevalence of malnutrition were targeted to reach the neediest children among those attending school. Attempts were made to develop community participation by involving parents in food production, preparation, and distribution activities at schools. And greater use was made of locally-produced, rather than imported, foods as a way of ensuring their continuity.

A reassessment of WFP assistance to education was carried out in 1990 and submitted to the *World Conference on Education for All* in Bangkok, Thailand (WFP, 1990a). A number of previous findings were reiterated, but with a new emphasis. It was reiterated that the effectiveness of WFP assistance depended crucially on the degree to which governments in developing countries were taking steps, within their capabilities, to improve basic education. The educational environment was a key factor to be taken into account in deciding whether to begin, or continue, WFP support for school feeding programmes. Many of the constraints in the education system could not be directly addressed with food aid. These problems needed to be removed with the help of external assistance, if the objectives of school feeding programmes were to be realized. The effective co-ordination of food aid with other forms of external assistance, and the inputs that governments in developing countries could provide, in a comprehensive package of resources with common objectives, would therefore be a key factor in planning and implementing school feeding programmes in the future. In 1997, the WFP's governing body agreed that the WFP could play a useful role by sharing its experience in school feeding programmes with other aid agencies, and by facilitating an exchange of expertise and experience among developing countries (WFP, 1997f).

WFP school feeding projects were, however, subjected to mounting criticism on grounds, *inter alia*, that: they were open-ended; created dependence on foreign aid; sometimes resulted in undesirable changes in food habits; did not encourage local agricultural production and greater self-reliance; and, overall, were not sustainable once foreign aid was withdrawn. The subject of long-standing food-aided projects and related issues of scaling down or phasing out such projects had caused legitimate concern for the WFP. It was recognized that school feeding interventions were open-ended by nature, but external support had to be structured in a more finite context.

However, phase-out had proved to be difficult when recipient governments, because of economic problems, experienced difficulties in assuming full responsibility for additional budgetary allocations to their social programmes. It was recognized that more phase-outs were necessary, particularly at a time when development assistance in general, and food aid resources in particular, were declining. This raised questions regarding the future focus of food aid for the development of human resources and the corresponding manner of utilizing food aid. In addition, there were not yet in place clear mechanisms, sufficiently concrete procedures, and a time frame for a phasing-out process with the active takeover of project activities recipient governments or local communities. It was also evident that the WFP phase-out strategies were not formulated in most project designs.

Against this background, a thematic evaluation of the WFP-supported national school feeding programme in Brazil was carried out (WFP, 1997b).[8] Brazil was selected as an appropriate case. At the time, its national school feeding programme, which reached 32.5 million children, was the largest in the world, to which the WFP had committed more than $64 million of assistance over a period of nine years (May 1985–February 1996). The evaluation focused on Brazil's attempt to decentralize the national programme, the WFP's contribution to that strategy, and the implications of decentralization for a successful phasing-out of WFP assistance.

The evaluation raised a number of issues for WFP assistance to future school feeding programmes. Such programmes were usually planned as social welfare activities, rather than seen and designed to achieve broader educational and human resource development aims. This approach had contributed to difficulties encountered in phasing out WFP assistance. Effective phase-out was more likely to succeed when governments, NGOs, and communities were active partners in the design and implementation of school feeding programmes. This partnership was a key ingredient in creating local ownership and sustainability. A more structured approach to addressing the phasing out of assistance was required, which should be explicitly addressed during the design, appraisal, and formulation of school feeding programmes, as well as during their evaluation. It was necessary to proceed in a way that such programmes would not collapse when assistance was scaling down and eventually phased out.

The evaluation found that the Brazilian experience pointed to certain key ingredients for successful external participation in school feeding programmes. These included: strong government commitment to allocating and protecting public funds for such programmes; a policy of decentralization of national programmes that led to increased effectiveness and sustainability; an adequate institutional framework and sufficient human resources to implement national programmes at the central, regional, and local levels; and appropriate infrastructure for purchasing food supplies and adequate food buffer stocks.

Concerning decentralization, the WFP had only limited impact on the evolution of policy and institutional considerations at the national level of large countries. In smaller and poorer countries, however, the WFP should concern itself more with the establishment of an appropriate institutional environment while, or even before, food aid resources were being allocated. Various forms of decentralization could be considered and assessed for effectiveness in reaching those most in need, and in making recipient institutions more responsible for continuation and sustainability. Regarding phasing-out of its assistance, the WFP should formulate an integrated strategy on how and when its aid should be phased out as recipient governments or local communities took over. A review of existing WFP long-standing and open-ended school feeding programmes should be conducted, and adequate training provided to WFP staff.

The turn of the new millennium witnessed a sea-change in national and international support for school feeding programmes. A number of key events came together to bring this about. The goal of extending a basic level of education to all, a major outcome of the 1990 *World Conference on Education for All*, was reconfirmed in the series of UN conferences throughout the 1990s. It was 're-specified' as six major goals at the *World Education Forum*, in Dakar, Senegal in April 2000.[9] An important complementary resolution adopt at Dakar was that governments and international agencies should be held accountable for progress towards achieving these educational goals. Two of the goals established at Dakar were incorporated into the MDGs that were adopted by world leaders at the UN Millennium Summit in New York in 2000, namely: to 'Ensure, by 2015, children everywhere, boys and girls alike, will be able to complete a full course of primary education'; and to 'Eliminate gender disparity in primary and secondary education, preferably by 2005, and in all levels of education no later than 2015'.

The G8 summit and the *New Partnership for Africa's Development* (NEPAD) both recognized the importance of school feeding in achieving these educational goals by listing it as a specific intervention in their action plans in 2002. In 2005, the UN Millennium Project recommended that school feeding using locally produced food be expanded to reach all children in 'hunger hotspots', and listed school feeding in ten key recommendations for achieving the MDGs (UNDP, 2005). Later, in its 'Fight against Hunger', the G8 summit in Bellagio, Italy in July 2009 identified social protection instruments and food-based safety nets, such as school feeding, as critical tools to tackle hunger and malnutrition that ensured that vulnerable, hungry children had access to food.

These policy pronouncements and specific targets were followed by actions to increase assistance to basic education. In 2000, as part of his initiative to end world hunger, George McGovern, then US Ambassador to the UN agencies in Rome, Italy, urged developed countries to ensure that every child in the world had a meal at school (McGovern, 2001).[10] At the G8 summit in Japan in 2000, US President Clinton made an initial contribution of $300 million to the McGovern initiative through the establishment of a two-year pilot programme (the *Global Food for Education Initiative*), and invited other nations to make contributions to school feeding as well. In May 2002, the *McGovern and Dole International Food-for-Education and Child Nutrition Programme* (the McGovern–Dole programme) was established by the US government to provide support to international school feeding and child nutrition improvement efforts until 2011, with an initial level of funding for 2003 set at $100 million.[11] In 2002, the Development Committee of the IMF and World Bank established a *Fast Track Initiative* to accelerate progress towards universal completion of quality primary education, supported by a partnership of all the major education donors, UNESCO, UNICEF, and the regional development banks.

In 2000, encouraged by these developments, and building on 37 years of experience, the WFP launched a global school feeding campaign with the objective of encouraging governments throughout the world to put in place national school feeding programmes that would provide nutritious food to all children who needed it. At the same time, a School Feeding Service was established at WFP headquarters to provide expertise and to find consultants. The service arranged, with UNESCO assistance, to compile a comprehensive list of the status of school feeding programmes in all developing countries, which could serve as a monitoring and evaluation tool and also facilitate sharing of experience among countries. It also established collaboration with other UN organizations, NGOs, and the private sector that contributed to the goals of 'Education for All', and undertook to present annual reports on progress made to the WFP's executive board.[12]

In April 2000, UNESCO, UNICEF, WHO and the World Bank agreed on a shared *Focusing Resources on Effective School Health* (FRESH) framework to strengthen school health, hygiene, and nutrition programmes. In partnership with the FAO, UNICEF and WHO, the WFP began providing food for education as part of an 'essential package' of health and education improvement initiatives. TNT, the Dutch global mail and logistics company, became the WFP's largest global corporate partner and donor to school feeding programmes (see Chapter 4). It sends volunteers to developing countries for three months to work directly with WFP-assisted school feeding programmes. TNT contributes a minimum of $500,000 directly to each country that hosts TNT volunteers. The funds are used for food and much needed school infrastructure. Due to the success of this volunteer programme, other large corporations contacted the WFP to discuss similar partner arrangements.

Supported by strong donor interest and contributions, the WFP expanded its school feeding programme, taking account of earlier WFP experience. As a result, the number of children and countries benefiting from the WFP school feeding programme has steadily increased to become the world's largest. At the same time, a number of countries previously benefiting from WFP assistance have 'graduated' to become self-sustaining in continuing their school feeding programmes (Table 5.1).

Table 5.1 WFP school feeding programmes, 2000–09

Year	Children (millions)	Number of countries
2000	12.3	54
2001	15.0	57
2002	15.6	64
2003	15.2	69
2004	16.6	72
2005	21.7	74
2006	19.1	71
2007	19.5	70
2008	20.6	67
2009	22.0	60

Source: WFP School Feeding Service.

The school meals provided are governed by local tastes and customs, nutritional needs, the availability of local foods, ease of operation, and available resources. School meals may take the form of a breakfast or midday snack, or lunch, and may be combined with take-home rations.

In 2003, the WFP reviewed its experience in phasing out its assistance to school feeding programmes in eight of the more than 20 countries where it had ended its involvement in such programmes (WFP, 2003a). The study concluded that a successful exit strategy was one that was developed in co-ordination with the relevant government authorities, implementing partners, and beneficiaries, and which was based on five key components: setting milestones for achievements; government commitment; technical support; strong management and communications; and involvement of the private sector. School feeding programmes varied, depending on the circumstances of each country in which they operated. A successful exit strategy required achievable milestones that were taken seriously by all concerned parties and monitored carefully, and ideally built into programme design at the outset. The WFP's school feeding service undertook to assist WFP country offices in putting in place and monitoring realistic exit strategies.

Between 2000 and 2004, the WFP studied more than one million students in over 4,000 schools in 32 countries in Africa. The results suggested the school feeding had strong impact on absolute enrolment in WFP-assisted schools. Average absolute enrolment increased by 28 per cent for girls and 22 per cent for boys during the first year of the programme. The combination of take-home rations for girls with on-school feeding saw a sustained increase in girls' absolute enrolment of 30 per cent from year to year (WFP, 2004l).

In 2007, a thematic evaluation of school feeding in emergency situations was carried out (WFP, 2007d).[13] The overall conclusion of the evaluation was that there was no clear distinction between school feeding in emergency situations or in a development context. It should be recognized, however, that the constraints to school feeding in non-emergency situations were exacerbated during emergencies. The WFP had, therefore, to provide comprehensive guidance and support in addressing such issues as: the foods to be provided when cooking facilities and clean water were limited; the choice of food delivery modality to avoid delays in providing rations; access to the most remote and vulnerable schools; and adjusting to the particular circumstances of an emergency, natural or man-made. The evaluation found that school feeding implemented in emergency situations was challenging in terms of constraints, such as security restrictions, limited access to afflicted areas, and limited capacities of governments and local partners in the stricken countries. Where WFP country offices could not manage these challenges, the response could be problematical, particularly regarding targeting, the alignment of emergency school feeding with educational support programmes, and implementation at the school level.

In responding to the evaluation report, the WFP executive board members indicated that the WFP needed a clear and coherent policy on school feeding in emergency situations that took into account its comparative advantage compared to other emergency activities, and which clarified the objectives that should be addressed (WFP, 2007e). School feeding in emergencies should be designed to respond to locally assessed needs. The nutritional benefits were most important in areas facing acute food insecurity and where HIV/AIDS was prevalent. For many board members, the most compelling argument in support of school feeding in emergencies was the need to meet children's psycho-social needs, for which attention should be given to the views of the affected communities, parents, and the children themselves.

The year 2009 saw the publication of four substantive reports, which led to the reformulation of WFP policy regarding school feeding. The WFP's School Feeding Service produced *Learning from Experience. Good Practices from 45 Years of School Feeding* (WFP, 2009b). The study was based on experience 'harvested' from 134 countries, case studies, an ongoing consultation process, and operational experience. It aimed to serve as a guide to all those engaged 'to design and implement high-quality, feasible, sustainable and cost-effective school feeding programmes'. Now the lead organization in this field, the WFP was 'committed to learn from and share its experience about what works and does not work in school feeding'.

School feeding was seen as a 'powerful hunger response' for children and their families. It was estimated that 66 million school children still went to school hungry. About $2 billion was needed to reach those children. It was noted that, perhaps for the first time, every country was now seeking to provide food, in some way and on some scale, to its school children. Few safety-net programmes provided so many multi-sector benefits in one single intervention as school feeding, which affected education, gender equality, food security, poverty alleviation, nutrition, and health. But school feeding remained least and weakest where it was most needed. The study showed that: intermittent funding and breaks in the food supply pipeline led to inconsistent outcomes; inadequately designed food rations resulted in costly operations and unsatisfied school children; and inappropriate geographical targeting resulted in children shifting between schools in the same district.

Four key factors were identified for good school feeding practice: nationally-led school feeding programmes backed by political will and strong policy statements (and commitments); sound analysis of the country context, leading to well-targeted and well-designed programmes; a planned transition to government ownership; and local food procurement, food processing and fortification – which stimulated local food economies and empowered smallholder farmers and women's group. The WFP was 'committed to working with partners in these ways, helping to ensure that no child goes to school hungry'.

Eight 'gold standards' or 'quality benchmarks' were identified for school feeding programmes: sustainability; sound alignment with national policy frameworks; stable funding and budgeting; needs-based, cost-effective quality programme design; strong institutional arrangements for implementation, monitoring, and accountability; a strategy for local production and sourcing; strong partnerships and inter-sector co-ordination; and strong community participation and ownership.

The main findings of the study were that: the quality and sustainability of school feeding is dependent on understanding and commitment to the programme at the decision-making levels of government and its incorporation in national policy frameworks; the costs of school feeding are high for most low-income countries; interim funding solutions are needed to support governments in those countries in their school feeding programmes, but those governments need to include school feeding in the national budget as early as possible; handover arrangements need to be planned well in advance with governments, and school feeding programmes may need to be periodically re-designed to allow a smooth transition; effective of school feeding programmes depended on four main design factors: sound, in-depth assessment; clearly defined programme objectives; targeting; and selection of the food basket and food delivery modalities; the institutional set-up and implementation arrangements should be directly linked and need to be adapted to the country context; and involving communities in programme design and implementation increased the prospects for programme sustainability.

The study made four recommendations: ensure that good practices and lessons are incorporated in project appraisal and design, and also in choosing target mechanisms, selecting food baskets, and identifying cost-containment options; incorporate the eight 'gold standards' in programme guidance and design – strategies to meet these standards should be elaborated in all programmes, and programme managers should regularly report on progress towards these standards during the life of the programme cycle; prioritized applied research on cost-effective solutions should be undertaken to enrich food baskets so that the nutritional value of food rations of school feeding programmes can be enhanced – this may include testing new nutritional products, many of which may be procured and processed locally; and creating a positive interaction between school feeding, local production and processing capacity, which links need to be studied and good experiences replicated across countries; and clear handover and transition strategies for school feeding are needed, including capacity assessment and capacity development plans.

The WFP's School Feeding Service also produced *Home-Grown School Feeding. A Framework to Link School Feeding with Local Agricultural Production* in 2009 (WFP, 2009c). The study defined home-grown school feeding as a 'school feeding programme that provides food produced and purchased within a country to the extent possible'. The study focused in particular on linking school feeding programmes with local small-scale farmer production by creating an ongoing market for small landowners. It noted that the WFP had collaborated with the Bill and Melinda Gates Foundation, the *New Partnership for Africa's Development* (NEPAD), and other partners in developing an approach to home-grown school feeding. It also noted that the value of home-grown school feeding programmes has been recognized consistently by many governments and organizations.

The study pointed out that African governments had endorsed such programmes in the *Comprehensive African Development Programme* in 2003. In the same year, NEPAD identified them as having an immediate impact on food insecurity in Africa, with a potential also to contribute to long-term development goals. The 2005 UN World Summit recommended 'the expansion of local school meals programmes, using home-grown foods were possible' as one of the 'quick-impact initiatives' to achieve the MDGs. The Africa Union Special Food Summit in December 2006 called for an expansion of home-grown school feeding to reach at least 20 per cent of member states by 2008.

Motivated by these strong endorsements, the NEPAD, WFP and the Millennium Hunger Task Force launched a pilot home-grown school feeding and health programme designed to link school feeding to agricultural development through the purchase and use of locally and domestically produced food, particularly by small-scale farmers, through activities in three distinct but linked focus areas: strategic food procurement through the purchasing process that supplies food to school feeding programmes in such a way that small-scale farmers benefit; agricultural development through activities intended to help small-scale farmers increase their productivity, produce better quality crops, manage natural resources, and mitigate risks in a sustainable way; and institutional and policy development to support appropriate design and implementation of home-grown school feeding programmes.

Other important issues identified in the study included: assuring minimum nutrition standards; maintaining continuous food supplies to schools; ensuring food quality and safety; reducing procurement costs and preventing price increases; protecting crop diversity and farmers' own food stocks; avoiding increasing communities' workloads and distracting teachers from other responsibilities; transporting food to food-insecure areas; countering corruption and bureaucratic inefficiency; facilitating institutional co-ordination; and balancing costs and benefits.

The study observed that home-grown school feeding programmes happened incrementally over three stages. The first stage was characterized by a relatively small proportion of food purchased from small-scale farmers. The existing food supply pipeline was protected while new procurement schemes with small-scale farmers were tested. Procurement was started in surplus agricultural production areas. Activities and investments were geared to establishing the feasibility of using food purchased from smallholders for the school feeding programme in terms of procurement practices and supply.

The second stage witnessed the gradual increase in the proportion of food purchased from small-scale farmers. At the same time, the amount of investment needed increased to its highest level precisely to support agricultural development and market access, and to overcome the barriers that prevent small-scale farmers from accessing the market.

In the third stage, a greater proportion of food was purchased from small-scale farmers. Ideally, these farmers would have developed sufficient capacity to deliver food to schools without sacrificing quality, quantity, and timeliness. At this stage, the focus shifts to institutional development.

The WFP and the Boston Consulting Group carried out a joint study, *School Feeding. A Sound Investment*, in 2009, which made the case for investing in school feeding programmes (the WFP and the Boston Consulting Group, 2009).[14] The monetary costs of providing school feeding were compared to their potential long-term economic benefits. Two case studies were carried out in Kenya and Laos to compare the costs related to the design and implementation of school feeding programmes and the delivery of food to the benefits derived from three major school feeding outcomes: increased education, improved nutrition and health, and value transfers to the beneficiaries.

The joint study found that school feeding: improved enrolment, attendance, and cognition; decreased drop-out rates and morbidity; and enhanced disease awareness, leading to increased wages and a longer productive life, which together led to increased lifetime earnings. School meals and take-home rations translated into savings at the household level, which could result in increased investment. The analysis also highlighted the reinforcing and multiplication effects between the various outcomes, which made school feeding a 'unique intervention'. Two conclusions were made from the study: investing in school feeding created significant economic value; and school feeding was a unique safety net driven by the interdependency between various outcomes, and combined short-, medium-, and long-term benefits.

The WFP also teamed up with the World Bank in producing *Rethinking School Feeding: Social Safety Nets, Child Development and the Education Sector* (Bundy *et al.*, 2009). In a foreword to the publication, WFP executive director, Josette Sheenan, and World Bank president, Robert B. Zoellick, wrote:

> What is so clear is that we are beyond the debate about whether school feeding makes sense as a way to reach the most vulnerable. It does. In the face of global crises, we must now focus on how school feeding programs can be designed and implemented in a cost-effective and sustainable way to benefit and protect those most in need of help today and in the future.

The four studies, and recent research and evaluation findings, were drawn upon in reformulating the WFP's policy for school feeding as a guide to WFP regional directors, country directors, and staff on how to implement school feeding programmes and budgets to meet specific safety-net, education, nutrition, health, and related objectives (WFP, 2009d).

The WFP's vision was 'to reduce hunger among school children so that it was not an obstacle to their development'. The rationale for school feeding programmes was defined as helping to:

> reduce vulnerability to hunger and protect and promote livelihoods by investing in human capital through better health, nutrition and education. By so doing, school feeding can bridge emergency and recovery measures with medium and longer-term development in an efficient manner.

In addition, school feeding was seen as leading to a sequence of outcomes that were mutually reinforcing, helping to lift households out of poverty and ending the inter-generational cycle of hunger and poverty. School feeding was regarded as facilitating education, which, particularly for girls, led to improved food security, health, and nutrition, the effects of which all contributed to ending hunger.

In implementing its school feeding policy, the WFP had an extensive field presence and capacity in policy formulation, needs assessment, vulnerability analysis and targeting, programme design and management, logistics, and food procurement. The breadth and depth of WFP expertise were regarded as crucial assets for the sound implementation of school feeding programmes on a global scale, and for providing informed advice and know-how to governments. As the leading co-ordinator of school feeding programmes, the WFP had developed good relations with, and commitments from, governments in support of such programmes, and had helped to increase capacity in developing countries to design and implement them.

The WFP also recognized that food could make a substantial impact on children's lives when it was part of a package of assistance to improve their education, health, and nutrition. As a result, a well-established network of co-operating partners had been created. The following gives an indication of the large and growing network that exists. The WFP supported the joint FRESH framework of UNESCO, UNICEF, WHO and the World Bank to improve school health, hygiene, and nutrition programmes. Following publication of their joint study in 2009, the WFP's strategic partnership with the World Bank would continue to gain momentum through a common research programme and provision of technical support in school feeding programmes for countries most in need, and where there was demand from low-income countries affected by the social shocks of the current global crises. Work with other UN agencies and NGOs would continue through education clusters, as well as co-ordination with partners in meeting the needs of children during emergencies. The WFP was an active member of the humanitarian response education cluster in emergency situations, part of the Inter-Agency Network for Education in Emergencies (INEE), and a member of the UN Standing Committee on Nutrition (SCN).

The WFP chaired the SCN's working group on the nutrition of school-age children, which shared information on the latest programmes, innovations, and evidence in this field. The WFP remained actively engaged in the IMF/World Bank *Fast Track Initiative*, a compact among donors designed to ensure that countries with sound education policies and agreed education plans receive adequate and predictable donor funding. The WFP would also participate in the formalized network on school feeding, led by Joint Aid Management, that was agreed at the *NGO School Feeding Roundtable* and the *Global Child Nutrition Forum* held in May 2009. And partnerships would continue and develop with a number of academic and development research institutes, foundations, and the private sector.

This new policy statement had emerged at a critical time. The ongoing global economic crisis had presented many challenges at all levels. The WFP was under greater pressure to help those most in need and was adapting to the challenging global environment. With its *Strategic Plan (2008–13)* in effect, the WFP had a 'unique opportunity' to enhance school feeding as a tool to reach the most vulnerable children as it made the transition from a food aid to a food assistance programme (see Chapter 6). In 2008, 20 governments had looked to school feeding programmes as a safety-net response to the food crisis. The WFP had scaled up is school feeding programmes to reach five million more school children in 17 countries. The World Bank launched a *Global Food Crisis Response* facility that mobilized $2 billion to help countries respond to the food and fuel crises, which included scaling up school feeding.

During its long experience with school feeding, the WFP had helped millions of children become educated and productive adults, who, in turn, had created greater food security for their families, with healthier and better educated children. In this way, the benefits of school feeding had translated to the next generation and helped to stop the inter-generational sequence of hunger and poverty. Experience had shown that school feeding could be an effective safety net, helping to protect vulnerable children during times of crises.[15] Properly designed and implemented, school feeding could safeguard nutrition, education, and gender equality, and provide a range of socio-economic benefits.

When putting food on the family table today took priority over a child's potential tomorrow, a daily meal served as a strong incentive to send children to school and ensure that they attended regularly. When local food production contributed to school feeding programmes, there were benefits for the local economy. More national governments were acknowledging the importance of school feeding programmes in removing obstacles to their development as a valuable 'social safety-net mechanism' to improve livelihoods. School feeding served as an 'exceptional platform' at the community level for long-term investment in human capital to reduce hunger while achieving nutrition, education, and gender equality outcomes.

Experience had also shown that school feeding programmes were sustainable. The WFP had helped in capacity development in developing countries, with the result that such programmes had been handed over to 31 national governments, including the two largest in the developing world in Brazil and India, which continue to operate them today. With an estimated 66 million children still going to school hungry in 2009, the WFP aimed to meet the change by helping the most needy, and strengthening school feeding as a 'hunger-reduction tool'. The WFP's policy aimed to make school feeding programmes meet the standards of: sustainability; alignment with national policies; stable funding and budgeting; cost-efficient quality programme design; strong institutional arrangements for implementation, monitoring, and accountability; local food production and sourcing, where feasible; strong partnerships and inter-sectoral co-ordination; and strong community participation and ownership. The WFP undertook to ensure that a rigorous monitoring and evaluation system was in place to measure progress and results.

The WFP would assist governments in meeting these standards and foster better understanding among governments, donors, and stakeholders of the benefits of school feeding as a hunger solution and safety net. In co-operation with partners, the WFP would also help governments to: develop national school feeding policies and strategies; establish national co-ordination mechanisms for school feeding; provide multi-sector technical assistance to design good-quality and cost-effective programmes; provide capacity development to ensure sustainability; resource school feeding programmes and their implementation; support a knowledge base of best practices, innovation, and research; and promote the sharing of information and learning.

As the largest implementer of school feeding programmes in the world, investing almost half a billion dollars per year in such programmes, the WFP now supported the provision of meals to an average of 22 million children each year, half of whom were girls. A global coalition of governments, the WFP, the World Bank, other UN agencies, and NGO partners, and research and academic institutions, and the private sector was now emerging to ensure that 'no child is hungry at school'.

The WFP's executive board approved the reformulated school feeding policy and requested the WFP secretariat to keep it informed about progress in its implementation. The WFP's Office of Evaluation was asked to conduct a comprehensive evaluation of school feeding programmes and present its findings to the first session of the board in 2012 (WFP, 2009f). What remains is to build capacity in developing countries to hand over the school feeding programmes currently assisted by the WFP.

HIV/AIDS-related programmes

The onset of the HIV/AIDS pandemic radically changed and added to the world's emergencies. The WFP made addressing this pandemic a 'cornerstone' of its operations. High prevalence rates in poor countries exacerbated food emergencies as well as chronic hunger among the poor, especially in sub-Saharan Africa. In consultation with its governing body, deliberate and protracted consideration was given as to exactly how WFP assistance should be focused and used to combat the disease.[16]

The target of 'halting by 2015 and beginning to reverse the spread of HIV/AIDS' was included among the MDGs approved by world leaders at the UN Millennium Summit in 2000. At the UN General Assembly Special Session on HIV/AIDS in September 2001, the UN secretary-general made a clarion 'Call to Action', and challenged the entire UN system to expand substantially its efforts to confront the pandemic. A Joint UN Programme on HIV/AIDS (UNAIDS) was established as a global partnership programme to fight the disease. Earlier, in May 2000, the WFP's executive board had agreed that the WFP 'should explore with its partners, and consistent with its mandate, specific areas of WFP intervention concerning HIV/AIDS'. In its response, the WFP secretariat pointed out that its entry point in counter-HIV/AIDS activities was rooted in nutrition and food security, because the pandemic 'could be both a cause and a consequence of food insecurity' (WFP, 2001a). In April 2001, the UNAIDS secretariat and the WFP made a joint presentation to the WFP's executive board on the global AIDS situation and on the

WFP's approach to it. A joint publication by IFPRI and the WFP entitled *HIV/AIDS, Food and Nutrition Security: Impacts and Action* (IFPRI/WFP, 2001) was also made available to executive board members, and an information note was produced updating the WFP's fight against HIV/AIDS (WFP, 2002b).

All this was prelude to a policy paper that the executive board requested on the subject (WFP, 2003b), which was summarized as follows: HIV/AIDS threatened food and security in ways that were significantly different from other crises. For those affected, its impact could be as devastating as war, drought, or other catastrophes. In food-insecure communities affected by the disease, the WFP should take it into account in its project design and adapt its programming as and when new information on the disease became available. The *WFP's strategy should always concentrate on food insecurity brought about by HIV/AIDS, and not on the disease itself* (emphasis added), which lay in the comparative advantages of other agencies, especially the WHO. In areas of high food insecurity and high HIV prevalence, WFP food assistance could provide a safety net to catch affected families before they became destitute and, thus, even more vulnerable to the risk of infection. AIDS was a long-term emergency that had to be tackled both within the immediate needs of the most vulnerable and with a longer-term recovery approach.

When associated with other inputs, WFP food assistance could: create opportunities for less risky livelihoods, and strengthen household and community capacities to respond to the impact of HIV/AIDS on food security through initiatives such as food-for-training and food-for-asset creation; improve and maintain human capital through nutrition programmes, food-for-training, school feeding, and disease control programmes; reduce the vulnerability of families to food insecurity through safety-net initiatives, such as home-based care projects, mother and child health programmes, and initiatives targeted to child-headed households; and through partners, it could be used as a conduit for the dissemination of HIV/AIDS prevention messages and information. The policy paper recommended that the WFP should: incorporate HIV/AIDS concerns in all its programme categories; work with local and international partners, NGOs, governments, and UN agencies, and particularly with UNAIDS co-sponsors and the UNAIDS secretariat, to ensure that food was incorporated into HIV activities, when and where appropriate; adjust its programming tools, such as needs assessment, vulnerability analysis, the design of rations, and other nutrition-related activities as information and results became available to reflect the new reality presented by HIV/AIDS; and when HIV/AIDS threatened food security and influenced mortality in ways similar to other disasters, the WFP would consider HIV/AIDS as a basis for a PRRO, consistent with current WFP policy on PRROs.

The executive board welcomed the policy paper, in particular the mainstreaming of HIV/AIDS concerns in all WFP programming activities, focusing on the WFP's comparative advantage, the WFP's co-sponsorship of UNAIDS, and co-operation with the WHO through a *Letter of Intent*, but called for clarification on the use of HIV/AIDS as a basis for a PRRO (WFP, 2003c).

Having established its policy, the WFP turned to strengthening its operations related to HIV/AIDS, and took to advocating its food and nutrition role. In 2003, a

HIV/AIDS Unit was created at WFP headquarters to pursue WFP policy objectives and to report to the WFP's executive board. In October 2003, the WFP became a co-sponsor of UNAIDS along with nine other organizations. In December 2003, over 100 participants from WFP country and regional offices and WFP headquarters attended the first-ever programming meeting on HIV/AIDS and school feeding in Geneva, Switzerland. The WFP made over $1 million available to inter-agency contributions to deploy UN volunteers (UNVs) to strengthen HIV/AIDS programmes in the field. The WFP also joined forces with several organizations to carry out operational research, studies, and reviews of best practices to improve the understanding of the relationship between HIV/AIDS, food security, and nutrition, and to amplify nutrition programmes. By the end of 2003, the WFP was active in 41 countries, 30 of them in Africa, where HIV/AIDS was prominent.

In his capacity as special envoy to the UN secretary-general for Humanitarian Needs in Southern Africa, the WFP's new executive director, James Morris, conducted missions to the region in September 2002 and January 2003 to review the situation and make recommendations to the secretary-general. The missions generated attention among humanitarian agencies and the media regarding the role of HIV/AIDS in the crisis in southern Africa, where the disease was particularly severe.[17] The WFP co-sponsored a Satellite Session on *HIV/AIDS and the Southern African Crisis* at the 13th International Conference on *AIDS and Sexually Transmitted Infections in Africa* in Nairobi, Kenya in September 2003. The WFP's advocacy was also conveyed in 2003 through a series of publications and brochures. The WFP published *Widening the Window of Hope: Using food aid to improve access to education for orphans and other vulnerable children in sub-Saharan Africa*. Three brochures were prepared: *Putting it on the Table: Why food and nutrition matter in the fight against HIV/AIDS*; *HIV/AIDS and Children: Bringing hope to a generation*; and *The First Line of Defense: Why food and nutrition matter in the fight against HIV/AIDS*. The brochures were published in English, French, Spanish, Italian, and Japanese. A corporate message was published on HIV/AIDS to inform WFP staff about the WFP's approach and response to the disease, outline advocacy goals, and provide updated information for media and resource mobilization. Also, an HIV/AIDS page was developed for the WFP's website.

The year 2004 saw a rapid change in the international community's response to the global HIV/AIDS pandemic, bringing new opportunities and challenges for the WFP (WFP, 2005). The rapid increase in the number of aid agencies appearing to confront the disease resulted in an urgent need for co-ordination, for which the 'Three Ones' principles were established: one HIV/AIDS action framework that provided the basis for co-ordinating the work of all partners; one national AIDS co-ordinating authority, with a broad-based multi-sectoral mandate; and one country-level monitoring and evaluation system.

The WFP worked to ensure that food and nutrition support related to HIV/AIDS interventions were integrated into national-level planning and programming, and national AIDS strategies, policies, and budgets. The main focus was on providing this support in treatment and care programmes, for orphans and children affected by HIV/AIDS, and by including prevention education linked to school feeding and relief operations. In 2004, 8.3 million people were targeted through the WFP's HIV/AIDS-related programmes.

A number of questions remained regarding the interaction between food and nutrition interventions and HIV/AIDS. The challenges for the WFP and its partners were to expand the evidence base, to ensure that it was well-targeted in effective programmes, and used in areas of greatest need. The WFP provided guidance material, training programmes, and advocacy, all of which increased awareness. But despite recognition of the importance of food and nutrition in HIV/AIDS prevention, mitigation, care, and treatment, the WFP did not receive adequate financial support from donors to meet the rapid increase in the number of people affected by the disease.

In 2005, the WFP's HIV/AIDS-related programmes continued to grow. By the end of the year, the WFP was working in 21 of the 25 most seriously affected countries and had programmes of assistance in a total of 51 countries. Addressing gender issues was regarded as being essential for successful programmes. The WFP therefore developed a technical guidance document entitled *Getting Started: HIV, AIDS and Gender in WFP programmes*. The WFP also stepped up its involvement in operational research with academic and specialist institutions. WFP field offices were given access to updated technical information, and assisted in the start-up and implementation of HIV/AIDS-related activities to reduce HIV transmission and mitigate its impact on WFP staff, their families, and their workplaces.

In 2005, the UN system reached a new level in its response to the pandemic. Its efforts were consolidated and co-ordinated. The Three Ones principles were reaffirmed, and a global task team on improving AIDS co-ordination among multilateral institutions and international donors (GTT) was established. GTT produced a set of recommendations for the multilateral system to simplify and harmonize procedures and practices, and align effectors more closely with national needs and priorities.[18] As part of the GTT-agreed division of labour, the WFP was identified as the lead organization for dietary and nutrition support for national governments, including during emergencies. At the UN World Summit in September 2005, member states committed to scaling up comprehensive HIV responses, with country ownership and leadership. The WFP undertook to advocate for food and nutritional programmes in support of universal access to prevention, care, and treatment of HIV/AIDS through its country offices and regional bureaux.

By 2006, five years after the beginning of its response to the HIV/AIDS pandemic, the WFP had scaled up its programming to provided food and nutrition support to over 2.3 million people in 51 countries through care, treatment, and mitigation interventions (WFP, 2006g). Advocacy efforts were intensified to gain recognition that food and nutrition were an essential part of the global fight against HIV and AIDS. The rationale was that good nutrition could delay the onset of AIDS-related illness and improve the quality of life of those living with the disease. Food assistance could help vulnerable children stay in school and keep affected families together. Food aid, combined with drug treatment, could help people living with HIV, or other diseases such as tuberculosis and malaria, feel better and help them adhere to the treatment. When family members were sick with HIV, they were less able to work. As incomes decline, less money was available to buy food or pay for health care. Without assistance, the likely and serious consequence was malnutrition for the sick wage earner and the rest of the family. When poor and hungry people were affected by HIV, food assistance helped to mitigate the impact. For these reasons, the WFP advocated that food assistance should be part of treatment and care programmes: medicines alone are not enough.

The WFP found that orphans were more likely to suffer from chronic malnutrition than children with parents. The WFP's food for education programmes could help give orphans and other vulnerable children the nutrition, skills, and confidence they needed to lead healthy and productive lives. The WFP's experience was that education was an effective way of mitigating both the impact and spread of HIV/AIDS. The WFP and its partners therefore used school feeding programmes as a platform for HIV/AIDS awareness and prevention education. In addition, home-based feeding programmes that target the chronically ill could be used to identify and reach vulnerable children by helping them access education and training opportunities.

In an effort to mitigate the impact of HIV/AIDS in families and communities, the WFP ensured that food assistance was part of a larger package of assistance provided to afflicted households.[19] Food aid in asset-creation and training programmes also encouraged longer-term livelihood security, providing children with a better chance of survival. A *Junior Farmer Field and Life Schools* initiative was an innovative programme implemented with the FAO in several countries. It provided vulnerable adolescents with agricultural skills, and crucial information about health and nutrition. To help strengthen agriculture, the WFP also supports conservation farming in countries such as Zambia and community-based agricultural activities in Swaziland.

With persistence and perseverance, WFP advocacy efforts began to pay off. At the beginning of the new millennium, food and nutrition were rarely mentioned in the context of HIV/AIDS intervention programmes. Many questioned the WFP's relevance in the global response to the pandemic. By 2006, 'there was widespread recognition of the central role of nutrition in maintaining the health and quality of life of people living with HIV/AIDS' (WFP, 2006g). The WHO resolution on *Nutrition and HIV/AIDS*, adopted at the World Health Assembly in January 2006, urged member states to integrate nutrition into their HIV/AIDS responses and called for strengthened political commitment and intensified action on nutrition in HIV/AIDS programmes. The WHO assessed that HIV-infected adults had a 20–30 per cent increase in emergency nutrition support and children a 50–100 per cent increase, and recommended that these needs by met by food-based programmes, wherever possible.

Significantly, two major institutional sources of funds for HIV/AIDS programmes now included nutrition in their guidance for programme managers: the World Bank's guidance to its field managers on nutrition in care and treatment programmes; and the *Global Fund to Fight AIDS, TB and Malaria*, which placed nutritionists on its technical review panel. At the UN General Assembly's 2006 *High-Level Meeting on AIDS*, countries committed to revising their national AIDS plans 'to integrate food and nutrition support, with the goal that all people at all times will have access to sufficient, safe and nutritious food to meet their dietary needs and food preferences, for an active and healthy life, as part of a comprehensive response to HIV/AIDS'. This acknowledgement of the role of food and nutrition in responding to the HIV/AIDS epidemic was an important milestone for the WFP and its partners. After years of absence from international conference agendas, food and nutrition received strong support from the AIDS community at the *XVI International AIDS Conference* in Toronto, Canada in 2006, and the WFP received recognition for the lead role it played in getting food and nutrition into national AIDS strategies and care, treatment, and support programmes.

The WFP's response to the HIV/AIDS pandemic had developed considerably over the past five years (2000–05), 'but not nearly enough' to meet the rapid increase in the disease. The WFP was encouraged to document its experience and encourage others to do so to facilitate the sharing of knowledge and replication of good practice. But if the WFP were to do more, 'it must acknowledge that current activities were inadequate'. Larger funding and greater co-operation with other agencies was required. The UK Government's Department of International Cooperation (DFID) funded a consortium of humanitarian organizations to scale up HIV/AIDS services for populations of humanitarian concern and expanded its country-level work with partners. Since becoming a co-sponsor of UNAIDS in 2003, the WFP had worked with partners to strengthen community, national, and global responses to the pandemic. The WFP strengthened its collaboration with the WHO and jointly prepared nutritional guidelines for the care and treatment of people living with HIV/AIDS. The WFP's programming in support of children affected by HIV/IDS was central to its work in this field, but it was recognized that its effectiveness was dependent on the commitment, capacity, and actions of governments. The WFP therefore worked to strengthen national responses by providing technical advice to governments and NGOs on how to programme and estimate the cost of food and nutrition support for people living with HIV/AIDS and other infectious diseases, and orphans and vulnerable children, and assisted governments in developing their proposals to the *Global Fund to Fight AIDS, TB and Malaria* for financing.

In 2007, the HIV/AIDS epidemic showed no signs of abating and it was realized that responses to it must adapt to its evolving nature (WFP, 2007f). The WFP was chair of the UNAIDS Committee of Co-sponsoring Organizations for the year June 2006–June 2007 and worked with the UNAIDS secretariat to put together the 2008–09 UNAIDS Unified Budget and Workplan and proposals for the *XVII International Conference on AIDS* to be held in Mexico City in August 2008. In 2006, about 1.2 million people received WFP food and nutrition support as part of HIV/AIDS and TB care and treatment packages. Some 1.1 million orphans and children affected by HIV/AIDS were also supported in 25 countries. Many more beneficiaries affected by HIV/AIFS were reached through various mitigation activities. In southern Africa, for example, which was regarded as the 'epicentre' of the global AIDS pandemic, the WFP assisted 7.2 million people affected by HIV/AIDS through social protection platforms. The WFP also worked with governments to ensure that costed food and nutrition support was included in their national HIV/AIDS programmes, and 32 countries had done so.

The WFP adopted a social protection approach to provide short-term assistance to HIV/AIDS-affected households at extreme risk of losing livelihood assets or resorting to negative coping strategies. Community and household surveillance in southern Africa showed improvements in the coping strategy capacity and dietary diversity of beneficiary households. The WFP, together with its partners, also scaled up interventions such as HIV prevention and AIDS education by incorporating them into food-for-work and food-for-training, mother and child health programmes, and emergency operations, and particularly school feeding activities.

At the same time, the need to develop clear exit strategies for assistance to HIV/AIDS programmes became a major concern. For care and treatment programmes, the exit strategy needed to be strengthening livelihoods by enlisting partners to provide income-generating activities, micro-credit, training, and other forms of livelihood support. Sustainable measures should also be put in place at the initial programme design stage to ensure that activities continued after food assistance came to an end. It was observed that most patients were sufficiently well after six to nine months' treatments and food and nutrition support to return to their former livelihoods and to continue their treatment without support.

About two-thirds of the global burden of HIV infection occurred in countries affected by complex emergencies with limited access to HIV services. The WFP was part of a UN system-wide initiative to scale up HIV/AIDS services for populations of humanitarian concern. The WFP worked to improve monitoring and evaluation of its HIV/AIDS food-based interventions. It also engaged in operational research projects in collaboration with university and research institutions to provide evidence-based programming, support advocacy, and raise funds with donors and the international community. In collaboration with UN agencies and IFPRI, the WFP continued to disseminate guidance documents to increase national government commitments, assist WFP country offices to improve HIV programming, and for WFP staff and their families.

By 2010, evidence had been accumulated and analyzed by the World Bank in sub-Saharan Africa, which supported the WFP's conviction and commitment to the education sector as a means of responding to the HIV/AIDS pandemic (Bundy *et al.*, 2010). The education sector became increasingly recognized as paying a key 'external' role in preventing and reducing the disease, and an important 'internal' role in providing access to care, treatment, and support for teachers and support staff, a group that, the World Bank pointed out, represented more than 60 per cent of the public sector workforce in many developing countries.

In 2002, UNAIDS' Inter-Agency Task Team on Education (IATT) established an 'Accelerate Initiative Working Group' to support countries in sub-Saharan Africa as they accelerated their education sector response to HIV/AIDS. This was done by establishing programmes with strong local ownership, capable of accessing suitable funding, at all levels of the education sector. The networks of Ministry of Education HIV/AIDS focal points, established by an accelerated initiative under the auspices of the African Union Regional Economic Communities, rapidly took over ownership of the programme.

The experiences of the education sector across sub-Saharan Africa were explored as they speeded up their response to HIV/AIDS. This demonstrated that leadership by the Ministries of Education has become 'crucial' in mobilizing activities, and that full participation by all stakeholders is needed for effective implementation. Since 2002, 37 countries in the region have participated, four networks have been established, and 1,350 education staff members and 76 development partners have participated in training programmes. Three-quarters of the participating countries are now accessing funds through their national AIDS committees. Over three-quarters have an HIV/AIDS education sector strategy and plan, and over 90 per cent of the teachers have been trained to protect themselves. All countries are now implementing HIV prevention education, and over 70 per cent provide free education for orphans and vulnerable children.

In 2010, the WFP updated its policy regarding HIV/AIDS (WFP, 2010g). It would address its obligations under the *UNAIDS Joint Outcome Framework* through two main objectives: by ensuring nutritional recovery and treatment success through nutrition and/or food support, which in 2009 had reached 1.83 million beneficiaries; and by mitigating the effects of AIDS in individuals and household through sustainable safety nets, which in 2009 had benefited 1.13 million people. It was recalled that the WFP had spent seven years designing, implementing, and evaluating progress relating to HIV and TB. A desk review in 2010 found that three million people living with HIV in 47 countries had benefited from nutritional rehabilitation, safety nets, or a combination of the two – either through clinics, or by reduction in the burdens on households. Many more may have also benefited from other WFP programmes, such as school feeding and food-for-asset programmes.

The WFP had worked with its partners in research to build an evidence base. *Monitoring and Evaluation Guidelines for Food-Assisted HIV Programmes* had been developed, which define the main HIV and AIDS programming categories and results frameworks. The guide helps programme staff to design their own monitoring and evaluation systems in line with national systems. The organization also recognized the importance of handover strategies, recognizing that HIV was a life-long chronic disease, while its food and nutrition interventions were finite and addressed the acute phase of the clinical stage of HIV and related income shocks. The WFP and governments therefore needed to work together in developing handover strategies with the following principles: know your epidemic, know your response, and tailor each assistance programme to the specific epidemiological and socio-political context; keep in mind the 'Three Ones' principles and the objective of national ownership; integrate food and nutrition into comprehensive HIV/AIDS responses; implement evidence-based, cost-effective programmes with sound monitoring and evaluation systems; incorporate collaboration and partnership; include community partnership and ownership; buy food locally; maintain predictable and reliable funding; consider gender concerns; and 'do no harm' that could make a bad situation worse and recognize that food insecurity could lead to negative coping strategies that could increase exposure to HIV.

The WFP has made substantive progress in its HIV/AIDS programme over the past decade. Much more remains to be done with its partners, which will depend on the level of support and resources it receives from donors, the international community, and the private sector. Above all, a combined effort is now required to increase the capacities of government in the affected countries – and, especially, the affected communities – to address the disease themselves.

Gender policy

Research and experience have shown that women play pivotal roles in the health, social, and economic development of their families, communities, and nations. This has often been achieved in the face of formidable constraints. Nowhere is this more evident than in maintaining the three pillars of food security: sustainable food production; economic access to available food; and nutrition security for all family members.[20]

Improvements in household welfare depend not only on the level of income, but also on who earns and controls that income. In many developing countries, women, relative to men, tend to spend their income disproportionately on food for the family and improvements in their children's nutrition, health, education, and general growth and development. Ensuring household nutrition security through the combination of food and other factors – such as child care, and access to clean water and sanitation – are almost the exclusive domain of women. This raised the question of how to take gender-sensitive factors into account in the design, implementation, and evaluation of WFP-assisted development projects. Although women's roles had been recognized, there remained a great deal of tokenism in supporting and strengthening their activities. Women continued to be 'helped' often through projects exclusively for them, thereby marginalizing their impact.

The *United Nations Decade for Women* (1976–85) provided the impetus and opportunity that helped to make a difference. In common with other aid agencies, both within and outside the UN system, the WFP was stimulated, for the first time, to take stock of what it had done to improve the status of women, enhance their contribution to development, and identify what more might be done in future. The WFP's first policy paper on the subject was presented to its governing body in 1975.[21] Two important facts emerged: the inclusion of women in the development process could not be taken for granted but, rather, had to be a deliberate and conscious concern; and because of the close affinity between women and food, food aid had a special potential for improving women's status, providing as it did a vehicle for bringing new ideas, particularly in rural areas, and offering possibilities to women for assuming new roles in addition to their traditional tasks. The WFP declared its full commitment to meeting the aims of *International Women's Year* in 1975. The executive director at the time, Francisco Aquino, stated that: 'Common sense urges it; common humanity demands it. Not just for this year but for all the years to come' (WFP, 1975b).

A number of studies and reports were presented to the WFP's governing body throughout the *United Nations Decade for Women*, making it one of the most documented of any single issue. Surveys showed the high proportion of women engaged in the labour force of WFP-supported food-for-work projects. When linked with a package of development services, functional literacy, training in income-generating activities, and access to savings and credit schemes, poor women had the chance, for the first time, to break the cycle of abject poverty and join the mainstream of development. However, two sets of obstacles and imperatives emerged from the WFP's ten-year experience during the UN Decade for Women. The first were institutional factors within the WFP, which were shared by other aid organizations. These mainly related to conceptualizing the issues for the advancement of women during the various phases of the project cycle. The second consisted of factors conditioning the roles and status of women within the countries receiving WFP assistance and linking national macro-economic policies to actual living conditions at the family and village levels.

A WFP strategy to the year 2000 was approved in 1985 to assist governments in developing countries in the fuller integration of women in national development programmes, particularly in the field of food security.[22] This included: improving support for women in food production; establishing priorities in food-for-work programmes; intensifying support for female education and training; supporting community-based skills training for employment, income generation, and nutritional improvement; strengthening collaboration with other aid agencies both within and outside the UN system; and improving the operational dimensions of WFP activities.

Other issues were subsequently highlighted. One cross-cutting concern was the need for greater recognition and appreciation of the 'continuum' in women's productive and reproductive roles. Both roles are performed in a continuum of labour time allocations that have a finite limit. A major failure of both national policies and programmes, and of international assistance, was that by addressing women's reproductive roles in the social sector, and their production roles in the economic sector, separately and dysfunctionally, they dichotomized what was not separated in reality. The resultant additional burdens placed on women tended to lower their productivity and diminish their capacity to fulfil their domestic responsibilities, including child care (Hammam and Youssef, 1986).

Another issue concerned whether development projects should be designed and supported exclusively for women. It was recognized that, under certain conditions, it made sense to limit eligibility for project benefits primarily or solely for females (WFP, 1980: 14–15). However, experience showed that improving women's status was best obtained in projects targeted at the family as a whole. These findings underlined that successful policy formulation and projects required gender analysis, and should involve gender mainstreaming in all WFP activities.

By the beginning of the 1990s, the WFP had emerged as the largest single source of grant assistance in the UN system for development projects that involved and benefited women in the rural areas of the developing world. Of the $3 billion of WFP assistance invested in operational development projects at that time, over half directly supported the advancement of poor rural women. This did not include the substantial emergency relief food provided to the victims of natural and conflict-induced disasters, most of whom were women and children.

Impressive changes were made when, for the first time, a woman, Catherine Bertini, was appointed as the WFP's executive director in 1992. The WFP's strong and persistent attempts to enhance the status of women and their role in development over a period of two decades were capped by far-reaching commitments made on its behalf by her at the *Fourth World Conference on Women* in Beijing, China in 1995 (WFP, 1995b, 1996: 4–5). The WFP would use its food aid to change behaviour and improve the status of women. While beliefs and prejudices that did so much damage to women worldwide could not be quickly changed: 'Each small change in behaviour will one day pay-off in a change in attitude'. In countries with major gaps in literacy, education, and basic skills between the sexes, the WFP would commit at least 60 per cent of its resources to women and girls. In emergencies, the WFP would see to it that women took the lead in managing the relief food provided in co-operation with NGOs and other UN agencies.[23] More than 50 per cent of WFP school feeding resources would be allocated to girls. WFP funding for women's literacy projects would be doubled. The WFP would also expand the use of food aid in refugee camps to support training for women in basic education, work skills, family planning, health, and nutrition. The WFP would target food aid better to overcome vitamin and mineral deficiencies among women by fortifying or adjusting WFP food rations. WFP staff would be more attuned to women's issues and would be assessed for their performance on gender issues. Also, more women would be employed and promoted by the WFP with the minimum aim of attaining the UN secretary-general's goal of 25 per cent of high-level posts for women and full gender equality by 2000.

By the end of 2006, nearly 40 per cent of WFP professional staff were women. An action plan was drawn up to meet WFP commitments by 2001. Consultations were held with WFP operating partners on how to carry out its policy to distribute a targeted 80 per cent of relief food in emergencies directly to the senior female of a household. And an MOU was signed with NGOs which included reference to the involvement of women at all levels of food aid planning, management, distribution, and monitoring.

This consultation process resulted in the WFP's *Gender Policy 2003–07,* approved by the WFP's executive board in 2002, which established eight 'enhanced commitments' to women to ensure food security.[24] The specific nutritional requirements of expectant and nursing mothers and adolescent girls should be met, and their awareness health and nutrition should be heightened. Activities that enable girls to attend school should be expanded and it should be ensured that women benefit at least equally from the assets created through food-for-training and food-for-work. Women's control of food in relief food distribution of household rations should be supported and it should be ensured that women are equally involved in food distribution committees and other programme-related local bodies. Gender should be mainstreamed in programming activities. There should be contribution to an environment that acknowledges the important role women play in ensuring household food security, and both men and women should be encouraged to participate in closing the gender gap. Finally, progress should be made towards gender equality in staffing, opportunities, and duties, and ensure that human resources policies are gender sensitive and provide possibilities for staff members to combine their personal and professional priorities.

A survey was conducted in 48 countries in 2004–05 to see how the WFP's *Gender Policy 2003–07* was being implemented and to provide a baseline for future surveys. The survey showed some impressive gains, but also a number of shortcomings. Micronutrient-fortified food was provided to all mothers at 89 per cent of the project sites visited. At 90 per cent of the project sites, at least half the assisted mothers attended awareness-raising sessions on nutrition, health, and child-caring practices. But de-worming medications were provided at only 19 per cent of project sites. At many sites, adolescent girls were not targeted at all, and awareness-raising sessions on HIV/AIDS prevention were offered at only 61 per cent of the sites. In school feeding projects, 48 per cent of students provided with WFP food in 2004 were girls, close to the 50 per cent target set. But the gender gap persisted with boys exceeding girls by more than 15 per cent in primary schools in one-third of the countries visited, and by 25 per cent in secondary schools in one-quarter of the countries visited.

In food-for-training projects, women made up 61 per cent of the trainees, approaching the target set of 70 per cent. However, data on adolescent girls were rarely available and, at 88 per cent of the projects, they were not involved. In food-for-work projects, 55 per cent of the workers were women and adolescent girls. To enhance women's participation, flexible timing and working shifts were offered at 74 per cent of the project sites. In 36 per cent of cases, there was no participatory consultation to define work activities. In emergencies, both men and women were well-aware of food distribution modalities, but consultations on the location of food distributions took place in only 48 per cent of the relief sites. Beneficiary food distribution committees existed in 92 per cent of the food-for-work projects, with women comprising at least half of the representative- and more than half of the executive-level members, at about 70 per cent of the work sites. Leadership training for women participating in committees was not sufficiently provided in all activities: only 28 per cent at relief sites, 31 per cent at food-for-work sites, and 54 per cent in the training programmes. In only half the WFP country offices in the countries visited did contingency plans prepared since January 2005 explicitly reflect and address gender issues. Clearly, the survey showed that, while progress had been made in implementing WFP gender policies, much remains to be done.

Ending Child Hunger and Undernutrition Initiative and transformation to Renewed Efforts Against Child Hunger and Undernutrition (REACH)

The WFP and UNICEF joined forces in 2006 to spearhead a global initiative, *Ending Child Hunger and Undernutrition* (ECHUI), based on their long and profound practical experiences.[25] They were also stimulated to take this initiative by efforts to reform the UN system and the international consensus afforded by the *UN Millennium Summit* of 2000, and the adoption of the MDGs. This provided an opportunity for UN bodies supporting food and nutrition-related programmes to strengthen their capacities and serve as catalysts to address the global problem of child hunger and malnutrition.

The size and complexity of the problem, and the failure of past efforts to mount a broad and sustained attack on the problem, indicated that a strong global partnership was needed, focused on action, to achieve progress for children. It was estimated that 400 million children under 18 years of age suffered from hunger and undernutrition. The WHO and UNICEF estimate that 149 million children under five years are underweight, a key indicator of undernourishment. More than 3.5 million child deaths and 35 per cent of the total burden of children aged under five years can be attributed to undernutrition. Experience over many years had shown that not only was access to more food required, but also that provision of a package of assistance was needed. Health, education, and other related concerns, and the social, human rights, and political environment into which children were born and in which they were brought up, together with the grinding poverty of their economic condition, needed to be addressed.

The initiative had four intended outcomes: increased awareness of hunger and undernutrition, and an understanding of potential solutions; strengthening national policies and programmes affecting hunger and nutrition; increased capacities for direct community action on child hunger and nutrition; and increased efficiency and accountability of global efforts to reduce child hunger and undernutrition through monitoring and evaluating the initiative's interventions and impact on children (WFP, 2007h). Four groups would work to reduce child hunger and malnutrition over a ten-year period: individual initiative members; a steering committee to provide oversight and direction; a high-level partners group consisting of key UN agencies, NGOs, and members of civil society and the private sector to provide strategic guidance at the global level; and a secretariat, based in Rome, Italy, with a senior UNICEF official as team leader, staff provided by the WFP and UNICEF, and technical guidance from the FAO, with a budget of $2.2 million a year. The WFP and UNICEF would act as advocates and catalysts in pursuing the goals of the initiative.

The aim was to satisfy immediate needs while addressing systemic problems. The size of the global problem is daunting, but is highly concentrated. Almost three-quarters of the world's underweight children live in 10 countries: 80 per cent live in 16 countries. About 85 million families affected by child hunger live in countries where the prevalence of underweight among children under five years of age is greater than 10 per cent. The experiences of UNICEF and the WFP had shown that the problem can be tackled operationally given adequate, sustained, and co-ordinated resources and programmes. The focus would be on the most affected countries for the first two years, during which strategies and priorities would be formulated for later action. The initiative would distinguish between 'child hunger' and 'family hunger', and promote various interventions targeting poor households to enable them to bring up healthy children.

The UN Standing Committee on Nutrition (SCN) estimated that the direct cost of inaction on child hunger and undernutrition was between $20 billion and $30 billion per year. The estimated annual cost of providing a set of interventions for 85 million families in countries with severe child underweight problems was put at $8 billion. This could not be absorbed immediately, but an additional $1 billion raised internationally could be programmed immediately. The WFP and UNICEF executive boards authorized the WFP and UNICEF secretariats to continue to develop the initiative and approved their roles in the 2007–08 workplan and first year of the initiative, with a budget of $1.31 million from each organization (WFP, 2007m).

A new sense of urgency, globally and within many countries, to address the problems of hunger and undernutrition resulted in the ECHUI initiative being replaced by a new initiative called REACH (*Renewed Efforts Against Child Hunger and Undernutrition*) by the initiating partners of the FAO, WHO, UNICEF and WFP. A REACH Global Coordinator, Bjorn Ljungquist, has been appointed to coordinate work from REACH headquarters in Rome, Italy, hosted by the WFP. He was seconded from UNICEF and has over 40 years' involvement in global, country-level and community work around the problems of hunger and undernutrition. As with its predecessor initiative, REACH is a country-led approach to scale-up proven and effective interventions addressing child undernutrition through partnerships and the co-ordinated action of UN agencies, civil society, donors, and the private sector.

The UN secretary-general on Food Security and Nutrition chairs the task team formed to develop an action plan. The team comprises representatives from developing country governments, civil society organizations, bilateral agencies, the World Bank, the Bill and Melinda Gates Foundation, and the business community. To date, partnerships have been established with the Center for Global Health at George Washington University, the Johns Hopkins Bloombery School of Public Health, and the School of Nutritional Science and Policies at Tufts University, IFAD and the UN Volunteers programme, the NGOs Micronutrient Initiative, the Mercy Corps, Helen Keller International, Save the Children, the Global Alliance for Improved Nutrition (GAIN), World Vision, and the private sector company the Boston Consultancy Group.

By December 2010, REACH was supporting nutrition and food security activities in Bangladesh, Laos, Mauritania, Mozambique, Rwanda, and Sierra Leone. These high priority countries have been targeted based on each government's stated commitment and readiness to develop and implement a national strategy and to mobilize resources. The REACH process builds consensus about the magnitude of nutritional challenges and the need for a new approach to scaling-up coverage for the most disadvantaged. REACH engages all stakeholders to improve breastfeeding, complementary feeding, hygiene, micronutrient intake, parasite control, treatment of acute malnutrition, and household food security. REACH intends to expand its operations to 36 of the world's most highly-burdened countries, in which a country-led process will last about four years at a cost of about $2.5 million per country. A key objective is to create monitoring and evaluation frameworks that government counterparts can manage on their own.

REACH is a direct outcome of the *Paris Declaration on Aid Effectiveness* (2005) and the *Accra High-Level Forum on Aid Effectiveness and Agenda for Action* (2008) that recommended local ownership, donor alignment and co-ordination, and division of labour and management for the maximum effectiveness of aid to support country development strategies. Within the UN system, there are distinct linkages to other global strategies and initiatives on nutrition and food security, including the SCN, the UN High Level Task Force on the Global Food Security Crisis, and the reformed Committee on World Food Security. REACH's technical advisory committee meets once a month via videoconference. Its secretariat provides technical expertise, and programme, managerial, and administrative support from its headquarters in Rome, currently hosted through a co-operative agreement with the WFP. REACH is considered to be a strategic vehicle to advance the *Scaling-up Nutrition* (SUN) policy framework and corresponding roadmap to action, and is regarded by the UN secretary-general on Food Security and Nutrition as a major resource for scaling-up nutrition action and delivering capacity at the country level.

Chapter 6 will turn to the commitment expressed in the WFP's *Strategic Plan (2008–13)* of transforming food aid as provided by the WFP since the start of its operations in 1963 into food assistance programmes to end hunger in sustainable ways through innovative interventions, which is currently in progress.

6
Transforming Food Aid to Food Assistance

Background

The WFP's *Strategic Plan (2008 – extended to 2013)*:

> marks a historical shift from WFP as a food aid agency to WFP as a food assistance agency, with a more nuanced and robust set of tools to respond to critical hunger needs. Its overarching goal is to reduce dependency and to support governmental efforts to ensure long term solutions to the hunger challenge. The global context in which WFP operates is rapidly changing... Deploying WFP most effectively within this broader global context is what the *Strategic Plan* is all about. (WFP, 2008k: 3)

The WFP's *Annual Performance Report* for 2009 clarified further:

> The *Strategic Plan (2008–2013)* shifted WFP's focus from delivering food aid to providing hunger solutions that are not limited to food aid and other direct food transfers. It implies that WFP would no longer start with the food aid tool and determine how to use it to support humanitarian and development objectives. Instead it would begin with the problem – hunger – and identify the most appropriate tools to address it in each context. (WFP, 2010c:15)

In 2009, three new initiatives reflected the new approach: improving approaches – to address malnutrition; *Purchase for Progress* (P4P) – to improve market opportunities for small-scale farmers; and using cash transfers and vouchers – to address food needs while supporting markets. This was not the first time that the WFP had broken out of its food aid modality of delivering food commodities in kind directly from donors to beneficiaries. It was, however, the first time it was announced in advance that this was what it explicitly endeavoured to do. There were many occasions in the past when different modalities were developed to deliver the benefits of food aid to poor and hungry people. The lessons derived from these early initiatives should be taken into account in charting the new way forward.

Early initiatives

As we saw in Chapter 1, from the WFP's inception preference was given by its governing body to the direct distribution of food from donors to the hungry poor. But other modalities were also developed to overcome some of the difficulties facing direct distribution in specific situations, adding to the flexibility, but also the complexity, of resource management.

Monetization

The complex question of monetization came to assume pronounced importance in the international debate on food aid. Some analysts and practitioners argued that the most efficient use of food aid was to sell (monetize) the food aid commodities provided by donors and use the proceeds to help finance well-designed development projects. Others reasoned that the hungry poor could be better targeted if food were directly distributed to them, particularly in situations of food insecurity where food markets functioned inefficiently. The debate assumed practical and operational importance.

There had been 15 years of experience with monetization in the United States food aid programme before WFP operations began in 1963. Through Title 1 of the PL480 food aid legislation, which came into force in 1948, the United States sold substantial quantities of programme food aid to developing countries. This resulted in the accumulation of large amounts of counterpart funds in the recipient countries, and controversy over their use, until the unspent funds were eventually written off. The academic literature also warned about the 'myths' of counterpart funds and drew attention to the fact that their economic effect was related to their first use, that their value could be significantly reduce by maladjusted exchange rates, and that they were subject to fungibility (Singer, 1961; Singer *et al.*, 1987).

Ground-rules for monetization

At the inception of WFP operations in 1963, preference was given to the direct distribution of food aid commodities, in kind and free of charge, from donors to beneficiaries that represented additional consumption to meet nutritional standards. Under these arrangements, it was considered easier to verify that the commodities provided by the WFP neither discouraged agricultural production in food aid recipient countries nor displaced existing supplies on international or local markets, thereby complying with the *FAO Principles of Surplus Disposal*. It was recognized, however, that for administrative and operations convenience, and to meet some specific requirements of WFP-assisted development projects, it would be expedient, in certain circumstance, to sell some of the food commodities provided. Soon after the WFP began operations, ground rules were established for WFP's sales policy in a circular letter sent out by the WFP's first executive director, Addeke Boerma, on 19 March 1963 (WFP, 1963b). Projects involving sales were to be exceptions to the general rule of direct distribution of free food. Each proposal for sales of WFP supplies had to be examined on its own merit and cleared by the FAO's Consultative Subcommittee on Surplus Disposal (CSD), which had been specifically set up to monitor adherence to the FAO *Principles*.

The principal consideration was to guard against sales depressing local market prices, which could discourage domestic agricultural production. Proceeds from the sales were to be spent on implementing the specific project that had been approved by the WFP's governing body. They should neither go to meeting the costs of other projects, nor should they go to augmenting the general budget of the recipient government as US programme food aid did, from which the WFP had been precluded. Three categories of sales were envisaged:

Category A – which allowed sales on the open market in a recipient country;

Category B – where sales were inherent in the purpose of the WFP-assisted project, such as in dairy development schemes in which the toned milk containing WFP-supplied dry skim milk was sold, or in price stabilization schemes in which the WFP-supplied grains provided to establish food reserves were sold to stabilize prices and the proceeds used to replenish the reserves; and

Category C – which involved close-circuit sales to designated project beneficiaries outside the normal market at subsidized prices as an incentive to attract and retain workers at work sites in remote and difficult locations, where the availability of food was limited and at high prices.

Sales proceeds could be used to buy locally produced tools, materials, and equipment required for the implementation of the WFP-assisted development project, thereby creating additional employment and income, which would be spent mostly on food. Sales proceeds could also be used to help offset the internal transport, storage and handling (ITSH) costs of the food commodities provided by the WFP.

Increasing monetization

A number of reports were presented to the WFP's governing body by the WFP secretariat to keep it informed of the number, extent, and types of projects involving sales in the three categories in which sales were allowed. By 1977, after 15 years of operations, projects with open market sales had involved less than 2 per cent of the total quantity of food committed to all operational projects at that time (WFP, 1977a). The governing body:

> agreed that WFP's policy of restricting sales on the open market to recipients of limited quantities of food in exceptional circumstances, applied judiciously and with caution, could help recipients to raise the necessary local funds and facilitate project implementation.…the Committee therefore endorsed the Executive Director's recommendation that a greater degree of flexibility was justified in the practical application of that policy. (WFP, 1977b)

By the beginning of the 1980s, the WFP's Achilles' heel, the shortage of cash resources, began to hurt seriously, resulting in an increase in monetization. The WFP's *General Regulations* stipulated that at least one-third of contributions to the

Programme 'in the aggregate' should be in cash and services. This formula was fixed on the understanding that those donors with food surpluses would contribute mainly food commodities, while others with no surpluses would contribute cash or services, such as shipping. The formula was adopted at a time when the WFP was mainly engaged in development projects. While some donors complied, other, particularly the larger donors, did not, with the result that the WFP began increasingly to face the problem of cash shortages. Other factors exacerbated the problem. One was that the WFP became increasingly involved in emergency operations, which required more cash to implement. Another was that, in 1972, the WFP's governing body agreed to the proposal of the Canadian delegation that the WFP should help meet the ITSH costs in least-developed countries related to the receipt of WFP food aid. The WFP's increasing involvement in emergency operations required higher ITSH costs.

To address the problem, executive director Ingram proposed, and the governing body agreed, that the sale of grain or other commodities donated to the WFP should be permitted to generate funds to offset up to 50 per cent of the ITSH costs in selected countries with large WFP food aid programmes (such as Bangladesh, Ethiopia, Mozambique, Somalia, and Sudan) through what was called an 'experimental sales procedure' (ESP) (WFP, 1982a). But before taking this action, Ingram suggested that a detailed study be conducted of the ESP in one country, Ethiopia, to determine whether such sales: had any displacement effects on commercial imports; any disincentive effects on local agricultural production or disruption of domestic markets; and any effects on long-term national development. The ESP would be reviewed by the governing body after the study had been completed and its results were known.

A study, which was conducted by FAO's Commodities and Trade Division with the support of the FAO's Investment Centre, found no significant negative effects on all three counts (WFP, 1983b). The study made three recommendations: the timing of the delivery of food commodities designated for sale should be negotiated in advance on an annual basis; and a more rigorous system of monitoring actual ITSH costs should instituted; and an undertaking should be obtained from the food aid recipient government to maintain procurement cereal prices at levels consistent with long-term import parities.

The executive director concluded that, taking into account the favourable findings and recommendations of the FAO study, 'the sale of grain or other commodities to generate funds for internal transportation is useful in conserving the cash resources of the Programme, and that the Executive Director should have the flexibility to adopt this practice in appropriate circumstance' (WFP, 1983c: 15). He also concluded, however, that the technique should be used only in those countries where the savings in WFP cash resources were substantial. He added that country-specific safeguards were required, with particular reference to domestic food supplies and pricing policies, to monitor the possible adverse impact of such sales on local agricultural production and/or import markets, and that the practice should be abandoned if negative effects were detected. WFP agreements involving sales would incorporate reference to usual marketing requirements (UMRs) – that is, a commitment by the recipient government to maintain the normal level of commercial imports of the commodities concerned, in addition to the food aid imports provided under concessional transactions.

Following the recommendations of the FAO study, more rigorous and systematic procedures would be adopted for determining the value of commodities delivered for sale to help meet ITSH costs and for monitoring, over time, the actual transport and handling costs incurred. These procedures would allow a simplification in the administration of the ITSH subsidy, preferably by abolishing the detailed procedure for deposit and disbursement of generated funds in favour of simple delivery at port of the equivalent value in commodities of the WFP's ITSH subsidy obligation without requiring any further accountability. CSD members had expressed concern that the sale of WFP commodities to help meet ITSH costs might contravene the *FAO's Principles of Surplus Disposal*. The practical effectiveness of safeguards adopted by the WFP was seen as the key to the continuation of such sales. The governing body agreed with the executive director's recommendations for the future application of the ESP in least-developed countries and specifically endorsed continuation of the sales procedure in Bangladesh and Ethiopia (WFP, 1983c: vii).

By 1986, after 24 years of operations, sales had been permitted in 16 per cent of all WFP-assisted projects, involving 15 per cent of the total quantity of WFP food aid committed to that date (WFP, 1987a). Open market sales were 1.5 per cent of total WFP commitments. The governing body agreed with the executive director's recommendation to allow monetization to take place where the free distribution of food aid to the poor was inappropriate. Two examples were given. First, schemes to improve access of the poor to food – such as supplementary feeding, rationing, price subsidy, and food coupon programmes targeted on the poor – particularly to mitigate the impact of changes in macro-economic policies through structural adjustment measures undertaken by governments in developing countries, often with donor governments and IMF and World Bank encouragement.[1] Second, in small countries heavily dependent on food imports where the cost of food aid shipments and internal administration of food aid and transport costs in recipient countries did not warrant direct distribution, but where the funds generated by the sale of food aid commodities could be used to finance development activities of direct benefit to the poor.

At the same time, new guidelines were drawn up on the programming and management of funds generated through WFP-assisted development projects (WFP, 1987b). The guidelines stressed the importance of the monetization process itself – that is, the ways in which food aid commodities were sold; the valuation of WFP commodities, which should reflect their real market value; and the speedy expenditure of sales proceeds on agreed items of expenditure in order to avoid erosion of their value through inflation.

World Bank/WFP joint study

WFP experience showed that monetization was not an easy option to bring the benefits of food aid to poor, food-insecure people. A study carried out jointly by the World Bank and the WFP of food aid in sub-Saharan Africa revealed that a number of issues required particular attention (WFP, 1991c: 23–5).[2] The study noted that direct distribution of food was not an end in itself. It was a method of targeting an available resource to malnourished or food-insecure people. But it was not the only method of targeting. As a general principle, resources should be transferred in ways that allowed the greatest flexibility and efficiency. When the targeted beneficiaries benefited more from local currency generated from monetized food aid, such an approach should be considered. Much depended on whether local conditions were conducive to efficient monetization and whether the funds generated could be effectively channelled to the target group. Effective use of monetized food aid depended on a number of conditions. Donors should be fully informed about, and responsive to, the requirements of recipient countries. Also, to maximize the local currency generated, recipient governments should value monetized food aid at import parity prices.

The study identified various issues concerning monetization that required particular attention: exchange rates, food subsidies, local markets, intra-household distribution, dependency, poverty focus, and the monetization process.

Exchange rates. If the exchange rate correctly reflected real scarcity values, food aid sold in the market at the import price would generate funds that reflected the real resource transfer. If the exchange rate were overvalued, the local currency fund would be less than the real value of the food aid. This had been a constraint on monetization. One solution was devaluation. Another alternative was to find a different basis for valuing food aid. If neither were possible, direct distribution of food aid may be preferred.

Food subsidies. When food prices in urban markets were subsidized, food aid may not be monetized at its full value, since part of the sales value was transferred directly to consumers. When the food subsidy was directed to the poor, there was no problem. In more frequent cases, the subsidy may be captured by less-needy groups, or used for the purchase of wheat or rice, which risked taste changes and dependency (Pinstrup-Andersen, 1988). In these cases, monetization faced the same problems as direct distribution of food. The provision of food aid in such cases may make it more difficult to reform the food system. The best solution would be to use food aid in support of food policy reform, which may include a targeted subsidy to needy groups in place of a general subsidy.

Local markets. As a general principle, the more autonomy given to beneficiary households, the better. Where a resource transfer to households was the primary objective, and where the local currency was reasonably stable and local markets were functioning, food would, as a rule, be less valuable to the beneficiaries than cash. If the commodities do not fully correspond to the local diet, food aid in kind was often 'monetized' at the household level. This may be more efficient than monetization at the national level. Stable currencies and well-functioning local markets were conspicuously absent in many developing countries. Food-aided projects were typically targeted at the most-needy and food-insecure people, and were therefore often located in remote areas. In such circumstances, transferring cash may simply raise local food prices. And, thus, delivering food directly may be preferable.

Intra-household distribution. Increasing the food intake of vulnerable groups, such as infants and pregnant and nursing women, can make a direct contribution to the development of human resources. It was argued that additional food was more likely to be directly controlled by women than cash. A target group may be more effectively assisted, however, through other measures, such as improved public health care and nutrition education, using local cash from monetization. The choice of direct distribution or monetization required careful analysis of local conditions.

Dependency. All aid carried the risk that it may create dependency. Part of project food aid was used as an incentive for activities that beneficiaries were expected to continue on their own. Food may be more appropriate for this purpose than cash.

Poverty focus. All aid faced the problem of fungibility. Governments may direct monetized resources to the general budget, which may thwart the donors' and aid agencies' intention to see it used for poverty alleviation. To the extent that national development policies and plans were perceived as sound by all concerned, fungibility should not be a problem. In such situations, donors and aid agencies should support policies and sectoral programmes, rather than attempt to direct their aid to specific purposes. This reinforced the need for food aid to be fully integrated into national plans and donor strategies.

The monetization process. How food aid is monetized has important effects on the benefits from monetization. While monetization through the private sector might stimulate development, sales through the public sector might support high-cost parastatals with a monopoly on grains marketing. The evidence showed that monetization was most effective when food aid was sold at full market prices. Careful consideration should also be given to how the funds generated are used. Experience suggested that the funds were best placed in a special interest-bearing account and used promptly for priority items agreed upon at the design and approval stages of a programme or project.

The joint study recommended that a review of the performance of monetizing food aid was needed. Taking into account the problems that had led to inefficiencies in the monetization process, and also in the management and use of the funds generated, the review should examine all aspects of monetization, including the benefits that could be derived from the establishment of a common counterpart fund derived from food aid from all sources. It also led to wider interest in the subject, including an international workshop at the Institute of Development Studies at the University of Sussex, UK on *Commodity Aid and Counterpart Funds in Africa* in 1991 (Maxwell and Owens, 1991). It also led to a proposed set of practical criteria for determining the conditions under which food aid to individual projects should be distributed in kind or monetized (Schulthes, 1992: 37).

Review of monetization

Between 1987 and 1996, about 13 per cent of the total value of WFP commitments was monetized (WFP, 1997d). From the beginning of the 1990s, over one-third of the funds generated from the sales of commodities supplied by the WFP were used to finance project activities, such as strengthening of market infrastructure in dairy development projects, and the purchase of tools and materials. However, the most common reason for monetization was to meet WFP commitment to help meet ITSH costs.

At the same time, monetization was taking place in a markedly changing WFP resource situation. There was a sharp reduction in the volume of food commodities made available by donors. The sale of increasingly scarce food aid commodities on the open market in recipient countries therefore became harder to justify than at a time when the WFP had large commodity contributions at its disposal and limited cash resources. The share of cash contributions to the WFP's resources also rose steadily. At the end of the 1980s, about 70 per cent of the total value of WFP commitments was in the form of food commodities. By 1995, more than half was in the form of cash tied by donors in varying degrees to the purchase of food commodities in specified markets. The WFP increasingly purchased food, mainly in developing countries, to use as food aid (see pp. 000–00). This implied less need for monetization in order to help meet ITSH costs. In addition, the cost of non-food items to implement WFP-assisted development projects was written into project proposals, thereby obviating the need for monetization to meet those costs.

As a result, it was decided that the WFP would *not* (emphasis added) undertake projects involving full open market monetization to fund activities that were not directly related to food aid. However, when some donors, particularly developing countries governments, did not have the flexibility to provide sufficient or timely cash resources, and when alternative financing was not available, some monetization could still be undertaken. The WFP would also continue to used 'closed-circuit' monetization to bring the benefits of food aid to project beneficiaries when it was considered to be the most appropriate modality. Monetization was also to be a considered option in: emergency operations where direct distribution of food aid to disaster victims was not feasible; when beneficiaries had the resources to pay for the food they received; or where local monetization would help promote a return to normal conditions following the end of an emergency.[3] In all cases involving monetization, however, the WFP undertook to establish the cost- effectiveness of the monetization process in advance, and to avoid any market displacement, domestic production disincentives, or risk of creating lasting dependency among beneficiaries.

Against this background, in May 1993 the WFP's external auditor recommended that the WFP's Evaluation Service should consider conducting a broad review of the achievements and impact of monetization projects (WFP, 1993b).[4] The review identified the main advantages and problems of monetization (WFP, 1994e). Regarding the advantages, monetization could help to meet the real needs of projects and their beneficiaries that could not be met by food aid alone. Monetization could also make food aid more flexible and adaptable. It could act as an investment resource, financing project activities when government budgets did not allow activities to be carried out at the expected pace. The funds generated could supplement government allocations in order to make the necessary equipment and inputs available, and to employ additional workers to increase project outputs.

Monetization could support credit schemes and concomitant services for project beneficiaries. It was less lengthy and costly in delivering benefits. Commodities could be sold at the port of entry or delivery points, thereby saving time and ITSH expenses. It could help augment local demand for food, thus creating an incentive for domestic food production; it could also strengthen local, regional, and national trade. The presence of additional food for sale could help to reinforce markets, and it could contribute to the integration of people into the economy, rather than isolating them by setting up special, temporary systems of food distribution.

But the review also revealed a number of problems. Market displacement was mentioned in the food aid literature as one of the dangers inherent in monetization. There were no cases of market displacement reported during the review, however, confirming that the key factors were: knowledge of the market structure and of competing import/export interests; a good understanding of consumer behaviour, demand, and consumption patterns; good timing and size of shipments, in order that sales did not coincide with harvest/post-harvest periods, and to avoid competition with local food production; good co-ordination among donors, in order to avoid the risk of flooding the market with large quantities of food products to be sold; and the choice of food commodities to be sold. The choice of commodities to be sold was sometimes more donor- than recipient-oriented. As a result, the commodities provided did not always fit either country requirements or market policies, causing retarded sale, low priorities, and consequent delays or failures in attaining project objectives.

The review found that monetization could not be cost-effective in countries where food prices were cheaper than in the donor country, including the cost of transport. Similarly, it was not cost-effective where cheap, subsidized prices were in force, unless the subsidy was financed out of the government budget and not supported by the donor. Consignments of food commodities were usually small, as external transport was often made in liner vessels with high freight rates, resulting in a prohibitive price for cost, insurance, and freight in the recipient country. Shipment of larger consignments at one time on charter vessels with lower freight rates entailed either storing food for gradual release over longer periods, or selling large amounts on the recipient markets, and leaving the generated funds in bank accounts, often without interest-bearing provisions, with the risks of losses through deterioration and depreciation of their value.

In order to achieve high-efficiency through monetization, the review suggested that the donated food commodities should be treated as a full-cost resource. Too often, commodities for sale were not of the same quality or not presented in packaging similar to the ones sold through commercial channels, resulting in difficulties in selling and differences in prices. Funds generated through open-market sales were often not deposited immediately in bank accounts, thereby losing potential interest. Funds were not always deposited in interest-bearing accounts or in commercial banks that offered the most advantageous interest rates but, rather, were kept in state-owned banks where they could be more easily drawn upon, on a temporary basis, for purposes outside those for which they had been generated.

Funds were usually disbursed much more slowly than foreseen as their generation, and deposit into the project's account were often delayed, resulting in the planned level of funds at the disposal of the project was not reached. Disbursement was often subject to cumbersome and/or inefficient government bureaucracy with lengthy procedures. In addition, disbursements were not always carried out in line with agreed project objectives but, rather, were sometimes used by governments for other general purposes. Poor management of the funds generated was often due to lack of training, which affected control over the funds and problems in accounting, reporting, and monitoring.

In the case of open-market sales, revision of the prices of commodities provided for sale was not always carried out in a timely manner, resulting in difficulties in selling or loss of earnings. The particular technical skills required to conduct sales operations were not always available in WFP country offices. In closed-circuit sales, the value of wage deductions was not reviewed and adjusted regularly in accordance with prevailing local prices and minimum wages, generally resulting in excessive income transfers to the beneficiaries that did not necessarily translate into increased productivity.

The review concluded that, in the majority of the cases analyzed, the sale of commodities could advantageously have been replaced by the direct supply of cash. If cash were available, it could be transferred more quickly, efficiently, and cost-effectively than through the monetization process. The potentially positive aspects of monetization could be outweighed by negative effects resulting from a poorly-organized and managed operation. The risks involved in both the sales and expenditure aspects on monetization needed equally good justification from the beginning of a project and be clearly stated in it plan of operation.

In sum, monetization of a small proportion of WFP-supplied food aid had positive results in achieving project objectives and supporting certain project costs. But recourse to monetization was sometimes seen as the easiest and quickest way of ensuring the availability of the cash required for a project. It should be the last resort after all other possible sources of funding had been examined, including the provision of non-food items, bilateral contributions, and support and co-operation from other UN agencies, NGOs, and the private sector. Food sold to generate funds was no longer available for direct distribution to poor and food-insecure people. And the dual objective of monetization, to benefit local markets and to meet cash requirements, could not always be confirmed.

Monetization policies

The last time the WFP's governing body discussed monetization was in response to a requested policy paper to determine whether, and under what conditions, the WFP ought to be involved in the sale of food aid commodities (WFP, 1997d). The paper was presented in a changed global food aid context in which food aid resources had decreased considerably and the demand for WFP assistance was greater than its supply.

The policy paper proposed that the WFP would *not* (emphasis added) undertake projects involving full open-market monetization to fund activities that were not related to direct food assistance, and where the generation of funds was the primary objective. Open-market monetization to cover support costs of a directly distributed WFP food intervention would, normally, *no longer be necessary* (emphasis added), in accordance with the WFP's resources and long-term financing policies. However, where some donors did not have the flexibility to provide sufficient or timely cash resources for this purpose, and in the absence of any alternative financing, some monetization might still need to be undertaken.

Open-market sale of WFP food commodities to finance the purchase of locally produced food for direct distribution to beneficiaries as food aid would be managed in the same way as open-market sales for other purposes and should be *demonstrably cost-effective* (emphasis added). The initial commodity sale *should not disrupt* (emphasis added) the normal markets of recipient countries. The WFP should *continue* to use closed-circuit monetization *where it is considered the most appropriate modality* (emphases added) in line with past practice. In emergency operations, the WFP would consider monetization where it was *clearly demonstrable* that the monetization process itself had benefits *over and above the income transfer* to the beneficiaries and where the generation of funds was *not* (emphases added) the primary object of commodity sales.

The WFP would monetize on behalf of donors as a bilateral service as long as the intervention was consistent with the WFP's ongoing programmes and its *Mission Statement* (WFP, 1994b), and did not distort local markets, cause import displacement or price disincentives, or infringe the *FAO Principles of Surplus Disposal*. In all cases where projects that involved monetization were envisaged: the cost-effectiveness implications of the monetization process would be made explicit through an *ex ante* analysis comparing the cost of procuring, transporting, and selling food commodities with alternative methods of supporting interventions; the WFP would have sufficient prior knowledge of market conditions, actors, and mechanisms to determine the likely impact of monetization, and the most appropriate and cost-effective way of undertaking the process; and there would be no market displacement, production disincentive, or risk of creating lasting dependency among beneficiaries.

The governing body approved these policy proposals (WFP, 1997f).

Other modalities: triangular transactions, commodity purchases and commodity exchanges

Faced with the difficulties and costs of direct distribution of food aid commodities, shortage of cash resources, and the limitations placed on monetization, the WFP looked for other modalities to transfer food aid resources to the hungry poor in developing countries, which might have additional food aid and developmental benefits. These modalities added further to the flexibility, but also the complexity, of resource management.

In addition to monetization, three modalities were used:

Triangular transactions – whereby a donor bought food in a developing country and shipped it to another developing country, where it was used as food aid;

Commodity purchases – in a developing country for use as food aid in the same country;

Commodity exchanges – by which a food commodity, say wheat, supplied as food aid to a developing country was exchanged for another commodity produced in that country, say maize, which was used as food aid in the same country.

The resolution adopted by the 1974 World Food Conference, 'An Improved Policy for Food Aid', among other things urged donor countries to 'provide, as appropriate, to food aid programmes additional cash resources for commodity purchases from developing countries to the maximum extent possible' (UN, 1975: 16). The Guidelines and Criteria for Food Aid, unanimously agreed to by the WFP's governing body in 1979, also recommended that:

> Donor countries should make efforts to provide whenever possible cash resources with a view to financing food aid through triangular transactions between themselves, developing food exporting countries and recipient countries, including coverage of the shipping costs, wherever applicable, and further diversifying the varieties of food provided as aid. Such arrangements would increase the participation of developing exporting countries in food aid. (WFP, 1979b)

These modalities were perceived as having a wide array of potential important benefits for food aid, including: reducing transfer costs; increasing the speed and timeliness of food aid deliveries; and providing food commodities more in keeping with the food tastes and habits of recipients than those provided directly by donors. In addition, they could bring with them potentially wider developmental benefits, including: stimulating increased food production in food aid recipient countries; promoting exports; fostering intra- and inter-country trade; supporting food strategies and food security programmes by helping developing countries manage their food surpluses; assisting in the restructuring, revivication, and liberalization of domestic food markets; encouraging and assisting improvements in transportation, storage, and logistics infrastructure in food exporting developing countries, and neighbouring developing countries; and strengthening food management and administration capacity in association with technical assistance and training.

An opportunity for the WFP to engage in triangular transactions on a large scale in sub-Saharan Africa occurred at the beginning of the 1980s. Zimbabwe had two successive bumper maize harvests. At this time, many neighbouring countries faced acute food shortages, and the WFP was called upon to provide food aid to alleviate the threat of widespread hunger and malnutrition. The WFP purchased over 250,000 tons of maize not only from its own limited cash resources, but also with financial assistance provided by 16 donor countries, organizations, and NGOs. The maize purchased in Zimbabwe was transported to 15 countries in sub-Saharan Africa to support emergency operation and development projects, mainly for agricultural and rural development. At the same time, with the co-operation of donor countries, the WFP helped in the improvement of transport and logistics infrastructure both within Zimbabwe and with neighbouring countries (WFP, 1982b; Shaw, 1983).[5]

Despite the potential benefits, procuring food aid commodities in developing countries remained a modest, but growing, part of total WFP food aid deliveries. In 1998, about 900,000 tons of foods were procured by the WFP in developing countries for use as food aid. As total food aid deliveries fell, however, an increasing share came from procurement in developing countries. In 1998, that share was 11 per cent. Cereals made up over 90 per cent of the food commodities obtained in developing countries. Just over half was procured through local purchases and slightly under half from triangular transactions. More than 60 per cent took place in sub-Saharan Africa (WFP, 1999f).

Ultimately, the amount of food procured in developing countries for use as food aid depended on the cash resources donors were prepared to invest in these food aid modalities. This, in turn, was influenced by donors' assessments of the benefits food purchases brought to them in economic and political terms, and the opportunity costs of using their limited financial aid for these purposes rather than for other developmental uses. The experience of both the WFP and donor agencies showed that there were formidable barriers and difficulties to procuring food aid commodities in developing countries (RDI, 1987, 1990; WFP, 1989b, 1990b; Clay and Benson, 1990).[6] There were significant differences between 'regular' food-exporting developing countries and those 'non-regular' food exporters with only intermittent food surpluses. These differences arose from such factors as: assurance of the availability of the food commodities required; their timely supply through efficient marketing systems; and uncertainties in food aid programming because commodities were not regularly available, which could result in additional costs to the WFP and donors. These difficulties were compounded by non-tariff barriers, such as: limited administrative and managerial capacities; transport, storage, and logistics bottlenecks; and inadequate quality control.

Concern was also expressed about how to manage surplus production in developing countries given the uncertainties in food availabilities and prices on world markets, and the undernourished state of a high proportion of their populations. The disposal of surpluses above the current level of effective demand could lead to inadequate investment in stocks, storage, and targeted food subsidy programmes for the hungry poor. Another major concern was that donors and aid agencies carried out these food aid modalities separately, at different prices and exchange ratios, through different marketing channels, and at different times of the year. Insufficient consideration was also given to their potential developmental benefits, or to building up capacity in developing countries to undertake them more efficiently and on a larger scale. The country office staffs of the WFP, bilateral donors, and NGOs in developing countries were often inadequately trained to engage in these food aid modalities, were insufficiently informed of market prices and conditions, and their administrative overheads were often underestimated.

Two overriding lessons emerged from WFP experience in carrying out these food aid modalities. First, donors and aid agencies should develop with governments a common strategy, based on a common code of conduct, for each developing country in which these modalities were regularly implemented. A common information and market intelligence system should also be established and maintained for individual developing countries on food availabilities and prices for traditional staples, as well as cereals and other food commodities that were not so widely traded. Standard guidelines would facilitate co-ordinated purchasing and exchange negotiations and operations, marketing channels, transport and logistics arrangements, and monitoring and evaluation systems that would facilitate the assessment and comparison of individual food aid transactions and their aggregate effects. Without these provisions, unco-ordinated food aid transactions carried out with different criteria and guidelines could be in competition and therefore counterproductive for recipient countries and donor and aid agencies alike.

Second, the full developmental benefits derived from these food aid modalities might be achieved if a co-ordinated programme of financial, technical and food assistance could be provided to improve the capacities of developing countries to undertake their operation. Such a programme might include: technical assistance and training services to strengthen administrative and managerial support; development of trading skills and market analysis; improved grading, handling and storage techniques to improve the quality of food products; and financial assistance to improve transport and logistics infrastructure.

There was general agreement that countries in sub-Saharan Africa would require help in meeting their food import requirements in the years ahead, whether as food aid or aid for food. It was therefore proposed that the WFP should organize, as a matter of priority, an international conference to reconcile the significant differences in outlook, perspective, and practices that existed among donor countries on both sides of the Atlantic. The aim of the conference would be to arrive at a comprehensive policy and programme of food assistance that would take into account the lessons learned (WFP, 1991c; Shaw, 2000: 210–30, 2001: 251–2).

From food aid to food assistance

Local and regional food purchases

By the late 1990s, procurement of goods and services had become a major part of the WFP's overall activities, accounting for about 25 per cent of total UN purchases, making the WFP the largest procurement organization in the UN system (WFP, 1998f). Originally, the WFP food supplies came from donor countries' pledges of food commodities in-kind. Over time, an increasing share of contributions to the WFP came in cash so that, by 1997, the WFP purchased about 50 per cent of the 2.7 million tons of food aid it delivered. There were two main reasons for this increasing trend. First, was the marked increase in emergency operations for which donors pledged more cash than food, which was increasingly used for local and regional food purchases to speed up deliveries, and to meet transport and handling costs. Second, was the change in donor policies, which allowed more local purchases and triangular transactions.

WFP food procurement activities were governed by provisions in the WFP's new *General Rules and Regulations*, which came into force in 1992 (WFP, 1992b). Rule XII.4 (Responsibility for optimum use of resources) states:

> The Executive Director shall be responsible for making the optimum use of available resources...To this end the Executive Director may use unrestricted cash resources to purchase commodities to the maximum extent possible from developing countries, and shall report such purchases to the Board.

Rule XII.6 (Safeguarding exporters, international trade and producers in recipient countries) states:

> In the assessment of prospective economic and social development programmes and projects, in their implementation and subsequent evaluation, full consideration shall be given to the prospective and actual effects of programmes and projects upon local production, including possible ways and means of increasing such production, and upon the markets for agricultural products produced in the country.

WFP procurement was based on competitive bids. For large purchases, formal tenders were issued and strict procedures were closely scrutinized by the WFP's Office of Internal Audit. Limited procurement authority was also devolved to WFP country offices as part of the devolution process and to improve the response to emergencies. Governments in supplying developing countries were encouraged to promote trade, establish trade laws consistent with international commercial practices, improve basic infrastructure and support services, and provide credit facilities. Potential suppliers were encouraged to indicate their interest in supplying food commodities to the WFP by completing a registration form. Following a screening process, successful applicants were placed on a roster for future invitations to make bids when goods and services were required.

At its annual session in 1998, the WFP's executive board emphasized its support for local purchasing of food and non-food items and triangular transactions, and requested the WFP secretariat to present a document explaining the analytical process carried out in making local purchases under optimal conditions and avoiding negative effects (WFP, 1998g).

The secretariat responded by conducting a review of WFP methodology for effecting purchase of food in developing countries. This involved missions to countries in east and west Africa to identify any possible negative consequences of past purchase on local markets (WFP, 1999g). The WFP was generally guided by three basic principles when purchasing food in developing countries to avoid driving up local food prices. To the extent possible: food purchases were made through competitive tenders to ensure that prices were in line with those in prevailing markets; purchases were avoided in the agricultural lean season; and purchases were not made in food-deficit areas.

The review found no evidence that WFP purchases had either adversely disrupted markets or had negative effects on local consumption. The WFP *Food Procurement User Guide*,[7] introduced in 1996, and the appointment of specialized staff in WFP country offices to undertake procurement, helped to increase and improve local purchase activities. The general approach of using import parity pricing ensured that prices paid were not above prevailing international prices. But the review found that WFP food purchases in developing countries did not always follow a systematic approach. It was recommended that current procedures be strengthened to help ensure that WFP food purchases were undertaken in a well-planned and co-ordinated manner, with the fullest possible knowledge of the prevailing market conditions.

This could be done by: developing country situation analysis; maintaining up-to-date market intelligence; preparing an annual food procurement plan; establishing systems to co-ordinate food purchases with those of other significant food purchases; and reviewing prices before finalizing purchases. Other ways were proposed to avoid adverse market effects, including: intensifying efforts to improve market intelligence as the WFP's share of the market increased, including, if necessary, funding studies to obtain pricing data; avoiding tendering for large allotments, and tender overlapping; and limiting WFP purchases to stocks actually held by suppliers at the time of tender, to prevent drawing food from subsistence farming households in poorly-developed food markets.

The executive board expressed appreciation and support for local purchases conducted by the WFP (WFP, 1999h). It noted that 60 per cent of WFP purchases were made in developing countries. It recommended that periodic market reviews, the advice of local governments, the concept of 'least delivered cost', and import parity pricing of substitute commodities should contribute to successful and economic local procurement conducted in ways that did not disrupt local economies.

By the turn of the new millennium, food procurement had reached such levels that the WFP began to review not only how it could contribute to improved food aid, but also to development in developing countries through food assistance programmes. The WFP's firmly established policy was to procure food in developing countries to the maximum extent possible, in a manner that was cost-effective, timely, and appropriate to beneficiary needs, and in ways that avoided causing negative effects on markets, including price rises that would harm the food security of the poor. By 2006, food procured in developing countries accounted for about 20 per cent of global food aid. The WFP was historically the largest single procurer of food aid on a global scale. From 2001 to 2004, the WFP bought an average of 1.25 million tons of food a year at a cost of $263 million in developing countries.

To produce another paper for the executive board on food procurement in developing countries, the WFP commissioned six case studies of its local and regional food procurement in Bolivia, Burkina Faso, Ethiopia, Nepal, South Africa, and Uganda (WFP, 2006l). They showed that a serious limitation on the WFP's ability to contribute to market development in developing countries was that it was not a regular or reliable buyer on many markets. As an uncertain and often unpredictable buyer, the WFP had a responsibility to intervene in markets without creating false expectations. All case studies showed that, when cash was in hand and could be used flexibly and without restriction, local and regional purchases were more cost-effective and timelier than other sources of food aid. When procurement took place in markets that were not well-developed, however, administrative costs and risks increased. The studies also showed that, under its normal procurement procedures, the WFP could have important impacts on market development by promoting competitive behaviour, raising business standards, and improving the quality of food supplied by traders. The WFP could also support the development of the local food processing sector. However, the WFP had not been successful in promoting market development through procuring directly from farmers or farmer groups.

The WFP aimed to achieve a balance between its procurement objectives and its programmatic objective of promoting the development of food markets and food security in food aid recipient counties. Various conclusions were drawn from analysis as a precursor to its *Purchase for Progress* (P4P) programme (see pp. 281–6).

Market development as an implicit objective. The WFP sought to strengthen developing country markets, wherever this could be achieved consistently, with purchasing efficiency and the optimal use of scarce cash resources. Incorporating an explicit food security or market development objective into the procurement activity could, in some cases, compromise the WFP's primary objective of addressing beneficiary food needs. Nevertheless, analysis had identified important lessons on the WFP's development impact. These warranted the WFP's consideration of a greater emphasis on market development in its procurement and programming activities.

Flexible and timely cash contributions. The provision of untied donor resources would allow the WFP to procure at the local, regional, or international level, promoting market competitiveness and ensuring cash was used to provide food in the most timely and efficient manner. Early confirmation of cash contributions enabled the WFP to plan its procurement better, particularly in local markets, where substantial cost savings could be achieved by procuring at harvest time.

Encouraging small traders and farmer groups. When food needs were not urgent, the WFP could do more to encourage small traders and farmer groups that could trade competitively in the formal sector. The amount that the WFP could purchase in this way was limited, however, as it was necessary to balance benefits with the administrative costs of monitoring a large number of contracts for small quantities. Also, there was a risk to WFP beneficiaries, if a supplier defaulted on a contract.

Preferential treatment for farmers and farmer groups. The WFP was not well-placed to use procurement as a means to support farmers and farmer groups in entering the marketplace. There may be limited opportunities for support as part of a broader partner-led strategy to link groups with larger traders or national grain reserves. The WFP face high administrative costs and risks with such procurement, however, while the benefits go to farmers that had surpluses rather than to food-insecure households. In particular, purchasing premiums resulted in a transfer of resources from WFP beneficiaries to relatively better-off surplus-producing farmers.

Developing food processing capacity. The WFP should continue to support the creation of processing capacity to produce fortified and blended foods in countries where local processors had the potential to become market competitive. However, further study of the developmental impact in relation to the costs and risks of this support was required.

Procurement office capacities at the country and regional levels. The WFP was able to secure the primary objective of its food procurement – to purchase in a cost-efficient and timely manner. To promote local and regional purchases further, particularly in countries where markets were not well-developed, and procurement required significant market analysis and administrative efforts, the WFP would need to expand the capacity of its specialist food procurement staff. The required increase should be considered in relation to the potential supply capacity of market, the cost-savings that local and regional procurement could bring, and the WFP's overall needs.

The executive board's reaction to the secretariat's paper was to encourage local, sub-regional and regional purchases 'to the extent possible' (WFP, 2006m). In addition, it urged donors to provide more unrestricted, timely, and predictable funding, so that the WFP could more effectively plan and undertake procurement. It also requested that due consideration be given to optimizing the potential development benefits by: working closely with national governments, the FAO, IFAD and others; ensuring that WFP country offices and regional bureaux had the necessary staff; and providing the executive board with annual reports on procurement activities (Table 6.1).

Table 6.1 WFP food procurement, 2002–09 (million tons/$ millions)

Year	Total quantity	Total cost	In developing countries			In developed countries		
			No.	Quantity	Cost	No.	Quantity	Cost
2002	1.5	307.5	57	1.0	204.3	20	0.5	103.1
2003	2.7	634.2	69	2.0	443.6	15	0.7	190.6
2004	3.5	1,051.4	79	2.3	725.5	12	1.2	325.9
2005	2.5	712.4	75	2.0	548.0	10	0.5	164.4
2006	2.0	601.0	70	1.5	460.3	14	0.5	140.7
2007	2.1	767.4	69	1.6	612.4	13	0.4	155.0
2008	2.8	1,407.9	73	2.1	1,092.9	12	0.7	314.9
2009	2.6	965.2	75	2.1	771.7	17	0.5	193.5

Source: WFP Food Procurement Annual Reports.

Since the beginning of the new millennium, increasing cash contributions for donors have made it possible for the WFP to become a stable and substantial purchaser of tradable food internationally, particularly in developing countries. Since 1990, the WFP has tripled the quantity and value of its food purchases globally. Procurement has markedly increased since 2002, even discounting the massive food purchases for Iraq under the *UN Oil for Food Programme*.[8] In 2009, 2.6 million tons of foods were purchased by the WFP at a cost of $965 million in 92 countries. About 80 per cent in value terms was purchased in 75 developing countries; about one-third in least-developed and other low-income countries. About two-thirds of the food purchased consisted of cereals (wheat, maize and rice). Over one million tons of food were purchased in Asia and 0.6 million tons in Africa. The main developing countries where WFP food purchases took place in 2009 are given in Table 6.2.

The WFP was found to have performed well in its local and regional procurement operations in Africa (Tschirley, 2007). From 2001 to 2005, the WFP's maize procurement in Kenya, Uganda, and Zambia was calculated to have made savings of $67.7 million compared to the supply of US food aid, and deliveries were faster. The saving made was sufficient to purchase an additional 437,700 tons of maize. Local procurement may also produce less obvious benefits, such as high farm-gate prices, strengthened formal markets, and increased investment by traders and processors (Sserunkuuma, 2005).

As food procurement in developing countries began to grow significantly, the WFP and donors asked what developmental benefits such purchases could bring in addition to the advantages it brought for providing food aid. Such procurement could offer more than financial savings in transfer costs, more appropriate commodities, and faster delivery It also presented an opportunity for bringing benefits to poor farmers and farming communities, thereby helping to break the generational cycle of poverty and hunger, and dependency on food aid. The WFP had engaged in small but irregular food purchases from farmers and farmer groups in a number of developing countries, and had supported food processing

Table 6.2 Main developing countries for WFP food purchase, 2009

Country	Quantity ('000 million tons)	Value ($ millions)
Pakistan	267.1	91.4
India	253.4	61.6
South Africa	210.3	60.8
Uganda	117.2	49.8
Malaysia	50.2	41.6
Ethiopia	73.6	40.4
Indonesia	41.5	33.8
Bangladesh	44.3	21.3

Source: WFP Food Procurement Annual Report 2009.

plants as part of its assisted development projects. However, there was no overarching policy or operational framework to conduct these activities; there was also little assessment of their results.

Purchase for Progress Programme (P4P)

A number of factors came together that resulted in the launch of the *Purchase for Progress* (P4P) initiative to capture the developmental benefits of the WFP's growing food procurement activities (Davies and Menage, 2010: 125–38).[9] Strategic objective (SO) 5 of the WFP's *Strategic Plan (2008–13)*, on 'Strengthening the Capacities of Countries to Reduce Hunger, including through Hand-Over Strategies and Local Purchase', states:

> Food and non-food local purchasing activities are supporting the capacity of countries and communities to enhance employment opportunities and develop sustainable livelihoods. WFP is committed to utilizing its purchasing power, when and where possible, to develop suppliers' capacities and build up with other partners' complementary interventions aimed at reinforcing the supply side. Pilot local procurement activities can be mainstreamed into WFP procurement practices and, more importantly, adopted and scaled up by national governments and other actors in agricultural sectors. (WFP, 2008k: 20)

The WFP's procurement activities are described as being a 'central mechanism' through which SO 5 will be achieved. Three goals are identified. Purchasing power should be used to support the sustainable development of food and nutrition security systems, and transform food and nutrition assistance into a productive investment in local communities. Clear handover strategies should be developed to enhance nationally-owned hunger solutions. There should be strengthening of the capacities of countries to design, manage, and implement tools, policies, and programmes to predict and reduce hunger.

P4P has the potential of bringing together the WFP's work in improved nutrition, school feeding, HIV/AIDS, and gender policy. It is also aligned with other national, regional, and global efforts to address food insecurity by promoting smallholder agricultural production and access to markets, such as the *New Partnership for Africa's Development* (NEPAD); the *Comprehensive African Agricultural Development Programme* (CAADP); the *Alliance of Commodity Trade in East and Southern Africa* (ACTESA); the *Comprehensive Framework for Action* (CFA); and the *Alliance for a Green Revolution in Africa* (AGRA), whose goals include helping smallholder farmers lift themselves out of poverty. An MOU was signed on 4 June 2008 between AGRA (which is supported by the Rockefeller Foundation and the Bill & Melinda Gates Foundation), the UK's Department for International Development and other donors, and the three Rome-based UN agencies (the FAO, IFAD and WFP). This underpinned the critical importance of working together to scale up farmers' access to inputs and markets to trigger their increased food production. At the signing ceremony, the WFP executive director Josette Sheeran said:

> WFP is delighted to work with AGRA, a critical player who will help stimulate agricultural production. Together with FAO and IFAD, we can bring major improvements in the lives of small-scale producers and food-insecure farmers all across Africa, and help reduce hunger and vulnerability.[10]

In essence, the P4P initiative is designed to allow the WFP to help those who have little or no food while also supporting local small-scale farmers who have little or no access to markets to sell their crops. It builds on the WFP's local food procurement and takes it a step further by enabling smallholder and low-income farmers to supply food to the WFP, and to gain more by doing so. P4P aims to identify and share best practices for governments, the WFP, NGOs, and agricultural market stakeholders to increase profitable engagement in markets. It plans to expand small-scale farmer capacities to increase their incomes from agricultural markets, and to identify and implement best practices for increasing low-income farmers' sales to the WFP. P4P also aims to transform WFP food purchases programmes to provide better support to sustainable production and to address the root causes of hunger.

A five-year pilot P4P initiative was launched at the UN General Assembly in September 2008. Its aim is to promote the development of agricultural markets in such a way that, by 2013, at least half a million low-income, smallholder farmers (most of whom are women) will produce food surpluses and sell them at a fair price to increase their income, thereby turning WFP local procurement into a vital tool to address global hunger. The initiative is funded by the Bill & Melinda Gates Foundation and the Howard G. Buffett Foundation (which together have committed $92 million as of 30 November 2010), the European Commission, and the governments of Belgium, Canada, France, Ireland, Luxembourg, and the United States. $137 million have been allocated to the WFP and partners for the five-year period for capacity-building activities, such as strengthening farmer associations, constructing warehouses, facilitating farmers' access to credit, providing training in P4P procedures, and ensuring the participation and empowerment of women. Pilot projects are being conducted in 21 countries: 15 in sub-Saharan Africa, two in Asia, and four in Latin America.[11]

P4P is an integral part of the WFP's local and regional procurement programme. It will use part of the WFP's regular procurement through the P4P pilot projects to test new ways for the WFP to purchase food in order to promote marketing opportunities for smallholder farmers. These include competitive processes, direct contracting, and forward contracting.

Competitive processes. These take place under conditions favourable to farmer organizations and small/medium traders, for example: pro-smallholder tendering practices with less stringent conditions, including smaller quantity bids, and those not requiring performance bonds and special bag markings; delivery points closer to the suppliers' warehouses; cereal fairs where producers and traders gather to market their commodities at which the WFP would be able to select sellers based on quality, prices offered and past performance; and commodity exchanges where sellers register their produce and describe the location and quality of commodities, and the WFP place bids to purchase.

Direct contracting. These are negotiations between the WFP and farmer organizations to purchase food commodities in order to 'bring demand down the value chain', while maintaining food quality and grade standards, such as a warehouse receipt system whereby farmers may deposit their commodities in a certified warehouse in return for a receipt, which could be exchanged for cash at a local institution. The commodities would meet certain quality and grade standards, and the value of the receipt would be equivalent to 60 per cent of the market value, the balance to be paid after the commodities were sold.

Forward contracting. These are contracts which commit the WFP to purchase a specified quantity and quality of a food commodity at some point in the future at a minimum guaranteed price. Food purchased through forward contracts may be for the WFP school feeding or nutrition improvement programmes, where demand could be more easily predicted, or for the development of local food processing with raw materials supplied by smallholders.

A crucial factor in P4P operations is that the WFP links its potential food purchasing capacity with partners who can supply the expertise, knowledge, and resources that support small-scale farmers to increase and improve the quantity and quality of their production. Over 150 partners are working with targeted farmer organizations to support P4P activities, and national co-ordination or steering committees have been established. The P4P initiative has also provided a focus for collaboration among the three Rome-based UN agencies. Through training and capacity-building, smallholder farmers are expected to develop the skills and tools to participate in agricultural markets by selling to the WFP and others. Access to credit, greater knowledge and understanding of how markets operate, and technical support provided by WFP partners are expected to facilitate farmers' engagement in markets that goes beyond selling their produce to the WFP.

Through P4P, the WFP is exploring ways of leveraging its presence in agricultural markets to promote market development, market access, and increased incomes for smallholder farmers; and how, when, and under what conditions to buy locally so as to maximize development impact without compromising food assistance objectives. A monitoring and evaluation system has been developed to track progress and assess results. Baseline surveys have been conducted in the countries where P4P pilot projects are being carried out. The lessons learned about effective approaches to help smallholder farmers benefit from the sale of their agricultural production through the P4P pilot projects will be widely shared with WFP partners and others. The objective would be for the best practices to be mainstreamed into government and aid agency policies and programmes, and shared with other public and private stakeholder in the agricultural sector. A technical review panel has been established to support the learning and sharing process by providing high-level independent advice to the WFP and to the P4P pilot projects. Its ten members have been selected to ensure individual and institutional diversity.

WFP procurement and market support staff undertake continuous market analysis in collaboration with external partners. Through P4P, this analysis is being strengthened at the local level to manage micro-level market distortions and to assess the impact of WFP market engagements. Independent surveyors/superintendents are employed to ensure product quality standards before WFP purchases are undertaken.

By 31 December 2010, P4P assessments had been completed in all 21 pilot countries, and 19 country implementation plans had been approved. By that date, over 125,000 tons of food was contracted by the WFP, either directly from farmer organizations or through other marketing arrangements, including commodity exchanges and the warehouse receipt system. Defaults were less than 13 per cent, caused mainly by side-selling due to price fluctuations within the contract lifetime or to the inabilities of farmer organizations to aggregate supplies owing to lack of access to credit. Over 140 farmer organizations had sold food commodities to the WFP.

The number, size, and typology of farmer organizations targeted vary greatly across countries, from 172 grass-roots level associations targeted in the Democratic Republic of the Congo, 99 in Guatemala who extended P4P to new districts under new donor funding, and 92 in Uganda to seven or eight farmer organizations in Afghanistan, Burkina Faso, Liberia, and Mozambique. The average number of farm organizations targeted by country is 15 to 20. Depending on the country context and specific P4P country goals, grass-roots level or higher-level organizations, including farmer unions and federations, can be targeted. This explains the important heterogeneity of country P4P models, which widens the spectrum of learning generated by the P4P pilot.

Purchasing from smallholder farmers has been carried out in line with the WFP's principles of quality and cost-efficiency. Local purchases under the P4P initiative have saved some $19 million, compared to importing the same commodities from abroad. Under the P4P initiative, the WFP has purchased food commodities for the first time in post-conflict countries, such as Liberia and Sierra Leone, where the aim is to re-energize markets. Purchases in Kenya, Malawi, Mali, Tanzania, and Zambia aim to support the development of innovative marketing arrangements, including the warehouse receipt system, that present new opportunities for smallholder farmers. The WFP and its P4P partners have trained more than 25,000 farmers and small and medium-size traders in warehouse operations. Faster delivery is another advantage of local or regional purchases. Other benefits include higher farm-gate prices, strengthened formal markets, and increases in investment by traders and processors.

In the implementation of P4P, a number of challenges have emerged for which donor and partner support is required. Market development is an important part of the support for smallholders to increase their productivity. But there are many other impediments that have to be addressed that are beyond the WFP's comparative advantages, of which market development is an important one, and which the WFP partners must simultaneously confront. Although donors have made funds available for implementing the technical aspects of P4P, timely cash contributions for commodity purchases from the smallholder farmers engaged in the P4P pilot projects are a necessary and fundamental part of the initiative. In addition, limited access to credit for funding crop aggregates and for the purchase of food commodities from participating farmers, farmer groups, and organizations is hindering their ability to market their products. This, together with a lack of storage facilities and crop cleaning equipment, is the cause of most side-selling-out of contract. Lack of credit has been identified as a major constraint in nearly all of the P4P pilot projects. Lack of storage and post-harvest handling equipment are other major problems facing farmers in many of the P4P pilot projects, leading to high post-harvest losses and encouraging side-selling.

Weak business management skills and lack of experience in handling and marketing their products is yet another major limitation for farmer organizations. Strengthening these organizations – including – their internal management, business plans, and record keeping – is an area requiring more WFP partner support. Misunderstandings regarding the ultimate goal of P4P persist among some partners, giving rise to concern that P4P's focus on smallholders might lead the WFP to compromise on product quality and/or pay above market prices. Another problem is that it has taken longer than expected to translate various agreements with partners, such as the MOU between AGRA and the Rome-based UN agencies, into action in the P4P pilot project in African countries. Potential and existing P4P partners that support farmer organizations are facing resourcing problems, and P4P has limited financial capacity to support their activities.

P4P pilot projects have also struggled to translate the WFP's gender targets for the advancement of women farmers within farmer organizations into action. More efforts are required and additional partners found to work specifically to enhance women farmers' positions within farmer organizations in order to ensure that women reap more of the economic benefits generated.

P4P is, essentially, a catalyst that offers an opportunity to ensure that food assistance is part of a long-term solution to the hunger challenge. It is based on the perception that lack of market access has been a major impediment to smallholder agricultural development. The initiative contributes to a much broader programme of efforts and investment in agricultural and market development. The WFP's role is to demonstrate how its purchases of food in local markets in developing countries can help to promote the development of small-scale agriculture and stimulate the growth of nascent markets.

Strategic priorities have been identified for P4P's development. The WFP's procurement processes and practices should be adapted and adjusted to allow experimentation in how the WFP does business for the benefit of smallholder farmers and organizations, including through engagement in emerging markets. The capacity of WFP staff, partners, and farmer organizations should be developed in critical areas, such as the reduction of post-harvest losses. Efforts should be co-ordinated so that the WFP's demand-side contribution through food commodity purchases is matched with supply-side support in order to increase productivity and prevent food price rises. Study should be made of what works, and the lessons learned shared widely. Finally, the crucial planning for exit and handover by the WFP should be put in place by ensuring strong links are established with buyers in the public sector (schools, hospitals, and such) and the private sector, in place of WFP purchases, so that smallholder farmers and organizations have the ability and choice to sell their products on a permanent basis.

The president of the World Bank, Robert B. Zoellick, has suggested that the G20 could help smallholder farmers become a bigger part of the solution to food security by helping them benefit from tenders from humanitarian purchasers, such as the WFP. He pointed out that this may require flexibility to allow development benefits – such as building local markets – to be taken into account in sourcing decisions, as envisioned in the P4P programme (Zoellick, 2011).

Voucher and cash transfer schemes

Background

There has been considerable experience in the past of both the benefits and problems of using voucher and cash transfer schemes to reach the hungry poor, in developed and developing countries, and in emergency situations, and development programmes and projects. Such schemes have long been used for welfare payments and in response to emergencies in developed countries, and through the insurance system and as part of relief action. China and India have a long history of their use (Dreze and Sen, 1989), and they were an important feature of famine response in African countries in the 1980s.

United States Food Stamps Programme

The United States federal food stamps programme (FSP) is the world's largest and longest-standing programme of its kind. The FSP was established in 1964 to provide basic nutrition to low-income individuals and families by supplementing their incomes with food stamp benefits. The FSP is administered by the Food and Nutrition Service of the United States Department of Agriculture (USDA) but implemented by the individual states, each of which is responsible for determining eligibility and benefit levels. It reached 36.5 million people in 2009 – one in eight Americans, and nearly one in four children – as the economic depression and job losses took effect. Past studies showed that an additional $1 of food stamps increased food consumption by between 17 and 47 per cent, as opposed to between 5 and 13 per cent induced by cash. The effect on nutrient availability was roughly between 2 and 7 times greater for food coupons than cash (Fraker, 1990).

Despite the fact that the FSP has an effective administration and infrastructure, with an estimated $90 million spent annually on the management of the programme, two reports of the US Government Accounting Office (GAO) illustrated some of the problems of its implementation. In 2001, a GAO report showed that many individuals and families who were eligible to receive benefits from the

FSP did not do so (GAO, 2004). While an average of about 16 million people per month received food stamps benefits, almost 11 million did not. Various reasons were given for the shortfall including: lack of knowledge about the FSP and of its eligibility criteria; the burdensome bureaucratic process and procedures, and the stigma attached to receiving food stamps. It was recommended that steps be taken to better inform the public about the FSP, and their eligibility, to ease the administrative process, to demonstrate the value of its benefits, and to reduce the attached stigma.

In 2005, a GAO report noted that states had made progress in reducing errors in paying out benefits from the FSP but that further challenges remained (GAO, 2005). In FY 2003, the FSP made payment errors totalling about $1.4 billion in benefits (about 7 per cent of the total $21.4 billion in benefits provided to a monthly average of 21 million low-income beneficiaries). It was recommended that steps be taken to minimize the errors, as they represented a misuse of public funds and could undermine public support for the programme. Almost two-thirds of the payment errors were found to be caused by case workers who failed to keep up with reported changes in entitlements, or made mistakes in applying programme rules. Almost one-third of the errors were cause by participants failing to report complete or correct information, such as household income and composition. State implementing officials said that the programme's complexity, lack of administrative resources, and staff turnover also contributed to the errors. An additional factor was that FSP beneficiaries received benefits from other welfare programmes with different rules and procedures, adding to the complexity of determining and monitoring eligibility and benefits received from all sources.

Consumer food subsidy programmes

Interest in consumer food subsidy programmes was accentuated during the 1980s because of concern with the increasing number of hungry people in developing countries as their access to food deteriorated during the world economic recession. Those concerns were exacerbated by the economic structural adjustment programmes that countries were force to implement, assisted by the World Bank and the IMF, and the need to find effective compensatory measures to protect the poor and address the social costs of the adjustment process.

Research undertaken by IFPRI over a period of almost ten years (1978–86) provided the results of consumer-oriented food subsidy programmes in a number of developing countries (Pinstrup-Andersen, 1988). It showed that these programmes could be a double-edged sword. They could be a powerful and cost-effective tool to reach certain social, economic, and political goals, or they could be harmful to growth and equity. As with so many other policy measures, the question was not whether they were good or bad, but when and how they were applied. They were also not the only means of keeping consumer prices low, and were open to abuse.

The programmes had different objects. These included: improving the real purchasing power or nutritional status of low-income groups; maintaining low urban nominal wages; reducing energy and nutrient deficiencies, or assuring social and political stability by protecting poor households from deteriorations in their already low standard of living while structural adjustment programmes were implemented. They also took different forms: directly government-financed, or indirectly supported through fiscal or exchange rate policy; and generally applied across the population, or highly targeted at specific population groups.

IFPRI's research showed that, used imaginatively, food subsidy programmes could be an effective way of reaching specific and limited policy goals with little or no negative effects in economic growth. They could result in healthier children, more productive adults, and stronger economic growth in the long run. Conversely, indiscriminately used, they were unlikely to be a cost-effective means by which to improve the welfare of the poor in the short run, and could have adverse effects on economic growth in the longer term. While consumer food subsidies had a positive role to play, in many cases that role was not properly specified. Failure to design or modify subsidy programmes to achieve objectives in the most cost-effective manner, and failure to discontinue or replace inappropriate programmes, resulted in high fiscal and economic costs, and misallocation of resources and transfers. In Egypt, for example, the annual costs of subsidy programmes during the first half of the 1980s were $2 billion (about 6 per cent of GNP).

The effectiveness and efficiency of a food subsidy programme depended, crucially, on its design and how it was implemented. A food stamps programme, such as that in the United States, was best suited to more-developed economies with effective administrations and infrastructure. Modifying existing programmes may improve their performance. Pursuing rationing or price stabilization may require programmes that were different from those needed to ensure efficient income transfer or the efficient achievement of nutrition improvement goals. Many existing programmes and policies changed over time from public distribution schemes, aimed at assuring poor households access to certain rations of basic food staples at fixed prices, to food-linked income-transfer programmes. Some changes were cause by default rather than design, such as when inability to increase the price of food rations at the same rate as price increases in the open market rendered the subsidy programme cost-ineffective.

Targeting poor households was found to be a key element in achieving income-transfer or nutritional gaols at reduced costs. But this was often logistically difficult, and could result in economic losses for non-targeted households, also incurring political opposition. The political costs of reducing subsidies, especially if undertaken without appropriate political preparation, could be higher than the economic gains. The benefits of food subsidies to political leaders could be important and sufficient to sustain them when other redistribution programmes were ended. But they could also result in their abuse. A further consideration was that there was a point beyond which increases in administrative staff and costs involved in reaching poor households could not be economically supported.

Often, a balance had to be struck between criteria that focused on the poorest households and less exacting criteria that focused on a community or area basis, without dissipating scarce resources and impact, or biasing benefits in favour of any one particular group. Many of the difficulties involved may be overcome if the target population itself were involved in the design, implementation, and evaluation of subsidy programmes. Risk assessment and vulnerability mapping could provide useful operational tools for focusing attention on those most in need, and for determining the types and amounts of assistance required. In the absence of reliable data, appropriate rapid appraisal and beneficiary participation techniques could be used to establish the parameters for targeting, which could be further defined through the operation of intervention measures.

The IFPRI research findings concluded that 'consumer food subsidy programs should be seen as a temporary but important means of ensuring that the poor can acquire sufficient food for nutritional requirements while such capacity [for them to acquire such food for themselves] is being created'. But opportunities for using food subsidies to create self-sustaining income-generating capacity among the poor 'have not been fully exploited and should be pursued'. To be cost-effective, 'it is essential that the programme be targeted'. The most important lesson learned was that consumer food subsidies could be a 'powerful and cost-effective policy tool to reach certain social, economic, and political goals, or they can be harmful to growth and equity'. This depended on when and how they were applied.

Cash-based responses in emergencies

Over the past decade, the perception of voucher and cash-based schemes in humanitarian relief has shifted dramatically from 'radical and risky' to a mainstream programming approach (ALNAP, 2009). Food aid represents the largest proportion of humanitarian aid, accounting for over half of all contributions to UN appeals since the start of the new millennium (GHA, 2008: 27). However, longstanding and widespread dissatisfaction and criticism of the large-scale distribution of food, and of in-kind goods in general, as a 'default response' during humanitarian crises, persisted. While it doubtless saved many lives, it was also perceived to have been 'over-used, irrespective of needs and contexts'. The drivers of food aid were seen to be political and economic as well as humanitarian, with the needs and well-being of food aid recipients being just one of a number of competing and often incompatible interests. The view was expressed that a re-casting of food aid's role, and the roles played by the main stakeholders, could:

> substantially reduce the negative effects of food aid and contribute substantively to development and humanitarian policy objectives... [but]... the global constellation of agencies and actors engaged in food aid programmes has been insufficiently proactive in engaging these debates so as to bring about the sorts of reforms that could render food aid a far more effective and less controversial instrument of development and humanitarian policy. (Barnett and Maxwell, 2005: 223–4)

The rationale for using vouchers and cash in dispensing humanitarian aid was increased markedly by the work of Amartya Sen on famines and his finding that the problem was not so much lack of food but, rather, poor people's access to it (Sen, 1981). In 2000, a groundbreaking study by the British Red Cross noted:

> the practical experience so far, limited as it is, provides evidence that direct cash distribution, in the right circumstances and with careful planning and monitoring, can be more timely, less costly and more empowering to local communities than traditional food distribution. (Peipiat *et al.*, 2000)

Reluctance to adopt voucher and cash distribution schemes was attributed to incentives and inertia that perpetuated the dominance of food aid, combined with a paternalistic perception that they were not feasible because recipients and governments could not be trusted to use them effectively. Several important events and initiatives occurred in the early part of 2000 that led to the acceptance of voucher and cash schemes. The Indian Ocean tsunami of late 2004 led to money becoming available to implement more cash programmes and to document them, and to promote learning activities to embed practices. A series of reports and publications helped to bring vouchers and cash transfers back to the top of the policy agenda (Harvey, 2005, 2006; Harvey and Lind, 2005; Farrington and Slater, 2006). Also, advances in information and communication technology (CTC) provided a breakthrough for their adoption. They could be applied to every sector of humanitarian assistance – food, shelter, health, water, and sanitation. In May 2007, a joint statement by the WHO, WFP, UNICEF and the SCN endorsed the community-based management of severe acute malnutrition among children, stating: 'properly combined with a family-based approach for those malnourished children with complications and implemented on a large scale, CTC could prevent the death of hundreds of thousands of children' (WHO *et al.*, 2007).

Early WFP experience

The WFP has supported a number of development projects in the past in which vouchers and cash transfers were employed.[12] In India, for example, it was common practice for workers engaged on the construction of irrigations systems to receive their WFP food-for-work rations through government fair-price shops located in the project area, where they collected their entitlements in exchange for food-wage vouchers issued by the executing agency for the work performed. To improve the social and economic conditions of the poorest people living and working in the forest areas of India, workers were given food coupons with their cash wages according to their entitlement. They were given the option of voluntarily surrendering a portion of their cash wages in return for a WFP family ration. The funds generated were deposited in an interest-bearing account and used for various works, such as the provision of drinking water, school repairs, construction of a hotel for schoolboys, and the construction of storage facilities.

In an innovative paper to the WFP's governing body on 'Anti-Hunger Strategies of Poor Households and Communities: Roles of Food Aid' (WFP, 1989c), it was noted the food aid could help to stabilize farmer income fluctuations by financing credit schemes for poor farmers with funds created from food aid sales. In a WFP-supported project in Colombia, for example, the constraints faced by smallholder farmers through lack of low-interest credit was overcome by creating a special credit fund. This was achieved by selling WFP commodities to the Colombian Institute of Family Welfare (WFP, 1987c). The credit fund was used to promote the production, processing, and marketing activities of the farmers associations. Credit was also given to enable women's associations to engage in activities such as small animal production units, and milk and cheese processing; and fruit and vegetable production, processing, and marketing. Once the farmer associations assisted by the credit scheme became consolidated and achieved profitable activities, they were able to meet the collateral required of other credit institutions charging higher interest rates. In the meantime, promotional work with the farmer associations involved organizational skills, training, and the provision of technical assistance.

A particularly innovative project involved WFP support for the development of human resources in five island nations in the Eastern Caribbean. This was undertaken through health and nutrition centres for mothers and pre-school children, day-care centres, primary education, vocational training, improvements in environmental health and sanitation, and smallholder farmer agricultural development (WFP, 1990c). The five island nations were Antigua and Barbuda, Dominica, Grenada, Saint. Kitts and Nevis, and Saint Vincent and the Grenadines. They were all members of the Organization of Eastern Caribbean States, established in 1981 as sub-regional group to consolidate efforts in economic integration and co-operation in agriculture and industry, and in foreign policy. They all have smaller populations and fewer human, financial, and natural resources than other Caribbean countries.

The WFP faced severe operational constraints in helping these states. It was complex and costly to ship small tonnages of food to each country separately. It was difficult to provide a complete food basket on a timely basis. And there was the risk of deterioration of commodities with a limited shelf-life. To overcome these problems, the WFP arranged with a donor to monetize food commodities in the donor country. The funds generated were transferred by the WFP to the projects in the five countries and placed in interest-bearing accounts with commercial banks. Withdrawals from the accounts were authorized by project management committees, which included representatives from the Ministries of Health and Education, in consultation with the WFP. The funds were used mainly to purchase locally-produced food commodities. A small part was used to complement government investments in upgrading the health and education infrastructure.

During the 1980s, developing countries faced a world economic recession of unprecedented magnitude since the Great Depression of the 1930s. Often encouraged and supported by the IMF and the World Bank, they sought to adjust their economies to the realities of their internal and international conditions. Unless far-reaching structural and sectoral adjustments were made, drastic demand-restricting measures would have to be imposed in order to avoid total economic, and perhaps political, collapse. At the same time, particular concern was expressed about the 'social costs' of the adjustment process on the poor, and the need for what came to be called 'adjustment with a human face' to protect the vulnerable and promote economic growth with equity (Cornia *et al.*, 1987).

A number of food aid donors and the WFP began to work closely and systematically with the World Bank in relating food aid to the Bank's adjustment lending programmes. The issues were complex, and the parties involved sought collaboration with different motives in mind. But it was generally understood that mutual benefits could be forthcoming from an association of food aid with adjustment measures (Shaw and Singer, 1988, Singer, 1991). An example was the food entitlement programme in Jamaica, for which WFP food aid was approved in 1988. The government had embarked on a programme of progressively restructuring the economy, including the removal of basic food subsidies and the full liberalization of the exchange rate. To mitigate the negative effects on the most vulnerable groups of the population, the government instituted a safety-net programme. This included a food stamps scheme (FSS) to provide basic food items to 200,000 expectant and nursing mothers, children up to five years of age, and 200,000 elderly, indigent, and very poor people. WFP commodities were provided for sale to generate funds to cover about 25 per cent of the face value of the overall monthly cost of the FSS and to provide budgetary support. An evaluation of the project found that WFP assistance had achieved the twin objectives of income support to the most vulnerable and budgetary support to the government (WFP, 1993c).

The Prime Minister of Jamaica, Edward Seaga, addressed the WFP's governing body in the WFP's 25th anniversary year in June 1988. Referring to his country's five-year 'social well-being programme', he said that food aid had the capability simultaneously to: address the problems of the most vulnerable groups; provide balance of payments support; be doubly advantageous to recipient countries, if given in grant form; and be particularly useful, if monetized, in providing up-front cash to meet the expenditure needs of social programmes.

In a world recession calling for harsh economic adjustments, he felt that the WFP's governing body had:

> the opportunity, through innovation and imaginative approaches, to press home the greater awareness of the flexibility of food aid as a multi-purpose mechanism to increase the momentum of economic development and enhance the quality of life. (WFP, 1988)[13]

However, there were conflicting signals in the WFP's governing body. While many delegations welcomed the use of WFP assistance in structural adjustment programmes, others cautioned against what they perceived as a policy of pursuing greater monetization of WFP commodities or various forms of programme aid in support of World Bank structural lending programmes with which they did not agree. The WFP secretariat was therefore requested to prepare a study on the roles of food aid in structural and sectoral adjustment programmes (WFP,

1986d: 14). Meetings were held between World Bank and WFP staff in August and December 1986 in preparation for the requested paper, which was presented to the governing body session in May/June 1987 (WFP, 1987d).

Four major roles were identified for food aid: providing general financial support through savings in foreign exchange or budgetary support; supporting reform measures within a particular sector of the economy, particularly the food and agricultural sector, which could involve partial or full monetization and a multi-year commitment; as an investment resource in special development projects and programmes that supported adjustment measures; and, perhaps most obviously, as compensation for the social costs of those adversely affected by the adjustment reform measures. The most serious concern was that food-aided compensatory measures should not be used to try to make politically and socially palatable adjustment measures that involved disproportionate cost for the poor. The WFP was adamant in its discussions, both with the World Bank and later with the IMF, that this should not happen.[14]

The WFP secretariat suggested that the governing body might wish to respond to its paper in the form of a resolution, which recommended that: the potential roles of food aid should be given explicit attention from the inception of preparations for structural and sectoral adjustment programmes, and not as an add-on or afterthought; the CSD should make use of the existing provisions in the *FAO Principles of Surplus Disposal* to waive UMRs for low-income, food-deficit countries that were heavily burdened by debt and facing severe balance of payments problems while undergoing economic structural adjustment measures; donors should provide additional food aid to those countries on a multi-year basis with flexible drawing rights; food aid used in compensatory projects should not be automatically subject to suspension if adjustment reforms were not carried out on schedule; and food aid should be used particularly to support the productive capacity and the well-being of the poor, promote equitable adjustment with growth, and thereby reduce the social costs and enhance the human dimension of adjustment (WFP, 1987e: 20–1).

The governing body did not adopt the proposed resolution. It was clear that insufficient discussion had taken place with governing body members to dispel misunderstandings before the paper was presented, a lesson that was later closely followed. Most delegations could not give definitive views without fuller consideration with their governments. Several delegations interpreted the paper as a call for additional food aid, with increasing monetization, and with conditionality imposed by the World Bank, which they could not accept. The governing body did, however, agree that 'the matter would be the subject of continuing discussion over time in the light of practical experience and the secretariat would submit a report in that regard at a future session' (WFP, 1987e: 13), which was never done.

An evaluation of ten years of World Bank experience with adjustment lending at the end of the 1980s concluded that: 'Adjustment lending ... is both a potentially high pay-off and high risk instrument. There is, therefore, the need to continue to adapt and improve policies and procedures of structural lending to increase its effectiveness' (World Bank, 1988: 9). Adjustment programmes were also considered to have a negative effect on food security (FAO, 1989). A history of the World Bank found that the bank and its critics were guilty of 'overkill' in their assessments of adjustment lending. 'In many cases, the critics let ideological predilections turn correlations into causality. For the World Bank's part, too much was claimed' (Kapur *et al.*, 1997: 544). Adjustment programmes as supported by the World Bank and IMF remained controversial. Negative effects of adjustment on the poor were often certain and immediate, while positive effects remained uncertain and long-term. They also tended to be more contractionist (exacerbating income inequality), rather than expansionist (involving the poor in the development process, and contributing to equitable and sustainable development).

Voucher and cash transfer schemes revisited

A number of factors on the demand and supply side of the equation came together that resulted in the WFP re-examining the appropriateness of direct in-kind food distribution or voucher and cash transfer schemes in any given situation. On the demand side, some of these factors applied to advances in developing countries that have now made it more possible to consider the alternatives, including: improvements in the functioning of markets; the integration of food systems; the pace of urbanization; and, critically, improvements in financial services and their spread into rural areas, which, together with the evolution in information and communications technology, have made it possible for agricultural and rural communities to access these services for the first time. Additional factors have been: increasing interest in social protection programmes; the effect of the sharp increase in international food and energy prices; combined later with the global financial crisis; and the effects of in-kind food distribution or voucher and cash transfer schemes on living standards in the developing world. On the supply side, donors have shown greater flexibility in their aid budgets, including increased provision of cash, as opposed to in-kind food transfers, in support of food security and social protection programmes; and in emergency operations and development projects. They have, in part, been motivated by the continuing debate in the World Trade Organization (WTO) on the future of food aid.

The debate has been energized by a remarkable outpouring of studies, reports, and conferences on both theoretical and operational aspects, and the response to major disasters, including the Indian Ocean tsunami. Prominent in this work have been the Humanitarian Policy Group (HPG) at the Overseas Development Institute (ODI) in London; the Institute for Development Studies (IDS) at the University of Sussex, UK; and NGOs. The HPG carried out a three-year research project looking into when the option of giving people money instead of, or as well as, in-kind food assistance was feasible and appropriate (Harvey, 2007). This built upon a discussion paper published in early 2005 on the role of cash and voucher schemes in emergencies (Harvey, 2005), a document on learning from cash-based responses to the Indian Ocean tsunami (Adams and Harvey, 2006), and a conference held at ODI in January 2006 (ODI, 2006).[15]

The HPG study pointed out that humanitarian aid agencies still overwhelmingly provided disaster-affected people with food aid and other material items, rather than money to enable them to invest in their own priorities for recovery. Obstacles to the use of appropriate cash were perceived to be partly institutional in that donors (and aid agencies) continued to tie their assistance to food aid, and to its use in the objectives and countries they favoured. Reluctance to use cash was also seen as a function of the attitudes of aid providers and the sense that providing cash was threatening because it implied handing over power from the aid agency to the beneficiary.

Nevertheless, the HPG group welcomed the growing interest in the use of cash and considered that there was a strong case for continuing to expand its use in emergencies. At the same time, it cautioned that cash-based responses were neither a panacea nor universally appropriate. They were one element of what was called the 'humanitarian toolbox', and were a complement to in-kind assistance, not a replacement. Furthermore, cash-based responses had their own risks. They could trigger inflation in local markets, and suffer from poor implementation and management; they also faced problems of exclusion, poor targeting, and corruption, as with any other form of aid. Another consideration was that much remained to be done to build the skills and capacities of staff to deliver this relatively new form of aid, both in aid agencies and in developing countries. This should be achieved through training programmes, and by learning from experience through appropriate monitoring and evaluation systems.

The study concluded that a strong body of evidence was starting to emerge that indicated that providing disaster victims with cash or vouchers worked. It was possible to target and distribute cash or vouchers safely, and recipients used them sensibly on basic essentials and on rebuilding their livelihoods. Cash transfers and vouchers could also provide a stimulus to local economies and, in appropriate contexts, could be more cost-effective than commodity-based alternatives. As part of the UN reform process, the study recommended that consideration be given to where responsibility for implementing cash-based responses to food insecurity should lie, and to allow for the inclusion of cash and voucher responses in the UN emergency assistance appeals. Cash-based welfare safety nets may also be a more appropriate mechanism for addressing chronic and long-term food insecurity and poverty. Ways should therefore be investigated to link cash-based emergency responses more closely with emerging social protection systems and safety nets.

The growing body of evidence that emerged from the increasing number of detailed empirical studies not only challenged the arguments against cash transfer and voucher schemes, but also revealed that they could take many forms. For example, cash grants or relief could be given to destitute people with no conditions or work requirements. Cash-for-work could be given to people engaged in public works programmes. Conditional cash transfers could be provided to people on the condition that they performed some specific task, such as attending school, or planting crops, or if they were being demobilized from armed service.

Also, vouchers could be given to people to provide access to a particular good or service, or a bundle of them, often at subsidized rates.

Research work confronted two prominent views that were at the forefront of the debate about providing social assistance in developing countries. The first was that it caused disincentives to work, as was part of the controversy over the *Rural Employment Guarantee Scheme* in India (Dreze, 2005). In response to such concern, work requirements were imposed on beneficiaries of social assistance programmes in Africa. The second, more prominent view was that social assistance payments had purely consumption effects and no effect on productivity, representing what was described as 'money down the drain'. The results of a growing number of research studies showed that they need not be wasteful and could achieve a positive impact on production.

Not surprisingly, in view of the results of field research there was an upsurge of policy interest in cash transfers and voucher schemes. They were the central theme of the OECD/DAC/Povnet Social Protection thematic group. They were made a central plank of the social protection strategies of donors. International conferences took place on cash transfers. And the World Bank had a growing cadre of headquarters and country-based staff working on a range of cash transfer issues. A World Bank policy research team supported by an advisory committee of American and British academics produced a report on conditional cash transfers (CCTs) in 2009 (Fiszbein and Schady, 2009). The report noted that CCTs had become increasingly popular in developing countries for reducing income-poverty, while requiring beneficiaries to make pre-investments in child health and education, which had been adopted, or were being considered, 'at a prodigious rate'. Virtually every country in Latin America had a CCT programme, and there were large-scale programmes in other developing regions. Interest had also spread to developed countries and to donor agencies. The impact of the global financial crisis of 2008 on living standards in the developing world had given renewed emphasis to the importance of social safety-net programmes, such as CCTs.

Drawing on a number of evaluations of the impact of CCTs on poverty, education, health, and nutrition, the report concluded that CCTs had been generally successful in reducing poverty and in encouraging parents to invest in their children's health and education. Poverty had been 'substantially reduced', especially when the cash transfer had been adequate, well-targeted, and structured in a way that did not discourage recipients from taking other actions to escape poverty. By providing a steady stream of income, CCTs helped buffer poor households from the worst effects of unemployment, illness, and other sudden income shocks. Also, as they particularly targeted women, they increased their bargaining power, considered to be an important goal in many contexts. The report also notes, however, that even the best-designed CCTs could not meet all the needs of a social protection system, and are only one element of a wider approach that should include many other features, including work, employment, and social pension programmes. Experience showed that targeting was easier to implement than conditionality. CCTs should therefore fit within a country's social protection strategy, and are not the only programmes appropriate for that purpose.

A group of researchers at the Brooks World Poverty Institute and the Chronic Poverty Research Centre at the University of Manchester, and at the International Development Centre of the Open University, UK have taken the argument to its ultimate conclusion (Hanlon *et al.*, 2010). They recommend that simply giving money to the poor with no strings or conditions attached may be the most promising approach not only to avoiding hardship and reducing poverty, but also for long-term development as well. They identify five principles: cash grants must be seen to be fair, in the sense that most citizens agree on the choice of who receives them and who do not. Recipients must be convinced that the money will really arrive regularly and that families can depend on it. A practical and reliable system should be in place to identify legitimate recipients and to ensure that they receive their grants regularly. Grants must be large enough to cause a real change in behaviour, such as growing new crops or sending children to school. And any grant programme must be politically acceptable and popular, and a vote-winner. They point out that cash transfer programmes are now prominent in six major developing countries (Brazil, China, India, Indonesia, Mexico, and South Africa) and that at least 45 developing countries give cash transfers to more than 110 million families.

WFP's reaction

The developments described above encouraged the WFP to re-examine its own policy and programming regarding cash transfers and voucher schemes compared to direct in-kind food assistance (Gentilini, 2007). Building on WFP experience and the work of others, five key determinants were identified in selecting food or cash/voucher transfers: first, was the importance of clearly defining a programme's objective at the outset, be it to save lives, transfer income, or improve nutrition. The second key determinant was the relevance of assessing the status of markets to determine whether to provide food or cash. For example, where local markets functioned well, cash transfers or vouchers should be provided to targeted recipients rather than food aid. Where markets did not function well but sufficient food was available, food aid should be provided based on local purchases or triangular transactions. Where insufficient food was available, food aid should be shipped in from outside (Barrett and Maxwell, 2005: 202).[16] But as markets did not function perfectly, a flexible approach should be adopted that could be adjusted to changing market conditions. Cost effectiveness and efficiency of cash transfers or food aid comprised the third key determinant, as these should take into account the specific circumstances that existed at the time when aid was to be provided. Fourth, the administrative capacity required to deliver and implement food or cash/voucher transfers should be assessed, drawing from actual experience across countries. Finally, beneficiary preferences should be taken into account, disaggregated spatially, temporally, and by gender.

A central conclusion was that the appropriateness of food or cash/voucher transfers could not be predetermined before examining these key determinants. A number of factors warned against drawing definitive conclusions, including: the robustness of the evidence; the short-term perspective of, and the problems of scaling up from, pilot projects; the need to consider not only the cash versus food option, but also the possibility of cash and food alternatives, to see them as components of broader social protection strategies, and to remove the outdated dichotomy of food in emergency operations and cash in development projects; and consideration of cross-cutting issues that applied to both kinds of transfers, including sound needs assessments, monitoring of markets, emergency preparedness mechanisms and contingency plans, the attachment of conditionalities, and targeting modalities. A 'productive and balanced debate' on cash and food transfers 'should be anchored to policies for addressing the root causes of food insecurity' (Gentilini, 2007). A pragmatic approach was needed in order to better understand factors generating vulnerability *in a given context* (original emphasis) to identify the most appropriate options, ensure that conditions were in place for effective implementation and monitoring, and embed such programmes within broader development and social protection strategies.

We saw in Chapter 4 that the WFP secretariat presented a policy paper to the WFP's executive board in 2008 containing proposals for the use of cash and voucher transfer schemes that could be used as complements or alternatives to existing food assistance modalities. This was part of the WFP's move towards more flexible tools for addressing hunger issues (WFP, 2008h). The executive board agreed that such schemes could serve to maximize the efficiency of food interventions, and help markets and farmers in recipient countries. They cautioned, however, that the WFP should proceed with care, given the risks involved and the need to ensure that they complemented national programmes. They reasoned that cash and voucher transfer schemes were likely to be more efficient in transition and development situations, and where markets were functioning; they could, however, be used in emergencies in appropriate implementing conditions.

It was agreed that such schemes would be used only in the context of food assistance for vulnerable people. Where appropriate market and implementing capacities were in place, it was felt that they could foster economic advancement, empower beneficiaries, and improve the cost-effectiveness of interventions. Cash and voucher transfer schemes could also give opportunities for new WFP partnerships, including with the private sector. However, they should be used wherever possible with country-led initiatives, such as social protection and safety-net systems.

Innovations in food assistance

The first and immediate impact of the adoption of cash and voucher transfer schemes and other food assistance tools was to lead to increasing the WFP's innovations in providing food assistance, as portrayed in *Revolution: From Food Aid to Food Assistance. Innovations in Overcoming Hunger* (Omamo *et al.*, 2010a).[17]

The book contains 21 chapters on innovative pilot projects and experience written by 46 contributors, mainly WFP staff, working on the front line in the battle against world hunger. It provides an account of some of the most imaginative and innovative approaches now being tried, and of the lessons learned so far in finding sustainable solutions to overcoming hunger and malnutrition. It makes a compelling case for partnerships between the WFP and a wide range of actors and agencies, and provides a rich reference source for researchers, practitioners, and policy-makers in the search for food security for the hungry poor.

In her foreword to the book, WFP executive director Sheeran states that, with the unveiling of the WFP *Strategic Plan (2008–13)*: 'WFP has moved from a food aid to a food assistance agency that delivers in emergencies and empowers the hungry to overcome food insecurity'. She points out that never before has the need for innovation and tested hunger solutions been greater, with conflict-induced and natural disasters, and economic crises pushing the number of hungry and malnourished people to historically high levels. With staff in more than 70 developing countries, and over 45 years of working with the people and governments in developing nations and the donor governments, aid agencies, and private sector in the developed world, the WFP aims to build resilience in responding to 'the world's most challenging disaster' – hunger. In doing so, she describes the WFP as 'one of the foremost incubators in designing and testing programmes that deliver results for hungry people'.

In her view, it is essential to take proven solutions to the field, scale them up, and constantly innovate to improve, in order to reverse the negative trend in the fight against hunger. Therefore, food assistance, not food aid, must meet dual objectives: to deploy safety nets to beat hunger sustainably and comprehensively, and to cushion vulnerable people from inevitable shocks; and to respond to emergencies caused by conflict and nature, so that they do not turn into humanitarian tragedies. Within a comprehensive and linked strategy, these two approaches can help build resilience to future disasters; provide jobs, education, nutrition, and health; and help move people and nations to sustainable food security – the *leitmotiv* of food assistance.

In their overview, the book's editors state that the ultimate aims of the book are:

> to identify and document innovative interventions from WFP's work around the world, drawing lessons from these initiatives, yield further advancements in food assistance knowledge and practice, and thereby enhance evidence-based food assistance policy making and programming. (Omamo *et al.*, 2010: 3)

In so doing, the book shows WFP not only as a provider of food, but also as a deliverer of solutions to the hunger problem. This historical shift – the 'revolution' in the book's title – has, in the editors' opinion, positioned WFP as a 'catalyst of practical hunger innovations with fundamental changes in the way WFP implements programs, shapes key policy debates, and engages strategically with actors and partners'.

The term 'innovation' is used to refer to the sweeping changes brought about by the application of novel products and processes, and the refinement of existing routines, within the WFP's action arena. 'Food assistance' is defined as a set of interventions designed to provide access to food by vulnerable and food-insecure people. Three dimensions of food assistance are covered in the book. The first is in terms of instruments, such as in-kind food, vouchers or cash transfers, to assure access to food of a given quantity, quality or value. These instruments can be used to pursue specific objectives, such as improving nutrition and education, or reducing risk reduction. The second is in terms of the WFP's engagement in various thematic areas of work or sectors, including agricultural development, disaster risk reduction, nutrition, education and protection, especially of women – which throw up challenges as diverse as their objectives, requiring a varied set of innovations. And third, supportive activities and institutional arrangements are required to implement innovations, including technical support, capacity-building, and partnerships with a wide range of actors and agencies. Space restrictions allow only a brief description of the 21 innovations included in the book, but sufficient to give an idea of the wide-ranging case studies provided.

Instruments

Seven examples are given of permutations of voucher and cash transfer schemes in diverse situations. The WFP's food voucher scheme in Burkina Faso is the first of its kind in sub-Saharan Africa (Ouattara and Sandström, 2010: 19–32). This initiative was set up to respond to high food prices that severely affected the poor and food-insecure. The initiative features two areas in which the WFP is gaining experience: the implementation of relatively large-scale voucher programmes; and operations in urban areas. These two approaches pose several operational challenges, such as targeting in urban areas where 'everybody is poor', and dealing with constraints caused by fragile markets. But the lessons learned from this pilot venture illustrate that – carefully designed and implemented – voucher schemes can be successful even when administrative capacity is limited.

In the Occupied Palestinian Territory, the WFP is implementing a voucher programme to mitigate the impact of high food and fuel prices on food-insecure households in a protracted conflict situation (Galluzzi and Natsheh, 2010: 33–52). In an economy weakened by the restricted movement of foods, trade, and people, distributing vouchers has two objectives: to improve dietary diversity and nutrition among urban households; and to stimulate the business and farming sectors, as the vouchers are used to obtain mainly locally-produced protein-rich food commodities.

In Pakistan, through the longest operating voucher programme in Asia (set up in 1994 to address the high logistic costs associated with direct food aid transfers) several objectives are being explored (Brinkman *et al.*, 2010: 53–64). These include: scaling up from a pilot venture; carrying out joint programming; engaging intra-community support in programme execution; testing vouchers in other

WFP programmes using index-based vouchers; participating in national social protection initiatives; and undertaking a rigorous impact evaluation. A national disaster caused by flooding of large parts to the country in 2010 had devastating effects of crops, livestock, and livelihoods. It remains to be seen if and when voucher schemes can be used effectively in the process of relief, recovery, and rehabilitation.

An electronic voucher scheme in Syria has shown that innovative delivery mechanisms can provide opportunities for efficient and secure management, and prompt monitoring and reporting (Elguindi, 2010: 65–74). The scheme, the first of its kind to operate though mobile phones, serves Iraqi refugees who have access to markets but no legal income-generating opportunities. The first phase of this pilot project confirmed that the voucher scheme reduced the re-sale of food items, a major problem with in-kind food aid programmes.

The cash transfer initiative in post-tsunami Sri Lanka is one of the first of its kind in the aftermath of a major emergency (Sandström and Tchatchua, 2010: 75–88). An evaluation carried out as part of this pilot project, comparing the impact of cash and food transfers, provided important insights, particularly on positive changes in households' consumption patterns, and gender-related controls and preferences.

A combined food and cash transfer initiative in Malawi provided information into the cost-efficiency versus cost-effectiveness of the two transfer modalities (Audsley *et al.*, 2010: 89–102). A detailed cost/benefit analysis showed that, while in rural Malawi food is cheaper to deliver than cash, households receiving cash transfers showed considerable improvements in food consumption and dietary diversity.

Pilot weather-index insurance schemes have been implemented in China and Ethiopia (Balzer and Hess, 2010: 103–20). These schemes, which are gaining increased interest under the threat of global climate change, seek to build resilience to the likely effects of extreme weather events that displace or wipe out food security assets and result in negative coping strategies that have led to generational poverty and hunger. The objective is that climate risk insurance can facilitate adjustments to climate change that protect natural, ecological, human, and economic assets from degradation and displacement, thereby safeguarding food security.

Thematic areas

Examples are given of WFP innovations in contributing to agricultural development, disaster risk reduction, improvements in nutrition, education and health, and protection of the beneficiaries of its food assistance.

The WFP's contribution to agricultural development through what has become a flagship programme, *Purchase for Progress* (P4P), has been described (pp. 000–00). An example of disaster risk reduction measures is given in the WFP's multiannual experience with the *Managing Environmental Resources to Enable Transition* (MERIT) programme in Ethiopia (Nedessa and Wickrema, 2010: 139–56).[18] Experience from this programme shows how food assistance can support effective disaster risk reduction over wide areas. While meeting the immediate food needs of food-insecure people, the programme strives to address the factors causing their vulnerability. This is achieved by supporting sustainable land management and increased productivity measures through watershed management, participatory approaches, and technical rigour that enhance poor communities' livelihoods and resilience.

Two examples are given of the WFP's initiatives to improve nutrition. One involves the introduction of new and improved food products (de Pee *et al.*, 2010: 157–75). Specially formulated foods have opened up new ways of improving nutrition, but a thorough understanding of the causes of malnutrition is crucial, as well as advances in food technology. With partners in the private sector, food commodities are being developed, improved, and added to the WFP food basket to meet the nutritional needs of beneficiaries more effectively. Recent developments include addressing the needs of specific target groups, including infants aged under two years, moderately malnourished children, pregnant and lactating women, and people living with HIV/AIDS or TB. New strategies are being implemented, including fortification of food at home to address micronutrient deficiencies, ready-to-use supplementary foods for treating malnourished children, and food supplements to complement the diets of infants aged six to 23 months to prevent malnutrition.

The second example concerns the use of food technology to produce safe and nutritious food (Bounie *et al.*, 2010: 177–94). Advances in food technology have enabled the WFP to improve the quality, taste, convenience, and safety of the commodities in its food basket. Fortified foods, fortified blended foods, and ready-to-use foods for children can now be prepared according to local habits and tastes. Many can be easily produced using basic technologies that require low technical know-how and capacity. A continuing challenge is to develop ready-to-eat meals to complement fortified high protein biscuits during the early stages of emergencies. In this area of development and innovation, WFP food technologists are co-operating with universities and the food industry to develop technological and associated innovations that may be used in humanitarian crises, such as new processes, equipment, technological skills, and regulations, and evolving scientific theories.

The evolution of the WFP's decade of food assistance in the care and treatment of HIV/AIDS victims (see Chapter 5) is reviewed (Erdelmann *et al.*, 2010: 195–216). Special attention is paid to the institutional innovations and scientific advances that have taken place in the past ten years that have shaped the directions and approaches of interventions. The WFP's approach and assistance has been shaped by rapid scientific, epidemiological, and political development, and has contributed to national and global priority-setting.

Through its school feeding programmes, the WFP has been a contributor to the spread and strengthening of education throughout the developing world from the inception of its operations in 1963. In its new approach, the WFP is seeking to change its role from direct implementer of these programmes to that of enabler, capacity-builder, adviser, and repository of best practice in fostering national ownership and county-led approaches (Molinas and Regnault de la Mothe, 2010: 217–30). The ultimate aim is to align school feeding programmes more closely with national development strategies, education polices, and financing provisions. The multiple impacts of school feeding are summarized from growing empirical evidence.

Working in complex emergencies and conflict situations, the WFP faces serious and different protection concerns ranging from violence during food delivery and distribution to human rights abuses by the afflicted population as well as its own staff and other humanitarian workers, as shown in the examples of complex emergencies. The steps taken by the WFP in promoting protection, safety, and dignity are described, which demonstrate that the WFP can use its food assistance to address protection concerns (Crawford *et al.*, 2010: 231–54).

Supportive activities and institutional arrangements

In order for WFP innovations to work, a number of supportive and preparatory activities have first to be performed and institutional arrangements made.

To gauge the impact of global economic crises on household food security, the WFP has developed leading methods to gather, analyze, and interpret macro- and micro-level data, and outline the findings and lessons learned from these studies (Sanogo and Luma, 2010: 259–73). The objectives of these assessments were: to determine country-specific transmission channels of the impacts of global food, fuel, and financial shocks on changes in the food security of households; and to determine what mitigating responses might be appropriate. In-depth studies of food markets were central because in most contexts key impacts are transmitted through these markets.

Emergency preparedness tools and activities are crucial in mitigating the impacts of disasters. The ways in which information is managed and organized when preparing for emergencies in the Latin American and Caribbean region, where natural disasters are frequent, are critical to organizing a response (Balletto and Wertheimer, 2010: 275–93). Innovations centre on preparedness tools and response capacities in the region, including the pre-positioning of food and non-food items in sub-regional depots based on geographic information systems, early warning, target training, strengthening co-ordination; and south–south co-operation within the region.

We saw in Chapter 4, and again earlier in this chapter, that the WFP had pioneered information and communications technology (ICT) and has been designated as co-lead agency in the ICT global cluster. Details are given of how the WFP uses state-of-the-art ICT to support its food assistance activities (Yu, 2010: 295–306). ICT not only supports food assistance initiatives, but also changes their nature through innovations, thereby enabling new capabilities. Innovations cover the range of food assistance activities from individual action to system-wide co-ordination and integration cross the world.

One of the WFP's outstanding contributions has been through the development of its expertise and experience in logistics, which led to it being designated as the lead agency for the global logistics cluster (Chapter 4). The WFP's central role in humanitarian logistics is described (Quinn, 2010: 307–28). Complex operating situations and increasingly sophisticated food assistance arrangements demand logistics operations that are innovative, dynamic, and multi-modal, ranging from the organization and management of a network of collection points from many remote locations (as required in the P4P initiative) to responding to large-scale unpredictable emergencies (such as earthquakes, floods, and tsunamis) and getting food through to the civilian population caught up in a war zone in complex conflict situations.

A particularly innovative area of the WFP's work has been in food-based safety-net schemes. The largest scheme of this type in sub-Saharan Africa is the *Productive Safety Net Programme* (PSNP) in Ethiopia (Gebru *et al.*, 2010: 329–49). The evolution, achievements and challenges of the PSNP are described. And the innovations and principles that define the PSNP approach and have shaped its design and implementation are outlined, including its multi-actor platform, strong government ownership and guidance, multi-annual approach, and integration within a broader food security framework.

The WFP's *Strategic Plan (2008–13)* sets out the WFP global strategy for the five-year period. But how has this global strategy been applied at the country level? The example of Uganda's experience is given (Samkange *et al.*, 2010: 351–64). The key steps undertaken by the WFP country office in Uganda to translate the global strategy into a country-specific strategy are laid out. A path-breaking consultative process for priority setting, forging partnerships, establishing institutional linkages, and formulating a programme portfolio has resulted in an internally consistent and widely embraced strategy that brings together previously disparate investments in Uganda's food system in an operationally feasible way.

The ultimate aim of all WFP activities is that they should be adopted and sustained as their own by governments and communities in developing countries. This 'handover' process is clarified in the case of Namibia (Osmani, 2010: 365–76). A programme for orphans and vulnerable children was designed from the outset with an exit strategy entailing the integration of beneficiaries into the national social safety-net programme. The modalities, arrangements, and steps for effective handover of food assistance interventions from international actors to the Namibian government are described.

A wider view: study of food aid and food assistance in emergency and transitional contexts

The WFP was not alone in seeking the transformation from food aid to food assistance. In 2010, the German government announced its intention to revise its food assistance policy in emergency and transitional contexts. To assist the process of revision, a study of changes in food aid and food assistance policies and strategies within the international aid system was commissioned by the German Federal Ministry for Economic Cooperation and Development (BMZ).

The study was conducted by the Humanitarian Policy Group (HPG) at the Overseas Development Institute in London (Harvey *et al.*, 2010).[19] It was circulated widely throughout the international aid system by the German government to 'contribute to our ongoing discussion and provide ... a stimulating and thought-provoking overview of current key issues and debates in the field of food aid and food assistance', after it was assessed that:

> The study comes to the conclusion that a broader concept of food assistance is gradually emerging, replacing the increasingly obsolete notion of food aid. In addition, the context in which food assistance is being provided, the international architecture by which it is financed and delivered, and the way in which it is being delivered have been shifting dramatically. (Faehmann, 2010)

Reasons for the study

The study was prompted for a number of reasons. One was the shift from food aid to food assistance by key donors, UN agencies, and NGOs. Significant trends included the move from in-kind food aid transfers to local and regional food procurement, increased use of cash transfers, and an increasing role for social protection and hunger safety nets. Another was changes in the context in which food assistance was provided. The global food, financial and fuel crises, and climate change, as well as the more protracted nature of some internal conflicts, were putting pressure on the international community for a change of focus in food assistance policies and practices. Yet another reason was the changes in the international architecture for the delivery of food assistance. The humanitarian reform agenda and the future financing of external assistance, currently in debate, were also critical areas of change in the international humanitarian and food security architecture.

Significant changes had also taken place in the contexts of crises. The past decade had seen a rise in the number and severity of natural disasters, persistent protracted conflicts, and major humanitarian emergencies. More frequent extreme weather-related disasters, related to climate change, were anticipated. In reaction, the need for disaster preparedness, response, and mitigation measures had concomitantly increased. Other factors, such as rapid urbanization and an ageing population, added to the complexity of crises. In addition, global food and fuel price rises were likely to remain volatile as a result of increasing climatic variability, continuing instability in the global financial system. Also, the growing demand for cereals and meat in major emerging economies such as China called for changes in international food security. And the debate in the WTO on the future of food aid had still to be resolved.

Against this background, an increasing number of donors and aid agencies are using the term 'food assistance' as an alternative to 'food aid'. We have seen how the WFP saw itself as transforming from a food aid to a food assistance agency within the context of its *Strategic Plan (2008–13)*. The European Commission talked about a gradual and important shift over the last 15 years from using in-kind commodity food aid as a response to emergencies towards considering a broader and more effective set of humanitarian food assistance tools. The commissioned study found a major reason for the evolution in terminology was to allow aid agencies to include the provision of cash for food-related purposes within definitions of food assistance.

The study found that the definition of what constituted 'food assistance' varied considerably among different stakeholders. Some definitions embraced all interventions that addressed food and nutrition insecurity, including in-kind food aid, cash transfers, some forms of production, and market support. Others, such as the WFP, limited food assistance to direct food, and cash-based and voucher transfers. The study pointed out that the lack of a clear and common definition of food assistance raises conceptual and practical issues, including the forms and level of food assistance currently being provided, because there is no widely accepted definition on the basis of which data can be collected and reported. Another ongoing debate is whether food assistance is, primarily, a humanitarian instrument, or whether it can also be used in transition and development programmes. The study suggests that it may be more helpful to think about how the objectives and modalities of different food assistance and food security instruments shift with transitions from humanitarian to development approaches. Another emerging development are the longer-term approaches to provide social protection, including food assistance, as an alternative or complement to emergency relief; this is gaining currency, particularly in places with chronic food insecurity, repeated periods of acute food insecurity, or both.

Trends in food aid

Major changes have taken place in food aid over the past decade, during which global deliveries have fallen to half their previous level. Food aid-commodity market interconnections are now weak so that food aid levels are even more contingent on short-term political and administrative considerations, and are sensitive to not only food price volatility, but also currency fluctuations and aid budgetary pressures. Recent extreme cereals market volatility underscores these concerns. To give an example, at the time of the earthquake in Haiti in January 2010, wheat suitable for humanitarian assistance for early delivery from US Gulf ports could be obtained for under $200 a ton. By the time of the massive humanitarian operations required to respond to the widespread flooding in Pakistan in August 2010, prices has risen by almost 50 per cent. The FAO food price rose sharply in the latter part of 2010 to approach levels reached during the 2007–08 food crisis, pushing more people into hunger.

The study identified three main trends in food aid. First, emergency relief has accounted for an increasingly larger percentage of overall food aid, with a decline in its use for development purposes. Between 1996/98 and 2006/08, the share of emergency aid rose from 38 per cent to 66 per cent of all food aid, while programme food aid for balance-of-payment or budgetary support declined from 33 per cent to 12 per cent. Project food aid fell from 28 per cent to 22 per cent. Food aid has traditionally formed a large part of humanitarian sectoral requirements in the UN Consolidated Appeal Process (CAP). Humanitarian assistance levels have increased since 2000, with growth accelerating from 2005 onwards coinciding with the inception of pooled funding mechanisms for humanitarian aid contributions (CERF). Overall, food aid levels have declined but food aid remains the largest component (25–30 per cent) of humanitarian assistance.

The second main trend has been the dramatic increase in local and regional procurement, both in absolute terms and as a share of food aid. This resulted in a change in the composition of food aid from predominantly wheat towards maize and other coarse grains. A growing number of donors are making their funding more flexible to allow for local and regional purchases, and other triangular transactions. This has been found to be cheaper and faster than tied in-kind aid, and to have the potential of delivering development benefits to local markets and small farmers, as in the WFP's P4P.

The third main trend is that non-DAC/OECD governments are becoming increasingly important funders of food aid, although less predictable. In 2008, they accounted for 20 per cent of all food aid, including a major contribution from Saudi Arabia. An increasing number of developing country governments are providing contributions to food aid operations in their own countries. But, for the most part, the major food aid donors remain unchanged. The United States provides around half of all food aid. Other major donors include the EU and its member states, Canada and Japan. The main food aid recipients are countries in sub-Saharan Africa and Afghanistan. Five countries (Afghanistan, Ethiopia, Somalia, Sudan, and Zimbabwe) received over half the total food aid deliveries in 2008.

Food security architecture

The global increases in food and fuel prices, and the world financial crisis and economic recession gave impetus to re-examining food security at the international level. A number of initiatives have taken place that could have an impact on future food assistance and the ways in which it is provided. It remains to be seen how these various pieces of the architecture will fit together.

In April 2008, the UN secretary-general established a *High Level Task Force on the Global Food Security Crisis* consisting of 13 UN bodies, including the WFP, under the co-ordination of the UN under-secretary-general for Humanitarian Affairs, together with a *Comprehensive Framework of Action* to enhance the efforts of the UN system and the international financial institutions to respond to the crisis.

In April 2008, in the face of soaring food prices, the newly appointed president of the World Bank, Robert B. Zoellick, appealed for what he called a 'new deal for global food policy' (Zoellick, 2008). The new deal would incorporate a number of initiatives, including:

- meeting the WFP's call for at least $500 million of additional food supplies to meet current emergencies, and to support the WFP's proposal to shift from traditional food aid to a broader concept of food and nutritional assistance; invest more to meet the first MDG, what Zoellick called the 'forgotten MDG', of reducing the proportion of poor and hungry people by half by 2015, which he thought would have the greatest multiplier effect;

- creating a stronger delivery system to overcome fragmentation, which would intertwine agriculture, water, sanitation, rural infrastructure, and gender policies;
- increasing food production through a 'green revolution' in sub-Saharan Africa that would help smallholders out of poverty, for which the World Bank would almost double it lending from the current $450 million; and
- scaling-up the advisory services of the International Finance Corporation (IFC) to support agribusiness.

For his proposal to be successful, Zoellick recognized that there would be need to integrate and mobilize a diverse range of partners, including the WFP and IFAD, other multilateral development bodies, private donors (such as the Bill and Melinda Gates Foundation), agricultural institutes, developing countries with successful agricultural experience, and the private sector. Zoellick linked three other immediate measures to his proposed new global food policy: a 'global trade deal' that would break the *impasse* in the Doha development agenda (see p. 343); devising a 'one per cent solution' for equity investment in Africa, which would draw on the sovereign wealth funds of emerging developing countries that currently held about $3 trillion in assets; and reversing the 'resource curse' of developing countries by launching an *Extraction Industries Transparency Initiative*.

In May 2008, the World Bank Group set up a *Global Food Crisis Response Programme* (GFRP) to mitigate the effects of soaring food prices and to help countries adapt to higher and more volatile food prices. It was designed as a fast track facility with a total initial ceiling of $1.2 billion. In April 2009, the ceiling was raised to $2 billion to enable a continued rapid response to the food crisis, if demand for assistance were to increase. By September 2010, the total amount of World Bank and externally-funded operations under the GFRP was $1.4 billion.

A *High-Level Conference on World Food Security* was held in Rome, Italy in June 2008, convened by the FAO, IFAD, WFP, and the Consultative Group on International Agricultural Research (CGIAR), to address the challenges of higher food prices, climate change, and bioenergy. The conference adopted a declaration:

> to use all means to alleviate the suffering caused by the current crisis, to stimulate food production and to increase investment in agriculture, to address obstacles to food access, and the use of the planet's resources sustainably, for present and future generations.

The declaration ended:

> We commit to eliminate hunger and to secure food for all today and tomorrow.' (FAO, 2008)

The UN secretary-general, Ban Ki-moon, identified the 'right to food' as a third track of the *Comprehensive Framework for Action* at the *High Level Conference on Food Security* in Madrid in January 2009. The UN *High-Level Task Force on Global Food Security* emphasized the need to address all aspects of the food systems from a human rights perspective. As a result, the Office of the UN High Commissioner for Human Rights (OHCHR) joined the *High Level Task Force* (UN, 2009).

At the G8+ summit in L'Aquila, Italy in July 2009, more than $20 billion was pledged for what became known as the 'Agriculture and Food Security Initiative'. Leaders at the G20 summit in Pittsburgh in the United States in September 2009 called on the World Bank Group to 'work with interested donors and organizations to develop a multilateral trust fund to scale up agricultural assistance to low income countries'. The World Bank's Board of Executive Directors approved a *Global Agricultural and Food Security Programme* (GAFSP) in January 2010 as a multilateral financing mechanism. The programme will allow the immediate targeting and delivery of additional funding to public and private entities to support national and regional strategic plans for agricultural and food security in poor countries. It aims to put the countries themselves in the driver's seat. Plans are designed and implemented by developing country governments and their regional partners. The decision-making body of the GAFSP is a steering committee which includes representatives from the FAO, IFAD, WFP, the World Bank, and other multilateral development banks, with civil society organizations as active but non-voting participants. The GAFSP was launched in April 2010. The Steering Committee allocated $224 million to five countries (Bangladesh, Haiti, Rwanda, Sierra Leone, and Togo) in the first round of allocations in June 2010. The next allocations were scheduled to be made in November 2010.

The World Bank's mission is described as:

> To fight poverty with passion and professionalism for lasting results, to help people help themselves and their environment by providing resources, sharing knowledge, building capacity, and forging partnerships in the public and private sectors. (World Bank, 2007a)

The inscription over the entrance to the World Bank's offices at 1850 I Street in Washington, DC reads 'Our dream is a world without poverty'. The Bank has long recognized that poverty exists mostly in rural areas, where agricultural is the main livelihood. The institution has received growing contributions to its resources, while those of other multilateral organizations have declined. Yet, the enigma has been a fall, not a rise, in its assistance to the agricultural sector over the past twenty years.[20]

In 2005, a process of redressing this long-term declining trend was initiated with the publication of a major report, *Agricultural Growth for the Poor. An Agenda for Development*. The report concluded that 'the agricultural sector can command greater attention by clearly communicating the impact of agricultural investments on economic growth and the welfare of the poor' (World Bank, 2005). The scene was therefore set for a major review of the role and importance of agriculture in economic development, which was taken up in the *World Development Report 2008. Agriculture for Development*, published by the World Bank in 2007, the first time in 25 years that the *World Development Report* was devoted to the subject (World Bank, 2007b). The expectation was therefore created that a significant increase in bank lending to agricultural and rural development would take place.

That expectation was fulfilled with the publication in 2009 of the World Bank Group's *Implementing Agriculture for Development. Agricultural Action Plan: FY 2010–2012* (World Bank, 2009). The publication is particularly useful in that it shows the many, interrelated factors at work in creating problems for food security in the future. The proposed three-year work programme draws attention to food security issues caused by recent and projected food price volatility. It responds to the main message of the 2008 *World Development Report* that 75 per cent of the world's poor are in rural areas; most are involved in farming; and agriculture remains fundamental for poverty reduction, economic growth, and environmental sustainability in the twenty-first century. The World Bank Group projects a significant increase in support to agriculture from the International Development Association (IDA), International Bank for Reconstruction and Development (IBRD) and International Finance Corporation (IFC) from a baseline average support in FY 2006–08 of $4.1 billion annually to between $6.2 billion to $8.3 billion annually between FY 2010 and 2012, a rise of between 13 per cent and 17 per cent of total projected World Bank commitments.

Relatively greater attention is projected to be given to: the critical need to increase agricultural productivity, especially of food smallholder farmers, in order to make headway in the alleviation of rural poverty; differentiating the mix of support across the 'three worlds of agriculture' (agriculture-based, transforming, and urbanized countries), as described in the 2008 *World Development Report*; and the role of agriculture in providing environmental services, including in the context of climate change. The Bank's agricultural action plan is organized around five focal areas: raising agricultural productivity; linking farmers to markets and strengthening value addition; reducing risk and vulnerability; facilitating agricultural entry and exit, and rural non-farm income (including improved rural investment, with a focus on empowering farmers, livestock-keepers, and fishers, especially women, and upgrading skills to adjust to climate change); and enhancing environmental services and sustainability.

In these ways, the bank has made a renewed commitment to agriculture. With partners in developing and developed countries, it seeks to harness fully the power of agriculture to promote poverty alleviation and economic growth, and to protect the environment. It also recognizes that the changing global context adds new urgency to the task and shows the compounded effects of negative trends. The sudden increase in food prices in 2008 drove an estimated 100 million more people into poverty (Ivanic and Martin, 2008). The seasonal nature of agriculture resulted in a lagged production response. Global food prices more than double from 2006 to mid-2008, and then declined by 30–40 per cent to the end of May 2009. Global food prices are now increasing again, driven by events outside the food sector; future prices are expected to remain higher than in the 1990s and to be more volatile. High price volatility may dampen supply response to higher average prices, negatively impacting both poor producers and consumers. In addition, the financial crisis has slowed both economic growth and trade.

The resultant declines in revenue have curbed the ability of governments to respond. Exchange rate depreciators have kept food prices high for many developing country importers. Higher lending practices of commercial banks have led to higher interest rates on farmers and agribusinesses borrowing, and lower subsequent investment in agriculture. Lower remittances and migration back to rural areas from cities and towns as unemployment increased have lowered purchasing power and have affected the household budgets of the poor, the greater part of whose expenditure is spent on food.

The severity of the impact of the food and financial crises has been amplified by broader trends that need to be acknowledged to a greater extent in future action. These include the ability of institutions, policy, and investment to respond to accelerated and changing demand for food, globalization of markets and associated risks, rising urbanization, growing land and water scarcity, and climate change. Each has implications for the role of agriculture in the broader economy, and the associated priorities for action. By 2050, there will be an estimated 2.3 billion more people in the world to feed, one third more than today. Demand for cereals and meat will increase. Competing uses of food are growing rapidly, as in the production of livestock and biofuels, and water scarcity will increase. Climate change adds to the uncertainty. Yet, global annual growth rates in yields of major gains have declined from around 3 per cent in 1980 to 1 per cent in 2009. These trends place upward pressure on food prices, on further deforestation for crop area expansion, and associated climate change impacts.

Overall GDP growth originating in agriculture has been, on average, two to four times as effective in raising the incomes of the poor as growth generated in the non-agricultural sectors. Concerted efforts are required to integrate smallholder farmers into growing affordable food. Market driven rural-to-urban shifts of land and labour all facilitate economic growth and transformation in a process in which agriculture must play its significant role. Income growth to spur demand, productivity growth to provide affordable food and raise real wages, and market-driven release of land and labour for urban development, all require further investment in agriculture.

Climate change is likely to expose more people, more frequently, and for longer periods, to threats to their livelihoods. Agriculture can play a significant role in mitigating climate change effects, but adaptation remains important. Productivity growth potentially reduces the need for deforestation. More drought-tolerant crops and livestock breeds can improve resilience. Education and training can improve management of climate-induced changes in pests, weeds, and diseases. Better-managed agricultural intensification can reduce greenhouse gas emissions, as can sequestering more carbon in the soil. Rapidly rising rural–urban income disparities, particularly in south and east Asia, coupled with continuing extreme rural poverty, are major sources of social and political tensions and unrest.

The additional amount of global public investment required to meet the first MDG of halving poverty and hunger by 2015 is estimated to be $14 billion annually for all developing countries, of which $3.8 billion to $4.8 billion is required annually for sub-Saharan Africa (Fan and Rosegrant, 2008). Recent policy reforms have improved price incentives for agricultural producers in developing countries that can strengthen future investment returns. The World Bank Group considers that it has a comparative advantage to respond to the challenge of achieving global food security. It will respond to the short-term effects of the food and financial crises, but has embedded these within the response to the longer-term challenges with the focus on the five key areas outlined (p. 310).

In the meantime, other parts of the global food security architecture are being strengthened and modified. Both the FAO and IFAD were subject to independent external evaluations, the first in their histories, in 2007 and 2005, respectively (FAO, 2007; IFAD, 2005). Efforts are now being made to reform and reshape these important multilateral institutions in the light of their recommendations. Nominations for the director-general of the FAO for the period 2012–15 have been called for by 31 January 2011, thus signalling the end of the 18-year period of office of the present director-general, Jacque Diouf, (1994–2012), the same length of time the position was held by his predecessor, Edouard Saouma (1976–93). The FAO *Committee on World Food Security* (CFS) has been substantially changed with the aim of it becoming the 'central UN political platform dealing with food security and nutrition', supported by a *High Level Panel of Experts in Food Security*, an *Advisory Group* composed of representatives of the FAO, WFP and IFAD, and other non-member CFS participants, and by a secretariat headed by a secretary from the FAO and staff from the WFP and IFAD (FAO, 2009). Also, deliberate steps are being taken to strength co-operation between the three Rome-based UN food-related agencies, the FAO, IFAD, and WFP.

The continuing debate concerning the future of the *Food Aid Convention* (FAC) is also relevant. The FAC is the only legal instrument for ensuring minimum levels of food aid. Six FACs have been approved since the first was signed in 1967. Signatories agree to provide a guaranteed minimum quantity of food in physical terms, irrespective of fluctuations in production, stocks, and prices. Aggregate minimum commitments reached a peak of 7.6 million tons in the 1980 FAC but declined to 4.9 million tons in the 1999 FAC, although many signatories surpassed their minimum obligations in many years. The conventions gradually became more flexible in terms of the food commodities included and the ways in which they could be acquired. Substantive changes were made in the 1999 FAC, which was signed by 23 members.

Discussion and decision on the revision and continuation of the 1999 FAC was put on hold pending the outcome of the WTO Doha development agenda agreed in 2001, which included substantially reduced barriers to agricultural trade. But progress on the commitments made at Doha have proved to be difficult, and negotiations stalled in 2007. The United States called for substantial cuts in farm import tariffs to open markets for its farmers. Others called on the United States, first, to cut its agricultural subsidies. The ways in which the United States conducted its food aid programme were criticized as adversely affecting international agricultural trade, calling into question the future of food aid, which question still remains to be resolved.

Against this background, a proposal has been made to reach agreement on a new 'food assistance convention' as part of the global food security architecture discussed earlier (pp. 307–13) (Clay, 2010). Following the G8 development ministers' meeting in Canada in April 2010, the chair's summary made public after the main report was drafted stated: 'Ministers believe in a Food Aid Convention for the 21st Century that focuses on providing appropriate and effective food assistance to vulnerable populations', confirming that the term 'food assistance' is being adopted in preference to 'food aid'. Details of an agreement would need to be carefully worked out to ensure effective linkages to the wider humanitarian system, as well as food security agencies.

Another proposal has been made for incorporating agricultural inputs into a renegotiated FAC in recognition of the importance they play in the recovery and rehabilitation of the agricultural sector following disasters (Konandreas, 2010). In addition, the proposal suggests raising the FAC minimum commitment, broadening the FAC donor base, earmarking and prioritizing FAC resources to emergency operations, introducing flexibility in funding arrangements, and ensuring compatibility with WTO rules.

Opinions differ widely on a future FAC. Some consider that the above proposals merit consideration as providing a safety net of support for food assistance and becoming a key component of the new global food security architecture. Others consider this irrelevant and the product of a previous era of surplus food disposal and in-kind food aid. One analyst found the FAC in its current form too small and to be reduced at crucial periods, and therefore 'contributed little to international food security', and suggested a shift away from 'minimum quantitative commitment... towards some form of obligation linked to need' (Benson, 2000: 116–18). The expectation that the WFP would benefit from successive FACs remained largely unfulfilled, as only a small amount of FAC commitments have been channelled through the Programme (Shaw, 2001: 72–4).

Other changes are being implemented or proposed for the new global food security architecture. The IASC cluster approach is a key component of the 2005 Humanitarian Response review and ongoing reform initiative for improved efficiency, increased predictability, and higher accountability in international responses to humanitarian emergencies (see Chapter 4). The WFP has been fully engaged in the reform process from the outset. At the country level, the decision to establish food security clusters reflected the heightened recognition being given to food security in humanitarian crises. In recognition of their value, the FAO and WFP initiated a consultative process to explore options for the possible establishment of a co-led global food security cluster (GFSC), for which broad support was given. The FAO and WFP therefore submitted a proposal to the IASC for the establishment of a co-led GFSC to complement existing global clusters and country co-ordination mechanisms (IASC, 2010). There is now broad convergence among practitioners and stakeholders at the global and country levels for strengthened co-ordination of humanitarian food security responses in crisis situations. A GFSC cell has been established at WFP headquarters headed by an experienced team leader. Cluster partners have been invited to second staff to the cell.

IFPRI held a global consultation in its 2020 conference series on 'Leveraging Agriculture for Improving Nutrition and Health', unleashing the potential of agriculture to reduce malnutrition and ill-health, in New Delhi, India between 10 and 12 February 2011.[21] A new revised edition of *The Sphere Project. Humanitarian Charter and Minimum Standards in Disaster Response* will be published in 2011.[22] The qualitative and quantitative indicators and guidance notes are being updated. The *Humanitarian Charter* is being rewritten to reflect significant changes since the *Sphere Handbook* was first published in 2004, with the common standards significantly changed, and a stronger focus on protection introduced.

An open letter signed by 16 eminent humanitarian advocates was sent to member states of the UN at the start of the 2010 session of the UN General Assembly, marking the fifth anniversary of the adoption of the *Responsibility to Protect* (R2P), calling them to honour the 2005 pledge to uphold the responsibility to protect, and for R2P to be 'right at the top of the lists of concerns' (GCFR2P, 2010). The *Second World Conference on Humanitarian Studies* will be hosted by Tufts University in the United States in June 2011.

Chapter 7 looks at the way ahead for the WFP, as revealed in its *Strategic Plan (2008–13)*, analyzes the challenges and opportunities that the organization is likely to face in the future, and offers proposals for action.

7
The Way Ahead: Challenges and Opportunities

The way ahead

Strategic Plan (2008–13)

The framework for WFP action over the six years between 2008 and 2013 was laid down in its *Strategic Plan (2008–11)*, extended to 2013 (WFP, 2008k). Five strategic objectives (SOs) were identified.

Save lives and protect livelihoods in emergencies. Three goals were set: to save lives in emergencies and reduce acute malnutrition caused by shocks to below emergency levels; to protect livelihoods and enhance self-reliance in emergencies and early recovery; and to reach refugees, internally displaced persons (IDPs), and other vulnerable groups and communities whose food and nutrition security had been adversely affected by shocks. The WFP's four main tools for achieving these objectives are: general and targeted food assistance and emergency nutrition interventions; emergency needs assessments; emergency logistics, special operations, and information and communications technology (ICT) capacity; and the WFP's leadership role for logistics and emergency ICT in the UN cluster leadership system.

Prevent acute hunger and invest in disaster preparedness and mitigation measures. Two goals were recognized: to support and strengthen governments' capacities to prepare for, assess, and respond to acute hunger arising from disasters; and to support and strengthen communities' resilience to shocks through safety nets or asset creation, including adaptation to climate change. The WFP's four main tools for reaching these objectives are: vulnerability analysis and mapping (VAM); early warning products and tools; disaster preparedness and mitigation programmes; and programmes to help communities reinforce their essential food and nutrition security systems and infrastructures, and their adaptability to climate change, including voucher-, cash- and food-based safety nets.

Restore and rebuild lives and livelihoods in post-conflict, post-disaster, or transition situations. Three goals were established: to support the return of refugees and IDPs through food and nutrition assistance; to support the re-establishment of livelihoods and food and nutrition security of communities and families affected by shocks; and to assist in establishing or rebuilding food supply or delivery capacities of countries and communities affected by shocks and to help avoid the resumption of conflicts. The WFP's five main tools for achieving these objectives are: targeted programmes that facilitate the re-establishment of livelihoods; special operations to rebuild essential hunger-related infrastructure; food distribution programmes that facilitate re-establishment of food and nutrition security; voucher- and cash-based programmes that facilitate food access; and capacity strengthening for the re-establishment of community service infrastructure.

Reduce chronic hunger and undernutrition. The three goals are: to help countries bring undernutrition up from below critical levels and break the inter-generational cycle of chronic hunger; to increase levels of education and basic nutrition and health through food and nutrition assistance and food and nutrition security tools; and to meet the food and nutrition needs of those affected by HIV/AIDS, tuberculosis (TB), and other pandemics. The WFP's four main tools for addressing these objectives are: mother-and-child health and nutrition (MCHN) programmes; school feeding programmes; programmes addressing and mitigating HIV/AIDS, tuberculosis and other pandemics; and policy and programme advice.

Strengthen the capacities of countries to reduce hunger, including through handover strategies and local purchases. The three goals are: to use the WFP's purchasing power to support the sustainable development of food and nutrition security systems, and transform food and nutrition assistance into a productive investment in local communities; to develop clear handover strategies to enhance nationally-owned hunger solutions; and to strengthen the capacities of countries to design, manage, and implement tools, policies, and programmes to predict and reduce hunger. The WFP's four main tools for addressing these objectives are: the WFP's procurement activities; handover of WFP hunger tools; policy and programmatic advice; and advocacy.

The five SOs are derived from the WFP's mandate, its *Mission Statement*, and the MDGs agreed upon by all UN member states. The *Strategic Plan* reflects 'the changing nature of food aid and hunger, and WFP's history, experience and comparative advantage'. The overarching goal is defined as: 'to reduce dependency and to support governmental and global efforts to ensure long term solutions to the hunger challenge'. This would involve a 'historical shift from WFP as a food aid agency to WFP as a food assistance agency, with a more nuanced and robust set of tools to respond to critical hunger needs'. The four main tools for achieving its overarching objectives are identified as: the WFP's procurement activities; handover of WFP hunger tools; policy and programmatic advice; and advocacy.

Changing strategic context

The WFP faces serious challenges in implementing the *Strategic Plan*, as significant changes are taking place in the world environment in which it works since the plan was adopted in 2008 (WFP, 2010c: 8). By 2009, the fall in the number of hungry people that had previously taken place was reversed by a surge in their number to over one billion, the highest level on record. A global economic crisis and sharply rising food prices contributed to the surge, exacerbated by 245 natural disasters that affected 58 million people. Although the number of hungry poor has subsequently fallen to below one billion, food prices remain high and volatile, and major disasters, such as the massive flooding in Pakistan and the earthquake in Haiti, threaten to keep their number at historical levels. The FAO estimated that the total number of undernourished people in 2010 was 925 million, higher than before the food and economic crises of 2008–09 (FAO, 2010).

Substantial increases in the WFP's resources were required to respond to the challenge. Donors responded by providing a larger proportion of their contributions in cash, as opposed to food commodities. This enabled the WFP to begin the transition from a focus on food aid to food assistance programmes to provide hunger solutions including: improved approaches to tackling malnutrition; launching P4P to improve market opportunities for smallholder farmers; and cash transfers and voucher schemes to address food needs and protect markets. At the same time, the WFP experienced increasing attacks on its staff and contractors in a number of countries, including Afghanistan, Pakistan, the Occupied Palestinian Territory, Sudan, and Somalia, as terrorists deliberately targeted humanitarian aid workers (see p. 364).

Looking forward: future challenges

Looking ahead, WFP faces a number of challenges. Some of the main ones are mentioned here (WFP, 2010c: 85–7).

Resourcing. The WFP aims to reach the most destitute and vulnerable, who often have no other means of food security or support, and who account for about 10 per cent of the estimated total number of hungry people. This raises a serious resourcing challenge. The WFP is committed to obtaining the resources required to meet its assessed needs. Mobilizing funding on this scale, particularly at a time of economic downturn, and rising food and energy prices, will be a complex challenge. In 2009, for the first time in recent history, the WFP was not able to meet a high percentage of its assessed needs, even though WFP country offices were able to mitigate this by drawing on stocks carried over from 2008. Early provision of predictable cash or in-kind contributions enables the WFP to plan and assist the vulnerable in the most efficient way. Opportunities for expanding multi-year funding agreements, such as those completed with Australia, Canada, Luxembourg, the Russian Federation, and the United States, will be pursued. And the WFP's financing policies and regulations are being reviewed to identify the optimum arrangements to enable it to respond to future challenges. But resource-related problems remain, including the position of the United States, the WFP's largest donor (see pp. 341–6).

Emergency response. The challenge of responding quickly and efficiently to emergencies continues. To meet this challenge, the WFP has undertaken to meet its responsibilities as lead agency or co-lead agency of the UN global logistics cluster, the UN global telecommunications cluster, and the UN global food security cluster. It will maintain special units at WFP headquarters to supports field-level clusters in these fields to drive initiatives that contribute to preparedness and response capacity not only that of the WFP, but also of the humanitarian community as a whole. Training will be provided for personnel from the WFP, UN agencies, and NGOs to expand the roster for the deployment of inter-agency response teams, and preparedness information will be increased through the development of a digitized form of capacity assessments.

Nutrition. The WFP will continue to address the nutritional needs of various target groups, but in ways that convey the best possible and lasting nutritional benefits to individuals and communities by providing 'the right foods, at the right time, to the right beneficiaries'. The number of children and pregnant and lactating women receiving new nutritionally enhanced food products is being rapidly increased. More focus on children under two years of age is being given to prevent chronic malnutrition. In emergencies, more attention is being given to the quantity and quality of relief rations, including special foods with micronutrients for mothers and young children to support child growth and development. The WFP will also continue to explore and advocate the linkages between HIV, food, and nutrition. Innovative cash transfers and voucher schemes are being tested to enable the WFP to respond to government needs in the quest for HIV social protection. In areas where malaria is endemic, the WFP and its partners are testing the use of a sodium-iron compound in combination with a high dosage of vitamin C, mixed with food containing a micronutrient powder with a high iron content. In all these areas, specific attention will be needed to increase capacity in WFP-assisted countries to take over these advances in appropriate handover strategies.

School feeding. In pursuing its policy on school feeding, the WFP will increase its focus on the development of national capacity and technical support, and handover strategies. Strategies for sustainable school feeding will be developed, and new tools and processes tested in a number of countries in partnership with the World Bank, the *New Partnership for Africa's Development* (NEPAD), the *Partnership for Child Development*, the *Global Child Nutrition Foundation*, and others.

Performance and risk management. While activities are being undertaken to improve the quality of its programmes, measures are also being pursued to strengthen the WFP's management. Work is in progress to reinforce results-based management under the *Strategic Plan (2008–13)*. The capacity of WFP country offices to carry out performance management will be increased. And a management results framework is being developed, along with an enterprise risk management framework, to improve the WFP's ability to manage risks proactively.

The international humanitarian system

The WFP does not act alone but with an impressive array of partners as part of the international humanitarian system (see Chapter 4). Since the end of the Second World War in 1945, and more particularly since the end of the Cold War at the beginning of the 1990s, the system has grown and diversified in an astonishing way. The system was never designed but, instead, evolved and 'like most products of evolution, it has its anomalies, redundancies, inefficiencies, and components evolved from one task being adapted to another' (Walker and Maxwell, 2009: 2). To call it a 'system', with its amazing number of local, national, international, and

UN organizations and networks, 'risks implying a degree of cohesion and uniformity of objectives that simply is not the case' (Harvey *et al.*, 2010: 13). But, by their shared broad goals and humanitarian principles, and their interdependence in field operations, they do comprise a 'system', even though loosely configured.

The international context within which the system works is constantly changing, and appears to be worsening. There were 52 major humanitarian disasters for which UN consolidated and flash appeals were launched in the two years 2007 and 2008, an eight per cent increase over the previous six years. The major part of international humanitarian aid continues to be focused on protracted, complex, humanitarian crises, such as in the Sudan and the Democratic Republic of the Congo, and the high-profile conflict situations, involving major powers military intervention, such as those in Afghanistan, Iraq, and Somalia. And humanitarian funding per individual emergency operation has increased significantly as emergencies have increasingly involved not only relief, but also post-disaster recovery and rehabilitation action.

The humanitarian system faces a number of new and ongoing challenges. These include: high food prices, a world financial crisis, HIV/AIDS and other pandemics, and longer-term issues, notably rapid urbanization, an ageing population, and climate change. While controversy remains over the likely effects of climate change, there is growing realization that this is likely to result in more and larger-scale climate-related disasters, and greater need for a corresponding humanitarian response (Webster *et al.*, 2008; Schümer-Cross and Taylor, 2009). The massive flood in Pakistan in 2010 – which affected some 20 million people and inundated about 10 per cent of the country, destroying crops, livestock, food stocks and homes, and threatening an epidemic of water-born diseases – may be an indication of things to come. Responding to a UN appeal and others, donor governments and the general public pledged over $1 billion of emergency aid to respond to this emergency.

The main elements of the international humanitarian system may be defined as[1]

The donor community. DAC/OECD member governments, particularly the US and EU members, are the largest source of humanitarian aid funding, but non-DAC governments, including Saudi Arabia, have shown the largest increases of reported contributions in recent year. In addition, there are the contributions of the private sector and citizens in the developed world, and of the community-based organizations, and national and local NGOs in developing countries, which are considerable and often critical, but remain unquantified.

The International Red Cross and Red Crescent Movement. This movement, which is neither a non-governmental nor an inter-governmental organization, encompasses all 186 national Red Cross or Red Crescent Societies, a Federation which brings them together, and the International Committee of the Red Cross.

International non-governmental organizations (INGOs). About 250 organizations and multinational federations, each with their multiple national affiliates, comprise the global INGO community. The majority, based in North America, particularly the United States, and western Europe, are secular in orientation, and engage in humanitarian action across a range of sectors.

UN humanitarian and international agencies. These are the nine members of the Inter-Agency Standing Committee (IASC): the FAO, UNDP, UNFPA, UNHCR, UNICEF, UNRWA, WFP, WHO, and OCHA. However, 39 other UN bodies make contributions to emergency operations, as well as international organizations outside the UN system, such as the IOM.

Only now are estimates of the full dimensions of the international humanitarian system becoming available (Harvey *et al.*, 2010: 18–22). In 2008, the total number of aid workers in the field employed on providing both relief and development assistance was estimated at roughly 595,000. A more conservative estimate, including only those working on crisis response and rehabilitation activities, was 210,800. Of those, 112,900 (53 per cent) worked for international NGOs, 48,400 (23 per cent) for the ICRC, IFRC, and their national societies, and 49,500 (24 per cent) for the UN humanitarian agencies and the IOM. On average, the humanitarian fieldworker population has increased by about 6 per cent per year over the past ten years (Stoddard *et al.*, 2009).

Estimates of funding for humanitarian action have ranged considerably from $15 billion in 2007 and around $18 billion in 2008 (Development Initiatives, 2009) to $4.4 billion and $6.6 billion (excluding the responses to the Iraq and Indian Ocean tsunami emergencies) (OCHA Financial Tracking Service) for the same years. Taking the latter figures, estimates indicate that humanitarian flows to emergencies have more than doubled since the beginning of the new millennium.

A major pilot study that assessed performance and progress in the international humanitarian system has begun the process of revealing its strengths and weaknesses (Harvey *et al.*, 2010).[2] The pilot study covered six key aspects of the system. Its findings are summarized here because of their relevance both for the WFP's own assistance programme and its membership of the system.

Coverage/sufficiency. While humanitarian funding had increased and was being distributed more equitably, it still fell short of requirements. On average, total humanitarian contributions equalled over 85 per cent of total stated requirements in 2007 and 2008, compared to 81 per cent in 2006, and only 67 per cent in 2005. The needs of the affected population had also gone up. Humanitarian access was also seen to be declining in some locations owing to insecurity and/or host government restrictions, and insecurity for aid workers had markedly increased.

Relevance/appropriateness. The study also examined the question whether humanitarian needs were adequately assessed and resources appropriately allocated. While improvements had taken place, humanitarian needs assessment remained a key weakness within the system. Beneficiaries continued to be inadequately consulted and involved in assessments, and the subsequent design and implementation of humanitarian operations. An impressive amount of innovation had occurred recently in both inter-agency needs assessment methodologies and mechanisms for strategic prioritization, causing concern that too many parallel initiatives could have counter-productive effects, and possibly needed some consolidation. An array of new types of programming was started to be considered, including voucher and cash transfer schemes, and new interventions to support livelihoods and promote market development.

Effectiveness. The study focused on the issues of preparedness/timeliness, co-ordination, monitoring and human resources, and institutional capacity. Investments in standby capacity and new mechanisms, notably the CERF and the UN cluster approach, had enabled more rapid action. While improvements in sectoral co-ordination had occurred, overall co-ordination was a noted weakness. The strengthening of the UN humanitarian co-ordinator (HC) system was seen as vital, with too many HCs lacking sufficient knowledge of the humanitarian system to co-ordinate and advocate effectively.

A growing role in co-ordination was seen for regional bodies, and for increased investments in aid consortia approaches, promoting greater collaboration among NGOs. Although improving, monitoring continued to be identified as a particular weakness within the system. While many agencies had made real efforts to increase investment in operational capacity and the quality of human resources, leading to improvements in the professionalism of humanitarian staff, problems of high staff turnover and the need to invest more in the management of human resources and the development of national staff remained. The capacities of national governments were growing and needed to be considered in advance of launching response efforts.

Connectedness. Lack of investment in local and national capacities to contend with emergencies was noted, as were the top-down orientation of the system and the risk of undermining local capacities. But there were signs of improvement in how international agencies worked with local humanitarian actors, and efforts at local capacity-building were increasing. There was also recognition of the need for greater downward accountability and participation, and investments in feedback and complaints mechanisms, and greater transparency.

Efficiency. Efficiency issues, including the risk of corruption, continued to be relatively unaddressed in the literature and evaluations, although Transparency International was developing an anti-corruption toolkit. There was widespread concern about agency overheads and programme support costs, but concern was also expressed that the constant drive to minimize administrative costs was leading to chronic under-investment in key capacities that could serve to improve performance. In terms of the transaction costs of co-ordination, the consensus was that the benefits of co-ordination exceeded the costs of the new administrative burdens.

Coherence. There seemed to be a growing concern about the lack of respect for international humanitarian law and core humanitarian principles in many recent conflicts on the part of warring parties, and by some donor governments and their militaries, by integrating humanitarian action within their broader foreign policy goals.

Aid agencies felt that they were not doing enough to maintain principled approaches or to advocate effectively for respect for humanitarian principles and international humanitarian law. Integrated UN missions caused concern for some aid agencies regarding the challenge they posed to humanitarian independence, although in some contexts integration was seen to provide real opportunities. The role of UN integrated missions and UN peacekeeping forces was considered to be significantly less threatening than the growing involvement of the militaries of western governments in conflicts in which they were involved.

An increasing focus on the issue of protection of the victims of conflict and humanitarian aid workers has taken place. Guidelines and policies have been developed, and an unprecedented number of humanitarian organizations are now undertaking protection activities. But there was confusion over what 'protection' meant and which actors were responsible for providing protection. The quality of the protection work that had been provided was criticized, including the deployment of inexperienced staff, breaches of confidentiality of affected populations, and inconsistent knowledge and application of relevant laws. There was also a tendency within the humanitarian system towards sudden bursts of attention to particular issues, such as HIV/AIDS and gender streamlining, followed by a relative lull with difficulty in maintaining sufficient and prolonged attention.

The humanitarian system has come under bitter criticism (e.g., Polman, 2010a, 2010b). The response of the Humanitarian Policy Group (HPG) at the Overseas Development Institute in London to the criticisms is instructive (HPG, 2010). The HPG recognizes that many of the criticisms of the practice of humanitarian action are valid and echo those levelled against aid workers in the 1990s. Humanitarian assistance has become a 'vast industry'. There have been occasions when aid has had perverse and catastrophic effects, as in the much quoted case in the huge refugee camps in Goma during the Rwandan genocide (see Chapter 3). Competition among aid agencies forces them to go where the money is, not necessarily where the greatest needs are.

In complex conflict-induced emergencies, aid is entangled with political and strategic motives and efforts. The living conditions of aid workers are often markedly different from those of the people they seek to help, and there have been cases of sexual abuse. Relief aid is diverted by insurgents, militias, politicians, and agency staff. Targeting help on the poorest and most vulnerable and affected remains an incomplete art, resulting in everyone receiving something in the belief that 'a little is better than nothing', and in defence of the principle of 'doing no wrong'. Donors are pressed to give more aid when giving too much creates aid dependency. Lack of 'contextual knowledge and cultural insensitivity' can lead to inappropriate and unsustainable projects. Herding IDPs into camps can make it easier and cheaper to deliver aid and provide protection, but the same camps can become incubators of disease and crime, and sitting targets for terrorists in the absence of adequate security personnel. And, ultimately, humanitarian aid may become a substitute for the state, freeing governments of their responsibility to their own people.

Aid workers are aware of these problems but are accused of being unwilling to address them because of competition among agencies. But new mechanisms are trying to improve co-ordination and cut out wasteful duplication. Agencies are more aware of the need to work with local government and the victims of disasters themselves, following the international evaluation reports of the response to the Rwanda crisis and the Indian Ocean tsunami. By hiding behind the humanitarian principles of humanity, impartiality, neutrality, and independency, aid workers are accused of being impudent and immune to criticism. But a commitment to these principles neither allows humanitarian agencies to behave as they wish, nor gives them permission to duck responsibility and accountability for what they do.

In the ultimate analysis, no standards or codes can guarantee effective action on the ground, and humanitarianism remains 'messy and imperfect'. Yet, progress has been made over the past decade. Humanitarian assistance alone, however, cannot ensure that belligerents will behave well towards the victims of conflict and to aid workers, or listen to calls to respect human rights and international humanitarian law, and provide protection. 'Influencing the course and conduct of conflict is ultimately the business of politicians, diplomats and soldiers, not aid workers, whose main concern is with the victims of conflict and abuse' (HPG, 2010). Failure to appreciate this has led to much of the misguided and incorrect criticism of the humanitarian system.

The WFP can now benefit from the considerable amount of analytical work that has appeared in the recent past on its target group, the world's bottom billion, both in appreciating the causes of their problems and identifying solutions to them. Particularly helpful is the work of Paul Collier at Oxford University, UK (Collier, 2007, 2008, 2009), IFPRI (Akhter *et al.*, 2007; Von Braun and Pandya-Lorch, 2007; and Von Braun *et al.*, 2009; and work on IFPRI's global hunger index (Von Grebmer *et al.*, 2010), fixing failed states (Ghani and Lockhart, 2008), and the Brookings Institution on IDPs (Cohen and Deng, 1998a and 1998b,) and on the effects of climate change on global poverty (Brainard *et al.*, 2009). And the WFP's partnerships with leading authorities of humanitarian aid, such as the ALNAP, HPG, IFPRI, and the Feinstein International Center at Tufts University, has significantly increased its analytical capacity.

Leadership and co-ordination

In Chapter 4, we saw that the WFP was caught up in a series of reform measures that took place during the 1990s to improve the co-ordination both of emergency and development assistance provided through the UN system. This led to an institutional arrangement through which humanitarian assistance is provided at present (UN, 2008b).

Growing frustration with a lack of co-ordination of humanitarian assistance provided through the UN system led the UN General Assembly to pass a resolution in 1991 that resulted in the creation of the post of emergency relief co-ordinator (ERC) at the UN undersecretary-general level, the establishment of a UN Department of Humanitarian Affairs (DHA) to assist the ERC in carrying out his functions, and the appointment of a UN Inter-Agency Standing Committee (IASC) for emergencies (UN, 1991b)

The ERC has been described as the UN system's 'principal policy adviser, co-ordinator and advocate on humanitarian emergencies', and the 'focal point' for the co-ordination of the international response to humanitarian crises (UN,

2008b: 267). The ERC determines which humanitarian emergencies are complex and require co-ordinated action by the UN agencies, assigning responsibility in the field, mobilizing contributions for emergency responses through a consolidated appeals process (CAP), allocating funds from a central emergency revolving fund (CERF), and ensuring that emergency relief operations are conceived and implemented in such a way that rehabilitation and reconstruction stem naturally from those operations.

The IASC brings together all the major humanitarian agencies both within and outside the UN system to co-ordinate the international response to humanitarian crises. The UN agencies include the FAO, UNDP, UNFPA, UNHCHR, UNHCR, UNICEF, WFP, WHO, and the World Bank. Also included are the major humanitarian intergovernmental organizations, the IOM, ICRC, and IFRCRC, the UN secretary-general's representative for internally displaced persons, and three international consortia of NGOs: Inter-Action, the International Council of Voluntary Agencies, and the Steering Committee for Humanitarian Response. Other agencies may be invited on an *ad hoc* basis.

The IASC is chaired by the ERC who also heads the DHA, which was renamed and reorganized as the Office for the Coordination of Humanitarian Assistance (OCHA) in 1998, following the UN secretary-general's UN reform measures of 1997 (Annan, 1997). The OCHA co-ordinates assistance in humanitarian crises that go beyond the capacity and mandate of any single agency. Its role is to ensure that, when a disaster strikes, there is a coherent framework within which all agencies can contribute promptly and effectively to the overall humanitarian response. It undertakes consultations with member states and members of the IASC at headquarters and in the field to determine priorities for action. The OCHA then provides support for the co-ordination of activities in the affected countries through a network of regional and field offices, country teams, and UN humanitarian coordinators. The humanitarian coordinators have overall responsibility for ensuring coherent relief efforts in the countries in which they serve.

The DHA got off to an inauspicious start and encountered a number of problems (Cohen and Deng, 1998a: 144). One was its constantly changing leadership. In its first five years, between its founding in 1992 and 1997, it had three executive heads. Another problem was poor co-ordination within the DHA, exacerbated by bureaucratic rivalries in the department, further complicated by divisions located in New York and Geneva, Switzerland. There was also resistance from other UN agencies to its co-ordination function. The DHA had minimal authority, and inadequate staff and resources, with which to direct the activities of the UN agencies it was supposed to co-ordinate, including large operational organizations with their own mandates, governing bodies, and extensive staff and funding. In addition, the ERC was outranked by the heads of other UN agencies, and so found it difficult to exercise the kind of leadership needed in large-scale, complex, international relief efforts.

Yet another problem was the DHA's cautious approach in dealing with human rights and protection issues. The UN General Assembly resolution that led to the appointment of the ERC specified only that assistance should be co-ordinated.

The DHA's mandate gave it no human rights or protection responsibilities *per se*. The needs of the victims of disasters were therefore defined by the DHA and its assessment missions in terms of basic relief items – food, water, medicines, shelter – not protection or civil and human rights requirements. As a result, DHA staff generally had expertise in providing basic humanitarian needs but not on how to deal with the personal security and human right of the affected population. The UN consolidated appeal process (CAP) rarely included funding for protection and human rights activities, although the UN secretary-general's 1997 UN reform programme did say 'funding requirements for human rights field operations will be included in the CAP, where appropriate' (Annan, 1997: para. 191). This was done in the case of Rwanda and the former Yugoslavia, but not in Liberia and Angola where massive and serious violations of human rights occurred.

To forge a more integrated approach between humanitarian assistance, human rights, and protection, it was decided in 1994 that the UN High Commissioner for Human Rights and the UN secretary-general representative on Internally Displaced Persons (IDPs) would be invited to meetings of the IASC and its sub-bodies when issues relating to their mandates were discussed. In 1997, they were made standing members of the IASC; however, protection issues did not receive the attention they deserved until they were embraced by a UN General Assembly resolution at the UN World Summit in 2005 (Evans, 2008: 4). The IASC acknowledged the importance of addressing both protection and relief needs in urgent situations of internal displacement, as was shown in the humanitarian crises in Rwanda and Bosnia (IASC, 1993). An Inter-Agency Task Force on Internally Displaced Persons was created by the IASC in 1992, but was discontinued in 1997.

In the complex and highly political emergency situations, the questions of leadership and co-ordination in the international response were confused. This arose because of the number of personalities involved, and the lack of clear definitions of the roles and responsibilities of those assigned to lead and co-ordinate including: the UN resident co-ordinator, the UN humanitarian co-ordinator, the special representative of the UN secretary-general, the heads of the UN peace-keeping operations, the commanders of the military forces and ambassadors of the major donor countries, and representatives of the major NGOs. UN resident co-ordinators are often given responsibility for co-ordinating humanitarian assistance and for linking relief efforts with rehabilitation and development activities after disasters are over, for which they could appoint disaster management teams (DMTs). But DMTs were not always set up; also, when they were, they did not always meet regularly.

UN agencies and NGOs often undercut the initiatives of the UN secretary-general's representative in their endeavour to provide humanitarian assistance as quickly as possible, within the glare of the world's media, without reference to the overall political, human rights and protection objectives being pursued. The joint evaluation of emergency assistance to Rwanda noted that 'perhaps the most important finding was that humanitarian action cannot substitute for political action' (Eriksson, 1996: 4). Or, to quote the now famous observation of the former

UN High Commissioner for Refugees, Sadako Ogata, 'There are no humanitarian solutions to humanitarian problems... Humanitarian action may create space for political action but on its own can never substitute for it' (Ogata, 2005: 25–6).

In complex emergencies, UN resident co-ordinators may also serve as the UN humanitarian co-ordinator, for which training and experience are required. They also need to strengthen relations with authorities in their country of residence, with UN agencies, NGOs, and military forces, which often play an important role in facilitating the delivery of humanitarian assistance and providing protection. And adequate funding for post-conflict rehabilitation and development activities should be assured. The joint evaluation report on the lessons from the Rwanda experience characterized co-ordination within the UN system as a 'hollow core', where co-ordination remained 'more of a concept than an effective reality', and the organizational centre was described as 'weak, poorly resourced and lacking organizational clarity' (Eriksson, 1996: 132–3).

In the chaos that too often existed at the epicentre of the international response to large-scale, complex emergencies, the DHA and its successor the OCHA were often swept aside. The experience of the DHA under the best of circumstances has been described as 'coordination by consensus', and that of the OCHA, under the worst of circumstance, as 'coordination by default' (Weiss, 2009: 95). In the Tsunami Evaluation Coalition report on co-ordination of international humanitarian assistance in the tsunami-affected countries, the conclusion was that: 'Despite the best efforts of OCHA to harness and broadcast information and technical know-how within the humanitarian community, it had neither the authority nor in some cases the influence to direct events' (Bennett *et al.*, 2006: 76). A comprehensive external evaluation in January 2004 damned – in no uncertain terms – what it described as the OCHA's 'lack of strategic vision' in responding to internal displacements, but recommended a few years of grace by stating: 'If, on the other hand, after a period of two to three years there is still no progress in the collaborative approach, the Unit [now Division] should be shut down – at that point it will have become a veil masking inherent failures of the system' (Stites and Tanner, 2004: 12).[3]

A number of suggestions have been made to improve the current system (Cohen and Deng, 1998a: 172–86). One is that principal responsibility for providing assistance and protection for IDPs should be assigned to one UN operational agency in each emergency. Experience has shown that when no one agency was so designated, IDPs did not receive adequate attention. Co-ordination mechanisms alone have been generally ineffective in ensuring the protection of, and assistance to, IDPs. On the other hand, a warning was given that:

> An existing agency deputized to deal with IDPs or an agency newly created solely for that purpose might simply add more bureaucracy to an already overly bureaucratic system. A single agency responsible for IDPs might duplicate efforts, heighten competition for donor resources, and provoke more debates over definitions relating to the displaced. Any single humanitarian entity would probably also lack the authority and capacity to integrate

essential political, human rights, humanitarian, and peacekeeping elements. (Minear and Kent, 1998: 83)

Recommendations were made to minimize overlap and duplication between resident and humanitarian co-ordinators and UN secretary-general special representatives, with the co-ordinators acting as deputies to the latter, and all UN humanitarian and development organizations reporting to the office of the special representative. The special representative should have a second deputy, drawn from the UN peacekeeping structure, thereby bringing under one umbrella all the different components in an emergency situation. Other suggestions included: strengthening co-ordination, establishing a locus of responsibility in the IASC, integrating protection and humanitarian assistance more effectively, strengthening the position of the UN secretary-general's representative, and integrating relief and development assistance more effectively. One way to build closer working relationships between humanitarian and human rights bodies might be to draw up agreements on protection, such as that signed between the UNHCR and the Human Rights Operation in Rwanda (HRFOR).[4]

In 2005, the ERC launched an independent review of the global humanitarian system to assess the capacity of the system, identify gaps, and make recommendations to address them. The review considered both complex emergencies and natural disasters, and sought to establish benchmarks for accountability and performance, preparedness and response capacity, co-ordination, and financing. Following the review, the IASC undertook humanitarian reform measures in 2005 and 2006 to address three areas of continuing concern: improved humanitarian response capacity, leadership, accountability and predictability in specific sectors or areas of response through what was called a 'cluster approach'; adequate, timely and flexible humanitarian financing; and improved humanitarian co-ordination and leadership though the UN humanitarian co-ordinator system.

We saw in Chapter 4 that, in 2006, the IASC designated the WFP as the lead agency for the global cluster on logistics, and co-leader for the global clusters on emergency telecommunications (ETC) and food security. Although a global food sector cluster was not established, the IASC reaffirmed the WFP's global lead in the food sector. And the IASC agreed to apply the approach in all emergency situations where there was a UN humanitarian co-ordinator. At the same time, a *Global Humanitarian Platform* was created in 2006 to cultivate more effective partnerships between the UN and non-UN humanitarian actors. 'Principles of Partners' were formulated in 2007, which called for greater inclusiveness of NGOs and a shift from UN country teams to humanitarian country teams, including NGOs. The first evaluation of the cluster approach, completed in late 2007 following the major earthquake in Kashmir/Pakistan, recognized that it had improved co-ordination, allowed for better engagement with the humanitarian community, and led to greater predictability in the international response to emergencies. It noted that the emergency telecommunications cluster co-led by the WFP was considered to be one of the most productive of the global clusters, and recognized the WFP's expertise in leading the logistics food security cluster.

In 2009, the WFP's executive board requested the WFP secretariat to prepare a document on the WFP's role in the humanitarian system, as it had evolved since the humanitarian response review in 2005 (WFP, 2009m). The secretariat took the opportunity to seek the executive board's support for the WFP's engagement in humanitarian reform, particularly in the further development of the cluster approach, which it considered to be 'one of the most important humanitarian reforms' (WFP, 2010d). It also considered that the cluster approach was in accordance with the WFP's *Strategic Plan (2008–13)*, which clearly stated that the WFP's partnerships with other UN agencies, NGOs, and others 'were central to its work'.

In 2006–07, the WFP-led logistics cluster had responded to 11 new emergencies, and nine in 2008. These field clusters had made use of the 167 logisticians from 30 different organizations that the WFP had trained for deployment as part of the logistics cluster response. The WFP had 'always recognized the fundamental role that the logistics function plays in carrying out humanitarian operations'. This awareness led the WFP to build, maintain, and constantly seek ways to improve its ability to deliver assistance effectively and efficiently (see Chapter 2).

As a result, the WFP was assigned a number of inter-agency mandates (see Chapter 4). In 2000, the UN secretary-general designated the WFP as the manager of the UN humanitarian response depot (UNHRD) network. In 2003, the UN High-Level Committee on Management selected the WFP as the pioneer of the UN humanitarian air service. Recognizing its logistics expertise and experience, the IASC gave the WFP responsibility to provide logistics services to the UN and non-UN partners in the humanitarian community through the global logistics cluster. The IASC also reaffirmed the WFP's global lead in the food sector in the humanitarian context and requested the WFP to consider the establishment of a food security cluster, possibly with the FAO as co-leader. Executive director, Josette Sheenan, announced the establishment of the cluster at WFP headquarters, co-led by the WFP and FAO, in February 2010 (WFP, 2010e).

In 2006, in order to provide the logistics cluster with guidance on strategy and policy, training, mobilization of support, and surge capacity for start-up operations and ongoing humanitarian programmes, a Global Logistics Cluster Support Cell was established in the Logistics Division at WFP headquarters. The cell consisted of a group of logisticians with different skills drawn from UNICEF and the international NGOs World Vision International, Action contre la Faim, and CARE. The WFP also offered free storage services to UN agencies, governments, and NGOs through the UNHRD network. By February 2009, 30 UN agencies, international organizations, and NGOs had signed agreements with the WFP to use the network.

Since 2007, the global ETC cluster had provided co-ordination and technical support in seven major emergencies that had occurred in 2007, another seven in 2008, and a further five in 2009. In 2009, the WFP became sole leader of the cluster to provide training and a focal point for telecommunications issues. In addition, 19 of the food clusters created by UN country teams have been led or co-led by the WFP.

The WFP is active in the Humanitarian Financing Working Group, whose overall objective is to strengthen the Central Emergency Response Fund (CERF), country-based funds and other humanitarian funding mechanisms. The WFP had been the largest recipient of the CERF since it was established in 2005. In 2009, the WFP received $163 million (38 per cent) of the total funding to agencies in support of new emergency operations or those that were under-funded. Common humanitarian funds and other funds pooled at the country or regional levels have also financed WFP humanitarian operations.

Concerned to strengthen co-ordination in humanitarian operations, the WFP has taken part in the IASC and through the Humanitarian Coordinator's Issues Group. A pool of candidates from which to select UN humanitarian coordinators was initiated in 2005, but without thorough appreciation and selection criteria, and sufficient agency commitments. As a result, it failed to produce a roster of strong candidates ready for deployment as UN humanitarian co-ordinators. The WFP has expressed its interest in selected WFP staff being appointed as humanitarian coordinators, and supports the establishment of a second pool of candidates. The leadership capabilities of its staff are being built up through targeted training programmes to assume the humanitarian coordinator role.

The executive board acknowledged the WFP's valuable contributions to the international humanitarian response through the cluster system (WFP, 2010e). It welcomed the formation of the new food security cluster, and called for discussions with WFP partners and the High-Level Task Force in the Committee on Global Food Security. An annual update on the WFP's role in humanitarian assistance and progress in humanitarian system reform was requested.

Conflict of priorities

In conflict situations, three overriding priorities have been recognized: saving lives, maintaining human rights, and protecting the afflicted and vulnerable. While these priorities are regarded as sacrosanct, recent experience has shown that they are often difficult to achieve, and especially to achieve together. Two major obstacles, among others, have created problems. First, and foremost, is the principle of national sovereignty, enshrined in the *Charter of the United Nations* (UN, 1945), which states:

> Nothing contained in the present Charter shall authorize the United Nations to intervene in matters which are essentially within the domestic jurisdiction of any state or shall require the Members to submit such matters to settlement under the present Charter. (Article 2.7)

The Charter does go on to say that: 'this principle shall not prejudice the application of enforcement measures under Chapter VII' on 'Action with respect to threats to peace, breaches of the peace, and acts of aggression'. Such acts, and what measures are to be taken to respond to them, are determined by the UN Security Council. These provisions have made it difficult to gain access to countries engaged in internal conflicts or conflicts with their neighbours. And despite traumatic acts of appalling travesty, ranging from Cambodia, Rwanda, the Balkans, to Darfur, the international community has failed to respond quickly and effectively, calling for clarity on what became known as 'the right to intervene'.

But there is a second major factor that often hindered or limited the response. No single multilateral body has the mandate, resources, and ability to address the three priorities together. The WFP and other agencies may intervene to save lives, but do not have the mandates to maintain human rights and protect the oppressed. The UNHCR was created specifically to protect the rights of refugees; UNICEF, to protect the rights of children. It is therefore necessary to establish close working relationships among these agencies, for which MOUs have been signed. The separation of functions and responsibilities has led to the three priorities being considered separately and individually, which has created additional problems.

During the first decade of the new millennium, a spate of books appeared on the subject of human rights in humanitarian interventions. Written mainly by academics and specialists in the legal aspects of human rights, they have contained surprisingly little reference to the work of the operational agencies involved in humanitarian interventions. An unfortunate gap (some may say gulf) has therefore appeared between them and the practitioners of humanitarian operations that has resulted in the discussion of human rights, and the search for effective solutions, being taken out of the context of the realities of operational humanitarian action. An important part of the agenda for the immediate future should therefore be to bring the sides together.

Similarly, discussion and action on the 'Right to Protect' (R2P) has tended to be removed from that of the realities of the other two priorities, particularly that of saving lives.[5] Throughout the 1990s, fierce argument raged between the advocates of humanitarian intervention and the right to intervene, militarily if necessary, against the will of the government of a country, and defenders of the UN Charter's principle of national sovereignty that outside intervention was unnecessary and unwarranted. Inability to agree on an appropriate response to each humanitarian crisis became increasingly more frustrating and damaging as incidents of genocide and mass atrocities occurred, and the phrase 'never again' was oft repeated (Slim and Bonwick, 2005).

What was called a breakthrough came with the emergence of the concept of the 'responsibility to protect' (R2P) in the Canadian government sponsored International Commission on Intervention and State Sovereignty (ICISS) in 2001, which was embraced by the UN General Assembly at the UN World Summit in 2005 (Evans, 2008). The concept turned the language on 'the right to intervene' on its head by forcing, instead, a responsibility of all states to meet the needs of the powerless and most vulnerable. It pointed out that responsibility for action lay, first, with the government of a country. But if unable, or unwilling, to do so, a wider responsibility lay with other members of the international community to assist, preventively before a crisis occurred, and to rebuild after it, as well as to react during the crisis, with the emphasis on non-military action, although military intervention remained an option in extreme cases.

The concept was first articulated in the report of the ICISS entitled 'The Responsibility to Protect' in 2001. A key issue was whether a 'coalition of the willing' should be able to bypass the UN Security Council if a veto by one or more of the five major powers on the Council blocked action that most of the world community thought appropriate and diffusible. The ICISS report was published in the aftermath of the al-Qaeda terrorist attacks on New York and Washington, DC on September 11, 2001 that started the war on international terrorism. This led to the UN secretary-general's report *High-Level Panel on Threats, Challenges, and Change* (UN, 2004) and the UN secretary-general's report *In Larger Freedom: Towards Development. Security and Human Rights for All* (Annan, 2005). At around the same time, the *Rome Statute of the International Criminal Court* (ICC), adopted in July 1998, entered into force in July 2002, and now has over 100 signatories. An International Crisis Group (ICG) was established in 2000 to work on issues related to conflict prevention and resolution. A Global Centre for the Responsibility to Protect (GCRP) was created in 2008. The centre is a research and advocacy body with a strong North–South character to act as a catalyst to ensure that R2P is effectively implemented and practiced.[6]

With so many bodies involved in the three priorities of saving lives, maintaining human rights, and protecting the oppressed and vulnerable, it is essential to establish close co-operation among them. Failure to do so could have serious negative consequences, as was demonstrated in the prolonged humanitarian crisis in Darfur, Sudan. The issue of a warrant for the international arrest of the president of Sudan for crimes against humanity and war crimes in the Darfur region of Sudan, to which was later added the crime of genocide, led, predictably and immediately, to the expulsion of humanitarian aid agencies from Sudan, threatening to exacerbate the already serious humanitarian situation existing in the region. At the same time, there was concern that the national referendum to decide the outcome of the civil war that had existed in the Southern Sudan might be jeopardized, leading to the newspaper headline 'Justice or Peace'. In the meantime, the Sudanese president has visited Chad and Kenya, both signatories to the ICC and the Geneva Convention on Genocide, without being arrested and sent to The Hague, Netherlands for trial, as called for as signatories.

Although it has no mandate in the areas of human rights and protection, the WFP has undertaken to inform the responsible mandated agencies of transgressions in human rights that it observes in the conduct of its work, and to take measures to protect the beneficiaries of its assistance as well as its staff and those of its partners. For the WFP, protection is not about changing its mandate and providing legal advice or monitoring human rights. It is about working within its mandate of saving lives and ending hunger to contribute to the protection of people, which it considers is the primary responsibility of states (WFP, 2008l). For the WFP, therefore, protection is when its food interventions help people to stay safe and preserves their dignity, and the emotional and material quality of their safety. It is also in explicitly recognizing that addressing hunger is often not sufficient to help people enjoy life in its fullness or its integrity. Violations or deprivations not directly related to food or hunger can diminish the effectiveness of, or even render meaningless, the WFP's food assistance.

Internally displaced people (IDPs)

While a separate UN body, the UNHCR, was set up in 1950 specifically to 'provide international protection of refugees and to seek durable solutions to refugee problems' (UN General Assembly resolution 428 (V) of 14 December 1950), no such body has been established to address the problems of people displaced from their home within their own countries, referred to as internally displaced persons (IDPs), despite a number of attempts to do so. This failure is a major indictment of the UN system.[7]

Subsequent resolutions of the UN General Assembly, ECOSOC, and the Executive Committee of the UNHCR itself have called on the organization, in the context of its basic mandate, to protect and assist other groups of persons regarded as falling within its competence including: refugees, asylum seekers, returnees, and IDPs. But the UNHCR's involvement with IDPs is selective. It applies to persons displaced internally for reasons that would make them of concern to the UNHCR had they crossed an international boundary. In line with relevant UN General Assembly resolutions, the UNHCR's involvement with IDPs is based on a specific request from the UN secretary-general or competent organ of the UN, the consent of the state, or other entities concerned, and the availability of adequate resources.

The UNHCR's definition of IDPs is:

> persons who have had to leave their homes for refugee-like reasons and are in a refugee-like situation, but who remain within the borders of their own country. They have fled persecution, situations of general violence or massive violations of human rights and do not enjoy the full protection of their own government. (UNHCR, 1996: 2)

The most widely used definition of IDPs, presented in a report of the UN secretary-general in 1992, identifies them as:

> persons who have been forced to flee their homes suddenly or unexpectedly in large numbers, as a result of armed conflict, internal strife, systematic violation of human rights or natural or man-made disasters, and who are within the territory of their own country. (UN, 1992b: para. 17)

Over the years, a number of proposals have been made to reform the structure of the UN system in order to improve co-ordination of both development and emergency activities. In 1969, a study under the direction of Sir Robert Jackson to improve the capacity of the UN development system proposed the amalgamation of UNICEF, the UNHCR and WFP, under the leadership of the UNDP (UN, 1969). In 1995, the United States proposed the consolidation of the emergency functions of UNICEF, the UNHCR, WFP and the DHA into a new entity. As in the case of the

1969 study, the suggestion was met with considerable resistance from the agencies concerned, as well as governments. US officials acknowledged that the proposal was not 'thought through enough' and it was withdrawn (US, 1995).

With neither the political will nor the resources to support the establishment of a new agency, another alternative was to enlarge the mandate of an existing UN agency to protect and provide assistance to IDPs. The UNHCR seemed the best equipped legally and operationally to take on these additional responsibilities.[8] But when the Netherlands made this proposal in 1993, neither the UNHCR nor its executive committee endorsed the idea (UNHCR, 1993). The UN High Commissioner for Refugees, Sadako Ogata, observed: 'the magnitude of the problem far exceeds the capacity and resources of any single agency. It calls for a comprehensive and concerted effort of the United Nations and other humanitarian organizations' (Ogata, 1993).

The matter was discussed again in 1994 by the Sub-Committee of the Whole of the High Commissioner's Programme (EXCOM). On this occasion, Ms Ogata clearly defined the extent and conditions under which the UNHCR was prepared to undertake activities on behalf of IDPs: 'when they were in a refugee-like situation, or intermingled with refugees, or when it could prevent a refugee flow, and when specifically requested by the United Nations'. The UNHCR executive committee endorsed those criteria for IDP interventions (UN, 1994b).

In the meantime, the rapid growth in the number of IDPs around the world was to place a challenging issue on the international agenda. At first count in 1982, there were 1.2 million IDPs in 11 countries. By 1997, there were over 20 million IDPs in at least 35 countries (Cohen and Deng, 1998b: 1). The main reason for the increase was internal conflict, which became far more prevalent than inter-states wars in the post-Cold War era. From fewer than 10 internal conflicts in 1960, there were 50 in 1992. The number of IDPs began to exceed those of refugees over this period. Their condition was often worse than that of refugees, as the general public saw by means of the telecommunications revolution that brought the issue to world attention.

Against this background, the UN Commission for Human Rights (CHR) requested an analytical report on IDPs. The report was presented to the CHR in 1992 by the newly-appointed UN secretary-general, Boutros Boutros-Ghali (CHR, 1992b). The Commission's controversial response was to authorize the UN secretary-general to appoint a representative to explore the:

> views and information from all Governments on the human rights issues related to internally displaced persons, including an examination of existing international human rights, humanitarian and refugee law and standards of their applicability to the protection of and relief assistance to internally displaced persons. (CHR resolution 1992/73)

But the CHR limited the scope for reporting to existing laws and mechanisms. New ways to address the needs of IDPs were not to be covered. Many states were uneasy, however, with this potential intrusion into their domestic affairs, which went against the principle of national sovereignty enshrined in the UN Charter. Also, many humanitarian agencies were concerned with the possible bureaucratic fallout, perhaps in the form of a new UN agency (Weiss and Korn, 2006: 2).

Shortly thereafter, Boutros-Ghali announced the designation of what might have been to many the surprise choice of his representative for IDPs. Francis M. Deng, a former senior Sudanese diplomat from the southern Sudan, and a senior fellow at the Brookings Institution in Washington, DC, was appointed to serve as the UN secretary-general's representative on IDPs. Both knew and respected each other from the time when Deng was Sudanese minister of state for foreign affairs and Boutros-Ghali was Egyptian foreign minister. Deng had subsequently been Sudanese ambassador to Canada, the United States, and Scandinavia, before becoming a senior fellow at the distinguished Brookings Institution in 1988 to head its Africa programme. Deng agreed to take up his new appointment on the understanding that he would maintain his independent base and salary at the Brookings Institution (Weiss and Korn, 2006: 30–1).

Deng's mandate largely focused on developing legal and institutional frameworks for providing international protection and assistance to IDPs, and engaging governments and other actors in dialogues in an effort to improve IDPs' conditions. In addition, Boutros-Ghali requested him to conduct an in-depth examination of the problem and to develop a comprehensive global strategy for providing effective protection, assistance, and re-integration support to IDPs. In response to this request, the Brookings Institution undertook a collaborative project with the Refugee Policy Group (RPG), an independent centre for policy research and analysis concerning refugee and elated humanitarian emergency issues. Roberta Cohen, a US human rights advocate and senior adviser to the RPG, joined the Institute as guest scholar. Together with Deng, they co-directed the Institute's Project on Internal Displacement (PID) with a small secretariat. Deng's mandate was extended by the CHR until July 2004, the maximum time allowed by the UN under such mandates. He was replaced by Walter Kalin, a Swiss law professor whose title became the UN Secretary-General's Representative on the Human Rights of IDPs. Kalin has continued the direction of the PID at Brookings since 2004 under a similar arrangement as that enjoyed by Cohen and Deng.

Cohen and Deng were prolific in their work. Not only was a series of eminent annual reports presented to the CHR and two major publications produced by the Bookings Institution, which became the principal reference works on IDPs (Cohen and Deng, 1998a; Cohen and Deng (eds), 1998b), but they also played an important role in the formulation and acceptance of *Guiding Principles on Internal Displacement* in 1998 (Weiss and Korn, 2006: 55–70). The conceptualization of internal displacement brought about by the PID made a notable contribution to contemporary thinking about international relations, in particular by reframing the central component of theory and practice of state sovereignty, and UN bodies and NGOs established special programmes for this largely ignored category of war victims (Weiss, 2009: 200).

All this left its mark, but there was still no decision on which UN institution should take the lead on IDP issues, and provide protection and assistance. That opportunity came when the UN secretary-general, Kofi Annan, decided to undertake a reform of the UN system in 1997, which he described as 'the most extensive and far-reaching reforms in the 52-year history of our Organization' to 'prepare the United Nations to meet the major challenges and needs of the world community in the 21st century' (Annan, 1997).

In his preface to Cohen and Deng's seminal book on *Masses in Flight. The Global Crisis of Internal Displacement*, Annan wrote:

> Internal displacement has emerged as one of the great human tragedies of our time. It has also created an unprecedented challenge for the international community: to find ways to response to what is essentially an internal crisis. The severity of the problem, both in intensity and scope, is obvious from the numbers of the displaced, now estimated [in 1998] at between 20 and 25 million, and the fact that virtually no region of the world is spared from the epidemic. (Cohen and Deng, 1998a: xix)

As part of preparations for his UN reform proposals, Annan ordered a UN system-wide review with special attention to humanitarian and human rights operations.[9] The penultimate draft proposals for UN reform recommended handing responsibility for IDPs to the UNHCR, which was favoured by Cohen and Deng. An appendix to the draft UN reform proposals even fleshed out the possibility of creating a consolidated UN humanitarian agency over the long term. Other UN agencies, especially UNICEF and the WFP, and the NGO consortium InterAction, voiced their objections (Weiss and Korn, 2006: 80–1; Weiss, 2009: 77–80). In the UNHCR itself, the proposal met a mixed reception. While some welcomed the proposal as strengthening the UNHCR's role and resources, and saw it as a natural expansion of the UNHCR's responsibilities for refugees, others thought it would undermine the organization's capacity to fulfil its mandate for refugees. They also remembered the mauling the organization had experienced in carrying out its role as lead agency in dealing with the displacement and suffering caused by the wars in Yugoslavia in the early part of the 1990s (Weiss and Pasic, 1998: 175–231).

Faced with fierce opposition backed by governments who 'preached coordination but had their own agendas as well, including protecting the territory and budget allocations of their favourite intergovernmental and nongovernmental organizations in quintessential patron–client relations', Annan backed down (Weiss, 2009: 80). In the final version of his 1997 UN reform measures, the DHA was repackaged as the Office for the Coordination of Humanitarian Affairs (OCHA) under the ERC. And 'coordination' was reaffirmed as the UN mechanism for dealing with urgent IDP crises through the IASC, even though an Inter-Agency Task Force on Internally Displaced Persons created by the IASC in 1992 was closed down in 1997. The rationale for proposing the establishment of a new agency was to ensure that there was accountability in dealing with IDP issues.

Still no organization has been made responsible. And while everyone currently supports co-ordination, 'no one wishes to be "coordinated" if that entails any loss of autonomy' (Weiss, 1998: 11).

As the largest provider of food assistance to IDPs, what were the WFP's views on the subject (WFP, 1996a)? The WFP recognized its responsibility to assist IDPs by providing food through governments or NGOs in the form of relief, rehabilitation, recovery, and development programmes. But it found that access of IDPs to material assistance and protection was often less secure than that afforded to refugees. Four reasons were identified by the WFP for difficulties in assisting IDPs. First, was the lack of clear institutional responsibility for ensuring the international protection and material needs of IDPs. The reasons of internal displacement were often complex, and assistance for them was addressed on an *ad hoc* basis. Second, national sovereignty constrained efforts to protect the physical safety and human rights of IDPs, and access for delivering assistance to them. IDPs remained under the responsibility of the national authority, but their suffering was often denied or not recognized by their own government. Third, not having crossed an international frontier, IDPs were likely to remain vulnerable to the causes of their displacement, usually civil conflict. Their situation was therefore characterized by greater instability and insecurity than that of refugees. And finally, the international community's approach to sovereignty and human rights often needed to be reviewed to provide satisfactory and safe access to IDPs.

As there were no clearly established rules, guidelines, and modalities, the WFP found itself having to become involved in what came to be called 'humanitarian diplomacy' between the warring parties in order to gain access to IDPs (Minear and Smith, 2007).[10] This was often a delicate matter. While the WFP did not have a mandate to protect IDPs, it was fully supportive of the need to ensure their protection. If negotiations were protracted, the provision of emergency food aid may precede the finalization of protection arrangements. Such action should not be seen as undermining negotiations on protection but merely the WFP fulfilling its primary mandate, the alleviation of hunger among the poor and needy. On other occasions, in fulfilling it mandate, the WFP had to adopt protection measures for the beneficiaries of its assistance, as well as for its own staff and those of its partners, including transport and logistics officers, and other humanitarian workers.

The WFP's approach was based on what needed to be done, rather than on a formal interpretation of mandates. Its framework of intervention was flexible and tailored to each individual circumstance. The WFP arranged for the distribution and monitoring of food aid to IDPs through NGO implementing partners. Food may be the most prominent need but, in other cases, protection, drinking water supplies, shelter, medicines, and other essential needs may be more crucial; these were supplied by other agencies, making co-ordination of assistance critically important.

In response to ECOSOC resolution 1995/56 concerning strengthening the co-ordination of emergency humanitarian assistance of the United Nations, the WFP felt that the humanitarian system could be improved by designating an operational lead agency for each emergency. That agency would have responsibility to: organize the assessment of all needs; co-ordinate all technical support and services; and negotiate with governments and local authorities. The requirements of the lead agency were specified. These included: a predictable and reliable emergency role and response capability; the necessary operational field presence; the capacity to operate without the request of the government and in areas where the government may not be recognized; a rapid standby emergency response capacity; and ability to engage in rehabilitation programmes.

Without explicitly saying so, in listing these requirements, the WFP was implicitly stating that it was ready to assume a lead agency role. It recognized the ICRC's mandate to assist in complex emergencies and its important role in protecting IDPs, but pointed out that its constitution did not allow it to engage in longer-term assistance programmes. The WFP suggested that the ERC could develop the parameters for collaboration and division of labour among UN agencies for addressing the needs of IDPs and the procedures to determine the operational lead agency in each emergency situation. It recognized that inter-agency co-ordination had been improved through the creation of the DHA, but a forum for inter-agency co-ordination that included political and military questions in preparing for, planning, and responding to emergencies was required. Co-ordination between the DHA, the UN Department of Peacekeeping Operations, and the UN Department of Political Affairs could be expanded to cover regular consultations with operational agencies, such as the WFP, the UN Security Adviser, and the UN Security Council.

The WFP considered that there had been marked progress in the international response to emergencies since the sub-Saharan drought in 1984/85. However, it felt that further improvements still needed to be made to protect the world from the risks of hunger, malnutrition, and starvation resulting from calamities. The WFP also supported the UN resident co-ordinator system. Executive director, Catherine Bertini, wrote a letter to all WFP country directors underlining the importance of support, in which she stated:

> the success of the Resident Coordinator system depends as much on the commitment of the WFP country offices, and those of our sister agencies, as it does on the Resident Coordinators themselves. We must re-commit ourselves to strengthen the system, and I want you to make it a top priority. (Executive director letter to WFP country directors, 5 March 1995)

She also wrote a letter to all WFP country staff on the WFP's support for IDPs (Letter, 18 August 1995). As we have seen (pp. 326–9), the WFP gave its full support to the cluster approach designed by the IASC. In these various ways, the WFP demonstrated it commitment to improve co-ordination in the response to emergencies and the implementation of quick and effective action, which included meeting the needs of IDPs.

Resources and resource-related problems

Despite global food aid deliveries falling to a record low of 5.7 million tons in 2009 (less than half its level of ten years previously) and a global financial and economic crisis, contributions to the WFP reached a record high of over $5 billion in 2008, almost as much as the combined resources of the other global food and agricultural institutions – the FAO, the Agricultural and Rural Development Department of the World Bank, IFAD, and the CGIAR (Shaw, 2009: 2). In the face of what WFP executive director Josette Sheeran described as the 'perfect storm' of higher food and fuel prices, climate change, population growth, and rising absolute numbers of the hunger poor, the donor community responded strongly to the WFP's 'extraordinary appeal' to donate at least $500 million, later raised to $750 million, for ongoing emergency operations to avoid rationing food aid in response to the spiralling costs of food, fuel, and shipping. The donor community more than met the appeal: Saudi Arabia alone made a contribution of $500 million. Confidence in the WFP, and the recognized importance of its mandate, has resulted in over 100 countries making voluntary contributions to its resources at one time or another, added to by increasing contributions from the private sector. But the world's largest humanitarian agency still does not have an adequate, assured, predictable, and flexible resource base from which to conduct its operations quickly and effectively. In 2009, $4.4 billion in total revenue was received, 65 per cent of the planned funding required.

Some of the WFP's resource problems are also faced by many UN agencies. But, in many ways, the resource problems of the WFP are more serious, many-sided, and complex. Food aid flows have been influenced by the interplay of three factors: food production, stocks, and prices. Flows have been highest when production and stocks have been high and prices low, and lowest when production and stocks have been down and prices high, just when poor food-importing countries have needed them most. In the past, donors pledged their contributions to the WFP's resources in monetary terms, used mainly to draw food commodities from their own food stocks. While the WFP secretariat gives donors an indication of the kinds and amounts of food commodities required for WFP operations, a high degree of mutual self-interest has been shown in the commodities that each donor has actually provided, including high value-added products, such as canned meat and fish, and where and how they should be used. In 2009, only 8 per cent of the total value of contributions to the WFP were designated as 'multilateral' to be freely and flexibly used, and 6.5 per cent as 'unrestricted', defined as 'multilateral cash contributions to food-based operations without procurement restrictions'. The majority of contributions were tied by donor to specific uses (WFP, 2010c: 58).

A study commissioned by the OECD in 2005 on the tying of food aid by donors to the commodities they supplied, and the destinations they selected, found that the transfer costs involved were on average about 50 per cent more than food aid was provided through local food purchases, and 33 per cent more than through triangular transactions (OECD, 2005).[11] The overall results of the study showed that there were substantial cost inefficiencies associated with tying food aid. The most resource transfer-efficient forms of food aid were likely to be flexibly sourced, either within the recipient country or from third countries, but not necessarily always from a developing country, although it was noted that greater donor flexibility in sourcing food aid could benefit agricultural development in many low-income developing countries.

In recent years, the WFP has appealed to donors to provide more of their contributions in cash to purchase food in developing countries, especially for emergency operations. A number of donors have responded, including the European Union, which now provides most of its contributions to the WFP in cash. About 59 per cent of total contributions to the WFP in 2009 were made in cash. While helpful, the sudden and substantial increases in the prices of basic food commodities have created further problems, in that smaller quantities of food could now be purchased with the cash contributions. Increased oil prices have also had their effect on food production, through increasing the costs of running agricultural machinery and transportation, and especially the manufacture of fertilizers. These increased costs have resulted in record shipping rates and transport costs to deliver food to poor, food-importing countries, and to the hungry poor within them. In most years since the turn of the millennium, world grain production fell below consumption and stocks declined. The situation in sub-Saharan Africa is particularly disquieting; food production has actually fallen, increasing the problems of food insecurity and malnutrition. Investment in agriculture has lagged where hunger is most prevalent. And external assistance to agriculture is far below the levels of the 1980s, and does not target the neediest countries.

These factors are having a compounded effect on the WFP's resources. It has forced attention on how the WFP operates in order to respond to the needs of the hungry poor and the victims of natural and conflict-induced disasters, and on its ability to transform from a food aid into a food assistance agency. As if this were not enough, the WFP also faces a peculiar financial problem concerning the staffing and administration of the world's largest humanitarian agency.

The WFP's management plan rests on the basic and crucial assumption that the UN and its member states require, and are ready to fund on a voluntary basis, WFP global humanitarian operations and programme activities (WFP, 2007a). The funding model differs significantly from that of most UN bodies, in that the WFP has no predictable income for its programme support and administrative (PSA) expenditures. The PSA budget covers all staff and non-staff costs at WFP headquarters and liaison offices, the majority of costs at its regional bureaux, and some management costs of its country offices. These costs are solely funded by income derived from a certain percentage of the voluntary contributions received from donors, currently set at 7 per cent. This low percentage, the lowest in the UN system, was set when the WFP was first established as a three-year experimental programme with an uncertain future; when administrative and management costs were kept to a minimum, consistent with operational efficiency; and when most of its resources were invested in development projects. It proved to be diseconomic when the WFP was transformed into a mainly emergency agency.

Given the uncertainties inherent in this funding model, a main challenge facing WFP member states and leadership is to maintain a managerial and operational support capacity that has certain basic features. It has to be robust and flexible; able to meet the commitments made to the beneficiaries of its assistance in operations and programmes approved by its governing body; and maintain a rapid response and preparedness capacity in terms of people, equipment and systems, ready to be mobilized immediately at the onset of unforeseen emergencies.

The funding model operated well in years when the volume of the WFP's work and resources rose considerably with the increased occurrence and frequency of major natural and conflict-induced disasters. But when fewer or no major emergencies occurred, the 7 per cent formula was unable to sustain the management costs that had been built up in crisis years, and which would be required when major disasters occurred again. A related problem was that the funding model lacked a mechanism to compensate for significant exchange rate variations. When the US dollar exchange rate against the European euro fell in recent years, this caused additional problems. Most of the WFP's PSA expenditures are incurred at its headquarters in Rome, Italy and are thus based on euro costs. A fixed 7 per cent of overall income has therefore been unable to cope with PSA cost increases related to the transformation of WFP operations from development projects to emergency operations, the increased volume of work and real costs, and exchange rate variations. As a result, as we saw in Chapter 4, the PSA budget for the 2008–09 biennium was reduced by 21 per cent in real terms and WFP staffing, mostly at its headquarters, was cut by around 290 posts. With retirements and voluntary early separations, about 50 staff did not have their contracts extended. The decision has now been made to rely more on short-term staff and short-term consultancies.

Yet another problem remained to be addressed. In 1996, the WFP adopted the principle of full-cost recovery, whereby donors are now expected to meet all the operational and support costs of their contributions to the organization (General Regulation, article XII.2). This principle applied to the in-kind food aid in which the WFP had traditionally been involved in the past. But what of the new food assistance programmes that were now being developed under its *Strategic Plan (2008–13)*? The WFP secretariat proposed that the principle of full-cost recovery adopted in 1996 be applied to non-commodity based activities, such as vouchers and cash transfers, local production of nutritionally enhanced food, and local capacity development, outlined in the *Strategic Plan* (WFP, 2010h). The executive board agreed to segregate non-commodity activities within programmes and projects and, exceptionally, allow separate financing streams. It also agreed to modify the current direct funding model to a percentage of the operational budget, rather than as a rate per metric ton.

While every effort is being made to ensure that these measures will not impair the efficiency of WFP operations, they may not be sufficient to ensure adequate resourcing of all critical areas. New ways are now being explored to maintain a sustainable core budget, including specific funding for initiatives that the WFP has been asked to undertake on behalf of the humanitarian community or costs arising from global United Nations decisions, such as cluster leaderships and the UN 'delivering as one' initiative. Ultimately, this will require the international community to decide on how the world's largest humanitarian agency is to be adequately, securely, and flexibly funded to undertake the vital roles that it is being requested to perform, quickly and efficiently.

The United States' position

The United States position is of special concern to the WFP. As we saw in Chapter 1, the United States played a prominent role in the establishment of the WFP. Since its inception, the United States has been the WFP's major donor, contributing 40–50 per cent annually to the WFP's resources, significantly more than contributions provided by other donors, including the members and commission of the European Union, although the difference between them is narrowing (see Tables 7.1 and 7.2). United States continued interest in the WFP is shown by the fact that its last two executive directors and the present one are US citizens. But the United States has insisted on deciding where, and for what purposes, its contributions should be invested, and that they are tied to US interests. Under US legislation, all food commodities provided as food aid must come from stocks declared to be in surplus from US agricultural production. In addition, three-quarters of the food aid commodities should be in the form of bagged, fortified, or processed products. And under US cargo preference legislation, three-quarters of its food aid commodities must be shipped in US vessels at rates significantly above the international level.

In 2006, a study of the US food aid programme undertaken by the US Government Accounting Office (GAO) showed that, despite growing demand for food aid, rising business and transport costs contributed to a 43 per cent decline in the average volume of US food aid delivered over the past five years (GAO, 2006). These costs represented about 65 per cent of total food aid expenditure, highlighting the need to maximize the efficiency and effectiveness of US food aid deliveries, and impeding the goal of 'getting the right food to the right people at the right time'. By donating food aid that is US-sourced and US-shipped, US taxpayers lose more than half the value of their food aid dollars in costs by the time it reaches destination ports. The GAO recommended that the USAID and the

Table 7.1 Top ten donors to WFP, 2005–09 ($ millions)

Donor	2005	2006	2007	2008	2009	2010
USA	1,174	1,123	1,184	2,076	1,761	1,045
Canada	152	149	161	275	225	248
European Commission	264	266	250	355	350	229
Japan	160	71	119	178	203	213
United Kingdom	112	100	67	169	128	103
Australia	62	61	62	108	82	80
Germany	69	60	66	101	132	75
Sweden	84	58	65	82	72	74
Netherlands	115	80	76	117	77	68
Spain	11	17	30	117	214	48
Grand total	2,718	2,699	2,715	5,046	4,034	2,882

Note: Position of donors as at 26 September 2010.

Source: WFP WINGS data warehouse.

Table 7.2 Annual contributions to WFP resources by the United States and European Union, 1998–2009 ($ millions)

Year	Total number of contributors	Total contributions	United States	European Union*
1998	49	1,704.4	873.0	516.3
1999	52	1,512.5	721.2	463.7
2000	59	1,694.2	795.9	443.2
2001	53	1,906.6	1,201.2	449.3
2002	60	1,821.6	939.3	562.8
2003	67	2,555.1	1,458.9	662.9
2004	70	2,242.0	1,065.0	695.5
2005	80	2,718.2	1,173.7	876.2
2006	96	2,698.8	1,123.2	747.6
2007	88	2,714.9	1,184.2	745.7
2008	98	5,046.2	2,076.4	1,265.0
2009	79	4,033.6	1,761.0	1,172.7

Note: *Includes European member states and the European Commission.
Source: WFP.

US federal departments of agriculture and transportation should work together to institute measures to improve logistical planning, transportation contracting, and monitoring of the US food aid programmes.

A number of factors have accounted for the steep increase in international food prices in recent years, among them the use of food crops to produce biofuels, which may be characterized as providing fuel security for the rich at the expense of food security for the poor. It is now on the agenda of both US political parties to reduce dependence on imported oil. In 2000, about 15 million tons of the US maize (corn) crop was used to produce ethanol. In 2007, it was 85 million tons. The US is largest exporter of corn, a staple food in many developing countries as well as a major livestock feed product. The US now uses more of its corn production for ethanol than it sells abroad. The dramatic rise in demand for corn, stimulated further by government subsidies, has encouraged farmers to switch from other cereals used for food and has reduced food stocks to record low levels. The US Department of Agriculture (USDA) predicts that 38 per cent of the 2010 corn crop will become ethanol fuel. The US corn ethanol export business has emerged as a force in global energy markets. In the first nine months of 2010, 251 million gallons of ethanol were exported, more than double the total for 2009, and corn futures reached a two-year high. Government support for ethanol totalled $7.7 billion in 2009.

The environmental benefits of biofuel and its contribution to solving the US energy problem are ambiguous and controversial (Runge and Senauer, 2007; Daschle *et al.*, 2007). The US *Energy Independence and Security Act* of 2007 calls for the annual production of 36 billion gallons of renewable fuels by 2012, a fivefold increase in ethanol production, leading to a long-term diversion of farm land from food crops to the production of ethanol and other synthetic fuels, and to food price increases. The IMF estimated that corn ethanol production in the US accounted for at least half the rise in world corn demand. IFPRI estimated that the rapid increase in global biofuel production could push global corn prices up by 20 per cent by 2010 and 41 per cent by 2020.

While other donors such as the EU, Canada, and Australia have made significant steps to untie their food aid, they have put pressure on the US to move away from its in-kind food aid programmes. This push has come, in part, via the WTO negotiations on agriculture as part of the discussions on the implementation of the agreed Doha development agenda. The EU has played a key role in arguing for a primarily cash-based food assistance system on the grounds that the US in-kind food aid programmes are distorting trade, both in recipient countries and in other food-exporting countries. At the same time, the political process around the 2008 US Farm Bill in the US has stirred calls from within the country, including by former US president George W. Bush, at least partially to untie US food aid in order to improve efficiencies and reach more people in need. The Bush administration tried to incorporate into the 2008 Farm Bill provision to allow up to 25 per cent of the funds appropriated under Title 11 of the PL480 legislation to be used for local and regional food purchases as part of the president's annual budget proposal to the US Congress. With little public debate, Congress rejected the proposal. The US House of Representatives Agricultural Appropriations Committee pointedly stated:

> We are pleased that the Committee rejected an ill-advised administration proposal to move $300 million of international food aid to USAID, rather than continuing to fund it through the PL 480 program. The USAID funds would be used to buy food abroad, instead of American commodities, thus undermining the historically broad support for international food aid in this country. (US House of Representatives, Agricultural Appropriations Committee, 2005)

President Bush repeated the proposed reform in his budget requests of 2006 and 2007, but each time it was rejected by Congress (Hanrahan, 2007). Instead, only a four-year $60 million pilot programme for local and regional food purchases to be administered by the USDA was approved. These developments sparked off considerable debate within the US over its future food aid policy. At the same time, halting discussions are taking place on food aid reform at the WTO in Geneva, Switzerland as part of the stalled Doha Round trade negotiations. The US has resisted any new rules, arguing that food aid as a development and humanitarian instrument is beyond the competencies of the WTO to determine.

In response to President Bush's emergency package for the food crisis sparked off by rising international food prices, Congress enacted approximately $1.8 billion for food crisis-related international assistance, including substantially more funding for food aid for development and disaster relief to 'alleviate world hunger' (US House of Representatives, Committee on Appropriations, 2008). The Congressional funding package included $200 million for a new 'Food Security

Initiative', which was meant to provide support for agricultural research and development activities. Of this amount, Congress specified that $50 million was to be used for 'local and regional purchases'. In total, the emergency funding package included $125 million in funds from various sources for local and regional food purchase programmes over a period of about 18 months, in contrast to the reform in the 2008 Farm Bill, which provided for $60 million over five years. Neither represented a dramatic shift in US food aid policy, being less than 10 per cent of the overall food aid budget.

However, one analyst has optimistically stated that: 'the trend is clear that after years of inaction, policy-makers in Washington are taking steps to reform the US food aid program to include local and regional purchase' (Kripke, 2009: 122). He adds that:

> ideas, research, and analysis do contribute to reform, but that the processes by which reform will occur are likely to be irregular and sometimes require a catastrophic event. Creating the pressure for reform can be a long exercise and very gradual. It can be frustrating to practitioners to find that regular process is unsuccessful. It is useful to keep this in mind and seek opportunities in crises to advance existing reform agendas. (Kripke, 2009: 124)

In May 2008, in response to the growing food crisis, the US Center for Strategic and International Studies (CSIS) launched a bi-partisan task force to assess the rising humanitarian, security, developmental, and market impacts of rising food costs and shortages. Its co-chairs were Republican senator Richard G. Lugar and Democrat senator Robert P. Casey. The task force grew out of extensive prior work CSIS had carried out with the WFP on global food relief issues, particularly in Afghanistan, Myanmar, Somalia, Sudan, and Zimbabwe.[12]

The task force called for a strategic US approach to the global food crisis (Morrison and Tuttle, 2009). Among its recommendations, it proposed that the US annual commitment to emergency food relief be doubled from $1.6 billion to $3.2 billion, and that no less than 25 per cent and as much as 50 per cent of these expanded emergency funds be available for local and regional purchases. US food security diplomacy was called upon to press for more stable and predictable international financing mechanisms for supporting the WFP and agricultural productivity in the developing world in the next decade, and to significantly reduce hunger, poverty, and malnutrition. Also, it was proposed that a White House-led standing interagency mechanism on global food security should be created.

Former WFP executive director, Catherine Bertini, and former US secretary of Agriculture, Dan Glickman, have made a compelling case for bringing agriculture back to US foreign policy (Bertini and Glickman, 2009).[13] They point out that US policy has been to treat the symptoms of hunger with food aid, have called for greater investment of money and talent in combating the root causes of hunger, and suggest that President Obama should move hunger and malnutrition to the top of his list of aid priorities.

How this debate plays out in the United States is important on an international scale generally, and to the WFP in particular, as the US is by far the world's largest food aid donor and contributor to the WFP. It is necessary to understand how US food aid policy is formulated and enacted to find an answer.[14] Corporate actors have traditionally played a prominent role in the internal debates on US food aid reform. It is argued that 'corporate concentration and the historic importance of the grain, milling, and shipping industries to the US economy give these actors a degree of structural power in setting the addenda for discussing food aid reforms' (Clapp, 2009: 126–7). These same industries have also actively lobbied the US Congress. And they have sought to influence perceptions of the role of food aid by engaging in public debate over questions of world hunger and food security, and the role of US food aid.

These corporate actors have a complex relationship with other non-state actors that also have a stake in food aid policy. A number of key US NGOs, as part of their Coalition for Food Aid, have historically supported a similar position as that of the corporate actors because of their own economic interests in food aid policy, which has lent a degree of legitimacy to corporate opposition to food aid policy reform. This tripartite alignment of interests has been called the 'iron triangle' (Barrett and Maxwell, 2005: 87–106). But a growing number of US NGOs are increasingly moving away from the corporate position towards food aid policy reform. The most spectacular case is that of CARE, one of the largest international NGOs. In 2006, this NGO decided to stop receiving US food aid commodities, which it had used for many years for sale in developing countries to generate cash for its humanitarian programmes, in view of the potential harm to markets and local food production in developing countries, as well as the high management costs involved (CARE, 2006). The only exceptions would be where it was clearly demonstrated that food aid sales could be used to address the underlying causes of chronic food insecurity with reasonable management costs and without causing harm to markets or local food production.

The institutional context within which US food aid policy is made is particularly susceptible to the influence of powerful individuals and interest groups. Food aid policy and appropriations in the US are governed by protracted debates around successive farm bills covering between four and five years and annual presidential budget requests, which means that the US Congress must approve changes in policy. This enables private actors to engage in the public debate. The mixture of political, economic, social, and humanitarian objectives, which were brought to bear in originally fashioning the US food aid programme largely in the form that remains today, also enables a range of actors and interest groups to have their say (Austen and Wallerstein, 1978; Ruttan, 1996).[15]

Rather than trying to fund more local and regional procurement of food through the established food aid process using USDA funds, the Obama administration has proposed that up to $300 million appropriated by the US Congress in FY 2010 for international disaster assistance be made available for local and regional food procurement, and cash transfers and voucher schemes. Another possible provision of cash for local and regional food procurement is under the proposed senators Lugar-Casey 'Food Security Bill' (S.384). This bill is an effort to support the administration in implementing a comprehensive food security policy and covers many issues. Title IV calls for establishing a $500 million 'emergency rapid response to food crises' fund that would provide cash for local and regional food procurement, and other emergency cash assistance to address food emergencies. In sum, at the time of writing (March 2011), in-kind food aid remains the bulk of US food assistance and is likely to remain so for the foreseeable future. But cash for local and regional food procurement is growing and could become a potentially significant complement to traditional US food aid, both for the WFP and US-funded food assistance NGOs.

Climate change and disaster risk reduction

The WFP is gearing up to what could be its greatest challenge in the future, responding to the effects of climate change, and reducing the risks and mitigating the effects of disasters. Climate change is now generally regarded as one of the greatest challenges facing humankind. Potentially, it could pose a serious threat not only to world food security, but also to the existence of life on earth. But opinions are deeply divided both on an assessment of the dimensions of this global threat, and on developing and implementing a common and united response to address it.

International concern about the possible negative interaction between human activity and climate change was voiced at the first World Climate Conference organized by the World Meteorological Office (WMO) in 1979, which expressed the view that 'continued expansion of man's activities on earth may cause significant regional and even global changes in climate' and called for 'global cooperation in exploring the possible future course of global climate'. In 1988, the WMO and the United Nations Environment Programme (UNEP) jointly agreed to set up an Intergovernmental Panel on Climate Change (IPCC), a worldwide network of some 2,500 leading scientists and experts, to review scientific research in three working groups: the available scientific information on climate change, the environmental and socio-economic impacts, and the formulation of response strategies.

Since 1990, the IPCC has produced four major assessment reports, each showing increasing concern about the potential widespread negative effects of global warming caused by climate change. The final report in March 2007 declared, for the first time, that warming of the world's climate system was 'unequivocal' and caused by human activity. The linear warming trend over the past 50 years was found to be nearly twice that for the last 100 years. Eight of the warmest years on record had occurred in the previous decade.

If unchecked, the report painted a picture of a world of starvation, mass migration of people, rampant diseases, and the extinction of many animal species. Ironically, the worst effects would be felt in regions that were already poor, had contributed least to climate change, and were least able to address the problem. An estimated 250 million people would face hunger. Diseases, such as malaria, dengue fever, yellow fever, and Nile fever, would spread. Billions of people in Asia would be at risk from flooding. On the other hand, wealthier countries in the higher latitudes could benefit from higher temperatures, leading to increased agricultural production, open Arctic seaways, and fewer deaths from cold. The report warned that the world should begin to adapt immediately, or face a bill of many billions of dollars more and a heavy cost in human suffering within a few decades. It suggested that most of the cost should be met by the private sector and business rather than by governments.

A comprehensive review of the economics of climate change commissioned by the UK government was published in October 2006 (Stern, 2006). At the launch of the review, its author, Sir Nicholas Stern, head of the UK Government Economic Service, and formerly chief economist at the World Bank, said:

> The conclusion of the Review is essentially optimistic. There is still time to avoid the worst impacts of climate change, if we act now and act internationally. Governments, businesses and individuals all need to work together to respond to the challenge. Strong, deliberate policy choices by governments are essential to motivate change. But the task is urgent. Delaying action, even by a decade or two, will take us into dangerous territory. We must not let this window of opportunity close.

Climate change was described in the review as 'the greatest market failure the world has seen'. All countries would be affected by climate change, but the poorest would suffer earliest and most. Climate change threatened the basic elements of life for people around the world – access to water, food production, health, the use of land and the environment – and the damage caused by climate change would accelerate as the world got warmer (Table 7.3).

In the meantime, intergovernmental action had been increased. A *United Nations Framework Convention on Climate Change* entered into force in March 1994, ratified by 189 of the 192 UN members. The convention aims 'to achieve ... stabilization of greenhouse gas concentrations in the atmosphere at a level which would prevent dangerous anthropogenic interference with the climate system'. It sets an overall framework for intergovernmental efforts to tackle the challenges posed by climate change. The convention recognizes that the world's climate system is a shared resource whose stability can be affected by industrial and other emissions of carbon dioxide and other greenhouse gases. Under the convention, developed countries agreed to reduce their emissions to 1990 levels by 2000 and to transfer to developing countries technologies and information to help them respond to the challenges of climate change.

The *Kyoto Protocol* was adopted in Japan in 1997, which strengthened the UN convention by committing parties to individual, legally binding targets to limit or reduce their greenhouse gas emissions. The Protocol, which entered into force in February 2005 and runs until 2012, is ratified by 165 countries. Of these, 35 countries and the EU are required to reduce their emissions below levels specified for each country. Total emission cuts add up to at least 5 per cent from 1990 levels.

A major impediment to co-ordinated and binding international action to meet the challenges of climate change has been the marked difference between the

Table 7.3 Possible impacts of climate change on economic growth and development

Temp. rise (C)	Water	Food	Health	Land	Environment	Abrupt and large-scale impacts
1	Small glaciers in the Andes disappear completely, threatening water supplies for 50 million people.	Modest increases in cereal yields rise in temperate regions.	At least 300,000 people each year die from climate-related diseases (predominantly diarrhoea, malaria, and malnutrition). Drop in winter mortality in higher latitudes (northern Europe, USA).	Permafrost thawing in Canada and Russia damages buildings and roads.	At least 10% of land species face extinction (according to one estimate), 80% bleaching of coral reefs, including the Great Barrier Reef.	Atlantic thermo-haline circulation starts to weaken.
2	Potentially 20–30% decrease in water available in some vulnerable regions, e.g. southern Africa and Mediterranean.	Sharp declines in crop yields in tropical regions (5–10% in Africa).	40–60 million more Africans exposed to malaria.	Coastal flooding affects up to 10 million more people each year.	15–40% of species face extinction (according to one estimate). High risk of extinction of Arctic species, including polar bear and caribou	Potential for Greenland ice sheet to begin melting irreversibly accelerating sea levels rise to possibly seven metres.
3	Serious droughts in southern Europe occur once every 10 years. 1–4 billion more people suffer shortages, while 1–5 billion gain water, which may increase flood risk.	150–550 million more people at risk of hunger (if carbon fertilization weakens). Agricultural yields in higher latitudes likely to peak.	1–3 million more people die from malnutrition (if carbon fertilization weak).	Coastal flooding affects 1–170 million more people each year.	20–50% of species face extinction (according to one estimate). Onset of Amazon forest collapse (some models only).	Rising risk of abrupt changes to atmos-pheric circulations, e.g. the monsoon. Rising risk of collapse of west Antarctic ice sheet threatened with collapse.

4	Potentially 30–50% decrease in water availability in southern Africa and Mediterranean.	Agricultural yields decline 15–35% in Africa, and entire regions out of production (e.g. parts of Australia).	Up to 80 million more Africans exposed to malaria.	Coastal flooding affects 7–300 million more people each year.	Loss of around half Arctic tundra. Around half of the world's nature reserves cannot fulfil objectives.	Rising risk of collapse of Atlantic thermohaline circulation.
5	Possible disappearance of large glaciers in the Himalayas, affecting one-quarter of China's population and hundreds of millions of people in India.	Continued increase in ocean acidity seriously disrupting marine ecosystems and possibly fish stocks.		Major cities such as London, New York and Tokyo and low-lying coastal areas such as Florida threatened by rising sea levels.		
More than 5	This level of global temperature rise would be equivalent to the amount of warming that occurred between the last ice age and today – and is likely to lead to major disruptions and population movements. Such 'socially contingent' effects could be catastrophic but are currently very hard to capture with current models as temperature are so far outside human experience.					

Note: The table shows illustrative impacts of different degrees of warming. Temperatures represent increases relative to pre-industrial levels. The impacts are expressed for a 1 degree C band around the central temperature, e.g. 1 degree C represents the range 0.5C–1.5 degree C.

Source: Adapted from Stern (2006).

United Sates and other countries. The United States has neither ratified the UN convention nor the Kyoto Protocol, despite being the world's largest source of global greenhouse gas emissions (GGEs). With 5 per cent of the world's population, the United States accounted for 24 per cent of global carbon dioxide emissions and for 36 per cent of 1990 emissions. Uncertainty or unacceptance of the scientific evidence and predictions of the severity of the problem, and the estimated cost of the proposed solutions, have been quoted as reasons for US reluctance to co-operate. Aspects of domestic US politics also play a role. Many attribute the US reluctance to take action on climate change to politically powerful industrial and energy interest and lobby groups. These groups argue that imposing cuts in GGEs is a ploy to impose a tax burden on them, which would handicap their competitiveness in domestic and international markets. Another factor is seen as the separation between the executive and legislative branches of the US federal political process, which requires a super-majority of Congress plus presidential approval to take on international obligations.

Despite three UN Conferences on climate change (Nairobi, Kenya in November 2006; Bali, Indonesia in December 2007; and Copenhagen, Denmark in December 2009), each with their non-binding action plans, a binding agreement on co-ordinated global action to confront climate change has yet to be achieved. The former US vice president Al Gore has played his part in helping to turn public opinion against the sceptics in the US and elsewhere with his commentary on the film, and his book *An Inconvenient Truth* (Gore, 2006), for which he shared the 2007 Nobel Peace Prize with the IPCC.

In the meantime, the global financial and economic crises have diverted attention away from the global issue of climate change, and time is running out before the *Kyoto Protocol* ends in 2012. Despite lack of global agreement, certain scientific facts are now irrefutable. The ten warmest years on record have occurred since 1997. Data from the National Oceanic and Atmospheric Administration (NOAA) in the United States show that 2010 is set to be the warmest year globally since its records began in 1880. June 2010 was the 304th consecutive month with land and ocean temperatures above the twentieth-century average. All ten indicators from 50 independent records monitoring climate change involving ten separate indices showed a clear pattern of warming over the past half century. Carbon dioxide (CO_2) levels in the atmosphere have gone up significantly, induced by human activity. The IPCC says that we need to stop the world getting more than two degrees warmer, if we want to avoid dangerous climate change. Global sea levels have already started to rise as a result of melting ice and warming oceans. And severe droughts and widespread flooding are now more common than they were in 1970.

The World Resources Institute and the Earth Policy Institute, both located in Washington, DC, have declared that the effects of climate change are already upon us and that adaptation will be necessary to survive. Rising temperatures are said to have contributed to increasing food prices through heat, drought, and failed harvests in Australia and Russia. Disproportionate effects will be felt on two particular groups, the poorest and island populations, who make up over one billion people in 100 countries. The IFPRI has analyzed the potential effects of climate change on agriculture and the costs of adaptation (IFPRI, 2009). It concludes that the 'accelerating pace of climate change, combined with global population and income growth, threatens food security everywhere'. Agriculture is extremely vulnerable to climate change. The results of IFPRI analysis suggests that agriculture and human well-being will be negatively affected by climate change. In developing countries, climate change will cause yield declines for the most important crops. South Asia will be particularly hard hit. Climate change will have varying effects on irrigated yields across regions, but irrigated yields for all crops in South Asia will experience large declines.

Climate change will result in additional price increases for the most important agricultural crops – rice, wheat, maize, and soybeans. Higher feed prices will result in higher meat prices. Calorie availability in 2050 will not only be lower, but will also decline relative to 2000 levels throughout the developing world, increasing child malnutrition by 20 per cent and eliminating much of the improvement in child malnourishment levels that has occurred. The IFPRI estimates that investment in increasing agricultural productivity of $7.1–$7.3 billion is needed to raise calorie consumption sufficiently to offset the negative effects of climate change on the health and well-being of children.

A report by the UK government's Department of International Development (DFID) points out that sub-Saharan Africa has done least to contribute to climate change but will be hard hit by its impacts (DFID, 2009). Africa already has a highly variable and unpredictable climate, and many countries are ill-equipped to respond to existing climate pressures such as periodic drought and floods. The impacts on a region in which 333 million people already live in extreme poverty threaten to be devastating. Innovations – social, economic, and technological – will be central to combating the effects of climate change, but the actions needed to translate to a life dependent on clean and efficient energy will create new economic opportunities (Rees and Giddens, 2010).

The FAO, WFP, IFAD and Bioversity International on behalf of the CGIAR convened a High-Level Conference on *World Food Security: The Challenges of Climate Change and Bioenergy* in Rome, Italy in June 2008 to seek ways to achieve world food security and address challenges of higher food prices, climate change, and bioenergy. The conference, which was attended by representative of 180 countries and the European Community, adopted a declaration outlining immediate, short-term, medium-term and long-term measures to achieve the objectives of the World Food Summit of 1996 and the MDGs established at the UN World Summit of 2000 (FAO, 2008).

In a report commissioned by the WFP on *Climate Change and Hunger*, climate change is seen as one among a range of risks applying to food security of poor people and developing countries (Parry *et al.*, 2009).[16] It points out that the effects of climate change are not always easily discernable from the effects of other risks, partly because the indirect consequences of climate change – such as those affecting livelihoods, health, and migration – have the greatest impacts on poor people. Accordingly, the challenge of adapting to climate change is not a stand-alone area of focus and attention. The central requirement is defined as to 'mainstream adaptation in national development programmes and to focus on ways of replacing vulnerability with resilience'. The report discusses the entry points for mainstreaming adaptation, the governance of food production and natural resources, access to food, risk reduction, and social protection, and institutional implications.

The authors find that climate change is likely to exert a critical influence on the prospects for food production and food security, and to pose a major challenge for citizens, states, and international actors alike. But climate change cannot be tackled in isolation. The fundamental challenge is 'to identify the sources of vulnerability among poor people and focus on replacing vulnerability with resilience'. The challenge of building resilience will have to involve entire governments and the whole international system, from farms where food is produced to where it is consumed. It will involve policy-makers working in radically different ways, abandoning preoccupations with organizational territory, and developing new partnerships and mechanisms for co-operation. Recent attempts to improve coherence in the international system are a modest first step, but the real work remains to be done. The first and most obvious institutional requirement is adequate and predictable financing. There was also need to upgrade systems for risk surveillance and early warning, for capacity-building, and for organizational coherence at the national and international levels.

Concerning the projected impacts on the risk of hunger, studies using a variety of models were consistent on certain major issues. Climate change will reduce agricultural productivity in most of the world, leading to increased food prices, food insecurity, and malnutrition. The scale of the impacts was in the order of tens to hundreds of millions of additional people at risk of hunger due to climate change, an increase of roughly 10–20 per cent. Developing countries will be hit harder than developed countries, and the most food insecure regions, sub-Saharan Africa and South Asia, will be hit hardest. Adaptation of farming practices could halve the impact. And reform of institutions could reduce the impact further.

In a foreword to the report, David Stephenson, former director of the WFP's Policy, Planning and Strategy Division, states: 'WFP has a crucial role to play in the global response to climate change'. He points out that the WFP's work in vulnerability analysis and mapping (VAM), early warning systems, and weather-based insurance programmes helps governments and partners predict the onset of natural disasters and take appropriate measures to mitigate their impact. The WFP also provides emergency relief food assistance when disasters strike, helping devastated families to recover and rebuild, while assisting vulnerable communities to adapt in more difficult and uncertain times. He predicts that responding to increased hunger and malnutrition caused by the effects of climate change will be a major focus of the WFP's work in the 21st century. The WFP and its partners would do well to adopt a strategy and a plan of action to position themselves to respond immediately to the challenges arising from climate change as they adapt their economies and livelihoods.

The World Bank devoted its World Development Report 2010 to *Development and Climate Change* (World Bank, 2010). In his foreword to the report, the president of the Bank, Robert B. Zoellick, wrote:

> Climate change is one of the most complex challenges of our young century. No country is immune. No country alone can take on the interconnected challenges posed by climate change, including controversial political decisions, daunting technological change, and far-reaching global con sequences. As the planet warms, rainfall patterns shift and extreme events such as droughts, floods, and forest fires become more frequent. Millions in densely populated coastal areas and in island nations will lose their homes as the sea level rises. Poor people in Africa, Asia, and elsewhere face prospects of tragic crop failure; reduced agricultural productivity; and increased hunger, malnutrition and disease.

The report states that tackling the immense and multidimensional challenge of climate change demands extraordinary ingenuity and co-operation. A 'climate-smart' world is possible in our time, yet effecting such a transformation required all to act now, act together, and act differently. Many of the ways to address adaptation to, and mitigation of, climate change are already known. A major problem will be overcoming behavioural and institutional inertia.

In his foreword to the book *Climate Change and Global Poverty. A Billion Lives in the Balance?* (Brainard *et al.*, 2009), the president of the Brookings Institution, Strobe Talbott, states:

> Although climate change is a global threat, it is especially menacing to the world's poor. As the mean temperature of the Earth rises, the impact of climate change…will be greater in those regions that are already struggling. Waves of 'climate refugees', damage to traditional cultures, increasingly frequent and severe floods and droughts – these and other results of global warming will constitute a humanitarian disaster on top of the environmental one.

The costs of climate change will be political – and geopolitical – as well. Weak states will become failed ones, and failed states will erupt in chaos across borders. Hard-fought human development gains will likely be compromised with serious implications for global security, political stability, and world prosperity.

Another UN summit on climate change was held in Cancun, Mexico in December 2010, an important point in international negotiations for a global climate change agreement. Achieving progress will be crucial to tackling global poverty. The UK International Development Secretary, Andrew Mitchell, said in a speech on climate change at the Climate and Development Knowledge Network event in London on 18 November 2010:

> If we fail to act today then we will pay the price tomorrow not just in pounds and dollars but in human life. As we look ahead, our role – in partnership with

developing countries – must be to find a solution that tackles the challenges of climate change, while meeting development goals and facilitating long-term growth.

The Cancun summit reached agreements which invigorated the international process and put the move towards a global deal back on track. A 'green fund' that will distribute money to help poor countries cope with climate change, a mechanism for international co-operation on low-carbon technology, and a way to help developing nations preserve their forests emerged from the two weeks of negotiations. Countries will now continue to work towards agreement on other elements, such as the legal form a new deal could take, while climate change will continue to be felt on the ground in some of the world's most vulnerable communities.

A review of 188 WFP programmes and projects in execution in 2009 revealed that 85 (45 per cent) contained a climate change and/or disaster risk reduction activity in 53 (75 per cent) of the 71 countries where the WFP operated. The highest number of such projects was in southern, central and eastern Africa. The main activities involved support for agriculture (26 per cent), water conservation (23 per cent), and forestry, infrastructure and capacity-building in the assisted countries (WFP, 2009o). A review of ongoing experience of the WFP and climate change, undertaken by an independent consultant and commissioned by the WFP's Climate Change and Disaster Risk Reduction Office in 2010, found that 'WFP has a strong foundation upon which to build a coherent response to climate change', and that 'WFP County Offices are acutely aware of growing impacts of increasing climate variability and climate change on their target populations' (Urquhart, 2010: 2–3).

The WFP has also joined forces with other partners in conveying five key messages for *UN Framework Convention on Climate Change* negotiators about the interrelations between climate change, food security and hunger. Climate change will act as a multiplier of existing threats to food security: by 2050, the risk of hunger is projected to increase by 10–20 per cent and child malnutrition is anticipated to be 20 per cent and higher compared to a no-climate change scenario. Achieving food security under a changing climate requires substantial increases in food production on the one hand, as well as improved access to adequate and nutritious food, and capacities to cope with the risks posed by climate change on the other. Governments must be assisted in enhancing food production and access, scaling up social protection systems and improving their ability to prepare for and respond to disasters. Community-based development processes need to be fostered in order to enable the poorest and most vulnerable to build sustainable and climate-resilient livelihoods and to move out of chronic poverty and food insecurity. The humanitarian community must prepared itself for more extreme weather events and for protecting the already food-insecure better by strengthening both crisis response and crisis prevention (WFP *et al.*, 2009: 2).

At its second regular session in November 2010, the WFP's executive board requested that a revised policy on disaster risk reduction be presented for its approval by the end of 2011, incorporating elements emerging from the WFP's consultations and recent developments.

Comparative advantage and partnerships to end hunger

At the special session of the UN General Assembly in September 2010 to discuss progress in meeting the MDGs, the WFP executive director, Josette Sheeran, said it was time to put hunger 'on top of the global agenda' (Sheeran, 2010b).[17] Calling hunger 'the most severe face of poverty', she warned that only swift and committed action by global leaders will make the difference for millions of people worldwide. She felt that 'we knew what to do but we have to do it, and we have to do it vigorously. There was nothing more basic than hunger'. Although the number of chronically hungry people had fallen for the first time in 15 years, she said that 'this was no time to relax'. The recent global financial and food crises had exposed structural weaknesses in the battle against hunger. Many vulnerable people in poor countries had been priced out of the market for basic foods, which she called the 'silent tsunami' of hunger. Hunger fell disproportionately on women and children, and especially on the most vulnerable, infants under the age of two years. New scientific evidence had reinforced the crucial importance of getting adequate nutritious food to them at the right time.

The rationale for setting the elimination of hunger as a central goal for humankind is based on the fact that food is a fundamental human need – and, therefore, a basic human right. Ending hunger is both an important outcome of, and a vital contributor to, the development process, and to the achievement of the MDGs. Yet, it is essential to understand and appreciate the multi-dimensional and multi-sectoral dimensions of the causes of global hunger in order to reduce and eventually eliminate it (Shaw, 2007: 383–461).

Since the 1974 World Food Conference, the concept of food security has: 'evolved, developed, multiplied and diversified' (Maxwell, 1996). After the conference, the tendency to equate the world food security problem with the world food problem continued by concentrating attention on increasing food production, stabilizing food supplies, and using food surpluses – despite the efforts of the World Food Council, which was disbanded in 1993, to broaden the focus of attention (Shaw, 2010). The ILO World Employment Conference of 1976, with its 'basic needs' concept (ILO, 1976), and the work of Amartya Sen and his 'food entitlement' concept (Sen, 1981), led to an understanding and acceptance of the importance of assuring access to food by the hungry poor. This led to moving the concept of food security out from a purely agricultural sector concern into the broader arena of poverty and development problems. This process was carried further by the series of international conferences of the 1990s (Shaw, 2007: 274–380).

In essence, food insecurity is now seen as the eye of the storm of interlocking local, national, and global concerns, to which it contributes and whose solution lies in tackling those concerns holistically. This broader concept of world food security may be depicted graphically in many ways. It is represented in Figure 7.1 as a series of concentric circles. The innermost circle – the eye of the storm – includes

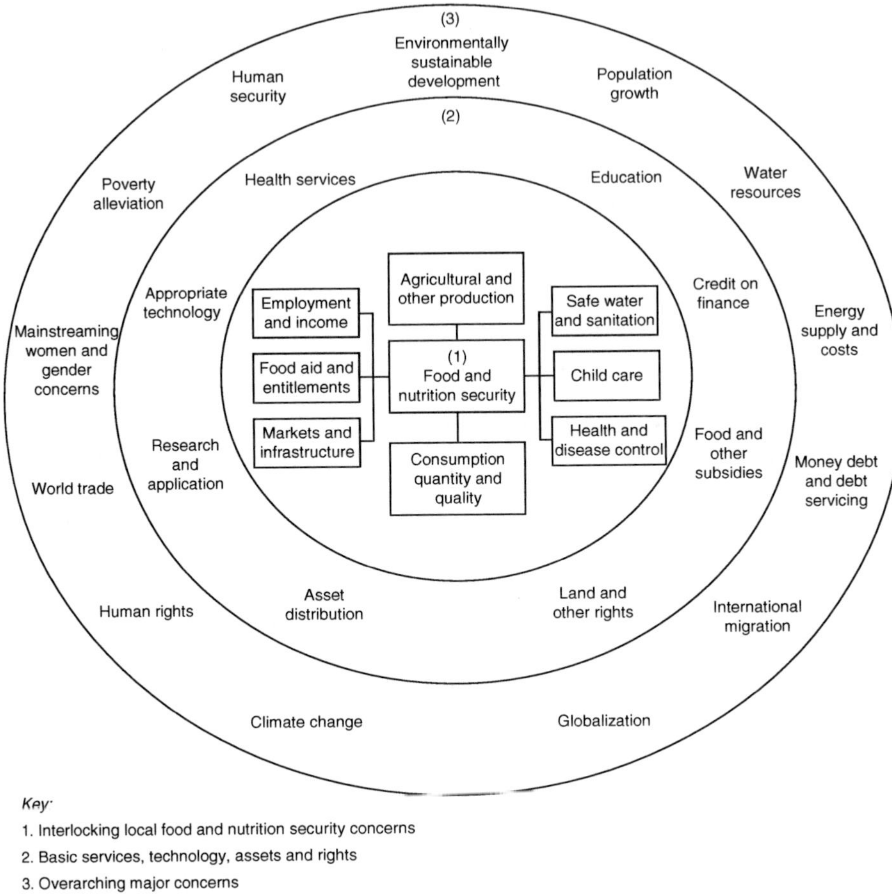

Figure 7.1 The broad concept of food and nutrition security: the eye of the storm
Source: Shaw (2007): table 42.1.

a series of interlocking food and nutrition security concerns, the relative importance of which varies from specific location to location. Those local concerns are surrounded by a number of wider regional and national concerns – such as basic services, access to technology, asset accumulation, and human rights – that impact on how the local concerns are played out. They, in turn, are affected by overarching major global concerns, such as environmentally sustainable development, water resources, world trade, human security and rights, climate change, and the current pattern of globalization; these penetrate and affect the concerns in the two inner circles.

This enlarging, refining, and redefining process carries with it two important implications. First, it highlights the problem of institutional incoherence. With so many multilateral, bilateral, and non-governmental organizations involved, food security has become everybody's concern and so, in reality, no one's responsibility

(WFC, 1990; Maxwell and Shaw, 1995; Delisle and Shaw, 1998; Shaw and Clay, 1998). Second, it has made the problem of developing common and coherent policies, priorities, and programmes to attain world food security and end world poverty and hunger especially difficult. Hunger, malnutrition, and poverty are intricately interlinked. Poverty is now generally regarded as the root cause of hunger and malnutrition. As pointed out in Chapter 4, what is not always understood is that hunger and malnutrition can be major causes of poverty. They affect the capabilities and capacities of individuals attempting to escape from poverty in several ways (FAO/IFAD/WFP, 2002). But poverty also has various dimensions including: food and nutrition insecurity, the population dimension, the income factor, the importance of education, employment and productivity, international trade, human security – in turn, affected by the global concerns such as climate change and global warming, and globalization (Shaw, 2007: 387–461). And the elimination of hunger and poverty is being sought through a human rights approach that would establish legally binding international obligations (Eide and Kracht, 2005, 2007).

The WFP has recognized the complexity of finding sustainable solutions to ending hunger. As stated in its *Strategic Plan (2008–13)*, the WFP's effort is an important 'building block' in the fight against hunger, but 'its effectiveness will be maximized only if it is accompanied by other actors' efforts or integrated into a broader alliance' (WFP, 2008k: 10). The WFP's overall strategy has been, therefore, to combine its own comparative advantages with those of partners in national governments, other UN organizations, NGOs, and the private sector, in precursor efforts, emergency response, or during the transition to sustainable solutions to hunger. To do this effectively, the WFP will need to define where its comparative advantages lie and then, rather than extend the boundaries of its expertise, combine with the comparative advantages of other organizations. An example would be to fill the WFP's 'nutritionist profile' through co-operation with other UN organizations that already have nutrition experts, rather than advertise for qualified individuals to undertake short-term assignments (ALNAP, 2010).

However, with so many organizations involved, the many initiatives proposed, and the changing architecture of aid in trying to achieve food security described in Chapter 6, a more deliberate focus is necessary. An effective way of demonstrating solidarity and establishing co-ordination would be for the five global food and agricultural organizations – the CGIAR, FAO, IFAD, World Bank and WFP – to declare a common initiative on world hunger in which they would share their comparative advantages (Shaw, 2009: 215).This initiative could be part of the 'new deal on global food policy' called for by the president of the World Bank (see Chapter 6). The initiative could take the form of a Global Partnership Programme against World Hunger, similar to those that already exist in the fight against the communicable diseases of AIDS, tuberculosis, and malaria; the global environment facility; and international agricultural research. As in the other global partnership programmes, the five organizations would pool their resources (financial, technical, staff, skills, and reputations) towards achieving agreed objectives over time, with a common governance and management structure. They may also invite other organizations to join them in joint endeavours.[18]

The UK government has proposed another approach. In its response to the UK House of Commons International Development Committee's report on *The World Food Programme and Global Food Security* (IDC, 2008), which was reproduced as an annex to the committee's report, the UK government believes that:

> identifying WFP as lead UN agency on hunger offers a route towards quick gains without substantial system-wide reforms being necessary. Making the role of lead agency explicit and official would assist the WFP in securing additional resources it would need to fulfil this role. (IDC, 2008, para. 101)[19]

In the UK government's opinion, the 'One UN' approach, currently in its pilot stage, was 'a necessary but insufficient condition' for achieving more efficient collaboration and greater UN coherence on food security. Given that the WFP already led the frontline response to hunger, that its mandate was expanding to include social protection work, and with an increasing focus on nutrition, it would seem the 'obvious candidate' for this role. Furthermore, linking this leadership role to hunger, rather than to the broader area of food security, would also make sense, as there were many long-term developmental aspects to food security that required inputs based on the agricultural and environmental expertise of the FAO and IFAD, among other agencies.

The UK government considered that the WFP deserved credit for its role at the centre of the UN's response to humanitarian emergencies, including its leadership of the global food aid sector and the global logistics cluster. It acknowledged the difficult and often dangerous job that WFP staff did in difficult environments, especially in conflict-prone and conflict-affected states. But priority should be given to ensuring coherence with other UN agencies in line with the 2005 Humanitarian Reform Agenda, and the WFP should continue to support the OCHA in its role in overseeing the co-ordination of the responses to emergencies.

The WFP's broadening of its activities from food aid to food assistance, and its associated increasing use of cash and food transfer schemes, was welcomed. These social protection schemes offered a flexible and effective approach to building up vulnerable communities' resilience to food insecurity over time. The WFP was therefore encouraged to continue to evaluate different elements within social protection packages, including striking the right balance between food aid and the best techniques for targeting transfers, to ensure that an optimal package can be provided. Specifically, the WFP was encouraged to explore options for replicating lessons from the Productive Safety Net Programme in Ethiopia elsewhere. Strong support was given for the WFP's activities in nutrition. It was noted that work in this area was fragmented across different UN bodies with no agency taking overall responsibility. It was therefore vitally important for the WFP to continue its nutrition activities. As an agency working at the point of delivery in humanitarian emergencies, it was essential for the

WFP to raise its profile as a major implementation agency for nutrition-focused work.

The WFP has been called upon to play yet another important role. In the face of increasing and volatile food prices, attention has returned to the need to establish a global system of food stocks. Over half a century ago, in December 1954, the UN General Assembly passed a resolution on the 'Establishment of a World Food Reserve' (827 (IX)). The FAO was requested to conduct an in-depth study of what was a popular concept at the time, but the idea was not pursued due to lack of political support (FAO, 1956; Shaw, 2007: 37–48). As was said at the time, the concept would give importing countries confidence that supplies would always be for sale when prices spiked, calming panic-buying and reducing pressure to retreat into a counter-intuitive view of self-sufficiency as the only way of ensuring food security. The FAO study pointed to practical difficulties, such as who would control the sale of stocks and when, but these were not consider insuperable. *The Economist* has suggested that the WFP could run such a system (*The Economist*, 2010). This would be a major undertaking on top of the WFP's already considerable tasks.

The president of the World Bank, Robert B. Zoellick, has suggested a different role for the WFP, to be supported by the G20 (Zoellick, 2011). He suggests that small regional humanitarian reserves should be established in disaster-prone, infrastructure-poor, areas where food crises are likely to recur and transport links are weak, such as in the Horn of Africa. These small pre-positioned strategic reserves would get food to the hungry fast, probably at lower cost. He suggests that the WFP could manage this system.

The third transformation: building capacity in developing countries

As this account has shown, the WFP has completed its transformation from a largely developmental to a mainly emergency assistance programme. Its transformation from a food aid to a food assistance programme is also in progress. But there is a third transformation explicit in SO 5 of the WFP *Strategic Plan (2008–13)*, described at the beginning of this chapter, that remains outstanding. This requires strengthening the capacities of developing countries, and the hungry poor themselves, to reduce and end hunger. It is now generally realized that only when governments, people, and communities in developing countries take ownership and responsibility for programmes initiated and supported by aid agencies can real and lasting progress be made in the fight against hunger and undernutrition. This requires sufficient policy and operational capacities at the national and local levels, as is recognized in SO 5.

The WFP has acquired 'an unparalleled experience and strong expertise' in the issues involved, reinforced by the knowledge it has gained from close contact with the beneficiaries of its assistance. Its 'deep field presence', particularly with the decentralization of its staff and the creation of its regional bureaux and country offices, was completed a decade ago. Also, the WFP has undertaken to design a clear 'handover strategy' to enhance nationally-owned hunger solutions as a crucial component of its interventions at the design phase of its programmes and as part of national poverty reduction strategies. What is suggested here is that the WFP adopt what may be called a VAM + approach. VAM directs attention to the people and communities that are most food-insecure and vulnerable. One step further would be to see their problems and priorities through their eyes, and to plan and implement strategies and programmes of assistance that support their aims and objectives. In so doing, their capacities to take care of their own future would be increased.[20]

One experienced analyst and practitioner has identified four 'drivers of change' that are required in order to bring about the desired transformation outlined in SO 5 (Walker, 2008: 5–6).[21] First, of crucial importance to the humanitarian system are the partnerships that international agencies make with local organizations, citizen groups, and the like in the crisis-affected areas where they seek to deliver assistance. Second, these partnerships can be particularly 'problematic', however, as they happen across such power imbalances. The external aid agencies have the money and political power, but the local agencies have the knowledge so essential to understanding and acting on the specific context. Similarly, a relationship of mutual trust and responsibility must be built up, based on the understanding that change in organizations is created by individuals at all levels, inspired by 'evidence-driven narratives'.

Third, change requires momentum and mass to reach the tipping point. Working with local communities to better understand crises has to go hand-in-hand with working with agents of service and change in the crisis area – extension workers, local politicians, landlords or warlords, and national politicians, corporation boards, and key religious leaders. Lobbying only at the top or at the bottom of the power structure is insufficient. Finally, change in human and natural systems is driven by positive feedback. Reward the behaviour you want to promote and promote it where it makes the most difference.

The third transformation that is sought is essential not only for effective emergency operations in which the aid agencies support the actions that the victims seek to perform, but also to hand over nutrition-improvement, school feeding, gender policies and mainstreaming, and HIV/AIDS programmes to national and local authorities, and to executive and scale up innovations made possible by food assistance schemes. It also helps to deliver the appropriate message by the most appropriate messenger. Too often, national politicians have been turned off by attempts to improve nutrition by aid agencies, which they have interpreted as a sign of their failed political policies.[22]

The example of India is instructive. Despite its impressive economic growth and the fact that India has produced some of the world's leading thinkers about undernutrition, India is home to one-third of the world's undernourished children (Haddad, 2009). In 1992–93, 52 per cent of Indian infants under three years of age were underweight. In 2005–06, 46 per cent were still underweight (Deaton and Dreze, 2009). India has received much assistance over many years from donor countries and aid agencies, including the WFP. It is now in a position to provide more of its own resources to improve the nutrition of its children. But it is argued that additional resources must be accompanied by a complementary effort to strengthen governance at all levels to improve: the capabilities to deliver services; the responsiveness of the state to the needs of all its citizens; and accountability to those the interventions are intended to benefit. A number of institutional and incentive roadblocks have been identified in the effort to improve infant nutrition. And there are choices to be made about resource levels and their deployment, mediated by the governance of nutrition resources.

For the first time, the WFP's *Annual Performance Report* for 2009 reported on the direct expenses made for SO 5 (WFP, 2010c: 23, 52–4). The activities involved accounted for 3 per cent of the direct expenses in projects and were mainly related to capacity-building, compared to 61 per cent for SO 1, 9 per cent for SO 2, 23 per cent for SO 3, and 4 per cent for SO 4. The WFP grants and trust funds were an important source of funding for its role in enhancing the capacity of governments to prepare for and respond to emergencies, and to pilot new initiatives.

Some examples of initiatives taken were given. The Latin America and Caribbean Emergency Response Network (LACERN) reduced response times from seven days to between one and three days in countries where the WFP did not have a presence. Emergency preparedness and response capacities in countries in the Middle East where the WFP did not have a presence were increased through capacity-building and partnerships with UN agencies, local governments, and regional networks. The WFP assisted the Ministry of Social Solidarity in Egypt to increase its capacity to improve targeting and cost-effectiveness in the national food subsidy programme, which resulted in increased budget allocations to improve the food subsidy system.

In 2009, the WFP's local purchases amounted to $364 million. The WFP country offices have been requested to increase local purchases as a percentage of the total quantity of food distributed annually by the WFP. In Indonesia, for example, all food distributed by the WFP in 2009 was purchased locally. The main advantages have been more timely availability, a reduction in handling costs and losses, and the delivery of food more readily acceptable to the beneficiaries. Local purchases have also helped to develop capacity to manufacture fortified foods. As a result of WFP support, eight countries had developed national micronutrient plans and programmes by the end of 2009, and 17 partnership agreements between the WFP and stakeholders were in operation to address micronutrient deficiencies.

It would now be appropriate for the WFP secretariat to present a report to its executive board giving details of achievements and problems encountered in pursuing SO 5. The case should be made for higher priority to be assigned to, and with a higher proportion of its resources to be devoted to, SO 5, which should be the ultimate goal of all WFP activities.

WFP staff: professionalism and security

The dedication and motivation of its workforce is the WFP's greatest asset. The professionalism of the organization depends on the people who steer and staff it. It also requires having the right staff, in the right place, at the right time.

Considerable pressures have been exerted on WFP staff as its mandate, and the way in which it is organized, have changed significantly. Recruiting, training, and retraining the right leadership at all levels in the operational chain are vital for a successful operational structure.

Mobility of staff constitutes a fundamental expectation of WFP staff and forms an integral part of the contractual employment conditions of its staff members. The WFP introduced and applied an internal geographical mobility concept almost from its inception in 1963. Subsequently, mobility, both professional/functional and geographical, was recognized as a key element of UN reform, promulgated by the UN secretary-general in 1997. A WFP human resources policy document on reassignment, rotation, and mobility of international professional and higher-category staff was approved by executive director James Morris, which took effect from 1 October 2005 (Morris, 2005b).

To implement its *Strategic Plan (2004–07)*, the WFP was defined as 'the employer of choice with the required staff, with the right skills, to meet the challenges'.

As recommended in a global staff survey, a WFP office of Ombudsman located in the office of the executive director was opened in September 2005 by executive director Morris.[23] With the objective of fostering a harmonious and productive work environment, the office provides to staff and management the services of an impartial and independent function where employment-related complaints and grievances can be informally addressed in a totally confidential setting. All interactions are voluntary and no action is taken without the permission of the plaintive. The ombudsman is not an advocate and has no decision-making powers, but can propose options to settle conflicts through direct access to the executive director.

The reports of the ombudsman for the four years 2006–09 provide an instructive source for management concerning the well-being of WFP staff (Shaver, 2006–09). They show the number and types of grievances of a growing organization now with a total staff of over 14,000; over 90 per cent are located in developing countries. The majority of WFP staff are nationally recruited, and there are general service staff in almost 100 country offices and sub-offices throughout the developing world, where decentralization and delegation are actively embedded in the work principles (Table 7.4). At the heart are strong internal communications, now strengthened through WINGS II, inclusion, evaluative learning, transparency, empowerment, and due process.

Table 7.5 shows the number of issues raised with the ombudsman by WFP staff annually between 2006 and 2009. During this time, WFP staff and activities have grown significantly. Its mission has been changed with the approval of *Strategic Plan (2008–13)*, which includes the transformation of the WFP from a food aid to a food assistance programme, and the quest for innovative solutions to ending hunger.

The caseload compares with other UN agencies of similar size and geographic distribution. In 2009, the majority of cases (37 per cent) related to evaluative relationships between supervisors and staff, and complaints of harassment and abuse

Table 7.4 Number of WFP staff by type and location, as at 31 December 2009

Location		Type of staff[1]			
		Total	International employees[2]	Locally recruited employees[3]	Miscellaneous[4]
Grand total		14,628	2,221	12,172	235
HQ and Liaison Offices		1,356	787	460	109
Staff on Special Status[5]		73	67	6	
Field Offices – Subtotal:		13,199	1,367	11,706	126
Brindisi Office		38	4	33	1
ODB[6]	Subtotal:	3,016	256	2,728	32
ODC[6]	Subtotal:	764	106	647	11
ODD[6]	Subtotal:	1,791	236	1,539	16
ODJ[6]	Subtotal:	3,768	467	3,255	46
ODP[6]	Subtotal:	879	75	785	19
ODS[6]	Subtotal:	2,943	223	2,719	1

Notes: [1]Data extracted from WINGS2; [2]Including: International Professional Staff, JPOs, International General Service, Consultants and UNVs; [3]Including: National Officers, General Service at HW, General Service Field, Service Contract Holders, SSAs HQ and SSAs Field; [4]Including: Author's Contract, Fellowship Holders, Interns and WFP Volunteers; [5]Staff on leave without pay or on loan/secondment to other agencies; [6]Manually derived from the actual duty station countries in order to reflect the actual staffing situation within the regions; for example, employees who are located in Kenya but report to Sudan, are counted under the Kenya duty station.

Key:
ODB Asia
ODC Middle East, Central Asia and Eastern Europe
ODJ Southern, Eastern and Central Africa
ODP Latin America and Caribbean
ODS Sudan

Source: WFP Human Resources Division.

Table 7.5 Number of cases examined by the WFP Ombudsman, 2006–09

Year	Number of cases			
	Cases opened	Cases closed	IRP staff	LRN/GS staff
2006[1]	259	232	114	145
2007	257	239	116	141
2008	265[2]	250	139	124
2009	259[3]	255	123	133

Note: [1]Started from 1 September 2005; [2]Includes two cases with external parties; [3]Includes three cases with external parties.

Key:
IRP Internationally recruited professional staff
LRN/GS Locally recruited national and general service staff

Source: Reports on the activities of the Office of the WFP Ombudsman.

of power. The next highest category (28 per cent) related to career progression and development, with 17 per cent of the cases relating to organizational, strategic, and mission-related questions and policies, procedures, ethics, and standards. Surprisingly, only 3 per cent of the cases examined related to safety, health, and physical environment issues, when staff safety has become a major concern (see p. 364).

The WFP has zero tolerance for all forms of harassment. In the past, barriers have existed between different categories of staff, especially between internationally recruited professional staff and locally recruited national staff, and steps are being taken to remove them. A management plan is being developed to provide a comprehensive framework for all locally recruited personnel in which equity in contractual terms and conditions is being addressed. As part of the overall policy of capacity creation in developing countries and handover strategies, consideration is also being given to upgrading the training provided for nationally recruited staff for them gradually to take over many of the tasks now undertaken by internationally recruited staff.

Clarity and training are also required in WFP policies and strategies. In many ways, the change from a food aid to a food assistance programme will require many of the elements that were involved in the transformation of the WFP from a development to an emergency programme including: a redeployment of regional bureaux and country offices, training in food assistance methods, and implementation and scaling up of innovative programmes, new transportation and logistics expertise, and new partners to implement food assistance programmes. With greater reliance on short-term staff and consultants, priority should be given to completing a comprehensive WFP policy statement on emergencies and associated developments (described in Chapter 4) that were individually approved at different times by the WFP's executive board in order to show the linkages and avoid overlap and duplication. Also, greater investment should be made in knowledge management and the WFP's institutional memory. This should include applying to all the documentation presented to the WFP's executive board since 1996 the same computer retrieval system that the head of the WFP's library, Andreas Psoroulas, has applied to all documentation presented to the WFP's governing bodies between 1963 and 1995. WFP staff have declared that they are proud to work for a WFP whose mandate is important and inspiring. But, as the work of the ombudsman has shown, it is everyone's responsibility to ensure that performance is strong and effective, starting at the top and permeating throughout the organization.

At the same time, there is increasing concern for the safety of WFP staff in developing countries. The WFP, along with other UN and other humanitarian organizations, was targeted during 2009 by various armed and disenfranchised groups (WFP, 2010a: 4). The situation was further exacerbated by a disinformation campaign waged by militants that urged violence against humanitarian organizations in general, and UN agencies in particular, who were seen to be a threat to their plans to take over countries or regions within them.

More than 600 security incidents involving WFP staff or installations were reported during 2009, including, harassment, detention, theft, abduction, and violent death. The most serious incident occurred in October 2009, when a suicide bomber killed himself and five WFP staff at the WFP's office in Islamabad, Pakistan. In all, 15 people lost their lives while working for the WFP in 2009, and another 35 were injured.

For the WFP, staff security remains paramount. At the same time, the WFP also recognizes its mandate as a front-line humanitarian agency with responsibility for the lives of millions of victims of war and civil unrest. In response to these two competing concerns, the WFP has chosen to adopt a 'how to stay' security culture, as far as practicable, to ensure that the WFP continues to address the critical hunger needs of affected populations anywhere in the world.

Independent external evaluation of the WFP

This account has shown the many vital and important roles that the WFP currently plays, and the perceived roles it will be called upon to play in the future, not only in meeting its own mandate, but also for the benefit of the entire humanitarian community. It is essential to have a clear and commonly approved agreement on what those roles will be, and how they will be performed and funded. As was done for the FAO, IFAD and the CGIAR, one way of reaching a unified and common understanding and full appreciation of the WFP's future tasks as the world's largest humanitarian agency would be for the WFP's executive board to call for, and supervise, an independent external evaluation, which would be presented to it for consideration and approval.[24] The evaluation should focus on redefining: the WFP's mandate; its comparative advantages; the formation of effective partnerships with other organizations; and the establishment of an adequate, assured, and flexible funding arrangement to support all the tasks the WFP will be requested to perform. The evaluation should be carried out by a peer group of recognized and independent analysts and practitioners drawn from recipient and donor governments, other appropriate UN organizations, NGOs, the private sector, civil society organizations, and leading development institutions.

Postscript

Significant developments have taken place since this book was completed. Food and oil prices have continued to escalate, eroding further the gains made in reducing the number of hungry poor and adding significantly to the import bills of food-deficit, low-income countries. In addition, there are increasing signs that the effects of climate change and global warming are already taking effect as massive unstable weather systems create widespread flooding, drought, and forest fires, affecting the homes and livelihoods of many people and the harvests in major agricultural producing countries. A large earthquake in Haiti and an even larger one in Japan, accompanied by a massive tsunami, caused widespread destruction. In Japan, nuclear electricity power plants were disabled, resulting in the danger of radioactive leakage.

The global financial and economic recession has limited the amount of assistance that the developed countries provide to poor countries. In 2009, the G8 richest nations pledged more than $20 billion to aid agriculture in developing countries, including $6 billion for a food security fund housed at the World Bank. As at March 2011, only $925 million of the pledges have been paid, because of the financial problems of donor countries. As chair of the talks at the International Grains Council, Canada is endeavouring to break the deadlock to reach a new agreement among the signatories for a new food aid or food assistance convention.

To add further to significant developments, political upheaval in North Africa and the Middle East, fuelled at least in part by rising basic food prices, has resulted in the overthrow of long-established repressive regimes and the demand for political, economic, and social reform. The uprising of the population in Libya against their leader who came to power in a *coup d'état* over 40 years ago has resulted in many deaths among the civilian population and the exodus of large numbers of foreign migrant workers, causing a major humanitarian crisis. The UN Security Council adopted a resolution which called for imposing a no-fly zone over Libya and taking 'all necessary measures' to protect the civilian population, short of a foreign ground invasion.

The FAO reported in January 2011 that, for the seventh month in a row, food prices had increased, predicting that, with some basic food stocks low, prices will probably continue to reach new heights until the harvests of next summer are known. Uncertainty itself is a new factor in the market that pushes up prices. The FAO price index, which tracks 55 food commodities for export, rose 3.4 per cent in January 2011, reaching the highest level since tracking began in 1990. Countries not dependent on food imports are less affected by global volatility but, even in the United States, food prices are expected to rise between 2 and 3 per cent in 2011. The World Bank's food price index rose by 15 per cent between October 2010 and January 2011, and was only 3 per cent below the 2008 peak, driving an estimated additional 44 million people into poverty in developing countries since June 2010, and increasing malnutrition as poor people eat less and are forced to buy food that is both less expensive and less nutritious.

Several factors are seen as driving food prices higher including: weather, higher demand, smaller yields, volatile weather patterns – increasingly attributed to climate change – that are wreaking havoc on some harvests, and diversion of food crops to produce bio-fuels. Severe drought is threatening the wheat crop in China, the world's largest wheat producer, and resulting in shortages of drinking water for people and livestock. China is also the world's largest producer of rice and the second largest producer of corn (maize) after the United States. China has been essentially self-sufficient in grain for decades for national security reasons and an obsession with food self-sufficiency. Any move by China to import large quantities of food in response to the drought could send shock waves through the world's grain markets, driving international prices even higher than the record levels reached recently. China's wheat industry has existed in almost total isolation from the rest of the world with virtually no imports or exports until 2010, when modest imports began. Yet, it showed that China produced almost twice as much as the United States or Russia, and more than five times as much as Australia. China also grows one-fifth of the world's corn, mostly in the country's northern provinces, where the drought has been worst. China is already the world's largest importer of soybeans, mainly used as animal feed as the Chinese diet shifts towards increased meat and dairy product consumption. In India, lack of investment in modern agricultural systems has meant that domestic agricultural production struggles to feed the large population and high basic food prices has resulted in persistent undernutrition, particularly among children, despite the country's impressive economic performance.

A record heatwave and drought in Russia has also seriously reduced the country's wheat harvest. Heavy rains in Australia damaged the wheat crop to the extent that much of its usually high quality was downgraded to animal feed. These events pushed the demand and price for American wheat much higher, with the best grades selling at 100 per cent more than they were in 2009/10. The autumn soybean harvest in the United States was poor, so strong demand resulted in stocks being at the lowest level in fifty years. Brokers are waiting to see how acreage in the United States will be divided between soybeans, corn (maize), and cotton (with cotton fetching record prices), and how much of the corn crop will be diverted to bio-fuel production.

Increasing demand for food caused by population growth and changing diets in developing countries, stemming from higher incomes in countries such as China and India, are also driving food prices higher. Close to 80 million people are being added to the world's population each year, the majority in countries where cropland is scarce, soils are eroding, and irrigation wells are drying up. Some three billion people are trying to change their diets as their incomes rise, consuming more grain-intensive livestock and dairy products in countries where inflation is becoming a greater problem. Countries such as Pakistan have had their agricultural production obliterated by widespread flooding. Others face the increasing risk of drought. It remains to be seen how much of the food crops will be used to produce bio-fuel, to support the energy security of the rich at the expense of the food security of the poor. However, rising oil prices will take their toll through increased costs of agricultural and fertilizer production and transportation.

Restoring food security for all will require action on many fronts, and the co-operative action of all countries and aid agencies, to a much greater extent than has been achieved to date. World leaders and international bodies have many times made a commitment to end hunger and poverty, and have acknowledged that there are sufficient resources and know-how to do so, although it is appreciated that, while producing enough calories can be achieved, the task of producing adequate nutrition for all for a healthy and productive life will be more difficult. In a globalizing world of increasing prosperity, in which the richest tenth owns 85 per cent of the world's assets, the scourge that so many should live in dehumanizing conditions is not only morally unacceptable, but is also a serious impediment to equitable and sustainable economic and social development, and to world peace.

The emerging world food crisis has been caused by a mixture of factors but, ultimately, it is the outcome of prolonged neglect by governments in developing countries and donors to invest in agricultural development, particularly that of smallholder farmers. International trade should also be stimulated by avoiding food export restriction, providing better information on food stocks worldwide, and developing less food-intensive biofuels. At the same time, nutritional and safety-net programmes should be expanded where food prices rise fastest, and poor countries should be helped to adapt to the effects of climate change. Political stability will be essential, brought about not by repressive regimes but, rather, by democratically elected bodies that respond to the needs and demands of the people who elected them. And the multilateral system designed after the Second World War to manage and regulate the world's financial and economic development will need to be adapted and reformed to reflect the major changes that are taking place in the new world economic order. About half of global growth is now from developing countries, and China's economic assistance to sub-Saharan Africa is greater than that of the World Bank.

Against this background, the activities of the world's largest humanitarian agencies in responding to emergencies, supporting innovative action to end hunger, and providing vital services for the entire humanitarian community will become increasingly important. Adequate, flexible, and assured funding will be essential. The dimensions of recent natural and conflict-induced disasters indicate the need for a significant change of strategy and mindset on the part of the international humanitarian system from managing poverty and hunger to helping people in ways that avoid dependency. Action should be particularly focused on building the capacities of poor hungry people and food-insecure countries to achieve their own food security, and for aid agencies to support their actions to end hunger.

The main messages to emerge from the World Bank's *World Development Report 2011. Conflict, Security and Development* are that some 1.5 billion people live in countries affected by repeated cycles of political and criminal violence, causing human misery and disrupting development. To break these cycles, it is crucial to strengthen national institution and governments in order to provide citizens with security, justice and employment, as well as alleviating the international stresses that increase the risk of violent conflict. The same applies to measures to end world hunger and the interplay with terrorism, national and international. A major lesson that has emerged is the need for far closer co-operation and coordination of action between humanitarian and developmental agencies and assistance.

Dramatis Personae

WFP executive directors[1]

James C. Ingram

Executive director for two terms from April 1982 to April 1992.

An Australian citizen, born in 1928, he studied economics and political science at Melbourne University. He began a career in the Australian Foreign Service in the Ministry of Foreign Affairs, and served in the Australian representations to the EEC, Indonesia, and the UN before being appointed as assistant secretary to the ministry's Asian and Pacific Department. Appointed ambassador to the Philippines (1970–73), high commissioner to Canada and several Caribbean states (1973–74), and director-general of the Australian Development Assistance Bureau (1975–82), during which he served as Australia's alternate governor of the World Bank, the Asian Development Bank, and IFAD, and Australian representative at the high-level meetings of the OECD's Development Assistance Committee, a member of the Australian National Commission for UNESCO, and a member of the North–South Round Table and the Tidewater Group. He was the first Australian to head a UN body. At the time of his appointment as WFP executive director, he received Australia's highest civil honour for services to his country.

He delivered the Joyce Pearce Memorial Lecture at the University of Oxford in 1988 on *Sustaining Refugees' Human Dignity: International Responsibility and Practical Reality*, which was published in the *Journal of Refugee Studies* in 1989. He served as the UN secretary-general's special representative to conduct humanitarian negotiations on behalf of the UN in the Horn of Africa (1989–91). He received the Alan Shawn Feinstein World Hunger Award for his work as WFP executive director and was the first recipient, with George McGovern, of WFP's Food for Life Award in 2000. He served on the governing body of the International Food Policy Research Institute and was distinguished visitor at the Watson Institute of International Affairs at Brown University in the United States, where he wrote his views on an improved arrangement for international humanitarian assistance. Since retirement he has continued to write on an improved system for providing humanitarian assistance, and was chairman of the Crawford Fund Task Force report on *A Food Secure World: How Australia Can Help* (2008). He was pressed on more than one occasion to head the UN Department for Humanitarian Affairs, later the UN Office for the Coordination of Humanitarian Affairs, and to join the Refugee Studies programme at the University of Oxford and a similar organization at the University of Toronto, Canada, but declined the offers.

Catherine Bertini

Appointed as the first woman WFP executive director in April 1992 and served two terms until April 2002.

A United States citizen, born in 1950, she graduated from New York State University at Albany and was later fellow at the John F. Kennedy School of Government at Harvard University. She worked for ten years in the private sector as a manager with the Container Corporation of America, where she was responsible for the firm's government and community relations and public affairs. She began her career in public office by holding a variety of positions in the state governments of New York and Illinois. She served for two years with the US Department of Health and Human Services, first as director of the Office of Family Assistance and later as acting assistant secretary of the Family Support Administration. Prior to her appointment as WFP executive director, she was assistant secretary of agriculture for Food and Consumer Services in the US Department of Agriculture in Washington, DC, which involved the management of all US federal food assistance programmes. She displayed a special interest in child nutrition and the advancement of women. She was appointed by the UN secretary-general as his special envoy for drought in the Horn of Africa (2000–01). She was chair of the UN Standing Committee on Nutrition for four years (2002–06), and served as under-secretary-general for Management at the United Nations (2003–05). She is a senior research fellow at the Bill and Melinda Gates Foundation, and is currently professor of public administration at the Maxwell School of Citizenship and Public Affairs at Syracuse University in the United States. She has received honorary degrees from seven universities in four countries.

James T. Morris

Appointed as WFP executive director in April 2002, he served for one term until April 2006.

An American citizen with a degree in Political Science at Indiana University and an MBA from Butler University in the United States, he combined a distinguished career of business, philanthropic, and humanitarian leadership with a personal life of public service. His principal interests have been building communities, serving vulnerable children at risk, and leadership development. After serving six years in city government in Indianapolis, Indiana, he moved to the Lilly Endowment, Inc., one of the world's largest charitable foundations, in 1973 and became president for six years until 1989. He then became chairman and chief executive officer of IWC Resources Corporation and Indianapolis Water Company, which under his leadership became a multi-million dollar holding company. While serving in these leadership roles and on several corporate boards, he was affiliated with the US Olympic Committee as treasurer and chairman of the audit and ethics committee. He was also chairman of the NCAA Foundation, a member of the Board of Governors of the American Red Cross, and chairman of the Board of Trustees in Indiana University, during which he contributed time and guidance to many civil and community organizations. His four years as executive director witnessed a dramatic increase in the WFP's activities in emergency operations and in WFP partnerships with NGOs and the private sector. He was appointed by the UN secretary-general in July 2002 as his special envoy for Humanitarian Needs in Southern Africa. He has received 11 honorary degrees.

Josette Sheeran

Appointed WFP executive director in April 2007.

An American citizen, she came to the post after serving as under-secretary for economic, energy, and agricultural affairs at the US Department of State. There, she was responsible for economic issues including development, trade, agriculture, finance, energy, telecommunications, and transportation, with much of her focus on economic diplomacy to help developing nations advance towards economic self-sufficiency and prosperity. She was appointed by the UN secretary-general in 2006 to the High-Level UN Panel on System-wide Coherence in the areas of development, humanitarian assistance, and the environment. As part of the UN panel, she conducted hundreds of interviews with development and humanitarian experts, NGOs, and national leaders throughout the world, and found WFP to be 'a gem in the UN system'. She had also served as deputy US trade representative in the Office of the US Trade Representative (USTR), where she advanced the Africa Growth and Opportunity Act, which helps African countries develop trade capacity to compete successfully in international markets. She was responsible for trade negotiations in Asia and Africa, and was instrumental in launching the first USTR trade capacity-building department. She also oversaw the US Department of State's economic diplomatic corps of 2,000 officers. Before joining USTR, she was managing director of Starpoint Solutions, a leading Wall Street technology firm that works with Fortune 500 clients. She also served as president and chief executive officer of Empower America, a Washington, DC think tank, where she advanced the agenda of economic development for inner cities and developing nations. She was a member of the Council on Foreign Relations for more than a decade and served on its Washington, DC advisory board. She also served on a number of other boards, including the Washington, DC boards of the Urban League and the United Negro College Fund. She had a distinguished background in media and, as managing editor of a major US newspaper, received numerous awards, including the Press Award for Journalistic Achievement by the National Order of Women Legislators, and a national award for developing and promoting African-American journalists. Believing that effective policies to address global issues such as hunger and poverty must focus on long-term solutions in addition to urgent responses, she developed several important US initiatives and aided development on critical multilateral projects in aid reconstruction in Afghanistan, Pakistan after the 2005 earthquake, and in the Lebanon after the 2006 war. She launched WFP's Strategic Plan (2008–2011), which was extended to 2013, and which provides the framework for the WFP's activities, including the transformation of the WFP from a food aid to a food assistance programme, over the six-year period.

WFP deputy executive directors[2]

Salahuddin Ahmed

WFP deputy executive director from December 1982 to his retirement in April 1994.

A citizen of Bangladesh, born in 1932, he graduated from Dhaka University, and received training in public administration and development economics at the University of Oxford, UK. He had a long career in his government's development administration and policy planning, particularly in the agricultural sector. He joined his country's civil service in 1956 and served as permanent secretary for Agriculture from 1969 to 1973. He was then appointed head of the Bangladesh embassy in Rome, Italy and the first permanent representative of Bangladesh to the FAO. He served as chairman or vice-chairman of several FAO committees. From 1976 to 1978, he was permanent secretary for Home Affairs in Bangladesh. He was appointed deputy executive director of the UN World Food Council in October 1978 until his appointment as WFP deputy executive director in 1982. His name was put forward as his country's candidate at the election of the director-general of the FAO in 1993.

A. Namanga Ngongi

WFP deputy executive director from June 1994 to April 2002.

A citizen of Cameroon, born in 1945, he studied agriculture at the California State Polytechnic University and received a PhD in agronomy at Cornell University in the United States, where he was a research associate and head of a joint research programme with the Soil Research Institute of Ghana to develop low-cost technologies for the production of basic food crops. Returning to the Cameroon, he held various posts in the Ministry of Agriculture, including chief of the Service of Projects. He then became first-secretary and counsellor at the Cameroon embassy in Rome, Italy, and was charged with Cameroon's relations with the Rome-based UN agencies: the FAO, IFAD, and WFP. He joined the WFP in 1984 and served in a number of positions, including regional bureau manager for the West and Central Africa region, head of the External Relations Division, associate director of the Operations Department, and director of the Development Division. He was vice-president of the Rome International chapter of the Society for International Development, and chairperson of the UN Administration Committee on Coordination Subcommittee on Nutrition. On leaving the WFP, he was appointed as the UN secretary-general's special representative to the Democratic Republic of the Congo, and later as the first president of AGRA in Nairobi, Kenya.

Jean-Jacques Graisse

Appointed as WFP senior deputy executive director in charge of its Development Department in January 2004. He retired in 2007.

He was appointed after 40 years as an international civil servant in the UN system, having served as WFP assistant executive director from 1996 and for two years as WFP deputy executive director. Before joining WFP, he worked at the UNDP in New York as assistant administrator and director of the Bureau for Resources and External Affairs. A Belgian national, he was born in Brussels in 1940. Prior to joining the UN system he was assistant professor in International Politics and Commerce in Antwerp, Belgium. He began his UN career as the first junior professional officer ever recruited in the UN system, working in Tunisia for the UN Technical Assistance Board before it was absorbed into the UNDP in 1956. His UN assignments included serving with UNDP in Côte d'Ivoire, at its headquarters in New York and at its European office until 1973. He then joined the newly established United Nations Environment Programme (UNEP) in Nairobi, Kenya from 1973 to 1980, before transferring to the International Trade Centre (UNCTD/GATT), which he left as director of Programmes, Finance and Personnel in 1988. He then became director of the Office for the Coordination of UN Humanitarian and Economic Assistance Programmes relating to Afghanistan (1988–89), before becoming UN resident coordinator in Kenya (1989–91).

Sheila Sisulu

Appointed WFP deputy executive director for Hunger Solutions in the Office of the Executive Director in January 2008.

A South African national, she was appointed as WFP deputy executive director of the Policy and External Affairs Department in 2003 before becoming WFP deputy executive director for Hunger Solutions in the Office of the Executive Director in January 2008. Before joining the WFP, her diplomatic career began in 1997 as consul general in New York, before becoming South Africa's ambassador to the United States. She had 25 years of experience in South African politics and government. After graduating in 1974, she started work as a high school teacher in Soweto. At the same time, she became closely involved with the radical opposition to the apartheid system. With the end of apartheid and the advent of black majority rule, she moved from being a force for change from outside to being an implementer for change from within as a special adviser to the national minister of education and a member of the team assigned with drawing up new legislation. She was responsible, in particular, for policy on gender equity, youth development, and early childhood care and education. She holds honorary degrees from the University of Maryland and the City University of New York.

John M. Powell

Appointed as WFP deputy executive director of the External and Resources Development Department in April 2003. He retired in 2009.

An Australian national, born in 1945, he is a graduate of the University of Canberra and was a barrister prior to joining the WFP in 1990. He assumed a number of senior positions at WFP headquarters including: regional manager of the Asia and Pacific Bureau (1990–93), director of the Strategic and Policy Division (1993–99), and director of the Asia and Eastern Europe Bureau (2000–01). He also held various positions in developing countries, including: regional manager of the West and Central Asia Bureau and country director in Pakistan (1999–2000), and regional director for the Asia Bureau (2001–03), where he was responsible for setting up a newly established decentralized bureau in Bangkok, Thailand for overseeing all WFP operations in Asia. Before joining the WFP, he spent three years in the World Bank's Latin America and Caribbean Division, and more than 25 years with the Australian government.

Amir Mahmoud Abdulla

Appointed WFP deputy executive director and chief operating officer in March 2009.

A Sudanese national, born in Khartoum in 1957, he is a graduate of Imperial College in London. His career with the WFP began as a logistics officer in 1991. He then went on to serve in a variety of field and headquarters posts including project manager responsible for implementing the WFP's corporate information management system (2000–01) and director of budget (2001–04). He was regional director for the WFP's Middle East, Central Asia and Eastern Europe Bureau (2004–06), and regional director for Southern Africa (2006–08). Prior to joining the WFP, he was branch manager for Juba and Port Sudan for the shipping and forwarding company Transintra, and assistant area manager in the Sudan for the engineering company Burmeister & Wain Scandinavian Contractor. He also taught at the American School and Comboni College in Khartoum.

Gina Casar

Appointed WFP deputy executive director for Resources Management and Accountability and chief financial officer in April 2009.

A Mexican national, born in Mexico City in 1959, with a Masters degree in Business Administration, she served as the WFP's chief financial officer from 2004 to 2006. She was the Treasurer of Mexico (2006–09) and chief financial officer of the Banco Nacional de Servicios Fincieros (Bansefi) (2001–04). Her professional financial experience includes service with Mexico's Ministry of Finance, as director of Financial Analysis, and deputy director of Financial Analysis at the Banking and Securities Commission of Mexico. She was a professor and head of the School of Accounting and Administration at the Instituto Tecnologico Autonomo de Mexico in Mexico City.

Staffan de Mistura

Appointed WFP deputy executive director for External Relations from July 2009 to February 2010.

This appointment was held between completing an assignment as the UN secretary-general's special representative in Iraq and taking up the assignment of the UN secretary-general's special representative in Afghanistan. A dual citizen of Italy and Sweden, he was born in Stockholm in 1947 and graduated from the University of Rome, Italy in Political Science and Development Economics. He began his 40-year career in the UN system with the WFP as project officer in the Sudan. Over the years, he helped organize food aid and relief operations there and in Ethiopia, the Balkans, and Rwanda. He has also served in complex, crisis-driven emergency operations in Bosnia, Croatia, Kosovo, Somalia, and Tirana, Albania. As an emergency relief officer in Chad, he led the first ever UN airdrop operations in 1973. He served in the FAO for 14 years until returning to the WFP in 1987 as director of operations in Sudan. He also served as director of Fundraising and External Relations of the UN Office of the Coordinator for Afghanistan (1989–91). He held a variety of posts in UNICEF, including director of the Division of Public Affairs at its headquarters in New York. His other UN posts include deputy special representative of the UN secretary-general in Iraq, personal representative of the UN secretary-general for Southern Lebanon, and director of the UN Information Centre in Rome, Italy.

Ramiro Lopes da Silva

Appointed as WFP deputy executive director for External Relations in March 2010.

A Portuguese national, born in Beira, Mozambique, with a Masters degree in Electrical Engineering from the University of Mozambique, prior to his appointment, he served as the WFP's director of emergencies and deputy chief operating officer. He began his career with the WFP in 1985 as food aid logistics coordinator, during the drought emergencies in the Horn of Africa and the Sahelian countries of West Africa. Since then, he has held other senior management roles in WFP operations in many countries including, Ethiopia, Pakistan, Afghanistan, Iraq, Angola, and Sudan. He has held other senior positions with the WFP, including director of transport and logistics (1998–2002), special envoy of the WFP executive director for the Afghanistan crisis (2001–02), and regional director of the newly established WFP bureau in Sudan (2004–06). He was UN assistant secretary-general and humanitarian coordinator for Iraq (2002–04), subsequently becoming, in 2004, senior adviser to the UN under-secretary-general for Humanitarian Affairs. Before joining the WFP, he worked for the Mozambique Port and Railways (CFM) (1975–83), starting as a port equipment maintenance engineer. By 1978, he was the director general of CFM-South, with 17,000 workers reporting to him and a budget of over $100 million.

Presidents of WFP's executive board[3]

Name	Country	Year
Beatrice Damiba	Burkina Faso	1996
Louis Dominici	France	1997
Maria Eulalia Jiménez	El Salvador	1998
Laurie Tracy	USA	1999
Mohammed Saeed Nouri-Naeeni	Iran	2000
Ulla-Maija Finskas-Aho	Finland	2001
Georges Ruphin	Madagascar	2002
Anthony Beattie	UK	2003
Miguel Barreto	Peru	2004
Poul Skytte Christoffersen	Denmark	2005
Mirzaz Qamal Beg	Pakistan	2006
James Melanson	Canada	2007
Jose Eduardo Dantas Ferreira Barbosa	Cape Verde	2008
Vladmir V. Kuznetsov	Russian Federation	2009
Sabas Pretelt de la Vega	Colombia	2010

Notes

Introduction

1. I am grateful to the head of the WFP Library, Andreas Psoroulas, for confirming that this was the first time that WFP so described itself in an official document.
2. The book is a personal account of the author's ten-year leadership of the WFP, based mainly on detailed records kept in his diaries throughout the period.

1 Historical background

1. The highlights of the historical background that are given here are drawn from more detailed treatments I have written elsewhere (Shaw, 2001: 19–36; 2007: 12–14, 85–111; 2009: 59–63, 76–82).
2. One of the best accounts of United States food aid up to 1976 in given in Wallerstein (1980); for the later period, see Barrett and Maxwell (2005) and Shaw (2007: 85–111).
3. Later, when European countries formed the European Economic Community, which later became the European Union, they produced their own agricultural surpluses stimulated by a Common Agricultural Policy, which led to their national and common food programmes that competed with that of the United States.
4. For a detailed account of the domestic politics of United States foreign economic aid, including food aid, see Ruttan (1996) and Clapp (2009).
5. A selective and annotated bibliography on the food aid literature commissioned by the WFP in 1964 listed 423 items. In a foreword to the bibliography, WFP executive, director, Addeke Boerma, noted: 'Ideas on the whole subject (of food aid)...are in a state of flux and evolution. Theoretical and empirical contributions to the literature are appearing so fast that it is sometimes difficult to keep track of them, let alone evaluate them. In these circumstances, an annotated bibliography – the first in this field – would seem to fulfil a useful purpose' (Henderson, 1964).
6. The WFP commissioned surveys of the food aid literature in 1978 and 1985, see WFP (1978b; 1985a). They were carried out by Hans Singer alone and Edward Clay and Hans Singer, respectively, both at the Institute of Development Studies at the University of Sussex, UK at the time they were conducted. These surveys were used to produce: S. Maxwell and H. W. Singer (1979) 'Food Aid to Developing Countries. A Survey', *World Development* 7: 225–46, and Singer *et al.*, (1987).
7. For a detailed description of these two proposals, and the discussions leading to their rejection, see Shaw (2007: 15–36).
8. Details of the numerous pioneering FAO studies and reports are given in Shaw (2007: 37–76).
9. The expert group consisted of Dr M. R. Benedict, Professor of Agricultural Economics, University of California at Berkeley, United States; Dr J. Figueres, Ex-President of the Republic of Costa Rica; Dr V. K. R. V. Rao, ex-Vice Chancellor, University of Delhi, and Director of the New Delhi Institute of Economic Growth. India; Dr P. N. Rosenstein-Rodan, Professor of Economics, Massachusetts Institute of Technology, United States; and Dr H. W. Singer, Principal Officer, Office of the Under-Secretary for Economic and Social Affairs, United Nations, New York, who was designated as chairman of the group.
10. See, Memorandum to President Kennedy from Adlai Stevenson, US Ambassador to the United Nations, 31 November 1961, in which Stevenson described the expert group's

report as 'One of the most remarkable documents on the subject', in *Adlai Stevenson, Ambassador to the United Nations, 1961–65*, Vol. VIII (Boston: Little, Brown & Co., 1979): 149. See also, Memorandum to US Secretary for Agriculture, Orville Freeman, from Willard W. Cochrane, Director, Agricultural Economics Service, United States Department of Agriculture, 21 June 1961 in which Cochrane found it 'an excellent report. The analysis of the role of food aid in economic development is in my opinion highly competent and informative. I know of no better analysis in the literature on economic development'. (Secretary's Record Section, Food for Peace Program, File IX, US Department of Agriculture, National Agricultural Library, Beltsville, Maryland, United States).

11. Executive Order 10914 'Providing for an Expanded Program of Food Distribution to Needy Families' and Executive Order 10915 'Amending Prior Executive Orders to Provide for the Responsibilities of the Director of the Food-for-Peace Program' in *Code of Federal Regulations Title 3 – The President. 1059–1963 Compilation* (Washington, DC: Office of the Federal Register: 443–4). See also 'Memorandum to Federal Agencies on the Duties of the Food-for-Peace Program' in *Public Papers of the Presidents of the United States. John F. Kennedy, 20 January to 31 December 1961* (Washington, DC: US Government Printing Office, 1962: 6).
12. Memorandum to President Kennedy from McGovern of 28 March 1961 and attached report on *Recommendations for Improvements in the Food for Peace Program*: 35–6. (McGovern Papers, Box TK-5, Seeley G. Mudd Manuscripts Library, Princeton University, United States).
13. 'Annotated Agenda for the Meeting on Use of Surplus Food for Emergency and Development Purposes through Multilateral Channels (FAO and UN)' with Annexes on the two food aid proposals of McGovern and the US representatives at the UN at the State Department, Washington, DC on 25 October 1961. (Copy in the McGovern Papers, Box TK-3, Seeley G. Mudd Manuscript Library, Princeton University).
14. A detailed account of the birth of the WFP is given in Shaw (2001: 2–18).
15. File EC342 (1-1), PT-A, RAG-3/2, Box 468, UN Archives and Records Centre, New York.
16. To give some idea of the intense and concerted effort required of a small band of pioneers (led by the executive director, Addeke Boerma, and the director of the WFP's Programme Development and Appraisal Division, Sushil Dey), visits were made to over 60 countries between July 1962 and March 1963 to acquaint governments with the new opportunities provided by the WFP. Mainly as a result of these visits, the number of requests for WFP assistance stood at 193 at the beginning of November 1964. These requests had to be examined, processed, approved or rejected, implemented and evaluated as far as experience allowed before the end of the three-year experimental period in 1965.
17. The ILO Convention of 1949 lays down a number of principles to be observed for payment of wages in kind, namely, that: allowances in kind are in a form appropriate for the personal use and benefit of the workers; partial payment of wages in kind should be permitted only in those occupations where it is customary or desirable because of the nature of the occupation concerned; payment in kind should also be authorized by national laws or regulations, collective agreements or arbitration awards; and the value attributed to payment in kind should be 'fair and reasonable' (ILO, 1949).
18. The studies were prepared by: Professor V. M. Dandekar, Gokhale Institute of Politics and Economics, Poona, India (Study No. 1); G. R. Allen, in association with R. G. Smethurst, Agricultural Economics Institute, University of Oxford, England (Study No. 2); Professor S. Chakravarty and Professor P. N. Rosenstein-Rodan, Center for International Studies, Massachusetts Institute of Technology Cambridge, United States (Study No. 3); Dr D. A. FitzGerald, Brookings Institution, Washington, DC, United States (Study No. 4); and Professor J. Dessau, Institute de Science Economique Appliquée, Paris, France (Study No. 5).

19. A small number of dedicated WFP staff members were responsible for establishing and building up the WFP's experience and reputation in transportation and logistics including: Dirk Sintobin (Belgium), Deputy Director, Resources Management Division; Erik Moller (Denmark), Chief, Transport Branch; Per Ivarsen (Norway), Shipping Officer; Tun Myat (Burma, now Myanmar), Director, Transport and Logistics Division; Andrew Toh (Singapore), Logistics Officer; and John Murphy (UK), Logistics Officer.
20. The joint views of the UN secretary-general and the FAO director-general were drafted by Dr H. W. Singer, Principal Officer, Office of the Under-Secretary for Economics and Social Affairs, United Nations, New York, and chairman of the expert group appointed by the FAO director-general, which prepared a report on an *Expanded Program of Surplus Food Utilizations* (FAO, 1961), who enjoyed the confidence of both executive heads (World Food Programme, Series RAG-3/2, Box 468, UN Archives and Records Centre, New York).
21. The proposals of the Israeli and Argentine governments to modify the WFP are given in WFP 1965a; 1965b.
22. Jens Schulthes joined the WFP in 1969 and served a director of the Regional Bureau of Asia and the Pacific until his retirement in 1997.
23. Fifteen different types of development projects received WFP assistance. For a description of each type, see Shaw (2001: 88–137).
24. Chr. Michelsen Institute (1994). The evaluation, which took three years to complete, at a cost reported to be over $3 million, was conducted by 16 international consultants, assisted by national consultants in nine country case studies. The first phase of the evaluation, completed in late 1992, was conducted by the North–South Institute of Canada. The second phase, completed in December 1993, was co-ordinated by the Chr. Michelsen Institute of Bergen, Norway. The evaluation report consisted of an abridged version, a main report, and nine country case studies. See also J. Faaland, Diana McLean and Ole Koht Norbye (2000) 'The World Food Program (WFP) and International Food Aid', in Clay and Stokke (eds): 221–55.
25. In its Resolution 2768 (XXVI) of 18 November 1971, the UN General Assembly singled out the poorest countries for special attention. They were called the 'least-developed countries' (LDCs) and were defined as 'countries with severe long-term constraints on development assessed on three basic criteria: per capita GDP of $100 or less at 1970 prices; of share of manufacturing of 10 per cent or less of GDP; and 20 per cent or less *literate* persons aged 15 years or more'. New criteria established in 1991 defined LDCs as 'those countries that are suffering from long-term handicaps to growth, in particular low levels of human resource development and/or severe structural weaknesses'. Low-income, food-deficit countries (LIFDs) include all net cereal-importing countries with a per capita GNP not exceeding the level used by the World Bank to determine eligibility for soft lending from its International Development Association (IDA).
26. The evaluation of the WFP's enabling development policy consists of two volumes. The main report (DMZ, 2005: 80pp) can be downloaded at www.depevaluation.com. The second volume, on CD ROM, (119pp.) gives details of the composition of the evaluation team, the evaluation tools used, the scale of WFP interventions in 2003, WFP development expenditure 2001–03, and the key findings from the desk and country studies.

2 From development projects to emergency operations: tipping points in the WFP's transformation

1. For a detailed description of the 1974 World Food Conference and its outcomes, see Shaw, 2007: 121–49.
2. I am grateful to Julian Lefevre, who spent almost six years as WFP project officer and the first UNBRO field co-ordinator based in Aranyaprathet, Thailand, and Kampuchea

in two assignments between 1979 and 1987, for his perceptive comments on an early draft of my description of the Kampuchean relief operation. Among other things, he spent a week in early 1981 travelling between Bangkok, Thailand, and Burma (now Myanmar) to supervise the WFP's first rice shipment to Kampuchea.

3. I am grateful to former WFP executive director, James Ingram, for clarifying his intentions in his personal correspondence to me during 2008 and the early part of 2009, which amplified those given in his book *Bread and Stones. Leadership and the Struggle to Reform the United Nations World Food Programme* (2007).
4. Personal correspondence for Trevor Page, 18 October 2008.
5. FAO director-general Edouard Saouma objected to the title of director of the WFP's Emergency Service, as Page had not been interviewed and accepted by him. Eventually, he interviewed Page and agreed with the designation of director. (Personal correspondence from Trevor Page, 29 December 2008.) Speaking at a seminar on food aid and emergencies in December 1984, Page referred to emergency relief operations as 'the last bastion of unprofessionalism' (Page, 1985).
6. A graphical account of WFP emergency operations during the African food crises of the 1980s is given in Fraser (1988).
7. The United States Marshall Plan contained large food aid shipments, but to European countries with strong absorptive and administrative capacities. US food aid shipments to India reached over eight million tons in 1966, but this was from one donor to one recipient country with good administration and logistics, and a well-functioning public food distribution system.
8. Erik Moller, chief of the WFP's Transport Branch, organized the trucking fleet in Ethiopia, the first such venture by WFP. He became ill there and died shortly afterwards from cancer.
9. The evaluation was led by Bronek Szynalski, then chief of the WFP's Operational Evaluation Branch, who wrote most of the evaluation report. It comprised a desk study of all WFP emergency operations in sub-Saharan Africa approved between 1983 and 1985, field missions to six countries (Chad, Ethiopia, Mozambique, Senegal, Sudan, and Uganda) between March and July 1985 and in January 1986, with FAO and WHO officers, and a questionnaire to 19 other African countries. Its objective was defined as 'to assess the efficiency of all aspects of the WFP response to the emergency which resulted from drought and other factors in 1983 and 1984'.
10. Personal correspondence from Bronek Szynalski, 21 December 2008 and 26 January 2009.
11. A detailed review of Operation Lifeline Sudan is given in Minear (1991).
12. *WFP General Regulations, Article IX: Eligibility for assistance*, 2008 edn: 14.
13. The Joyce Pearce Memorial Lecture is delivered annually at the University of Oxford, UK under the auspices of the Refugee Studies Programme and the Ockenden Venture, founded by Joyce Pearce as a charitable agency concerned with providing humanitarian assistance for refugees, mainly those entering Britain.
14. Personal correspondence from James Ingram, 8 December 2008.
15. Personal correspondence from James Ingram, 14 February 2009.

3 Emergency assistance: transformation accomplished

1. Guidelines on food rations for refugees have been agreed between the WFP and UNHCR. When refugees are dependent entirely on external food aid, the total food available to them from all sources should provide an intake of no less than 1,900 kilocalories of energy per person per day, of which at least 8 per cent should be in the form of protein and 10 per cent in the form of fat. The calories of energy can be modified depending on the circumstance of the refugee population.
2. In a review of the literature published between 1989 and 1996, about one-quarter of the 2,200 entries related to outside military forces under UN auspices in complex

emergencies of the post-Cold War period in 'operations other than war' (Collins and Weiss, 1997).

3. Development Initiatives (DIs), as part of the *Global Humanitarian Assistance* (GHA) programme, produces an annual *Global Humanitarian Assistance* report, funded by a number of donor countries. In a new phase of the GHA programme, DIs are also researching data on humanitarian assistance from other sources, as well as those of DAC/OECD countries. Further information on the GHA project and the complete set of GHA reports is available from www.globalhumanitarianassistance.org.
4. No operational guidelines were issued for PROs.
5. Most evaluations are managed by the WFP's Office of Evaluation (OEDE) and conducted by teams of independent external consultants. On a few occasions, the OEDE both manages the evaluation and has one of its evaluation officers on the evaluation team. (Personal correspondence from Julian Lefevre, former Chief Evaluation Officer, OEDE, 28 March 2009.)
6. The evaluation team was led by an independent consultant, and included a nutritionist who spoke fluent Bahasa Indonesian, which facilitated interviews with disaster victims, and health and logistics specialists, and a WFP evaluation officer, who also acted as evaluation manager. The evaluation took place over four weeks in May/June 2005, and included interviews with government officials in Indonesia and Sri Lanka, and UN and NGO representatives, and informal group discussions with affected people, local government officers, and leaders.
7. The *Joint Evaluation of the International Response to the Indian Ocean Tsunami* was carried out by the Tsunami Evaluation Coalition (TEC), a multi-agency learning and accountability initiative in the humanitarian sector established in February 2005, in the wake of the disaster. The TEC produced five thematic evaluations of different aspects of the international response on: co-ordination; needs assessment; capacities; linking relief, rehabilitation, and development; and the funding response. The WFP contributed $25,000 to the overall cost of the evaluation and the WFP's Office of Evaluation participated in two of the five thematic evaluations.
8. The evaluation team leader was a former UNICEF senior public health and nutrition officer. The WFP's chief evaluation officer was the evaluation manager.
9. The evaluation team consisted of an economist (team leader), a nutritionist, a vulnerability assessment expert, and an agricultural economist.
10. I am grateful to Ron Ockwell for providing me with a copy of his report. The report was based on previous evaluation reports, field visits to Uganda and Kenya, and interviews with a large number of WFP staff and those of other UN agencies, NGOs, institutes, private researchers, and consultants in Rome, Geneva, and London. While in Kenya, Ockwell interviewed staff working in the Great Lakes region of Africa, northern Uganda, Somalia, and southern Sudan who had experience in several different emergency operations. I also appreciated the personal correspondence from Ockwell of 14 October 2008, in which he described the work he carried out in preparing much of the early training material for WFP staff on emergencies and his taking part in training programmes.
11. Ten WFP staff were killed, apparently deliberately, in complex emergencies between July 1997 and June 1998, and an unknown number of staff of WFP contractors and NGO partners were killed or injured.
12. The evaluation was initially proposed by the Danish Government's international development agency, DANIDA, and was managed by a steering committee consisting of 37 members drawn from governments, UN agencies, and NGOs, who guided the work and provided the $1.7 million to carry it out. It was released after more than a year of work by some 52 consultants and researchers. The evaluation contains four separate studies on: Historical Perspective; Early Warning and Conflict Management; Humanitarian Aid and Effect; and Rebuilding Post-War Rwanda, and a Synthesis Report. The evaluation, which includes a review of bibliographical material,

represented the most exhaustive review of any major humanitarian operation, and provided an example for the international Evaluation of the Indian Ocean tsunami (2005).

13. Personal correspondence from Trevor Page, 22 April 2009, who was head of the WFP's rapid response team in Rwanda.
14. At the time, Larry Minear was a co-director on the *Humanitarian and War Project* at Brown University in the United States and its principal researcher. Randolph Kent served as United Nations humanitarian co-ordinator in Rwanda between October 1994 and November 1995, as special adviser on post-conflict recovery of the UN Special Emergency Programme for the Horn of Africa, and as co-ordinator of the Inter-Agency Support Unit of the Inter-Agency Standing Committee.
15. Further information on ALNAP can be found at www.alnap.org, e-mail, alnap@alnap.org. Its flagship annual publication, the *Review of Humanitarian Action*, provides detailed research and analysis on performance, and occasional papers are produced on thematic issues.
16. The evaluation mission was led by a WFP consultant and included a consultant on food security and nutrition, and part-time technical support. The evaluation was managed by the WFP's Office of Evaluation. The mission's report was prepared by the mission leader on the basis of the mission's field work. The mission spent 35 days in the field visiting the five countries involved, meeting with representatives of government and other UN agencies, donors, and NGOs. Particular efforts were made to obtain the perspectives of the beneficiaries of WFP assistance. Travel in each country was severely restricted by the security situation. In Côte d'Ivoire, the mission was confined to its hotel for four days for security reasons.
17. The review was conducted by an independent consultant as mission leader and a WFP policy officer, with a WFP staff member as review manager.
18. The evaluation mission was led by a staff member of the FAO's Investment Centre and included four consultants, a WFP resources officer, an evaluation manager and a government representative. The mission visited Afghanistan between 16 May and 7 June 2004, when the staff of government departments, donor, and UN agencies, and implementing partners were interviewed. Visits were made to all five WFP area offices and three sub-offices, and beneficiaries were met at 65 project sites in 13 provinces. The evaluation report was prepared by the mission leader on the basis of the mission's field work.
19. Much has been written about the history of conflict in Darfur; see, for example, De Waal (1989), (2005), (2007); Cheadle and Prendergast (2007), DFID (2005); Flint and De Waal (2008); Young *et al.*, (2005). For an intimate account of the conflict seen from the perspective of an aid worker and a Sudanese translator, see Marlowe (2006) and Hari (2008).
20. The charge of genocide was led by the United States, which had led interventions into Afghanistan and Iraq, as well as the pursuit of the global war on international terrorism. This called into question the *bona fides* of the world's sole remaining superpower and the largest aid donor to the Sudan (Minear, 2004: 98).
21. The WFP is by far the largest provider of food assistance to Darfur, although some food is provided from other sources, mainly through the ICRC.
22. The WFP's co-operating partners included CARE International, CRS, German Agro Action, Samaritan's Purse, Save the Children (USA), Solidarites, United Methodist Committee on Relief, and World Vision.
23. The evaluation team consisted of consultants in humanitarian response and logistics (team leader), public health and nutrition, rural development and food security, and organizational management and community empowerment, the latter two being Sudanese nationals. Preparations for the evaluation centred largely on documents gathered by a preparatory study undertaken by the Feinstein International Center at Tufts University in the United States on behalf of the WFP Office of Evaluation.

Interviews were conducted with key informants in the Sudanese government, other UN agencies, co-operating partners, and the ICRC in Khartoum and Darfur. Group meetings were held with beneficiaries of WFP relief food in Darfur. Constraints included the delicate political situation and security in Darfur at the time of the evaluation team's visit, which precluded access to some parts of the region. The evaluation report followed the evaluation criteria proposed by the DAC/OECD in 1999 for the evaluation of humanitarian action.

24. The study included two weeks of field work in October 2008 to understand the ways in which participatory or community-based approaches to targeting had been attempted. The study's report was first drafted in December 2008 and reviewed in early 2009, before the Sudanese government expelled international and national NGOs from Darfur in March 2009.
25. The study listed their order of importance as: the WFP, co-operating partners, traditional leaders, camp leaders, food relief committees, the government's Humanitarian Aid Commission, the IOM/OCHA, recipient communities, local administration, armed groups, bandits, cereal traders, commercial truckers, non-targeted communities, and multiple food card holders.
26. Attempts were made to use high-tech approaches to improve registration and targeting through, for example, satellite imagery, but have so far been unsuccessful.
27. The international NGOs were: Action Contre la Faim (ACF); CARE International; Cooperative Housing Foundation (CHF); International Rescue Committee (IRC); Medecins Sans Frontiers – France and Holland (MSF-F and H); Mercy Corps; the Norwegian Refugee Council (NRC); Oxfam GB; the Planning and Development Collaborative International (PADCO), a development firm; Save the Children – UK and USA; and Solidarites. The national NGOs were: Amal Centre for Rehabilitation of Victims of Violence; the Khartoum Centre for Human Rights, Development and Environment; and the Sudan Social Development Organization (SUDO).
28. The forum was attended by 237 participants including academics, researchers, and representatives from civil society groups, the governments of Sudan and South Sudan, donor agencies, the United Nations, the African Union, the World Bank and the IMF. The participants included: 18 donor representatives; 85 government officials; 61 WFP staff (including 22 from sub-offices around the country); 56 NGO representatives; and 14 staff members from other UN agencies. A selection of the papers presented at the forum was contained in a special issue of the journal *Disasters*, 31, Supplement 1, March 2007.
29. A number of accounts of the war in Bosnia-Herzegovina can be found on the Internet. This summary is taken from *The History Place – Genocide in the 20th Century* at www.historyplace.com/worldhistory.genoci
30. The WFP was not involved in the allegations of corruption in the UN oil-for-food programme, which resulted in the dismissal of a UN official.
31. The UN House in Beirut, where many of the aid agencies had offices, was ransacked by angry demonstrators frustrated by the failure of the international community to bring a swift end to the conflict. On the previous day, Israeli bombing had demolished a village in southern Lebanon, killing at least 40 people. No UN staff were injured, and the 20 WFP staff in Beirut at the time moved their offices elsewhere.
32. During this time, the WFP also provided assistance to the Palestinian population in Gaza and support to UNRWA through innovative food assistance activities (see Chapter 6).
33. This description of the conflict and humanitarian action in Georgia is drawn largely from the study by Greg Hansen based on field research. He undertook this study in September 2008 and August 2009 as part of *The Humanitarian Agenda 2015* project of the Feinstein International Center at Tufts University in the United States. Details of the causes and history of the conflict between Georgia and two secessionist territories can be found in Hansen (1998).

34. *Guidelines on the Use of Military and Civil Defence Assets in Disaster Relief*, the 'Oslo Guidelines', updated November 2006. *Guidelines on the Use of Military and Civil Defence Assets to Support United Nations Humanitarian Activities in Complex Emergencies*, March 2003, revised January 2006.

4 Anatomy of WFP emergency operations

1. In 1994, the IASC agreed on the following definition of 'complex emergencies': 'a humanitarian crisis in a country, region or society where there is a total or considerable breakdown of authority resulting from internal or external conflict which requires an international response that goes beyond the mandate or capacity of any single agency and/or the ongoing UN country programme' (IASC, 10th meeting, December 1994).
2. Details of *Good Humanitarian Donorship*: The Challenge can be found at www.goodhumanitariandonorship.org
3. In 1991, the UN General Assembly agreed to a set of principles to guide the UN in providing humanitarian assistance in its Resolution 46/182 of 19 December 1991. Other notable efforts to standardize humanitarian principles included the *Code of Conduct* for the ICRC and NGOs in disaster relief, signed in 1994, which was recast as the *Humanitarian Charter* to underpin the *Sphere Project*. The project sought to improve the quality and accessibility of humanitarian work and set out minimum standards of food aid, nutrition, water supply and sanitation, shelter and site management, and health services. In 2000, the IASC endorsed the *Sphere Handbook* as an important tool for working with populations affected by disasters. The WFP provided technical support for the *Sphere Project*, including drafting a new chapter on food security and nutrition. The WFP's field-level agreements with implementing partners encourages adherence to the *Sphere Humanitarian Charter* and its standards.
4. The thematic review was conducted by four consultants. It included five country case studies in Darfur, Sudan, Ethiopia, Kenya, Malawi, and Myanmar that were carried out between January and June 2005, and a peer review workshop conducted in Rome in June 2005.
5. In preparing the document for consideration by the executive board, five case studies were carried out in Angola, Ethiopia, Indonesia, Mozambique, and Zambia to explore the WFP's experience in different types of urban food insecurity situations.
6. Livelihoods have been variously described but are generally understood to be the sum of the capabilities, skills, assets, and activities required for a means of living.
7. For a comprehensive review of the literature on safety-net programmes, see WFP (2004x).
8. Risk was defined as the combination of people's exposure (vulnerability) to a hazard or shock. Reducing disaster risk both lessened human vulnerability (by preventing or mitigating impact) and strengthened resilience.
9. Excluding operations in Iraq, over 46 per cent of the WFP's emergency operations costs between 1994 and 2005 were in response to natural disasters. In 2002, 103 out of the 207 approved emergency operations were developed in response to natural disasters, involving 62 per cent of emergency relief beneficiaries.
10. The WFP already provides support to the African Union in building networks for livelihood risk analysis, vulnerability mapping, and food security monitoring, with an emphasis on tracking the impact of climate change on agricultural productivity.
11. The WFP seconded disaster preparedness officers to the United Nations system influenza co-ordinator to draft the *Pandemic Planning and Preparedness Guideline for the United Nations System*, which guides UN country teams operating in a pandemic environment.
12. This framework built on studies in five countries – Bangladesh, Burundi, Haiti, Mozambique, and Tajikistan – and on the *Policy Guidance Framework on Disaster Risk*

Reduction: Strengthening WFP's Disaster Risk Reduction Capacity in Compliance with the Hyogo Framework for Action 2005–2015. This was funded by the Swedish government and is available at: http://epmaps.wfp.org/temp/drrpolicyguidance.zip

13. Important partners would include the International Strategy for Disaster Reduction (ISDR) an initiative of UN and non-UN stakeholders including the World Bank, WMP, IFRC, UNEP, and the ProVention Consortium. The main objectives of ISDR are: to increase public awareness; undertake risk, vulnerability, and disaster reduction globally; and obtain commitments from public authorities. In 2008, ISDR, the UN *Convention to Combat Desertification* and the WFP jointly launched a global drought risk reduction network. The ProVention Consortium is a global coalition of international organizations, governments, the private sector, civil society organizations, and academic institutions dedicated to increasing the safety of vulnerable communities and reducing the impact of disasters in developing countries. The Global Facility for Disaster Reduction and Recovery – managed by the World Bank and ISDR, with operations planned in 51 countries, to share information, conduct joint research, maintain integrated databases, and carry out joint planning and programming – allocated funds for WFP risk management work in Ethiopia. The Famine Early Warning System Network and the US Geological Survey, global leaders in early warning technology, will be important partners. Other major partners in the UN system include the FAO, IFAD, UNDP, UNICEF, and WMO. Major international NGOs, including the IFRC, are interlocutors from concepts and practices of disaster risk reduction.
14. Details of the major work and changes that took place are given in the authoritative account of executive director Catherine Bertini that was presented to the WFP's Executive Board at the end of her decade of leadership (WFP, 2002a). This account is fully drawn upon here.
15. WFP staff increased by 21 per cent between 1989 and 1992. With temporary staff recruited for emergency operations included, the increase was nearly 50 per cent.
16. According to one count, there were more than 43 key documents comprising reports to the executive board, executive decisions, and guidelines prepared by the executive directors, external partners, contracted consultants, and external auditors relating to the decentralization initiative (WFP, 2007k).
17. The WFP did not have its own standard set of administrative rules, regulations policies, and procedures. They were an amalgam of the United Nations common system and the rules and regulations of the FAO, the UN secretariat, UNDP, and WFP's own policies.
18. The evaluation took three years to complete at a cost reported to be over $3 million (excluding the costs of the extensive support and documentation provided by the WFP secretariat). It was conducted by 16 international consultants, assisted by national consultants for the nine country case studies. The first phase of the evaluation, completed in late 1992, was conducted by the North–South Institute of Canada. The second phase, completed in December 1993, was conducted by the Chr. Michelsen Institute of Bergen, Norway. The evaluation report consisted of an abridged version, the main report, and nine country case studies.
19. The seminar was chaired by Professor Paul Streeten, the eminent development economist and former director of the World Development Institute at Boston University in the United States.
20. The working group was composed of representatives of Brazil, Cameroon, China, Cuba, El Salvador, Ethiopia, France, Indonesia, Japan, Libya, the Netherlands, Norway, Saudi Arabia, and the United States. The group met four times between July and September 1994, and was chaired by the chairperson or vice-chairperson of the governing body.
21. The five task teams were: the field-headquarters team; the staffing and training team; the streamlining of procedures team; the communications team; and the advocacy and resources mobilization team. The teams held frequent meetings with

interested staff and presented their reports in late December 1995 and early January 1996.

22. These cluster or regional offices were located in Abidjan, Côte d'Ivoire; Addis Ababa, Ethiopia; Bangkok, Thailand; Islamabad, Pakistan; Lima, Peru; Managua, Nicaragua; Maputo, Mozambique; Nairobi, Kenya; New Delhi, India; Ouagadougou, Mauritania; Pristina, Kosovo; and Yaounda, Cameroon.
23. The West Africa regional bureau was located in Dakar, Senegal; the Central Africa regional bureau in Yaounde, Cameroon; the Eastern and Southern Africa regional bureau in Kampala, Uganda; and the Asia regional bureau in Bangkok, Thailand. The Eastern Europe regional bureau was kept temporarily at WFP headquarters. For operational and technical support (especially in programming, logistics, and information and communications technology), the regional cluster offices in Islamabad, Pakistan and Maputo, Mozambique were maintained. The cluster office in Lima, Peru was designated an outposted centre for resource mobilization, with the special role of raising awareness and mobilizing greater support for the WFP in Latin America and the Caribbean.
24. The WFP's External Auditor at the time was François Logerot, Premier President de la Court des Computes de la Republique Française.
25. See 'Review of the Decentralization Process – Results of the Survey Conducted' in, WFP, 2002: 78–112).
26. The review involved a study of documentation and interviews with WFP staff at headquarters. Regional directors took part in a half-day meeting in Rome during the annual session of the executive board in 2003 to discuss decentralization issues and priorities. In addition, more than 30 country directors from all regions were interviewed. The consultants travelled to regional bureaux in Cairo, Kampala, and Dakar, and to country offices in Senegal, Côte d'Ivoire, Ethiopia, and Uganda.
27. *The Food Insecurity Atlas of Rural India* was produced with the co-operation of the M. S. Swaminathan Foundation, which contributed the Indian government's planning document *A Hunger Free India*.
28. The WFP's external auditor at the time was Sir John Bourn, head of the United Kingdom National Audit Office.
29. This low percentage of income was set at a time when most of the WFP's activities were focused on development projects with much lower overhead costs than emergency operations, and to portray the image of a lean and efficient organization the bulk of whose voluntary contributions were for the benefit of poor and hungry people in developing countries.
30. The preparatory work for the WFP report was done by Bhim Mahajan, a former senior FAO staff member who knew the UN system well. He had extensive discussions with WFP staff in October 1991 and visited the WFP's major partners in the UN system and the country offices of WFP, and other agencies in El Salvador, Ghana, and India.
31. One immediate effect was that the meetings and documentation costs of the WFP's governing body were cut by 70 per cent from $8.0 million in 1992–93 to $2.4 million in 1996–97.
32. The evaluation was commissioned by the WFP's Office of Evaluation at the request of the WFP's Transport and Logistics Division. It was carried out by a UK company, ITAD Ltd., and a former WFP logistics officer, between April and July 2001, and was managed by the WFP's chief evaluation officer. The evaluation included visits to Ethiopia, Djibouti, Southern Sudan, Kenya, and Mozambique.
33. The UNHRD was established, in part, through the approval of four special operations between 2006 and 2009 at a total cost of $35.2 million.
34. The ICRC did not take part in the cluster approach but co-ordination with the UN continued 'to the extent necessary to achieve efficient operational complementarity and a strengthened response for people affected by armed conflict and other situations of violence' (IASC, 2006).
35. The review was conducted by the UK Audit Office for WFP's External Auditor, Sir John Bourn.

36. The FAO's mission is 'Helping to build a world without hunger'; IFAD's is 'To enable the rural poor to overcome poverty'; and the WFP's is 'To end hunger'.
37. The WFP's original *General Regulations* of 1961 (article 19(a)) stated 'NGOs should be encouraged, where appropriate, to co-operate with the Programme and support its activities. The WFP's revised *General Regulations* (Rule III-1) of 1997 states: WFP shall, whenever appropriate, associate its assistance with material, financial and technical assistance provided through other multilateral programmes and shall seek similar co-operation with bilateral programmes and non-governmental partners'.
38. The evaluation was planned and managed by the WFP's Office of Evaluation, and carried out by a team of four consultants in July and August 1999. Field reviews were conducted in eight countries in different regions (Afghanistan, Cambodia, Chad, Egypt, El Salvador, Gaza/West Bank, Nicaragua, and Tanzania) to gain a better understanding of the benefits and constraints within partnership arrangements in both development projects and relief operations. Due to visa and security problems, the Afghanistan case study was conducted from Pakistan, where the WFP country office for Afghanistan and many NGOs from Afghanistan were located.
39. The five countries were Indonesia (economic emergency), Ethiopia (chronic food insecurity and drought emergency), Mozambique (flood emergency and rehabilitation), Angola (complex emergency), and Guatemala (chronic food insecurity and disasters).
40. According to the ACC, sustainable capacity-building was viewed as:

    > encompassing the building of organizational and technical abilities, behaviours, relationships and values that enabled individuals, groups, and organizations to enhance their performance effectively and to achieve their development objectives over time. It included strengthening the processes, systems and rules that shape collective and individual behaviour and performance in all development endeavours as well as people's ability and willingness to play new development roles and to adapt to new demands and situations. (ACC, 2000)
41. These organizations included the Asian Development Bank, CARE, DFID, IFAD, USAID and the World Bank. The ACC had also issued a guidance note on partnerships.
42. The main author of the handbook was Camilla Knox-Peebles; the handbook was compiled and published with the financial support of the United Kingdom's DFID, together with a CD-ROM version.
43. For more information on the United Nations Global Compact, see: www.unglobalcompact.org
44. John Powell was appointed Deputy Executive Director, External Affairs and Resource Development Department in April 2003. He joined the WFP as regional manager of the Asia and Pacific Bureau (1990–93), and was director of the Strategic and Policy Division (1993–99), regional manager of the West and Central Asia Bureau and country director for Pakistan (1999–2000), regional director of the Asia and Eastern Europe Bureau (2000–01), and regional director for the Asia Bureau in Bangkok, Thailand, overseeing all WFP operations in Asia (2001–03).
45. The account of how the WFP–TNT partnership began is largely taken from Tomasini and Van Wassenhove (2009: 146–64). A similar account is given in Thurow and Kilman (2009).
46. A cup of nutritious corn-soya blend porridge is often the only meal children receive each day and costs $0.25 cents.

5 Associated development programmes and projects

1. FAO, *Disposal of Agricultural Surpluses. Principles recommended by FAO* (Rome, Italy: FAO, 1954). Subsequently revised and expanded in five versions, last edited in 2001. The

Principles are not legally binding but provide guidelines, a code of conduct, or what are called "consultative obligations". An FAO Consultative Subcommittee on Surplus Disposal (CSD) was created to monitor adherence to the *Principles.*

2. ACC/SCN, 'ACC/SCN Statement on Nutrition, Refugees and Displaced Persons', in ACC/ SCN (1993), *Nutritional Issues in Food Aid. Symposium Report. Nutrition Policy Discussion Paper* No. 12 (Geneva, Switzerland: ACC Subcommittee on Nutrition, 1993).
3. WFP (2004k) *Food for Nutrition: Mainstreaming Nutrition in WFP.* Document WFP/ EB.A/2004/5-A/1.
4. UN, *Report on the World Food Conference 1974* (1975): 9.
5. WFP (2004l) *Nutrition in Emergencies: WFP Experience and Challenges.* Document WFP/ EB.A/2004/5-A/3.
6. WFP (2004m) *Micronutrient Fortification: WFP Experience and the Way Forward* Mainstreaming nutrition in WFP, nutrition in emergencies, and micro-nutrient fortification were incorporated into the *Consolidated Framework of WFP Policies.* WFP/ EB.2/2009/4-E.
7. Memorandum to President Kennedy from McGovern of 28 March 1962 and attached report on *Recommendations for Improvements in the Food for Peace Program* (McGovern Papers, Box TK-5: 35–6, Seeley G. Mudd Manuscripts Library, Princeton University, NJ, USA.
8. The evaluation was undertaken in conjunction with the Brazilian government and assisted by a local team leader (consultant), the WFP, three senior government officers from the Ministry of Education, the Students Assistance Foundation, and the National Food Supply Company, and a representative from a local NGO.
9. The six goals were:
   - expanding and improving comprehensive early childhood care and education, especially for the most vulnerable and disadvantaged children;
   - ensuring that by 2015 all children, particularly girls, children in difficult circumstances, and those belonging to ethnic minorities, have access to and complete free and compulsory primary education of good quality;
   - ensuring that the learning needs of all young people and adults are met through equitable access to appropriate learning and life skills programmes;
   - achieving a 50 per cent improvement in levels of adult literacy by 2015, especially for women, and equitable access to basic and continuing education for all adults;
   - eliminating gender disparities in primary and secondary education by 2005, and
   - achieving gender equality in education by 2015, with a focus on ensuring the girls' full and equal access to and achievement in basic education of good quality; and improving all aspects of the quality of education, and ensuring excellence of all so that recognized and measurable outcomes are achieved by all, especially in literacy, numeracy, and essential life skills.
10. School feeding was one of McGovern's five-point strategies to end world hunger. The other four elements were: a worldwide special nutrition programme for mothers, infants, and children; the establishment of global food reserves; an assistance programme to help developing countries improve their own food production, processing, and distribution; and the dissemination of the results of high-yielding scientific agriculture, including genetically modified crops. McGovern estimated the cost of his strategy to be $5 billion a year, of which, he suggests, $1.2 billion could come from the United States. The US Agency for International Development (USAID) put the cost at $2.6 billion annually and the FAO at $6.0 billion a year (McGovern, 2001: 25–41).
11. This bipartisan bill was named after Democratic Senator George McGovern and Republican Senator Robert Dole 'for their tireless efforts to encourage a global commitment to school feeding and child nutrition'. Funding levels must be approved annually by the US Congress and are made mainly in the form of US agricultural commodities

and their shipment, although the internal transport, storage, and handling costs in recipient countries, certain administrative costs, and the cost of activities that enhance programme effectiveness may also be met. Funding is administered by the Foreign Agricultural Service of the US Department of Agriculture, which invites NGOs and international organizations to submit proposals for funding under this programme for priority countries, listed annually – generally low-income, food-deficit countries that have demonstrated a commitment to universal education, with an increasing focus on Africa and some concentration on Asia. Some 30 priority countries were listed for FY 2008. Proposals are selected on several criteria including: implementing organizations' experience; additional resources being available from other sources to complement multi-year sustainable programmes based on assessed needs, with a clear exit strategy; targeting on low-income areas with low school enrolment or attendance, especially for girls; co-ordination of supplementary feeding with nutrition programmes; and involvement of local institutions and communities. Further details are available at http://fas.usda.gov/excredits/FoodAid/FFE/mcdfactsheet.asp

12. Annual reports on WFP school feeding programmes were presented to the WFP executive board between 2000 and 2006.
13. The evaluation team consisted of an evaluation specialist, two experts on education in emergencies, and a nutritionist. The evaluation involved a desk study; visits to three countries with emergency school feeding operations, Sudan, Pakistan, and the Democratic Republic of the Congo; an e-mail survey to emergency school feeding project managers in WFP country offices; and an analysis, including a workshop, to review and process the data collected.
14. Background papers and inputs for this report were produced by staff from the WFP, Cardiff University, UK, and IFPRI. The report was possible thanks to a grant provided by the Bill and Melinda Gates Foundation.
15. Safety nets were defined as a sub-set of broader social protection systems. They mostly include non-contributory transfers in cash or in kind, conditional or unconditional, (including, for example, conditional cash transfers, school feeding, food-for-work, cash-for-work, and vouchers) and other interventions to improve access to food and basic essentials, such as price subsidies. Depending on programme objectives and design features, safety nets could generate a variety of outcomes – including, for example, improved nutrition, enhancements in education, or the transfer of income to targeted households (WFP, 2004q).
16. Papers were presented by the WFP secretariat to the WFP's executive board every year from 2000 to 2007, inclusive.
17. An editorial jointly signed by the WFP's executive director and the WHO's director-general on the importance of combining food assistance with ARV drugs was published in the *International Herald Tribune* on World AIDS Day, 1 December 2003.
18. The Global Task Team (GTT) was established at the high-level meeting held in London in March 2005 on 'Making the Money Work'. Its draft recommendations were submitted to the WFP's executive board at its annual session in 2006 under four main headings: empowering national leadership and ownership; alignment and harmonization; reform for a more effective multilateral response; and accountability and oversight. The recommendations were welcomed by the board, especially the emphasis on country-level action. The WFP's role in the fight against HIV/AIDS was widely acknowledged, as was the need for food and nutrition in care and treatment programmes. Concern was expressed, however, that insufficient emphasis was placed on co-ordination among the agencies involved, and an amendment was agreed. (*Summary of the Work of the Annual Session of the Executive Board, 2006*, WFP/EB.A/2006/17).
19. WFP (2004v) *People Living With AIDS. Food as the First Line of Defence* (Rome, Italy: WFP).
20. Quisumbing, A. R., L. R. Brown, H. S. Felstein, L. Haddad and C. Pina (1995) *Women: The Key to Food Security* (Washington, DC: International Food Policy Research Institute).

21. WFP (1975a) *The Contribution of Food Aid to Improving Women's Status*. Document WFP/IGC: 27/15.
22. WFP (1985b) *Breadwinners at Home and at Work. World Food Programme Support during the Decade for Women*. Document WFP/CFA: 20/INF/5. Also published as *WFP Occasional Paper* No. 4 (1985).
23. The Refugees Studies Programme at the University of Oxford, UK produced a comprehensive document for the WFP on improving social and gender planning in emergency operations.
24. WFP (2002d) *Gender Policy 2003–2007. Enhanced Commitments to Women to Ensure Food Security* (Rome, Italy: WFP).
25. WFP (2007h), *Ending Child Hunger and Undernutrition Initiative*. Document WFP/EB.1/2007/5-A and WFP (2007m) *Global Framework for Action: Ending Child Hunger and Undernutrition Initiative*. Document WFP/EB.1/2007/5-A/Add.1.

6 Transforming food aid to food assistance

1. At the time, UNICEF was campaigning for 'Adjustment with a Human Face': see Cornia *et al.* (1987).
2. The study was carried out under the direction of Shlomo Reutlinger for the World Bank and me for the WFP. It was prepared by Charles Paolillo, Robert Chase, and me of the WFP and Shlomo Reutlinger, Robert Hindle, and Harry Walters of the World Bank. The study took seven drafts and over two years to complete. The differences between the two sides – particularly concerning the scale, conditions, and issues relating to monetization – were reconciled at a meeting at the Institute of Development Studies at the University of Sussex, UK, with Simon Maxwell as convener.
3. There was nothing in the WFP's *Basic Documents* that precluded the sale by the WFP of commodities in emergency operations. It was in the criteria and procedures for handling requests for WFP emergency assistance, drawn up by the director-general of the FAO in 1967, that it was stipulated that recipient governments would assume 'full responsibility for distributing food *free* to the designated beneficiaries' (emphasis added) (WFP, 1963a: paragraph 14 (A) (vii)).
4. The review was based on a representative sample of 25 per cent of projects involving monetization approved and in operation since 1987. Between 1987 and 1992, 122 projects were approved involving monetization. The value of the commodities monetized was $406.4 million, representing 13.3 per cent of the total value of all projects approved during that period. The review provided additional reference material for the preparation of a policy paper on monetization presented to the governing body in 1997 (WFP, 1997d). The FAO was requested to review WFP-assisted projects that involved the creation of credit schemes, which involved a desk study of 19 such projects and a detailed study of seven other projects, involving visits to project sites in four countries.
5. Zimbabwe, which was the cereal supplier for neighbouring countries at the time, is now one of the WFP's main food aid recipient countries.
6. The WFP commissioned studies by the Relief and Development Institute (RDI) in London on triangular transactions and commodity purchases in 1987 (RDI, 1987) and on commodity exchanges in 1990 (RDI, 1990). Both studies were carried out by Edward Clay and Charlotte Benson, who were respectively the director and research officer of RDI. The results of both studies were presented to the WFP's governing body (WFP, 1989; 1990). The RDI was later absorbed into the Overseas Development Institute in London.
7. The WFP *Food Procurement User Guide* of 1996 superseded the *Procurement User Guide* of 11 December 1996 and RD 96/001 'Operational Procedures for the Purchase of Foodstuffs' of 25 March 1996.

8. In 2003, the WFP purchased over 0.5 million tons of food at a cost of $182 million for Iraq. In 2004, WFP purchases for Iraq increased to over 1.5 million tons at a cost of $540 million.
9. I am grateful to Ken Davies, Co-ordinator P4P, for a copy of the paper on P4P that was presented to the Borlaug Symposium on 'Taking it to the Farmer' in Addis Ababa, Ethiopia, 13–14 July, 2010.
10. With its headquarters in Nairobi, Kenya, AGRA's goal is to end the poverty and hunger of Africa's small-scale farmers. Kofi. A. Annan, former UN Secretary-General, is chairman of its Board of Directors. Dr Namanga Ngongi, the former WFP deputy executive director, is its first president. Former WFP executive director Catherine Bertini is a senior fellow of the Agricultural Development Team at the Bill and Melinda Gates Foundation, working on the Foundation's Agricultural Development Initiative, including the importance of gender in agricultural development, particularly in South Asia and sub-Saharan Africa.
11. The 21 P4P pilot countries are: Burkina Faso, Democratic Republic of Congo, Ethiopia, Ghana, Kenya, Liberia, Malawi, Mali, Mozambique, Rwanda, Sierra Leone, Sudan, Tanzania, Uganda, and Zambia in sub-Saharan Africa; Afghanistan and Laos in Asia; and El Salvador, Guatemala, Honduras, and Nicaragua in Latin America.
12. I am particularly grateful to Andreas Psoroulas, Head of the WFP Library, for identifying past WFP-assisted development projects containing voucher or cash transfer arrangements from project documents submitted to the WFP's governing body for approval.
13. I am grateful to Maurizio Gnocchi, former director of WFP's Bureau for Latin America and the Caribbean, for reminding me of the address of the Jamaican Prime Minster to the WFP's governing body.
14. For more details, see Shaw (2001): 114–17. The IMF held a seminar at its headquarters in Washington, DC in October 1990 on the 'Social Aspects of Adjustment Programs', the first time it had a meeting with the non-Bretton Woods organizations of the UN system. The aim of the meeting was to establish closer co-operation before adjustment programmes, supported by the IMF and World Bank, were carried out in order to take account of the needs of the poor from the outset of such programmes and not as a 'little sweetener' to make adjustment programmes more palatable.
15. Some of the evidence of the growing volume of field research on cash transfer and vouchers schemes was published in special issue of the journal *Development Policy Review*, 24(5) 2006, edited by John Farrington and Rachel Slater, complemented by the simultaneous publication of papers in the journal *Disasters*, 30(3) 2006, which gave experience with cash transfers in emergencies.
16. A variant 'decision tree' was suggested for the UK NGO Oxfam by Creti and Jaspars (2006). Food aid would be more appropriate than cash transfers if there were problems of market accessibility, government restrictions on food movement, market competitiveness and integration, trader behaviour, and possible inflation effects.
17. I am grateful to the editors of the book, Steven Were Omamo, Ugo Gentilini, and Susanna Sandström, respectively deputy director, policy advisor, and policy officer of the WFP's Policy, Planning and Strategy Division, for making an advance copy of the book available to me.
18. This is reminiscent of the call for a doubly-green agricultural revolution, which would be more productive and sustainable than the first Green Revolution, and even 'greener' in terms of conserving natural resources and the environment (see: Conway *et al.*, 1994 and Conway, 1997).
19. The study was conducted between January and May 2010 and involved interviews with a representative selection of officials, ranging from bilateral donors to international and UN agencies and NGOs and a review of recent literature and organizational policies.

20. Some of the reasons for this decline in World Bank assistance to agriculture are given in Shaw (2009): 115–20.
21. Details of the conference can be found at http://2020conference.ifpri.info/.22. For information see http://www.sphereproject.org
22. For information see http://www.sphereproject.org

7 The way ahead: challenges and opportunities

1. This classification of the component parts of the international humanitarian system is drawn from Walker and Maxwell (2009) and Harvey *et al.* (2010).
2. The study was conducted by an ALNAP humanitarian outcomes team led by Paul Harvey. It involved interviewing 89 humanitarian aid specialists, including three from the WFP, synthesizing 499 responses to a questionnaire (48 per cent from INGO staff, 21 per cent from UN agency staff, and 42 per cent from field-level workers in Africa), 100 recent evaluation reports, staffing and budget information of over 200 aid organizations, and a financial analysis of global humanitarian aid flow. The resulting report is described as representing 'a pilot effort to broadly assess the "state of the system" with the intent, if found useful, to repeat the exercise once every two years' (Harvey *et al.*, 2010: 9).
3. The notion that within a few years the OCHA would improve its performance called to mind Oscar Wilde's characterization of second marriages as being 'the triumph of hope over experience' (Weiss, 2009: 86).
4. 'Note on co-operation between UNHCR and HRFOR', 29 September 1995.
5. Gareth Evans, formerly Australian foreign minister and founder president and CEO of the International Crisis Group, is generally credited with launching and propagating the R2P concept. He was co-chair of the International Commission on Intervention and State Sovereignty, which initiated the concept, and led the movement for its worldwide adoption and application. He has served on the UN secretary-general's High-Level Panel on Threats, Challenges and Change (2003–04), the UN secretary-general's Advisory Committee on the Prevention of Genocide and Mass Atrocities (2006 to the present), and is co-chair of the International Commission on Nuclear Non-Proliferation and Disarmament (since 2008).
6. For information on the International Crisis Group, see www.crisisgroup.org, e-mail: brussels@crisisgroup.org; and for the Global Centre for the Responsibility to Protect, see www.Globalr2p.org, e-mail: inform@globair2p.org
7. I am most grateful for the work of Thomas Weiss on this subject: see Weiss, 1998; 2009; and Weiss and Korn, 2006.
8. I am indebted to Roberta Cohen and Francis Deng for their detailed account of the response of the UNHCR to the proposal that it assumed responsibility to protect and assist IDPs in addition to their work for refugees (Cohen and Deng, 1998a: 169–70).
9. Maurice Strong, the Canadian businessman and special representative to UN secretaries-general, who had made his mark as secretary-general of two major UN conferences on the environment in 1972 and 1989, and as head of the Office of Emergency Operations in Africa, was put in charge of the UN reform effort.
10. See the chapters in Minear and Smith (eds) (2007) on the 'Steep learning curves in the DPRK' by David Morton (pp. 194–214). Morton served in the country from 1998 to 2002 as WFP representative and UN humanitarian co-ordinator and later, in addition, as UN resident co-ordinator and UNDP resident representative. See also 'Nurturing humanitarian space in Sudan' by Masood Hyder (pp. 239–57) (Hyder served as WFP representative and deputy UN humanitarian co-ordinator in Sudan from 2002 to 2004), and 'Steering through insurgencies in Nepal' by Erika Joegensen (pp. 215–36). Joergensen worked with the WFP between 2000 and 2006. She was the WFP representative in Armenia

and Nepal and then deputy regional representative in the WFP Regional Bureau in Bangkok, Thailand.

11. The study was undertaken by Edward Clay, senior research associate at the Overseas Development Institute, London in collaboration with Barry Riley and Ian Urey.
12. WFP executive director Josette Sheeran delivered a keynote address to the CSIS on 18 April 2008 on 'The New Face of Hunger'. The evening before, CSIS hosted a dinner at which Ms Sheeran engaged with representatives from the Senate Appropriations Committee, the US Department of States, USAID, USDA, CARE, the Center for Global Development, IFPRI, the Bill and Melinda Gates Foundation, and the military. Sentiment at that session was strongly in favour of CSIS launching the task force, which was financed by a grant from the Connect US Fund.
13. Catherine Bertini and Dan Glickman are co-chairs of the Chicago Council on Global Affairs' Global Agricultural Development Project. The project's final report is available online at www.thechicagocouncil.org/globalagdevelopment
14. I am grateful to Jennifer Clapp, CIGI Chair in International Governance and Professor of Environmental and Resource Studies at the University of Waterloo, Canada for providing me with an advance copy of her chapter of the book she wrote on 'Corporate Interests in US Food Aid Policy: Global Implications of Resistance to Reform' (Clapp and Fuchs, 2009: 125–52) and for copies of the two books she co-edited (Clapp and Fuchs, 2009 and Clapp and Cohen, 2009).
15. One of the best accounts of the personalities and interest groups involved in determining US food aid policy up to 1976 is given in Wallerstein (1980).
16. The report was written by authorities from the IFPRI, the New York University Center on International Cooperation, the Grantham Institute at Imperial College, London and the Walker Institute, University of Reading, UK, and evaluates current knowledge on climate change, assesses responses to the challenge, and estimates the potential impacts.
17. Executive director Sheeran identified 'ending hunger' as the WFP's mission on taking up her appointment in April 2006. She was no doubt strongly motivated by the experience of her ancestors, who were tenant farmers in Ireland caught up in the great famine of the 1840s and who emigrated to the United States (Sheeran, 2008).
18. The UK government supported the establishment of an International Partnership for Agriculture and Food proposed by the G8 at its summit meeting in Japan. It also encouraged the WFP, FAO, and IFAD to carry out a review of how their global operations could be better integrated, building on the 2007 report on improving co-operation over administrative processes (IDC, 2008).
19. WFP executive director Josette Sheeran gave evidence before the UK House of Commons International Development Committee on 22 April 2008. Its report was published on 23 July 2008. On 6 October 2008, the UK government made its response, which was annexed to the report.
20. This would be in keeping with the Mahatma Gandhi's principle of *antyodaya*: 'Recall the face of the poorest and the weakest man whom you may have seen, and ask yourself if the steps you contemplate are going to be of any use to him' (*Collected Works of Mahatma Gandhi*, Vol. 96, Government of India, 1958–82). It is also in keeping with the view of the distinguished development economist Professor Sir Hans Singer, who devoted his long and prolific career to addressing and finding solutions to the problems of developing countries. In recalling how he developed his analytical abilities, he stated: 'One tries to look at the world from the viewpoint of the underdog – of the recipient, the victim. You may get insights into the world that are not open to people who look at the world from the top down' (Emmerij *et al.*, 2001: 51; Shaw, 2002: 274).
21. Peter Walker is director of the Feinstein International Center (FIC) at Tufts University in the United States. From 1979, he has worked for British-based NGOs and environmental organizations in African countries, and has been a university lecturer and director

of a food wholesaling company. From 1990 to 2000, he was director of disaster policy and head of regional programmes for Southeast Asia at the International Federation of Red Cross and Red Crescent Societies in Geneva, Switzerland. He founded and managed the *World Disaster Report*, and initiated and developed the Code of Conduct for disaster workers and the *Sphere* humanitarian standards. He has co-written *Shaping the Humanitarian World* (Walker and Maxwell, 2009) with Daniel Maxwell, a research director at FIC.

22. I am grateful to WFP deputy executive director for Hunger Solutions, Sheila Sisulu, for emphasizing this point during my interview with her at WFP headquarters on 16 September 2008.
23. Georgia Shaver was appointed as the WFP's first ombudsman. She is a certified mediator and has completed thirty years of service with the WFP, including a tour of duty in eastern and southern Africa, and as WFP representative and country director in Mozambique (1996 and 2001) and Ethiopia (2001–05).
24. This proposed arrangement would differ from the previous evaluations of the WFP, which were conducted by small groups of donor countries outside the WFP's governing body. It would ensure that all WFP members agreed to, and were involved in, the proposed independent external evaluation, and in approving its recommendations, and monitoring their implementation. The independent external evaluation of the FAO was carried out in 2007 (FAO, 2007), IFAD in 2005 (IFAD, 2005), and the CGIAR in 2004 (World Bank, 2004).

Dramatis personae

1. Details of the WFP executive directors before the appointment of James Ingram in 1982 are given in Shaw (2001: 291–3).
2. Details of previous deputy executive directors before the appointment of Salahuddin Ahmed in 1982 are given in Shaw (2001: 293).
3. The chairpersons of the WFP's previous governing bodies, the Intergovernmental Committee (IGC), and the Committee on Food Aid Policies and Programmes (CFA) are listed in Shaw (2001: 294–5).

Bibliography

Primary references

WFP documents (Rome, Italy: UN World Food Programme) – unless otherwise stated

(1963a) *World Food Program. Basic Documents. General Regulations. Financial Regulations. UN/FAO Intergovernmental Committee Rules of Procedure.* 1st edn.

(1963b) Executive Director, Circular Letter on Sales Policy. WFP/16, 19 March.

(1964) Synopsis of World Food Program Policy. FP1/1.

(1965a) *A New Approach to the World Food Program. Proposal of the Israeli Government.* WM/IGC: 7/94.

(19965b) *A Multilateral World Food Fund. Proposal of the Government of Argentina for the conversion of the World Food Program.* WM/IGC: 7/1 Add.2.

(1965c) *Report on the World Food Program*, by the Executive Director.

(1965d) 'Food Aid and Education'. *WFP Study* No. 6.

(1966a) *Report on the Jamaica Mission. Study of the Feasibility of Multilateral Food Aid for National Development Programs.* WFP/IGC: 9/18.

(1966b) *Comments on the Methodology adopted in the Jamaica Mission Report* WFP/IGC: 10/17 Add.3.

(1968) *WFP Assistance to Education in Africa.* WFP/IGC: 13/6 Add. 26.

(1969) *Scope for Expansion of WFP Assistance in the Spheres of Improved Nutrition, Education and Training. Development of Human Resources.* WFP/IGC: 15/16.

(1970) *Food Aid and Related Issues during the Second Development Decade.* WFP/IGC: 17.5 Rev. 1. para. 78 and *Report of the Seventeenth Session of the Intergovernmental Committee.* WFP/IGC: 17/16, para. 22.

(1973) *Ten Years of World Food Programme Development Aid, 1963–72.*

(1975a) *The Contribution of Food Aid to Improving Women's Status.* WFP/IGC: 27/15.

(1975b) *Executive Director's Statement and Declaration on International Women's Year.* WFP/IGC: 27/INF/5.

(1975c) *The World Food Programme and Women's Involvement in Development.* WFP/IGC: 28/11 Add. 1.

(1977a) *Sales and Exchange of Commodities.* WFP/CFA: 4/9.

(1977b) *Report of the Fourth Session of the UN/FAO Committee on Food Aid Policies and Programmes.* WFP/CFA: 4/26.

(1978a) *Modalities of Operation of the International Emergency food Reserve. Report of the Sixth Session of the UN/FAO Committee on Food Aid Policies and Programmes*, Annex IV.

(1978b) *A Survey of the Studies of Food Aid.* WFP/CFA: 5/5A.

(1978c) *Food Aid and Education.* WFP/CFA: 5/9 Add. 1.

(1979a) *WFP's Contribution to the United Nations Decade for Women.* WFP/CFA: 7/8.

(1979b) *Report of the Seventh Session of the UN/FAO Committee on Food Aid Policies and Programmes.* WFP/CFA: 7/21. Annex IV.

(1980) *The Contribution of the World Food Programme to the United Nations Decade for Women.* WFP/CFA: 9/16.

(1981) *Report of the Twelfth Session of the UN/FAO Committee on Food Aid Policies and Programmes.* WFP/CFA: 12/22.

(1982a) *Report of the Thirteenth Session of the UN/FAO Committee on Food Aid Policies and Programmes.* WFP/CFA: 13/20.

(1982b) *WFP Zimbabwe Maize Train Operations.* WFP/CFA: 13/INF/6.

(1983a) *Annual Report of the Executive Director on the Development of the Programme.* WFP/CFA: 15/4.

(1983b) *Sales of Grain to Help Meet Internal Costs in Least Developed Countries (with particular reference to a case study analysis of experience in Ethiopia).* WFP/CFA: 15/8.

(1983c) *Report of the Fifteenth Session of the UN/FAO Committee on Food Aid Policies and Programmes.* WFP/CFA: 15/20.

(1984) *Review of Proposals for Improvement of WFP's Project Cycle.* WFP/CFA: 17/10.

(1985a) 'Food Aid and Development: Issues and Evidence. A Survey of the Literature since 1977 on the Role and Impact of Food Aid in Developing Countries'. *WFP Occasional Paper* No. 3.

(1985b) *Breadwinners at Home and at Work. World Food Programme Support for Women during the UN Decade for Women.* WFP/CFA: 20/INF/5. Also *WFP Occasional Paper* No. 4.

(1986a) *Lessons Learned from the Africa Food Crisis: Summary Evaluation of the WFP Emergency Response.* WFP/CFA; 22/7 Add.1. See also *Note* by the Executive Director. WFP/CFA: 21/12 and WFP/CFA: 22/7.

(1986b) *Report on WFP management review.* WFP/CFA: 23/5.

(1986c) *Criteria for the Provision of Food Aid.* WFP/CFA: 21/10 Add. 1.

(1986d) *Report of the Twenty-first Session of the UN/FAO Committee on Food Aid Policies and Programmes.* WFP/CFA: 21.24.

(1987a) *The Management of Funds Generated by Food-Assisted Projects.* WFP/CFA: 23/5, Add.2.

(1987b) *Monetization of Food Aid.* WFP/CFA: 24/5.

(1987c) *Colombia. Rehabilitation of Small Farmers.* WFP/CFA: 23/13-A (ODL) Add/1.

(1987d) *Roles of Food Aid in Structural and Sectoral Adjustment.* WFP/CFA: 23/5 Add.1.

(1987e) *Report of the Twenty-third Session of the UN/FAO Committee on Food Aid Policies and Programmes.* WFP/CFA: 23/22.

(1988) Address by the Rt. Hon. Edward Seaga, Prime Minister of Jamaica to the Twenty-Fifth Session of the World Food Programme's Committee on Food Aid Policies and Programmes. WFP/CFAS: 25/INF/18.

(1989a) *Review of Protracted Emergency Operations for Refugees and Displaced Persons.* WFP/CFA: 27/P/7.

(1989b) *Food Aid Triangular Transactions and Food Purchases: A Review of Experience.* WFP/CFA: 27/P/INF/3.

(1989c) *Anti-Hunger Strategies for Poor Households and Communities: Roles of Food Aid.* WFP/CFA: 27/P/INF/1 Add/1.

(1990a) 'Food Aid for Education. Past Experience and Future Directions'. Paper presented to the World Conference on Education for All, Bangkok, Thailand.

(1990b) *A Review of WFP and Bilateral Food Commodity Exchange Arrangements.* WFP/CFA: 29/P/INF/2.

(1990c) *Development of Human Resources in the Eastern Caribbean.* CFA:30/SCP/5.

(1991a) *Report of the Thirty-Second Session of the Committee on Food Aid Policies and Programmes.* WFP/CFA: 32:13

(1991b) *Basic Documents for the World Food Programme.* 5th edn.

(1991c) *Food Aid in Africa: An Agenda for the 1990s. A Joint Study by the World Bank and the World Food Programme.* CFA: 32/P/6-D.

(1991d) *The Role of WFP in the Nineties.* CFA: 31/P/5-A.

(1992a) *Annual Report of the Executive Director,* 1991, WFP/CFA: 33/P/4.

(1992b) *General Rules and Regulations of the World Food Programme.*

(1993a) *Annual Report of the Executive Director, 1992.* CFA: 35/P/4.

(1993b) *Audited Accounts for 1990–91 and Report of the External Auditor.* CFA: 35/P-A: 17.

(1993c) *Jamaica. Food Entitlement Programme. Interim Evaluation Summary Report.* CFA: 36/SCP/11/5E Add.1.

(1994a) *The World Food Programme and the Programme Approach.* CFA; 38/P/6.

(1994b) *WFP Mission Statement.* CFA: 38/P/5.

(1994c) *Emergency Operations in Southern Africa during the Drought of 1992–93. Report of the WFP Evaluation Mission.*
(1994d) *Cost Measurement Study.* WFP/CFA: 37/8/INF.1.
(1994e) *Evaluation of Achievements and Impact of the Monetization Components of WFP Development Projects.* CFA: 37/SCP/12/6-C.
(1994f) 'Food Aid for Development'. World Food Programme Asia and Pacific Regional Seminar, Beijing, China, March 1994 (Beijing: China Agriculture Press).
(1994g) *Review of WFP Policies, Objectives and Strategies.* CFA; 37/P/7
(1995a) *Linking Relief and Development. Annual Report of the Executive Director.* CFA: 37/P/7/INF.1.
(1995b) 'Statement of Catherine Bertini', Executive Director of the World Food Programme. *Fourth World Conference on Women*, 6 September 1995, Beijing, China.
(1995c) *Food for Humanitarian Assistance.* Proceedings of the United Nations World Food Programme Africa regional Seminar, Addis Ababa, Ethiopia, February.
(1995d) 'Efficiency in Food Aid. Using Food to Address Hunger and Poverty'. World Food Programme Americas Seminar, Cartegena de Indias, Colombia, August.
(1995e) *Linking Relief and Development. Annual Report of the Executive Director.* CFA: 37/P/7/INF.1/
(1996a) *Reform and Revitalization Measures.* WFP/EB.A/96/6/Rev.1.
(1996b) *Ending the Inheritance of Hunger. Annual Report of the Executive Director,* 1996. WFP/EB.A/96/4.
(1997a) *WFP Support to Countries in Establishing and Managing National Food Assistance Programmes.* WFP/EB.2/97/3-A.
(1997b) *Thematic Evaluation of Project Brazil 2732 (Exp.1) – Feeding Pre-school and Primary School Children in Depressed Areas.* WFP/EB.2/97/5/Add. 3
(1997c) *Measures to enhance WFP's programming with the poorest countries.* WFP/EB.3/97/3-A.
(1997d) *Policies on the Use of Food Aid in Relief and Development Activities: Monetization.* WFP/EB.A/97/5-A.
(1997e) *Policies on the use of WFP food aid in relief and development activities.* WFP/EB.A/97/5-A.
(1997f) *Discussions and Decisions of the Annual Session of the Executive Board, 1997.* WFP/EB.A/97/9.
(1997g) *Reform and Revitalization Measures in the World Food Programme.* WFP/EB.A/97/5-B.
(1997h) WFP/UNHCR Memorandum of Understanding on the Joint Working Arrangements for Refugees, Returnees, and Internally Displaced Persons. Revisions with effect from 31 March 1997. WFP/EB.2/97/3-C/Add.1.
(1998a) *From Crisis to Recovery.* WFP/EB.A/98/4-A.
(1998b) *Gender Mainstreaming in WFP: An Integrated Assessment.* WFP/EB.2/98/9.
(1998c) *Summary of the Work of the Second Regular Session of the Executive Board,* 1998. WFP/EB.2/98/13.
(1998d) *Decision of the Annual Session of the Executive Board, 1998.* WFP/EB.A/98/10.
(1998e) *UNHCR/WFP Joint Evaluation of Emergency Food Assistance to Returnees, Refugees, Displaced Persons and Other War-Affected Populations in Bosnia and Herzegovina.* WFP/EB.2/98/3/1.
(1998f) *Local Purchases of Food and Non-Food Items.* WFP/EB.A/98/87-B.
(1998g) *Decisions and Recommendations of the Annual Session of the Executive Board,* WFP/EB.A/98/10.
(1998h) UNICEF/WFP Memorandum of Understanding in Emergency and Rehabilitation Interventions. WFP/EB.1/98/12.
(1999a) *Enabling Development.* WFP/EB: A/99/4-A.
(1999b) *Summary of the Work of the Annual Session of the Executive Board, 1999* (WFP/EB.A/99/11), 27 October 1999: 2–3.
(1999c) *Discussions and Recommendations of the Annual Session of the Executive Board, 1999* (WFP/EB.A/99/10), 20 May, 1999.

(1999d) *Guidelines for PRROs.*
(1999e) *Partnerships with NGOs.* WFP/EB.1/99/3-A.
(1999f) *The Food Aid Monitor.1998 Food Aid Flows.* Special Issue. May.
(1999g) *Review of the Methodology on Local Purchases.* WFP/EB.3/99/10-A.
(1999h) *Summary of the Work of the Third Regular Session of the Executive Board, 1999.* WFP/EB.3/99/14.
(1999i) Aide-Memoire for Field Arrangements between the International Committee of the Red Cross and the World Food Programme. Geneva and Rome, 23 December
(2000a) 'Emerging Issues Relevant to WFP: Working with the Military'. WFP/EB.A/2000/4-A.
(2000b) *Thematic Evaluation of WFP–NGO Partnerships.* WFP/EB.1/2000/5/2.
(2000c) *Disaster Mitigation. A Strategic Approach.* WFP/EB.1/2000/4-A
(2000d) *Disaster Mitigation. Guidelines for WFP Assistance* (Rome, Italy: WFP).
(2001a) *WFP, Food Security and HIV/AIDS.* WFP/EB. 3/2001/INF/18.
(2001b) *WFP Working with NGOs: A Framework for Partnership.* WFP/EB.A/2001/4-B.
(2001c) *Decisions and Recommendations of the Annual Session of the Executive Board 2001.* WFP/EB.A.2001/1/9.
(2002a) *A Decade of Change: Renewal and Transformation of the World Food Programme, 1992–2002.* WFP/EB.1/2002/9.
(2002b) *Update on the WFP's Role in the Fight against HIV/AIDS.* WFP/EB.3/2002/INF/22.
(2002c) *Thematic Evaluation of WFP's Commitment to Women (1996–2001).* WFP/EB.3/2002/6-C.
(2002d) *Gender Policy 2003–2007. Enhanced Commitments to Women to Ensure Food Security.* WFP/EB.3/2002/4-A.
(2002e) *Food Assistance in Urban Areas.* WFP/EBa/2002/5-B.
(2002f) *Gender Policy 2003–2007. Enhancing Commitments to Women to Ensure Food Security.*
(2002g) *Full Report of the Evaluation of WFP's Special Operations.* OEDE/2002/10.
(2002h) *World Food Programme Annual Report for 2001.*
(2002i) *Progress Report on the Implementation of the Recommendations in the 2000–2001 Report of the External Auditor.* WFP/EB.3/2002/5-A/1/5.
(2002j) *Tribute to the Executive Director.* WFP/EB.1/2002/25.
(2003a) *Exit Strategies for School Feeding: WFP Experience.* WFP/EB.1/2003/4-C.
(2003b) *Programming in the Era of HIV/AIDS: WFP's response to HIV/AIDS.* WFP/EB. 1/2003/4-B.
(2003c) *Summary of the Work of the First Regular Session of the Executive Board, 2003.* WFP/EB.1/2003/11.
(2003d) *Food Aid and Livelihoods in Emergencies: Strategies for WFP.* WFP/EB.A/2003/5-B.
(2003e) *Summary of the Work of the Third Session of the Executive Board, 2003.* WFP/EB.3/2003/14.
(2004a) *Definition of Special Operations. Amendment to General Regulation V.2 (d).* WFP/EB.A/2004/5-D.
(2004b) *Assistance to Populations in Southern Africa Vulnerable to Food Insecurity and the Impact of AIDS.* WFP/EB.3/2004/8-B/7.
(2004c) *Full Report of the Evaluation of the West Africa Coastal Region Protracted Relief and Recovery Operation.* Document OEDE/2004/6. Summary Evaluation Report in document WFP/EB.3/2004/6-C.
(2004d) 'Review of the Protection Issues in West Africa Coastal Countries', in WFP, 2004c, Annex 8.
(2004e) *Humanitarian Principles.* WFP/EB.A/2004/5-C.
(2004f) *Full Report of Evaluation of the Afghanistan Protracted Relief and Recovery Operation 10233.* Document OEDE/2005/1. Summary Evaluation Report in document WFP/EB.1/2005/6-A.
(2004g) *Full Report of the Evaluation of the WFP EMOP 10048.00/01/02 in the Sudan. Food Assistance to Populations affected by War and Drought.*

(2004h) *Iraq: WFP's Biggest Ever Operation*. WFP/EB.A/2004/4-3: 3
(2004i) *World Food Programme Annual Report 2004.*
(2004j) 'ACC/SCN statement on nutrition, refugees and displaced persons' in *ACC/SCN Nutrition Issues in Food Aid*. Symposium Report. Nutrition Policy Discussion Paper No. 12 (Geneva, Switzerland: ACC Subcommittee on Nutrition, 1993).
(2004k) *Food for Nutrition: Mainstreaming Nutrition in WFP.* WFP/EB.A/2004/5-A/1.
(2004l) *Nutrition in Emergencies: WFP Experiences and Challenges*. WFP/EB.A/2004/5-A/3.
(2004m) *Micronutrient Fortification: WFP Experience and the Way Forward.*
(2004n) 'Information Note on School Feeding'. WFP/EB.3/2004/4-D.
(2004o) *WFP and Food-Based Safety Nets.*
(2004p) *Humanitarian Principles*. WFP/EB.1/2004/4-C.
(2004q) *WFP and Food-Based Safety Nets: Concepts, Experiences and Future Programming Opportunities*. WFP/EB.3/2004/4-A.
(2004r) *Proposed Programme of Work of External Auditor for the 2004–2005 Biennium* (WFP/ EB.3/2004/INF/8).
(2004s) *Vulnerability Analysis and Mapping – VAM.*
(2004t) *New Partnerships to Meet Rising Needs – Expanding the WFP Donor Base*. WFP/ EB.3/2004/4-C.
(2004u) *Summary of the Work of the Third Regular Session of the Executive Board, 2004*. WFP/ EB.3/2004/16.
(2004v) Exchange of Letters between the International Committee of the Red Cross and the World Food Programme of 11 and 19 August, and attached documents on Common Principles of Humanitarian Action and Terms of Cooperation between the United Nations World Food Programme and the International Committee of the Red Cross, and Technical Arrangements and Provisions of Food Commodities between the International Committee of the Red Cross and the United Nations World Food Programme.
(2004w) *People Living With AIDS. Food as the First Line of Defence* (Rome, Italy: WFP)
(2004x) *Vulnerability, Livelihood Protection and Food-Based Safety Nets. Theory, Evidence and Policy Underpinnings* (Rome).
(2005a) *Strategic Plan 2006–2009* (WFP/EB.2005/5-A/Rev.1.), 9 June 2005.
(2005b) *Real-Time Evaluation of WFP's Response to the Indian Ocean Tsunami*. WFP/ EB.2/2005/6-C Rev.1.
(2005c) *Answering the Call to Action: An Update on WFP's Response to HIV/AIDS*. WFP/ EB.A/2005/5-D.
(2005d) *Definition of Emergencies*. WFP/EB.1/2005/Rev. 1.
(2005e) *Decisions and Recommendations of the First Regular Session of the Executive Board, 2005*. WFP/EB.1/2005/13.
(2005f) *Exiting Emergencies. Programme Options for Transition from Emergency Response*. WFP/ EB.1/2005/4-B.
(2005g) *Review of the Dubai Support Office and Fast Information Technology and Telecommunications Emergency and Support Team (FITTEST)*. WFP/EB.2/2005/5-G/1.
(2005h) *How to Work with WFP. A Handbook for Non-Governmental Organizations.*
(2006a) *Summary Report of the Evaluation of the Central American Protracted Relief and Recovery Operation*. WFP/EB.2/2006/6-A.
(2006b) Information Note on the Inter-Agency Real Time Evaluation of the Application of the Inter-Agency Standing Committee Cluster Approach in the South Asia Earthquake. WFP/EB.2/2006/6-D.
(2006c) *Post-Earthquake Relief and Recovery Operation in South Asia*. WFP/EB.2/2006/8/Rev.1.
(2006d) *World Food Programme Annual Report 2006.*
(2006e) *Global School Feeding Report.*
(2006f), *Hunger and Learning. World Hunger Series 2006*. A co-publication of WFP and Stanford University Press, California, USA).
(2006g) *Five Years Later – An Update on WFP's Response to HIV/AIDS*. WFP/EB.A/2006/ 5-D/1.

(2006h) 'Global Task Team Recommendations on Improving AIDS Coordination Among Multilateral Institutions and International Donors'. WFP/EB.A/2006/5-D2.(2006i) *Ending Child Hunger and Undernutrition. Global Framework for Action*. WFP/EB.2/2006/4-A.
(2006j) *Thematic Review of Targeting in Relief Operations. Summary Report*. WFP/EB.1/2006/7-B.
(2006k) *Targeting in Emergencies*. WFP/EB.1.2006/5-A.
(2006l) *Food Procurement in Developing Countries*. WFP/EB.1/2006/5-C.
(2006m) *Decisions and Recommendations of the First Regular Session of the Executive Board, 2006*. WFP/EB.1/2006/14.
(2007a) *WFP Biennial Management Plan (2008–2009)*. WFP/EB.2/2007/5-A/1.
(2007b) *Summary Report of the Mid-Term Evaluation of the Southern Africa Regional Protracted Relief and Recovery Operation*. WFP/EB.A/2007/7-B.
(2007d) *Summary Report of the Thematic Evaluation of School Feeding in Emergency Situations*. WFP/EB.A/2007/7-A.
(2007e) *Summary of the Work of the Annual Session of the Executive Board, 2007* WFP/EB.A/2007/16.
(2007f) *Time to Deliver – An Update of WFP's Response to HIV/AIDS*. WFP/EB. A/2007/5-B.
(2007g) *Gender and Geographical Diversity: A Way Foreword for Meeting Established Targets*. EFP/EB.2007/4-B.
(2007h) *Ending Child Hunger and Undernutrition Initiative*. WFP/EB.1/2007/5-V.
(2007i) *Summary of the Work of the First Regular Session of the Executive Board, 2007*. WFP/EB.1/2007/17.
(2007j) *Collaboration among the United Nations Rome-based Agencies*. WFP/EB.2/2007/12-b.
(2007k) *Has Decentralization Met the World Food Programme's Operational Need?* WFP/EB.2/2007/5-C/1.
(2007l) *Hunger and Health. World Hunger Series 2007*(Rome, Italy: WFP).
(2007m) *Global Framework for Action: Ending Child Hunger and Undernutrition Initiative*. WFP/EB.1/2007/5-/Add.1.
(2008a) *Summary Report of the End-of-Term Evaluation of WFP's Gender Policy (2003–2007): Enhanced Commitments to Women to Ensure Food Security*. WFP/EB.2'2008/6-B.
(2008b) *Preparing for Tomorrow Today; WFP Strategy for Managing and Developing Human Resources (2008–2011)*. WFP/EB.2/2008/4-C.
(2008c) *WFP's Gender Policy (2003–2007). A Desk Review on Human Resources*. March.
(2008e) *Summary of the Work of the Second Regular Session of the Executive Board, 2008*. WFP/EB.2/2008/16.
(2008f) *Progress Report on Ending Child Hunger and Undernutrition*. WFP/EB.2/2008/4-E.
(2008g) *WFP General Regulations and Rules. Eligibility for assistance: 14*. 2008 edn.
(2008h) *Vouchers and Cash Transfers as Food Assistance Instruments: Opportunities and Challenges*. WFP/EB.2/2008/4-B.
(2008i) *WFP's Private-Sector Partnership and Fundraising Strategy*. WFP/EB.1/2008/5-B/1.
(2008j) *Summary of the Work of the First Regular Session of the Executive Board, 2008*. WFP/EB.1/2008/16.
(2008k) *Strategic Plan (2008–11)*. WFP/EB.A/2008/5-A/1/Rev/1.
(2008l) 'WFP Protection Project. Ten Minutes to Learn About'. *WFP Humanitarian Policy and Transitions Unit*, Vol. 1, No. 9, July.
(2009a) *WFP Biennial Management Plan (2011–2011)*. WFP/EB.2/2009/5-A/1.
(2009b) *Learning from Experience. Good Practices from 45 Years of School Feeding*.
(2009c) *Home-Grown School Feeding. A Framework to Linking School Feeding with Local Agricultural Production*.
(2009d) *WFP School Feeding Policy*. WFP/EB.2/2009/4-A.
(2009e) *WFP Gender Policy. Promoting Gender Equality and the Empowerment of Women in Addressing Food and Nutrition Challenges*. WFP/EB./2009/5-A/Rev.1.
(2009f) *Summary of the Work of the Second Regular Session of the Executive Board, 2009*. WFP/EB.2/2009/EB.1.3.

(2009g) *WFP Gender Policy. Corporate Action Plan (2010–2011).* WFP/EB.2.2009/4-C.
(2009h) *Consolidated Framework of WFP Policies.* WFP/EB.2/2009/4-D.
(2009i) *Summary of the Work of the Second Regular Session of the Executive Board, 2009.* WFP/EB.2/2009.4-D.
(2009j) *WFP Policy on Disaster Risk Reduction.* WFP/EB.1/2009/5-B.
(2009k) *Summary of the Work of the First Session of the Executive Board, 2009.* WFP/EB.1/2009/17.
(2009l) *WFP's Operational Relationship with NGOs. Annual Report 2009.*
(2009m) Decisions and Recommendations of the First Regular Session of the Executive Board 2009. WFP/EB.1/2009/16.
(2009n) *World Food Programme Annual Report for 2008.*
(2009o) *Review of Climate Change and Disaster Risk Reduction in WFP. A strategic analysis of standard project reports.* (Rome, Italy: WFP Climate Change and Disaster Risk Reduction Office).
(2010a) *Annual Report for 2009 to ECOSOC and FAO Council.* WFP/EB.1/2010/4/Rev. 1.
(2010b) *Final Report on the WINGS II Project* (WFP/EB.1/2010/6-G/1).
(2010c) *Annual Performance Report for 2009.* WFP/EB.A/2010/4.
(2010d) *WFP's Role in the Humanitarian Assistance System.* WFP/ED1/2010/5-C.
(2010e) *Decisions and Recommendations of the First Regular Session of the Executive Board 2010.* WFP/EB.1/2010/Rev.1.
(2010f) 'World Food Programme announces bold partnership with private sector to cut hunger'. WFP News Release, 22 September.
(2010g) *World Food Programme HIV and Aids Policy.* WFP/EB.2/2010/4-A
(2010h) *Financial Framework Review.* WFP/EB.2/2010/5-A/1+Corr.1.

Other references

ACC (2000) *Guideline Note on Capacity-Building* (Geneva: Administrative Committee on Coordination, March).
ACC/SCN (1993) *Nutritional Issues in Food Aid. ACC/SCN Symposium Report. Nutrition Policy Discussion Paper* No. 12 (Geneva, Switzerland: ACC/SCN).ACC/SCN (1993) 'ACC/SCN Statement on Nutrition, Refugees and Displaced Persons', in ACC/SCN (1993): 86.
Adams, L. and P. Harvey (2006) 'Learning from Cash Based Responses to the Tsunami', *Issues Paper* (London: Overseas Development Institute).
Akhter, U. A., R. V. Hill, L. C. Smith, D. M. Wiesmann and T. Trankenberger (2007) *The World's Most Deprived. Characteristics and Causes of Extreme Poverty and Hunger* (Washington, DC: International Food Policy Research Institute).
Allen, G. R. (with R. G. Smethurst) (1965) 'The Impact of Food Aid on Donor and Other Exporting Countries'. *WFP Study* No. 2 (Rome, Italy: UN and FAO).
ALNAP (2001) *ALNAP Annual Review 2001. Humanitarian Action/Learning from Evaluation* (London: Overseas Development Institute).
ALNAP (2008) *Responding to Earthquakes 2008. Learning from Earthquake Relief and Recovery Operations* (London: Overseas Development Institute).
ALNAP (2009) *ALNAP 8th Review of Humanitarian Action, Performance, Impact and Innovation* (London: Overseas Development Institute).
ALNAP (2010) *Jobs and Consultancies. WFP Nutritionist Profile.* 1 September (London: Overseas Development Institute).
ALNAP/HPG (2009) *Where to Now? Agency Expulsions in Sudan: Consequences and Next Steps* (London: Overseas Development Institute).
Annan, K. A. (1997) *Renewing the United Nations. A Programme of Reform* (New York: United Nations).
Annan, K. A. (1999a) *Preventing Wars and Disasters. A Growing Global Challenge. 1999 Annual Report on the Work of the Organization* (New York: United Nations).

Annan, K. A. (1999b) 'Two Concepts of Sovereignty', *The Economist*, 18 September: 81–2.

Annan, K. A. (2001) *Cooperation between the United Nations and All Relevant Partners, in particular the Private Sector* (New York: UN, 28 August).

Annan, K. A. (2005) *In Larger Freedom: Towards Development, Security, and Human Rights for All* (New York: United Nations).

Audsley, B., R. Halme and N. Balzer (2010) 'Comparing Cash and Food Transfers: A Cost-Benefit Analysis from Rural Malawi', in Omamo, Gentilini and Sandström (eds): 89–102.

Austin, J. E. and M. B. Wallerstein (1978) *Towards a Development Food Aid Policy* (Cambridge, MA: MIT INP Discussion Paper).

Baker, J. E. (1979) *Food for Peace, 1954–1978. Major Changes in Legislation* (Washington, DC: Congressional Research Service, Library of Congress).

Balletto, R. and S. Wertheimer (2010) 'Emergency Preparedness Tools and Activities in Latin America and the Caribbean', in Omamo, Gentilini and Sandström (eds): 275–93.

Balzer, N. and U. Hess (2010) 'Climate Change and Weather Risk Management: Evidence from Index-Based Insurance Schemes in China and Ethiopia', in Omamo, Gentilini and Sandström (eds): 103–20.

Barrett, C. B. and D. G. Maxwell (2005) *Food Aid After Fifty Years. Recasting its Role* (London: Routledge).

Barnett, M. and T. G. Weiss (eds) (2008) *Humanitarianism in Question. Politics, Power, Ethics* (Ithaca, NY and London: Cornell University Press)

Benedict, M. and E. Bauer (1960) *Farm Surpluses: U.S. Burden or World Asset?* (Berkeley, CA: University of California Press).

Bennett, J., W. Bertrand, C. Harkin, S. Samarasinghe and H. Wickramatillake (2006). *Coordination of the International Humanitarian Assistance in Tsunami-Affected Countries* (London: Tsunami Evaluation Coalition).

Benson, C. (2000) 'The Food Aid Convention: An Effective Safety Net?' in E. Clay and O. Stokke, *Food Aid and Human Security* (London and Portland, OR: Frank Cass: 102–119).

Bertini, C. (1994) 'WFP Statement to the Forty-Fifth Session of the Executive Committee for the High Commissioner's Programmes' (Geneva, Switzerland: UNHCR), October 3.

Bertini, C. and D. Glickman (2009) 'Bringing Agriculture Back to U.S. Foreign Policy' *Foreign Affairs* 88(3): 93–105.

Bertrand, M. (1984) *Report on Personnel Problems in the World Food Programme*. Document JIU/REP/84/8 (Geneva, Switzerland: United Nations Joint Inspection Unit).

Bounie, D., C. Bienfait, S. Prigge and B. Salvignol (2010) 'Food Technology for Safe and Nutritious Food', in Omamo, Gentilini and Sandström (eds): 177–94.

Boyd Orr, J. and D. Lubbock (1953) *The White Man's Dilemma* (London: Unwin Books).

Brainard, L., A. Jones and N. Purvis (eds) (2009) *Climate Change and Global Poverty. A Billion Lives in the Balance?* (Washington, DC: Brookings Institution Press).

Brinkman, H.-J., U. Gentilini and Z. Majeed (2010) 'Climbing Mountains and Crossing Deserts: Insights from a Multi-Annual Voucher Programme in Pakistan', in Omamo, Gentilini and Sandström (eds): 53–64.

Bundy, D., C. Bubano, M. Grosh, A. Gelli, M. Jukes and L. Drake (2009) *Rethinking School Feeding: Social Safety Nets, Child Development and the Education Sector* (Washington, DC: WFP and the World Bank).

Bundy, D., A. Patrikios, C. Mannathoko, A. Tembon, S. Manda, B. Sarr and L. Draka (2010) *Accelerating the Education Sector Response to HIV: Five Years of Experience from Sub-Saharan Africa* (Washington, DC: World Bank).

Burgess, A (!982) 'Evaluation of Nutrition Interventions: An Annotated Bibliography and Review of Methodologies and Results'. *FAO Food and Nutrition Paper* No. 24. 2nd edn (Rome: FAO).

CARE (2006) *White Paper on Food Aid Policy: CARE USA* (New York: Cooperative for American Relief Everywhere).

Chakravarty, S. and P. N. Rosenstein-Rodan (1965)'The Linking of Food Aid with Other Aid'. *WFP Study* No. 3 (Rome, Italy: UN and FAO).
Charlton, M. W. (1992) 'Innovation and Inter-Organizational Politics: The Case of the World Food Programme', *International Journal* (XLVII), summer: 630–65.
Charlton, M. W. (1997) 'Famine and the Food Weapon: Implications for the Global Food Aid Regime', *Journal of Conflict Studies* XVII(1): 28–54.
CHR (1992a) 'Internally Displaced Persons'. *Commission on Human Rights, Resolution 1992/73,* requesting the UN secretary-general to appoint a representative to undertake a comprehensive study on the issue of internally displaced persons (Geneva, Switzerland: UN Commission on Human Rights).
CHR (1992b) *Analytical Report of the Secretary-General on Internally Displaced Persons.* Document E/CN.4/1992/3 (Geneva, Switzerland: United Nations Commission on Human Rights).
Chr. Michelsen Institute (1994) *Evaluation of the World Food Programme* (Bergen, Norway: Chr. Michelsen Institute).
Clapp, J. (2009) 'Corporate Interest in US Food Aid Policy: Global Implications of Resistance to Reform', in J. Clapp and D. Fuchs (eds): 125–52.
Clapp, J. and M. J. Cohen (eds) (2009) *The Global Food Crisis. Governance Challenges and Opportunities* (Waterloo, Canada: Centre for International Governance Innovation and Wilfrid Laurier University Press).
Clapp, J. and D. Fuchs (eds) (2009) *Corporate Power in Global Agrifood Governance* (Cambridge, MA and London: MIT Press).
Clay, E. (2010) 'A Future Food Aid or Food Assistance Convention?' *ODI Background Paper on Food Aid* No. 6 (London: Overseas Development Institute, July).
Clay, E. and H. W. Singer (1985) 'Food Aid and Development: Issues and Evidence. A Survey of the Literature since 1977 on the Role and Impact of Food Aid in Developing Countries'. *WFP Occasional Paper* No. 3 (Rome: WFP).
Clay, E. and C. Benson (1990) 'Acquisition of Commodities in Developing Countries for Food Aid', *Food Policy* 15(1): 27–43.
Clay, E., N. Pillai, and C. Benson (1998) *The Future of Food Aid: A Policy Review* (London: Overseas Development Institute).
Clay, E. and O. Stokke (eds) (2000) *Food Aid and Human Security* (London: Frank Cass).
Cochrane, W. W. (1959) 'Farm Technology, Foreign Surplus Disposal, and Domestic Supply Control', *Journal of Farm Economics* 41(5): 885–99.
Cochrane, W. W. (1962) 'Contributions of the New Frontier to Agricultural Reform in the United States', *Journal of Farm Economics* 24(1): 93–108.
Cohen, R. and F. M. Deng (1998a) *Masses in Flight: The Global Crisis of Internal Displacement* (Washington, DC: Brookings Institution Press).
Cohen, R. and F. M. Deng (eds) (1998b) *The Forsaken People. Case Studies of the Internally Displaced* (Washington, DC: Brookings Institution Press).
Collier, P. (2007) *The Bottom Billion: Why the Poorest Countries are Failing and What Can be Done About It* (Oxford, UK: Oxford University Press).
Collier, P. (2008) 'The Politics of Hunger', *Foreign Affairs*, November/December: 67–79.
Collier, P. (2009) *Wars, Guns, and Votes. Democracy in Dangerous Places* (New York: HarperCollins).
Collins, C. and T. G. Weiss (1997) 'An Overview and Assessment of 1989–1996 Peace Operations Publications'. *Occasional Paper* No. 28 (Providence, RI: Watson Institute).
Conway, G. (1997) *The Doubly Green Revolution. Food for All in the 21st Century* (London and New York: Penguin Books).
Conway, G., U. Lele, J. Peakcock, and M. Pineiro (1994) *Sustainable Agriculture for a Food Secure World. A Vision for International Agricultural Research* (Washington, DC and Stockholm, Sweden: Consultative Group on International Agricultural Research and Swedish Agency for Research Cooperation with Developing Countries).

Cornia, G. A., R. Jolly and F. Stewart (eds) (1987) *Adjustment with a Human Face. Protecting the Vulnerable and Promoting Growth. A Study by UNICEF* (Oxford, UK: Clarendon Press).

Crawford, N., G. Pattugala and K. Dale (2010) 'Protection and Food Assistance Programmes: Promoting Safety, Dignity and More Effective Hunger Outcomes in Humanitarian Crises', in Omamo, Gentilini and Sandström (eds): 231–54.

CRED (2004) *Thirty Years of Natural Disasters, 1974–2003: The Numbers* (Brussels, Belgium: International Disaster Database, Catholic University of Louvain).

Dallaire, R. (2003) *Shake Hands with the Devil* (Toronto, Canada: Random House).

Dandekar, V. M. (1965) 'The Demand for Food and Conditions Governing Food Aid during Development'. *WFP Study* No. 1 (Rome, Italy: UN and FAO).

Daschle, T. and C. F. Runge, and B. Senauer (2007) 'Food for Fuel? Debating the Tradeoffs of Corn-Based Ethanol', *Foreign Affairs* (September/October): 157–62.

Davies, K. and N. Menage (2010) 'Connecting Farmers to Markets: Insights from the Purchase for Progress Initiative', in Omamo, Gentilini and Sandström (eds): 125–38.

de Pee, S., T. van den Briel, J. van Hees and M. W. Bloem (2010) 'Introducing New and Improved Food Products for Better Nutrition', in Omamo, Gentilini and Sandström (eds): 157–75.

De Waal, A. (1989) *Famine that Kills: Darfur, Sudan, 1984–1985* (Oxford, UK: Studies in African Affairs, Oxford University Press).

De Waal, A. (2005) *Famine that Kills: Darfur, Sudan* (Oxford: Studies in African Affairs, Oxford University Press).

De Waal, A. (ed.) (2007) *War in Darfur and the Search for Peace* (Cambridge, MA: Global Equity Initiative, Justice in Africa, Harvard University).

Deaton, A. and J. Dreze (2009) 'Food and Nutrition in India: Facts and Interpretation' *Economic and Political Weekly* XLIV(7): 14.

Delisle, H. and D. J. Shaw (eds) (1998) 'The Quest for Food Security in the Twenty-First Century'. *Canadian Journal of Development Studies* XIX. Special Issue.

Deng, F. (2004) Specific Groups and Individuals: Mass Exoduses and Displaced Persons. Report of the Secretary-General on Internally Displaced Persons (Geneva, Switzerland: ECOSOC).

Dessau, J. (1965) 'The Role of Multilateral Food Aid Programs'. *WFP Study* No. 2 (Rome, Italy: UN and FAO).

Development Initiatives (2009) *Global Humanitarian Assistance 2009* (Wells, UK: Development Initiatives).

DFID (2009) *Climate Change in Sub-Saharan Africa* (London: Department of International Development).

DMZ (2005) *Joint Evaluation of the Effectiveness and Impact of the Enabling Development Policy of the World Food Programme. Synthesis Report.* Vol. 1. Main Text, February 2005 (Berlin, Germany: Federal Ministry for Economic Cooperation and Development (DMZ) on behalf of the Steering Committee of the Evaluation).

Dreze, J. (2005) 'Employment Guarantee Act: Promise and Reality'. Paper for the International Conference on Employment and Income Security in India. New Delhi: 2–8 April. Convened by the Institute for Human Development.

Dreze, J. and A. K. Sen (1989) *Hunger and Public Action* (Oxford: Clarendon Press).

Easterly, W. (2008) 'Foreign Aid Goes Military', *New York Review of Books*, LV(19): 51–4.

ECOSOC (1990) 'Operational Activities of the United Nations System'. Document E/1990/85, 18 May (Geneva, Switzerland: United Nations).

Eide, W. B. and U. Kracht (2005) *Food and Human Rights in Development. Vol. 1, Legal and Institutional Dimensions and Selected Topics* (Antwerp, Belgium and Oxford, UK: Intersentia).

Eide, W. B. and U. Kracht (2007) *Food and Human Rights. Vol. 2. Evolving Issues and Emerging Applications* (Mortsel, Belgium: Intersentia).

Elguindi, T. (2010) 'New Technologies in Food Assistance: Electronic Vouchers for Iraqi Refugees in the Syrian Arab Republic', in Omamo, Gentilini and Sandström (eds): 65–74.
Emmerij, L., R. Jolly and T. Weiss (2001) *Ahead of the Curve? UN Ideas and Global Challenges* (Bloomington, IN: Indiana University Press. United Nations Intellectual History series).
Epstein, S. B. (1987) *Food for Peace, 1954–1986: Major Changes in Legislation* (Washington, DC: Congressional Research Service, Library of Congress).
Erdelmann, F., M. Njoroge and A. Isler (2010) 'The Evolution of Food Assistance for HIV Care and Treatment 2000 to 2009: A Decade of Institutional Innovations', in Omamo, Gentilini and Sandström (eds): 195–216.
Eriksson, J. (1996) *The International Response to Conflict and Genocide: Lessons from the Rwanda Experience. Synthesis Report* (Odense, Denmark: Strandbery Grafisk for the Steering Committee on the Joint Evaluation of Emergency Assistance to Rwanda).
Evans, G. (2008) *The Responsibility to Protect. Ending Mass Atrocity Crimes Once and For All* (Washington, DC: Brooking Institution Press).
Faaland, J., D. McLean and O. K. Norbye (2000) 'The World Food Program (WFP) and International Food Aid', in Clay and Stokke (eds): 221–55.
Faehmann, K. (2010) Transmittal letter circulating commissioned study (Harvey *et al.*, 2010) (Berlin: Head of Development-oriented Emergency and Transitional Aid, German Federal Ministry for Economic Cooperation and Development).
Fan, S. and M. Rosegrant (2008) 'Investing in Agriculture to Overcome the World Food Crisis and Reduce Poverty and Hunger'. *Policy Brief* 3 (Washington, DC: International Food Policy Research Institute).
FAO (1946) 'Proposals for a World Food Board'. Prepared for Submission to the Second Session of the FAO Conference, Copenhagen, Denmark, 2 September 1946 (Washington, DC: FAO).
FAO (1954) *Disposal of Agricultural Surpluses. Principles Recommended by FAO* (Rome, Italy: FAO). Subsequently revised and expanded in five versions, last edition 2001.
FAO (1955) 'Uses of Agricultural Surpluses to Finance Economic Development in Under-Developed Countries: A Pilot Study in India'. *Commodity Policy Studies* No. 6 (Rome, Italy: FAO).
FAO (1956) 'Functions of a World Food Reserve. Scope and Limitations'. *FAO Commodity Study* No. 10 (Rome, Italy: FAO).
FAO (1961a) 'Development through Food: A Strategy for Surplus Utilization'. *FFHC Basic Study* No. 2 (Rome, Italy: FAO).
FAO (1961b) 'Utilization of Food Surpluses. World Food Programme'. *FAO Conference Resolution* 1/61, adopted on 24 November 1961 (Rome, Italy: FAO).
FAO (1965) 'Continuation of the World Food Programme'. *FAO Conference Resolution 4/65*, adopted on 6 December 1965 (Rome, Italy: FAO).
FAO (1989) 'The Effects of Stabilization and Structural Adjustment Programmes on Food Security. *Economic and Social Development Paper* No. 89 (Rome: FAO).
FAO (1991) 'Revision of the General Regulations of WFP and Membership of the WFP Committee on Food Aid Policies and Programmes'. *FAO Conference Resolution 9/91*, adopted on 26 November 1991 (Rome, Italy: FAO).
FAO (1992) *Principles of Surplus Disposal*. Revised Edition (Rome, Italy: FAO).
FAO (1993) 'Food and Nutrition in the Management of Feeding Programmes'. *Food and Nutrition Paper* No. 23, Rev. 1 (Rome, Italy: FAO).
FAO (1996) World Food Summit. Rome Declaration on World Food Security and World Food Summit Plan of Action (Rome, Italy: FAO).
FAO (2000) *Guidelines for National FIVIMS. Background and Principles* (Rome: FAO).
FAO (2002) *Report of the World Food Summit: Five Years On* (Rome: FAO).
FAO (2004) *The State of Food Insecurity in the World* (Rome: FAO).
FAO (2005) 'Voluntary Guidelines to Support the Progressive Realization of the Right to Adequate Food in the Context of National Food Security'. Adopted by the 127th Session of the FAO Council, November 2004 (Rome, Italy: FAO).

FAO (2007) *FAO: The Challenge of Renewal. Report of the Independent External Evaluation of the Food and Agriculture Organization of the United Nations* (Rome, Italy: FAO).

FAO (2008) *Declaration of the High-Level Conference on World Food Security: The Challenges of Climate Change and Bioenergy.* Rome, 5 June 2008 (Rome, Italy: FAO).

FAO (2009) 'Reform of the Committee on World Food Security'. Document CFS: 2009/2 Rev. 1 (Rome, Italy: FAO).

FAO (2010) *The State of Food Insecurity in the World 2010* (Rome, Italy: FAO)

FAO/IFAD/WFP (2002) 'Reducing Poverty and Hunger: The Critical Role of Financing Food, Agriculture and Rural Development'. Paper prepared for the International Conference on Financing Development, Monterrey, Mexico March 2002 (Rome, Italy: FAO/IFAD/WFP).

Farrington, J. and R. Slater (eds) (2006) 'Cash Transfers Theme Issue'. *Development Policy Review* 24(3) (London: Overseas Development Institute).

Figa-Talamanca, I. (1985) 'Nutritional Implications of Food Aid: An Annotated Bibliography'. *FAO Food and Nutrition Paper* No. 33 (Rome: FAO).

Fiszbein, A. and N. Schady (2009) *Conditional Cash Transfers: Reducing Present and Future Poverty. A World Bank Policy Research Report* (Washington, DC: World Bank).

FitzGerald, D. A. (1965) 'Operational and Administrative Problems of Food Aid'. *WFP Studies* No. 4 (Rome, Italy: FAO).

Flint, J. and A. De Waal (2008) *Darfur: A New History of a Long War* (London and New York: Zed Books).

Fraker, T. (1990) *The Effects of Food Stamps on Food Consumption: A Review of the Literature* (Washington, DC: United States Department of Agriculture).

Fraser, C. (1988) *Lifelines for Africa Still in Peril* (London: Hutchinson).

Galluzzi, C. and S. Natsheh (2010) 'Market-Based Food Assistance in Protracted Crisis: Vouchers in the Occupied Palestinian Territory', in Omamo, Gentilini and Sandström, eds.: 33–52.

GAO (2004) *Food Stamps Program.* GAO-04-346 (Washington, DC: United States General Accounting Office).

GAO (2005) *Food Stamps Program.* GAO-05-245 (Washington, DC: United States General Accounting Office).

GAO (2006) Foreign Assistance. U.S. Agencies Face Challenges to Improving the Efficiency of Food Aid (Washington, DC: United States General Accounting Office).

GCFR2P (2010) Open Letter to Member States of the United Nations Marking the Fifth Anniversary of the Adoption of the Responsibility to Protect (New York: Global Centre for the Responsibility to Protect, 23 September).

Gebru, F., U. Gentilini and S. Wickrema (2010) 'Engaging in a Multi-Actor Platform: WFP's Experience with the Productive Safety Net Programme in Ethiopia' in Omamo, Gentilini and Sandström (eds): 329–49.

Gelsdorf, K. P. Walker and D. Maxwell (2007) 'Editorial: The Future of WFP Programming in Sudan', *Disasters*, 31, March 2007: S1-S8.

Gentilini, U. (2007) 'Cash and Food Transfers: A Primer'. *WFP Occasional Paper* No. 18 (Rome, Italy: WFP).

GHA (2008) *Global Humanitarian Assistance* (Wells, UK: The Global Humanitarian Assistance Team, Development Initiatives). Available at www.globalhumanitarianassistance.org

Ghani, A. and C. Lockart (2008) *Fixing Failed States. A Framework for Rebuilding a Fractured World* (Oxford, UK: Oxford University Press).

Gore, W. (2006) *An Inconvenient Truth* (New York: Rodale).

Government of India, (1958–82) *Collected Works of Mahatma Gandhi, Volume 96.*

Greaves, J. P. and D. J. Shaw (eds) (1986) *Food Aid and the Well-Being of Children in the Developing World* (New York: UNICEF and WFP).

Guruge, A. (1983) *School Feeding as a Potential Source for Learning* (Paris and New Delhi: UNESCO and UNICEF).

Haas, E. B. (1969) *Tangle of Hopes. American Commitments and World Order* (Englewood Cliffs, NJ: Prentice-Hall, Inc.).

Haddad, L. (ed.) (2009) 'Lifting the Curse. Overcoming Persistent Undernutrition in India'. *IDS Bulletin* 40(4) (Brighton, UK: Institute of Development Studies).

Hall, C. (2010) *UN Global Compact Annual Review – Anniversary Edition. Annual Review 10 Years 2000–2010* (New York: United Nations Global Compact Office).

Hammam, M. and N. Yousef (1986) 'The Continuum in Women's Productive and Reproductive Roles: Implications for Food Aid and Children's Well-Being' in J. P. Greave and D. J. Shaw (eds): 85–104.

Hanlon, J., A. Barrientos and D. Hume (2010) *Just Give Money to the Poor. The Development Revolution from the Global South* (Sterling, VA: Kumarian Press).

Hanrahan, C. (2007) *International Food Aid and the 2007 Farm Bill* (Washington, DC: Congressional Research Service).

Hansen, G. (1998) 'Humanitarian Action in the Caucasus: A Guide for Practitioners. Humanitarianism and War Project and Local Capacities for Peace Project' (Providence, RI: Thomas J. Watson Jr. Institute for International Studies, *Occasional Paper* No. 32, Brown University).

Hansen, G. (2009) *Politics and Humanitarian Action in the Georgia Conflicts* (Medford, MA: Feinstein International Center, Tufts University).

Hari, D. (2008) *The Translator. A Tribesman's Memoir of Darfur* (New York: Random House).

Harvey, P. (2005) 'Cash and Vouchers in Emergencies: An HPG Discussion Paper' (London: Humanitarian Policy Group, Overseas Development Institute).

Harvey, P. (2006) 'Editorial: Mini Special Issue on Cash Transfers'. *Disasters* 30(3): 273–6 (London: Overseas Development Institute).

Harvey, P. (2007) 'Cash-Based Responses in Emergencies'. *Humanitarian Policy Group Report* No. 24 (London: Overseas Development Institute).

Harvey, P. and J. Lind (2005) 'Dependency and Humanitarian Relief: A Critical Analysis', *PHG Report* 19 (London: Humanitarian Policy Group, Overseas Development Institute).

Harvey, P., A. Stoddard, A. Harmer, G. Taylor with V. DiDomenico and L. Brander (2010) *The States of the Humanitarian System: Assessing Performance and Progress. A Pilot Study* (London: ALNAP, Overseas Development Institute).

Harvey, P., K. Proudlock, E. Clay, B. Riley and S. Jaspars (2010) *Food Aid and Food Assistance in Emergency and Transitional Contexts: A Review of Current Thinking* (Berlin, Germany and London: German Federal Ministry for Economic Cooperation and Development and Overseas Development Institute).

Henderson, E. (1964) *Food Aid: A Selected Annotated Bibliography* (Rome, Italy: United Nations and FAO).

Hess, U. and S. Y. Im (2007) 'Saving Livelihoods through Weather Risk Management – A Case Study of Ethiopia', *Journal of Rural Development* 40(1): 21–30.

HPG (2010) 'Aid and War: A Response to Linda Polman's Critique of Humanitarianism'. *Opinion* 144 (London: Overseas Development Institute)

Humphrey, H. H. (1958) 'Food and Fiber as Force for Freedom'. Report to the Committee on Agriculture and Forestry, United States Senate (Washington, DC: US Government Printing Office).

Herbinger, W., B. Crawshaw and D. J. Shaw (1999) 'Beneficiary Participation in Context: Practical Experience from a Food-Aided Project in Ethiopia', in J. Mullin (ed.) *Rural Poverty, Empowerment and Sustainable Livelihoods* (Aldershot, UK: Ashgate): 1–13.

Hoskins, A. (2004) *Targeting General Food Distributions: Desk Review of Lessons from Experience* (Rome, Italy: WFP).

IASC (1993) *Internally Displaced Persons: The Next Stage* (New York: Inter-Agency Standing Committee).

IASC (2005) *Cluster Approach* (New York: United Nations).

IASC (2006) 'Guidance Note on Using the Cluster Approach to Strengthen Humanitarian Response' (New York: Inter-Agency Standing Committee).

IASC (2010) 'Proposal for the Creation of a Global Food Security Cluster'. Document WO/1006/3505/7 (Geneva, Switzerland: Inter-Agency Standing Committee.
IDC (2008) 'The World Food Programme and Global Food Security'. Document HC 593-1 (London: UK House of Commons International Development Committee).
IFAD (2005) *An Independent External Evaluation of the International Fund for Agricultural Development* (Rome, Italy: Office of Evaluation, International Fund for Agricultural Development).
IFPRI (1998) 'The Changing Outlook for Food Aid', *News and Views*, November (Washington, DC: International Food Policy Research Institute).
IFPRI (2009) *Climate Change. Impacts on Agriculture and Costs of Adaptation Food Policy Report* (Washington, DC: International Food Policy Research Institute).
IFPRI/WFP (2001) *HIV/AIDS, Food and Nutrition Security: Impacts and Action* (Washington, DC and Rome, Italy: International Food Policy Research Institute and WFP).
ILO (1930) *Forced Labour Convention*, No. 29 (Geneva, Switzerland: International Labour Office).
ILO (1949) *Protection of Wages Convention*, No. 95 (Geneva, Switzerland: International Labour Office).
ILO (1957) *Abolition of Forced Labour Convention* (Geneva, Switzerland: International Labour Office).
ILO (1976) *Tripartite World Conference on Employment, Income Distribution and Social Progress and the International Division of Labour* (Geneva, Switzerland: International Labour Office).
Ingram, J. (1989) 'Sustaining Refugees' Human Dignity: International Responsibility and Practical Reality', *Journal of Refugee Studies* 2(3), 1989: 329–58.
Ingram, J. (1993a) 'The Future Architecture for International Humanitarian Assistance' in T. G. Weiss and L. Minear (eds) *Humanitarianism Across Borders. Sustaining Civilians in Times of War* (Boulder, CO and London: Lynne Rienner Publishers: 171–93).
Ingram, J. (1993b) 'The Politics of Human Suffering', *National Interest*, spring.
Ingram, J. (1994) 'The International Response to Humanitarian Emergencies', in K. Clements and R. Ward (eds) *Building International Community* (St Leonards, NSW: Allen & Unwin.
Ingram, J. (1997) 'Re-thinking the Future Architecture for International Humanitarian Assistance' in N. Azimi (ed.) *Humanitarian Action and Peace-Keeping Operations: Debriefing and Lessons* (London: Kluwer Law International Ltd.: 231–6).
Ingram, J. (2007) *Bread and Stones. Leadership and the Struggle to Reform the United Nations World Food Programme* (Charleston, SC: BookSurge).
Isenman, P. and H. W. Singer (1977) 'Food Aid: Disincentive Effects and their Policy Implications', *Economic Development and Cultural Change* (25), January: 205–37.
Ivanic, P. and R. Martin (2008) 'Implications of Higher Global Food Prices for Poverty Reduction in Low-Income Countries', *Agricultural Economics* 39: 405–16.
Jackson, T. (1982) *Against the Grain. The Dilemma of Project Food Aid* (Oxford, UK: Oxfam).
Jaspars, S. and H. Young (1996) *General Food Distribution in Emergencies: From Nutritional Needs to Political Priorities* (London, UK: Overseas Development Institute).
Kapur, D., J. P. Lewis and R. Webb (1997) *The World Bank. Its First Half Century. Vol. 1. History* (Washington, DC: Brookings Institution Press).
Keen, D. *et al.* (2000) 'The Political Economy of War with Special Reference to Sudan and Bhar el Ghazal' in G. Loane and T. Schümar (eds) *The Wider Impact of Humanitarian Assistance: The Case of Sudan and the Implications for European Policy* (Baden-Baden, Germany: SWP-Conflict Prevention Network).
Kennedy, P. (2006) *The Parliament of Man. The United Nations and the Quest for World Government* (London: Allen Lane).
Konandreas, P. (2010) *Promoting Agricultural Inputs under the Food Aid Convention to Increase Food Production in Emergency-Prone Developing Countries* (Rome, Italy: FAO).
Kripke, G. (2009) 'The Uses of Crisis. Progress on Implementing US Local/Regional Procurement of Food Aid', in Clapp and Cohen (eds): 113–26.

Levinger, B. (1983) *School Feeding Programs in Less Developed Countries: An Analysis of Actual and Potential Impact* (Washington, DC: Agency for International Development).

Levinger, B. (1984) 'School Feeding Programs: Myths and Potential', *Prospects* XIV(3): 369–76.

Macrea, J. and A. Zwi (eds) (1994) *War and Hunger. Rethinking International Responses to Complex Emergencies* (London, UK: Zed Books with Save the Children (UK)).

Margous, Jon (2002) *Building the World's Largest Humanitarian Agency* (Rome, Italy: World Food Programme).

Marlowe, J. (2006) *Darfur Diaries: Stories of Survival* (New York: Nation Books).

Maxwell, D., K. Sadler, A. Sim, M. Mutonyi, R. Egan and M. Webster (2009) 'Emergency Food Security Interventions'. *HPN Good Practice Review* 10 (London: Overseas Development Institute).

Maxwell, S. (1978) 'Food Aid for Supplementary Feeding Programmes: An Analysis', *Food Policy* 3(4): 289–98.

Maxwell, S. (1996) 'Review Article: Perspectives on a New World Food Crisis', *Journal of International Development* 8(6): 859–67.

Maxwell, S and T. Owens (1991) 'Commodity Aid and Counterpart Funds in Africa'. *IDS Discussion Paper* 291.

Maxwell, S. and D. J. Shaw (1995) 'Food, Food Security and UN Reform', *IDS Bulletin* 26(4): 41–53.

Maxwell, S. and H. W. Singer (1979) 'Food Aid to Developing Countries. A Survey', *World Development* 7: 225–46.

McGovern, G. S. (1964) *War Against Want. America's Food for Peace Program* (New York: Walkers & Co.).

McGovern, G. S. (2001) *The Third Freedom. Ending Hunger in Our Time* (New York: Simon & Schuster. [Also published in paperback, Lanham, MD: Rowman & Littlefield, 2002]).

Melvern, L. (2000) *A People Betrayed: The Role of the West in Rwanda's Genocide* (New York: Zed Books).

Melvern, L. (2004) *Conspiracy to Murder: The Rwanda Genocide* (London: Verso).

Minear, L. (1991) *Humanitarianism Under Siege. A Critical Review of Operation Lifeline Sudan* (Trenton, NJ and Washington, DC: Red Sea Press and Bread for the World Institute on Hunger and Development).

Minear, L. (2004) 'Lessons Learned: The Darfur Experience', in *ALNAP Review of Humanitarian Action in 2004* (London: Overseas Development Institute: 73–122).

Minear, L. and R. C. Kent (1998) 'Rwanda's Internally Displaced: A Conundrum within a Condunrum', in R. Cohen and F. M. Deng (eds): 57–95.

Minear, L. and H. Smith (eds) (2007) *Humanitarian Diplomacy: Practitioners and their Craft* (Tokyo, New York, Paris: United Nations University Press).

Mitchell, J. (1997) 'Collective Action and Performance: A Personal View', in ALNAP, *7th Review of Humanitarian Action* (London: Overseas Development Institute: 11–16).

Molinas, L. and M. Regnault de la Mothe (2010) 'The Multiple Impact of School Feeding: A New Approach for Reaching Sustainability', in Omamo, Gentilini and Sandström (eds): 217–30.

Morris, J. (2003) 'Opening Statement to the Third Session of the Executive Board', 2003. WFP/ED.3/2003/14.

Morris, J. (2004) 'Preface'. *Annual Performance Report for 2003*. WFP/EB.A/2004/4-A.

Morris, J. (2005a) 'Foreword'. *How to Work with WFP. A Handbook for Non-Governmental Organizations* (Rome: WFP).

Morris, J. (2005b) 'Reassignment, Rotation and Mobility of International Professional and Higher Category Staff'. *WFP Human Resources Policy Document* (Rome, Italy: WFP Human Resources Division, 1 October).

Morrison, J. S. and J. N. Tuttle (2009) *A Call for a Strategic U.S. Approach to the Global Food Crisis. A Report of the CSIS Task Force on the Global Food Crisis. Core Findings and Recommendations* (Washington, DC: Center for Strategic and International Studies).

Nedessa, B. and S. Wickrema (2010) 'Disaster Risk Reduction: Experience from the MERET Project in Ethiopia', in Omamo, Gentilini and Sandström (eds): 139–56.

Nordic UN Project (1990) 'Responding to Emergencies: The Role of the UN in Emergencies and Ad Hoc Operations'. Report No. 14, in *The United Nations. Issues and Options* (Stockholm, Sweden: Almqvist & Wiksell International).

Ockwell, R. (1999) *Full Report of the Thematic Evaluation of Recurring Challenges of Food Assistance in Complex Emergencies. The Problems and Dilemmas faced by WFP and its Partners* (Rome, Italy: WFP/OEDE, September).

ODI (1998) *The Future of Food Aid: Summary of Findings and Recommendations* (London: Overseas Development Institute).

ODI (2006) 'Cash and Emergency Relief'. An Overseas Development Institute Conference (London: Overseas Development Institute).

OECD (2005) *The Development Effectiveness of Food Aid. Does Tying Matter?* (Paris, France: Organisation for Economic Cooperation and Development).

Ogata, S. (1993) Statement of the UN High Commissioner for Refugees to the World Conference on Human Rights, Vienna, June 15 (Geneva, Switzerland: UNHCR).

Ogata, S. (2005) *The Turbulent Decade. Confronting the Refugee Crises in the 1990s* (New York: Norton).

Omamo, S. W., U. Gentilini, and S. Sandström (eds) (2010a) *Revolution: From Food Aid to Food Assistance. Innovations in Overcoming Hunger* (Rome, Italy: WFP).

Omamo, S. W., U. Gentilini and S. Sandström (2010b) 'Innovations in Food Assistance: Issues, Lessons and Implications', in Omamo, Gentilini and Sandström (eds): 1–15.

Osmani, B. (2010) 'Hand-Over in Namibia: From Food Aid to Social Protection for Orphans and Vulnerable Children', in Omamo, Gentilini and Sandström (eds): 365–76.

Ouattara, A. and S. Sandström (2010) 'Responding to High Prices: Evidence from a Voucher Programme in Burkina Faso', in Omamo, Gentilini and Sandström (eds): 19–32.

Page, T. (1985) 'Issues in Emergency Food Aid: A Personal View', in E. Clay and E. Everitt (eds) 'Food Aid and Emergencies. A Report of the Third IDS Food Aid Seminar', *IDS Discussion Paper* No. 206: 3–9.

Parry, M., A. Evans, M. W. Rosegrant and T. Wheeler (2009) *Climate Change and Hunger* (Rome, Italy: WFP, IFPRI, New York University Center on International Cooperation, Grantham Institute at Imperial College, London, and the Walker Institute at University of Reading, UK).

Peipiat, D., T. Mitchell and P. Allen (2000) *Buying Power: The Use of Cash Transfers in Emergencies* (London: British Red Cross).

Pinstrup-Andersen, P. (ed.) (1988) *Food Subsidies in Developing Countries. Costs, Benefits and Policy Options* (Baltimore, MD: Published for the International Food Policy Research Institute by Johns Hopkins University Press).

Pollitt, E. (1984) 'Nutrition and Educational Achievement'. *Nutrition Education Series* Issue 9 (Paris: UNESCO).

Pollitt, E. (1990) *Malnutrition and Infection in the Classroom* (Paris: UNESCO).

Polman, L. (2010a) *War Games. The Story of Aid and War in Modern Times* (London: Viking).

Polman, L. (2010b) *The Crisis Caravan. What's Wrong with Humanitarian Aid?* (New York: Metropolitan Books).

Quinn, E. (2010) 'Logistics for Food Assistance: Delivering Innovations in Complex Environments', in Omamo, Gentilini and Sandström (eds): 307–28.

Quisumbing, A. R., L. R. Brown, H. S. Felstein, L. Haddad and C. Pina (1995) *Women: The Key to Food Security* (Washington, DC: International Food Policy Research Institute).

RDI (1987) 'A Study of Triangular Transactions and Local Purchases in Food Aid'. *WFP Occasional Paper* No. 11 (Relief and Development Institute, London for WFP).

RDI (1990) 'A Review of Commodity Exchanges in WFP and Other Food Aid Operations'. *WFP Occasional Paper* No. 12 (Relief and Development Institute, London for WFP).

Rees, M. and A. Giddens (2010) 'Whoever said global warming was dead. Overall scientific findings remain intact'. *The Times*. No 70077: 24. (London).

Reutlinger, S. (1999) 'From "Food Aid" to "Aid for Food": Into the 21st Century' *Food Policy* 24(1): 7–15.
Reynell, J. (1989) *Political Pawns. Refugees on the Thai-Kampuchean Border. A RSP study* (Oxford, UK: Refugees Programme).
Runge, C. F. and B. Senauer (2007) 'How Biofuel Could Starve the Poor', *Foreign Affairs* (May/June): 41–53.
Ruttan, V. M. (ed.) (1993) *Why Food Aid?* (Baltimore, MD: Johns Hopkins University Press).
Ruttan, V. W. (1996) *United States Development Assistance Policy. The Domestic Politics of Foreign Economic Aid* (Baltimore, MD: Johns Hopkins University Press).
Samkange, S., P. Howe and M. Cavalcante (2010) 'Country Implementation of the Strategic Plan: The Case of Uganda', in Omamo, Gentilini and Sandström (eds): 351–64.
Sandström, S. and L. Tchatchua (2010) 'Do Cash Transfers Improve Food Security in Emergencies? Evidence from Sri Lanka', in Omamo, Gentilini and Sandström (eds): 75–88.
Sanogo, I. and J. K. Luma (2010) 'Assessments of the Impacts of Global Economic Crises on Household Food Security: Innovative Approaches, Lessons and Challenges', in Omamo, Gentilini and Sandström (eds): 259–73.
Schümer-Cross, T. and B. Taylor (2009) *The Right to Survive: The Humanitarian Challenge for the Twenty-first Century* (Oxford, UK: Oxford Professionals).
Schultz, T. W. (1960) 'Value of US Farm Surpluses to Underdeveloped Countries', *Journal of Farm Economics* 42(5): 1019–30.
Schuh, E. (1983) 'Increasing the Effectiveness of Food Aid: Offsetting the Opportunity Cost of Schooling', in WFP and Government of the Netherlands, *Report of Food Aid Seminar*, The Hague 3–5 October 1983 (Rome: WFP and Government of the Netherlands).
Schulthes, J. (1992) 'Monetisation of Project Food Aid?' *IDS Bulletin* 23(2): 36–40.
Schulthes, J. (2000) 'Is There a Future for the WFP as a Development Agency? Or Does Food Aid Still Have a Comparative Advantage' in, Clay and Stokke (eds): 256–73.
Seaman, J., and J. Rivers (1988) 'Strategies for the Distribution of Relief Food', *Journal of the Royal Statistical Society* 151(3): 464–72.
Sen, A. K. (1981) *Poverty and Famine. An Essay on Entitlement and Deprivation* (Oxford, UK: Clarendon Press).
Sen, B. R. (1982) *Towards A Newer World* (Dublin, Ireland: Tycooly).
Sen, S. R. (1960) 'Impact and Implications of Foreign Surplus Disposal on Underdeveloped Economies – The Indian Perspective', *Journal of Farm Economics* XLII: 1031–42.
Shaver, G. (2006–09) *Report on the Activities of the Office of the Ombudsman* (Rome, Italy: WFP).
Shaw, D. J. (1983) 'Triangular Transactions in Food Aid: Concepts and Practice' *IDS Bulletin* 14(2): 28–31.
Shaw, D. J. (2000) 'Food Aid in Sub-Saharan Africa: Policy Lessons for the Future', in D. Belshaw and I. Livingstone (eds) *Renewing Development in Sub-Saharan Africa: Policies and Prospects* (London: Routledge: 235–56) and *Canadian Journal of Development Studies* XXIII(3): 571–99.
Shaw, D. J. (2001) *The UN World Food Programme and the Development of Food Aid* (Basingstoke, UK and New York: Palgrave Macmillan).
Shaw, D. J. (2002) *Sir Hans Singer. The Life and Work of a Development Economist* (Basingstoke, UK and New York: Palgrave Macmillan).
Shaw, D. J. (2007) *World Food Security. A History since 1945* (Basingstoke, UK and New York: Palgrave Macmillan).
Shaw, D. J. (2009) *Global Food and Agricultural Institutions* (London and New York: Routledge Global Institutions Series).
Shaw, D. J. (2010) The World Food Council. The Rise and Fall of a UN Body', *Canadian Journal of Development Studies* 30(3–4): 663–94.

Shaw, D. J. and E. Clay (eds) (1993) *World Food Aid: Experiences of Recipients and Donors* (Rome, Italy, London, UK, and Portsmouth, NH; World Food Programme in association with James Currey and Heinemann).

Shaw, D. J. and E. Clay (1998) 'Global Hunger and Food Security after the World Food Summit', *Canadian Journal of Development Studies* XIX, Special Issue: 55–76.

Shaw, D. J. and H. W. Singer (eds) (1988) 'Food Policy, Food Aid and Economic Adjustment', *Food Policy* 13(1), Special Issue.

Shaw, D. J. and H. W. Singer (1995) 'A Future Food Aid Regime: Implications of the Final Act of the GATT Uruguay Round', *IDS Discussion Paper* No. 352 (Brighton, UK: Institute of Development Studies).

Shawcross, W. (1984) *The Quality of Mercy. Cambodia, Holocaust and Modern Conscience* (New York: Simon & Schuster).

Shawcross, W. (2000) *Deliver Us from Evil: Warlords and Peacekeepers in a World of Endless Conflict* (London, UK: Bloomsbury).

Sheeran, J. (2007a) Opening Statement to WFP's Executive Board, 4 June 2007 (Rome. Italy: WFP).

Sheeran, J. (2007b) Speech at the International Affairs Luncheon, Cosmos Club, Washington, DC, 1 August 2007.

Sheeran, J. (2008) 'Challenges and Opportunities in Meeting the New Face of Hunger' Keynote Address, International Food Aid Conference. 15 April, Kansas City, USA.

Sheeran, J. (2010a) Opening Statement. Annual Session of the Executive Board. 23 June, Rome, Italy.

Sheeran, J. (2010b) No time to relax in the fight against hunger, top UN official warn', *UN News Centre*, 20 September (New York: United Nations).

Singer, H. W. (1961) 'The Use and Abuse of Local Counterpart Funds', *International Development Review* 3(3): 1–10.

Singer, H. W. (1972) 'Children in the Strategy of Development'. *Executive Briefing Paper* No. 6 (New York: United Nations Centre for Economic and Social Information).

Singer, H. W. (1991) 'Food Aid and Structural Adjustment in Sub-Saharan Africa' in Clay and Stokke (eds): 180–90.

Singer, H. W., J. Wood and T. Jennings (1987) *Food Aid: The Challenge and the Opportunity* (Oxford, UK: Clarendon Press).

Slim, H. and A. Bonwick (2005) *Protection: An ALNAP Guide for Humanitarian Agencies* (London: Overseas Development Institute).

Sserunkuuma, D. (2005) 'Local and Regional Procurement in Uganda. An Analytical Review'. Paper prepared for the WFP Economic Analysis Unit (Rome, Italy: WFP).

Stern, N. (2006) *The Economics of Climate Change* (Cambridge, UK: Cambridge University Press).

Stevens, C. (1979) *Food Aid and the Developing World. Four African Case Studies* (London: Overseas Development Institute).

Stites, E. and V. Tanner (2004) *External Evaluation of OCHA's Internal Displacement Unit: Final Report* (New York: Office for the Coordination of Humanitarian Assistance).

Stoddard, A., A. Harmer and V. DiDomenico (2009) *Providing Aid in Insecure Environments: 2009 Update. Trends in Violence against Aid Workers and the Operational Response* (London: Humanitarian Policy Group, Overseas Development Institute).

TechEcon (1992) *Food Aid Transport Costs and Options* (London: Economic and Transport Consultants for the Commission of the Economic Communities).

Telford, J. and J. Cosgrove (2006) *Joint Evaluation of the International Response to the Indian Ocean Tsunami: Synthesis Report* (London: Tsunami Evaluation Coalition).

The Economist (2007) 'Dealing with disasters. Flood, famine and mobile phones', July 28: 65–6.

The Economist (2010) 'Don't starve thy neighbour. How to rebuild confidence in food markets after this summer's spike in wheat prices', September 11: 14–16.

Thurow, R. and S. Kilman (2009) *Enough. Why the World's Poorest Starve in an Age of Plenty* (Philadelphia, PA: Public Affairs: 227–31).

Toole, M. (1993) 'Protecting Refugees' Nutrition with Food Aid', in ACC/SCN (1993): 87–90.
Tomasini, R. and L. Van Wassenhove (2009) *Humanitarian Logistics* (Basingstoke, UK and New York: Palgrave Macmillan and INSEAD Business Press)
Tschirley, D. L. (2007) 'Presentation on WFP Local and Regional Food Procurement – An Assessment of Experience in Africa and Elements of Good Donor Practice (Rome, Italy: WFP).
UN (1945) *Charter of the United Nations* (New York: United Nations).
UN (1948) *Universal Declaration of Human Rights.* Adopted by the UN General Assembly on 10 December 1948 (New York: United Nations).
UN (1960) 868th Plenary Meeting. United Nations General Assembly. Fifteenth Session. Official Records (Part 1). Plenary Meetings Vol. 1. *Verbatim Records of Meetings* 20 September –17 October 1960 (New York: United Nations).
UN (1961a) 'World Food Programme'. *General Assembly Resolution 1714 (XVI)*, adopted on 19 December 1961 (New York: United Nations).
UN (1961b) Statements to the Second Committee of the General Assembly on 8 December 1961. Document A/C.2/L.623-4 (New York: United Nations).
UN (1965) 'Continuation of the World Food Programme'. *General Assembly Resolution 2095 (XX)*, adopted on 20 December 1965 (New York: United Nations).
UN (1966) *International Convention on Economic, Social and Cultural Rights* (New York: United Nations).
UN (1969) *A Study of the Capacity of the United Nations Development System* (Geneva, Switzerland: United Nations).
UN (1975) 'Report of the World Food Conference', Rome 5–16 November 1974. Document E/CONF. 65/20 (New York: United Nations).
UN (1976) 'Development and International Economic Cooperation'. *Resolution 3362 (S-VII)* adopted by the General Assembly during its Seventh Special Session: 1–16 September. *UN General Assembly Official Records*, Supplement No. 1 (A/10301 (New York: United Nations).
UN (1991a) 'Revision of the General Regulations of the World Food Programme and the Enlargement of the Committee on Food Aid Policies and Programmes of the World Food Programme'. *United Nations General Assembly Resolution 46/22*, adopted on 5 December 1991 (New York: United Nations).
UN (1991b) 'Strengthening of the Co-ordination of Humanitarian Emergency Assistance of the United Nations'. *United Nations General Assembly Resolution 46/182*, adopted on 19 December 1991 (New York: United Nations).
UN (1992a) 'Triennial Policy Review of the Operational Activities of the United Nations Development Assistance'. *United Nations General Assembly Resolution 14/199*, adopted on 22 December 1992 (New York: United Nations).
UN (1992b) 'Commission on Human Rights. Analytical Report of the Secretary-General on Internally Displaced Persons'. Document E/CN.4/1992/23 (New York; United Nations).
UN (1993) 'Further Measures for the Restructuring and Revitalization of the United Nations in the Economic, Social and Related Fields'. *United Nations General Assembly Resolution 48/162*, adopted on 20 December 1993 (New York: United Nations).
UN (1994a) *Report of the Secretary-General on the Situation in Rwanda* (New York: United Nations).
UN (1994b) 'Conclusions of the Executive Committee on the High Commissioner's Programme'. UN General Assembly Document A/AC.94/XLV/CRP.3 (New York: United Nations).
UN (1995) *Report of the Fourth World Conference on Women*, Beijing 4–15 September 1995 (New York: United Nations).
UN (2000) 'United Nations Millennium Declaration'. *United Nations General Assembly Resolution 55/2* (New York: United Nations).
UN (2003) 'The Human Rights Based Approach to Development Cooperation. Towards A Common Understanding Among the UN Agencies'. Report of the Second Interagency

Workshop on Implementing a Human Rights-based Approach in the Context of UN Reform. Stanford, USA, 5–7 May 2003 (New York: United Nations).

UN (2004) 'A More Secure World: Our Shared Responsibility'. Report of the High-Level Panel on Threats, Challenges and Change. Document A/59/565 (New York: United Nations).

UN (2006) *High-Level Panel Report on United Nations System-Wide Cohesion* (New York: United Nations).

UN (2008a) *The Least Developed Countries Report 2008. Growth, Poverty and the Terms Development Partnership*. Prepared by the UNCTAD Secretariat (New York and Geneva, Switzerland: United Nations).

UN (2008b) 'Humanitarian Action', in *The United Nations Today* (New York: Department of Public Information, United Nations).

UN (2009) 'UN High-Level Task Force on the Global Food Security Crisis'. Progress Report, April 2008–October 2009 (New York: United Nations).

UN and FAO (1965) Report of the Secretary-General of the United Nations and the Director-General of the Food and Agriculture Organization of the United Nations on the Future Development of the World Food Programme with reference to *General Assembly Resolution 1714 (XVI)*. Document WM/IGC: 7/4 Add. 8, 1 March (New York and Rome, Italy: United Nations and FAO).

UNDP (1994) *Human Development Report 1994* (New York: Published for the United Nations Development Programme by Oxford University Press).

UNDP (2001) *Disaster Profile of Least Developed Countries* (New York: United Nations Development Programme).

UNDP (2004) 'Unleashing Entrepreneurship. Making Business Work for the Poor'. Report to the Secretary-General of the United Nations Commission on the Private Sector and Development (New York: United Nations Development Programme).

UNDP (2005) *UN Millennium Project 2005: Investing in Development: A Practical Plan to Achieve the Millennium Development* (New York: United Nations Development Programme).

UNESCO (1980) 'School Feeding as a Service to Children. Guidelines for Planning School Feeding Programmes'. *Basic Education Series* No. 3 (Paris: UNESCO).

UNESCO (1983) Workshop on School Feeding and Education. Sri Avinashilingam Home Science College for Women, Coimbatore, India, December 1983 (Paris: UNECO).

UNHCR (1993) Representative of the Kingdom of the Netherlands Statement to the Forty-Fourth Session of the UNHCR Executive Committee (Geneva, Switzerland: UNHCR).

UNHCR (1996) *International Legal Standards Applicable to the Problem of Internally Displaced Persons: A Reference Manual for UNHCR Staff* (Geneva, Switzerland: UNHCR).

UNHCR (1997) *The State of the World's Refugees 1997–98: A Humanitarian Agenda* (Oxford, UK: Oxford University Press).

UNHCR/WFP (2004) *Joint Assessment Guidelines with Tools and Resource Material* (Geneva, Switzerland and Rome, Italy: UNHCR Technical Support Service and WFP Emergency Needs Assessment Unit).

UNICEF (1999) *The State of the World's Children, 1999* (New York: Oxford University Press for UNICEF).

Urquhart, P. (2010) *WFP and Climate Change. A Review of On-going Experience and Recommendations*. Commissioned by the WFP Climate Change and Disaster Risk Reduction Office (Rome, Italy: WFP).

US (1961) Congressional Record. Proceedings and Details of the 87th Congress, 1st Session. Volume 107, Part 1 (Washington, DC: US Government Printing Office).

US (1962) Public Papers of the Presidents of the United States. John F. Kennedy, 20 January to 31 December 1961 (Washington, DC: US Government Printing Office).

US (1963) President Kennedy Speeches (Papers of the President's Office Files. Box 34. John F. Kennedy Library, Boston, MA: United States).

US (1995) *Readjusting the United Nations for the Twenty-first Century: Some UN21 Proposals* (Washington, DC: United States Department of State).

Van den Briel, T., E. Cheug, J. Zewari and R. Khan (2006) 'Fortified Food in the Field to Boost Nutrition: Case Studies from Afghanistan, Angola and Zambia'. *WFP Occasional Paper* No. 16 (Rome: WFP).

Vayrynen, R. (1996) *The Age of Humanitarian Emergencies. Research for Action 25* (Helsinki, Finland: World Institute for Development Economic Research).

Von Braun, J. and R. Pandya-Lorch (2007) 'Taking Action for the World's Poorest and Hungry People'. Synopsis of an International Consultation, Beijing, China, 2007 Washington, DC: International Food Policy Research Institute).

Von Braun, J. R. V. Hill and R. Pandya-Lorch (eds) (2009) *The Poorest and Hungry. Assessments, Analysis and Actions* (Washington, DC: International Food Policy Research Institute).

Von Grebmer, K., B. Hestorova, A. Quisumbing, R, Fertiger, H. Fertziger, R. Pandya-Lorch, and Y. Yohannes (2010) *2010 Global Hunger Index: The Challenge of Hunger: Focus on Financial Crisis and Gender Inequality* (Bonn, Germany, Dublin, Ireland and Washington, DC: Deutsche Welthungerhilfe, Concern Worldwide, and the International Food Policy Research Institute).

Walker, P. (2008) 'Complexity and Context as the Determinants of the Future'. *Opinion Paper,* 7 July (Medford, MA: Feinstein International Center, Tufts University).

Walker, P. and D. Maxwell (2009) *Shaping the Humanitarian World* (London and New York: Routledge Global Institutions Series).

Wallerstein, M. B. (1980) *Food for War – Food for Peace. United States Food Aid in a Global Context* (Cambridge, MA: MIT Press).

Webster, M., J. Ginnetti, P. Walker, D. Coppard and R. Kent (2008) *The Human Cost Of Climate Change* (Medford, MA: Feinstein International Center, Tufts University).

Weiss, T. G. (1998) 'Humanitarian Shell Games: Whither UN Reform?' Security Dialogue: 29(9): 9–23 (Oslo: International Peace Research Institute). Also available online at http://sdi.sagepub.com

Weiss, T. G. (2009) *What's Wrong with the United Nations and How to Fix It* (Malden, MA and Cambridge, UK: Polity Press).

Weiss, T. G. and A. Pasic (1998) 'Dealing with the Displacement and Suffering caused by Yugoslavia's Wars: Conceptual and Operational Issues' in Cohen and Deng (eds): 175–231.

Weiss, W. G. and D. A. Korn (2006) *Internal Displacement. Conceptualization and Its Consequences* (London and New York: Routledge Global Institutions Series).

WFC (1990) 'Improving Co-ordination of National and International Action towards a More Concerted Attack on Hunger'. Document WFC/1990/5 (Rome, Italy: World Food Council).

WFP *et al.*, (2009) 'Climate Change, Food Security and Hunger: Key Messages for UNFCCC Negotiators'. *Technical Paper for the IASC Task Force.* Submitted by WFP, FAO, IFRC and OXFAM as well as WHO, WVI, CARE, Caritas, and Save the Children (Rome, Italy: WFP).

WFP and the Boston Consulting Group (2009) *School Feeding. A Sound Investment. Results from Investment Case Studies* (Rome: WFP).

WFP and UNU (1997) *Ending the Inheritance of Hunger* (Rome, Italy: WFP and United Nations University).

WHO and World Bank (2006) *A Global Burden of Disease Study* (Geneva, Switzerland and Washington, DC).

WHO, WFP, UNICEF, and SCN (2007) *Joint Statement on Community-Based Management of Severe Acute Malnutrition among Children* (Geneva, Rome, and New York: WHO, WFP, UNICEF and UNSCN).

Wilmshurst, J., P. Ackroyd and R. Eyben (1992) 'Implications for U.K. Aid of Current Thinking on Poverty Reduction', *IDS Discussion Paper* No. 307 (Brighton, UK: Institute of Development Studies, University of Sussex).

Witt, L. M. (1964) 'Development through Food Grants and Concessional Sales', in C. Eicher and L. W. Witt (eds) *Agriculture in Economic Development* (New York: McGraw-Hill): 334–59.

Wood, D. H., A. Baron and V. W. Brown (1986) *The U.S. Response to the African Famine 1984–1986. Vol. 1. An Evaluation of the Emergency Food Assistance Program: Synthesis Report. A. I. D. Program Evaluation Report No. 16* (Washington, DC: U.S. Agency for International Development).

Woodbridge, G. (1950) *UNRRA: The History of the United Nations Relief and Rehabilitation Administration* (New York: Colombia University Press).

World Bank (1986) *Poverty and Hunger. Issues and Options for Food Security in Developing Countries* (Washington, DC: World Bank).

World Bank (1988) 'Adjustment Lending: An Evaluation of Ten Years of Experience', *Policy and Research Series* No. 1 (Washington, DC: Country Economics Department, World Bank).

World Bank (2000) *Entering the 21st Century. World Development Report 1999/2000* (New York: Published for the World Bank by Oxford University Press).

World Bank (2004) *The CGIAR at 31: An Independent Meta-Evaluation of the Consultative Group on International Agricultural Research* (Washington, DC: World Bank Operations Evaluation Department).

World Bank (2005) *Agricultural Growth for the Poor. An Agenda for Development* (Washington, DC: World Bank).

World Bank (2007a) *A Guide to the World Bank*. 2nd edn (Washington, DC: World Bank).

World Bank (2007b) *World Development Report. Agriculture for Development* (Washington, DC: World Bank).

World Bank (2009) *Implementing Agriculture for Development. World Bank Group Agriculture Action Plan FY 2010–2012* (Washington, DC: World Bank).

World Bank (2010) *World Development Report 2010. Development and Climate Change* (Washington, DC: World Bank).

World Bank (website) 'Natural Disasters. Counting the Costs', www.worldbank.org

World Bank and WFP (1991) *Food Aid in Africa. An Agenda for the 1990s* (Washington, DC and Rome, Italy: World Bank and World Food Programme).

Young, H., A. Monim Osman, Y. Aklilu and R. Dale (2005) *Darfur – Livelihoods under Siege* (Medford, MA: Feinstein International Center, Tufts University).

Young, H. (2007) 'Looking beyond Food Aid to Livelihoods, Protection and Partnerships: Strategies for WFP in the Darfur States', *Disasters*, 31, March 2007: S40-S56.

Young, H. (2009) *IDPs, Migration and Remittances: Case-Studies from the Darfur Region* (Medford, MA: Feinstein International Center, Tufts University).

Young, H. and D. Maxwell (2009) *Targeting in Complex Emergencies: Darfur Case Study* (Medford, MA; Feinstein International Center, Tufts University).

Yu, E. (2010) 'Information and Communication Technology in Food Assistance', in Omamo, Gentilini and Sandström (eds): 295–306.

Zoellick, R. B. (2008) 'A Challenge of Economic Statecraft'. Center for Global Development, Washington, DC, 2 April.

Zoellick, R. B. (2011) 'Free markets can still feed the world', *Financial Times*, 4 January: 9.

Index